Financial accounting
GROUPS

CW00728655

Financial accounting
GROUPS

Ilse Lubbe • Goolam Modack • Shelly Herbert • Andrew Hyland

OXFORD

UNIVERSITY PRESS

SOUTHERN AFRICA

OXFORD
UNIVERSITY PRESS

Oxford University Press is a department of the University of Oxford.
It furthers the University's objective of excellence in research, scholarship,
and education by publishing worldwide. Oxford is a registered trade mark of
Oxford University Press in the UK and in certain other countries

Published in South Africa by
Oxford University Press Southern Africa (Pty) Limited

Vasco Boulevard, Goodwood, N1 City, P O Box 12119, Cape Town
South Africa

© The Authors 2014
Questions in this textbook are the copyright of University of Cape Town,
reprinted with permission

The moral rights of the author have been asserted

First published 2014

All rights reserved. No part of this publication may be reproduced, stored in
a retrieval system, or transmitted, in any form or by any means, without the
prior permission in writing of Oxford University Press Southern Africa (Pty) Ltd,
or as expressly permitted by law, by licence, or under terms agreed
with the appropriate reprographic rights organisation, DALRO, The Dramatic, Artistic
and Literary Rights Organisation at dalro@dalro.co.za. Enquiries concerning
reproduction outside the scope of the above should be sent to the Rights Department,
Oxford University Press Southern Africa (Pty) Ltd, at the above address.

You must not circulate this work in any other form
and you must impose this same condition on any acquirer.

Financial Accounting: Groups

ISBN 978 0 19 599863 4

Typeset in Palatino Lt Std 10 pt on 12 pt
Printed on 70 gsm woodfree paper

Acknowledgements
Publishing manager: Alida Terblanche
Publisher: Marisa Montemarano
Project manager: Kelly Williams
Editor: Louise Banks
Indexer: Michel Cozien
Typesetter: PH Setting cc
Designer: Gisela Strydom
Cover design: Shaun Andrews
Printed and bound by ABC Press, Cape Town
122432

The authors and publisher gratefully acknowledge permission to reproduce copyright material in this book.
Every effort has been made to trace copyright holders, but if any copyright infringements have been made,
the publisher would be grateful for information that would enable any omissions or errors to be corrected in
subsequent impressions.

Links to third party websites are provided by Oxford in good faith and for information only.
Oxford disclaims any responsibility for the materials contained in any third party website referenced in this work.

Contents

Preface

Financial statements are intended to communicate information about an entity's financial position, financial performance and cash flows for a specific reporting period. They also provide information about the entity's future net cash inflows and their associated risks. If financial statements achieve all of these aims, the information presented in them is said to be decision useful. In other words, the information is useful to users of the entity's financial statements because it allows these users to make decisions about providing financial capital to the entity. The users in question could be existing or potential investors, lenders or creditors, and they could be individuals or other entities.

In this publication, we focus on an **investor that is an entity**. The investor buys shares in another entity, the investee. The investor may acquire anything from 0.1% to 100% of the equity of the investee. The point is that a relationship is established when one entity invests in another. The nature of that relationship depends on the nature of the investment. Why is this important?

There are many reasons why an investor would want to invest and there are many ways in which it could obtain a return on its investment. These reasons include dividends, gains from selling its investment in the future, the ability for the investor to grow its own business by accessing the investee's markets (products, location and customers) or the ability of the investor to manage its existing business better because the investee has skills, processes and so on that the investor can access. In addition, there are many reasons why the investee may want the investor to invest in its business, for example, access to financial capital, or access to the investor's markets or skills, which would benefit the investee.

Entities are required to maintain accounting records, so the investor and the investee would most likely prepare individual financial statements. The investor may be required to structure its operations through different entities for legal, tax or regulatory reasons. In your studies up to now, you have learnt how to prepare the financial statements of a single legal entity. So in our example above of an investor that is an entity, you would have looked at the individual financial statements of the investor and those of the investee. In the investor's financial statements, you would probably have reflected the investor's investment in the investee as an asset and measured that asset at fair value, perhaps even at cost.

Take a step back and think about the investor's financial statements. How would and could the information in these financial statements be decision useful? In some instances, reflecting only an investment in the investee as an asset is appropriate, but in many other instances, it may not be.

For example, what if, as a result of the investor's investment in the investee, the investor obtains control over the assets of the investee and assumes obligations for its liabilities? Would it not be more useful for the investor's financial statements to report the assets and liabilities of the investee? What happens if the investor does not obtain control of the investee's assets or assume its liabilities, but the nature of the investment is such that reporting the investor's investment in the investee as an asset at cost or at fair value is not appropriate? Would it not be more useful if the investor reported its investment in the investee at some other amount?

You may have seen examples of financial statements of an investor that achieve this. They are referred to as **group financial statements**. Think of the many large companies that exist, for example, Apple, Microsoft, Facebook, Pick n Pay and Shoprite. These companies do not comprise one single legal entity, but consist of a number of different entities. In many instances, the group has been structured through one entity (the investor) investing in many other entities (the investees). So Pick n Pay does not comprise a single legal entity; it is a group of companies, made up of many different legal entities, some of which are even incorporated in different countries. However, when Pick 'n Pay reports to its users, it reports as one single entity in a manner that reflects all of the assets, liabilities, income, expenses and equity of these different entities appropriately so that the information is decision useful.

From the discussion above, it is clear that there are many reasons why one entity may invest in another entity as well as various reasons why the nature of the investment may differ. In addition, the investment in the other entity may change the expectation about the investor's future cash flows and their associated risks. How, then, does the investor prepare a single set of financial statements that combines all of the financial information of each of the individual entities in a way that is appropriate and that makes sense to the users of that single set of financial statements? How does the investor do this in a way that makes it possible to achieve the objective of financial reporting?

These are the questions that this publication will answer. You will learn to identify and understand the nature of investments in the equity of other entities, the implications of these investments and the process for preparing a single set of group financial statements that provides decision-useful information to the users of the financial statements.

Authors

Ilse Lubbe

Associate Professor, College of Accounting, University of Cape Town
B.Com (Hons), HDTE, M.Phil (Higher Education Studies), CA(SA)

Goolam Modack

Senior Lecturer, College of Accounting, University of Cape Town
B.Com, PGDip (Tax Law), M.Com, CA(SA)

Shelly Herbert

Lecturer, College of Accounting, University of Cape Town
B.Com (Hons), CA(SA)

Andrew Hyland

Lecturer, College of Accounting, University of Cape Town
B.BusSc, B.Com (Hons), CA(SA)

Acknowledgements

We would like to thank our colleagues and students in the College of Accounting at the University of Cape Town for their comments and contributions. We would also like to thank our families for their support, patience and encouragement.

Pedagogy

How to use this book

This publication adopts a principles-based approach in terms of the structure of the content, which is supported by discussions of reporting issues, case studies and accounting challenges that are unique to the preparation and presentation of group financial statements.

The book contains a number of features in each chapter to help the reader, whether he or she is a student, a tutorial group leader or a lecturer.

Prior knowledge

This publication focuses on the preparation and presentation of group financial statements. In order to understand the principles of preparing group financial statements, you should have a thorough understanding of the IASB **Conceptual Framework** and be able to prepare **general purpose financial statements** for a single entity in accordance with IFRS.

IFRS principles

Within each chapter, you will find regular reminders of the applicable IFRS in order to emphasise the key principles in the IFRS standards relating to financial reporting for groups.

Where applicable, attention is drawn to the IFRS for SMEs standards.

Learning objectives

At the beginning of each chapter, you will find a bullet-point list of skills-orientated learning objectives. After studying the chapter, you should have enough information at your disposal to be able to express an informed opinion on the objective in question and to demonstrate a related skill if this is relevant.

At the end of every chapter, there is a reminder to go back over the learning objectives to ensure that all of the outcomes for a specific chapter have been achieved.

Test your knowledge

There is a list of learning objectives at the beginning of this chapter. Go back to this list and check whether you have achieved these outcomes. If not, reread the appropriate section.

Examples

Short examples illustrating concepts and principles feature in every chapter, providing a valuable study and revision tool.

Features

The study of the content of this book is made more interesting by the inclusion of boxes called 'Think about it', which contain interesting research facts, debates and anomalies, or provide clarity on the specific detail of an accounting principle or standard.

 Think about it

Why is it not appropriate for an investment entity to prepare group financial statements?

An investment entity acquired its interest in another entity with the main purpose of receiving dividend income and benefitting from increases in its fair value. It is not the intention of the investment entity to acquire a controlling interest in the operations and activities of the other entity.

Reporting information about the fair value of its investment in a subsidiary is more relevant than consolidation of its individual assets and liabilities.

These features can also be used by tutorial leaders and lecturers as discussion points in a classroom situation.

Exercises and case studies

Each chapter includes worked examples and comprehensive case studies. As a student accountant, you will know that the best way to promote your complete understanding of the principles and applications involved is to practise using various exercises or examples. Additional questions and answers have been made available to lecturers using this textbook. These can be used as the basis of tutorials, further classroom discussion or assignments.

Free CD!

A CD containing a series of additional examples and case studies, including additional questions at an advanced level, together with selected solutions and helpful comments, is supplied free with every textbook purchased.

Ancillary material

An Instructor's Manual to accompany this first edition of *Financial Accounting: Groups* will be made available by Oxford University Press Southern Africa to lecturers prescribing this textbook.

The Instructor's Manual contains the following materials:
1 Solutions to all questions in the textbook and on the student CD
2 A teaching plan
3 A set of PowerPoint® slides.

The Instructor's Manual is available on CD with the ISBN 978 0 19 040020 0 and can be obtained from Oxford University Press SA through the Higher Education sales administrator.

Further contact

Should you have any comments about this textbook, the publisher and authors would be pleased to receive them. Contact the Commissioning Editor, Higher Education Division, Oxford University Press Southern Africa or contact Oxford University Press Southern Africa through the website at www.oxford.co.za.

Introduction

In financial accounting, where entities form relationships with other entities, it is important that the financial information that is presented and reported clearly reflects and communicates these relationships as well as the economic substance of the financial performance and financial position of the entities involved. This is necessary so that users of the financial statements are able to identify these relationships, and are able to make informed economic decisions and draw conclusions from this information. In the modern financial world, there are several forms of relationships that exist between different entities, for example, where one entity has an investment in another entity that results in a controlling interest in that entity or is able to influence the decisions of another entity significantly, or has a non-controlling investment in another entity. Based on the nature of the relationship, some entities are classified as subsidiaries, others as associates and others as joint ventures, and these entities together are often referred to as a 'group' of companies.

When preparing group financial statements, certain recording and reporting principles need to be applied in terms of the **International Financial Reporting Standards** (IFRSs), depending on the nature of the relationships that exist. These group financial statements are statements that are prepared in addition to the separate financial statements that are prepared by the individual entities (that is, the parent, subsidiary and so forth) as separate legal entities.

One type of relationship that can exist is a **parent–subsidiary relationship**. The existence of this type of relationship between two entities is established when one entity has control over the other. In order to determine the existence of control, it is necessary to assess the power that one entity has over another entity, and whether the investor is exposed to or has the rights to variable returns from its involvement in the investee. In addition, you must consider the ability of the investor to use its power over the investee to influence its financial decisions and returns.

Furthermore, a parent entity may have investments in subsidiaries that are incorporated in countries other than that of the parent. A subsidiary of this nature is referred to as a **foreign operation**. A foreign operation generally records its transactions using its functional currency, which is the currency of the primary economic environment in which it operates. When a foreign subsidiary is consolidated, or included in the group financial statements, the financial statements of the foreign operation may need to be translated into the presentation currency of the group, using the translation method.

Besides subsidiaries, an entity may have a special relationship through its investments in other entities, such as **associates** and **joint ventures**. A relationship of this nature may give the investor significant influence in the determination of the financial and operating policy decisions (as in the case of an associate) or be in the form of a contractually agreed sharing of control (as in the case of a joint venture). The equity method of accounting is used to provide more information about an investment of this nature when preparing the group financial statements.

A **joint arrangement** relationship is usually not structured through a separate vehicle or entity and is thus referred to as a joint operation. A joint arrangement exists when two or more parties have joint control over an operation, that is, when decisions about relevant activities require the unanimous consent of all of the parties sharing the control.

Parties in a joint operation must recognise their share of the assets and liabilities of the arrangement as well as any revenues or expenses associated with the arrangement.

When it comes to financial reporting, **parent** entities are responsible for the preparation of the group financial statements. Group financial statements include the consolidation of subsidiaries as well as the inclusion of the results of associates and joint ventures subsequent to the acquisition date, in accordance with the equity method.

The following IFRSs cover the preparation and presentation of group financial statements:
- IAS1: *Presentation of Financial Statements*
- IFRS3: *Business Combinations*
- IFRS10: *Consolidated Financial Statements*
- IFRS11: *Joint Arrangements*
- IFRS12: *Disclosures of Interests in Other Entities*
- IAS21: *The Effects of Changes in Foreign Exchange Rates*
- IAS27: *Separate Financial Statements*
- IAS28: *Investments in Associates and Joint Ventures.*

The IFRSs for SMEs also require the preparation of group financial statements. These standards apply to small- and medium-sized entities that do not have public accountability, and that publish general purpose financial statements for external users. An entity has public accountability if its debt or equity instruments are traded in a public market or it is in the process of issuing instruments of this nature for trading in a public market. The following sections in the IFRS for SMEs deal with the preparation and presentation of group financial statements:
- IFRS for SMEs Section 9: *Consolidated and Separate Financial Statements*
- IFRS for SMEs Section 14: *Investments in Associates*
- IFRS for SMEs Section 15: *Investments in Joint Ventures*
- IFRS for SMEs Section 19: *Business Combinations and Goodwill.*

There are a few differences between the accounting treatment required in terms of the IFRS standards the accounting treatment required in terms of the IFRSs for SMEs. Examples include the allowed option in the IFRSs for SMEs that investments in associates and joint ventures be recognised at cost or at fair value in the group financial statements as alternatives to the equity method, and the subsequent treatment of goodwill. These differences are highlighted throughout this publication, where appropriate.

This publication focuses on the accounting treatment for group accounting in compliance with the IFRSs. Owing to the variety of currencies used in different countries, a standard **Currency Unit** (CU) is used in this publication.

The following abbreviations are used frequently in this publication:
- IFRS: International Financial Reporting Standards
- IAS: International Accounting Standards (these form part of the IFRSs)
- IASB: International Accounting Standards Board
- FASB: Financial Accounting Standards Board (based in the United States of America)
- CU: Currency Unit.

PART I

The reporting entity

1

An introduction to group accounting

The following topics are included in this chapter:

- An overview of general purpose financial statements
- An overview of the reporting entity
- An introduction into the preparation of group financial statements
- Recognising investments in the separate financial statments of the parent.

Learning objectives

By the end of this chapter, you should be able to:

- Describe the objective of financial reporting
- Identify the reporting entity
- Explain what is meant by a group and why group financial statements are prepared
- Understand the purpose of preparing group financial statements and who the users of these financial statements are
- Identify a parent entity and know how to account for investments in other entities in the separate financial statements of the parent.

1. Objective of financial reporting

An entity could be a company, a partnership, a trust or another form of business. Information about the entity's financial performance and position is important to providers of financial capital (investors, owners, lenders and other creditors). The objective of financial reporting is to provide financial information that is useful to the users of that information. The tool through which this information is communicated is the financial statements of the entity. These financial statements provide financial information about the entity that is useful to present and potential investors as well as to lenders and other creditors in making decisions about whether they should provide resources to the entity (refer to the *Conceptual Framework for Financial Reporting* of the International Accounting Standards Board [IASB]). We refer to these as **general purpose financial statements** as they are intended to meet the information needs common to a range of users who are unable to command the preparation of reports tailored to satisfy their own particular needs.

Information about the entity's economic resources and claims that exist against those resources can help users identify and evaluate the entity's strengths and weaknesses. Financial statements provide information about the entity's ability to generate future cash flows and the associated risks. They also make it possible to hold those people charged with governance accountable, giving information on how effectively and efficiently they have discharged their responsibilities to use the entity's resources appropriately.

You should be familiar with the preparation of general purposes financial statements. Refer to Chapters 1 to 3 in *Financial Accounting: IFRS Principles* by Lubbe *et al.* (2014) for a detailed description of the purpose of financial reporting, the information needs of the users of financial statements and the qualitative characteristics of financial reporting information.

The objective of financial reporting is to provide decision-useful information. Information is 'decision-useful' if users can base their decisions on it, which means that they must be able to use the information to predict the future cash flows of the entity as well as to assess the risks attached to these cash flows. The most important group of users of financial information is current and potential future investors

2. The reporting entity

Definition

What is 'the reporting entity'?

In March 2010, the IASB released an exposure draft titled *Exposure Draft ED/2010/2 Conceptual Framework for Financial Reporting – The Reporting Entity.* This is a joint project between the IASB and the American accounting standard-setting body, the Financial Accounting Standards Board. The two boards are in the process of determining what constitutes a 'reporting entity' in the context of general purpose financial statements.

This is an extract relating to the description of a reporting entity from that exposure draft:

> *'A reporting entity is a circumscribed area of economic activities whose financial information has the potential to be useful to existing and potential equity investors, lenders and other creditors who cannot directly obtain the information they need in making decisions about providing resources to the entity and in assessing whether the management and the governing board of that entity have made efficient and effective use of the resources provided.'*

2.1 A look at the reporting entity

We will adopt the description given above and describe a **reporting entity** as a separate business operation (circumscribed area of economic activities) with the following characteristics:

- Its economic activities can be objectively distinguished from other entities.
- It needs to provide financial information about its economic activities that has the potential to be useful to investors, lenders and other creditors in making decisions

about the effective and efficient use of the resources provided to that entity by its owners and lenders.

This means that a reporting entity is not limited by legal boundaries, but rather by the characteristics outlined above. For example, consider an entity, A Ltd, that manufactures and sells goods:

- A Ltd's manufacturing and retailing operations occur in the single legal structure that is A Ltd. Thus, A Ltd is a reporting entity.
- A Ltd is a single legal entity, but its manufacturing operations and its retailing operations occur in two separate divisions. Thus, A Ltd, the manufacturing division and the retailing division are all reporting entities.
- A Ltd is a single entity. Its manufacturing operations and its retailing operations occur in two separate divisions. In addition, each retailing operation occurs through a number of branches. Thus, A Ltd, the manufacturing division, the retailing division and the branches are all reporting entities.

In the three scenarios above, we identified a number of reporting entities. The divisions or branches may prepare their own financial statements; these are likely to be used internally by divisional management for reporting to the head office. The financial statements could also be useful if a third party wanted to buy a division. In reality, however, the financial statements of the reporting entity that will be most useful to a broad range of users are A Ltd's financial statements. These are likely to be closest to what we consider general purpose financial statements. They reflect the economic reality of A Ltd's operations and the related risks, irrespective of how the entity is structured (legally or internally). In this case, the legal boundary (A Ltd as a separate entity) and the reporting boundary that may be most useful (A Ltd as a reporting entity) are the same.

Will this always be the case? What would happen if A Ltd's operations were structured such that A Ltd, which is a retailer, also sets up and acquires all of the equity of another entity, B Ltd, which manufactures the inventory that is sold by A Ltd? The legal boundaries have now been drawn up differently. A Ltd and B Ltd are both legal entities, and they are both reporting entities. The economic reality, however, is that A Ltd is directly and indirectly exposed to the risks associated with manufacturing and retailing as it owns all of the equity of B Ltd. The risks relating to manufacturing and retailing impact on the resources of A Ltd as well as on the claims against those resources. Users of A Ltd's financial statements have to understand this economic reality if the information in the financial statements is going to be useful. In this case, the legal boundaries and the reporting boundary that may be most useful are not the same.

In the scenario above, IFRS terms A Ltd the '**parent**' entity and B Ltd the '**subsidiary**'. You will learn more about what these terms mean and their implications for financial reporting as you progress through this publication. For now, think about them much like you would think of a family. We could consider each member of the family as an individual, but it makes more sense to look at the whole family in order to get a feeling for the family dynamics when planning for the future, budgeting and so on.

For the purposes of financial reporting, the family is known as a **group**, which comprises a parent entity and its subsidiaries. As with any family, there are the extended family members. You will learn more about them as you go along as well. For now, focus on the parent and the subsidiary. IFRS requires the parent (in this case, A Ltd), with limited exceptions, to prepare consolidated (or group) financial statements.

We will use the terms 'group' and 'consolidated' interchangeably. These are financial statements that combine the assets, liabilities, income, expenses and cash flows of the parent (A Ltd, in our scenario above) and its subsidiary (B Ltd, in our scenario above) into one single economic entity. In this case, that entity is the A Ltd group. We have now added another reporting entity to our list: the group. The group financial statements will reflect the financial position, performance and cash flows of the group as a single economic entity (irrespective of the fact that the group may comprise different legal entities). The group will recognise the assets, liabilities, income, expenses and cash flows that meet the definitions and recognition criteria in accordance with the Conceptual Framework and the specific IFRSs that pertain to the situation in question.

2.2   The reporting entity in context

Consider the following real-life example: Truworths is a fashion retail group, with Truworths International Ltd ('Truworths') being the parent entity. The annual report for the financial year ended 30 June 2013 described the entity as follows: 'Truworths International Ltd is an investment holding and management company ... Its principal trading entities, Truworths Ltd and YoungDesigners Emporium (Pty) Ltd, are engaged either directly or through agencies, franchises or subsidiaries, in the retailing of fashion apparel and related merchandise' (Truworths, 2013). The group comprises Truworths International Ltd as a parent entity and various subsidiaries, including Truworth Ltd and YoungDesigners Emporium (Pty) Ltd.

When we look at the annual financial statements of Truworths, we see that it presents company (or separate) financial statements as well as group financial statements. Refer to the group statements of financial position that follows.

Figure 1.1 Group statements of financial position

Group Statements of Financial Position

	Note	at 30 June 2013 Rm	at 1 July 2012 Rm
ASSETS			
Non-current assets		1 280	1 197
Property, plant and equipment	2	857	775
Goodwill	3	90	90
Intangible assets	4	103	94
Derivative financial assets	5	19	34
Available-for-sale assets	6	4	3
Loans and receivables	7	118	143
Deferred tax	16	89	58
Current assets		5 991	5 720
Inventories	9	787	670
Trade and other receivables	10	3 766	3 421
Derivative financial assets	5	42	7
Prepayments		71	62
Cash and cash equivalents	11	1 325	1 560
Total assets		7 271	6 917
EQUITY AND LIABILITIES			
Total equity		6 219	5 981
Share capital and premium	12,13	293	205
Treasury shares	14	(2 028)	(1 274)
Retained earnings		7 825	6 944
Non-distributable reserves	15	129	106
Non-current liabilities		97	97
Post-retirement medical benefit obligation	17.1	53	47
Cash-settled compensation obligation	26.6.2	8	12
Straight-line operating lease obligation	18.1	36	38
Current liabilities		955	839
Trade and other payables	19	719	598
Provisions	20	71	73
Tax payable		165	168
Total liabilities		1 052	936
Total equity and liabilities		7 271	6 917

Source: Truworths International. Annual Financial Statements 2013. [Online], Available: https://www.truworths.co.za/assets/investor/2013/Truworths_2013_AFS.pdf Accessed 9 June 2014.

A quick glance at the group statement of financial position shows the line items that we would expect from a fashion retailer (for example, inventory and trade receivables). This information is useful as it gives an indication of the future cash flows and associated risks of an entity that sells fashion. This reflects the economic reality even though Truworths International Ltd is not the trading entity (retailing occurs through Truworths Ltd and YoungDesigners Emporium (Pty) Ltd. If you invested in Truworths International

Ltd, you would mostly be exposed to the risks associated with fashion not selling and customers not paying.

How do the statements of financial position presented relate to the description of the nature of the Truworths provided in its annual report? It is described as 'an investment holding and management company'. There are no investment balances relating to investments in the equity of other entities in the group statement financial position. Legally, the group owns investments in the subsidiary companies listed below.

Figure 1.2 Details of subsidiary companies

DETAILS OF SUBSIDIARY COMPANIES

Name	Main business	Ordinary share capital and premium		Percentage held (effective interest)		Book value of shares		Amounts owing to subsidiaries (refer to note 8 in company annual financial statements)	
		2013	2012	2013 %	2012 %	2013 Rm	2012 Rm	2013 Rm	2012 Rm
Direct subsidiary companies									
All (Pty) Ltd companies unless otherwise stated									
Incorporated in South Africa									
Truworths Ltd	R	R23 883 152	R23 883 152	100	100	37 806	38 660	(1 076)	(1 215)
Young Designers Emporium	C	R200	R200	100	100	513	540	–	–
Uzzi	D	R100	R100	100	100	36	36	–	–
SRG International	D	R2	R2	100	100	–	–	–	–
Truworths Trading	D	R60	R60	100	100	–	–	–	–
Truworths International Limited Share Trust	E	N/A	N/A	100	100	N/A	N/A	–	–
Truworths Investments	I	R120	R120	100	100	562	585	–	–
Truworths Investments Two	I	R120	R120	100	100	464	505	–	–
Truworths Investments Three	I	R120	R120	100	100	458	491	–	–
Truworths Investments Four	I	R120	R120	100	100	493	524	–	–
Incorporated in Guernsey									
Truworths International Trust	I	N/A	N/A	100	100	N/A	N/A	–	–
Truworths Worldwide Ltd	I	US$5 386 039	US$5 386 039	100	100	–	–	–	–

C = Commission agent, D = Dormant, E = Employee share scheme, I = Investment holding, R = Retailing

Source: Truworths International. Annual Financial Statements 2013. [Online], Available: https://www.truworths.co.za/assets/investor/2013/Truworths_2013_AFS.pdf Accessed 9 June 2014.

The carrying amount of these investments is presented in the separate statements of financial position of Truworths International Ltd, as shown on the next page.

Figure 1.3 Company statements of financial position

Company Statements of Financial Position

	Note	at 30 June 2013 R'000	at 1 July 2012 R'000
ASSETS			
Non-current assets			
Available-for-sale assets	2	40 332 041	41 341 234
Current assets		7 182	6 902
Prepayments		12	–
Tax receivable		110	135
Cash and cash equivalents	3	7 060	6 767
Total assets		40 339 223	41 348 136
EQUITY AND LIABILITIES			
Total equity		39 256 773	40 127 573
Share capital and premium	4,5	292 824	204 762
Retained earnings		97 717	47 386
Non-distributable reserves	6	38 866 232	39 875 425
Current liabilities			
Trade and other payables	8	1 082 450	1 220 563
Total equity and liabilities		40 339 223	41 348 136

Source: Truworths International. Annual Financial Statements 2013. [Online], Available: https://www.truworths.co.za/assets/investor/2013/Truworths_2013_AFS.pdf Accessed 9 June 2014.

Note 2 to the company statements of financial position shows that the non-current assets comprise the investments in subsidiaries. Note that it is referred to as 'available-for-sale assets' in accordance with IAS39, *Financial Instruments: Recognition and Measurement* (refer to 4.1 below).

Figure 1.4 Note to the company financial statements

Notes to the Company Annual Financial Statements

	2013 R'000	2012 R'000
2. **Available-for-sale assets**		
Shares in Truworths Ltd	37 805 873	38 659 562
Shares in Young Designers Emporium (Pty) Ltd	513 231	540 399
Shares in Uzzi (Pty) Ltd	35 918	35 918
Shares in Truworths Investments (Pty) Ltd	561 711	584 923
Shares in Truworths Investments Two (Pty) Ltd	463 983	504 995
Shares in Truworths Investments Three (Pty) Ltd	458 361	490 969
Shares in Truworths Investments Four (Pty) Ltd	492 964	524 468
Total	40 332 041	41 341 234

A detailed listing of all subsidiaries is contained in Annexure One.

During the period the value of the investments in subsidiaries decreased as a result of the Truworths International Ltd share price decreasing from R89.52 at 1 July 2012 to R86.95 at 30 June 2013.

Source: Truworths International. Annual Financial Statements 2013. [Online], Available: https://www.truworths.co.za/assets/investor/2013/Truworths_2013_AFS.pdf Accessed 9 June 2014.

The group statements of financial position reflect the economic entity, that is, one that is 'engaged either directly or through agencies, franchises or subsidiaries, in the retailing of fashion apparel and related merchandise.' The separate (company) statement of financial position largely reflects the legal nature of the entity, that is, 'an investment holding and management company'.

2.3 A comparison of the group and separate financial statements

Take a look at the line items presented by Truworths International Ltd. What do you notice? The group and separate statement of financial position are similar in that they reflect the assets, liabilities and equity of that reporting entity. This is important; if a reporting entity prepares a set of IFRS-compliant financial statements, the recognition and measurement criteria applying to the elements in the Conceptual Framework and/ or specific standards still apply. At the same time, however, the group and separate statement of financial position differ in terms of the types of assets and liabilities that are presented.

Each set of financial statements (the group statements and the separate financial statements) is useful to users. The separate financial statements of the parent may be useful if the investments in other entities are evaluated and considered on a fair value basis. In that instance, the legal boundaries of the group entities are important. In fact, under certain circumstances, IFRS terms these parent entities as 'investment entities' and does not require them to prepare group financial statements as reflecting investments at fair value reflects the economic reality. (Investment entities are explained in Chapter 2.) In other instances, it may be important to know the amount of dividends that could legally be distributed by the parent, so its unconsolidated profits are important.

The group and the separate and individual financial statements of the parent and its subsidiaries are therefore both important. The issue is which financial statements would most appropriately serve the needs of the broadest range of users.

You would already have considered the separate and individual financial statements of a parent or subsidiary when you dealt with the general purpose financial statements of a single legal entity. This publication focuses on the preparation and presentation of group financial statements.

Your understanding of the general purpose financial statements of a single legal entity is important. These individual entities are reporting entities. Legally, in most cases, they are required to prepare financial statements. So these financial statements are an existing source of financial information for these entities.

Where these entities are part of a group, this existing source of financial information is powerful. We can use the separate financial statements of the parent and the individual financial statements of its subsidiaries as a basis for the preparation of the single set of financial statements of the group. This publication will guide you through that process, which is referred to as the process of consolidation. This process involves preparing a group set of financial statements by using the individual and separate financial statements of the parent and its subsidiaries. In some instances, you may need to make adjustments to existing financial information. We will guide you through these adjustments in the chapters that follow.

3. Group financial statements

Group (or consolidated) financial statements are the financial statements of a parent and all of its subsidiaries presented as those of a single economic entity. They comprise a complete set of financial statements: the statement of financial position, the statement of profit or loss and other comprehensive income, the statement of cash flows and the statement of changes in equity as well as all of the related notes and comparatives.

The group financial statements reflect the assets, liabilities and equity of the group, irrespective of how the group is structured legally. The assets are resources that are controlled by the group and the liabilities are claims against the group's resources. The implication is that the elements recognised in the group financial statements must meet the definition and recognition criteria as normal in accordance with the Conceptual Framework and the applicable IFRSs. These elements will be measured and accounted for using the principles that you dealt with when learning to prepare financial statements for a single entity.

3.1 Subsidiaries

When we speak of a 'group', we are referring to the parent and all of its subsidiaries. Consequently, it is important to be able to identify a subsidiary. A subsidiary is an entity that is controlled by the parent. According to Section 3(1)(a) of the Companies Act, No.71 of 2008, a subsidiary can be defined as a company in which a juristic person 'directly or indirectly (is) able to control the exercise of the majority of the general voting rights associated with the issued securities of that company' or 'has the right to appoint or elect or control the appointment or election of directors of that company who control the majority of the votes at a meeting of a board.' IFRS has a similar but broader definition of **control**. You will learn more on this topic in Chapter 3.

Group financial statements are prepared by consolidating investments in subsidiaries. Consolidation is the process of combining 100% of the assets, liabilities, income and expenses of the parent as well as of all of its subsidiaries (irrespective of how much of the equity of a subsidiary the parent holds).

From this, it is clear that control exists even if the parent does not own all of the equity of the subsidiary. This equity is still consolidated in the parent's group financial statements, but is attributed to the **non-controlling interest**. The recognition and measurement of non-controlling interest is discussed in more detail in Chapter 7.

3.2 Associates, joint ventures and the equity method

Not all entities are controlled. In some instances, the investor owns shares in another entity over which it does not have control, but is able to exert more influence than, for example, an investor that buys some but not all of the shares in another entity (the investee). Carrying these investments at cost or fair value may not reflect the nature of the investor's interest or its ability to exert influence appropriately.

If the investor is able to exert significant influence over the investee, the investee is an associate.

In some instances, an investor may have control in the equity of another entity jointly with another party. These investees are generally referred to as joint ventures.

The investor, the associate and the joint venture are all possible reporting entities. For investments in associates and joint ventures, however, the investor does not control the associate or joint venture. The investor's group financial statements will therefore not reflect the assets and liabilities of the associate or the joint venture.

The investor has an asset: its investment in the associate or the joint venture. The investor is an owner that shares in the equity of that associate or joint venture. IFRS requires these investments to be accounted for on the **equity method** in the investor's group financial statements. The equity method results in the investment in the associate or the joint venture initially being recognised at cost and subsequently being adjusted by the investor's share in the changes in the associate or the joint venture's profit or loss and other comprehensive income. This approach results in an investment that is not carried at cost or at fair value, but on the equity method. You will learn more about associates, joint ventures and the equity method in Chapter 9.

3.3 IFRS requirements for group financial statements

Several IFRSs govern the preparation of group financial statements. The IASB issued IFRS10, *Consolidated Financial Statements*, in 2011, with its objective being 'to establish principles for the presentation and preparation of consolidated financial statements when an entity controls one or more other entities' (refer to paragraph 1 of IFRS10). In order to achieve this, IFRS10 requires a parent entity to present consolidated financial statements. IFRS10 establishes a single control model that applies to all entities and includes a new definition of control. The changes introduced by IFRS10 require management to exercise significant judgement to determine which entities are controlled and are therefore required to be consolidated by the parent.

Previously, the preparation of consolidated financial statements formed part of IAS27, *Separate Financial Statements* (amended in 2011). However, the issue of IFRS10 resulted in the revision of IAS27, which now only deals with the preparation of the separate financial statements of the investor. IAS27 outlines the accounting and disclosure requirements for the separate financial statements that are prepared by the investor (a parent company of a subsidiary, or an investor in a joint venture or an associate). This standard also outlines the accounting requirements for dividends and contains numerous disclosure requirements. The requirements for the preparation of separate financial statements are discussed in more detail in Section 4 of this chapter.

Although IFRS10 provides information on the preparation of consolidated financial statements, IFRS3, *Business Combinations*, provides guidance for the measurement of the underlying net assets of the acquiree and goodwill, if any, at the acquisition date. IFRS3 requires that in order for a business combination to occur, there has to be an economic transaction between two entities in which the control of a business is transferred from one business to another. The purpose of defining a business is to distinguish between the acquisition of a group of assets that does not constitute a business (such as a number of vehicles) and the acquisition of a business. For a group of assets to constitute a business, these assets must be capable of providing a return. Goodwill can only be recognised when assets are acquired as part of a business.

The required method of accounting for a business combination is the acquisition method (refer to paragraph 4 of IFRS3). The following four steps are required:
- Identify the acquirer.
- Determine the acquisition date.
- Recognise and measure the identifiable assets acquired, the liabilities assumed and any non-controlling interest in the acquiree.
- Recognise and measure goodwill or a gain from a bargain purchase.

Refer to Section 5 of Chapter 2 for a more detailed discussion of these steps.

The acquisition method is applied on the acquisition date, which is the date at which the acquirer obtains control of the acquiree. On this date, the business combination occurs. IFRS3 also outlines the requirements for the subsequent measurement and accounting of assets and liabilities recognised initially at acquisition date. There are many forms of business combinations. For example, A Ltd can acquire the net assets of B Ltd or A Ltd acquires the shares (and a controlling interest) in B Ltd. In this publication, the focus is on the acquisition of shares and a controlling interest in another entity, where both entities prepare separate financial statements and group financial statements are required.

IAS28, *Investments in Associates and Joint Ventures*, was issued by the IASB in 2011. This standard mainly deals with the nature of associates and joint ventures, and sets out how they are accounted for in group financial statements. The key characteristic determining the existence of an associate is that of significant influence (refer to the definitions in the next section). An investment where the investor is involved in a contractually agreed sharing of control is where the investor has joint control over the investee. This investee is referred to as a joint venture. The method of accounting used to account for an investor's interest in an associate or a joint venture is the equity method of accounting. Thus, when group financial statements are prepared, investments in associates and joint ventures are recognised using the equity method. The equity method is designed to provide more information about an investment than is generally supplied under the cost method, but less information than is supplied under the consolidation method. Interest in associates and joint ventures is discussed in detail in Chapter 9 of this publication.

The accounting for joint arrangements is covered by IFRS11, *Joint Arrangements*, which was also issued in 2011. The term 'joint arrangement' describes an activity, an operation or a specific grouping of assets and liabilities that may or may not form a legal entity (such as a company). A joint arrangement arises where two or more entities have an arrangement with each other such that these entities have joint control of the arrangement. The accounting for a joint operation is different from that of a joint venture. Where a joint operation is undertaken outside a formal structure, it is usually expected that the joint operation agreement requires separate accounting records to be kept for accountability reasons. Refer to Chapter 10 for a detailed discussion of identifying a joint arrangement and its accounting requirements.

The different requirements in terms of IFRSs for the recognition of business entities within group financial statements depend on the level of control or influence that the acquirer acquired in the acquiree. Table 1.1 is a summary of these requirements.

Table 1.1 IFRS requirements for the recognition of business entities within group financial statements

Type of influence	Acquirer	Nature of acquiree	Accounting basis	IFRS
Control	Parent company	Subsidiary	Consolidation	IFRS10
Joint control	Venturer	Joint venture	Equity method	IAS28
Significant influence	Investor	Associate	Equity method	IAS28
No significant influence[1]	Investor	Investee	Fair value	IAS32, IAS39 and IFRS9

[1] When an investor does not have any control or significant influence, the investment is classified as a financial asset. Investments in financial assets are not dealt with in this publication. Refer to Chapter 8 of Financial Accounting: IFRS Principles (2014) by Lubbe et al. for a detailed discussion of financial instruments.

IFRS12, *Disclosure of Interests in Other Entities,* issued in 2011, applies to an entity that has an interest in subsidiaries, joint arrangements, associates and/or structured entities. This standard replaces the disclosure requirements that were previously included in earlier versions of IAS27, IAS28 and IAS31. The revised IAS27, *Separate Financial Statements,* only sets out the disclosures required in the separate financial statements. The key objective of IFRS12 is to require an entity to disclose information that enables users of its financial information to evaluate the following:

- The nature of its interest in other entities and the risks associated with this interest
- The effects of those interests on its financial position, financial performance and cash flow (refer to IFRS12, paragraph 1).

The intention of these extended disclosure requirements is to assist users in making their own assessment of the financial impact if management were to reach a different conclusion regarding consolidation and to assist the users of financial statements in evaluating risks.

Some of the more extensive qualitative and quantitative disclosures in IFRS 12 include the following:

- Significant judgements used by management in determining control, joint control and significant influence, and the type of joint arrangement (that is, joint operation or joint venture), if applicable
- Summarised financial information for each of its subsidiaries that have non-controlling interest that are material to the reporting entity
- Summarised financial information for each individually material joint venture and associate
- The nature of the risks associated with an entity's interest in unconsolidated structured entities.

An entity is therefore required to disclose the significant judgements and assumptions that it has made in determining the nature of its interest in another entity, and in particular any judgements, assumptions and changes in these in relation to subsidiaries. The disclosure requirements are discussed within each section of this publication.

Figure 1.5 on the next page illustrates the interaction between the various IFRSs that you will encounter in this publication as you prepare group financial statements.

Figure 1.5 Illustration of the interaction between the various IFRSs

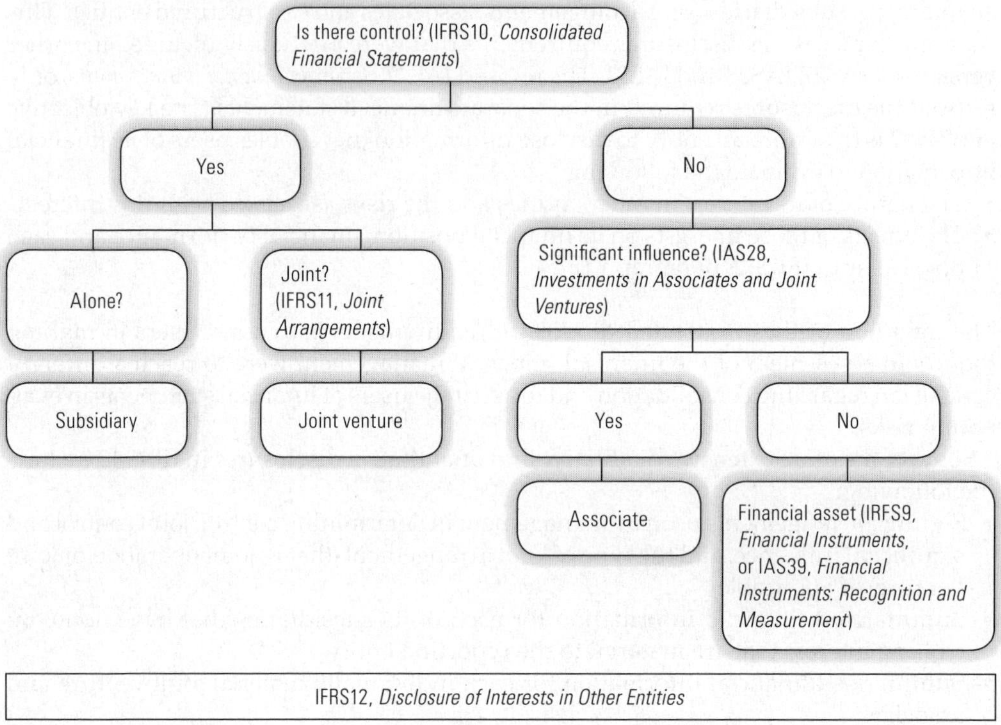

Is there control? (IFRS10, *Consolidated Financial Statements*)

Yes — No

Alone? | Joint? (IFRS11, *Joint Arrangements*) | Significant influence? (IAS28, *Investments in Associates and Joint Ventures*)

Subsidiary | Joint venture | Yes — No

Associate | Financial asset (IRFS9, *Financial Instruments*, or IAS39, *Financial Instruments: Recognition and Measurement*)

IFRS12, *Disclosure of Interests in Other Entities*

4. Recognising investments in the separate financial statements of the investor

An investor that is a parent entity or that owns investments in associates or joint ventures may choose to present separate financial statements. These are also known as company financial statements, as we saw in the example of Truworths earlier; the company is the legal reporting entity and not the economic entity, which is the group.

These separate financial statements are in addition to the parent's group financial statements. The parent entity may also be required to present these separate financial statements by law. For example, the JSE Listings Requirements generally require listed entities in South Africa to present company financial statements in addition to group financial statements (see Section 8.62(d) of the JSE Listings Requirements, Service issue 17).

IAS27, *Separate Financial Statements*, is the IFRS that deals with the parent entity's separate financial statements. IAS27 requires that an entity preparing group financial statements also present its own set of financial statements, referred to as the 'separate financial statements'. The objective of IAS27 is to set the standards to be applied in accounting for investments in subsidiaries, joint ventures and associates when an entity elects to present separate (non-consolidated) financial statements or is required to do so by local regulations. These statements should be prepared to include all of the assets and liabilities of the investor (as a separate entity).

There are two situations in which separate financial statements are prepared:
- Where a parent prepares separate financial statements in addition to consolidated financial statements
- Where a parent is exempted from preparing consolidated financial statements (refer to paragraph 4[a] of IFRS10).

These separate financial statements reflect the legal reality of the relationship between the investor and the investee (in other words, one entity [the investor] has purchased equity in another entity [the investee] in return for future economic benefits in the form of dividends). The separate financial statements of the investor will therefore reflect the investment and related dividend income accounted for in accordance with the Conceptual Framework and the applicable IFRSs.

These separate financial statements do not reflect the economic reality as discussed in Section 2 and Section 3 of this chapter.

4.1 Choice of accounting method

An investor that prepares separate financial statements in addition to its group financial statements accounts for investments in subsidiaries, associates and joint ventures by applying one of the following measurement bases in its separate financial statements:
- The cost model
- The fair value model in accordance with one of the standards that deal with the measurement of financial instruments (there are currently two IFRSs that could apply: IAS39, *Financial Instruments: Recognition and Measurement*, and IFRS9, *Financial Instruments*, which is the standard that is replacing IAS39; IFRS9 is effective from 1 January 2018, with early adoption permitted).

Initially, the investor recognises and records its investment at cost. The following journal entry would be required if an investor acquired an investee that was a subsidiary:

Dr		Investment in subsidiary
	Cr	Bank (or liability)

4.1.1 The cost model

Under the cost model, the investor does not change the carrying amount of the investment for changes in the investment's fair value. Investments accounted for on the cost model are initially measured at cost and subsequently impaired if the recoverable amount is below its carrying amount.

4.1.2 At fair value

It is acceptable to measure the investment at **fair value** in the separate financial statements of the parent at subsequent reporting dates. This is consistent with the treatment for investments in equity instruments. The table below summarises the options available to a parent entity in respect of investments in equity instruments.

Table 1.2 Recognising investments in equity instruments at fair value

IAS39	IFRS9
The investment is measured at fair value at the reporting date and gains or losses are recognised in profit or loss.	The investment is measured at fair value at the reporting date and gains or losses are recognised in profit or loss.
Investment is measured at fair value at the reporting date and gains or losses are recognised in other comprehensive income. When the investment is impaired or sold, cumulative gains or losses recognised in other comprehensive income are reclassified to profit or loss. These investments are termed 'available for sale' in IAS39.	At initial recognition, the parent makes an irrevocable election to measure the investments at fair value at the reporting date and gains or losses are recognised in other comprehensive income.

4.2 **Dividend income**

The parent also recognises dividend income in respect of its investment when its right to receive the dividend is established. This is consistent with reflecting only the investment in its separate statement of financial position; the dividend income reflects the return generated from that asset (the investment).

Example

Recognising investments in subsidiaries in separate financial statements

P Ltd acquired 10 000 shares in S Ltd on 1 January 20x5 for a cash consideration of CU2 000 000. P Ltd has control over S Ltd from that date. P Ltd prepares separate and group financial statements. The fair value of the investment is CU2 500 000 at 31 December 20x5.

On 1 January 20x5, P Ltd records the following entry in its accounts:

			CU	CU
Dr		Investment in S Ltd	2 000 000	
	Cr	Bank		2 000 000

Recording investment in subsidiary at the acquisition date, paid in cash

Accounting method 1: Cost model

The investment in S Ltd will be recognised at CU2 000 000 in the statement of financial position of P Ltd at 31 December 20x5. The investment is not increased for fair value changes, but could increase if P Ltd acquired more shares in S Ltd. The investment carrying amount will be reduced when the investment no longer meets the definition of an asset because P Ltd has sold the investment or the carrying amount of the investment is impaired.

Accounting method 2: Fair value model

The investment in S Ltd will be recognised at fair value in the separate statement of financial position of P Ltd at 31 December 20x5 and at each subsequent reporting date until it is sold. Therefore, at 31 December 20x5, the investment is reflected at CU2 500 000.

At 31 December 20x5, P Ltd will record the following entry if fair value gains or losses are recognised in profit or loss:

			CU	CU
Dr		Investment in S Ltd (CU2 500 000 – CU2 000 000)	500 000	
	Cr	Fair value gain (P/L)		500 000

Recognition of investment in subsidiary at fair value and fair value adjustment recognised in profit or loss

Alternatively, if fair value gains or losses are recognised in other comprehensive income, P Ltd will record the following entry at 31 December 20x5:

			CU	CU
Dr		Investment in S Ltd (CU2 500 000 – CU2 000 000)	500 000	
	Cr	Fair value gain (OCI)		500 000

Recognition of investment in subsidiary at fair value and fair value adjustment recognised in other comprehensive income.

For additional examples and explanations on the separate financial statements of the parent, refer to Chapter 24 of *Financial Accounting: IFRS Principles* (2014) by Lubbe *et al.* In addition, Chapter 8 of that publication deals with financial instruments and Chapter 12 deals with income taxes. These three chapters are useful in revisiting aspects dealing with accounting for investments in the equity of other entities and accounting for the related tax implications.

Irrespective of which measurement basis the parent applies, the parent recognises dividend income in its separate profit or loss when its right to receive dividends has been established. For example, if S Ltd declared a dividend of CU100 000 on 31 December 20x5, of which CU80 000 is declared to P Ltd, P Ltd will record the following entry on 31 December 20x5:

			CU	CU
Dr		Dividend receivable/Bank	80 000	
	Cr	Dividend income (P/L)		80 000

Dividends receivable from subsidiary

Test your knowledge

There is a list of learning objectives at the beginning of this chapter. Go back to this list and check whether you have achieved these outcomes. If not, reread the appropriate section.

Questions

Question 1
Explain, with reference to the Conceptual Framework, why group financial statements need to be prepared.

Suggested solution
Some of the reasons why group financial statements must be prepared include the following:
- Supplying of relevant information: The information presented in the consolidated financial statements is relevant to the investors in the parent entity. Remember that the parent is the investor in the

subsidiary and that group financial information is presented to the parent equity holders. These investors have an interest in the group as a whole, not just in the parent entity.

- Comparable information: Access to consolidated financial statements makes it easier for an investor to make useful comparisons between entities. In some cases, different operations or activities are located in a different group entity and the combining of all of the relevant information into one set of group financial statements enhances the comparability of the financial information of that group entity with other entities in the same industry, who may be organising their intra-group activities in a different way.
- Accountability: The management of the parent entity is equally accountable for the use of the resources and activities that are situated within the other group entities, for example, subsidiaries. As the parent entity controls the assets of all of the subsidiaries, the assets under the control of the parent entity's management are the assets of the group. The consolidated financial statements report the assets under the control of the group management as well as the group liabilities (claims against those assets).
- Reporting of risks and benefits: Consolidated financial statements include details of all assets and liabilities within the group of entities as well as the associated risks and benefits associated with these assets. This process provides for more information than just viewing the investment in the shares of a subsidiary or investee. It allows for an assessment of the associated risks of acquiring control of another entity as well as the significant benefits arising from that control.

Case study exercises

The extracts below, which are from the financial statements of two entities, P Ltd and S Ltd, for the year ended 31 December 20x5, have been presented to you.

Statements of the financial position of P Ltd and S Ltd on 31 December 20x5

	P Ltd CU	S Ltd CU
ASSETS		
Plant and machinery (carrying amount) (cost: CU400; CU350)	300	200
Investment in S Ltd	400	–
Loan to S Ltd (issued 1 Feb 20x5)	80	–
Current assets	140	500
	920	700
CAPITAL AND LIABILITIES		
Share capital	200	100
Retained earnings	620	500
Shareholders' equity	820	600
Loan from P Ltd	–	80
Current liabilities	100	20
	920	700

Statements of profit or loss and other comprehensive income of P Ltd and S Ltd for the year ended 31 December 20x5

	P Ltd CU	S Ltd CU
Gross revenue (including dividends and interest received)	1 870	1 600
Net operating costs	(1 050)	(920)
Profit from ordinary activities before interest	820	680
Interest paid	(200)	(50)
Profit on ordinary activities before taxation	620	630
Taxation	(250)	(230)
Profit for the year	**370**	**400**

Answer the questions that follow, which relate to these two entities and their relationship. In each case, motivate your answer.

Scenario 1

P Ltd acquired 100% of the issued ordinary share capital of S Ltd on 1 January 20x5.
1. How would you describe the relationship between P Ltd and S Ltd?
2. Based on your answer above, does P Ltd have to prepare group financial statements?
3. Will P Ltd still have to prepare its own, separate financial statements?
4. Prepare the journal entries in P Ltd relating to P Ltd's investment in S Ltd.
   a. Assume that P Ltd paid CU400 for the shares, in cash, on 1 January 20x5.
   b. Assume that P Ltd paid CU300 for the shares in S Ltd on 1 January 20x5 and that the fair value of the shares was CU400 at 31 December 20x5.
5. Assume that S Ltd declared and paid a dividend of CU50 at 31 December 20x5. Prepare the journal entry in the records of P Ltd and S Ltd respectively.

Suggested solution

Scenario 1
P Ltd acquired 100% of the issued ordinary share capital of S Ltd on 1 January 20x5.
1. **How would you describe the relationship between P Ltd and S Ltd?**
    As P Ltd acquired all of the issued ordinary shares in S Ltd, P Ltd acquired the controlling interest in S Ltd. P Ltd is therefore the parent and S Ltd is its subsidiary.
2. **Based on your answer above, does P Ltd have to prepare group financial statements?**
    Yes, as P Ltd has control of S Ltd, P Ltd has to prepare group financial statements.
3. **Will P Ltd still have to prepare its own, separate financial statements?**
    Yes, P Ltd has to prepare separate financial statements in accordance with IAS27.
4. **Prepare the journal entries in P Ltd relating to P Ltd's investment in S Ltd.**
    a. Assume that P Ltd paid CU400 for the shares, in cash, on 1 January 20x5.

    Acquisition of 100% of the shares in S Ltd, for cash

			CU	CU
Dr		Investment in S Ltd	400	
	Cr	Bank		400

    Acquisition of shares in subsidiary, for cash consideration

    b. Assume P Ltd paid CU300 for the shares in S Ltd on 1 January 20x5 and the fair value of the shares was CU400 at 31 December 20x5.
    *   On the assumption that the shares are recognised at fair value of CU400 at the reporting date (as per the statement of financial position) and that fair value adjustments are recognised in profit or loss, the journal entries that follow would be required.

    Acquisition of 100% of the shares in S Ltd, for cash

			CU	CU
Dr		Investment in S Ltd	300	
	Cr	Bank		300

    Acquisition of shares in subsidiary, for cash consideration

Fair value adjustment relating to investment in subsidiary, recognised in profit or loss

			CU	CU
Dr		Investment in S Ltd	100	
	Cr	Fair value gain (P/L)		100

Measurement of investment in subsidiary at fair value at reporting date, with fair value adjustments recognised in profit or loss

- On the assumption that the shares are recognised at fair value of CU400 at the reporting date (as per the statement of financial position) and that fair value adjustments are recognised in other comprehensive income, the journal entries that follow would be required.

Acquisition of 100% of the shares in S Ltd, for cash

			CU	CU
Dr		Investment in S Ltd	300	
	Cr	Bank		300

Acquisition of shares in subsidiary, for cash consideration

Fair value adjustment relating to investment in subsidiary, recognised in other comprehensive income (OCI)

			CU	CU
Dr		Investment in S Ltd	100	
	Cr	Fair value adjustment (OCI)		100

Measurement of investment in subsidiary at fair value at reporting date, with fair value adjustments recognised in other comprehensive income

5. **Assume that S Ltd declared and paid a dividend of CU50 at 31 December 20x5. Prepare the journal entry in the records of P Ltd and S Ltd respectively.**
   - The journal entry that follows is processed in the records of P Ltd.

Dividend received from subsidiary

			CU	CU
Dr		Bank	50	
	Cr	Dividend income (P/L)		50

Dividend income received from subsidiary

- The journal entry that follows is processed in the records of S Ltd.

Dividend declared and paid

			CU	CU
Dr		Dividend declared (equity)	50	
	Cr	Bank		50

Dividend declared and paid

References

Lubbe, I., Modack, G. & Watson, A. *Financial Accounting: IFRS Principles.* (4th ed.). 2014. Cape Town: Oxford University Press.
Truworths International. 2013. Annual Financial Statements 2013. [Online], Available: https://www.truworths.co.za/assets/investor/2013/Truworths_2013_AFS.pdf Accessed 9 June 2014.

2

Business combinations and group structures

The following topics are included in this chapter:

- Description of terminology for groups
- Business combinations
- Different forms of interests and group structures.

Learning objectives

By the end of this chapter, you should be able to:
- Identify a group of entities
- State which forms of business combinations constitute a group
- Say how you would identify and determine the following:
    - The acquirer and acquiree
    - The acquisition date
    - The cost of acquisition
- Identify the value at which we have to recognise and measure the assets acquired and liabilities assumed at the acquisition date, and explain why this is the case.

1. What constitutes a group of entities?

When a separate reporting entity acquires an interest in the equity of another entity and that interest represents control, joint control or significant influence, such a combination of different entities is referred to as a **group**. An entity is part of a group if the different entities are managed in a way that takes into account the interests of the group as a combined economic entity, rather than the needs of each individual entity.

A group typically includes some or all of the following entities:
- The investor, also known as a parent (if it owns a subsidiary) and a venturer (if it owns a joint venture)
- The subsidiaries of the investor.

The investor may also have other investments, including the joint ventures of the investor and the associates of the investor.

The preparation of **group financial statements** involves the combining of financial statements of the individual entities so that they show the financial position and performance of the group of entities, presented as if they are a single economic entity.

In this chapter, we will focus on the different forms of groups as well as the identification and measurement of the net assets acquired (including goodwill) in business combinations. The required method of accounting for business combinations is the **acquisition method** (refer to IFRS3, paragraph 4). The acquirer has to consider the recognition and measurement of the identifiable assets acquired and liabilities assumed as well as goodwill (or a gain from a bargain purchase) at the acquisition date.

2. Example of a group structure

Figure 2.1 represents the structure of the Tiger Brands group of companies. Tiger Brands is listed in the retail section of the Johannesburg Stock Exchange (JSE Ltd).

Figure 2.1 Group operations and markets of Tiger Brands

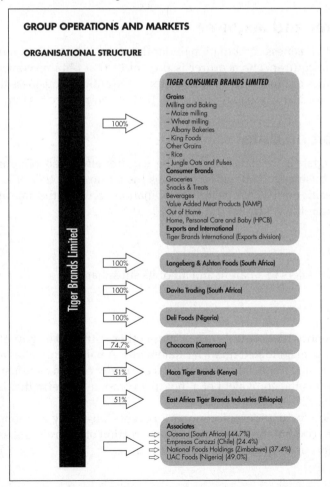

Source: Tiger Brands. 2012. Integrated Report. [Online], Available: http://financialresults.co.za/2012/tiger_ar2012/downloads.php Accessed 15 January 2014.

3. Definitions and descriptions

In order to understand the terminology used in group financial statements, the consolidation process and the equity method, you need to understand certain terms, which are explained below. Most of these terms are included as definitions in the various IFRSs, as discussed in Chapter 1.

3.1 Business and business combination

The term 'business' is defined as an integrated set of activities and assets conducted and managed for the purpose of providing a return to the acquirer. A business combination is the bringing together of separate entities or businesses into one reporting entity (refer to IFRS3, *Business Combinations*). In order for a business combination to occur, there has to be an economic transaction between two entities in which the control of a business is transferred from one business to another. A business combination is accounted for using the acquisition method.

3.2 Acquirer and acquiree

Accounting for a business combination under the acquisition method requires the identification of an acquirer. The acquirer is the entity that obtains control of the other combining entities or businesses. The acquiree is the entity or business that is acquired. A key criterion for identifying an acquirer is that of control (see Section 3.7 below).

3.3 Acquisition date

The acquisition date is the date on which the acquirer effectively obtains control of the acquiree. As a business combination involves the joining together of assets under the control of a specific entity, the business combination occurs at the date at which the net assets come under the control of the acquirer.

3.4 Group

The term 'group' refers to a parent and all of its subsidiaries.

3.5 Parent

A parent is an entity that controls one or more other entities. The parent is responsible for preparing the consolidated financial statements. A parent entity has an obligation to produce consolidated financial statements, except under certain circumstances and conditions. A parent is the equivalent of a 'holding company' (a term that is often used in some jurisdictions).

As the criterion for the identification of a parent–subsidiary relationship is control, when a business combination is formed by the creation of a parent–subsidiary relationship, the parent is usually identified as the acquirer.

3.6 **Subsidiary**

A subsidiary is an entity that is controlled by another entity. (The term 'control' is discussed in Section 3.7 below.) A subsidiary can be any type of business entity, whether it is an incorporated entity, such as a company, or an unincorporated entity, such as a partnership. (For easy reference, this publication refers to a subsidiary as a company.)

3.6.1 Wholly owned subsidiary

A wholly owned subsidiary is one in which an acquirer owns 100% of the shares, either directly or indirectly, through other subsidiaries. There are therefore no non-controlling shareholders.

3.6.2 Partly owned subsidiary

A partly owned subsidiary is one in which the parent, together with other subsidiaries, does not own all of the shares. The definition of a subsidiary requires ownership of sufficient shares to control the decision-making. In most cases, any shareholding of more than 50% constitutes control, and therefore a subsidiary–parent relationship and consolidation. Any entity that is a subsidiary but is not wholly owned is a partly owned (also known as partially held) subsidiary and will give rise to a non-controlling interest (refer to Section 3.9).

3.7 **Control (power and rights)**

As mentioned above, a parent is an entity that controls one or more entities, while a subsidiary is a controlled entity. An entity must thus determine when it is a parent and which entities it controls. The criterion for consolidation is **control** (refer to IFRS10) and the determination of whether control exists is a matter of judgement. IFRS10 provides numerous factors to be considered in making the decision concerning the existence of control. You need to consider all of the available facts and circumstances in order to determine whether control exists or not. For this, you need to understand the meaning of the term 'control' and the evidence that you need to accumulate in order to determine the existence or non-existence of control in specific circumstances. Then, if those circumstances change, you need to assess whether control still exists.

Definition

What is control?

Appendix A of IFRS10 defines the control of an investee as 'when the investor is exposed, or has rights, to variable returns from its involvement with the investee and has the ability to affect those returns through its power over the investee.'

Control is the power that an investor has over an investee to receive variable returns from its involvement with the investee from its exposure to, or rights, to receive those returns. As a guideline, control exists when an investor has all of the following three elements (refer to paragraph 7 of IFRS10):

- Power over the investee
- Exposure, or rights, to variable returns from its involvement with the investee

- The ability to use its power over the investee to affect the amount of the investor's returns.

Note that control is an exclusionary power. This means that in a group, there can only be one parent. If two or more investors can control an investee by joining together to direct the activities of the investee, neither investor controls the investee, as the decision-making ability is shared.

Control as the criterion for consolidation is discussed further in Chapter 3.

3.8 Consolidated financial statements

Consolidation is the process of combining 100% of the assets, liabilities, income and expenses of the parent as well as the assets, liabilities, income and expenses of all of its subsidiaries (including partly owned subsidiaries) and making adjustments necessary to remove the effect of any pre-acquisition and inter-company transactions. The consolidated financial statements should reflect non-controlling interest unless all subsidiaries are wholly owned.

A parent need not present consolidated financial statements if it meets all of the following conditions (refer to IFRS10):

- It is a wholly owned subsidiary or it is a partially owned subsidiary of another entity and all of its other owners, including those not otherwise entitled to vote, have been informed about and do not object to the parent not presenting consolidated financial statements.
- Its debt or equity instruments are not traded in a public market (for example, a domestic or foreign stock exchange) or an over-the-counter market, including local and regional markets.
- It has not filed, nor is it in the process of filing, its financial statements with a securities commission or other regulatory organisation for the purpose of issuing any class of instruments in a public market.
- Its ultimate or any intermediate parent produces consolidated financial statements that are in accordance with IFRS and are available for public use.

3.9 Non-controlling interest

Non-controlling interest is the equity in a subsidiary that is not attributable, directly or indirectly, to the parent. It is that portion of the profit or loss and net assets of a subsidiary that is attributable to equity interests that are not owned, directly or indirectly through subsidiaries, by the parent.

The non-controlling interest (also referred to as the 'outside shareholders' interest' or 'minority interest') is identified at the acquisition date and is the portion of the fair value of the net assets of the subsidiary at the date of acquisition that is not held by the parent. The non-controlling interest also includes their interest in the post-acquisition reserves of the subsidiary earned after the date at which it first became a subsidiary. The result is that the total non-controlling interest is the sum of their interest in the fair value of the net assets at the acquisition date and their share of the increase in the net assets (equity) since the date of acquisition. The total represents the non-controlling interest in the net assets of the subsidiary at the reporting date.

The recognition and measurement of non-controlling interest is discussed further in Chapter 7.

3.10 Associates and joint ventures

An associate is defined as an entity over which the investor has significant influence (refer to IAS28). The key characteristic determining the existence of an associate is that of **significant influence**, which is described as the power to participate in the financial and operating policy decisions of the investee, but is not control or only has joint control of those policies. For example, if an investor holds a 30% interest in an investee, this investment allows the investor to exert significant influence in the financial and operating policy decisions of the investee. However, it does not constitute control.

A **joint arrangement** is an arrangement between two or more entities whereby two or more entities have **joint control** of another entity. Thus a key feature of this relationship is that of joint control. For example, two entities each hold 50% of the shares of a third entity, resulting in joint control over the third entity. Joint control is described as the contractually agreed sharing of control of an arrangement, which exists only when decisions about the relevant activities require the unanimous consent of all of the parties that share the control.

Where a joint arrangement exists, the arrangement can either be classified as a joint operation or as a joint venture, depending on the rights and obligations of the parties to the arrangements (refer to IFRS11). A joint venture is an arrangement where the investor has a right to an investment in the investee. In this case, the legal form of the investee and the contractual arrangements are such that the investor does not have rights to the assets and obligations for the liabilities of the investee. Thus, the investee has been designed to trade on its own (and is able to do so). As such, it must face the risks arising from the activities that it undertakes (for example, credit risks) directly.

A **joint operation**, on the other hand, is not structured through a separate vehicle (or separate legal entity). It is an arrangement in which the parties that have joint control have rights to the assets and obligations for the liabilities relating to the arrangement. These parties are called joint operators.

3.11 Equity method

The equity method is a method whereby the investment in an investee is initially recognised at cost and adjusted thereafter for the investor's share of the post-acquisition equity of the investee. The post-acquisition equity includes movements in profit or loss as well as in other comprehensive income of the investee. The equity method of accounting is used to account for an investor's interest in an associate or a joint venture.

Investments in associates and joint ventures, and the equity method, are discussed in Chapter 9 and Chapter 10.

3.12 Investment entities

An investment entity is an entity whose business purpose is to make investments for capital appreciation or investment income, or both. An investment entity also evaluates the performance of those investments on a fair value basis. The concept of an investment entity is included in an amendment to IFRS10, which defines an investment entity as an entity that:

- Obtains funds from one or more investors for the purpose of providing those investor(s) with investment management services
- Commits to its investor(s) that its business purpose is to invest funds solely for returns from capital appreciation or investment income, or both
- Measures and evaluates the performance of substantially all of its investments on a fair value basis.

You are required to consider all of the facts, evidence and circumstances when determining whether an entity should be identified as an investment entity. For example, you must consider its purpose and design (think about an entity that makes investments in other entities on behalf of its clients, such as mutual funds). These entities typically have the following characteristics:

- They have more than one investment.
- They have more than one investor.
- They have investors that are not related to the entity or other members of the group containing the entity.
- They have ownership interests, typically in the form of equity or similar interests (for example, equity funds), to which proportionate shares of the net assets of the investment entity are attributed.

However, the absence of any of these typical characteristics does not necessarily disqualify an entity from being classified as an investment entity.

Investment entities are prohibited from consolidating particular subsidiaries. Where an entity meets the definition of an investment entity, it does not consolidate its subsidiaries or apply IFRS3, *Business Combinations,* when it obtains control of another entity. Instead, an investment entity is required to measure its investments (ownership interests in entities controlled) at fair value through profit or loss (in accordance with IFRS9, *Financial Instruments*). Therefore it is not an option but a requirement that where an entity qualifies as an 'investment entity', it does not consolidate all of its subsidiaries, but measures its investments at fair value.

In its separate financial statements, an investment entity is required to recognise its investments in subsidiaries in the same way. Because an investment entity is not required to consolidate its subsidiaries, intra-group related party transactions and outstanding balances are not eliminated.

 Think about it

Why is it not appropriate for an investment entity to prepare group financial statements?

An investment entity acquired its interest in another entity with the main purpose of receiving dividend income and benefitting from increases in its fair value. It is not the intention of the investment entity to acquire a controlling interest in the operations and activities of the other entity.

Reporting information about the fair value of its investment in a subsidiary is more relevant than consolidation of its individual assets and liabilities.

Note that an investment entity is still required to consolidate a subsidiary where that subsidiary provides services that relate to the investment entity's investment activities. Special requirements apply where an entity becomes an investment entity or ceases to be one (refer to IFRS10).

The exemption from consolidation only applies to the investment entity itself. Accordingly, the parent of an investment entity is required to consolidate all entities that it controls, including entities controlled through an investment entity subsidiary, unless the parent itself is an investment entity.

4. Business combinations and groups

For group financial statements to be prepared, there must be an acquirer who has acquired an interest in the form of shares in another entity, the acquiree. The **investment in the shares** in the acquiree as well as the power and rights that are associated with this investment (for example, controlling voting rights) determine the level of control that exists as well as the appropriate form of group reporting. The most common form of group reporting is the preparation of consolidated financial statements, when a controlling interest is acquired in another entity. Consolidated financial statements represent the 'adding together' of the financial statements of all of the entities within a group by adding together the assets and liabilities of all of these entities.

There is often criticism of the usefulness of presenting consolidated financial information, and the undue cost and effort required when preparing group financial statements. People who support this view often state that a similar measurement of the value of the net assets of the controlling entity can be obtained when the investment in the shares is measured at fair value. There is some merit in this argument in cases where the fair value of an investment would approximate the fair value of the underlying assets and liabilities plus goodwill that are acquired. However, a presentation of this nature would exclude the different classifications of underlying assets and liabilities that are controlled by the group, whether they are current or non-current, and the expected cash flows from these assets. The process of consolidation, which requires the underlying assets and liabilities of the controlled interests to be added together, provides this information.

4.1. Identifying different forms of groups

The primary purpose of a business is to create shareholder wealth. In order to do this, an entity must expand and grow its business. The entity purchases assets that will result in an increase of future economic benefits that will flow to it, thus enabling the entity to continue growing and expanding.

For example, if an entity wants to obtain control of a vehicle with the aim of securing the future economic benefits relating to that vehicle, it can obtain that control in a number of ways. It could purchase the vehicle directly, hire the vehicle under a long-term finance lease or purchase a business that owns the vehicle.

4.2 Different forms of business combinations and groups

The combination of separate businesses or entities requires 'joining' the assets and liabilities of the acquirer with those acquired from the acquiree. The following general forms of business combinations may occur:

a. A Ltd acquires all of the assets and liabilities of B Ltd, with B Ltd liquidating
b. C Ltd is formed to acquire all of the assets and liabilities of A Ltd and B Ltd, with A Ltd and B Ltd liquidating
c. A Ltd acquires all of the assets and liabilities of B Ltd in exchange for shares in A Ltd, with B Ltd continuing as a company, holding shares in A Ltd
d. A Ltd acquires all of the shares in B Ltd, with B Ltd being a subsidiary of A Ltd
e. A Ltd acquires the majority of the shares (and voting rights) in B Ltd, with B Ltd being a subsidiary of A Ltd
f. A Ltd acquires some of the shares in B Ltd; the number of shares acquired enables A Ltd to exert significant influence over B Ltd, with B Ltd being an associate of A Ltd
g. A Ltd acquires joint control over B Ltd with C Ltd, with B Ltd being a joint venture of A Ltd.

These different forms of business combinations each give rise to different forms of relationships between the entities involved. A business combination can either result in a single combined entity (as in points a and b above) or in a number of separate entities that together form a group.

When an entity acquires a controlling interest in another entity, the substance of the transaction is that the acquirer obtained control of the net assets of the acquiree, and it is therefore appropriate to join the assets and liabilities of the acquirer and acquiree.

In both point a and point d above, A Ltd obtained control of all of the assets and liabilities of B Ltd. However, there is a difference in the legal ownership of the assets and liabilities owned by A Ltd. In point a, A Ltd would include each asset and liability acquired from B Ltd in its financial statements. In point d, A Ltd would include its investment in the shares of B Ltd in its financial statements, but the economics of the situation are no different from the first scenario, where it owned all of the assets and liabilities. As a result of the fact that A Ltd owns all of the shares of B Ltd, it controls all of the assets and has an obligation relating to all of the liabilities of B Ltd.

For this reason, group financial statements are prepared in the case where an entity has a controlling interest in another entity. In the group financial statements, all of the assets and liabilities of the controlled entity, or subsidiary, are included with those of the acquirer, which results in financial statements reflecting the substance of the activities of the group.

Where an investor acquires an interest in an associate or joint venture (points f and g above), the results of the acquired entities are also included in the group financial statements in a way that reflects the degree of influence or joint control exercised over the acquired entity. The equity method of accounting, which is discussed in Chapter 9 of this publication, is used to accomplish this.

Group financial statements are prepared in addition to the separate entity financial statements, which are prepared as normal, and include those assets and liabilities that are legally attributable to the acquirer, including the investments in the various group entities.

4.3 Recognising assets and liabilities in terms of the Conceptual Framework

In terms of the Conceptual Framework, an asset can be recognised by an entity if it is a resource that is controlled by that entity and from which there are probable future economic benefits that will flow to the entity.

If an entity buys a piece of land, there is no dispute that the land meets the asset definition and recognition criteria in terms of the Conceptual Framework. But what if the entity buys shares in an entity that owns the piece of land?

By owning the shares in an entity, the acquirer is able to control the operations of that entity (refer to Chapter 3 for a detailed discussion of control). By virtue of that control, the asset definition is met in relation to that piece of land. The land is controlled as a result of the shareholding and there are probable future economic benefits that will flow to the acquirer as a result of the controlled operations of the acquiree.

It is therefore appropriate to recognise the land as well as any other assets and liabilities of a controlled entity in the group financial statements.

5. Accounting for a business combination

When a business combination has occurred, it is necessary to account for the assets and liabilities that are now under the control of the acquirer. IFRS3, *Business Combinations*, outlines the appropriate accounting of a business combination. The **acquisition method** consists of the following steps:

a. Identify the acquirer.
b. Determine the acquisition date.
c. Recognise and measure the identifiable assets acquired, the liabilities assumed and any non-controlling interest in the acquiree.
d. Recognise and measure goodwill or a gain from a bargain purchase.

Each of these steps is discussed briefly in this publication, but Chapter 22 of *Financial Accounting: IFRS Principles* (4e) by Lubbe, Modack and Watson contains a detailed discussion on business combinations.

5.1 Identify the acquirer and acquiree

When two or more businesses are combined in a business combination, one of the entities is identified as the acquirer, while the others are identified as acquirees. The acquirer is the entity that obtains control of the other entities. The acquirer is typically the entity that transferred cash or other assets in exchange for shares of the acquiree. In the case where an entity issues its own shares in exchange for shares in another entity, the entity issuing shares is typically the acquirer.

5.2 Determine the acquisition date

The acquisition date is generally the date when the acquirer legally transfers the purchase consideration, and then obtains control of the acquiree. However, the transfer of control could happen on a different date if a contractual agreement states that the acquirer will begin to control the acquiree either before or after the date on which the consideration is transferred. The important point is that the date of acquisition is the date on which the control of the entity is transferred.

5.3 Recognise and measure the assets acquired and the liabilities assumed

All assets and liabilities of the acquiree are included with those of the acquirer, according to the method of accounting that is most appropriate, depending on the level of control or influence that is exercised over the acquiree. But no matter the method of accounting, the assets and liabilities will be included to some degree and should be recognised appropriately.

When an asset is acquired by an entity, it is typically recognised and measured at the value of the consideration given in exchange for it. For example, if an entity buys a property and pays CU2 million for it, the property is measured at CU2 million in the financial statements of the entity.

In a business combination, the acquirer is acquiring a group of assets and liabilities, which need to be recognised individually in the case of an investment that is consolidated or included in the investment in the case of an investment that is equity accounted.

All **separately identifiable assets** acquired and liabilities assumed should be recognised separately from goodwill. This implies that all assets and liabilities recognised by the acquiree will be recognised by the acquirer. In addition, there may be assets (for example, intangible assets such as brand names) that are separately identifiable and therefore should be recognised by the acquirer, although the acquiree could not recognise them because they were internally generated. If the acquiree has contingent liabilities that it has not recognised in accordance with IAS37, *Provisions, Contingent Liabilities and Contingent Assets*, because the outflow of economic benefits is not probable, IFRS3 specifically requires that these contingent liabilities be recognised as part of the business combination if their fair value can be measured reliably.

The assets and liabilities are recognised in the financial statements of the acquiree according to IFRS and are measured using an historical cost-based measure or fair value, depending on the accounting policies of the acquiree. However, for the acquirer and the newly formed group, the historic cost of an asset has no relevance, and it would be inappropriate to recognise that asset using that basis.

At the acquisition date, it is necessary to measure each of the separately identifiable assets and liabilities of the acquirer. Although the purchase consideration was paid for the entire business, each of these assets and liabilities will be recognised separately and therefore require a value to be assigned to them.

All assets and liabilities of the acquiree are therefore recognised at their fair value at the date of acquisition, as this gives the fairest representation of the value of these assets and liabilities to the acquirer. Intangible assets and contingent liabilities that are recognised by the acquirer should also be recognised at their fair value at this date.

Where the fair value differs from the carrying amount recorded for an asset or liability by the acquiree, the acquirer is required to recognise a fair value adjustment for that asset or liability in order for it to be recorded at the appropriate fair value from the perspective of the group. For example, if a piece of land is recorded at a carrying amount of CU800 000 by the acquirer, but the fair value at the date of acquisition is CU900 000, it is necessary for the acquirer to adjust the carrying amount by CU100 000 in order to reflect the land at its fair value.

Any deferred tax asset or liability that arises from the business combination should be recognised and measured in terms of IAS12, *Income Taxes*. Any changes made to the carrying amount of an asset or liability result in a temporary difference because the underlying tax value is not changed, but it is now being carried at a different carrying amount.

The accounting treatment of acquisition adjustments is discussed in Chapter 5.

5.4 Cost of the acquisition

The total consideration transferred in exchange for control of the acquiree constitutes the **investment** in the acquiree. All assets transferred, including cash or other assets, liabilities assumed and equity issued, are measured at fair value at the date of acquisition. Where an asset was previously recognised at a different carrying amount, it is remeasured to fair value at this date. Any resulting gain or loss is recognised in profit or loss, in the same way that a gain or loss on disposal of an asset is normally recognised.

Any acquisition-related costs should be expensed, or included in profit or loss, in the year of the acquisition.

IFRS for SMEs update

Any costs relating to an acquisition are added to the cost of the acquisition and are not expensed (as is the case for full IFRS).

5.5 Goodwill and gain on bargain purchase

In many instances, an acquirer pays a different amount for a business from that of the fair value of the identifiable assets and liabilities. This difference results in **goodwill** being acquired, or a gain on a bargain purchase being recognised. The goodwill or gain on bargain purchase should be recognised by the acquirer at the acquisition date.

Goodwill represents all of those benefits that the acquirer identified in the acquiree that cannot be separately identified and therefore cannot be recognised. These include intangible assets such as a good customer base, loyal employees and market share as well as synergistic benefits that are expected to be realised between the acquirer and acquiree. The acquirer determines the value of these additional benefits and pays a premium for them, over and above the value of the recognised assets and liabilities. The acquirer may also be willing to pay a premium in order to acquire a controlling share of the acquiree.

Goodwill meets the asset definition and recognition criteria in terms of the Conceptual Framework because it represents future economic benefits that the acquirer considers probable, hence it was willing to pay the premium. Goodwill is recognised as a non-current asset in the group financial statements because the benefits are expected to be realised over an extended period of time.

In the case where the acquirer does not acquire the entire shareholding of the acquiree, but does exercise control nonetheless, non-controlling interest arises (refer to Chapter 7 for a detailed discussion). The non-controlling interest may also have a portion of goodwill attributable to its shareholding when non-controlling interest is recognised at its fair value at the acquisition date. In terms of IFRS3, *Business Combinations*, there is an option to recognise the portion of goodwill attributable to the non-controlling share-holders as well as the controlling shareholders. This is often referred to as the **full goodwill** method. Alternatively, the partial goodwill method can be applied when non-controlling interest is not measured at its fair value at the acquisition date. In this case, only the goodwill attributable to the interest of the acquirer is recognised. In other words, there is an option to recognise the non-controlling interest share of net assets either including or excluding goodwill. This option may be applied for each business combination.

Goodwill is measured as the difference between the fair value of the net assets of the acquiree at the date of acquisition, and the sum of the total consideration transferred for the business combination by the acquirer and the amount of non-controlling interest recognised (either including or excluding goodwill).

Subsequent to the date of acquisition, the goodwill recognised is accounted for in terms of IAS36, *Impairment of Assets*, with an annual impairment test being conducted. The goodwill is measured at cost less accumulated impairment. You will learn more about the recognition and measurement of goodwill and non-controlling interest in Chapter 7.

IAS12, *Income Taxes*, specifically states that the initial recognition of goodwill and any resulting taxable temporary differences are exempt from the recognition of deferred tax. The main reason for this exemption is the fact that no tax deductions are granted for goodwill and the goodwill therefore has a tax base of nil. The difference between the carrying amount recognised and the nil tax base will never reverse, and it is therefore inappropriate to recognise deferred tax.

In the case where an acquirer pays less than the fair value of the identifiable assets and liabilities, the result is a **bargain purchase**. In other words, the acquirer purchased the acquiree at a discount. This is sometimes referred to as 'negative goodwill'. The differ-ence between the fair value of assets and liabilities acquired and the sum of the purchase consideration and the non-controlling interest represents a gain on the purchase of the acquiree at a bargain price, and the resulting gain should be recognised in profit or loss immediately. However, if a bargain purchase arises, the acquirer is required to reassess the fair value of each of the assets acquired and liabilities assumed to ensure that it is appropriate to recognise a gain. Because the gain is recognised immediately, no subse-quent accounting relating to the gain on bargain purchase is required.

IFRS for SMEs update

Goodwill acquired as part of a business combination is amortised over its useful life. If the entity cannot determine the useful life of the goodwill, a period of ten years is assumed.

Note that this applies to the acquisition of a subsidiary, associate or joint venture, or the acquisition of a group of assets and liabilities that constitute a business.

Example

Applying the acquisition method to a business combination

Acquirer Ltd purchased all issued shares of Acquiree Ltd on 30 June 20x5 for a total cash purchase consideration of CU500 000. The statement of financial position of Acquiree Ltd at the acquisition date was as shown below.

Statement of financial position of Acquiree Ltd as at 30 June 20x5

	CU
ASSETS	
Property, plant and equipment	300 000
Inventory	72 000
Bank	81 000
	453 000
EQUITY AND LIABILITIES	
Share capital	262 000
Retained earnings	124 000
Total owners' equity	386 000
Accounts payable	67 000
	453 000

The identifiable assets and liabilities of Acquiree Ltd were considered fairly valued on 30 June 20x5, except for the following:

	CU
Trademarks	22 000
Property, plant and equipment	370 000
Inventory	80 000

The acquirer in this scenario is Acquirer Ltd because it paid cash for a controlling interest in Acquiree Ltd. The acquisition date is 30 June 20x5, which is the date on which control transferred.

The assets acquired and liabilities assumed should be recognised at their fair value at the date of acquisition. In this scenario, there is no non-controlling interest because Acquirer Ltd purchased all of the issued shares of Acquiree Ltd. The fair value of the identifiable and recognisable net asset acquired by Acquirer Ltd was as follows:

	CU
Property, plant and equipment	370 000
Trademarks	22 000
Inventory	80 000
Bank	81 000
Accounts payable	(67 000)
Net assets acquired	**486 000**

Acquirer Ltd paid CU500 000 for the net assets of Acquiree Ltd. Therefore the **goodwill** acquired amounted to CU14 000 (CU500 000 – 486 000).

Acquirer Ltd will recognised its investment in shares in its financial statements. However, each of the assets acquired (including goodwill) and the liabilities assumed will be included at their fair value in the financial statements of the newly formed group. Refer to Chapter 4 for an explanation of the consolidation process used to achieve this.

6. Interest acquired

An entity (acquirer) obtains its interest in another entity when purchasing shares in the investee (also referred to as the acquiree). The acquirer can either purchase all of the issued shares of the acquiree or a lesser number of shares, which can then result in a controlling interest, a significant influence or no influence.

When acquiring an interest, the acquirer can purchase shares that are issued directly by the acquiree to the acquirer, either at the date of incorporation or at a subsequent date, or it can purchase shares from the existing shareholders in the acquiree. In the case where shares are issued directly to the acquirer, the **acquiree** would record the following journal entry in its financial statements:

Dr		Bank
	Cr	Share capital

In the case where the acquirer purchases shares from existing shareholders, there will be no journal entry recorded by the acquiree. Because the transaction is between shareholders, it has no impact on the assets of the acquiree.

In both cases, the **acquirer** will record the following journal entry relating to its purchase of shares:

Dr		Investment in shares
	Cr	Bank

These same journal entries would apply regardless of the number of shares acquired by the acquirer. The investment recorded by the acquirer will represent its proportional investment in the acquiree.

Ownership of shares normally provides voting rights that enable the holder of the majority of shares to dominate the appointment of directors or an entity's governing board. Where the parent owns more than 50% of the shares of another entity, it is therefore expected that the parent holds more than half of the voting power of an entity. This level of ownership constitutes control and a parent–subsidiary relationship exists.

6.1 Direct and indirect interest

A direct interest arises where the parent has a direct investment in the subsidiary (in other words, it owns the shares itself). An indirect interest is an interest in a subsidiary that, in turn, is an investor in another entity. If the investor is able to control more than half of the votes attached to the shares, the controlled entity is a subsidiary. The parent controls the first subsidiary and is therefore able to control its shareholding in the second subsidiary. A parent could also obtain control of an entity if it has a combination of a direct and indirect interest in that entity. Direct and indirect interest is discussed further in Chapter 11.

6.2 Effective versus controlled holdings

For a company to be a subsidiary, the investor needs to control **more than half of the votes** of the entity, but this does not necessarily mean that the investor holds more than half of the issued shares or that it would receive more than half of the profits of the subsidiary. (Note that control can be demonstrated in ways other than voting rights. Refer to paragraph 7 of IFRS10.)

The percentage of profits that would be received is known as the 'effective interest' or the 'economic interest'. Once you have established that control exists, you should determine the parent's effective interest in the profits of a subsidiary by calculating its shareholding as a percentage of the total issued share capital of the entity.

Where an entity owns share warrants or share call options, debt or any other type of equity instruments that are convertible into shares with voting rights, you should consider the existence and effect of the potential voting rights when assessing whether control exists. In other words, if a shareholder has options that could be converted into shares and the conversion of these options into shares would result in control, then the investment is a subsidiary. This is appropriate as the investor has the ability to control the entity.

Example
Effective interest

A Ltd owns 60% of B Ltd and therefore has control of B Ltd. B Ltd owns 40% of C Ltd and A Ltd owns 30% of C Ltd. A Ltd therefore has control of C Ltd by virtue of its direct ownership of 30% of the shares plus its control of an additional 40% of the shares, which are controlled indirectly. In total, A Ltd has control of 70% of the shares of C Ltd.

Figure 2.2 Illustration of a complex group

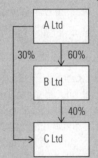

However, A Ltd's effective interest in C Ltd is not 70%. If C Ltd were to declare dividends of CU100, A Ltd would receive CU30 through its direct investment in C Ltd. CU40 would be paid to B Ltd, of which 60%, or CU24, would be attributable to A Ltd. In total, A Ltd therefore has an interest in CU54 of the CU100 dividend, or 54%. This represents its effective interest in C Ltd and can be calculated as follows:

30% direct holding + (40% × 60%) indirect holding = 54% effective holding

6.3 Special purpose entities

A **special purpose entity** (SPE) is set up for a specific purpose, often to borrow money, as the liability is limited to that entity. SPEs are normally designed so that no single entity holds the majority interest and therefore no group financial statements are considered necessary. One of the factors that caused the spectacular collapse of Enron was that it had managed to keep a lot of debt (liabilities) off the statement of financial position by holding them in SPEs. FASB, the US accounting body, reacted very swiftly and said that in many cases, SPEs were subsidiaries and should be consolidated. If you control an organisation from which you derive benefits, it is a subsidiary and it should be consolidated. This implies that 100% of all of the liabilities should be on the consolidated statement of financial position. Had this been the case with Enron, users would have realised sooner that Enron was not as financially sound as it appeared.

Example

Different group structures

In this structure, P Ltd has the ability to govern the financial and operating policies of S Ltd (in other words, control), based on the assumption that 60% interest = 60% voting rights. Note that the non-controlling interest is 40%.

Figure 2.3 Example of a simple group structure

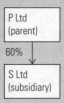

In this structure, P Ltd has the ability to govern the financial and operating policies of S Ltd (in other words, control) and SS Ltd. Both S Ltd and SS Ltd are subsidiaries of P Ltd. The non-controlling interest in S Ltd is 40% and the non-controlling interest in SS Ltd is 20%.

Figure 2.4 Example of a complex group structure (with direct interest)

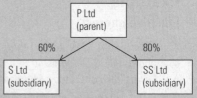

In this structure, P Ltd has the ability to govern the financial and operating policies of S Ltd (in other words, control). S Ltd has the ability to govern the financial and operating policies of SS Ltd.

Thus, S Ltd is both a parent of SS Ltd and a subsidiary of P Ltd. As SS Ltd is a subsidiary of S Ltd and S Ltd is a subsidiary of P Ltd, SS Ltd is an indirect subsidiary of P Ltd. The non-controlling interest in S Ltd is 40% and the non-controlling interest in SS Ltd is 20%.

P Ltd has an effective interest in SS Ltd of 48%. The non-controlling interest in SS Ltd (from the view of P Ltd) is 52% (100% – 48%).

Figure 2.5 Example of a complex group structure (with indirect interest)

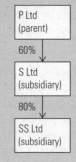

7. Direct acquisition of net assets as a business combination

In the case where an acquirer purchases the assets and liabilities of an entity, as opposed to the shares, the acquirer gets direct control of those assets and liabilities. Each asset and liability is recognised separately in the financial statements of the acquiree in the same way as if they had been acquired in a regular transaction.

The acquisition method in IFRS3 is applied to a transaction of this nature.

- The acquirer is the entity that has purchased the assets and liabilities.
- The acquisition date is the date on which the control and ownership of the net assets is transferred to the acquirer.

- The assets and liabilities are each recognised separately. Each asset and liability must be measured and recognised at its fair value at the date of acquisition. (There is no non-controlling interest owing to the fact that the net assets are all owned and controlled by the acquirer.)
- Goodwill or a gain on bargain purchase must be recognised and measured as the difference between the fair value of the net assets acquired and the purchase consideration.

Example

Direct acquisition of the net assets of a business

The facts are the same as the previous example where Acquirer Ltd purchased the shares in Acquiree Ltd, except that in this example, Acquirer Ltd acquired all of the assets and liabilities of Acquiree Ltd on 30 June 20x5 for a total cash purchase consideration of CU500 000.
Acquirer Ltd would record the following journal entry relating to the purchase:

			CU	CU
Dr		Property, plant and equipment	370 000	
Dr		Trademarks	22 000	
Dr		Inventory	80 000	
Dr		Bank	81 000	
Dr		Goodwill	14 000	
	Cr	Accounts payable		67 000
	Cr	Bank		500 000

Acquisition of individual assets and liabilities for cash consideration

After the business combination occurs, the acquirer will account for the acquired assets and liabilities in terms of the applicable IFRS standards. Any recognised goodwill will be tested for impairment in terms of IAS36, *Impairment of Assets*, or amortised in accordance with IFRS for SMEs.

An acquirer may purchase a portion of the assets and liabilities of an acquiree, as opposed to all of the net assets. If the portion acquired meets the definition of a business, in terms of IFRS3 (in other words, a group of assets that is capable of providing a return), it will be accounted for in the same way as discussed above. If the assets acquired do not meet the definition of a business, they will not be accounted for in terms of IFRS3, but rather as a normal purchase of assets.

The acquiree will record the disposal of its assets and liabilities as a normal sale of assets. It will derecognise each asset and liability at its carrying amount, and will recognise a profit or loss on the disposal.

If all of the assets of the acquiree are transferred to the acquirer, it is likely that the acquiree will no longer operate. The entity may either be liquidated, in which case the purchase consideration received will be distributed to its shareholders, or it may become dormant. If only a portion of the entity was disposed of, it is likely that the acquiree will continue operating with its remaining assets and liabilities.

Test your knowledge

There is a list of learning objectives at the beginning of this chapter. Go back to this list and check whether you have achieved these outcomes. If not, reread the appropriate section.

Questions

Question 1

P Ltd purchased 100% of the shares of S Ltd on 1 July 20x5 for an amount of CU1 600 000. The net assets of S Ltd were considered to be fairly valued at this date except for land, which was considered to be under-valued by CU50 000. Share capital amounted to CU400 000 and retained earnings to CU870 000.

1. Identify the acquirer.
2. Identify the acquiree.
3. Identify the purchase consideration.
4. Identify the acquisition date.
5. Calculate the fair value of the net identifiable assets at the acquisition date.
6. Calculate the amount paid for goodwill, if any.
7. If P Ltd decided not to acquire the shares in S Ltd, what alternative action could P Ltd take in order to acquire control of S Ltd's assets?

Suggested solution

1. P Ltd is the acquirer as P Ltd acquired the controlling interest in S Ltd.
2. S Ltd is the acquiree.
3. The purchase consideration amounts to CU1 600 000.
4. The acquisition date was 1 July 20x5.
5. The fair value of net identifiable assets at the acquisition date:

	CU
Fair value of net assets of S Ltd at acquisition date: Net assets = Equity (accounting equation) ∴ Net assets = CU400 000 + CU870 000	1 270 000
Land undervalued	50 000
Fair value of net identifiable assets of S Ltd	**1 320 000**

6. Goodwill acquired:

	CU
Purchase consideration	1 600 000
Less: Fair value of net identifiable assets (calculated in 5 above)	(1 320 000)
Goodwill acquired	**280 000**

7. Instead of acquiring the shares in S Ltd, P Ltd could have decided to acquire the individual assets and liabilities of S Ltd as a business operation.

Case study exercises

The extracts below, which come from the financial statements of S Ltd for the year ended 31 December 20x5, have been presented to you.

Statements of the financial position of S Ltd on 31 December 20x5

	20x5 CU'000	20x4 CU'000
ASSETS		
Plant and machinery	200	180
Current assets	500	130
	700	**310**
CAPITAL AND LIABILITIES		
Share capital	100	100
Retained earnings	500	200
Shareholders' equity	600	300
Loan from P Ltd	80	–
Current liabilities	20	10
	700	**310**

Statements of profit or loss and other comprehensive income of S Ltd for the year ended 31 December 20x5

	S Ltd CU'000
Gross revenue (including dividends and interest received)	1 600
Net operating costs	(920)
Profit from ordinary activities before interest	680
Interest paid	(50)
Profit on ordinary activities before taxation	630
Taxation	(230)
Profit for the year	**400**

Answer the questions below, which relate to the business combinations described in each scenario. In each case, motivate your answer.

Scenario 1

P Ltd acquired 100% of the issued ordinary share capital of S Ltd on 1 January 20x5 for CU400 000. The identifiable assets and liabilities of S Ltd were considered fairly valued at the date of acquisition.

1. Identify the acquirer.
2. Identify the acquiree.
3. Identify the purchase consideration.
4. Identify the acquisition date.
5. Calculate the fair value of the net identifiable assets at the acquisition date.
6. Calculate the amount paid for goodwill, if any.
7. What is the amount of dividends that S Ltd declared in the current year?
8. Prepare all of the journal entries that P Ltd would have recorded in its separate financial statements.
9. Prepare the journal entries that S Ltd would have recorded when P Ltd acquired 100% of the shares in S Ltd.
10. Why is no goodwill relating to its investment in S Ltd recognised in the separate financial statements of P Ltd?

Scenario 2

P Ltd acquired all of the assets and liabilities of S Ltd on 1 January 20x5 and paid CU400 000 in cash.
1. Prepare the journal entries that P Ltd would have recorded in its separate financial statements.
2. Prepare the journal entries that S Ltd would have recorded when P Ltd acquired all of its assets and liabilities.

Suggested solution

Scenario 1

P Ltd acquired 100% of the issued ordinary share capital of S Ltd on 1 January 20x5 for CU400 000. The identifiable assets and liabilities of S Ltd were considered fairly valued at the date of acquisition.

1. **Identify the acquirer.**
   P Ltd acquired the controlling interest in S Ltd, thus P Ltd is the acquirer.
2. **Identify the acquiree.**
   S Ltd is the acquiree.
3. **Identify the purchase consideration.**
   P Ltd paid CU400 000 for the shares in S Ltd.
4. **Identify the acquisition date.**
   The acquisition date is 1 January 20x5.
5. **Calculate the fair value of the net identifiable assets at the acquisition date.**
   Fair value of net assets of S Ltd at acquisition date　　　　　　　　　　　　CU300 000
   Net assets = Equity (accounting equation)
   ∴ Net assets = CU300 000
6. **Calculate the amount paid for goodwill, if any.**

	CU
Purchase consideration	400 000
Less: Fair value of net identifiable assets	(300 000)
Goodwill acquired	**100 000**

7. **What is the amount of dividends that S Ltd declared in the current year?**
   Reconstruct the 'retained earnings' column in the statement of changes in equity of S Ltd:

	CU
Opening balance	200 000
Profit after tax	400 000
∴ Dividend declared	(100 000)
Closing balance	**500 000**

8. **Prepare all of the journal entries that P Ltd would have recorded in the current financial year.**

			CU	CU
Dr		Investment in S Ltd	400 000	
	Cr	Bank		400 000

Acquisition of 100% of the shares in S Ltd, for cash

			CU	CU
Dr		Bank	100 000	
	Cr	Dividend income (P/L)		100 000

Dividends received from subsidiary, in cash

9. **Prepare the journal entries that S Ltd would have recorded when P Ltd acquired 100% of the shares in S Ltd.**

    P Ltd acquired the shares in S Ltd from S Ltd's shareholders. This is a transaction between the new and existing shareholders of S Ltd.

    There is no entry in the records of S Ltd.

10. **Why is no goodwill relating to its investment in S Ltd recognised in the separate financial statements of P Ltd?**

    P Ltd acquired the shares in S Ltd. Thus, in the separate financial statements of S Ltd, the asset acquired is the shares in S Ltd. The goodwill acquired in S Ltd is only recognised on consolidation.

Scenario 2

P Ltd acquired all of the assets and liabilities of S Ltd on 1 January 20x5 and paid CU400 000 in cash.

1. **Prepare the journal entries that P Ltd would have recorded in its separate financial statements.**

			CU	CU
Dr		Plant and machinery	180 000	
Dr		Current assets	130 000	
Dr		Goodwill	100 000	
	Cr	Current liabilities		10 000
	Cr	Bank		400 000

Acquisition of the individual assets and liabilities of S Ltd, acquired as a business combination

Note that, as P Ltd acquired the individual assets and liabilities of S Ltd, P Ltd is not a shareholder of S Ltd. Thus, any dividends declared by S Ltd since this acquisition date are not received by P Ltd, but by the existing shareholders of S Ltd.

2. **Prepare the journal entries that S Ltd would have recorded when P Ltd acquired all of its assets and liabilities.**

			CU	CU
Dr		Current liabilities	10 000	
Dr		Bank	400 000	
	Cr	Plant and machinery		180 000
	Cr	Current assets		130 000
	Cr	Profit on disposal of net assets		100 000

Sale of the individual assets and liabilities to P Ltd as a business combination

Think about it

What happens to S Ltd now?

As S Ltd sold all of its assets and liabilities to P Ltd, S Ltd only has one remaining asset: the cash received from the sale of its assets. The statement of financial position of S Ltd will therefore be as shown below immediately after this transaction.

Statements of financial position of S Ltd

	After 1 January 20x5 CU'000	Before 31 December 20x4 CU'000
ASSETS		
Plant and machinery		180
Current assets		130
CASH	400	
	400	310
CAPITAL AND LIABILITIES		
Share capital	100	100
Retained earnings (200 000 + 100 000 profit on disposal of net assets)	300	200
	400	310

We have ignored any taxation that may be payable resulting from the sale of the net assets. The shareholders of S Ltd can decide to:
- Distribute all of its profits in the form of a dividend and remain dormant
- Wind-up and close down the business after distributing all of its profits
- Start with new business operations.

PART II

The consolidation process

Consolidation: Controlled entities

The following topics are included in this chapter:

- The basic principles of consolidation
- Control as the criterion for consolidation
- Determining and assessing whether control exists
- The preparation of consolidated financial statements

Learning objectives

By the end of this chapter, you should be able to:
- Identify controlled entities and identify when it is necessary to prepare consolidated financial statements
- Understand what is meant by the term 'control' and be able to determine if control exists
- Understand the basic process of consolidation from the starting point, *pro-forma* journal entries and the end point.

1. Basic principles of consolidation

Consolidated financial statements are a **single set of financial statements** that involve combining the financial statements of separate, individual entities that are part of a group so that they show the financial position and performance of the group of entities, presented as if they were a **single economic entity**. At this stage of your studies, you should know how to prepare general purpose financial statements for a **single entity** in accordance with IFRS. The purpose of this chapter is to describe and explain the preparation of **consolidated financial statements**.

IFRS10, *Consolidated Financial Statements*, requires that any entity that is a parent should prepare consolidated financial statements. Because a **parent** is, by definition, an entity that has one or more subsidiaries, consolidated financial statements are required for every group that has subsidiaries. However, as discussed in Chapter 1, there are certain exemptions where a parent need not prepare consolidated financial statements.

The objective of financial reporting is to provide decision-useful information to users. Information is 'decision-useful' if users can use the information as the basis of their decisions, which means they must be able to use the information to predict the future cash flows of the entity as well as to assess the risks attached to these cash flows. The most important group of users of financial information is the group of current and potential future investors. These users are interested in the results of the group as a whole and not just the investor entity.

As the preparer of financial statements, you should ensure that the financial information reported meets the basic qualitative characteristics as set out in the **Conceptual Framework**. For financial information to be decision useful, it must possess two fundamental qualitative characteristics: relevance and faithful representation. The definition of an **asset** (refer to the Conceptual Framework) includes the phrase 'controlled by the entity'. If one entity controls another entity, this implies that the first entity is able to control the assets of the second entity. In Chapter 1 you learnt that the controlling entity is called a 'parent' and the controlled entity is called a 'subsidiary'. The process of consolidation involves recognising all assets **controlled by the group** and all liabilities that the group is responsible for settling. As the definition of a subsidiary implies, all assets and associated liabilities of the subsidiary are under the control of its parent. Group financial statements therefore include all assets and associated liabilities controlled by the group.

When preparing consolidated financial statements, the **reporting entity** is the group as a whole; this implies that the group is a business operation whose economic activities can be objectively distinguished from other entities. Furthermore, the group, as a single economic entity, is required to provide financial information about its economic activities that has the potential to be useful to investors, creditors and lenders in making decisions about the effective and efficient use of the resources provided to that entity by its owners and lenders. The parent prepares the consolidated financial statements for the group as the parent's equity holders (shareholders) are effectively the equity holders of the group. These are the primary equity holders to whom the group is reporting.

In order to prepare consolidated financial statements, you are required to add together, or combine, the financial statements of the individual legal entities in the group. A **group** consists of the parent and all of its subsidiaries (refer to IFRS10). A process of consolidation is used to recognise all of the **assets and associated liabilities controlled** by the group (in other words, those of both the parent and the subsidiary) and the group's share of post-acquisition reserves in the subsidiary.

2. **Control as the criterion for consolidation**

As mentioned in Chapter 1, a parent is an entity that **controls** one or more entities, while a subsidiary is a **controlled** entity. An entity must thus determine when it is a parent and which entities it controls. The criterion for **consolidation** is **control** (refer to IFRS10) and the determination of whether control exists is a matter of judgement. You need to consider all of the available facts and circumstances to determine whether control exists or not. For this, you need to understand the meaning of the term 'control' and the evidence that you need to accumulate in order to determine the existence or non-existence of control in specific circumstances. Then, if those circumstances change, you need to assess whether control still exists.

2.1 Determining whether control exists

For an entity to be classified as a subsidiary, that entity must be controlled by another entity. The definition of 'control' does not provide any percentage interest as an indication that control exists, but concentrates instead on **what control constitutes**.

IFRS principles

Determining whether control exists

An investor determines whether it is a parent by assessing whether it controls one or more investees. An investor considers all relevant facts and circumstances when assessing whether it controls an investee. An investor controls an investee when it is exposed, or has rights, to variable returns from its involvement with the investee and has the ability to affect those returns through its power over the investee (refer to IFRS10: 5–6 and IFRS10: 8).

An investor (parent) controls an investee (subsidiary) when it has rights to variable returns from its involvement with the investee and has the ability to affect those returns through its power over the investee. This power is defined (refer to IFRS10, Appendix A) as the 'existing rights that give the current ability to direct the relevant activities'. The key features of this definition are that power arises from rights, that power is the ability to direct, and that the ability to direct must be current and relevant to the activities that are directed.

Rights generally arise from some form of **legal contract**. For example, the rights that are held by the owner of an ordinary share in an entity may include voting rights, rights to dividends or rights on liquidation of the company. Rights can also exist because of a contract between one entity and another, for example, an entity that might engage another entity to manage its activities, which gives the latter management rights, but no rights to dividends.

The ability to direct the relevant activities of an investee constitutes the rights that are of importance when determining whether power exists. These relevant activities are activities that significantly affect the return to the investor, and include the buying and selling of goods and services, the decisions around investing in assets and the decisions relating to financing, amongst others (refer to IFRS10: B11). A parent must not only have power over an investee and exposure or rights to variable returns from its involvement with the investee; it must also have the ability to use its power over the investee to affect its returns from its involvement with the investee.

Table 3.1 Assessing control

Identifying relevant activities	Evaluating power	Assessing returns
Identify which activities of the investee are considered the 'relevant activities', in other words, those activities of the investee that significantly affect the investee's returns. Examples of relevant activities include: • Determining operating policies • Making capital decisions • Appointing key management personnel • Management of underlying investments.	Determine which party, if any, has power, that is, the current ability to direct those activities. Power arises from those rights that may include: • Voting rights • Potential voting rights (for example options or convertible instruments) • Rights to appoint key personnel • Decision-making rights within a management contract • Removal or 'kick-out' rights.	Assess whether the investor is exposed, or has rights, to variable returns from its involvement with the investee. Returns can be positive, negative or both. Examples of returns include: • Dividends • Remuneration • Returns that are not available to other interest holders (for example, economies of scale, cost savings, scarce products, proprietary knowledge or synergies).

Source: ey.com/IFRS, Issue 1/May 2011.

To control an investee, an investor must be exposed, or have rights, to variable returns from its involvement with the investee. Returns can be positive, negative, or both. **Returns are often an indicator of control.** This is because the greater an investor's exposure to the variability of returns from its involvement with an investee, the greater the incentive for the investor to obtain rights that give the investor power. However, the magnitude of the returns is not determinative of whether the investor holds power. The link between power over an investee and returns is essential to having control. An investor that has power over an investee, but cannot benefit from that power, does not control that investee. An investor that receives a return from an investee, but cannot use its power to direct the activities that significantly affect the returns of that investee, does not control that investee.

When assessing who has control over an investee, an investor considers the **voting rights** and potential voting rights that it holds as well as the rights and potential voting rights held by others. Common examples of potential voting rights include those that result from the exercise of an option or conversion feature of a convertible instrument. You should only consider potential voting rights if they are substantive, which means that the holder currently has the practical ability to exercise the right. Whether potential rights are substantive depends on facts and circumstances, for example, whether the option to acquire additional voting rights is 'in the money' or 'out of the money', or whether an investor would benefit for other reasons, such as realising synergies between the investor and investee.

2.2 Level of share ownership

Ownership of ordinary shares in another entity normally provides voting rights that enable the holder of the **majority** of shares (in other words, more than a 50% interest) to dominate the appointment of directors or an entity's governing board. Hence, in the absence of other evidence, you may assume that a majority of voting shares held by the investor indicates that the investor has power over the investee.

Example

Majority interest and majority of voting rights

An investor holds 70% of the shares in an investee. The voting rights are determined on a one-for-one ratio, based on the number of shares held. As the investor has the majority of voting rights in the investee, it has control. Thus, a parent–subsidiary relationship exists.

2.2.1 What happens if the investor holds less than a majority of voting rights, but still has control (*de facto* control)?

An investor may have control over an investee even when it has less than a majority of the voting rights of that investee. This is referred to as *de facto* control. In assessing whether *de facto* control exists, the following should be considered:

- The size of the investor's holding of voting rights relative to the size and dispersion of other vote holders. It will be more likely that the investor has power over the investee, specifically:
  - The more voting rights an investor holds
  - The more voting rights an investor holds relative to other vote holders
  - The more parties that would need to act together to outvote the investor.
- Voting patterns at the investee's previous shareholders' meetings, for example, the percentage of voters who attended past meetings, and whether that pattern is expected to be indicative of current voting behaviour.

In some cases, an investor might not have *de facto* control on its own. However, in assessing whether an investor has power, all facts and circumstances must be considered, including whether the investor has power through any (or a combination) of the following:

- A contractual arrangement, where the investor can direct other shareholders how to vote
- Rights arising from other contractual arrangements (for example, the ability to direct some of the manufacturing processes of an investee, or to direct other operating or financing activities of an investee that significantly affect the investee's returns)
- Potential voting rights, which is the option or conversion feature of a convertible instrument, as described above.

Applying the concept of *de facto* control is likely to require significant judgement of the facts and circumstances to establish an investor's interest relative to that of others. Conditions may exist where an investor finds itself in control of an investee simply because of circumstances that exist at a point in time, rather than because of deliberate action. In order to make these judgements, you need to gather and analyse all relevant information.

Example

Illustrations of *de facto* control

Consider these examples of *de facto* control:

- P Ltd owns 40% of the voting rights in S Ltd and enters into an **agreement with other shareholders** owning 15% of the voting rights. The agreement enables P Ltd to exercise 55% voting rights, giving it control over S Ltd.
- P Ltd owns 49% of the voting rights in S Ltd. The owners of the remaining 51% of the voting rights are **widely dispersed** (in other words, each owner only has a small number of shares). Traditionally, fewer than 75% of them attend annual general meetings, giving P Ltd control over S Ltd.

2.2.2 Principal-agency relationships

In determining whether control exists over an investee, an investor with decision-making rights needs to assess whether it is a principal or an agent (refer to IFRS10, paragraph B60). An **agent** is a party engaged to act on behalf of another party or parties (the principal), but it does not have control over the investee. A **principal** may delegate decision-making authority on some specific issues or on all relevant activities to the agent, but, ultimately, the principal retains that power. The terms and conditions of the arrangement that are considered to assess whether an entity is an agent or a principal include the following:

- Scope of decision-making authority
- Rights held by others, for example, the existence of removal rights
- Remuneration of the decision-maker
- Exposure to variability of returns through other interests.

An agent cannot be a parent. In a principal-agency relationship, the principal would be considered to be the parent.

> Note that for the remainder of this publication, we will assume that one share equals one vote. This means that when an investor acquires 80% of the shares in an investee, the investor also acquires 80% of the voting rights and thereby acquires a controlling interest.

3. What are consolidated financial statements?

The preparation of consolidated financial statements involves the combining of the financial statements of the parent and all of its subsidiaries. The process of consolidation results in all of the assets and associated liabilities of the subsidiary or subsidiaries that are controlled by the parent being included in the consolidated statement of financial position, thereby reporting the group results as **a single economic entity**. Where a subsidiary is not wholly owned by the parent, the shareholders who have the remaining interest in the net assets of the subsidiary, referred to as non-controlling interest, should be reflected as a separate group of shareholders (in other words, as an equity balance).

The consolidated financial statements of the parent and its subsidiaries include information about a subsidiary from the date the parent obtains control of the subsidiary, that is, from the **acquisition date**. A subsidiary continues to be included in the parent's consolidated financial statements until the parent no longer controls that entity, that is, until the date of the loss of control of the subsidiary, either through disposing of all or a portion of the shares, or through a change in the shareholding, which results in control being lost.

Consolidated financial statements are prepared by the parent. The process requires the adding together of the trial balances or financial statements of the parent and each subsidiary. The trial balances are added together so that the resulting consolidated financial statements include both the parent and the subsidiaries. Consequently, the consolidated statement of financial position, consolidated statement of profit or loss and other comprehensive income, and the consolidated statement of changes in equity will reflect all of the operations of the group. In addition, the information provided in the notes to the consolidated financial statements as well as the consolidated statements of cash flows will reflect both the parent and the subsidiaries.

A group does not record its transactions in a separate general ledger. Rather, the separate general ledgers of the group entities are used as the basis for preparing the group financial statements. The group financial statements are an additional set of financial statements. In essence, they represent a different way of presenting the financial information of the group entities. Group financial statements can be prepared in a number of different ways. One of these ways involves using a separate **group worksheet**, which combines the separate trial balances or financial statements of all of the entities in the group. In order to combine (add together) the separate financial statements of the parent and its subsidiaries, it is necessary to eliminate internal transactions and charges between the group entities, as the group financial statements should present the financial information of the group as a single reporting entity. These transactions are eliminated by using *pro-forma* **journal entries**, which are journal entries that are not actually recorded in any general ledger, but are used to record any group adjustments that may be necessary. The financial information of the parent and that of the subsidiary (or subsidiaries) are combined together in the **group worksheet**, which also reflects the *pro-forma* journal entries. The group worksheet is the basis from which the group financial statements are prepared.

The mechanics of preparing consolidated financial statements are based on basic procedures and although the application of these procedures may differ from one group of entities to another, they remain essentially the same. These basic procedures mainly comprise:

- Consolidating (adding together) the trial balances of each group entity, which will include all items and transactions
- Eliminating balances and transactions relating to other entities within the group.

This process is illustrated in the example that follows.

Example

Illustration of the consolidation process

IFRS10 (paragraph B86) lists the following **consolidation procedures** that should be followed in order to ensure that consolidated financial statements present financial information about the group as a single entity:

- Combine like items of assets, liabilities, equity, income, expenses and cash flows of the parent with those of its subsidiaries.
- Eliminate the carrying amount of the parent's investment in each subsidiary and the parent's portion of equity of each subsidiary.
- Eliminate in full intra-group assets and liabilities, equity, income, expenses and cash flows relating to transactions amongst entities of the group. This includes profits or losses resulting from intra-group transactions that are recognised in assets, such as inventory and fixed assets. Where these eliminations may give rise to temporary differences, you need to consider the deferred tax implications.

This process of adding the financial statements together is illustrated, in its simplest form, in the table that follows.

Table 3.2 Worksheet to illustrate the consolidation process

Trial balance of the parent	Trial balance of the subsidiaries	Adding together 100% of the like items in the trial balances of parent and subsidiaries	Adjustments and eliminations (by using *pro-forma* journal entries)	Consolidated financial statements
(A)	**(B)**	**(A + B)**	**(C)**	**(A + B) ± C**
Assets	Assets	Combined assets	Eliminate intra-group transactions	Consolidated assets
Liabilities	Liabilities	Combined liabilities	Consider deferred tax implications	Consolidated liabilities
Equity	Equity	Combined equity	Eliminate equity of subsidiaries at acquisition date against investment in subsidiaries (asset in parent) Recognise non-controlling interest	Parent equity plus group share of post-acquisition equity of subsidiaries plus non-controlling interest in subsidiaries
		⬆ Starting point	⬆ *Pro-forma* adjustments	⬆ End point

In Chapter 2, you learnt how to identify a business combination using the acquisition method. The acquirer obtains control of a business operation, either by acquiring the individual assets and liabilities of the business (as an economic unit) or by acquiring the shares of the entity that owns the individual assets and liabilities. The process of consolidation is required when the second option has been followed (that is, acquiring a controlling interest in the equity of the entity that owns the assets that are controlled and the liabilities to be assumed). This entity is then referred to as the subsidiary. The example that follows illustrates these options.

Example

Why is consolidation necessary?

The following are extracts from the **statements of financial position** of the two single legal entities, P Ltd and S Ltd:

P Ltd	CU'000
Land	900
Cash	1 000
	1 900
Share capital	200
Retained earnings	1 100
Long-term loan	600
	1 900

S Ltd	CU'000
Land	500
	500
Share capital	100
Retained earnings	100
Long-term loan	300
	500

P Ltd is interested in acquiring the land of S Ltd on 31 December 20x5. P Ltd can either buy the land of S Ltd or it can decide to buy the shares in S Ltd, which will give P Ltd a controlling interest in S Ltd, and thereby control of the land owned by S Ltd.

Scenario 1

P Ltd buys the land from S Ltd at its fair value of CU750 000 on 31 December 20x5.

Journal entries in P Ltd

			CU	CU
Dr		Land	750 000	
	Cr	Bank		750 000

Purchase of land for cash

The effect of this transaction is reported in the statement of financial position of P Ltd as shown below.

Statement of financial position of P Ltd after acquisition

	CU'000
Land (900 + 750)	1 650
Cash (1 000 – 750)	250
	1 900
Share capital	200
Retained earnings	1 100
Long-term loan	600
	1 900

The land was acquired as an asset by P Ltd. As P Ltd paid in cash, there is no change in net assets or equity of P Ltd.

Think about it

What is the entry in S Ltd?

S Ltd will recognise a profit on disposal of the land and will most likely settle the liability with the proceeds.

Scenario 2

P Ltd buys all of the shares in S Ltd for cash amounting to CU450 000 on 31 December 20x5. The land has a fair value of CU750 000, but as P Ltd acquires the equity of S Ltd, it also has to consider the liabilities of the subsidiary.

Think about it

What is P Ltd buying?

P Ltd acquires the shares in S Ltd (an equity instrument). The acquisition of the shares is reflected as an investment in the separate financial statements of P Ltd. P Ltd acquires these shares at fair value, which is influenced by the fair value of the land, but also the fact that P Ltd will assume responsibility for the liabilities of S Ltd as well.

Think about it

Can P Ltd show the land as an asset in its separate financial statements?

No, P Ltd did not legally acquire the land. The land is still owned by S Ltd. P Ltd acquired the right to **control** the land through its acquisition of the controlling interest in S Ltd.

Journal entries in P Ltd

			CU	CU
Dr		Investment in S	450 000	
	Cr	Bank		450 000

Purchase of shares in S Ltd for cash

The effect of this transaction is reported in the statement of financial position of P Ltd as shown below.

Statement of financial position of P Ltd after acquisition

	CU'000
Land	900
Investment in S Ltd	450
Cash (1 000 – 450)	550
	1 900
Share capital	200
Retained earnings	1 100
Long-term loan	600
	1 900

The shares in S Ltd are recognised as an asset. As P Ltd paid in cash, there is no change in the net assets or equity of P Ltd.

The statement of financial position of P Ltd does not report the underlying assets and liabilities of S Ltd that are controlled by P Ltd. The above statement reports land of CU900 000, while P Ltd actually controls land worth CU1 650 000 (CU900 000 + CU750 000). It is therefore not possible for the users of the financial statements of P Ltd to identify all of the assets that are controlled by P Ltd or to determine the risks and benefits associated with the controlling interest in S Ltd. The same applies to the liabilities, as P Ltd has assumed responsibility for the long-term loan, but it is not reported in its financial statements. For this reason, it is necessary that P Ltd prepare consolidated financial statements.

 Think about it

What is the entry in S Ltd?

S Ltd will not record any transaction. Changes in the shareholders of an entity are not recorded in the financial statements of the entity.

This example continues in Chapter 4, where the consolidation process is explained systematically.

In the sections that follow, we discuss the presentation in the consolidated statements of financial position, statements of profit or loss and other comprehensive income, and statements of cash flows. The **notes** to these consolidated financial statements should, in a similar way, be consolidated, which implies the adding together of the information presented in the notes of the parent and the subsidiaries, including the consolidation adjustments. Thus, the notes should support the consolidated financial information presented.

3.1 The consolidated statement of financial position

Simply stated, the consolidated statement of financial position is prepared by adding the assets, liabilities and equity of all of the subsidiaries to those of the parent, and eliminating the effects of internal transactions, or in other words, balances that relate to amounts owing between group entities rather than to external parties. The group statement of financial position should include assets and liabilities that are the result of transactions with outside parties and not those that are as a result of internal transactions between group entities.

Assets should be recognised only in the statement of financial position of the group when they meet the definition and recognition criteria of an asset of the group (in other words, when the asset is a resource controlled by the group that can be measured and that would probably result in the inflow of future economic benefits to the group). Similarly, group **liabilities** should be recognised only when the definition and recognition criteria of a liability are met (where there is a present obligation of the group resulting from a past event, which can be measured, and the settlement of which would probably result in an outflow of future economic benefits from the group).

The parent will, in its separate financial statements, recognise its investments in its subsidiaries. This represents an equity investment (that is an investment in the shares of the individual subsidiary companies). In the group statement of financial position, the **investment in the subsidiary** is eliminated against the **equity** of the subsidiary that existed at the acquisition date. Thus, in the group statement of financial position, there is no investment in subsidiaries. This investment is replaced with the underlying assets and liabilities of the subsidiaries.

Where **loans** are made to a subsidiary, the debit and the credit balances are set off against each other, as they are not owed to or receivable from parties outside the group. The same principle applies to receivables and payables arising from intra-group transactions. The adjusting entry would be a debit to the liability and a credit to the asset, resulting in the elimination of the balances held within the group.

The cost of **inventory** and other **non-current assets** would be the cost of the asset when it was first acquired by the group. If one group entity bought inventory and then sold it to another group entity, the gross profit recognised on that sale would have to be reversed and the cost of the inventory would have to be shown at its original cost to the group. The correcting entry would debit the profit and credit the inventory to reverse the profit and reduce the inventory to the original cost to the group.

3.2 The consolidated statement of profit or loss and other comprehensive income

The consolidated statement of profit or loss and other comprehensive income is prepared by adding all of the **income** and **expenses** of the parent and subsidiaries together on a line-by-line basis, and then eliminating any amounts that are internal to the group. The consolidated profit or loss is the difference between the total revenue and expenses of the parent and its subsidiaries. The profit is allocated between the two groups of shareholders: the equity holders of the parent and the non-controlling interest relating to the subsidiaries.

The income and expenses of a subsidiary are included in group profit or loss from the date of acquisition. If the **date of acquisition** is in the current year, the income and expenses relating to the period prior to the acquisition period should not be consolidated, but should be included in the net equity acquired at the acquisition date. In this case, it is necessary to determine the profit of the subsidiary at the acquisition date.

For example, where the profit of a subsidiary for the current financial year amounts to CU120 000, you have to determine what the actual revenue and related expenses of the subsidiary were at the acquisition date. If the subsidiary was acquired at the end of the fifth month of its current financial period and the profit at that date amounted to CU55 000, this profit would form part of the equity acquired when the investment was made, and should not be included in the consolidated statement of profit or loss and other comprehensive income. The profits of the subsidiary for the remaining seven months (CU120 000 – CU55 000 = CU65 000) were earned after the acquisition date, and should be included in the consolidated statement of profit or loss and other comprehensive income.

IFRS principles

Presentation of consolidated financial statements

A reporting entity includes the income and expenses of a subsidiary in the consolidated financial statements from the date it gains control until the date on which the reporting entity ceases to control the subsidiary. Income and expenses of the subsidiary are based on the amounts of the assets and liabilities recognised in the consolidated financial statements at the acquisition date (refer to IFRS10: B88).

Income and expenses of a subsidiary **disposed of during the current reporting period** should be identified in a similar way, and only those income and expenses relating to the period for which the entity was a subsidiary should be included in the consolidated statement of profit or loss and other comprehensive income. The statement of profit or loss and other comprehensive income should include the profit or loss and other comprehensive income of a subsidiary only for the portion of the financial year for which it was a subsidiary. Note that the profits earned after the subsidiary was acquired are referred to as 'post-acquisition profits'. The profits earned by the subsidiary before it was acquired are referred to as 'pre-acquisition profits'.

Internal charges between the parent and subsidiary should be eliminated when the consolidated statement of profit or loss and other comprehensive income is prepared (for example, where the parent has charged a subsidiary for management fees, interest or rental on the usage of a property).

Profits recognised by one of the group entities as a result of transferring goods to another group entity should be **eliminated**, as from a group perspective these are **unrealised**. The profit is only realised when it is as a result of a transaction with an outside party. For example, where the parent sells an asset to a subsidiary at a profit, the asset is still owned by the group and it is therefore inappropriate to recognise a profit on the sale. The profit should be reversed and the asset should be reduced to the carrying amount that the parent had recognised prior to the sale (in other words, the carrying amount to the group). Where the same asset has been sold to a third party, the profit is realised, as it was sold to a party outside the group and no adjustment is therefore required. As the parent and the subsidiary are part of the same group, profits from transactions between the parent and the subsidiary should be eliminated. However, if the asset that was sold by the parent to the subsidiary is subsequently sold by the subsidiary to a third party, the unrealised profit is now realised and can be recognised.

Normal corporate **taxation** charges are expenses relating to each entity that is registered for taxation. These amounts should not be adjusted for the effect of the elimination of internal charges between entities. In some jurisdictions, a group may become the taxable entity, resulting in a change in the tax base of the asset to its fair value. However, for purposes of examples in this publication, it is assumed that the tax bases of the subsidiary's assets and liabilities are unchanged as result of the parent's acquisition of the subsidiary. Thus, as the separate legal entities are taxed based on their individual profits (each legal entity is a tax entity) as opposed to the group profits, changing group profits will have no effect on the tax actually payable, as the group is not a taxable entity. Consequently, the taxation expense of each entity that is consolidated is added together to recognise the tax expense for the group. However, where the total group profit is adjusted as a result of the elimination of inter-entity transactions (and the carrying amounts of group assets and liabilities are adjusted as a result), a **deferred tax** adjustment will arise. This occurs because the carrying amount of the asset or liability is changing, while the tax base remains the same. This results in a temporary difference for which deferred tax needs to be recognised.

Where the parent has received **dividend income** from a subsidiary, the dividends received are normally included in the revenue figure recognised by the parent in its separate statement of profit or loss and other comprehensive income. The dividends were received by the parent from the subsidiary and should be eliminated against the dividends paid or declared by the subsidiary. If the dividends received were not eliminated, this would result in the double-counting of the distributed portion of the profits of the subsidiary. Consolidation results in the recognition of the profits earned by the subsidiary and therefore cannot also recognise the dividends received by the parent when these are a distribution of those profits.

3.3 The consolidated statement of changes in equity

The consolidated statement of changes in equity is prepared as a summary of the equity of the group as one economic entity. It divides the equity between the equity holders of the parent and the non-controlling interest. The **equity interest of the parent** includes the share capital and share premium of the parent only, as the equity of the subsidiary at the acquisition date is eliminated against the investment by the parent, after allocating the portion of the equity attributable to the **non-controlling shareholders**.

The **reserves** of the group (those attributable to the equity holders of the parent) are determined by combining the retained earnings and other reserves of the parent with the parent's share of the retained earnings and other reserves of the subsidiary since the date of acquisition.

The **dividends** declared by the subsidiary during the reporting period are eliminated against the dividends received by the parent, which are included in revenue. The consolidated statement of changes in equity should only include the dividends declared by the parent to its shareholders. The dividends declared by the subsidiary that are attributable to the non-controlling shareholders are allocated separately to the non-controlling interest.

4. Disclosure requirements

IFRS12, *Disclosure of Interests in Other Entities*, requires a wide range of disclosures about an entity's interests in subsidiaries, joint arrangements, associates and unconsolidated 'structured entities'. An entity is required to disclose information that enables users of its consolidated financial statements to understand the composition of the group, and the non-controlling interest in the group's activities and cash flows. The main disclosure requirements relating to **interests in controlled entities** (in other words, subsidiaries) are outlined below.

4.1 Significant judgements and assumptions

The entity must disclose information about significant judgements and assumptions the entity has made (and changes to those judgements and assumptions) in determining:
• That it has control over another entity

- That it has joint control of an arrangement or significant influence over another entity
- The type of joint arrangement (in other words, joint operation or joint venture) when the arrangement has been structured through a separate vehicle
- The non-controlling interest in the group's activities and cash flows.

An entity is required to disclose information that enables users of its consolidated financial statements to evaluate the nature and extent of **significant restrictions** on its ability to access or use assets, and to settle liabilities of the group. This includes the nature of and changes in the risks associated with its interests in consolidated structured entities, the consequences of changes in its ownership interest in a subsidiary that do not result in a loss of control and the consequences of losing control of a subsidiary during the reporting period.

Test your knowledge

There is a list of learning objectives at the beginning of this chapter. Go back to this list and check whether you have achieved these outcomes. If not, reread the appropriate section.

Questions

Question 1
P Ltd owns shares in S Ltd as follows:
- 45% of the 1 000 'A' class shares
- 70% of the 1 000 'B' class shares, where two 'B' shares are equivalent to one 'A' share in terms of voting rights.

Each class of shares has an equal share in the profits of S Ltd.
1. Calculate the percentage voting rights in S Ltd held by P Ltd.
2. Briefly explain how S Ltd should be accounted for in the group annual financial statements of P Ltd.

Suggested solution
1. Number of 'voting rights' in issue (equivalent): 1 000 'A' + 500 'B' (1 000 × ½) = 1 500
   Owns: (45% × 1 000) + (70% × 500) = 800/1 500 = 53.33%
2. S Ltd will be consolidated as it is a subsidiary (P Ltd owns > 50% of the voting rights in S Ltd).

Question 2
P Ltd has acquired the following investments in shares during the current year:

G Ltd	CU130 000 (40% of the issued share capital)
T Ltd	CU400 000 (32% of the issued share capital)

P Ltd is unsure how to account for these investments and has asked you for some advice. The information below is available about the two companies.
G Ltd:
- The remaining shares in G Ltd are owned by a diverse group of investors who each hold a small parcel of shares.
- In the past, only a small number of these shareholders attended the general meetings or questioned the actions of the directors.

- P Ltd has nominated three new directors and expects that they will be appointed at the next annual general meeting, replacing three of the existing directors. The current board of directors of G Ltd consists of five members.

T Ltd:
- The remaining shares in T Ltd are owned by a few investors who each own approximately 30% of the issued shares.
- The shareholders take a keen interest in the running of the company and attend all meetings.
- Two of the shareholders, including P Ltd, already have representation on the board of directors. These shareholders have indicated their intention of nominating these directors for re-election.

P Ltd is concerned that it may need to prepare consolidated financial statements under IFRS10.
For each of its investments, you are required to advise P Ltd whether control exists in terms of IFRS10. Motivate your answers.

Suggested solution

P Ltd's interest in G Ltd:
P Ltd has a 40% interest in G Ltd. The remaining 60% is held by a diverse group of investors who:
- Each hold a small parcel of shares
- Usually do not attend general meetings or question the actions of the directors.

In addition, P Ltd is able to appoint three of the five directors of G Ltd.
Even though P Ltd owns less than 50% of the issued shares in G Ltd, by further investigation it appears that P Ltd has the ability to control the financial and operating decisions of G Ltd. P Ltd has the ability to appoint key personnel (evaluating power).
Conclusion:
P Ltd has *de facto* control of G Ltd. As a result, it needs to prepare consolidated financial statements.

P Ltd's interest in T Ltd:
P Ltd has a 32% interest in T Ltd. The other shareholders each have similar interests. The evidence thereby indicates that there are at least two other shareholders that also hold approximately 30% interest in T Ltd.
P Ltd is able to appoint one director to the board of T Ltd, making it probable that P Ltd is able to exert significant influence over the operational and financial decisions of T Ltd.
Conclusion:
P Ltd does not have control over T Ltd, but the evidence shows that P Ltd has significant influence over T Ltd. T Ltd is therefore an associate and P Ltd's interest in T Ltd should be equity accounted in the group financial statements.

Case study exercises

Scenario 1
The extracts below, which are from the financial statements of two entities, P Ltd and S Ltd, for the year ended 31 December 20x5, have been presented to you.

Statements of financial position of P Ltd and S Ltd on 31 December 20x5

	P Ltd CU'000	S Ltd CU'000
ASSETS		
Plant and machinery (carrying amount)	300	200
Investment in S Ltd	400	–
Loan to S Ltd	80	–
Current assets	140	500
	920	700
CAPITAL AND LIABILITIES		
Share capital	200	100
Retained earnings	620	500
Shareholders' equity	820	600
Loan from P Ltd	–	80
Current liabilities	100	20
	920	700

Statements of profit or loss and other comprehensive income of P Ltd and S Ltd for the year ended 31 December 20x5

	P Ltd CU'000	S Ltd CU'000
Gross revenue (including dividends and interest received)	1 870	1 600
Net operating costs	(1 050)	(920)
Profit from ordinary activities before interest	820	680
Interest paid	(200)	(50)
Profit on ordinary activities before taxation	620	630
Taxation	(250)	(230)
Profit for the year	370	400

P Ltd acquired 100% of the issued ordinary share capital of S Ltd on 1 January 20x5. The identifiable assets and liabilities of S Ltd were considered fairly valued at the date of acquisition.

Answer the questions that follow, which relate to these two entities and their relationship. In each case, motivate your answer.

1. How would you describe the relationship between P Ltd and S Ltd?
2. Based on your answer above, does P Ltd have to prepare group financial statements?
3. Will P Ltd still have to prepare its own, separate financial statements?
4. Prepare the journal entry in P Ltd when it acquired its controlling interest in S Ltd.
   a. Assume that P Ltd paid CU400 000 for the shares, in cash, on 1 January 20x5.
   b. Assume that P Ltd paid CU300 000 for the shares in S Ltd on 1 January 20x5 and the fair value of the shares was CU400 000 at 31 December 20x5.
5. When preparing group financial statements for P Ltd for the year ended 31 December 20x5:
   a. What is the starting point?
   b. What is the end point?
   c. Describe the adjustments that you would make to move from the starting point to the end point.
6. Assume that P Ltd prepares group financial statements. What will be the following amounts recognised in the group financial statements at 31 December 20x5?
   • Investment in S Ltd
   • Current assets.
7. When will P Ltd not be required to prepare group financial statements?

Suggested solution

Scenario 1

P Ltd acquired 100% of the issued ordinary share capital of S Ltd on 1 January 20x5.

1. **How would you describe the relationship between P Ltd and S Ltd?**

   As P Ltd acquired all of the issued ordinary shares in S Ltd, P Ltd acquired the controlling interest in S Ltd. P Ltd is therefore the parent and S Ltd is its subsidiary.

2. **Based on your answer above, does P Ltd have to prepare group financial statements?**

   Yes. As P Ltd has control of S Ltd, P Ltd has to prepare group financial statements.

3. **Will P Ltd still have to prepare its own, separate financial statements?**

   Yes, P Ltd has to prepare separate financial statements in compliance with IAS27.

4. **Prepare the journal entry in P Ltd when it acquired its controlling interest in S Ltd.**

   a. **Assume that P Ltd paid CU400 000 for the shares, in cash, on 1 January 20x5.**

			CU	CU
Dr		Investment in S Ltd	400 000	
	Cr	Bank		400 000

   Acquisition of 100% of the shares in S Ltd, for cash

   b. **Assume P Ltd paid CU300 000 for the shares in S Ltd on 1 January 20x5 and the fair value of the shares was CU400 000 at 31 December 20x5.**

   - On the assumption that the shares are recognised at fair value of CU400 000 at the reporting date (as per the statement of financial position) and that fair value adjustments are recognised in profit or loss:

			CU	CU
Dr		Investment in S Ltd	300 000	
	Cr	Bank		300 000

   Acquisition of 100% of the shares in S Ltd, for cash

			CU	CU
Dr		Investment in S Ltd	100 000	
	Cr	Fair value adjustment (P/L)		100 000

   Fair value adjustment relating to investment in subsidiary, recognised in profit or loss

   - On the assumption that the shares are recognised at fair value of CU400 000 at the reporting date (as per the statement of financial position) and that fair value adjustments are recognised in other comprehensive income:

			CU	CU
Dr		Investment in S Ltd	300 000	
	Cr	Bank		300 000

   Acquisition of 100% of the shares in S Ltd, for cash

			CU	CU
Dr		Investment in S Ltd	100 000	
	Cr	Fair value adjustment (OCI)		100 000

   Fair value adjustment relating to investment in subsidiary, recognised in other comprehensive income (OCI)

5. **When preparing group financial statements for P Ltd for the year ended 31 December 20x5:**
   a. **What is the starting point?**

   The starting point is the separate financial statements of P Ltd and S Ltd for the year ended 31 December 20x5 combined. This means that the individual like items of assets, liabilities, income, equity and expenses and cash flows of the parent entity (P Ltd) and its subsidiary (S Ltd) are combined line by line.

   b. **What is the end point?**

   The end point is the consolidated financial statements of P Ltd for the year ended 31 December 20x5, reported as a single economic entity.

   c. **Describe the adjustments that you would make to move from the starting point to the end point.**

   From the starting point, being the combined like items of assets, liabilities, equity, income and expenses and cash flows of the parent and its subsidiary, I would eliminate (by using *pro-forma* journal entries) the carrying amount of the parent's investment in the subsidiary and the parent's portion of the equity of the subsidiary. I would also eliminate (by using *pro-forma* journal entries) any intra-group transactions amongst the entities in order to get to the end point, which is the consolidated financial statements reported as a single economic entity.

6. **Assume that P Ltd prepares group financial statements. What will be the following amounts recognised in the group financial statements at 31 December 20x5?**
   a. **Investment in S Ltd**

   There will be no investment in S Ltd in the group financial statements as this amount is eliminated on consolidation.

   b. **Current assets**

   CU640 000 (CU140 000 + CU500 000)

   The process of consolidation requires that the assets of the subsidiary be added to the assets of the parent.

7. **When will P Ltd not be required to prepare group financial statements?**

   P Ltd does not have to prepare group financial statements when all of the following criteria are met (refer to IFRS10):

   - When P Ltd is a wholly owned subsidiary or a partially owned subsidiary of another entity and all of its other owners, including those not otherwise entitled to vote, have been informed about and do not object to the parent not presenting consolidated financial statements.
   - When P Ltd's debt or equity instruments are not traded in a public market, for example, a domestic or foreign stock exchange, or an over-the-counter market, including local and regional markets.
   - When P Ltd has not filed, nor is it in the process of filing, its financial statements with a securities commission or other regulatory organisation for the purpose of issuing any class of instruments in a public market.
   - When P Ltd's ultimate or any intermediate parent produces consolidated financial statements that are available for public use and comply with IFRS.

Consolidation: Wholly owned subsidiaries

4

The following topics are included in this chapter:

- The basic consolidation process for a wholly owned subsidiary, with reference to:
  - The accounting equation
  - The consolidation worksheet and using *pro-forma* journal entries
  - The starting point and end point in the consolidation process.
- Preparing basic group financial statements for a parent with a wholly owned subsidiary in reporting periods subsequent to the acquisition date.

Learning objectives

By the end of this chapter, you should be able to:
- Apply the basic consolidation process principles for a parent with a wholly owned subsidiary
- Explain the consolidation process with reference to the accounting equation
- Identify the fair values of the net identifiable assets of the subsidiary at the acquisition date
- Identify the consolidation adjustments required at the acquisition date in order to eliminate the parent's interest in the subsidiary and recognise the net assets of the subsidiary at their fair values
- Understand that the starting point represents the individual financial statements of the parent and its subsidiary
- Prepare *pro-forma* journal entries required at the acquisition date and in the subsequent reporting periods to consolidate a wholly owned subsidiary
- Prepare the consolidation worksheet and understand that the end point represents the consolidated financial statements
- Explain what each of the amounts in the consolidated financial statements represents
- Analyse the equity of the subsidiary, for example, retained earnings, between the pre- and the post-acquisition periods.

1. Introduction

In this chapter, we will focus on the preparation of consolidated financial statements for a group consisting of a parent and a wholly owned subsidiary. This means that the parent acquired all the shares of the subsidiary at the acquisition date. In other words, the parent is the only holder of the subsidiary's equity and there are no other shareholders.

2. The consolidation process

The consolidation process starts with adding together the financial statements of the parent and its subsidiaries. These separate financial statements of the individual legal entities are prepared in accordance with IFRS. In the parent's separate financial statements (refer to Chapter 1), the parent initially records its investment in the subsidiary based upon the consideration transferred, which represents the cost of the shares. The end goal of the consolidation process is the group financial statements. The information included in the separate financial statements represents the starting point for consolidation. These financial statements are then added together in order to obtain the consolidated (or group) financial statements, which is the end point. Adjustments are required to the extent that the starting point and end point are different. These are the consolidation procedures.

IFRS principles

Consolidation procedures

The following consolidation procedures are required in terms of IFRS10 (refer to IFRS10: B86):
- Combine like items of assets, liabilities, equity, income, expenses and cash flows of the parent with those of its subsidiaries
- Offset (eliminate) the carrying amount of the parent's investment in each subsidiary and the parent's portion of equity of each subsidiary (IFRS3, *Business Combinations*, explains how to account for any related goodwill)
- Eliminate in full intra-group assets and liabilities, equity, income, expenses and cash flows relating to transactions between entities of the group (profits or losses resulting from intra-group transactions that are recognised in assets, such as inventory and fixed assets, are eliminated in full).

At the start of the consolidation process, we have a **business combination** (refer back to Chapter 2), which is when an acquirer obtains control of the acquiree. In this case, the parent obtains control of the subsidiary. In terms of IFRS3, *Business Combinations*, we need to identify the following elements relating to the business combination:
1. The acquirer (the parent)
2. The acquiree (the subsidiary)
3. The acquisition date (the date on which the parent obtains control of the subsidiary)
4. The consideration (the amount that the parent agreed to transfer or pay in return for the controlling interest)

5. The fair value of the separately identifiable assets acquired and liabilities assumed through this business combination
6. The fair value of any goodwill acquired
7. The non-controlling interest in the case when the parent did not acquire all of the shares in the subsidiary.

IFRS3 requires that the identifiable assets acquired and liabilities assumed of an acquired entity are recognised at fair value at the acquisition date. An initial adjustment needs to be made on consolidation concerning any assets or liabilities for which there are differences between the fair value and the carrying amount at the acquisition date. Furthermore, although some intangible assets and liabilities of the subsidiary may not have been recognised in the subsidiary's records, they are recognised as part of the business combination (for example, goodwill) (see Section 2.2 of this chapter).

When preparing consolidated financial statements, two important stages need consideration:

- The **acquisition date**: This is the date on which the parent acquired its controlling interest in the subsidiary. From the group perspective, this is the date on which the group acquires control of the underlying assets and liabilities of the subsidiary, and recognises these assets and liabilities for the first time. The parent would have considered the fair value of the identifiable assets and liabilities of the subsidiary at the acquisition date, and determined how much it was prepared to pay for this controlling interest.
- The **subsequent period**: This period is the period from the acquisition date until the current reporting date. The group reflects the changes in the assets and liabilities since the acquisition date. In other words, the group reflects the increases (or decreases) in the equity of the subsidiary subsequent to the acquisition date.

2.1 The acquisition date

The acquisition date is the date on which the parent obtains **control** of the subsidiary. The parent usually acquires the controlling interest when buying the shares in the subsidiary from its existing shareholders. The **purchase consideration** is determined through negotiation and is based on what the parent (the acquirer) considers the fair value of the investment to be. In order to determine the fair value of the investment, the parent considers the **fair value of the separately identifiable assets and liabilities** of the subsidiary. Any excess between the purchase consideration and the net fair value of the assets and liabilities of the subsidiary is recognised as **goodwill** acquired.

When a new company is registered (incorporated) and the parent acquires a controlling interest at the date of incorporation, the new subsidiary does not have any assets or liabilities. The parent therefore acquires the shares at the issue price.

The consolidation at acquisition involves replacing the cost of the investment in the subsidiary with the parent's share of the fair value of the identifiable assets and liabilities of the subsidiary, and recognising any excess payment as goodwill acquired. The parent identifies all of the assets and liabilities of the subsidiary **at the acquisition date** and determines whether the cost of acquisition of the shares includes any amount attributable to the fair value of any asset or liability that differs from its carrying amount. Where this is the case, the carrying amount of such an asset is adjusted so that the fair value of the asset or liability is recognised as the cost price to the group and the equity of the subsidiary is adjusted accordingly.

The equity of the subsidiary that exists at the date of acquisition is not recognised in the group financial statements.

2.2 Goodwill acquired at the acquisition date

When the parent acquires a controlling interest in a subsidiary, the purchase consideration may include an amount that was paid for goodwill. Goodwill at the acquisition date is the excess of a) over b) below (refer to IFRS3, paragraph 32):
  a)   The aggregate of the consideration transferred and the amount of non-controlling interest.
  b)   The net fair value of the identifiable assets acquired and the liabilities assumed of the subsidiary.

The goodwill arising on consolidation can relate to various synergies and **intangible assets** that have been acquired, but have not been recognised on the statement of financial position of the subsidiary (for example, a good customer base, loyal employees and market share). In addition, the mere fact that a controlling interest is obtained may result in the parent paying more than just the value of the net assets for an investment in a subsidiary.

The measurement of goodwill is discussed further in Section 3 of Chapter 7.

2.3 The subsequent period

The **subsequent period**, (also referred to as the post-acquisition period) refers to the financial reporting periods subsequent to the acquisition date. Consolidated financial statements are prepared at each reporting date of the parent. Thus, for each subsequent reporting period, we need to prepare consolidated financial statements that include the assets and liabilities of the subsidiary at that date as well as the equity attributable to the equity holders of the parent.

Changes in the assets and liabilities represent the changes in equity of the subsidiary income and expenses for the current reporting period, as well as profits recognised in prior periods, and gains and losses recognised in other comprehensive income in the current and prior periods. This equity is recognised in the form of reserves (retained earnings and any other type of reserve such as a revaluation surplus) that arose **after the subsidiary was acquired** and should be recognised in the consolidated financial statements.

The equity in the consolidated financial statements is based on the changes in the equity of the subsidiary **after the acquisition date**. This is represented by the difference between the cost of assets and liabilities to the group at the acquisition date and their carrying amount at the reporting date. Where the cost of the assets and liabilities to the group differs from their carrying amount at the acquisition date (in other words, the parent considers the fair value to be different from the carrying amount recognised by the subsidiary), that adjustment is recognised as part of the acquisition cost at the acquisition date and should not be taken into account when calculating the post-acquisition equity.

For financial years that are two or more years after the date of acquisition, the parent's interest in the profits (and changes in other comprehensive income) of the subsidiary relating to dates after the acquisition date until the beginning of the current year should be added to the parent's opening retained earnings balance to determine the correct group opening retained earnings balance in the consolidated statement of changes in equity.

The separate financial statements of the parent and its subsidiaries are complete and they are prepared in accordance with IFRS. This means that all of the necessary adjustments have been performed for each individual entity. The 'adding together' of the completed financial statements of each entity in the group is the **starting point** and the resulting group financial statements is the **end point**.

In the sections that follow, we will explain systematically how these consolidation procedures result in the reporting of consolidated financial statements. We assume that there is no consolidated general ledger, and that the consolidation process does not change any of the amounts recorded in the separate general ledgers of the parent and its subsidiaries, which have been prepared in accordance with IFRS. The consolidation process happens 'outside' of the general ledgers of the individual entities.

The preparation of consolidated financial statements can be done by using a consolidation **worksheet** or a computerised spreadsheet. The **adjustment** columns of the worksheet contain the consolidation adjustments, which adjust the amounts recognised in the individual financial statements of the parent and its subsidiaries (the starting point). As there is no general ledger that tracks the different adjustments, we need to keep a separate record of all of the consolidation adjustments; these are usually done by using *pro-forma* **journal entries**. The *pro-forma* entries have no effect on the actual financial records of the parent and its subsidiary.

In order to allocate the equity of the subsidiary between the pre-acquisition period and the subsequent period, we **analyse the equity** of the subsidiary to determine its equity at the acquisition date and any increases since the acquisition date.

3. The consolidation worksheet

Consolidated financial statements include a consolidated statement of financial position, a consolidated statement of profit or loss and other comprehensive income, a consolidated statement of changes in equity and a consolidated statement of cash flows. In addition, all of the notes presented in the financial statements should also include the consolidated balances. When consolidated financial statements are prepared, the financial statements of the parent and all of its subsidiaries are combined on a line-by-line basis.

The **consolidation worksheet** is a useful tool to assist in the preparation of the group financial statements. In a sense, the consolidation worksheet represents 'workings' associated with this process. Assets, liabilities, equity, income and expenses are added together on a line-by-line basis. This is normally done in a columnar format and a computerised spreadsheet is ideally used in practice. A consolidation worksheet (or group worksheet) is prepared by adding across the balances per line item for the parent and its subsidiaries, and by adjusting, where relevant, to determine the balances to be recognised by the group. For example, if the bank balance in the parent amounts to CU50 000 and the bank balance in the subsidiary amounts to CU20 000, the balances of the line item 'bank and cash balances' for the group would amount to CU70 000. This amount should then be recognised on the consolidated statement of financial position.

Example

Preparation of consolidation worksheet

In the example in Chapter 3, we asked why consolidation is necessary.

The parent acquired all of the shares in the subsidiary, S Ltd, for CU450 000. The equity of S Ltd consisted of:

- Share capital: CU100 000
- Retained earnings: CU100 000.

P Ltd considered the fair value of land to be CU750 000 (the cost to S Ltd was CU500 000), resulting in an adjustment to the equity of S Ltd, from a group's perspective, of CU250 000.

The worksheet that follows illustrates the basic steps in the consolidation process:

- The adding together of all of the assets and liabilities that are controlled by the group
- The elimination of the investment in the subsidiary (in P Ltd) with the corresponding equity of the subsidiary (S Ltd).

	P Ltd CU'000	S Ltd CU'000	Starting point CU'000	Adjustments CU'000	Consolidated CU'000
	(A)	(B)	(A) + (B)	(C)	(A + B) +/– (C)
Land	900	500	1400	250	1 650
Investment in S Ltd	450		450	(450)	–
Cash	550		550		550
	1 900	**500**	**2 400**		**2 200**
Share capital	200	100	300	(100)	200
Retained earnings	1 100	100	1 200	(100)	1 100
Long-term loan	600	300	900		900
	1 900	**500**	**2 400**		**2 200**

The **starting point** [(A) + (B)] is that 100% of the assets, liabilities and equity of the parent and subsidiary are added together. There are no consolidated ledger accounts.

The adjustments (C) are necessary to eliminate the investment that P Ltd acquired in S Ltd against the equity of S Ltd at the acquisition date. From a group perspective, there is no investment. In addition, the land should be recognised at its fair value at the acquisition date. An adjustment is needed to record the increase in value. The adjustments are recorded by using *pro-forma* journal entries.

The **end point** [(A) + (B) + (C)] represents the financial position of the group, which is made up of 100% of the assets, liabilities and equity of the parent and its subsidiary, plus or minus any adjustments made through the *pro-forma* journal entries.

In the **consolidated statement of financial position**, land is reported at CU1 650 000, which includes all of the land that is controlled by the group.

The consolidation worksheet is merely a tool to calculate the group balances. It does not form part of the consolidated financial statements, but supports the balances presented in the consolidated financial statements (together with the *pro-forma* journal entries) in a similar way to the way in which the trial balance of an entity supports the balances presented in the financial statements of an entity. The consolidation worksheet is a combination of many trial balances, all added together and adjusted to determine the group balances to be presented in the consolidated financial statements.

3.1 Starting point

As illustrated above, the starting point is the information presented in the individual financial statements of the separate legal entities in the group added together for the reporting period for which consolidated financial statements are now being prepared.

> ### Think about it
> **Why is this important?**
>
> Each entity prepares its own financial statements in accordance with IFRS. This means that the income and expenses, assets and liabilities, and equity, are recorded and reported for that specific entity.
>
> In the above example, the subsidiary will continue to recognise land at its cost of CU500 000, as that was the consideration paid when it was first acquired by S Ltd and land is recognised using the cost model.
>
> However, the cost of S Ltd's land amounted to CU750 000 when it was acquired by the group.

3.2 Understanding the end point

The consolidated financial statements should include all of the assets controlled and liabilities assumed by the group as a single economic entity, in accordance with IFRS. This is the end point.

3.3 Checking the end point

It is important that you are able to check that the **end point** makes sense.
- Is the equity of the subsidiaries at acquisition eliminated against the investment in the subsidiaries, as recognised in the parent's financial statements?
- Are all of the assets and liabilities of the group included?
- Where there were fair value adjustments to any assets at the acquisition date, is the cost of that asset to the group recognised after taking into account those fair value adjustments?
- In subsequent reporting periods, are the assets treated appropriately when considering the cost of those assets to the group? For example, depreciation for the group should be based on the cost of the asset to the group and not to the subsidiary.
- Has the effect of intra-group transactions been eliminated? This includes the fact that the results for the group should exclude any unrealised profits resulting from transactions within the group, and increases (or decreases) in the assets and liabilities that result from intra-group transactions should be eliminated. They should be measured at their fair value when they were first acquired (or assumed) by the group.

Throughout this publication, we will continue to emphasise the principles that you should check at the end point.

Example

Illustration of the consolidation process (for a wholly owned subsidiary)

In the example above, we prepared the consolidation worksheet in order to prepare the consolidated financial statements of P Ltd.

	P Ltd CU'000	S Ltd CU'000	Starting point CU'000	Adjustments and eliminations (by using *pro-forma* journal entries) CU'000	Consolidated CU'000
	(A)	(B)	(A) + (B)	(C)	(A + B) +/– (C)
Land	900	500	1 400	(Dr) 250	1 650
Investment in S Ltd	450		450	(Cr) (450)	–
Cash	550		550		550
	1 900	500	2 400		**2 200**
Share capital	200	100	300	(Dr) (100)	200
Retained earnings	1 100	100	1 200	(Dr) (100)	1 100
Long term loan	600	300	900		900
	1 900	500	2 400		**2 200**

Starting point   *Pro-forma* adjustments   End point

The following steps are illustrated in this worksheet:

- (A) represents the statement of financial position of the parent. Note that the parent has an investment in the subsidiary, representing a 100% controlling interest. This is a wholly owned subsidiary.
- (B) represents the statement of financial position of the subsidiary.
- (A) plus (B) represents the **starting point** of the consolidation process.
- (C) represents the adjustment entries that are required on consolidation. Note that these entries should always balance, resulting in a zero net balance.

P Ltd acquired all of the shares in S Ltd on 31 December 20x5 and paid CU750 000 for this investment. The substance of this transaction is that P Ltd acquired the equity of S Ltd on the acquisition date, consisting of share capital of CU100 000 and retained earnings of CU100 000. The consolidation process requires the **offsetting of the carrying amount of the parent's investment** in the subsidiary and the **equity of the subsidiary**. As P Ltd acquired this equity when acquiring its investment in S Ltd, it should be eliminated on consolidation.

As the consolidated statement of financial position represents the transactions of the group as a single entity, the consolidated financial statements of the group cannot recognise an investment in itself.

The **end point** of (A + B) +/– (C) is the consolidated statement of financial position. This statement combines the assets and liabilities of the group as a single entity.

A wholly owned subsidiary is an entity in which the parent holds all of the issued share capital. When a wholly owned subsidiary is consolidated, the share capital of the subsidiary and other pre-acquisition equity is eliminated against the investment in the subsidiary recognised in the statement of financial position of the parent. As there are no other shareholders in the subsidiary, no non-controlling interest is recognised.

The cost of the land in S Ltd when acquired by the group was CU750 000. The land in S Ltd should therefore increase by CU250 000 at the acquisition date. This is because P Ltd acquired the net assets of S Ltd at the acquisition date. These assets amounted to CU450 000, consisting of CU100 000 share capital, CU100 000 retained income and the fair value adjustment to land of CU250 000.

3.4 *Pro-forma* journal entries

Pro-forma **journal entries** are adjustments recorded on the consolidation worksheet for the following reasons (refer to IFRS10: B86):

- To eliminate the carrying amount of the investment in subsidiaries and the equity of the subsidiaries at the acquisition date
- To adjust the carrying amounts of the subsidiary's assets and liabilities to fair value, and to recognise goodwill, if any, at the acquisition date
- To eliminate the effect of intra-group transactions between the parent and its subsidiaries in subsequent periods.

It is assumed that *pro-forma* journal entries are never recorded in the separate general ledgers of any of the group entities. They are journal entries that can affect more than one trial balance at the same time. For example, a debit entry can refer to a balance in the parent's trial balance, while the related credit entry can refer to a balance in a subsidiary's trial balance. Because *pro-forma* journal entries are not recorded in a ledger, the financial statements of the group entities that are combined as the starting point do not include adjustments done in the prior period and thus need to be repeated at each reporting date.

This is an example of a *pro-forma* journal entry:

Dr		Loan from parent (in the trial balance of the subsidiary)
	Cr	Loan to subsidiary (in the trial balance of the parent)

Example

Preparation of *pro-forma* journal entries

In the example above, we illustrated why the preparation of consolidated financial statements is necessary. The worksheet enabled us to add together 100% of the assets, liabilities and equity of the parent and the subsidiary as the starting point.

The adjustments (C) are necessary to eliminate the investment that P Ltd has in S Ltd against the equity at the acquisition date of S Ltd and to recognise the assets at fair value. From a group perspective, there is no investment and the assets should be recognised at the cost to the group. The adjustments are recorded by using the following *pro-forma* journal entries:

			CU	CU
Dr		Share capital	100 000	
Dr		Retained earnings	100 000	
Dr		Land	250 000	
	Cr	Investment in S Ltd		450 000

Elimination of investment in subsidiary at the acquisition date

Note that this *pro-forma* journal entry affects the financial statements of the parent and the subsidiary. It eliminates the share capital and retained earnings of S Ltd at the acquisition date, increases the cost of the land at the acquisition date by CU250 000 and eliminates the investment in S Ltd, as recorded in the separate financial statements of P Ltd. It is also important to note that the debits and credits in the *pro-forma* journal entry are equal.

4. Consolidating a wholly owned subsidiary at the acquisition date

The example that follows is the first in a series of examples illustrating the process of consolidation. The example will be expanded to incorporate additional issues that are addressed in each chapter, which will allow you to identify the effect on a scenario with which you are already familiar.

 Example

Consolidating a wholly owned subsidiary at the acquisition date

The purpose of this example is to illustrate the consolidation process for a wholly owned subsidiary at the acquisition date. It includes a fair value adjustment of a depreciable asset at the acquisition date and the recognition of goodwill. It further illustrates the elimination of accumulated depreciation in the subsidiary at the acquisition date.

P Ltd acquired all of the shares in S Ltd at 1 January 20x4 for CU275 000. P Ltd considered all of the assets and liabilities of S Ltd to be fairly valued at the acquisition date, except for plant and machinery, of which the fair value is considered to be CU240 000. Ignore taxation.

Statements of the financial position of P Ltd and S Ltd on 1 January 20x4

	P Ltd CU	S Ltd CU
ASSETS		
Plant and machinery (carrying amount)	150 000	200 000
Cost	400 000	350 000
Accumulated depreciation	(250 000)	(150 000)
Investment in S Ltd	285 000	
Current assets	80 000	110 000
	515 000	310 000
EQUITY AND LIABILITIES		
Share capital	240 000	120 000
Retained earnings	90 000	115 000
Shareholders' equity	330 000	235 000
Current liabilities	185 000	75 000
	515 000	310 000

What is the acquisition date?

P Ltd acquired the controlling interest of 100% on 1 January 20x4. This means that consolidated financial statements should be prepared for every reporting period after and including this date. The first reporting date since this date is 1 January 20x4. Thus, we will prepare consolidated financial statements at the acquisition date.

When P Ltd acquired all the shares in S Ltd, what is the entry in S Ltd?

S Ltd does not record any entry in its own financial statements, as P Ltd acquired the controlling interest from the existing shareholders in S Ltd. P Ltd did not transact with the entity, it transacted with its owners. Furthermore, note that S Ltd will not adjust the cost of the plant and machinery in its own financial statements. The fair value of the assets at acquisition date does not affect the recording and reporting in S Ltd.

What is the equity of S Ltd at the acquisition date?

Equity/net asset value of S Ltd at acquisition:

	CU
Share capital	120 000
Retained earnings	115 000
Value of equity/net assets recorded by S Ltd:	235 000
Fair value adjustment to plant and machinery	40 000
Fair value of net assets of S Ltd:	275 000

What is the consideration that P Ltd paid for its controlling interest in S Ltd?

P Ltd paid CU285 000. Refer to the separate statement of financial position of P Ltd to see 'Investment in S Ltd'.

What is the difference?

The fair value of the net assets of S Ltd amounts to CU275 000. This is equal to the fair value of the equity of S Ltd at the acquisition date (CU275 000). However, P Ltd paid CU285 000 for this equity investment. The excess represents **goodwill** of CU10 000 (CU285 000 – CU275 000).

The statements of financial position of the parent and its subsidiary are used as part of the consolidation **worksheet** to determine the consolidated statement of financial position at the acquisition date.

Note that the value of the equity recorded by S Ltd needs to be adjusted for the fact that the plant and machinery recorded by S Ltd is recognised at a carrying amount of CU200 000, while it has a fair value of CU240 000. The net assets of S Ltd are therefore undervalued by CU40 000 (CU240 000 – CU200 000).

P Ltd and its subsidiary: Consolidated statement of financial position at 1 January 20x4

	P Ltd CU	S Ltd CU	Pro-forma journals CU	Consolidated CU
ASSETS				
Plant and machinery (carrying amount)	150 000	200 000	③ 40 000	390 000
Investment in S Ltd	285 000		⑤ (285 000)	–
Goodwill			④ 10 000	10 000
Net current assets	80 000	110 000		190 000
Total assets	**515 000**	**310 000**	**(235 000)**	**590 000**
CAPITAL AND LIABILITIES				
Share capital	240 000	120 000	① (120 000)	240 000
Retained earnings	90 000	115 000	② (115 000)	90 000
Total capital and reserves	330 000	235 000	(235 000)	330 000
Current liabilities	185 000	75 000		260 000
Total capital and liabilities	**515 000**	**310 000**	**(235 000)**	**590 000**

What is the starting point?

The statements of financial position of the separate, individual legal entities are included in the starting point.

Note the following:

- P Ltd's financial statements include the investment of CU285 000 in the subsidiary.
- S Ltd's financial statements do not record any transactions relating to the change in ownership, and include the plant and machinery at a carrying amount of CU200 000.

Checking the end point

The equity in the group is that of the parent only, CU330 000. The equity of S Ltd is eliminated on consolidation.

The **equity of S Ltd** at the acquisition date can therefore be summarised as follows:

	Total equity of S Ltd CU	Acquired by P Ltd 100% CU
At acquisition date:		
Share capital	120 000	
Retained earnings	115 000	
Plant and machinery (considered undervalued)	40 000	
Fair value of net assets at acquisition date	275 000	275 000
Goodwill acquired		10 000
Investment in S Ltd		285 000

Pro-forma journal entries

The process of consolidation requires that we eliminate the investment in P Ltd's financial statements with the equity of S Ltd at the acquisition date. This makes sense as the group cannot have an investment in itself.

			CU	CU
Dr		Share capital	① 120 000	
Dr		Retained earnings	② 115 000	
Dr		Plant and machinery	③ 40 000	
Dr		Goodwill arising on consolidation	④ 10 000	
	Cr	Investment		⑤ 285 000

Elimination of investment in subsidiary at acquisition date

The above *pro-forma* journal entry correctly adjusts the combined statements of financial position in order to derive the **consolidated statement of financial position**. It does this by eliminating the equity in the subsidiary that was 'purchased' with the investment in the subsidiary. In addition, the carrying amounts of the assets and liabilities in the subsidiary are increased (from a net carrying amount of CU235 000) to reflect all of the net assets at their fair values. By recognising the adjustment to plant and machinery and goodwill, the net assets that have already been included in the starting point are now reflected at their fair value. The recorded net assets, together with the fair value adjustments, represent what the parent invested in. The investment is therefore eliminated against the equity of the subsidiary at the acquisition date.

However, in the detailed notes and other financial information presented, the cost and accumulated depreciation of the plant and machinery need to be adjusted. This is required to report the plant and machinery correctly in the **notes to the consolidated financial statements**, as follows:

Property, plant and equipment note:

	P Ltd CU	S Ltd CU	*Pro-forma* journals CU	Consolidated CU
Cost	400 000	350 000	⑥ (150 000)	640 000
Accumulated depreciation	(250 000)	(150 000)	⑥ 150 000	(250 000)
Carrying amount	**150 000**	**200 000**		**390 000**

In order to record the cost of the plant and machinery of S Ltd correctly at CU240 000 in the group and not CU350 000 as it is recognised in the financial statements of S Ltd (the starting point), the **accumulated depreciation** of CU150 000 in S Ltd at the acquisition date needs to be reversed on consolidation, in addition to the increase of CU40 000 relating to the adjustment to fair value.

			CU	CU
Dr		Accumulated depreciation	⑥ 150 000	
	Cr	Plant and machinery		⑥ 150 000

Elimination of accumulated depreciation in subsidiary at the acquisition date

This makes sense, as the cost of the plant and machinery of S Ltd from the group's perspective amounts to CU240 000, which is the fair value at the date of acquisition. The financial statement of the subsidiary includes accumulated depreciation, which represents how the plant and machinery have been used by the subsidiary. However, this is a new asset for the group and it would not be appropriate to reflect any accumulated depreciation. It is therefore eliminated against the cost, to reflect a cost of CU200 000 (CU350 000, less accumulated depreciation of CU150 000 ⑥). This is not equal to the fair value of the plant and machinery, and an additional adjustment is required to increase the cost by CU40 000 ③ in order to arrive at the fair value of CU240 000.

5. Acquisition of a subsidiary during a reporting period

A parent may acquire its controlling interest in a subsidiary at a date that is not the same as the reporting date of the subsidiary, for example, where the reporting date of the subsidiary is 31 December and the acquisition date is 1 March. This means that the subsidiary would not have financial statements that are prepared and presented at the acquisition date. The purchase of an interest in a subsidiary at a date that is different from the reporting data requires that the profit or loss for the specific reporting period during which the interest was acquired be allocated between pre-acquisition and post-acquisition profits or losses. The parent would normally require the subsidiary to prepare financial statements at the date of the acquisition of a controlling interest, as these are needed by the parent in order to do the following:

- Identify the assets and liabilities of the subsidiary at the acquisition date, and verify their respective carrying amounts and fair values
- Identify the equity of the subsidiary at the acquisition date
- Identify any assets not recognised in the subsidiary's financial statements, such as internally generated trademarks and goodwill
- Use this information to conduct a due diligence of the financial position and performance of the subsidiary at the acquisition date.

As noted earlier, the parent acquires the equity of the subsidiary at the acquisition date. Where the acquisition date is at a date that is different from the reporting date, the profit or loss of the subsidiary for the period after its previous reporting date until the acquisition date needs to be determined. This profit or loss constitutes **pre-acquisition profits** and forms part of the equity of the subsidiary at the acquisition date. It is therefore necessary to allocate the profit or loss of the subsidiary to the pre- and post-acquisition periods with reference to the available information, as far as it is practical.

Income and expenditure must be examined individually and apportioned accordingly. Certain items, such as depreciation and interest, normally accumulate from day to day, and these should be included accordingly when determining the profit or loss of the subsidiary until its acquisition date. Taxation, both current and deferred tax, should be determined for the period until the acquisition date and included as a taxation expense.

Dividends are only recognised when declared. However, preference dividends relating to cumulative preference shares accrue to shareholders each year and should therefore be accounted for on a time basis. This means that a cumulative preference dividend should be accrued for, even if it has not yet been declared. Refer to Chapter 8 for a detailed discussion of preference shares in a subsidiary, and the accrual and declaration of preference dividends.

Example

The acquisition of a subsidiary during a reporting period and allocation of profits

P Ltd acquired the controlling interest in S Ltd on 1 April 20x4. The previous reporting date of S Ltd was 31 December 20x3. The current reporting date of both companies and the group is 31 December 20x4.

The retained earnings of S Ltd amounted to CU115 000 at 31 December 20x3. Its profit after tax for the 12 months ended 31 December 20x4 amounts to CU35 000.

Provided that the information is available and that it is feasible, the profits of S Ltd for the current 12 months should then be determined and allocated between the two periods:

- Pre-acquisition profits: 1 January 20x4 to 31 March 20x4
- Post-acquisition profits: 1 April 20x4 to 31 December 20x4.

An easier (but less accurate) way would be to split the profits evenly over the 12 months, as follows:

- Pre-acquisition profits: 1 January 20x4 to 31 March 20x4: CU35 000 × 3/12 = CU8 750
- Post-acquisition profits: 1 April 20x4 to 31 December 20x4: CU35 000 × 9/12 = CU26 250.

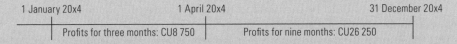

1 January 20x4	1 April 20x4	31 December 20x4
Profits for three months: CU8 750	Profits for nine months: CU26 250	

This means that the retained earnings and profits of S Ltd at the acquisition date amount to CU123 750 (CU115 000 + CU8 750).

Such a *pro rata* split, based on the months per annum, may not result in an accurate allocation of the profits between the periods, specifically if the subsidiary's profits are earned unevenly over the year, as is the case in seasonal trading.

6. Consolidation subsequent to the acquisition date

In the previous section, the consolidated financial statements were prepared on the same date that the parent acquired its controlling interest in the subsidiary. The consolidation process was illustrated on the acquisition date. The consolidation process needs to be performed at **every reporting date** subsequent to the acquisition date in order to prepare consolidated financial statements. At each reporting date, the consolidation starts with the individual financial statements of the parent and its subsidiaries (prepared in accordance with IFRS), and ends with the consolidated financial statements. It is necessary for this process to be repeated at each reporting date, as there is no 'consolidated' general ledger; each entity has its own general ledger and prepares its own financial statements. When consolidated financial statements are being prepared in periods after the acquisition date, the consolidation worksheet contains the financial statements of the parent and its subsidiaries at the current reporting date (the **starting point**). These include new transactions that occurred post-acquisition as well as transactions that occurred pre-acquisition (for example, sales in previous periods are included in retained earnings in the current financial statements). We need to reconstruct the adjustments arising on consolidation (using the *pro-forma* journal entries) to reflect the entries that should have been adjusted at the acquisition date as well as any adjustments required since the acquisition date correctly. In some cases, the adjusting entries that were originally done at the acquisition date may need to be adjusted, depending on the assets affected. For example, an asset with a fair value adjustment at the acquisition date may subsequently be depreciated, sold or revalued. Thus, if there have been changes to the assets and liabilities of the subsidiary since the acquisition date, these changes must be made against the profits of the subsidiary since the acquisition date. This is necessary so that the assets and liabilities are correctly measured and recognised from the group's perspective in the consolidated financial statements at the reporting date (the **end point**).

Refer to Chapter 5 for a further discussion of the effect of fair value adjustments at the acquisition date on subsequent reporting periods.

6.1 Important principles when preparing consolidated financial statements in the subsequent reporting periods

The consolidation process needs to be performed at **every reporting date** and the results of the subsidiary should be included in the consolidated financial statements from the acquisition date of the subsidiary.

The adjustments that were required at the acquisition date need to be repeated at each subsequent reporting date. Thus, consolidation adjustments (*pro-forma* entries) required in subsequent reporting periods consist of:
- Adjustments relating to the acquisition date
- Adjustments relating to the period since the acquisition date.

Refer to the example below for the preparation of consolidated financial statements for an investment in a wholly owned subsidiary subsequent to the acquisition date.

Example
Consolidating a wholly owned subsidiary

The purpose of this example is to illustrate the consolidation process one year after the reporting date. It includes the recognition of goodwill at the acquisition date, and illustrates the inclusion of the profits of the subsidiary since the acquisition date in the consolidated profit or loss.

The following extracts from the financial statements for P Ltd and its subsidiary, S Ltd, are presented at 31 December 20x4. P Ltd acquired all of the issued share capital of S Ltd on 1 January 20x4 (the acquisition date). P Ltd considered the net assets of S Ltd to be fairly valued at the acquisition date and any excess paid is attributable to goodwill. The retained earnings of S Ltd at the acquisition date amounted to CU115 000.

The following is an extract from the financial statements of P Ltd and S Ltd at 31 December 20x4 (in other words, the reporting date is one year after the acquisition date).

Statements of financial position at 31 December 20x4

	P Ltd CU	S Ltd CU
ASSETS		
Non-current assets	247 000	220 000
Current assets	145 000	130 000
Investment in S Ltd	288 000	
	680 000	**350 000**
EQUITY AND LIABILITIES		
Share capital	240 000	120 000
Retained earnings	300 000	150 000
Liabilities	140 000	80 000
	680 000	**350 000**

How is the retained earnings of S Ltd determined?
- At acquisition date: CU115 000
- Profit for current period: CU35 000
- Retained earnings at reporting date: CU150 000.

Statements of profit or loss for the year ended 31 December 20x4[1]

	P Ltd CU	S Ltd CU
Revenue	580 000	320 000
Cost of sales	(120 000)	(120 000)
Gross profit	460 000	200 000
Other operating expenses	(160 000)	(150 000)
Profit before tax	300 000	50 000
Taxation	(90 000)	(15 000)
Profit after tax	**210 000**	**35 000**

[1]Assuming there is no 'other comprehensive income' in any of the entities

To be able to prepare the consolidated financial statements of the group, you need to identify the following information (refer to IFRS3):
- The acquisition date: P Ltd acquired its controlling interest in S Ltd on **1 January 20x4**
- The reporting date: Consolidated financial statements need to be prepared at the same reporting date as the parent, which is **31 December 20x4**
- The purchase consideration: P Ltd paid **CU288 000** to acquire a 100% interest in S Ltd; this is recognised as the cost of the investment in the statement of financial position of P Ltd
- The fair value of the net identifiable assets of the subsidiary: When P Ltd acquired the controlling interest in S Ltd (1 January 20x4), it considered all the assets and liabilities of S Ltd to be fairly valued; this implies that the fair value of the net assets at the acquisition date is equal to the equity balance of S Ltd at 1 January 20x4 (share capital amounted to CU120 000, retained earnings amounted to CU115 000, so the total equity (net asset value) of S Ltd at acquisition date was **CU235 000**

- Goodwill acquired: The goodwill is determined as the excess paid, in other words, the difference between the purchase consideration of CU288 000 and the fair value of the net identifiable assets acquired of CU235 000; thus the goodwill acquired was **CU53 000**.

The process of consolidation requires that you combine the financial statements of the parent and its subsidiary, and eliminate the investment that the parent has in the equity of the subsidiary. As P Ltd paid an excess when acquiring a controlling interest in S Ltd, that excess is recognised on consolidation as **goodwill**.

The following *pro-forma* journal entry would eliminate the share capital and retained earnings of the subsidiary against the investment by the parent in the subsidiary at the acquisition date:

			CU	CU
Dr		Share capital	120 000	
Dr		Retained earnings	115 000	
Dr		Goodwill acquired	53 000	
	Cr	Investment in subsidiary		288 000

Elimination of investment in subsidiary at acquisition date

What is this?
The goodwill is the excess amount paid by the parent in order to acquire the controlling interest in the subsidiary. Goodwill is recognised on consolidation.

Consolidated statement of financial position at 31 December 20x4

	P Ltd CU	S Ltd CU	Pro-forma journals CU	Group CU
ASSETS				
Non-current assets	247 000	220 000		467 000
Current assets	145 000	130 000		275 000
Goodwill			53 000	53 000
Investment in S Ltd	288 000		(288 000)	–
	680 000	350 000	(235 000)	795 000
EQUITY AND LIABILITIES				
Share capital	240 000	120 000	(120 000)	240 000
Retained earnings	300 000	150 000	(115 000)	335 000
Liabilities	140 000	80 000		220 000
	680 000	350 000	(235 000)	795 000

What is the starting point?
The individual financial statements of the parent and its subsidiary at the reporting date, 31 December 20x4.

What is the end point?
The consolidated financial statements of the group at the reporting date, 31 December 20x4.

How is the retained earnings of the group determined?
- Retained earnings of P Ltd: CU300 000
- Retained earnings of S Ltd, since acquisition date: CU35 000, representing the profit for the current year
- Consolidated retained earnings: CU335 000.

The statements of financial position of the parent and the subsidiary have been combined in the consolidated worksheet above, and the investment in the subsidiary has been eliminated against the share capital and retained earnings of the subsidiary **at the acquisition date**. The group balances above represent the statement of financial position at 31 December 20x4.

In a similar way, we have to combine the statements of profit or loss and the statements of changes in equity of the parent and the subsidiary in order to prepare the consolidated financial statements for the year ended 31 December 20x4.

Consolidated statement of profit or loss for the year ended 31 December 20x4

	P Ltd CU	S Ltd CU	Pro-forma journals CU	Group CU
Revenue	580 000	320 000		900 000
Cost of sales	(120 000)	(120 000)		(240 000)
Gross profit	460 000	200 000		660 000
Other operating expenses	(160 000)	(150 000)		(310 000)
Profit before tax	300 000	50 000		350 000
Taxation	(90 000)	(15 000)		(105 000)
Profit after tax	**210 000**	**35 000**		**245 000**

Note that, as there are no intra-group transactions between P Ltd and S Ltd (for example, S Ltd did not declare any dividends that would be paid to P Ltd as its shareholder), there are no further *pro-forma* journal entries in the consolidated profit or loss. Furthermore, as P Ltd holds a 100% interest in S Ltd, there is also no non-controlling interest. The *pro-forma* journal entries relating to the elimination of intra-group dividends and the allocation of the appropriate portion of the profits to the non-controlling interest are illustrated in the examples in the following chapters.

Consolidated statement of changes in equity for the year ended 31 December 20x4

	Share capital CU	Retained earnings CU	Total group equity CU
Balance at 1 January 20x4	240 000	90 000	330 000
Profit or loss for the year		245 000	245 000
Closing balance at 31 December 20x4	**240 000**	**335 000**	**575 000**

Check your answer
Closing balance retained earnings include the following amounts:
- P Ltd: CU300 000
- S Ltd: CU35 000 (post-acquisition)
- Groups: CU335 000.

The parent acquired its controlling interest of 100% in S Ltd on 1 January 20x4. That is the date on which the subsidiary's results should be included in the consolidated financial statements. In other words, the parent equity holders share in the profit or loss of the subsidiary subsequent to the acquisition date. The retained earnings of the subsidiary prior to the acquisition date forms part of the equity interest acquired when the parent invested in the shares of S Ltd.

7. Analysing and differentiating between the pre- and post-acquisition profits of a subsidiary

A parent will share in the profits earned by a subsidiary after the date at which the parent obtains control of the subsidiary. It is therefore important to be able to identify what portion of the subsidiary's profits relate to the period prior to acquisition and what portion relates to the period after the acquisition date.

Example

Differentiating between the pre- and the post-acquisition profits of a subsidiary

P Ltd acquired all of the shares in S Ltd on 1 January 20x4, when its retained earnings amounted to CU115 000. Retained earnings in its current financial statements at 31 December 20x4 amounts to CU150 000. Retained earnings of S Ltd since the acquisition date therefore amounts to CU35 000 (CU150 000 − CU115 000).

Allocation of profits of subsidiary between pre- and post-acquisition periods

Pre-acquisition profits of S Ltd	Post-acquisition profits of S Ltd	Total retained earnings of S Ltd
CU115 000	CU35 000	CU150 000
Eliminated at acquisition date, as these profits were earned prior to the date on which P Ltd acquired control of S Ltd and 'belong' to the previous shareholders.	P Ltd shares in the profits of S Ltd after the acquisition date. The consolidated profit therefore includes this amount.	According to the separate financial statements of S Ltd.

The subsidiary accumulates profits (**retained earnings**) after its acquisition date as well as other reserves (for example, other comprehensive income in a **revaluation surplus**). As the previous year's retained earnings closing balance must equal the current year's opening balance, the opening balance of retained earnings in the statement of changes in equity must include the group's share of post-acquisition profits earned at the beginning of the current year. The current year's profits will be recognised in the current year's statement of profit or loss and other comprehensive income, and the balance will be transferred to the closing balance of retained earnings.

Example

Analysing retained earnings of the subsidiary after the acquisition date

The purpose of this example is to illustrate the allocation of profits between the pre- and post-acquisition date of a subsidiary. It shows how to calculate the amounts to be included in the consolidated financial statements for retained earnings and current year profits.

When P Ltd acquired the controlling interest of 100% in S Ltd on 1 January 20x4, the retained earnings of S Ltd amounted to CU115 000. The retained earnings of S Ltd recognised at 31 December 20x9 (six years after the acquisition date) amounts to CU665 000. The profit after tax for the current year, amounting to CU100 000, is included in this amount.

Summary of retained earnings of P Ltd and S Ltd

	P Ltd CU	S Ltd CU
Retained earnings at acquisition date	90 000	115 000
Retained earnings accumulated after the date of acquisition until the beginning of the current year (balancing figure)	500 000	450 000
Profit after tax for the current period	120 000	100 000
Retained earnings closing balance	**710 000**	**665 000**

How are the retained earnings of S Ltd recognised at the acquisition date?

The retained earnings of S Ltd at the acquisition date (CU115 000) is eliminated at the acquisition date by the investment in S Ltd. This makes sense as the retained earnings was earned prior to P Ltd's acquisition of the shares in S Ltd and was therefore included in the equity acquired by P Ltd.

What happens with the retained earnings of S Ltd after the acquisition date?

The consolidation process requires the adding together of all of the assets, liabilities and equity of the parent and its subsidiary. When all of the profits of the parent and the subsidiary are added together, the portion of retained earnings of S Ltd that has accumulated since its acquisition date is included in the group retained earnings. (The total retained earnings balance included in the starting point would have been CU565 000 [CU115 000 + CU450 000], which was the opening balance of retained earnings recorded by the subsidiary. However, the CU115 000 relating to the pre-acquisition period was eliminated against the investment.)

The **profit after tax** for the current period (CU100 000) is included in the consolidated statement of profit or loss for the current year by including all of the income and expense items.

Extract from group statement of changes in equity for 20x9

		Retained earnings CU
Balance at the beginning of the year	①	1 040 000
Profit after tax for the current period	②	220 000
Retained earnings closing balance	③	**1 260 000**

Explanations

① The opening retained earnings for the group consists of the retained earnings of P Ltd plus its share of the retained earnings of S Ltd since the acquisition date: P Ltd: (CU90 000 + CU 500 000 = CU590 000), S Ltd: CU450 000, Group: CU1 040 000.

② The group profit for the year includes the profits of both P Ltd (CU120 000) and S Ltd (CU100 000) = CU220 000.

③ Closing balance retained earnings consists of the retained earnings of P Ltd (CU710 000) plus P Ltd's share in the retained earnings of S Ltd since the acquisition date of CU550 000 (CU450 000 + CU100 000); closing retained earnings for the group amounts to CU1 260 000.

In addition to retained earnings, the parent also shares in the increases in other reserves, where gains are recognised in other comprehensive income, recognised by the subsidiary after the acquisition date if these adjustments are in line with the group policy (for example, if the subsidiary revalues owner-occupied land and the group policy is to apply the revaluation model). Where the subsidiary has revalued its non-current assets after the acquisition date, the parent shares in the post-acquisition movement in the revaluation surplus. This also implies that the asset be recognised at its revalued amount in the group financial statements. The revaluation gain is recognised in the group revaluation surplus when the value of the asset has increased after acquisition. This is explained in more detail in Chapter 5.

Test your knowledge

There is a list of learning objectives at the beginning of this chapter. Go back to this list and check whether you have achieved these outcomes. If not, reread the appropriate section.

Questions

Question 1

On 31 January 20x5, P Ltd acquired the entire issued share capital of S Ltd for CU62 000. The statements of financial position of the two companies at that date are set out below.

Statements of financial position at 31 January 20x4

	P Ltd CU	S Ltd CU
ASSETS		
Property, plant and equipment	40 000	30 000
Shares in subsidiary, at cost	62 000	
Current assets	108 000	50 000
Inventory	20 000	30 000
Accounts receivable	50 000	20 000
Bank	38 000	
	210 000	80 000
CAPITAL AND LIABILITIES		
Share capital	100 000	50 000
Retained earnings	60 000	10 000
Shareholders' equity	160 000	60 000
Current liabilities	50 000	20 000
Accounts payable	50 000	15 000
Bank overdraft		5 000
	210 000	80 000

You are required to do the following:
a. Prepare the *pro-forma* journal entries for consolidation.
b. Prepare the consolidated statement of financial position at 31 January 20x5, assuming that the identifiable assets and liabilities are fairly valued in the statement of financial position of the subsidiary at the date of acquisition.
c. Explain the amounts you have disclosed as share capital and retained earnings for the group.

Suggested solution

a. *Pro-forma* journal entries on consolidation

			CU	CU
Dr		Share capital	50 000	
Dr		Retained earnings	10 000	
Dr		Goodwill	2 000	
	Cr	Investment in S Ltd		62 000

Elimination of investment in S Ltd at the acquisition date

Workings: Goodwill purchased

	CU
Share capital	50 000
Retained earnings	10 000
Net asset value	60 000
Investment	62 000
Goodwill	2 000

b. P Ltd: Consolidated statement of financial position at 31 January 20x5

	Notes	CU	
ASSETS			
Non-current assets		**72 000**	
Property, plant and equipment		70 000	
Goodwill	3	2 000	
Current assets		**158 000**	
Inventories		50 000	
Trade and other receivables		70 000	
Cash and cash equivalents		38 000	
Total assets		**230 000**	
EQUITY AND LIABILITIES			
Capital and reserves		160 000	
Share capital		100 000	(P only)
Retained earnings		60 000	(Only post-acquisition reserves of S will be included)
Current liabilities		**70 000**	
Trade and other payables		**65 000**	
Bank overdraft		5 000	
Total equity and liabilities		**230 000**	

c. Share capital should only represent those shares issued to the parent equity holders. The share capital of the subsidiary is owned by the parent company and represents an investment in itself. It is eliminated against the investment.

Retained earnings should include only those profits earned by the group. All of the parent company's profits are included, but only those profits earned by the subsidiary after acquisition are included because the assets were not controlled before acquisition.

Case study exercises

Scenario 1

P Ltd acquired 100% of the issued ordinary share capital of S Ltd on 1 January 20x5. The identifiable assets and liabilities of S Ltd were considered fairly valued at the date of acquisition.

Statements of financial position of P Ltd and S Ltd on 31 December 20x5

	P Ltd CU'000	S Ltd CU'000
ASSETS		
Plant and machinery (carrying amount) (Cost: CU400 000; CU350 000)	300	200
Investment in S Ltd	400	–
Current assets	220	500
	920	**700**
CAPITAL AND LIABILITIES		
Share capital	200	100
Retained earnings	620	500
Shareholders' equity	820	600
Current liabilities	100	100
	920	**700**

Statements of changes in equity for the year ended 31 December 20x5

	P Ltd		S Ltd	
	Share capital CU'000	Retained earnings CU'000	Share capital CU'000	Retained earnings CU'000
Opening balance	200	400	100	200
Net profit for the year		370		300
Less: Dividends		(150)		–
Closing balance	**200**	**620**	**100**	**500**

Statements of profit or loss and other comprehensive income of P Ltd and S Ltd for the year ended 31 December 20x5

	P Ltd CU'000	S Ltd CU'000
Gross revenue	1 870	1 500
Net operating costs	(1 050)	(920)
Profit from ordinary activities before interest	820	580
Interest paid	(200)	(50)
Profit on ordinary activities before taxation	620	530
Taxation	(250)	(230)
Profit for the year	**370**	**300**

Net operating costs include depreciation of CU50 000 for P Ltd and CU50 000 for S Ltd for the year, respectively.

You are required to do the following:

1. Answer these questions before starting with the preparation of the consolidated financial statements:
   - What is the acquisition date?
   - What is the amount that P Ltd paid for the acquisition of all of the shares in S Ltd at the acquisition date?
   - What is the goodwill acquired, if any?
   - What is the reporting date?
   - What is the starting point for consolidation at the reporting date?
   - If the controlled net assets increase, does that meet the definition of income in the Conceptual Framework?
2. Prepare the *pro-forma* journal entries required in order to prepare the consolidated statements of P Ltd and its subsidiary at 1 January 20x5 (the date of acquisition).
3. Prepare the consolidated statement of financial position and the consolidated statement of comprehensive income for P Ltd and its subsidiary at 31 December 20x5. Your answer should include the note disclosure relating to property, plant and equipment.

Suggested solution

1. **Answer the following questions before starting with the preparation of the consolidated financial statements:**
   - **What is the acquisition date?**
     The acquisition date is the date on which the controlling interest was acquired, that is, 1 January 20x5.
   - **What is the amount that P Ltd paid for the acquisition of all of the shares in S Ltd at the acquisition date?**
     P Ltd paid CU400 000. (Tip: Refer to the amount of the investment in S Ltd, included in the statement of financial position of P Ltd.)
   - **What is the goodwill acquired, if any?**
     Goodwill is the residual between the net consideration paid and the fair value of the net identifiable assets acquired. This is calculated as follows:
     Consideration paid: CU400 000
     Fair value of net identifiable assets at the acquisition date: CU300 000 (equity of S Ltd at 1 January 20x5; no further adjustments are necessary, as the net assets were considered fairly valued at the acquisition date, thus net assets = equity at acquisition date)
     ∴ Goodwill acquired: CU400 000 – CU300 000 = CU100 000

Think about it

What is the equity acquired at the acquisition date?

	CU
Share capital	100 000
Retained earnings	200 000
FV of net assets	300 000
Investment (net consideration)	400 000
∴ Goodwill	100 000

- **What is the reporting date?**
  The current reporting date is 31 December 20x5. This means that we have to prepare the consolidated financial statements at this date and that S Ltd should be consolidated from 1 January 20x5.
- **What is the starting point for consolidation at the reporting date?**
  The starting point is the completed, separate financial statements of P Ltd and S Ltd at 31 December 20x5, as given in the case study.
- **If the controlled net assets increase, does that meet the definition of income in the Conceptual Framework?**
  Yes, as the controlled net assets of S Ltd were acquired on 1 January 20x5, the group shares in any increases in these assets since the acquisition date. This means that changes in the equity (net assets) of the subsidiary since the acquisition date meets the definition of income as per the framework.

2. **Prepare the *pro-forma* journal entries required in order to prepare the consolidated statements of P Ltd and its subsidiary at 1 January 20x5 (the date of acquisition).**

Pro-forma journal entries at 1 January 20x5

			CU'000	CU'000
Dr		Share capital	100	
Dr		Retained earnings	200	
Dr		Goodwill arising on consolidation	100	
	Cr	Investment in S Ltd		400

Elimination of investment in subsidiary, with equity of subsidiary at the acquisition date

			CU'000	CU'000
Dr		Accumulated depreciation	100	
	Cr	Plant and machinery		100

Elimination of accumulated depreciation relating to assets of subsidiary acquired at acquisition date, calculated as follows: (350 – [200 + 50])

3. **Prepare the consolidated statement of financial position and the consolidated statement of comprehensive income for P Ltd and its subsidiary at 31 December 20x5.**

Pro-forma journal entries at 31 December 20x5

			CU'000	CU'000
Dr		Share capital	100	
Dr		Retained earnings	200	
Dr		Goodwill arising on consolidation	100	
	Cr	Investment in S Ltd		400

Elimination of investment in subsidiary, with equity of subsidiary at the acquisition date

			CU'000	CU'000
Dr		Accumulated depreciation (S Ltd)	100	
	Cr	Plant and machinery		100

Elimination of accumulated depreciation relating to assets of subsidiary acquired at acquisition date, calculated as follows: (350 – [200 + 50])

Think about it

Why are these *pro-forma* journal entries the same as those at 1 January 20x5?

The process of consolidation requires us to consolidate the subsidiary from its acquisition date. This means that we need to 'process' the *pro-forma* journal entries at each reporting date, as the starting point includes the investment in the subsidiary.

P Ltd and its subsidiary

Consolidated statement of profit or loss and other comprehensive income for year ended 31 December 20x5

		CU'000
Gross revenue	(1 870 + 1 500)	3 370
Net operating costs	(1 050 + 920)	(1 970)
Profit on ordinary activities		1 400
Interest paid	(200 + 50)	(250)
Profit before taxation		1 150
Taxation	(250 + 230)	(480)
Net profit for year		**670**

P Ltd and its subsidiary

Consolidated statement of changes in shareholders' equity for year ended 31 December 20x5

	Share capital CU'000	Retained earnings CU'000	Total CU'000
Opening balance	200	400	600
Profit for the year		670	670
– Dividends		(150)	(150)
Closing balance	**200**	**920**	**1 120**

P Ltd and its subsidiary

Consolidated statement of financial position at 31 December 20x5

		CU'000
ASSETS		
Plant and machinery (carrying amount)	(See note 1 disclosure)	500
Goodwill		100
Net current assets	(220 + 500)	720
		1 320
CAPITAL AND LIABILITIES		
Share capital		200
Retained earnings	(P: 620 + S: 300)	920
Total capital and reserves		**1 120**
Current liabilities	(100 + 100)	200
		1 320

Note 1: Plant and machinery

		CU'000
Carrying amount: Opening balance		350
Cost	Only P Ltd	400
Accumulated depreciation		(50)
Additions		250
Depreciation	(50 + 50)	(100)
Carrying amount: Closing balance		**500**
Cost	(400 + 250)	650
Accumulated depreciation	(50 + 100)	(150)

Plant and machinery in S Ltd at acquisition date at fair value of CU250 00

5

Consolidation: Acquisition adjustments

The following topics are included in this chapter:

- Adjustments at the acquisition date of a subsidiary relating to:
  - Non-current assets
  - Current assets
  - Liabilities
  - Any related deferred tax implications.
- The impact of adjustment at the acquisition date on the measurement of goodwill
- The subsequent effect on consolidation when the assets of a subsidiary are measured at fair value at acquisition, which is different from their carrying amount in the subsidiary at that date, and are subsequently:
  - Depreciated and/or impaired
  - Revalued
  - Sold by the subsidiary.

Learning objectives

By the end of this chapter, you should be able to:
- Understand that the assets and liabilities of the subsidiary are measured at their fair values in the group financial statements at the acquisition date
- Identify the adjustments that are required at the acquisition date relating to the effect of fair value adjustments of assets and liabilities
- Identify the deferred tax implications, if any, of such fair value adjustments at the acquisition date
- Determine the goodwill acquired (or the bargain purchase gain recognised) after taking into account the fair value adjustments at the acquisition date, including the resulting deferred tax implications
- Understand what the effect is on subsequent reporting periods of fair value adjustments required at acquisition date when the assets are subsequently depreciated and/or sold by the subsidiary.

1. Introduction

In most of the examples in the previous chapters, the parent considered the net assets as recognised by the subsidiary to be fairly valued at the acquisition date. This implies that the parent agreed that the carrying amount of each of the assets and liabilities of the subsidiary was equal to its fair value at the time when the parent obtained the controlling interest. However, when the fair value of some of the individual assets or liabilities of the subsidiary is different (higher or lower) than the carrying amount of those assets as recognised by subsidiary, you need to take this difference into consideration when determining the goodwill acquired (or bargain purchase gain) at the acquisition date. The fair value of an asset of the subsidiary represents the cost price of that asset to the group and this is the amount at which the asset should be recognised initially in the group statement of financial position. The net assets acquired at the acquisition date must be recognised at their fair value in the consolidated financial statements.

 IFRS principles

Fair value of an asset acquired by the group

The fair value of an asset at the acquisition date represents the cost price of that asset to the group. The assets that the group acquires (by acquiring a controlling interest in a subsidiary) should be recognised at their fair value at the acquisition date.

At the acquisition date, the cost of each asset or liability to the group is the fair value at that date. The amount paid by the parent will be determined taking these amounts into account.

When a subsidiary is acquired, the emphasis is placed on getting the **correct fair value** of the assets and liabilities of the subsidiary. There are three main reasons for doing this:
- To determine the correct cost of the assets and liabilities to the group
- To calculate the goodwill correctly, as goodwill, simply stated, is the difference between the cost of the investment and the fair value of the net assets (or equity) acquired
- To determine correctly, from the group's perspective, the equity of the subsidiary at the date of acquisition (that equity, or increase in net assets, has been earned prior to acquisition by the group and is not a profit of the group; if the group considers an asset to be undervalued at the acquisition date, that increase in value took place before the asset was acquired by the group and it is therefore a pre-acquisition increase in equity of the subsidiary as opposed to a post-acquisition increase in equity; unless the subsidiary revalues the asset, the group's assessment of the subsidiary's equity will differ from that of the subsidiary itself).

2. Fair value adjustments of non-current assets at acquisition when the group applies the cost model

When the fair values of the assets and liabilities of the subsidiary differ from the carrying amounts in the records of the subsidiary, these carrying amounts must be adjusted for the purposes of preparing consolidated financial statements every time a consolidation is performed. In this section, we will consider fair value adjustments relating to non-current assets measured in accordance with the **cost model** at the acquisition date and the subsequent effect on the profits of the group as well as the deferred tax implications:

- Non-depreciating assets, for example, land
- Depreciating assets, for example, plant and machinery.

The fair value of a non-current asset at the acquisition date represents its cost to the group. The depreciation from the group's perspective is determined based on the cost to the group and not the amounts recorded by the subsidiary.

Later in this section, we will consider the situation when the subsidiary applies the **revaluation model** in its separate financial statements.

Example

A fair value adjustment at acquisition date for a non-depreciating asset

This example illustrates the consolidation process two years after the acquisition date as well as recognition of goodwill. The example ignores any deferred tax implications.

A similar example, which illustrates the effects of a partially held subsidiary, is included on the accompanying CD. Refer to the CD after you have worked through Chapter 7, *Consolidation: Partly owned subsidiaries and other consolidation considerations.*

P Ltd acquired 100% of the issued share capital of S Ltd at 1 January 20x4, when the retained earnings of S Ltd amounted to CU115 000. P Ltd considered the net assets of S Ltd to be fairly valued, except for the land, which had a fair value of CU125 000 at the acquisition date (no land was purchased or sold after the acquisition date). Any excess paid is attributable to goodwill.

You obtained the extracts that follow from the financial statements for P Ltd and its subsidiary, S Ltd, for the current reporting period, which ended 31 December 20x5.

Statements of financial position at 31 December 20x5

	P Ltd CU	S Ltd CU
ASSETS		
Land	150 000	100 000
Other non-current assets	375 000	130 000
Current assets	75 000	150 000
Investment in S Ltd	300 000	
	900 000	**380 000**
EQUITY AND LIABILITIES		
Share capital	240 000	120 000
Retained earnings	500 000	190 000
Liabilities	160 000	70 000
	900 000	**380 000**

Note that P Ltd acquired its controlling interest in S Ltd on **1 January 20x4**. The above balances represent the assets, liabilities and equity of the two entities at 31 December 20x5, which is two years after the acquisition date.
- Consolidated financial statements need to be prepared at the same reporting date as that of the parent, which is **31 December 20x4**.
- P Ltd paid **CU300 000** to acquire its 100% interest in S Ltd on 1 January 20x4.
- When P Ltd acquired its interest in S Ltd (1 January 20x4), it considered all of the assets and liabilities of S Ltd to be fairly valued, except for land.

What is the equity of S Ltd at the acquisition date?

Analysis of the equity of S Ltd

	Total equity CU	Acquired by P Ltd 100% CU
At acquisition date:		
Share capital	120 000	
Retained earnings	115 000	
Land	① 25 000	
Fair value of net assets of S Ltd	260 000	260 000
Investment in S Ltd		② 300 000
Goodwill acquired		**40 000**

① The fair value adjustment of the land should be included in the analysis of the equity of S Ltd at the acquisition date, as the cost of the land to the group is equal to CU125 000. This implies that the parent considered the net assets of the subsidiary to be worth CU25 000 more than the value reflected in the statement of financial position (CU125 000 – CU100 000). The equity of the subsidiary should therefore be adjusted by this understatement at the acquisition date to calculate the amount paid for goodwill correctly, assuming that there is no tax implication resulting from this adjustment. The subsidiary's equity of CU120 000 + CU115 000 = CU235 000 does not include the increase of CU25 000 in the carrying amount of the land. If the land is considered undervalued by CU25 000, the group considers the net assets as recognised by the subsidiary to be undervalued by CU25 000, and therefore equity is understated by CU25 000. This is because the cost of the land to the group is CU125 000. **Total equity** of S Ltd at the acquisition date from the group's perspective amounts to **CU260 000**.

② P Ltd paid CU300 000 for its 100% investment in the subsidiary. For this investment, P Ltd acquired all of the equity of S Ltd, which amounts to CU260 000. Thus, the difference relates to the goodwill of CU40 000 acquired by P Ltd.

The following *pro-forma* journal entry would eliminate the share capital and retained earnings of the subsidiary against the investment by the parent in the subsidiary at the acquisition date, and recognise the non-controlling interest at that date:

Pro-forma journal (1)

			CU	CU
Dr		Share capital	120 000	
Dr		Retained earnings	115 000	
Dr		Goodwill acquired	40 000	
Dr		Land	25 000	
	Cr	Investment in subsidiary		300 000

Elimination of investment in subsidiary at the acquisition date

> **What is this?**
> Land is recognised in S Ltd at its cost of CU100 000 (starting point). In the group, the cost of land is CU125 000. This entry increases land to its cost from a group perspective.

On consolidation, using the above *pro-forma* entry, the share capital and retained earnings of S Ltd are eliminated against the investment in S Ltd as recognised by P Ltd and goodwill is recognised.

How would you consolidate S Ltd in the financial statements two years after the acquisition date?

P Ltd acquired its controlling interest in S Ltd on 1 January 20x4, which is at the beginning of the prior reporting period. This means that the consolidated balances that are included in the current reporting period should include the profits of the subsidiary **since the acquisition date**. As you are required to prepare consolidated financial statements every year, you have to consider the effect of consolidation on the opening balances. For example, the profits of the subsidiary for the prior year should be included in the opening balance of retained earnings in the current year.

In order to allocate the appropriate portion of opening retained earnings to the group, you need to determine what portion of the profits of the subsidiary was earned subsequent to the acquisition date. The retained earnings of S Ltd and the allocation of the appropriate portions between the pre-acquisition and the post-acquisition earnings can be summarised as shown below.

Analysis of retained earnings of P Ltd and S Ltd

	P Ltd Total CU	S Ltd Total CU
Opening balance at 1 January 20x4 (acquisition date)	90 000	115 000
Profit or loss for year ended 31 December 20x4	210 000	35 000
Balance at 31 December 20x4	300 000	150 000
Profit or loss for year ended 31 December 20x5	200 000	40 000
Balance at 31 December 20x5 (see statements of financial position)	**500 000**	**190 000**

The consolidation worksheet, which contains the statements of financial position at 31 December 20x5, is shown below.

Consolidated statement of financial position as at 31 December 20x5

	P Ltd CU	S Ltd CU	*Pro-forma* journal (1) CU	Group CU
ASSETS				
Land	150 000	100 000	25 000	275 000
Other non-current assets	375 000	130 000		505 000
Current assets	75 000	150 000		225 000
Goodwill			40 000	40 000
Investment in S Ltd	300 000		(300 000)	–
	900 000	**380 000**	**(235 000)**	**1 045 000**
EQUITY AND LIABILITIES				
Share capital	240 000	120 000	(120 000)	240 000
Retained earnings	500 000	190 000	(115 000)	575 000
Liabilities	160 000	70 000		230 000
	900 000	**380 000**	**(235 000)**	**1 045 000**

How is 'land' of the group determined?
Land recognised by P Ltd is at a cost of CU150 000; the land of S Ltd was acquired by the group on the acquisition date, with a cost to the group of CU125 000 (end point).
The total land controlled by the group amounts to CU275 000.

Consolidated statement of profit or loss and other comprehensive income for the year ended 31 December 20x5

	P Ltd CU	S Ltd CU	Group CU
Revenue	580 000	320 000	900 000
Cost of sales	(120 000)	(120 000)	(240 000)
Gross profit	460 000	200 000	660 000
Other operating expenses	(160 000)	(150 000)	(310 000)
Profit before tax	300 000	50 000	350 000
Taxation	(100 000)	(10 000)	(110 000)
Profit after tax	**200 000**	**40 000**	**240 000**

P Ltd acquired its controlling interest in S Ltd on 1 January 20x4, which is at the beginning of the prior reporting period. This means that the consolidated opening balances included in the current reporting period should include the profits of the subsidiary since the acquisition date. The consolidated statement of changes in equity presented below includes the comparative figures in order to demonstrate the inclusion of S Ltd's profits after the date of acquisition.

Consolidated statement of changes in equity for the year ended 31 December 20x5

	Share capital CU	Retained earnings CU	Total group equity CU
Balance at 1 January 20x4	240 000	90 000	330 000
Profit or loss for prior year		245 000	245 000
Balance at 31 December 20x4	240 000	335 000	575 000
Profit or loss for the year		240 000	240 000
Closing balance at 31 December 20x4	240 000	575 000	815 000

Check your answer: Retained earnings at the beginning of the year
- P Ltd: CU300 000
- S Ltd (since acquisition date): CU35 000
- Attributable to parent equity holders: **CU335 000**.

Check your answer: Retained earnings at the end of the year
- P Ltd: CU500 000
- S Ltd (since acquisition date): CU35 000 + CU40 000
- Attributable to parent equity holders: **CU575 000**.

Applying the same principles as discussed above, the parent should also consider the fair values of depreciating assets held by the subsidiary at the acquisition date. The fair value of the depreciating asset represents the cost of the asset to the group. Any accumulated depreciation recognised in the statement of financial position of the subsidiary should be netted off against the cost price of the asset prior to considering its fair value.

This is done because the fair value of the asset when acquired by the parent is the cost of that asset to the group. You cannot acquire an asset with accumulated depreciation as the accumulated depreciation recognised relates to the usage of that asset prior to the acquisition date. Part of the consolidation process is therefore to eliminate accumulated depreciation against the cost of the asset.

This is normally done by processing the following *pro-forma* journal entry **at the acquisition date** (as discussed in Chapter 4):

Dr		Accumulated depreciation in subsidiary
	Cr	Asset in subsidiary

If the parent considers the carrying amount (the book value) at acquisition to be equal to its fair value, the cost to the group is the carrying amount of the asset at the date of acquisition.

Where the parent considers the fair value of the depreciating asset to be higher or lower than its carrying amount, the fair value of the asset should be recognised as the cost of the asset to the group (in reality, an asset may not be considered overvalued at the acquisition date, as this is a sign of impairment and the subsidiary should already have impaired the asset). The subsidiary can either react to such a fair value adjustment (by revaluing the asset in its separate financial statements if it applies the revaluation model) or it can continue to recognise the asset at its carrying amount (by applying the cost model), in which case an adjustment is required as part of the consolidation process.

Where the asset is depreciated, the annual depreciation of the asset in the group **since the acquisition date** differs from the annual depreciation charge recorded in the general ledger of the subsidiary. Depreciation is the allocation of the cost of the asset relating to the use of the asset in that period. If the cost of the asset differs, then the depreciation expense must also be different. You need to identify the difference between the depreciation expense to be included in the consolidated financial statements (the end point) and the amounts recorded by the subsidiary (included in the starting point), and adjust for any differences by way of *pro-forma* journal entries.

Thus, where the fair value of depreciable assets is different from their carrying amount, the depreciation charge for the group would be different from the depreciation recognised by the subsidiary (where the subsidiary has not recognised the fair value adjustment in its separate financial statements).

 ## Example

Wholly owned subsidiary, with fair value adjustment of depreciated assets at acquisition

This example illustrates fair value adjustment at the acquisition date of a depreciated asset (namely, plant and machinery), and the subsequent adjustment to prior years' profits (retained earnings) and the current year's profit (depreciation expense). The example ignores deferred tax implications.

 A similar example, which illustrates the effects of a partially held subsidiary, is included on the accompanying CD. Refer to the CD after you have worked through Chapter 7, *Consolidation: Partly owned subsidiaries and other consolidation considerations.*

P Ltd acquired 100% of the issued ordinary share capital of S Ltd on 1 January 20x4, when the financial statements of S Ltd included the following balances:

	CU
Share capital	120 000
Retained earnings	115 000
Shareholders' equity	235 000

At the date of acquisition, P Ltd considered the net assets of S Ltd to be fairly valued, except for the following:

Plant and machinery (carrying amount CU240 000)	CU350 000
The plant and machinery was acquired by S Ltd on 1 January 20x3 at a cost price of CU300 000. The estimated useful life was five years with no residual value. These estimates have been confirmed at each reporting date.	

The excess of the purchase price of the shares in S Ltd was paid for goodwill. You can assume that the goodwill is not impaired.

Statements of financial position of P Ltd and S Ltd on 31 December 20x6

	P Ltd CU'000	S Ltd CU'000
ASSETS		
Plant and machinery (note 1)	300	60
Investment in S Ltd	360	
Current assets	650	920
	1 310	**980**
CAPITAL AND LIABILITIES		
Share capital	240	120
Retained earnings	850	390
Shareholders' equity	1 090	510
Current liabilities	220	470
	1 310	**980**

Note 1: Plant and machinery

	P Ltd CU'000	S Ltd CU'000
Cost	500	300
Accumulated depreciation:		
Balance at 1 January 20x6	100	180
Depreciation	100	60
Balance at 31 December 20x6	200	240
Carrying amount at 31 December 20x6	**300**	**60**

Extract from statements of changes in equity of P Ltd and S Ltd for the year ended 31 December 20x6

	P Ltd CU'000	S Ltd CU'000
Retained earnings 1 January 20x6	500	190
Profit for the year	350	200
Retained earnings 31 December 20x6	**850**	**390**

Similar to the previous example, P Ltd acquired its controlling interest in S Ltd prior to the reporting date. The respective dates and activities include the following:

- The acquisition date: P Ltd acquired its controlling interest in S Ltd on **1 January 20x4**
- The reporting date: Consolidated financial statements need to be prepared at the same reporting date of the parent, which is **31 December 20x6**
- The purchase consideration: P Ltd paid **CU360 000** to acquire a 100% interest in S Ltd; this is recognised as the investment in the statement of financial position of P Ltd.

Think about it

Questions to consider

What is the cost of the plant and machinery for the group?

The plant and machinery of S Ltd were considered undervalued by CU110 000 ①. The cost of the plant and machinery for the group amounted to CU350 000 on the acquisition date.

What is the group depreciation for this asset?

The cost to the group amounts to CU350 000. S Ltd acquired this plant and machinery one year prior to the acquisition date. The plant and machinery had therefore been depreciated for one year when the group acquired it. From the group's perspective, this plant and machinery had a remaining useful life of four years at the acquisition date. Annual depreciation for the group amounted to CU87 500 (CU350 000/4 years).

What happens with the accumulated depreciation in S Ltd at the acquisition date?

As the cost of the plant and machinery for the group amounts to CU350 000 (CU240 000 + CU110 000), any accumulated depreciation in S Ltd prior to the acquisition date should be reversed as it relates to the use of the plant and machinery prior to its acquisition by the group.

Plant and machinery		S Ltd CU'000	Pro-forma journals CU'000	Group CU'000
1 January 20x3	Cost	300		
	Accumulated depreciation	(60)		
1 January 20x4	Carrying amount at acquisition	240	110	350
	Depreciation	(60)	(27.5)	(87.5)
31 December 20x4	Carrying amount 20x4	180	82.5	262.5
	Depreciation	(60)	(27.5)	(87.5)
31 December 20x5	Carrying amount 20x5	120	55	175
	Depreciation	(60)	(27.5)	(87.5)
31 December 20x6	Carrying amount 20x6	**60**	**27.5**	**87.5**

The plant and machinery is recognised in S Ltd's individual financial statements at CU60 000 at 31 December 20x6 (refer to the statement of financial position above). This is the **starting point**. The **end point** is that the plant and machinery should be measured at CU87 500 in the consolidated financial statements. The adjustments required on consolidation consist of the fair value adjustment at the acquisition date of CU110 000 and subsequent increases in the depreciation expense for this asset, amounting to CU27 500 per annum.

Pro-forma journal entries required to consolidate S Ltd

			CU	CU
Dr		Share capital	120 000	
Dr		Retained earnings	115 000	
Dr		Plant and machinery	110 000	
Dr		Goodwill arising on consolidation	15 000	
	Cr	Investment in S Ltd		360 000

Recognition of fair value adjustment relating to plant and machinery

			CU	CU
Dr		Accumulated depreciation	60 000	
	Cr	Plant and machinery		60 000

Elimination of accumulated depreciation existing at acquisition

			CU	CU
Dr		Retained earnings	55 000	
Dr		Depreciation	27 500	
	Cr	Accumulated depreciation		87 500

Recognition of additional prior year and current year depreciation

The above *pro-forma* journal entries relate to the fair value adjustments at the acquisition date, and then the subsequent consolidation adjustments resulting from these adjustments.

Analysis of the equity of S Ltd

	Total equity CU'000	Acquired by P Ltd (100%) CU'000	
		At acquisition	Since acquisition
At acquisition date (1 January 20x4):			
Share capital	120		
Retained earnings	115		
Plant and machinery	① 110		
Fair value of net assets of S Ltd	345	345	
Investment in S Ltd (fair value)		360	
Goodwill arising on consolidation		15	
Since acquisition date (1 January 20x4 – 31 December 20x5 = 2 years):	20		20
Retained earnings (190 000 – 115 000)	75		
Depreciation on plant and machinery (CU27 500 × 2 years)	(55)		
Current period (year ended 31 December 20x6):	172.5		172.5
Profit and loss after taxation	200		
Depreciation on plant and machinery	(27.5)		
	537.5		192.5

Extract from the consolidated statement of profit or loss and other comprehensive income for the year ended 31 December 20x6

Profit or loss:		CU
Depreciation	(100 000 + 60 000 + 27 500)	187 500
Profit after tax	(350 000 + 200 000 – 27 500)	**522 500**

Extract from the consolidated statement of financial position for the year ended 31 December 20x5

Non-current assets:	CU
Plant and machinery (note 1)	**387 500**

The worksheet that follows would be used to determine the note disclosure in the consolidated financial statements for the year ended 31 December 20x6.

Note 1: Plant and machinery

	Starting point		Group adjustments CU'000	End point group CU'000
	P Ltd CU'000	S Ltd CU'000		
Cost	500	300	+ 110 – 60	850
Accumulated depreciation:				
Balance at 1 January 20x6	100	180	– 60 + 55	275
Depreciation	100	60	+ 27.5	187.5
Balance at 31 December 20x6	200	240		462.5
Carrying amount at 31 December 20x6	**300**	**60**		**387.5**

Note that the adjustments to the closing balances of the cost and accumulated depreciation of plant and machinery are cumulative. The adjustment to the cost of CU110 000 would be repeated at each reporting date as well as the elimination of the accumulated depreciation of CU60 000 at the acquisition date. The additional depreciation of CU27 500 for each of the three reporting periods after acquisition is included in the closing balance of accumulated depreciation, amounting to a total adjustment of CU82 500. The opening balance would only have been adjusted by CU55 000, which relates to the two periods between the date of acquisition and the beginning of the current year.

Think about it

Would your answer above be different if the fair value of the plant and machinery were less than its carrying amount at the acquisition date?

When the fair value of an asset is below its carrying amount, it implies that the asset is impaired. In terms of IFRS (refer to IAS36, Impairment of Assets), the subsidiary should recognise an impairment loss when there is an indication that the asset is impaired. Thus, as the subsidiary is preparing its financial statements in accordance with IFRS, it will recognise the impairment in its individual financial statements prior to the acquisition date.

This will result in the carrying amount of the plant and machinery being equal to its fair value at the acquisition date.

3. Deferred tax implications

Fair value adjustments relating to assets acquired by the group may have deferred tax implications from a group's perspective. The amount of deferred tax arising in relation to the **acquisition of an entity or business** is recognised and included as part of the identifiable assets acquired and liabilities assumed when determining the goodwill or gain on bargain purchase arising on consolidation. Deferred tax liabilities and deferred tax assets that are associated with **temporary differences relating to business combinations** are recognised in accordance with IAS12, paragraphs 19 and 21. Such temporary differences arise when the tax bases of the identifiable assets acquired and liabilities assumed are not affected by the business combination. This applies when the carrying amount of an asset is increased to its fair value at the acquisition date, but the tax base of that asset remains at the cost to the existing legal owner (the subsidiary). A taxable (deductible) temporary difference arises on consolidation, which results in a deferred tax liability (asset). The resulting deferred tax liability (or asset) affects the measurement of goodwill.

Think about it

What are temporary differences?

Temporary differences (refer to IAS12: 46–56) arise from different treatments of transactions for accounting and taxation purposes. Such differences exist between accounting profit and taxable profit, when the period in which revenues and expenses are recognised for accounting purposes is different from the period in which such revenues and expenses are treated as taxable income and allowable deductions for tax purposes.

An asset can be recovered (for tax purposes) through use (by depreciating and impairing the asset), through use and sale (for example, by depreciating the asset and subsequently selling the asset) or only through sale (a non-depreciable asset).

The process of consolidation requires the preparation of financial statements for the group as a **single reporting entity**. For this purpose, the assets, liabilities and equity are recognised and reported for the group entity. From the group entity's perspective, we have to consider the fair value adjustments relating to the assets acquired and liabilities assumed in the subsidiaries at the acquisition date. In some jurisdictions, a group entity becomes the taxable entity. This means that the group determines a separate tax base for group assets as well as a separate taxable income for profit and loss purposes. However, in this publication, we assume that the **group entity is not a separate tax entity**, thus each entity in the group is a separate tax entity (as is the case in South Africa). In other words, we assume that the **separate entities are individually liable for tax**. The tax bases of the subsidiary's assets and liabilities are not affected by the parent's acquisition of the subsidiary. This is important as the assets and liabilities reported in the consolidated financial statements may have accounting carrying amounts that are different from those in the individual financial statements of the parent and its subsidiary.

Discussions and examples in this chapter assume a current tax rate of 28% and that the tax base of the assets in the subsidiary is not affected by the acquisition by the parent, which may result in temporary differences and deferred tax adjustments arising on consolidation. Thus, from the group's perspective, the assets acquired may have a fair value (which becomes the cost) that is different from that recognised in the individual financial statements of the subsidiary. As consolidated financial statements are prepared for the group entity, the **accounting carrying amount** of the asset in the group may thus be different from its **tax base** in the subsidiary, resulting in temporary differences and deferred tax implications arising on consolidation.

3.1 Deferred tax implications at acquisition date

Fair value adjustments at the acquisition date relating to the assets and liabilities of the subsidiary result in a different measurement of those assets in the group financial statements. Thus, for accounting purposes (consolidation), the cost of the assets for the group is its fair value at the acquisition date. However, the tax base of the assets remains unchanged as the subsidiary is the tax entity. This gives rise to a temporary difference at the acquisition date.

At the acquisition date, we need to consider the **future recovery** of each asset (or liability) measured at fair value in order to determine the existence of a temporary difference and the appropriate tax rate to use. This means whether an asset can be recovered (for tax purposes) through use (by depreciating and impairing the asset), through use and sale (for example, by depreciating the asset and subsequently selling the asset) or only through sale (a non-depreciable asset).

3.1.1 Fair value adjustment at acquisition date of non-depreciable asset

For a non-depreciable asset such as land that can only be recovered through sale, the effective capital gains tax rate may be the best rate at which to recognise deferred tax.

3.1.2 Fair value adjustments of depreciable assets at acquisition date

Depreciating assets (for example, machinery) are recovered through use (in other words, depreciated) or through sale (when sold). The current tax rate of 28% best reflects recovery through use (as the benefits arising from the use of the machinery are taxed at 28%), which is how the machinery is expected to be recovered at the date of acquisition, assuming that no decision has been made to sell the asset.

3.1.3 Fair value adjustments of inventory at acquisition date

Inventory is a non-depreciable asset and as such is recovered through sale. The current tax rate of 28% best reflects recovery through sale (as any gross profit arising from the sale of the inventory is taxed at 28%).

3.1.4 Implications for goodwill

As mentioned earlier, goodwill arising on consolidation is calculated as follows:

Consideration transferred **plus** the amount of non-controlling interest (if any) (refer to Chapter 7), **less** the net fair value of the identifiable assets acquired and liabilities assumed at the acquisition date.

The fair value of the net identifiable assets should therefore include any deferred tax liability (or asset) that is required to be recognised as a result of fair value adjustments arising at consolidation. The goodwill is then the residual value.

Example

Recognising deferred tax liability and goodwill at acquisition date

This example illustrates fair value adjustments at acquisition date, including deferred tax implications.

A parent acquires 100% of a subsidiary for CU1 million. At the date of acquisition, the carrying amount of the net assets of the subsidiary amounts to CU800 000. Goodwill of CU200 000 arises.

However, assuming the parent considers the machinery of the subsidiary to be undervalued by CU100 000, this has the effect of increasing the net assets of the subsidiary to CU900 000. Goodwill of CU100 000 arises. The effect of recognising the fair value adjustment at the acquisition date was that goodwill decreased.

> As the machinery is a depreciable asset, the carrying amount of which will be recovered through use, the related deferred tax liability must also reflect recovering the machine through use.

As the current tax rate (assumed at 28%) best reflects recovery through use (as it is the rate that will apply to the future economic benefits derived from using the asset), a temporary difference of CU100 000 exists on consolidation (the carrying amount of the asset increased by CU100 000, but the tax base remained unchanged). Thus a **deferred tax liability of CU28 000** arises at the acquisition date.

The **goodwill acquired** can therefore be determined as follows:
- Consideration paid: CU1 million
- Fair value of net identifiable assets of subsidiary: CU900 000 – CU28 000 (deferred tax liability) = CU872 000 (or: CU800 000 + (CU100 000 × 72%) = CU872 000)
- Goodwill at acquisition date: **CU128 000 (CU1 million – CU872 000)**.

The effect of recognising the deferred tax liability is that the net asset value of the subsidiary at the acquisition date has decreased. This in turn increases the goodwill arising on acquisition. The fair value adjustment, when recognised for the first time at a group level, therefore has no effect on group profit or loss. In jurisdictions where groups are not separate taxable entities, the group is not a taxable entity, but the individual entities within the group are separate taxable entities.

Furthermore, the recognition of the fair value adjustment at the date of acquisition has no effect on the taxable income of the subsidiary. The subsidiary will be allowed to deduct the cost (to the subsidiary) of the machine in the form of capital allowances. The fair value adjustment therefore has no effect on the tax base of the machine. As a result, a difference between the tax and accounting treatment of the fair value adjustment at the acquisition date arises in that the fair value adjustment has increased the carrying amount of the machine for accounting purposes (at a group level), but not the tax base. Even though this difference has no effect on accounting or taxable profit when recognised for the first time by the group, the temporary difference (being the fair value adjustment) is not exempt in terms of paragraph 15 of IAS12.

3.2 Deferred tax implications since the acquisition date

Fair value adjustments at acquisition date are reversed (or realised) subsequent to the acquisition date by depreciating the asset, impairing the asset or selling the asset to which the fair value adjustment related. When a deferred tax liability (or asset) is recognised at the acquisition date, the resulting changes in the deferred tax income (or expense) are recognised in the consolidated statement of profit or loss and other comprehensive income. The deferred tax adjustments (arising on consolidation) in the subsequent periods are recognised in the same place where the temporary differences originate and/or reverse, that is, through profit or loss, other comprehensive income or directly to equity.

For example, post-acquisition, the fair value adjustment will **reverse** as the machinery is depreciated. The additional depreciation recognised at a group level (as the group cost is higher than the carrying amount in the subsidiary as a result of the fair value adjustment not recognised by the subsidiary) is a post-acquisition expense. Similarly, the additional deferred tax liability relating to the fair value adjustment is reversed post-acquisition. As the carrying amount of the asset decreases, the temporary difference decreases. This results in a decrease in the deferred tax liability, which reduces the tax expense recognised in the group profit or loss. The deferred tax recognised at acquisition is effectively reversed as the machinery is depreciated. The logic is that group profits have decreased post-acquisition as a result of the additional depreciation, therefore group tax must reduce. If tax is an expense in profit or loss, it is reduced by crediting the tax expense. In terms of double entry, a corresponding debit is required. The debit adjusts the deferred tax liability.

 Example

Fair value adjustment of a depreciating asset at the acquisition date, including deferred tax implications

This example illustrates the measurement of the cost of a depreciable asset in the group and its subsequent treatment, including deferred tax implications.

 A similar example, which illustrates the effects of a partially held subsidiary, is included on the accompanying CD. Refer to the CD after you have worked through Chapter 7, *Consolidation: Partly owned subsidiaries and other consolidation considerations.*

When P Ltd acquired its 100% controlling interest in S Ltd on 1 January 20x4, S Ltd had the following depreciating asset in its statement of financial position:

	CU
Plant (at cost)	300 000
Accumulated depreciation	(60 000)
Carrying amount	**240 000**

The plant was acquired by S Ltd one year ago and had an expected useful life of five years. S Ltd depreciated this plant by CU60 000 in the prior year. S Ltd claims wear-and-tear allowances for tax purposes over a period of three years. As wear-and-tear allowances have already been claimed for one year, the tax base of the plant amounted to CU200 000 at the acquisition date (CU300 000 $\times \frac{2}{3}$).

P Ltd considered the fair value of the plant to be CU350 000 at the acquisition date and agreed with its remaining estimated useful life of four years.

What is the cost of the plant to the group?

The group acquired this plant at a fair value of **CU350 000** (the cost at which the plant should be recognised by the group at the acquisition date).

The accumulated depreciation of the plant at the acquisition date (CU60 000) should be reversed against the cost price of the plant by using *pro-forma* journal entries.

			CU	CU
Dr		Accumulated depreciation	60 000	
	Cr	Plant		60 000

Elimination of accumulated depreciation relating to the plant at the acquisition date

The cost price of the plant should then be increased by CU110 000 to recognise the fair value adjustment at the acquisition date (CU300 000 − CU60 000 + CU110 000 = CU350 000). Thus, the net effect of the fair value adjustment at the acquisition date amounts to CU110 000.

Dr/(Cr)	S Ltd CU	Pro-forma journals CU	Group carrying amount CU	Tax base (as per S Ltd) CU	Temporary difference S Ltd CU	Temporary difference group CU
Plant (at cost)	300 000	(60 000)				
Accumulated depreciation	(60 000)	60 000				
Carrying amount	240 000	−	240 000	200 000	40 000	40 000
Fair value adjustment at acquisition date		110 000	110 000			110 000
Carrying amount at acquisition date	**240 000**	**110 000**	**350 000**	**200 000**	**40 000**	**150 000**

The tax base of this asset remains unchanged at CU200 000. From a group perspective, the carrying amount has increased to CU350 000. The temporary difference of this asset from a group's perspective amounts to CU150 000 (CU350 000 − CU200 000). S Ltd would have recognised deferred tax for this asset in its own financial statements. Assuming that a normal tax rate of 28% applied, a deferred tax liability of CU11 200 (CU40 000 × 28%) was recognised by S Ltd. From a group's perspective, a deferred tax liability of CU42 000 (CU150 000 × 28%) exists at the acquisition date. This means that a **deferred tax liability adjustment** is required of **CU30 800** (CU110 000 × 28% or CU42 000 − CU11 200) as a result of the fair value adjustment of the plant of CU110 000.

Assuming the same information as in the previous examples, where P Ltd acquired 100% of the issued share capital of S Ltd at 1 January 20x4 for CU360 000, when the retained earnings of S Ltd amounted to CU115 000, the following *pro-forma* journal entry is required in order to adjust the fair value of the plant at the acquisition date, to allocate the appropriate portion to non-controlling interest and to determine goodwill:

		CU	CU
Dr	Share capital	120 000	
Dr	Retained earnings	115 000	
Dr	Goodwill acquired	45 800 ◄	
Dr	Plant	110 000	
	Cr Deferred tax liability		30 800
	Cr Investment in subsidiary		360 000

> **Goodwill** is the **residual**, being the excess amount paid, after determining the fair value of the net identifiable asset (including deferred tax).

Elimination of investment in subsidiary at the acquisition date

What is the depreciation expense relating to the plant for the group after the acquisition date?

The group confirmed the remaining useful life of the plant, but the cost price of the plant for the group amounts to CU350 000. The annual depreciation of the plant for the group amounts to CU350 000/4 = CU87 500.

	S Ltd CU	Pro-forma journals CU	Group CU
Plant (carrying amount)	240 000	110 000	350 000
Remaining useful life	4 years		4 years
Annual depreciation	60 000	27 500	87 500

As the carrying amount of the plant is higher in the group statement of financial position, the annual depreciation to be included in the group financial statements after the acquisition date should increase by CU27 500. The subsidiary will continue to claim wear-and-tear tax allowances and record the necessary adjustments for deferred tax in its separate financial statements. However, the increase in the depreciation expense in the group will result in a deferred tax adjustment on consolidation.

In the first year after the acquisition date of the subsidiary, the *pro-forma* journal entries that follow are required.

Pro-forma journal entry to adjust the depreciation

		CU	CU
Dr	Depreciation (P/L)	27 500	◄
	Cr Accumulated depreciation		27 500

> **What is this?**
> Additional depreciation resulting from the higher cost of the plant for the group is recognised in the group.

Adjustment to depreciation in subsidiary, from group's perspective $(\frac{CU110\,000}{4})$

Pro-forma journal entry to adjust the deferred tax, resulting from the increase in the depreciation expense

			CU	CU
Dr		Deferred tax liability	7 700	
	Cr	Deferred tax expense (reversal) (P/L)		7 700

Deferred tax adjustment, resulting from adjustment to deprecation in group (CU27 500 × 28%)

> **What is this?**
> The carrying amount of the plant changed (in the group), but its tax base remained the same (in S Ltd), resulting in a deferred tax adjustment on consolidation. As the expense is recognised in profit or loss, the deferred tax adjustment is also in profit or loss.

The two *pro-forma* journal entries above form a unit:
- The first *pro-forma* journal entry affects the adjustment for depreciation in the current year profit of S Ltd from a group's perspective, resulting from the higher cost of the asset in the group.
- The second *pro-forma* journal entry affects the deferred tax adjustment that is required as a result of the increase in the group's depreciation charge.

These *pro-forma* journal entries can also be combined in a single entry.

4. Fair value adjustments of non-current assets at acquisition when the group applies the revaluation model

When a group, being the parent and its subsidiary, applies the **revaluation model** to its property, plant and equipment, the subsidiary records a revaluation in its separate financial statements and the group recognises a revaluation surplus for its share of the revaluation in the consolidated statement of financial position. Financial assets that are measured at fair value through other comprehensive income may also give rise to a revaluation surplus in the subsidiary.

Where the subsidiary had previously revalued an asset at the acquisition date, the revaluation surplus at the acquisition date should be included in the equity of the subsidiary **at the acquisition date** when you determine the goodwill acquired. For example, where a subsidiary applies the revaluation model to its land, with a fair value of CU1 million at the acquisition date and a revaluation surplus of CU600 000 resulting from revaluations prior to the acquisition date, the revaluation surplus of CU600 000 forms part of the equity of the subsidiary at the acquisition date, meaning that it is a pre-acquisition reserve.

Revaluations **subsequent** to the acquisition date are recognised by the group in accordance with the group's policy.

Revaluations of property, plant and equipment are required at intervals. The acquisition date may not be the same date as the revaluation date of the subsidiary. In such cases, the group may recognise a fair value adjustment at the acquisition date, which will only be recognised by the subsidiary at its next revaluation date.

Example

The revaluation of an asset held by a subsidiary

This example illustrates the application of the revaluation model for property, plant and equipment. In this case, the fair value of the revalued asset is higher than its carrying amount at the acquisition date and the subsidiary revalues the asset after the acquisition date. The example ignores any deferred tax implications relating to such a revaluation.

A similar example, which illustrates the effects of a partially held subsidiary, is included on the accompanying CD. Refer to the CD after you have worked through Chapter 7, *Consolidation: Partly owned subsidiaries and other consolidation considerations*.

P Ltd acquired all of the ordinary shares in S Ltd on 1 January 20x4, when the retained earnings of S Ltd amounted to CU115 000 and there was a revaluation surplus of CU25 000. The trial balances of the two entities were as follows at 31 December 20x6:

	P Ltd		S Ltd	
	Debit CU	Credit CU	Debit CU	Credit CU
Ordinary share capital		240 000		120 000
Revaluation surplus (land)		200 000		50 000
Retained earnings (1 January 20x6)		500 000		190 000
Investment in S Ltd (200 000 shares)	320 000			
Land	500 000		110 000	
Other net assets (excluding investments)	470 000		450 000	
Revenue		840 000		600 000
Other expenses	325 000		314 000	
Tax expense	165 000		86 000	
	1 780 000	**1 780 000**	**960 000**	**960 000**

All of the assets and liabilities of S Ltd are considered fairly valued at the acquisition date, except for land, which had a carrying amount of CU100 000 and a fair value of CU110 000. Ignore deferred tax.

S Ltd revalued its land to CU120 000 at its next revaluation date, which was 31 December 20x4. Both P Ltd and S Ltd have always applied a policy of regular revaluation to non-current assets.

The balance on the revaluation surplus of S Ltd can be analysed as shown below.

Revaluation surplus of S Ltd: Land

	CU
Balance at 1 January 20x4	25 000
Increases in valuation since acquisition date until 31 December 20x5	20 000
Increases in valuation during the current period	5 000
Closing balance at 31 December 20x6	**50 000**

The parent did not revalue any of its own assets during the current year. The increases in the revaluation surplus of the subsidiary after the acquisition date should be included in the analysis of equity as shown below.

Analysis of the equity of S Ltd

		P Ltd's interest	
	Total of S Ltd's equity 100% CU	At acquisition 100% CU	Since acquisition 100% CU
At acquisition (1 January 20x4):			
Share capital	120 000		
Revaluation surplus	25 000		
Land (excess over carrying amount)	① 10 000		
Retained earnings	115 000		
	270 000	270 000	
Investment in S Ltd		(320 000)	
∴ Goodwill		50 000	
Since acquisition (January 20x4 to December 20x5):			
Retained earnings	75 000		75 000
(190 000 – 115 000)			
Revaluation surplus	② 10 000		10 000
(20 000 – 10 000)			
Current period (January 20x6 to December 20x6):			
Other comprehensive income	③ 5 000		5 000
Profit after tax	200 000		200 000
(600 000 – 314 000 – 86 000)			
Total equity of S Ltd	**560 000**		**290 000**

Check your workings

Analysis of the revaluation surplus of subsidiary:
- At acquisition date: CU35 000 (25 000 + 10 000)
- Since acquisition date: CU15 000 (10 000 + 5 000)
- Total revaluation surplus in S Ltd: CU50 000.

What is this?

The parent's interest in the equity of the subsidiary since acquisition date (CU290 000) consists of the following:
- Retained earnings of CU75 000 + CU200 000 = CU275 000
- Revaluation surplus of CU10 000 + CU5 000 = CU15 000.

Notes

① The revaluation surplus at the date of acquisition is included in the equity (or net assets) at the date of acquisition. This portion of the revaluation surplus is pre-acquisition equity and is not included in the group reserves as it was not earned while it was part of the group. The subsidiary did not revalue its land at the acquisition date. Thus, from a group's perspective, land is understated by CU10 000. This additional fair value adjustment is required at the acquisition date in order to reflect the fair value of the net assets of the subsidiary correctly at the acquisition date.

② The increase in the revaluation surplus subsequent to the acquisition date until the beginning of the current year would have been recognised in the prior year's group financial statements and should be included as part of the opening balances in the current year. However, the revaluation recognised for this period by the subsidiary (CU20 000) includes the fair value adjustment that was made by the group at the acquisition date. The revaluation since the acquisition date that is attributable to the group is only CU10 000 (CU20 000 – CU10 000 already recognised at the acquisition date). You should only include the group's portion in the opening revaluation surplus balance.

③ The current year's portion of the revaluation surplus has to be separately identified as it will be reflected in other comprehensive income. No adjustment is required to the CU5 000 recognised in the current year because the group agreed with the previous revalued carrying amount and with the new fair value. Therefore the full CU5 000 should be recognised. The CU10 000 attributable to 20x5 would be shown as comparative figures. In addition, the statement of changes in equity discloses the opening balance, the movement during the year and the closing balance.

Pro-forma journal entry at date of acquisition

			CU	CU
Dr		Share capital	120 000	
Dr		Revaluation surplus	25 000	
Dr		Retained earnings	115 000	
Dr		Land (fair value adjustment at acquisition date)	10 000	
Dr		Goodwill arising on consolidation	50 000	
	Cr	Investment in subsidiary		320 000

Elimination of investment in subsidiary at the acquisition date

This entry has the effect of reversing the equity that existed at the date of acquisition, specifically the revaluation surplus and the retained earnings, as that equity is purchased and not earned.

Pro-forma journal entries after the acquisition date

			CU	CU
Dr		Revaluation surplus	10 000	
	Cr	Land (fair value adjustment at acquisition date)		10 000

Reversing the fair value of the land at acquisition date, as the subsidiary has revalued its land since the acquisition date

The consolidation adjustments relating to the revaluation surplus in S Ltd are summarised as follows at 31 December 20x6:

	S Ltd (starting point) CU	Adjustments (*pro-forma* journal entries) above	Group (end point) CU
Revaluation surplus	50 000	Eliminate the balance at acquisition: (CU25 000)	
		Reverse fair value adjustment relating to land, as subsidiary has subsequently recorded this entry: (CU10 000)	15 000

The *pro-forma* journal entries are recorded on the consolidation worksheet as follows:

	P Ltd Dr/(Cr) CU	S Ltd Dr/(Cr) CU	Pro-forma at acquisition Dr/(Cr) CU	Pro-forma since acquisition Dr/(Cr) CU	Group Dr/(Cr) CU
Equity:					
Ordinary share capital	(240 000)	(120 000)	120 000		(240 000)
Revaluation surplus	(200 000)	(50 000)	25 000	10 000	(215 000)
Retained earnings (1 January 20x6)	(500 000)	(190 000)	115 000		(575 000)
Assets:					
Land	500 000	110 000	10 000	(10 000)	610 000
Other net assets (excluding investments)	470 000	450 000			920 000
Investment in S Ltd	320 000		(320 000)		–
Goodwill			50 000		50 000
Profit or loss:					
Revenue	(840 000)	(600 000)			(1 440 000)
Expenses	325 000	314 000			639 000
Tax expense	165 000	86 000			251 000

What is this?

The group's share of the revaluation surplus in the subsidiary at 31 December 20x6 amounts to CU15 000.
- Revaluation surplus in P Ltd: CU200 000
- Group: CU215 000.

The total of all the adjustments in the *pro-forma* journal entry column should **balance out to zero** as all of the journal entries balance.

Consolidated statement of profit or loss and other comprehensive income for P Ltd and its subsidiary for the period ended 31 December 20x6

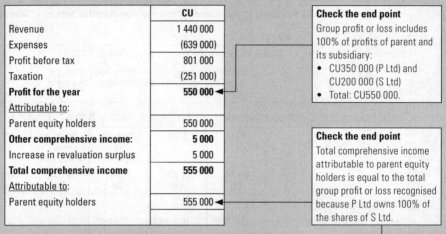

	CU
Revenue	1 440 000
Expenses	(639 000)
Profit before tax	801 000
Taxation	(251 000)
Profit for the year	**550 000**
<u>Attributable to:</u>	
Parent equity holders	550 000
Other comprehensive income:	**5 000**
Increase in revaluation surplus	5 000
Total comprehensive income	**555 000**
<u>Attributable to:</u>	
Parent equity holders	555 000

Check the end point

Group profit or loss includes 100% of profits of parent and its subsidiary:
• CU350 000 (P Ltd) and CU200 000 (S Ltd)
• Total: CU550 000.

Check the end point

Total comprehensive income attributable to parent equity holders is equal to the total group profit or loss recognised because P Ltd owns 100% of the shares of S Ltd.

Consolidated statement of changes in equity for P Ltd and its subsidiary for the period ended 31 December 20x6

	Share capital CU	Revaluation surplus CU	Retained earnings CU	Total parent equity CU
Opening balance at 1 January 20x6	240 000	210 000	575 000	1 025 000
Total comprehensive income		5 000	550 000	555 000
Closing balance at 31 December 20x6	**240 000**	**215 000**	**1 125 000**	**1 580 000**

Revaluation surplus (end point)
Opening balance: CU210 000
• P Ltd: CU200 000
• S Ltd: CU10 000 (refer to analysis of equity).
Closing balance: CU215 000
• P Ltd: CU200 000
• S Ltd: CU15 000.

Retained earnings (end point)
Opening balance: CU575 000
• P Ltd: CU500 000
• S Ltd: CU75 000 (refer to analysis of equity).
Closing balance: CU1 125 000
• P Ltd: CU850 000
• S Ltd: CU275 000.

Consolidated abridged statement of financial position for P Ltd and its subsidiary at 31 December 20x6

	CU
ASSETS	
Land	610 000
Other net assets	920 000
Goodwill	50 000
EQUITY AND LIABILITIES	1 580 00
Share capital	240 000
Revaluation surplus	215 000
Retained earnings	1 125 000
Share capital and reserves attributable to parent equity holders	**1 580 000**
Total equity and liabilities	**1 580 000**

Net assets
The land in the group statement of financial position is equal to the starting point (CU500 000 + CU110 000), in other words, the balances in the current trial balances of P Ltd and S Ltd, because the fair value adjustment to land at acquisition was reversed when the subsidiary revalued the land. The group carrying amount for the land is now equal to the carrying amount of the subsidiary.

5. Fair value adjustments of current assets at acquisition

The parent should consider the fair value of all the assets and liabilities of a subsidiary at the acquisition date in order to determine the cost of any goodwill acquired. This includes all of the current assets. The parent may consider the value of some **current assets** of the subsidiary, for example, inventory and trade receivable, to be higher (or lower) than their carrying amount at the acquisition date.

An entity recognises **inventory** at the lower of cost or net realisable value (refer to IAS2, *Inventories*). If the fair value of the inventory at the acquisition date is higher than its carrying amount, as recorded by the subsidiary, the fair value of the inventory represents the **cost** of the inventory for the group. For example, where a subsidiary is manufacturing inventory, it should recognise the inventory at the manufactured cost price, but the parent may consider the fair value of the inventory to be higher. The fair value of the inventory at the date that the parent acquires the interest in the subsidiary is the cost of the inventory to the group. Even though this is not the cost price for the subsidiary, it is the cost price of the inventory to the group, which is in agreement with the requirement of IAS2 that inventories should be recognised at the lower of cost and net realisable value in the entity (in this case, the group entity). The cost to the subsidiary is the amount paid when the subsidiary acquired the inventory, whereas the cost to the group is the fair value when the group acquired the subsidiary, thereby obtaining control of the inventory.

While the inventory is still held by the group, an adjustment has to be made to the subsidiary's inventory to increase it to the cost to the group. When the inventory is subsequently (after the acquisition date) sold by the subsidiary, the profit on the sale is the difference between the proceeds on the sale and the inventory cost. The cost to the group is the fair value at the date of acquisition, whereas the cost to the subsidiary is the original cost of the inventory. An adjustment has to be made to the cost of sales recognised by the subsidiary to get the correct cost of sales for the group.

A fair value adjustment to inventory at the acquisition date may give rise to temporary differences and thus have deferred tax implications on consolidation. As mentioned above, the carrying amount of the inventory in the group is its fair value at the acquisition date. However, the tax base is the cost of the inventory as recorded by the subsidiary.

 Example

Fair value adjustment on inventory at the acquisition date

This example illustrates fair value adjustment relating to inventory at the acquisition date and its deferred tax implications. The inventory is subsequently sold by the subsidiary.

 A similar example, which illustrates the effects of a partially held subsidiary, is included on the accompanying CD. Refer to the CD after you have worked through Chapter 7, *Consolidation: Partly owned subsidiaries and other consolidation considerations*.

P Ltd acquired a 100% interest in S Ltd at 1 January 20x4, at which date it considered the fair value of the inventory of S Ltd to be CU30 000 higher than its carrying amount. The cost price of the inventory in the statement of financial position of S Ltd at the acquisition date amounted to CU90 000 and the group therefore considered the fair value of the inventory to be CU120 000. Assume a current tax rate of 28%.

At acquisition date:

The inventory of S Ltd should be recognised in the group statement of financial position at the cost of CU120 000 to the group (CU90 000 + CU30 000). The tax base of the inventory is its cost of CU90 000 to the subsidiary. A taxable temporary difference of CU30 000 arises on consolidation and a deferred tax liability of CU8 400 should be recognised.

The following summarised trial balances are presented for P Ltd and its subsidiary, S Ltd, at 1 January 20x5, the acquisition date:

	P Ltd CU	S Ltd CU
Debits:		
Non-current assets	150 000	200 000
Other current assets	30 000	20 000
Inventory	50 000	90 000
Investment in S Ltd	270 000	
	500 000	**310 000**
Credits:		
Share capital	240 000	120 000
Retained earnings	90 000	115 000
Liabilities	170 000	75 000
	500 000	**310 000**

The goodwill acquired at the acquisition date is the difference between the cost of the investment and the fair value of the net assets (including the inventory valued at CU120 000) at the acquisition date.

Analysis of the equity of S Ltd

	Total CU	P Ltd (100%) CU
At acquisition date:		
Share capital	120 000	
Retained earnings	115 000	
Inventory	30 000	
Deferred tax liability	(8 400)	
Fair value of net assets of S Ltd	256 600	256 600
Investment in S Ltd		(270 000)
Goodwill acquired		13 400

The *pro-forma* journal entry at acquisition date would be as follows:

			CU	CU
Dr		Share capital	120 000	
Dr		Retained earnings	115 000	
Dr		Inventory	30 000	
	Cr	Deferred tax liability		8 400
Dr		Goodwill	13 400	
	Cr	Investment in subsidiary		270 000

Elimination of investment in subsidiary at the acquisition date

---

Think about it

The cost price of inventory for the group amounts to CU120 000. However, the starting point includes inventory recorded at its cost to the subsidiary of CU90 000. The adjustment required is therefore CU30 000 (CU120 000 − CU90 000). The net fair value adjustment at the acquisition date (after taxation) amounts to CU21 600 (CU30 000 × 72%) or (CU30 000 − CU8 400).

Since the acquisition date:

Assuming that S Ltd sold all of the inventory for CU140 000 in the year after the date of acquisition, S Ltd would recognise a gross profit of CU140 000 − CU90 000 = CU50 000 in that period. However, the group profit when the inventory was sold amounts to CU140 000 − CU120 000 = CU20 000. The gross profit of CU50 000 recognised by the subsidiary needs to be reduced by CU30 000 to get the correct group profit of CU20 000. The group cost of sales is CU120 000 (which is CU30 000 higher than that of the subsidiary) and therefore the gross profit is CU30 000 less.

The effect of these entries at the time that the inventory is sold by the group can be summarised as shown below.

Extract from profit or loss of S Ltd for the current year

	S Ltd (starting point) CU	Pro-forma journals CU	Group (end point) CU
Sales	140 000		140 000
Cost of sales	(90 000)	① (30 000)	(120 000)
Gross profit	50 000		20 000
Taxation expense:			
Normal tax	(14 000)		(14 000)
Deferred tax		② 8 400	8 400
Profit after tax	**36 000**	**(21 600)**	**14 400**

The inventory had a higher cost of CU120 000 for the group. This means that, the profit after tax of S Ltd should be CU21 600 less on consolidation.

The *pro-forma* journal entries when the inventory is sold are as follows:

			CU	CU
Dr		Cost of sales (P/L)	① 30 000	
	Cr	Inventory		30 000

Elimination of effect of increase in the carrying amount of inventory at the acquisition date, subsequently sold .

The credit in the entry above reverses the increase in inventory at the acquisition date. This makes sense, as the inventory is now sold. Cost of sales in the group is increased.

Dr		Deferred tax liability	8 400	
	Cr	Deferred tax expense (P/L)		② 8 400

Deferred tax implications relating to the elimination of the effect of the increase in the carrying amount of inventory at the acquisition date, subsequently sold

The debit in the entry above reverses the deferred tax recognised at the acquisition date. This makes sense, as the deferred tax should be reversed when the inventory is sold.

The parent can also consider the fair value of **trade receivables** to be an amount that is different from its carrying amount. This would happen as a result of a difference in opinion over the collectability of the debt. The net amount recognised on the statement of financial position is the difference between the gross debtors' listing and the doubtful debt allowance. Theoretically, the group could consider that the doubtful debt allowance was too low and consequently that the carrying amount of receivables was overstated. Where the subsidiary has adjusted its allowance for doubtful debts at the acquisition date, no consolidation adjustment is required. Where the subsidiary adjusts for the increase in the allowance for bad debts after the acquisition date (against post-acquisition profits), an adjustment is still needed at acquisition and the adjustment processed by the subsidiary should be reversed on consolidation; otherwise, the doubtful debt allowance would be double-counted, as the increase in the allowance for bad debts would be a *pro-forma* adjusting entry processed by the group at the acquisition date.

However, it could also happen that the subsidiary does not agree with the parent's fair value adjustment, and continues to recognise trade receivables and the allowance for bad debts as before. On consolidation, you have to adjust the carrying amount of trade receivables at the acquisition date to the fair value that the parent considers collectable from these debtors. Where the amount considered irrecoverable by the parent at the acquisition date has subsequently been settled, from a group's perspective this represents an income (that is, bad debt recovered). An adjustment at the date when the outstanding debt was settled should be recognised in the group financial statements. As both the parent and its subsidiary are required to prepare financial statements in accordance with IFRS, including the requirement to consider any impairment, it is unlikely that such differences would exist in practice.

Example

Wholly owned subsidiary, adjustments to trade receivables

In this example, the acquisition date was not at the reporting date of the subsidiary. The subsidiary has therefore not recognised its trade receivables at the recoverable amount at the acquisition date. The trade receivable was partly collected and partly written off post the acquisition date. The effects of tax are ignored in this example.

A similar example, which illustrates the effects of a partially held subsidiary, is included on the accompanying CD. Refer to the CD after you have worked through Chapter 7, *Consolidation: Partly owned subsidiaries and other consolidation considerations.*

P Ltd acquired 100% of S Ltd on 1 April 20x4 when the owners' equity of S Ltd amounted to CU243 750. P considered all of the assets of S to be fairly valued at the acquisition date, except for the following:

	Carrying amount in S Ltd	Fair value at acquisition date
Trade receivables	CU13 000	CU10 000

S Ltd collected CU11 000 from its trade receivable. The balance of CU2 000 was written off at 31 December 20x4.

Pro-forma journal entries (relating to trade receivable only)

			CU	CU
Dr		Goodwill	3 000	
	Cr	Trade receivables		3 000

Partial pro-forma *journal entry relating to the elimination of the investment in the subsidiary at the acquisition date*

What is this?
The carrying amount in S Ltd (starting point) for trade receivables is overstated, resulting in a credit adjustment of CU3000. The cost to the group at the acquisition date is CU10 000.

When S Ltd received CU11 000 from its debtor, it would have recorded a bad debts expense of CU2 000 (CU13 000 – CU11 000). However, the group had the trade receivable recorded at an amount of CU10 000 and reduced the equity of the subsidiary at the acquisition date accordingly. When CU11 000 was recovered from the debtor, the group should have recorded an income, bad debts recovered, of CU1 000. The bad debt expense of S Ltd should be reversed.

			CU	CU
Dr		Trade receivables	3 000	
	Cr	Bad debts expense		2 000
	Cr	Bad debts recovered		1 000

Reversal of adjustment to trade receivables at the acquisition date, subsequently recovered and written off by subsidiary

The effect of these consolidation adjustments on the group financial statements can be illustrated as follows:

At 31 December 20x4 Dr/(Cr)	S Ltd (starting point) CU	Pro-forma entries at acquisition date CU	Pro-forma entries since acquisition date CU	Group (end point) CU
Trade receivables	–	(3 000)	3 000	–
Profit or loss:				
Bad debts expense	2 000		(2 000)	–
Bad debts recovered			(1 000)	(1 000)

Think about it

The bad debts expense recorded by S Ltd was recorded by the group at acquisition when it decreased the carrying amount of the trade receivables. It would therefore be incorrect to record the expense a second time. It should be reversed.

Think about it

Trade receivables in the group at the acquisition date amounted to CU10 000. An amount of CU11 000 was collected from this debtor, resulting in a recovery of the bad debt (at acquisition date) of CU1 000.

Extract from the consolidated statement of profit or loss and other comprehensive income for the year ended 31 December 20x4

Profit or loss:	CU
Bad debts recovered	1 000

Extract from the consolidated statement of financial position at 31 December 20x4

	CU
Current assets: Trade receivables	Nil

6. Subsequent sale of an asset held at the acquisition date

When a subsidiary sells an asset that it held at the acquisition date, you should determine the group's profit arising from the sale of the asset. In the case where the parent considered the net assets of the subsidiary to be fairly valued at their carrying amount at the acquisition date and the subsidiary subsequently sells some of the assets, the group's profit on the sale of the assets equals the profit recognised by the subsidiary, as the cost of the asset to the group and the subsidiary is the same.

However, where the fair value of the net assets of a subsidiary has been adjusted **at the acquisition date**, the effect of such a fair value adjustment on the profits of the subsidiary **since the acquisition date** should be considered. For example, where a parent considered the fair value of an asset to be higher than its carrying amount at the acquisition date and that asset has subsequently been sold, the group profit on the sale of the asset is lower than the profit recognised by the subsidiary. This is because the group acquired that asset at a price higher than its carrying amount in the subsidiary at the acquisition date. The profit to the group must be calculated by using the cost of the asset to the group.

In the previous examples (refer to Section 2 above), we considered fair value adjustments at the acquisition date for depreciable assets. In these examples, you learnt that the subsequent depreciation in the group is based on the cost to the group, which is the fair value at the acquisition date. In a similar way, the profit in the group is based on the difference between the proceeds and the carrying amount in the group, which is the cost to the group less accumulated depreciation. The subsequent sale of an asset by the subsidiary, where the group cost was different from that of the subsidiary, results in **adjustments** to the profits of the subsidiary **after the acquisition date**. In effect, you have to reverse the fair value adjustment relating to the asset at the acquisition date against the subsidiary's profit since the acquisition date, as the subsidiary has subsequently sold the asset. As any adjustment to the carrying amount of the asset at the acquisition date may give rise to a temporary difference (and as a result, the recognition of **deferred tax** at the acquisition date), the subsequent depreciation and sale of such an asset then results in a **reversal of deferred tax** recognised at the acquisition date.

To include the group's profit on the sale of the asset correctly in the **group profit or loss**, the profits of the subsidiary (starting point) have to be adjusted by both the increased group depreciation for the period up to the date of disposal and the decreased profit on the sale of the asset for the current year. It is important that this is done in the correct periods: against opening **retained earnings** for those adjustments relating to prior years, and against the **correct line item** in the statement of profit or loss and other comprehensive income for adjustments relating to the current year. When group financial statements are prepared for the following financial year, all of the adjustments need to be made against opening retained earnings as the group's opening retained earnings for the current year should be the same as the group's retained earnings at the end of the prior year.

Example

The subsequent depreciation and sale of an asset held at acquisition date

This example illustrates the fair value of a depreciable asset at the acquisition date, its subsequent depreciation and sale, and the deferred tax implications.

A similar example, which illustrates the effects of a partially held subsidiary, is included on the accompanying CD. Refer to the CD after you have worked through Chapter 7, *Consolidation: Partly owned subsidiaries and other consolidation considerations.*

P Ltd acquired all of the ordinary shares in S Ltd on 1 January 20x4, when the retained earnings of S Ltd amounted to CU115 000. All of the assets and liabilities of S Ltd were considered to be fairly valued at the acquisition date, with the exception of a machine, which had a carrying amount of CU240 000 and a fair value of CU350 000. The accumulated depreciation of S Ltd relating to the machine amounted to CU60 000 at 1 January 20x4. The remaining useful life of the machine was estimated at four years, with a residual value of CU80 000 at the end of the period. These estimates were confirmed at each subsequent reporting date. The machine originally cost CU300 000 one year before the acquisition date and qualified for wear-and-tear allowances at 10% per annum. Wear-and-tear allowances are apportioned. S Ltd sold this machine to a third party on 30 June 20x6 for CU200 000.

These details can be summarised as follows:

Machine:	S Ltd CU	Difference CU	Group CU
At acquisition date (carrying amount/cost)	240 000	110 000	350 000
Residual value	(80 000)	–	(80 000)
Remaining useful life	4 years		4 years
Annual depreciation since the acquisition date	40 000	27 500	67 500
Tax base at acquisition date (recovery through usage)	270 000		270 000
Annual wear-and-tear allowances (at 10% per annum) on cost to S Ltd	30 000		30 000

The abridged trial balances of the two entities were as follows at 31 December 20x6:

	P Ltd		S Ltd	
	Debit CU	Credit CU	Debit CU	Credit CU
Ordinary share capital		240 000		120 000
Retained earnings (1 January 20x6)		500 000		190 000
Net assets	760 000		510 000	
Investment in S Ltd (200 000 shares)	330 000			
Profit after tax for the year		350 000		200 000
	1 090 000	1 090 000	510 000	510 000

Think about it

What are the tax implications?

S Ltd recognised deferred tax, being the difference between the carrying amount of CU240 000 and tax base of CU270 000 (CU300 000 × 90%), in its own financial statements. This is included in the starting point. Additional deferred tax, from a group's perspective, should be recognised only in relation to the group adjustment.

The difference between the carrying amount of the machine in S Ltd and the group can be summarised as follows:

	S Ltd CU	Difference CU	Group CU
Carrying amount at 1 January 20x4	240 000	110 000	350 000
Depreciation:			
20x4	(40 000)	(27 500)	(67 500)
20x5	(40 000)	(27 500)	(67 500)
Carrying amount at 31 December 20x5	160 000	55 000	215 000
Depreciation 20x6 (6 months)	(20 000)	(13 750)	(33 750)
Carrying amount when sold	140 000	41 250	181 250
Proceeds	(200 000)		(200 000)
Profit on disposal	**60 000**	**(41 250)**	**18 750**

S Ltd sold the machine before the current reporting date, which means that the machine is no longer recognised in S Ltd (starting point).
S Ltd recognises a profit on the sale of the machine in its own profit or loss of CU60 000.

Consolidation adjustments should be recorded every year from the acquisition date until the date on which the asset is sold. The profit of S Ltd should be reduced (debited) by CU41 250 in order to record the profit on the sale in the group correctly.

As the machine is no longer owned by the group, it should no longer be recognised in the group (end point). The profit on disposal in the group amounts to CU18 750.

Analysis of the equity of S Ltd

	Total of S Ltd's equity 100% CU	P Ltd's interest	
		At acquisition 100% CU	Since acquisition 100% CU
At acquisition:			
Share capital	120 000		
Machine	110 000		
Deferred tax (machine)	(30 800)		
Retained earnings	115 000		
	314 200	314 200	
∴ Goodwill		**15 800**	
Investment in S Ltd		330 000	
Since acquisition:	35 400		35 400
Retained earnings (190 000 – 115 000)	75 000		75 000
Depreciation (net of tax) (CU27 500 × 2 years) × 72%	① (39 600)		(39 600)
Current period:	160 400		160 400
Profit after tax	200 000		200 000
Depreciation (CU 27 500 x 6/12 × 72%)	(9 900)		(9 900)
Profit on sale of machine (CU41 250 × 72%)	(29 700)		(29 700)
Total equity of S Ltd	**510 000**		**195 800**

Think about it

The equity of the subsidiary is reported after tax. Any adjustments to the profits of the subsidiary should therefore be made net of tax. Thus, deferred tax adjustments arising on consolidation should be included in the analysis of the equity of the subsidiary when the underlying transaction affects the profits of the subsidiary, from the group's perspective.

Cost and depreciation of machine in the group:

The machine should be included in the group statement of financial position **at the acquisition date** at its fair value of CU350 000 (the cost to the group) and should be depreciated annually by CU67 500. The subsidiary has already depreciated the machine in its own records at CU40 000 per annum and you need to adjust for the increase of CU27 500 in the group depreciation after the acquisition date when preparing the consolidated financial statements.

At the acquisition date:

The equity at the date of acquisition is increased by the fair value adjustment of the machine at the date of acquisition (CU110 000). The fair value adjustment at the acquisition date gives rise to the deferred tax liability of CU30 800.

Pro-forma journal entries at date of acquisition

			CU	CU
Dr		Share capital	120 000	
Dr		Machine (fair value adjustment)	110 000	
Dr		Retained earnings	115 000	
Dr		Goodwill	15 800	
	Cr	Deferred tax liability		30 800
	Cr	Investment in subsidiary		330 000

Elimination of investment in subsidiary at acquisition date, and adjustments to recognise group assets and goodwill correctly

As the group acquired the net assets of the subsidiary, their carrying amounts represent the cost price of the assets for the group. The accumulated depreciation of these assets at the acquisition date should be deducted from their cost price recognised in the statement of financial position of the subsidiary to result in their carrying amount being recognised as the cost of the assets to the group. This is usually done by this *pro-forma* journal entry:

			CU	CU
Dr		Accumulated depreciation	xx	
	Cr	Buildings/machinery		xx

Reversal of depreciation of other assets in S Ltd at the acquisition date

In this example, the accumulated depreciation of the machine was CU60 000 at the acquisition date. However, as the machine is sold on 30 June 20x6, at 31 December 20x6, neither the machine nor its accumulated depreciation is in S Ltd (the starting point). It is therefore not necessary to reverse any accumulated depreciation relating to the machine.

Since the acquisition date:

The increased depreciation resulting from the increased cost to the group has to be recognised each year in which the machine was utilised. The depreciation for the period from the date of acquisition until the beginning of the year is recognised as an adjustment to opening retained earnings (CU27 500 × 2 years = CU55 000) and the current year's portion to the current year's statement of profit or loss (that is, the CU13 750 or CU27 500 × $\frac{6}{12}$ months). The post-acquisition profit of the subsidiary is reduced by an additional CU27 500 per annum before tax. As the subsidiary has already recognised depreciation at CU40 000, recognition of the additional CU27 500 results in the recognition of the total depreciation of CU67 500 per annum for the group.

As the depreciation adjustment is a consolidation adjustment and is not processed in the books of the subsidiary, the cumulative effect has to be adjusted each year in the form of *pro-forma* journal entries.

The accumulated depreciation is increased by the difference between the depreciation recorded by the subsidiary (starting point) and the depreciation expense for the group (end point). This is allocated to the retained earnings, net of tax, relating to prior years:

			CU	CU
Dr		Retained earnings	① 55 000	
	Cr	Accumulated depreciation		55 000
Dr		Deferred tax liability	15 400	
	Cr	Retained earnings		15 400

Recognition of additional depreciation attributable to the group, net of deferred tax

The increase in depreciation in the current year is recorded before tax in order to recognise the depreciation expense and tax expense in the group profit or loss correctly:

			CU	CU
Dr		Depreciation (P/L)	13 750	
	Cr	Accumulated depreciation		13 750

Recognition of additional depreciation attributable to the group

			CU	CU
Dr		Deferred tax liability	3 850	
	Cr	Deferred tax expense (P/L) (CU13 750 × 28%)		3 850

Deferred tax adjustment relating to additional depreciation in group profit or loss

The subsidiary sold this machine on 30 June 20x6. The machine is thus no longer included in the financial statements of the subsidiary at the reporting date. Any consolidation adjustments to the machine and accumulated depreciation (in the *pro-forma* journal entries above) should therefore be reversed when the machine is sold to a third party. The subsidiary recognised a profit on the sale of the machine of CU60 000 (starting point). This profit should be reduced by CU41 250 to result in the correct profit on the sale of the machine in the group of CU18 750 (end point).

			CU	CU
Dr		Profit on sale of machine	41 250	
Dr		Accumulated depreciation (CU55 000 + CU13 750)	68 750	
	Cr	Machine (cost)		110 000

Adjustment to the profit on the sale of the machine, and reversing the adjustment to its cost and accumulated depreciation

> **What is this?**
> Since the acquisition date, we recognised additional depreciation in the group relating to the machine that was sold by the subsidiary. The additional depreciation previously recognised on consolidation should be reversed when the machine is sold.

> **What is this?**
> The *pro-forma* journal entry at the acquisition date had a debit to the asset account, machine, resulting from the fair value adjustment at the acquisition date. However, S Ltd has sold this machine, so this debit should be reversed when the machine is sold.

			CU	CU
Dr		Deferred tax liability	11 550	
	Cr	Deferred tax expense (P/L) (CU41 250 × 28%)		11 550

Deferred tax adjustment relating to adjustment to profit on sale of machine in group profit or loss

The effect of these adjustments on the group results at 31 December 20x6, relating specifically to the machine, can be illustrated as follows:

At 31 December 20x6 Dr/(Cr)	S Ltd (starting point) CU	Pro-forma adjustments at acquisition date CU	Pro-forma adjustments since acquisition date CU	Pro-forma adjustments when the machine was sold CU	Group (end point) CU
Machine (cost)	–	110 000		(110 000)	–
Accumulated depreciation	–	–	(55 000) (13 750)	68 750	–
Deferred tax liability	–	(30 800)	15 400 3 850	11 550	–
Retained earnings	(190 000)	115 000	55 000 (15 400)		(35 400)
Profit or loss:					
Depreciation	20 000		13 750		33 750
Profit on sale of machine	(60 000)			41 250	(18 750)
Deferred tax expense	–		(3 850)	(11 550)	(15 400)

Think about it

Starting point versus end point

The **starting point** is that S Ltd has sold the machine. S Ltd would have recorded the sale in its own financial statements and recognised a profit on the sale of the machine, but the cost and accumulated depreciation are no longer reflected in its financial statements. S Ltd would also have recorded any tax consequences resulting from this sale correctly (for example, reversal of deferred tax resulting from the sale).

At the acquisition date of the subsidiary, the fair value of the machine (including deferred tax implications) had to be adjusted for in order to recognise the goodwill correctly. This resulted in a debit to the machine and a credit to deferred tax liability. However, at 30 June 20x6, the machine was sold to a third party. The machine and any related accumulated depreciation recognised in the consolidation adjustments (*pro-forma* journal entries) had to be reversed again at the time when the machine was sold. This makes sense as the adjustments had to be made against retained earnings and current year profits in order to recognise the opening balances in the consolidated financial statements correctly.

In the group (end point), there is no machine and the profit on sale is correctly recognised at CU18 750.

Think about it

What happens if the asset was sold in the prior year?

In the example above, the machine was sold in the current year. We had to adjust the depreciation expense in the current year first, and then, when the machine was sold, we adjusted the profit on the sale of the machine. These adjustments were made against the current year profit or loss. In the following financial year (in this case, 31 December 20x7), the adjustments will be against **retained earnings**.

These adjustments will be net of tax, as follows:

			CU	CU
Dr		Retained earnings	79 200	
Dr		Deferred tax liability (CU110 000 × 28%)	30 800	
	Cr	Machine		110 000

Reversal of the fair value adjustment of the machine at acquisition date, subsequently sold

As the machine was sold in the prior year, the adjustment to **retained earnings** since acquisition date consists of the following:

* Adjustments relating to depreciation for the two and a half years: CU68 750 (CU27 500 × 2.5 years)
* Adjustment to profit on the sale of the machine: CU41 250
* Total adjustment before taxation: CU110 000
* Adjustment net of tax: **CU79 200** (CU110 000 × 72%).

Note that there is no adjustment to accumulated depreciation, as this will contra out as a result of the sale of the machine.

Test your knowledge

There is a list of learning objectives at the beginning of this chapter. Go back to this list and check whether you have achieved these outcomes. If not, reread the appropriate section.

Questions

Question 1

A similar example, which illustrates the effects of a partially held subsidiary, is included on the accompanying CD. Refer to the CD after you have worked through Chapter 7, *Consolidation: Partly owned subsidiaries and other consolidation considerations.*

P Ltd acquired a 100% interest (and control) of the issued ordinary shares of S Ltd at 1 July 20x3 for CU550 000. At the acquisition date, S Ltd had the following equity balances:

Ordinary share capital	CU300 000
Retained earnings	CU300 000

P Ltd considered the net assets of S Ltd to be fairly valued at the acquisition date, except for machinery, which was considered to have a fair value of CU300 000 (carrying amount of CU200 000). S Ltd estimated the **remaining useful life** of the machinery at the acquisition date at five years and P Ltd agreed with this estimate. Ignore taxation.

Extracts from the respective trial balances of P Ltd and S Ltd for the year ended 30 June 20x5

	Dr/(Cr)	P Ltd CU	S Ltd CU
Ordinary share capital		(550 000)	(300 000)
Retained earnings at 30 June 20x5		(1 250 000)	(750 000)
Land		1 000 000	735 000
Machinery (cost)		600 000	240 000
Accumulated depreciation (machinery)		(120 000)	(160 000)
Investment in S Ltd		750 000	
Current assets		100 000	270 000
Current liabilities		(530 000)	(35 000)

You are required to do the following:

Prepare the group statement of financial position for P Ltd and its subsidiary at 30 June 20x5. Comparatives are not required. You should show the individual balances making up property, plant and equipment, including accumulated depreciation.

Suggested solution

Group statement of financial position at 30 June 20x5

	CU
ASSETS	
Land (1 000 000 + 735 000)	1 735 000
Machinery	600 000
Cost (600 000 + 240 000 + 100 000 – 40 000)	900 000
Accumulated depreciation (120 000 + 160 000 – 40 000 + 60 000)	(300 000)
Goodwill	50 000
Current assets (100 000 + 270 000)	370 000
Total assets	**2 755 000**
EQUITY AND LIABILITIES	
Ordinary share capital	550 000
Retained earnings (1 250 000 + 390 000)	1 640 000
Total equity	2 190 000
Current liabilities (530 000 + 35 000)	565 000
Total equity and liabilities	**2 755 000**

Workings

The consolidation adjustments in this question are illustrated by analysing the equity of the subsidiary.

Analysis of equity of S Ltd

	Total CU	P (100%) At CU	P (100%) Since CU
At acquisition:			
Class A share capital	300 000		
Retained earnings	300 000		
Machinery	100 000		
	700 000	700 000	
Investment in S Ltd		750 000	
Goodwill		50 000	
Since acquisition:			
(1 July 20x3–30 June 20x5)	390 000		390 000
Retained earnings (750 000 – 300 000)	450 000		
Depreciation (100 000 × 3/5)	(60 000)		
	1 090 000		390 000

Question 2

> A similar example, which illustrates the effects of a partially held subsidiary, is included on the accompanying CD. Refer to the CD after you have worked through Chapter 7, *Consolidation: Partly owned subsidiaries and other consolidation considerations.*

Part A

P Ltd acquired 100% (and the controlling interest) of S Ltd on 1 January 20x3, at which date it considered the land of S Ltd to be undervalued by CU50 000. All other assets were considered to be fairly valued at this date. S Ltd did not revalue the land in its own books at this date. On 31 December 20x4, S Ltd revalued the land by CU140 000 in its own books. S Ltd sold the land on 30 June 20x5 for a profit of CU80 000.

Assume that an income tax rate of 28%, and a capital gains inclusion rate of 66.6% apply.

1. Calculate the adjustment required to the land of S Ltd at the acquisition date.
2. Calculate the deferred tax adjustment (if any) at the acquisition date. Motivate your answer.
3. Show how the **revaluation gain** relating to the land (and related taxes) would be presented (on a gross basis) in the group statement of profit or loss and other comprehensive income for the year ended **31 December 20x4**.
4. Prepare the *pro-forma* **journal entry or entries** to consolidate S Ltd in the financial year ending **31 December 20x5**, relating **only** to the **sale of the land by S Ltd** (including tax implications, if any).

Part B

Assume the same information as in Part A above, **except** that P Ltd considered the machinery (instead of the land) of S Ltd to be undervalued by CU50 000 at the acquisition date. The machinery had an original cost of CU120 000 and accumulated depreciation of CU60 000 at the acquisition date, and its remaining useful life was estimated at four years. P Ltd agreed with S Ltd's estimate of the remaining useful life at the acquisition date.

Show how the machine should be included in the property, plant and equipment note disclosure in the group financial statements for the year ended 31 December 20x5. Ignore comparatives.

Suggested solution

Part A

1. **Calculate the adjustment required to the land of S Ltd at the acquisition date.**
   Adjustment to land: CU50 000
2. **Calculate the deferred tax adjustment (if any) at the acquisition date. Motivate your answer.**
   Deferred tax adjustment: CU50 000 × 28% × 66.6% = CU9 324
   Motivation: The future economic benefits of the land relating to the temporary difference arising at acquisition date is recoverable through sale. The future tax consequences arising from the temporary difference at the acquisition date is at the capital gains tax rate.
3. **Show how the revaluation gain relating to the land (and related taxes) would be presented (on a gross basis) in the group statement of comprehensive income for the year ended 31 December 20x4.**
   Other comprehensive income:

Revaluation gain (CU140 000 – 50 000)	CU90 000
Less deferred tax expense (90 000 × 28% x 66.6%)	(16 783)
Other comprehensive income after tax	CU73 217

4. **Prepare the *pro-forma* journal entry or entries to consolidate S Ltd in the financial year ending 31 December 20x5, relating only to the sale of the land by S Ltd (including tax implications and amounts attributable to non-controlling interest, if any).**

   No *pro-forma* journal entry is required owing to the fact that the land was revalued by the subsidiary between the acquisition date and the date of the sale. The result is that the carrying amount of the land is equal prior to the sale in both the separate and consolidated accounts, and no group adjustment is therefore required because both the subsidiary and the group will recognise the same profit.
   The profit relating to the sale of the land in the subsidiary is recognised in profit or loss. No further adjustments are required, as the land has now been sold.

Part B

Notes to the group financial statements for the year ended 31 December 20x5

Property, plant and equipment (relating to the machine in S Ltd only)	31 December 20x5 CU
Cost (120 000 – 60 000 + 50 000)	110 000
Accumulated depreciation:	
Balance at beginning of the year	55 000
Depreciation (110 000/4)	27 500
Balance at the end of the year	82 500
Carrying amount at beginning of the year	CU55 000
Carrying amount at end of the year	**CU27 500**

Case study exercises

A similar example, which illustrates the effects of a partially held subsidiary, is included on the accompanying CD. Refer to the CD after you have worked through Chapter 7, *Consolidation: Partly owned subsidiaries and other consolidation considerations.*

Scenario 1

P Ltd acquired all of the issued ordinary share capital of S Ltd on 1 January 20x3, when the financial statements of S Ltd included the following balances:

Share capital	CU170 000
Retained earnings	200 000
Shareholders' equity	CU370 000

At the date of acquisition, P Ltd considered the assets and liabilities of S Ltd to be fairly valued, except for the following items:

Market value of land (carrying amount of CU250 000)	CU310 000
Fair value of inventory (carrying amount of CU180 000)	CU200 000

(The inventory was sold within the 20x3 financial year.)

S Ltd did not change any of the balances recognised in its statement of financial position as a result of the fair values identified by P Ltd at the acquisition date. Ignore taxation.

Statements of financial position of P Ltd and S Ltd on 31 December 20x5

	P Ltd CU'000	S Ltd CU'000
ASSETS		
Land at cost		250
Plant and machinery (carrying amount)	300	120
Investment in S Ltd	480	
Inventory	400	350
Other current assets	210	460
	1 390	1 180
CAPITAL AND LIABILITIES		
Share capital	290	170
Retained earnings	900	900
Shareholders' equity	1 190	1 070
Current liabilities	200	110
	1 390	1 180

The cost price of the plant and machinery of S Ltd amounted to CU200 000 and accumulated depreciation at the acquisition date was CU60 000.

Statements of profit or loss and other comprehensive income of P Ltd and S Ltd for the year ended 31 December 20x5

	P Ltd CU'000	S Ltd CU'000
Revenue	2 320	1 700
Net operating costs	(1 440)	(1 000)
Interest expense	(100)	(50)
Profit before taxation	780	650
Taxation	(300)	(250)
Profit for the year	**480**	**400**

Extract from statements of changes in shareholders' equity of P Ltd and S Ltd for the year ended 31 December 20x5

	P Ltd CU'000	S Ltd CU'000
Retained earnings 1 January 20x5	620	500
Profit for the year	480	400
Dividends declared	(200)	–
Retained earnings 31 December 20x5	**900**	**900**

You are required to do the following:

1. Answer the following questions before starting with the preparation of the consolidated financial statements:
   - What is the fair value of the net identifiable assets of S Ltd at the acquisition date?
   - What is the goodwill acquired, if any?
   - What is the reporting date?
   - What is the starting point from a group's perspective?
2. Show the *pro-forma* journal entries required to prepare the consolidated financial statements of P Ltd Group for the year ended 31 December 20x5.
3. Prepare the following extracts from the consolidated financial statements of P Ltd for the year ended 31 December 20x5:
   - Profit after tax in the statement of profit or loss and other comprehensive income
   - Retained earnings column of the statement of changes in equity
   - Land and inventory in the statement of financial position.

Scenario 2

Use the information given in the first scenario and consider the taxation implications. Assume a current tax rate of 28% and that the land will be subject to capital gains tax at an inclusive rate of 66.6%, once sold.

1. Answer the following questions before starting with the preparation of the consolidated financial statements:
   - What is the fair value of the net identifiable assets at the acquisition date?
   - What is the goodwill acquired, if any?
2. Prepare the *pro-forma* journal entries required to prepare the consolidated financial statements of P Ltd Group for the year ended 31 December 20x5.
3. Prepare the following extracts from the consolidated financial statements of P Ltd for the year ended 31 December 20x5:
   - Profit after tax in the statement of profit or loss and other comprehensive income
   - Retained earnings column of the statement of changes in equity
   - Land and inventory in the statement of financial position.

Scenario 3

Use the information given in the first scenario above and consider the taxation implications. Assume a current tax rate of 28% and that the land is not subject to tax. S Ltd sold the land at 31 December 20x5 for CU400 000.

1. Answer the following questions before starting with the preparation of the consolidated financial statements:
   - What is the fair value of the net identifiable assets at the acquisition date?
   - What is the goodwill acquired, if any?
2. Show the *pro-forma* journal entries required to prepare the consolidated financial statements of P Ltd Group for the year ended 31 December 20x5.
3. Prepare the following extracts from the consolidated financial statements of P Ltd for the year ended 31 December 20x5:
   - Profit after tax in the statement of profit or loss and other comprehensive income
   - Retained earnings column of the statement of changes in equity
   - Land and inventory in the statement of financial position.

Suggested solution

Scenario 1

1. **Answer the following questions before starting with the preparation of the consolidated financial statements:**
   - **What is the fair value of the net identifiable assets of S Ltd at the acquisition date?**

	CU
Share capital	170 000
Retained earnings	200 000
Inventory (200 000 – 180 000)	20 000
Land (310 000 – 250 000)	60 000
Fair value of net identifiable assets at the acquisition date	**450 000**

   - **What is the goodwill acquired, if any?**
     Goodwill is the residual between the net consideration paid and the fair value of the net identifiable assets acquired. This is calculated as follows:

Consideration paid:	CU480 000 (investment in S Ltd)
Fair value of net identifiable assets	CU450 000
∴ Goodwill acquired:	CU480 000 – CU450 000 = **CU30 000**

   - **What is the reporting date?**
     The current reporting date is 31 December 20x5
   - **What is the starting point from a group's perspective?**
     The starting point is the financial statements of P Ltd and S Ltd, as presented in the question. It is important to note that the financial statements of the subsidiary do not recognise the net assets acquired at their fair values at the acquisition date, as they are recognised at historical cost.
     From a group's perspective, these assets are recognised at fair value. The fair value adjustments must be made at group level by using *pro-forma* journal entries.

2. **Show the *pro-forma* journal entries required to prepare the consolidated financial statements of P Ltd Group for the year ended 31 December 20x5.**

Pro-forma journal entries

			CU	CU
Dr		Share capital	170 000	
Dr		Retained earnings	200 000	
Dr		Inventory	20 000	
Dr		Land	60 000	
Dr		Goodwill	30 000	
	Cr	Investment in S Ltd		480 000

Elimination of equity and investment in S Ltd at acquisition, and investment in S Ltd

			CU	CU
Dr		Accumulated depreciation	60 000	
	Cr	Plant and machinery		60 000

Elimination of accumulated depreciation existing at acquisition

			CU	CU
Dr		Retained earnings (inventory sold)	20 000	
	Cr	Inventory		20 000

Reversal of fair value adjustment relating to inventory when sold

3. **Prepare the following extracts from the consolidated financial statements of P Ltd for the year ended 31 December 20x5:**
   - **Profit after tax in the statement of comprehensive income**
   - **Retained earnings column of the statement of changes in equity**
   - **Land and inventory in the statement of financial position.**

Extract from consolidated statement of profit or loss and other comprehensive income for year ended 31 December 20x5

		CU'000
Profit after tax	(480 + 400)	880

Extract from statement of changes in shareholders' equity for the year ended 31 December 20x5

	Retained earnings CU'000
Opening balance	(w1) 900
Profit for the year	880
– Dividends	(200)
Closing balance	(w2) 1 580

(w1): P: 620 000 + S: 280 000
(w2): P: 900 000 + S: 680 000

Extract from consolidated statement of financial position at 31 December 20x5

		CU'000
ASSETS		
Non-current assets:		
Land	(0 + 250 + 60)	310
Current assets:		
Inventory	(400 + 350 + 0)	750

Additional workings

Analysis of equity of S Ltd

			P Ltd (100%)	
	Total CU'000	At acquisition CU'000	Since acquisition CU'000	
At acquisition:				
Share capital	170			
Retained earnings	200			
Inventory (200 – 180)	20			
Land (310 – 250)	60			
	450	450		
Investment		480		
∴ Goodwill		30		
Since acquisition:	280		280	
Retained earnings	300			
Inventory (sold)	(20)			
Current year:				
Profit after tax	400		400	
	1 130		**680**	

Scenario 2

Use the information given in the first scenario and consider the taxation implications. Assume a current tax rate of 28% and that the land will be subject to capital gains tax at an inclusive rate of 66.6%, once sold.

1. Answer the following questions before starting with the preparation of the consolidated financial statements:
   - What is the fair value of the net identifiable assets at the acquisition date?

	CU
Share capital	170 000
Retained earnings	200 000
Inventory (200 000 – 180 000)	20 000
Less: Deferred tax (28% × 20 000)	(5 600)
Land (310 000 – 250 000)	60 000
Less: Deferred tax (28% × 66.6% × 60 000)	(11 200)
Fair value of net identifiable assets at the acquisition date	**433 200**

- ## What is the goodwill acquired, if any?
  Goodwill is the residual between the net consideration paid, and the fair value of the net identifiable assets acquired. This is calculated as follows:

Consideration paid:	CU480 000 (investment in S Ltd)
∴ Goodwill acquired:	CU480 000 – CU433 200 = **CU46 800**

2. **Show the *pro-forma* journal entries required to prepare the consolidated financial statements of P Ltd Group for the year ended 31 December 20x5.**

Pro-forma journal entries

			CU	CU
Dr		Share capital	170 000	
Dr		Retained earnings	200 000	
Dr		Inventory	20 000	
Dr		Land	60 000	
Dr		Goodwill	46 800	
	Cr	Deferred tax liability (5 600 + 11 200)		16 800
	Cr	Investment in S Ltd		480 000

Elimination of equity at acquisition, investment in S Ltd and raising non-controlling interest at acquisition

			CU	CU
Dr		Accumulated depreciation	60 000	
	Cr	Plant and machinery		60 000

Elimination of accumulated depreciation existing at acquisition

			CU	CU
Dr		Retained earnings (inventory sold)	14 400	
Dr		Deferred tax liability (20 000 × 28%)	5 600	
	Cr	Inventory		20 000

Reversal of fair value adjustment relating to inventory when sold

3. **Prepare the following extracts from the consolidated financial statements of P Ltd for the year ended 31 December 20x5:**
   - **Profit after tax in the statement of profit or loss and other comprehensive income**
   - **Retained earnings column of the statement of changes in equity**
   - **Land and inventory in the statement of financial position.**

Extract from consolidated statement of profit or loss and other comprehensive income for year ended 31 December 20x5

		CU'000
Profit after tax	(480 + 400)	880

Extract from statement of changes in shareholders' equity for the year ended 31 December 20x5

	Retained earnings CU
Opening balance	(w1) 905 600
Profit for the year	880 000
– Dividends	(200 000)
Closing balance	(w2) 1 585 600

(w1): P Ltd: 620 000 + S Ltd: 285 600
(w2): P Ltd: 900 000 + S Ltd: 685 600

Extract from consolidated statement of financial position at 31 December 20x5

		CU'000
ASSETS		
Non-current assets:		
Land	(0 + 250 + 60)	310
Current assets:		
Inventory	(400 + 350 + 0)	750

Additional workings

Analysis of equity of S Ltd

	Total CU'000	P Ltd (100%)	
		At acquisition CU'000	Since acquisition CU'000
At acquisition:			
Share capital	170		
Retained earnings	200		
Inventory (200 000 – 180 000)	20		
Deferred tax	(5.6)		
Land (310 000 – 250 000)	60		
Deferred tax	(11.2)		
	433.2	433.2	
Investment		480	
Goodwill		46.8	
Since acquisition:	285.6		285.6
Retained earnings	300		
Inventory (sold)	(20)		
Add back: Deferred tax	5.6		
Profit after tax	400		400
	1 130		**685.6**

Scenario 3

Use the information given in the first scenario above and consider the taxation implications. Assume a current tax rate of 28% and that the land is not subject to tax. S Ltd sold the land at 31 December 20x5 for CU400 000.

1. **Answer the following questions before starting with the preparation of the consolidated financial statements:**
   - **What is the fair value of the net identifiable assets at the acquisition date?**

	CU
Share capital	170 000
Retained earnings	200 000
Inventory (200 000 – 180 000)	20 000
Less: Deferred tax (28% × 20 000)	(5 600)
Land (310 000 – 250 000)	60 000
Fair value of net identifiable assets at the acquisition date	444 400

- **What is the goodwill acquired, if any?**

  Goodwill is the residual between the net consideration paid and the fair value of the net identifiable assets acquired. This is calculated as follows:

Consideration paid:	CU480 000 (investment in S Ltd)
∴ Goodwill acquired:	CU480 000 − CU444 400 = CU35 600

2. **Show the *pro-forma* journal entries required to prepare the consolidated financial statements of P Ltd Group for the year ended 31 December 20x5.**

   Pro-forma journal entries

			CU	CU
Dr		Share capital	170 000	
Dr		Retained earnings	200 000	
Dr		Inventory	20 000	
Dr		Land	60 000	
Dr		Goodwill	35 600	
	Cr	Deferred tax liability		5 600
	Cr	Investment in S Ltd		480 000

   Elimination of equity at acquisition, investment in S Ltd and raising non-controlling interest at acquisition

			CU	CU
Dr		Accumulated depreciation	60 000	
	Cr	Plant and machinery		60 000

   Elimination of accumulated depreciation existing at acquisition

			CU	CU
Dr		Retained earnings (inventory sold)	14 400	
Dr		Deferred tax liability (20 000 × 28%)	5 600	
	Cr	Inventory		20 000

   Reversal of fair value adjustment relating to inventory when sold

			CU	CU
Dr		Profit on disposal of land	60 000	
	Cr	Land		60 000

   Reversal of excess profit in group when land was sold

3. **Prepare the following extracts from the consolidated financial statements of P Ltd for the year ended 31 December 20x5:**
   - **Profit after tax in the statement of profit or loss and other comprehensive income**
   - **Retained earnings column of the statement of changes in equity**
   - **Land and inventory in the statement of financial position.**

   Extract from consolidated statement of profit or loss and other comprehensive income for the year ended 31 December 20x5

		CU'000
Profit after tax	(480 + 400 − 60)	820

Extract from statement of changes in shareholders' equity for the year ended 31 December 20x5

	Retained earnings CU
Opening balance	(w1) 905 600
Profit for the year	820 000
– Dividends	(200 000)
Closing balance	(w2) 1 525 600

(w1): P Ltd: 620 000 + S Ltd: 285 600
(w2): P Ltd: 900 000 + S Ltd: 625 600

Extract from consolidated statement of financial position at 31 December 20x5

		CU'000
ASSETS		
Non-current assets:		
Land	(60 – 60)	–
Current assets:		
Inventory	(400 + 350 + 0)	750

Additional workings

Analysis of equity of S Ltd

		P Ltd (80%)	
	Total CU'000	At acquisition CU'000	Since acquisition CU'000
At acquisition:			
Share capital	170		
Retained earnings	200		
Inventory (200 – 180)	20		
Deferred tax	(5.6)		
Land (310 – 250)	60		
	444.4	444.4	
Investment		480	
Goodwill		35.6	
Since acquisition:	285.6		285.6
Retained earnings	300		
Inventory (sold)	(20)		
Add back: Deferred tax	5.6		
Current year:	340		340
Profit after tax	400		400
Land (sold)	(60)		(60)
	1 070		625.6

Think about it

Why is the profit on the sale of the land in the group less than the profit in S Ltd?

	S Ltd starting point CU	*Pro-forma* adjustments CU	Group end point CU
Cost	250 000	At acquisition: 60 000	310 000
Proceeds	400 000		400 000
Profit	150 000	When sold: (60 000)	90 000

The cost of the land in S Ltd was CU250 000 and the profit in S Ltd when the land was sold amounts to CU150 000.

The cost of the land in the group was CU310 000 (when it was first acquired), thus the profit in the group is CU90 000.

At group level, the profit when the land is sold is reduced by the fair value adjustment of CU60 000 (CU150 000 – CU90 000) at the acquisition date.

6

Consolidation: Intra-group transactions

The following topics are included in this chapter:

- The entity concept and the requirement to eliminate the effects of intra-group transactions on consolidation
- The effect on consolidation of the following intra-group transactions between the parent and its wholly owned subsidiary:
  - Intra-group services
  - Intra-group borrowings
  - Intra-group dividends
  - Intra-group inventory transactions
  - Transfers of non-current assets intra-group
  - Any deferred tax implications resulting from intra-group transactions.

Learning objectives

By the end of this chapter, you should be able to:
- Explain, in terms of the accounting equation, the principle concerning the elimination of intra-group transactions when preparing group financial statements
- Understand why it is necessary to eliminate intercompany loans and interest charges when group financial statements are prepared, and how this is affected
- Understand how a dividend that it declared by the subsidiary is recognised in the group financial statements
- Understand that inventory that is transferred within the group is recognised at its cost when it was first acquired by the group
- Know how to eliminate unrealised profits included in the carrying amount of inventory when group financial statements are prepared
- Understand that the cost to a group of a non-current asset (for example, a machine) that was sold between two entities within the group is the cost when that asset was first acquired by the group
- Know how to eliminate unrealised profits resulting from intra-group sales of non-current assets, including any subsequent adjustments to depreciation, when group financial statements are prepared
- Understand how to determine the subsequent depreciation expense relating to an asset that was sold by the parent to its subsidiary at a profit, including any deferred tax implications
- Identify and eliminate the deferred tax implications of intra-group transfers.

1. Introduction

Whenever related entities trade with each other or lend money to each other, the separate legal entities disclose the effects of these transactions in the assets and liabilities recorded as well as the profits and losses reported. When consolidated financial statements are being prepared, the separate financial statements of the parent and its subsidiaries are initially added together without any adjustments for the effects of the intra-group transactions. This results in consolidated financial statements including not only the results of the group transacting with external parties, but also the results of transactions within the group. This is incorrect and conflicts with the purpose of the consolidated financial statements, which is to provide information about the financial performance and financial position of the group as a result of its dealings with external entities.

The effects of transactions amongst entities within the group must be adjusted for in the preparation of consolidated financial statements so that consolidated financial statements only include transactions with third parties. This implies that consolidation adjustments are required to eliminate intra-group transactions as well as any tax consequences that arise as a result of those adjustments or eliminations.

 IFRS principles

Intra-group transactions

Intra-group transactions between the parent and subsidiary (or between two or more subsidiaries) should be eliminated in full. Refer to IFRS10, paragraph B86(c), which requires the elimination, in full, of 'intra-group assets and liabilities, equity, income, expense and cash flows relating to transactions between entities of the group'.

IAS12, *Income taxes*, applies to temporary differences that arise from the elimination of profits and losses resulting from intra-group transactions.

The principle underlying the preparation of group financial statements is that the financial statements represent the results of the group as **one economic entity**. An entity cannot make profits by entering into transactions with itself. However, the parent's financial statements, which are included in the starting point, include all transactions entered into by the parent. These may include transactions entered into with a subsidiary because the parent is a separate legal entity. The subsidiary also prepares financial statements reflecting all of its transactions, including those entered into with its parent. From this, it should be evident that the starting point for preparing the group financial statements may not reflect the financial position and performance of the group as a single economic entity. Consolidation adjustments are therefore required for the transactions between the parent and subsidiaries in order to correct the starting point to what should appear in the group financial statements.

In terms of the accrual basis, income and expenses can be recognised only when earned or incurred. Group financial statements should reflect the effect of transactions between the group as a whole and third parties. For example, where the parent has charged the subsidiary interest on an internal loan, the parent should include the interest received in revenue, while the subsidiary should recognise the interest expense as finance costs. These two balances should be netted off on consolidation, otherwise the revenue and finance costs recognised would be overstated in the consolidated statement of profit or loss and other comprehensive income as a result of the internal charge. Interest revenue should only include amounts earned from outside the group and interest expense should only include amounts charged from outside the group. Similarly, the loan asset and loan liability should be eliminated as no amounts are receivable from or payable to third parties.

Other examples of similar internal charges between a parent and subsidiary are management fees, rental charges and royalties. Even though the net effect of these charges on the consolidated group profit or loss is zero because there are equal amounts included as an income and expense in the starting point, these charges should be netted off on consolidation to ensure that the line items disclosed on the face of the consolidated statement of profit or loss and other comprehensive income (for example, interest revenue) and the details included in the notes to the consolidated financial statements do not include transactions between entities within the same group.

 IFRS principles

Elimination of intra-group transactions

Intra-group balances, transactions, income and expenses shall be eliminated in full (IFRS10)

- Even though each legal entity (parent and its subsidiary) would have recognised the effects of the intra-group transactions in their own financial statements (as the items relate to parties that are external to the individual entity itself), the group is one economic entity, comprising 100% of the parent (P Ltd) and 100% of the subsidiary (S Ltd).
- These transactions have therefore arisen with other entities within the group and not with external parties.
- The effects must therefore be eliminated.

Elimination of unrealised profits or losses

- Where transactions between entities within the same group result in one entity recognising a profit, these profits do not arise from transactions with parties outside the group and must therefore be eliminated, as the profit is only realised when an item is sold outside of the group.
- However, these unrealised profits will be realised subsequently, either when the asset is used (depreciated) or when it is sold.
- Therefore, the unrealised profit will be realised subsequently through depreciating an asset (if depreciable) and/or selling the asset outside the group.

IAS12 applies to temporary differences that arise from the elimination of profits and losses resulting from intra-group transactions

- By eliminating unrealised intra-group profits, an adjustment is made to the carrying amount of an asset for accounting purposes at a group level without a corresponding adjustment to its tax base because the tax base remains the same as it was for the individual entity.
- This therefore gives rise to a temporary difference on which deferred tax must be recognised (as the resultant temporary difference is not exempt in terms of IAS12: 15; there has been an adjustment to accounting profit and the temporary difference does not arise from the initial recognition of the asset at a group level).

IFRS principles (continued)

Note that if one group entity sells to another at a loss, this may be an indication that the asset is impaired. Consequently, there may be no unrealised loss that needs to be eliminated. From a group's perspective, there may be a reclassification of the expense from, for example, loss on disposal of asset to impairment loss. The overall effect is that if the asset is impaired, the impairment loss must be recognised at a group level.

2. Intra-group services

It often makes sense for entities within a group to provide services to the other entities in the group in order to take advantage of synergies. For example, when the management and human resources competencies and activities are situated within one entity in the group, and that entity provides management and payroll services to other entities in the group. The entity that is providing the service, in turn, invoices its 'clients' (in other words, other group entities) for the management services provided. From a group perspective, the services provided are within the group and therefore an internal charge should be eliminated on consolidation as this does not represent income from a third party.

The elimination of such intra-group management fee charges and income has no effect on the group profit or loss. However, it does have disclosure implications. As the elimination has no effect on the total group profit or loss because an equal income and expense are either included or excluded, the elimination also has no effect on non-controlling interest, where applicable. This makes sense as we are not changing the profits or the net assets of the subsidiary or the parent. We are merely eliminating an intra-group transaction when combining the profits of the two entities in the group in order to report only the profit or loss that is achieved with outside parties.

Example
Elimination of intra-group management fees

P Ltd has a 100% controlling interest in S Ltd. As of 1 January 20x5, S Ltd pays P Ltd a monthly management fee of CU100. Each fee has been paid on time (at the end of each month). P Ltd recorded a profit of CU100 000 for the year ended 31 December 20x5, while S Ltd recorded a profit of CU50 000 for the same period.

What has each entity recorded in its separate financial statements regarding this transaction?

Journal entry in S Ltd

			CU	CU
Dr		Management fee expense	1 200	
	Cr	Bank		1 200

Recording the charge and payment of management fee expense to the parent company

Journal entry in P Ltd (the entity)

			CU	CU
Dr		Bank	1 200	
	Cr	Management fee income		1 200

Recording the charge and receipt of management fee income from the subsidiary

What are the implications for the group financial statements?

	Dr/(Cr)	S Ltd (starting point) CU	P Ltd (starting point) CU	Pro-forma journals CU	Group (end point) CU
Management fee expense		(1 200)		1 200	–
Management fee income			1 200	(1 200)	–

The following *pro-forma* journal eliminates the intra-group management fee:

			CU	CU
Dr		Management fee income	1 200	
	Cr	Management fee expense		1 200

Elimination of intra-group transaction

The scenario indicates that all amounts have been paid on time. This indicates that there are no intra-group balances (that is, management fee payable and management fee receivable) outstanding at the end of the year. If there had been, these would also have been eliminated via *pro-forma* journal entries.

 ## Think about it

Intra-group charges

What is the overall effect on group profit?

The consolidated profit or loss for the year amounts to CU150 000 (P Ltd: CU100 000 + S Ltd: CU50 000). The elimination of the management fees has no effect on the overall profit, either at the starting point (that is, when the income and expenses of the parent and its subsidiary are added together) or at the end point (that is, the group). The total profit of CU150 000 is both increased and decreased by CU1 200 as a result of the consolidation adjustment, leaving the profit at an amount of CU150 000 overall.

Then why do we have this *pro-forma* journal entry?

The elimination is for **disclosure purposes**. In the line items included in the consolidated statement of profit or loss and other comprehensive income, these amounts should be eliminated in order to avoid overstating the income and expenses of the group.

Why is there no deferred tax adjustment?

This is because the overall effect on group profit is nil.

How would this transaction be reported in the following reporting period?

When you prepare the consolidated financial statements for the 20x6 reporting period, the management fee income and expense are both included in retained earnings in the starting point. It is therefore not necessary to do a *pro-forma* journal entry to record the elimination of the intra-group transaction because both sides of the entry are within retained earnings and it would have no effect. However, when you prepare the comparative figures for the consolidated financial statements, the management fee income and expense should be adjusted to reflect the elimination done in the 20x5 reporting period.

3. Intra-group borrowings

Financial support between group entities is common, specifically where one entity (usually the parent) has excess cash and it makes business sense to use the group's cash resources to fund new initiatives that are situated within a subsidiary. These borrowings can either be at arm's length, for example, a market-related interest rate is charged on such loans, or alternatively, if it is a new venture, the loan may be interest free.

Viewed from a group's perspective, this is a loan within the same economic entity as the group is using its excess cash for 'internal' funding within the group. The individual entities within the group recognise the loan in their individual financial statements, either as an asset or as a liability. From a group perspective, the loan asset and liability should be eliminated. Similarly, the interest income and expense (given that interest is charged) should be eliminated on consolidation, even though the net effect on group profit is zero. This is important as both interest income (which is usually included in revenue) and the interest expense (finance cost) will be overstated in the consolidated profit or loss if this adjustment is not made.

 Example

Consolidation process to eliminate intra-group balances and transactions

Assume that P Ltd, having a 100% controlling interest in S Ltd, has granted a short-term loan to S Ltd of CU500 000. Interest of CU25 000 relating to this loan was incurred during the current period, ended 31 December 20x5. At the reporting date, the interest was added to the balance of the loan. P Ltd recorded a profit for the year ended 31 December 20x5 of CU100 000, while S Ltd recorded a profit of CU50 000 for the same period.

The following balances will be included in the financial statements of the separate legal entities:

	Dr/(Cr)	P Ltd (starting point) CU	S Ltd (starting point) CU	Pro-forma journals CU	Group (end point) CU
Current asset: Loan to S Ltd		525 000		(525 000)	–
Current liability: Loan from P Ltd			(525 000)	525 000	–
Profit or loss:					
Interest income		(25 000)		25 000	–
Interest expense			25 000	(25 000)	–

Both the loan to S Ltd (in P Ltd) and the loan from P Ltd (in S Ltd) need to be eliminated in the group financial statements. Similarly, the interest income and interest expense should also be eliminated.

If these balances are not eliminated, the group will overstate its current assets and current liabilities as well as interest income (included in revenue) and interest expense.

The consolidated group profit remains unchanged at CU150 000 (P Ltd: CU100 000 + S Ltd: CU50 000) as a result of the change and the total net assets of the group, which is equal to equity, is also unchanged. Since an asset and a liability of an equal value have been eliminated, the net asset value remains the same.

4. Intra-group dividends

When a subsidiary distributes profits earned after acquisition (in other words, declares a dividend), the portion of the distribution relating to the parent's shareholding is recognised by the parent as dividends received. The parent includes any dividend income received from the subsidiary in revenue, together with any other dividends received. The subsidiary recognises dividends declared as an appropriation of the profits within retained earnings in the statement of changes in equity. The portion of the dividend declared by the subsidiary and received by the parent represents an intra-group transaction, which should thus be eliminated as with all intra-group transactions.

The dividend declared by the subsidiary to the parent must be eliminated in the consolidated financial statements as an intra-group transaction so that the only dividends that are reflected as being declared are those payable to the shareholders outside the group. In other words, the only dividends disclosed are those paid to the shareholders of the parent and the non-controlling shareholders of the subsidiary, where applicable.

The *pro-forma* journal entry that follows is required to eliminate the intra-group dividends.

Dr		Dividend income (parent's share; in this chapter, 100%)
	Cr	Dividends (100%)

The consolidated statement of profit or loss and other comprehensive income should not include dividends received by the parent from the subsidiary entity. It should only include dividends received from outside the group. The statement of changes in equity should only include dividends declared by the parent as an adjustment to group retained earnings. This makes sense as the group retained earnings represents the accumulated profits of the group attributable to the shareholders of the group, who are in fact the shareholders of the parent. The dividend reflected as a distribution of those retained earnings should therefore only be the portion of the group profits paid to the group shareholders.

When the subsidiary declares a **dividend that has not yet been paid**, a liability (dividends payable) is recognised. The parent recognises dividend income once it is entitled to receive the dividend, at which stage an asset (dividends receivable) is recognised. The parent's dividends receivable should be eliminated with its portion of the dividends payable by the subsidiary.

Pro-forma journal entry

Dr		Dividends payable (parent's share)	
	Cr	Dividend receivable (parent's share)	

Example

Dividends declared by a subsidiary

This example illustrates the elimination of intra-group dividends.

P Ltd acquired a controlling interest of 100% in S Ltd on 1 January 20x4, when the fair value of the identifiable net assets of S Ltd amounted to CU235 000. At 31 December 20x4, the entities reported the profits and dividends shown below in their individual financial statements.

Statements of changes in equity for P Ltd and S Ltd for the year ended 31 December 20x4

	P Ltd			S Ltd		
	Share capital CU	Retained earnings CU	Total CU	Share capital CU	Retained earnings CU	Total CU
Balance at 1 January 20x4	240 000	90 000	330 000	120 000	115 000	235 000
Profit after tax		210 000	210 000		35 000	35 000
Less dividends		(150 000)	(150 000)		(10 000)	(10 000)
Balance at 31 December 20x4	240 000	150 000	390 000	120 000	140 000	260 000

P Ltd received 100% of the dividend declared by S Ltd, which is included in the profit after tax of P Ltd in the current reporting period. The effect of the elimination of the intra-group dividend results in a decrease in the profits of the parent.

The following *pro-forma* journal entry eliminates the intra-group dividend declared by S Ltd:

			CU	CU
Dr		Dividend income	10 000	
	Cr	Dividends (equity)		10 000

Elimination of dividend declared by S Ltd

In the consolidation worksheet, the effect of this *pro-forma* journal entry will be as follows:

	Dr/(Cr)	P Ltd (starting point) CU	S Ltd (starting point) CU	*Pro-forma* journals CU	Group (end point) CU
Dividend income		(10 000)		10 0000	–
Dividend declared and paid			10 000	(10 000)	–

Consolidated statement of changes in equity for the year ended 31 December 20x4

	Share capital CU	Retained earnings CU	Total equity CU
Balance at 1 January 20x4	240 000	90 000	330 000
Profit after tax		① 235 000	235 000
Less dividends		(150 000)	(150 000)
Balance at 31 December 20x4	**240 000**	**175 000**	**415 000**

① [P: CU210 000 – 10 000 (dividend income)] + [S: CU35 000] = CU235 000

What is this?
The total dividends declared by the group include all dividends declared to equity holders outside the group, which in this case is only the parent's shareholders.

Think about it

Dividends paid by the subsidiary

The subsidiary was acquired on 1 January 20x4; thus the parent only shares in the profits of the subsidiary subsequent to the acquisition date. Group profit after tax of CU235 000 was determined as 100% of P Ltd less the dividend income received from S Ltd plus 100% of the current year profit of S Ltd.

Notice that the group profit or loss for the year is reduced as a result of the elimination of the intra-group dividend, unlike the other intra-group transactions, which had no effect on the group profit. This is because the one side of the adjustment reduces dividend income within profit or loss, but the other side is directly in retained earnings. However, the closing balance of retained earnings is unaffected by the elimination because the total group net assets are unchanged when dividends are paid from one group entity to another. The assets (usually cash) have simply changed location.

Note that the dividend declared by the parent is not affected by the elimination of the subsidiary's dividends as this represents a distribution to the parent's shareholders. However, note also that the dividend deducted from retained earnings is CU150 000, which is **only** that relating to the dividends of the parent. The dividend declared by S Ltd was eliminated against the profit of the parent.

Refer to Chapter 7 for a discussion of the effects of dividends declared by a partly held subsidiary, attributable to non-controlling interest. Refer to Chapter 8 for a discussion of preference dividends declared and paid by the subsidiary.

5. Transfers of inventory

Parent–subsidiary relationships are often used to benefit the group as a whole. One of the methods used is that inventory is sold between group entities at favourable prices. Because the group is the reporting entity, the inventory should be recognised at the cost when it was first acquired by the group when consolidated financial statements are prepared. In this section, we will discuss the reversal of any unrealised profits that result from intra-group transfers of inventory and the deferred tax implications.

5.1 Intra-group inventory transactions

Where inventory is transferred between entities at a price different from the cost price, that price is referred to either as the 'transfer price' (which represents an agreed price between the parent and subsidiary) or as the 'selling price' (also referred to as the 'retail price'). This is similar to a head office transferring inventory to a branch. The head office can add a mark-up to the cost price of the inventory, thereby transferring it to the branch at a transfer price that differs from cost. It is important that, on consolidation, you reverse the effect of any such inventory transfers between the parent and subsidiary (or between subsidiaries) so that the consolidated financial statements recognise inventory on hand at the cost price to the group and only include transactions with parties outside the group. The group profit or loss should only recognise sales and the cost of sales as well as the related gross profit on the transactions when the goods are actually sold to a party outside the group.

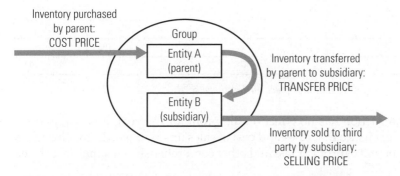

Figure 6.1 Illustration of possible transfer of inventory between group entities (note that inventory can be sold from the parent to a subsidiary, by a subsidiary to the parent or between subsidiaries)

Intra-group inventory transactions may result in various situations, including the following:

- Inventory was sold by the parent to a subsidiary and part of that inventory is still on hand at the reporting date. The effect of this transaction is that the **inventory (asset) is overstated** in the financial statements of the subsidiary that acquired the inventory because it includes a profit or mark-up that was added by the parent. This profit is unrealised as the inventory has not been sold outside the group yet and it should be reversed. In addition, the **sales and cost of sales** of the group are **overstated** as they include a transaction between group entities. In the same way as with other intra-group transactions, the sales and cost of sales should be eliminated against each other.
- Inventory was sold by the parent to a subsidiary and the subsidiary has sold all of the inventory to third parties. The effect of this transaction is that the profit is realised and should be recognised, and there is no overstatement of an asset (inventory) because the inventory has been sold. However, this transaction results in an **overstatement of sales and cost of sales** in the group as the intra-group sale results in the double counting of the sale of the same inventory in the group financial statements.

Where inventory was transferred between two group entities, but has subsequently been sold to a third party by the reporting date, no reversal of the internal mark-up is required as the group earned the internal profit at the time when the inventory was sold to a party outside the group. This applies to inventory transferred in the prior and current reporting periods. The total sales of inventory between the parent and subsidiary during the current financial year should be reversed (between sales and cost of goods sold) in order to avoid the overstatement of the income and expenses of the group. Where intra-group sales of inventory occurred in prior periods, the sales and costs of sales are included within retained earnings. It is not necessary to eliminate them because both the debit and credit would be to retained earnings and the *pro-forma* journal entry would have no effect. However, the comparative figures in the statement of profit or loss and other comprehensive income should be adjusted to reflect the elimination that should have occurred in the prior period.

When there are numerous transactions relating to inventory, you should first reverse the sales and cost of sales for all of the intra-group transactions that have taken place during the year, and then adjust for the unrealised profit included in the closing inventory on hand at the reporting date, as follows.

Pro-forma journal entry (1)

			CU	CU
Dr		Sales	100	
	Cr	Cost of sales		100

Reversing all of the intra-group sales that took place during the year

Even though this transaction has no effect on the profit for the year, it is required for disclosure purposes to ensure that sales and cost of sales (in other words, the line items on the face of the statement of profit or loss and other comprehensive income) are correct.

Pro-forma journal entry (2)

			CU	CU
Dr		Cost of sales	20	
	Cr	Inventory		20

Adjusting the unrealised profit included in closing inventory

As a result of the various adjustments done, the group **cost of sales** is therefore calculated as:

- 100% of the cost of sales recognised correctly by the parent and the subsidiary
- Less: The cost of sales relating to all inter-entity transactions during the current year (there is no effect on profits as sales are debited by the same amount; see *pro-forma* journal entry (1) above)
- Less: The reduction in the cost of sales for opening inventory to reduce the inventory from its transfer price to the cost price of the group (refer to the detailed discussion below)
- Plus: Increases in cost of sales for unrealised profits included in closing inventory (see *pro-forma* journal entry (2) above).

The net effect of *pro-forma* journal entries 1 and 2 is a credit (a reduction) of the original cost of sales as recognised by the parent (or the entity that sold the inventory to another group entity).

Example
Recording and eliminating intra-group inventory transactions (inventory sold by parent to subsidiary)

Where a parent sells inventory to a subsidiary at a mark-up of 20%, a typical sale of inventory at the transfer price of CU120 000 would be recorded as shown below (assuming a perpetual inventory system).

In the parent's general ledger

			CU	CU
Dr		Current account (receivable from S Ltd)	120 000	
	Cr	Sales		120 000

			CU	CU
Dr		Cost of sales	100 000	
	Cr	Inventory		100 000

In the subsidiary's general ledger

			CU	CU
Dr		Inventory	120 000	
	Cr	Current account (payable to P Ltd)		120 000

The inventory on hand would be recognised in the statement of financial position of S Ltd at CU120 000, while the cost price of the inventory to the group amounted to CU100 000, which was the cost of the inventory when it was first acquired by the group, in other words, when it was acquired by P Ltd. The mark-up of 20% included in the carrying amount of the inventory should be reversed on consolidation against the profit of the entity that recognised the sale (in this example, it is the parent as the parent sold the inventory to the subsidiary).

Assuming that the subsidiary has **not sold any of these inventories** at the reporting date, the following *pro-forma* journal entries need to be recorded on consolidation:

			CU	CU
Dr		Sales	120 000	
	Cr	Cost of sales		120 000

Elimination of the total intra-group sales for the period

			CU	CU
Dr		Cost of sales	20 000	
	Cr	Inventory		20 000

Removing the unrealised profit from closing inventory, thereby reducing the group profit or loss

The effect of these journal entries can be combined as follows. (You should be careful that you only remove the unrealised profit from inventory that has not been sold at the reporting date.)

			CU	CU
Dr		Sales	① 120 000	
	Cr	Cost of sales		② 100 000
	Cr	Inventory		③ 20 000

① and ② These entries reverse the amounts recognised by the parent as the transaction is an internal transaction. The effect is to reverse the gross profit of CU20 000 recognised by the parent as the inventory has not been sold to a third party.

③ Crediting inventory by CU20 000 reduces the carrying amount of CU120 000 in the subsidiary to the cost of the inventory to the group of CU100 000.

Assuming that the outstanding amount was not settled before year end and was included in the current accounts, you would need to eliminate the current accounts between the parent and subsidiary with the following *pro-forma* journal entry:

			CU	CU
Dr		Current account: Payable to P Ltd	120 000	
	Cr	Current account: Receivable from S Ltd		120 000

The extracts on the financial statements of the separate legal entities that follow would be included in the starting point and adjusted to arrive at the group figures as shown.

	P Ltd (starting point) CU	S Ltd (starting point) CU	Pro-forma journals CU	Group (end point) CU
	Dr/(Cr)			
Current asset: Inventory		120 000	③ (20 000)	100 000
Current asset: Intra-group current account	120 000		(120 000)	–
Current liability: Intra-group current account		(120 000)	120 000	–
Profit or loss:				
Sales	(120 000)		① 120 000	–
Cost of sales	100 000		② (100 000)	–

This makes sense as the cost of the inventory to the group amounts to CU100 000, as indicated in the group column (end point) and there has been no further transaction relating to the inventory from a group perspective that should be included within profit or loss.

In reality, there will usually be unrealised profit in **opening and closing inventory** because transfers of inventory would have occurred in the previous reporting periods as well and therefore a *pro-forma* journal entry is required to adjust the opening inventory.

Assuming that the inventory on hand at the previous reporting date that had been sold by the parent to the subsidiary is subsequently sold to a third party in the current reporting period, an adjustment is required to recognise that the amounts included in the starting point do not reflect the reality of the situation correctly from a group perspective. The prior year's retained earnings in the parent is overstated (as it includes profits unrealised from a group perspective) and the current year cost of sales in the subsidiary is overstated (and the profit is therefore understated) as it is based on the cost of inventory to the subsidiary, which is higher than the cost to the group as a result of the unrealised profit.

The following *pro-forma* journal entry is required to make the necessary adjustment:

Dr		Retained earnings (unrealised profit in prior year closing inventory)
	Cr	Cost of sales

Note that the effect of this journal entry is that the prior year profits are reduced by debiting retained earnings and the current year profit or loss is increased by crediting cost of sales. A reduction in cost of sales (an expense) results in an increase in profits. Therefore the internal profit has been adjusted to be recognised in the correct reporting period when the inventory was actually sold to external parties.

It is important to remember the following:

- The unrealised profit (the mark-up on goods transferred between group entities and unsold at the reporting date) gives rise to an entry debiting **retained earnings** and crediting cost of sales when that inventory is included in the opening inventory.
- When the goods are bought by the group and sold by the group in the same financial year, the only entry required is a debit to **sales** and a credit to **cost of sales**; if the goods are not in closing inventory at the reporting date, they must have been sold during that year and the profit is therefore realised.
- When the goods are still owned by the group at the reporting date (in other words, they appear in the closing inventory), the sale and cost of sales recorded by the parent (or the group entity making the sale) should be reversed and the **inventory** on hand should be reduced by the unrealised profit because it should be recognised at the cost price to the group).

Where a subsidiary is wholly owned by the parent, the consolidation adjustments required will be identical, regardless of whether the inventory was transferred by the parent to the subsidiary or from the subsidiary to the parent. Refer to Chapter 7 for an example of where inventory is sold to the parent by a partly owned subsidiary and the resulting effect on non-controlling interest.

5.2 **Deferred tax implications**

IAS12 applies to temporary differences that arise from the elimination of profits and losses resulting from intra-group transactions. The group adjustments required for eliminating unrealised profits and then subsequently realising those profits therefore have deferred tax implications. These deferred tax implications are based on how the asset (sold intra-group) is expected to be recovered, that is, through use or sale. In the case of inventory transactions, the reversal of the intra-group profits that are not realised results in a temporary difference. The asset (inventory) is overstated, resulting in a deductible temporary difference that is recovered through usage (in other words, at the normal tax rate), thus resulting in a reduction of the tax obligation (deferred tax).

Example

Intra-group sale of inventory, including deferred tax implications (inventory sold by subsidiary to parent)

This example illustrates the following key points:

- S Ltd has sold the inventory to P Ltd at a profit (which is unrealised).
- The profit will be realised through sale, in other words, when P Ltd (in this case) has sold the inventory outside the group.
- The carrying amount of inventory that has not yet been sold by P Ltd (in this case) is therefore overstated as it includes the unrealised profit.
- The tax base of the inventory is the cost to the entity that legally owns the asset, in this case, the parent.
- From the group's perspective, the cost of the inventory is what it was when it was first acquired by the subsidiary (in this case).

> A similar example, which illustrates the effects of a partially held subsidiary, is included on the accompanying CD. Refer to the CD after you have worked through Chapter 7, *Consolidation: Partly owned subsidiaries and other consolidation considerations.*

S Ltd (wholly owned subsidiary) bought inventory for CU200 000 and sold it for CU300 000 to P Ltd (its parent) in 20x4.

At the end of 20x4

The following entries were recorded in the separate financial statements of each entity assuming that none of the inventory acquired from S Ltd had been sold by P Ltd at the end of 20x4:

	Dr/(Cr)	S Ltd (starting point) CU'000	P Ltd (starting point) CU'000	*Pro-forma* adjustments CU'000	Group (end point) CU'000
Sales		(300)		300	–
Opening inventory		–	–		–
Purchases		200	300	(300)	200
Less: Closing inventory		–	(300)	100	(200)
Total cost of sales		200	–		–
Asset:					
Inventory		–	300	(100)	200

The starting point trial balance reflects a sale of CU300 000, which was recognised by S Ltd, but it is intra-group. The group profit or loss section of the statement of profit or loss and other comprehensive income must, therefore, reflect sales of nil (relating to the sale of inventory from S Ltd to P Ltd). Sales must, therefore, be debited with CU300 000.

In terms of double entry, a credit of CU300 000 is required. This credit goes to cost of sales. The reason for this is that the starting point trial balance includes purchases of CU300 000 (relating to the inventory purchased by P Ltd from S Ltd). It is inappropriate to reflect the purchases from another group entity and a credit to cost of sales of CU300 000 is therefore required.

Inventory affects the statement of financial position because it is recognised as an asset if still on hand at the reporting date. Similarly, as the inventory is not yet sold, it is deducted from cost of sales (where cost of sales is determined as opening inventory, plus purchases, less closing inventory). Changes in inventory thus affect both the asset account and profit or loss. The inventory is included in the starting point, both in inventory and in cost of sales, at an amount of CU300 000, being the cost of the inventory to P Ltd. This carrying amount includes the unrealised profit of S Ltd, which should be removed in order for the inventory to be reflected at the cost to the group of CU200 000. It is therefore necessary to credit the inventory to reduce its carrying amount and the debit goes to cost of sales to reduce the closing inventory used in the calculation of the total cost of sales expense.

Inventory is an asset. Deferred taxation should therefore be recognised if there is a difference between the carrying amount and the tax base. The tax base of the inventory is the cost of the inventory to the entity that legally owns it, in this case, the parent. When the group recognises the carrying amount of the inventory as CU200 000, which is different from the tax base of CU300 000, a deductible temporary difference is created. Therefore in respect of the inventory sold by S Ltd to P Ltd, none of which had been sold by P Ltd at the end of 20x4, the deferred taxation calculation shown below applies.

Deferred taxation (asset) at the end of 2014

	P Ltd (the entity)				Group			
	Carrying amount CU'000	Tax base CU'000	Temporary difference CU'000	Deferred tax CU'000	Carrying amount CU'000	Tax base CU'000	Temporary difference CU'000	Deferred tax asset CU'000
Inventory	300	300	–	–	200	300	(100)	28 debit

> **Why is this a deferred tax asset (debit)?**
> From the group's perspective, the asset's tax base is larger than its carrying amount, thus resulting in a deductible temporary difference. When the inventory is sold, the parent will be allowed a deduction of CU300 000, resulting in less tax to be paid.

The following *pro-forma* journal entry is required to eliminate the sale and purchase of inventory in P Ltd (acquired from S Ltd) at the end of 20x4:

			CU	CU
Dr		Cost of sales	300 000	
	Cr	Sales		300 000

Elimination of intra-group sale of inventory

This eliminates the intra-group transaction. The overall effect on group profits because of this adjustment is nil. Therefore, there is no deferred taxation adjustment for this *pro-forma* journal entry. This is essentially a disclosure adjustment.

			CU	CU
Dr		Cost of sales (unrealised profit in closing inventory)	100 000	
	Cr	Inventory		100 000

Elimination of unrealised profit included in inventory on hand in the group at the reporting date

The following *pro-forma* journal entry adjusts for the deferred tax implications of the above entry:

			CU	CU
Dr		Deferred tax (asset)	28 000	
	Cr	Deferred tax (P/L)		28 000

Deferred tax adjustment resulting from the elimination of unrealised profit included in inventory on hand in the group at the reporting date

As the inventory was sold by the subsidiary to the parent, from the group's perspective, the profit after tax of the subsidiary attributable to the parent is overstated by CU72 000 (CU100 000 – CU28 000), which is the after-tax adjustment of the intra-group sale of the inventory.

 Think about it

Inventory is recognised at the cost when it was first acquired by the group

The inventory has not yet been sold outside the group. It must therefore be reflected as an asset in the group statement of financial position as at the end of 20x4. The cost of the inventory to the group is CU200 000, being the cost to S Ltd (the entity that brought the inventory into the group for the first time). The inventory's cost in the starting point is CU300 000 (being the cost to P Ltd).

The cost of the inventory is thus overstated (by the effects of the intra-group profit). The cost of the inventory must be reduced, in other words, credited. Inventory affects the profit or loss section of the statement of profit or loss and other comprehensive income through cost of sales. If closing inventory is reduced, this has the effect of increasing the cost of sales. Therefore, cost of sales must be debited. Increasing cost of sales reduces group profit (think about it: cost of sales is an expense). Debiting the profit or loss section of the statement of profit or loss and other comprehensive income makes sense.

As a result of eliminating the unrealised profit, group profits (before taxation) have reduced, therefore group taxation must reduce. Consequently a credit is required to deferred taxation in the profit or loss section of the statement of profit or loss and other comprehensive income. (If you think about it, tax is an expense. If we wanted to reduce it, we would need to credit the expense). In terms of a double entry, a debit is required to deferred taxation in the statement of financial position.

We are adjusting group profits for the effects of a transaction (that is, the sale of the inventory from S Ltd to P Ltd) that originated in the subsidiary.

At the end of 20x5

During the 20x5 financial year, S Ltd sold additional inventory amounting to CU900 000 in total to P Ltd at a profit. P Ltd still has inventory on hand at the end of 20x5 acquired from S Ltd, amounting to CU450 000. The cost of the inventory when acquired by S Ltd was CU300 000.

We are interested in the intra-group inventory that has not yet been sold by P Ltd (in this case) at the reporting date. Inventory affects the profit or loss section of the statement of profit or loss and other comprehensive income through cost of sales, which equals opening inventory plus purchases (and other production costs) less closing inventory. We are therefore interested in the intra-group inventory that has not been sold by P Ltd, which is included in both the opening and the closing inventory.

Therefore, the following amounts in the starting point regarding these transactions are relevant (note as discussed above that at this point, we are only interested in the amounts within the opening and the closing inventory of the intra-group inventory that had not yet been sold by P Ltd):

	S Ltd (starting point) CU'000	P Ltd (starting point) CU'000	Pro-forma adjustments CU'000	Group (end point) CU'000
Opening inventory	–	300	(100)	200
Less: Closing inventory	–	(450)	150	(300)
Total effect on cost of sales	–	(150)	50	(100)

Deferred taxation (asset) at beginning and end of 20x5

	P Ltd (the entity)				Group			
	Carrying amount CU'000	Tax base CU'000	Temporary difference CU'000	Deferred tax CU'000	Carrying amount CU'000	Tax base CU'000	Temporary difference CU'000	Deferred tax asset CU'000
Opening inventory	300	300	–	–	200	300	(100)	28 debit
Closing inventory	450	450	–	–	300	450	(150)	42 debit

The following *pro-forma* journal entry is required to eliminate the sale of inventory between P Ltd and S Ltd for 20x5:

			CU	CU
Dr		Cost of sales	900 000	
	Cr	Sales		900 000

Elimination of intra-group sales

This eliminates the intra-group transaction. The overall effect on group profits because of this adjustment is nil. Therefore, there is no deferred taxation adjustment for this *pro-forma* journal entry. This is essentially a disclosure adjustment.

The following *pro-forma* journal entry removes the unrealised profit from the closing balance of inventory:

			CU	CU
Dr		Cost of sales (unrealised profit in closing inventory)	150 000	
	Cr	Inventory		150 000

Elimination of intra-group unrealised profit included in inventory still on hand in the group

The following *pro-forma* journal entry adjusts for the deferred tax implications of the above entry:

			CU	CU
Dr		Deferred tax (asset)	42 000	
	Cr	Deferred tax (P/L)		42 000

Deferred tax adjustment relating to elimination of intra-group unrealised profit in inventory

As we have to prepare *pro-forma* journal entries from scratch each year, bearing in mind that any adjustments made to the group profit and loss section of the statement of profit or loss and other comprehensive income in previous years will be adjusted through retained earnings, the following combined *pro-forma* journal entry can be done to remove the unrealised profit from the prior year profits and reallocate it to the current year:

			CU	CU
Dr		Retained earnings	72 000	
Dr		Deferred tax (P/L)	28 000	
	Cr	Cost of sales		100 000

Elimination of investment in subsidiary at the acquisition date

> **What is this?**
> The after-tax effect of the unrealised profit relating to the prior year (refer to the 20x4 year end above) is as follows: CU100 000 × 72% = **CU72 000**.

Think about it

Unrealised profits resulting from intra-group transfer of inventory should be adjusted in profit or loss

From the table in 20x5, we can see that opening inventory is overstated at a group level (as a result of the intra-group profit). Opening inventory must therefore be reduced. This has the effect of reducing cost of sales (see the calculation of cost of sales) by CU100 000. To achieve a reduction in cost of sales, we credit cost of sales. A reduction in cost of sales increases group profits. As group profits have increased, we expect group taxation to increase; therefore, we debit deferred taxation in the profit and loss section of the statement of profit or loss and other comprehensive income with CU28 000 (that is, CU100 000 × 28%). Group net profit has increased by CU72 000 (that is, CU100 000 – CU28 000) relating to a transaction that originated in the subsidiary (in other words, the original sale from S Ltd to P Ltd).

What if the inventory was sold from the parent (P Ltd) to its subsidiary (S Ltd)?

The *pro-forma* journal entries will be similar to those illustrated above because the subsidiary is wholly owned. Refer to Chapter 7 for a discussion of the impact of non-controlling interest.

6. Transfers of non-current assets

The sale of a non-current asset between a parent and its subsidiary is an internal transaction, and the effect of such a sale should be reversed when consolidated financial statements are prepared as the group cannot sell an asset to itself. In this section we will discuss the reversal of the effect of intra-group transfers of non-current assets and the deferred tax implications.

6.1 Intra-group transactions relating to property, plant and equipment

The cost to the group of an asset is the cost when it was first acquired by the group. This is the acquisition cost if the entity that first bought the asset was part of the group when the asset was acquired or the fair value of the asset at the date on which the subsidiary was acquired by the parent if it was an asset held by the subsidiary when the parent obtained control of it. The asset should be recognised in the consolidated statement of financial position at its **cost to the group**. Where an asset has been sold by a subsidiary to a parent (or by a parent to a subsidiary) at a profit, the profit should be eliminated on consolidation.

Example

Intra-group sale of land (subsidiary sold to parent)

A wholly owned subsidiary acquired land after the date on which the parent obtained control of the subsidiary. The land had a cost price to the subsidiary of CU1 000 000. The subsidiary sold the land to the parent for CU1 500 000, realising a profit of CU500 000.

The following consolidation worksheet is prepared in order to consolidate P Ltd and S Ltd:

	Dr/(Cr)	P Ltd (starting point) CU	S Ltd (starting point) CU	Pro-forma journals CU	Group (end point) CU
Non-current asset: Land		1 500 000		(500 000)	1 000 000
Profit or loss:					
Profit on sale of land			(500 000)	500 000	–

The required adjustment is recorded in the following *pro-forma* journal entry:

			CU	CU
Dr		Profit on disposal of land	500 000	
	Cr	Land		500 000

Reversal of intra-group profit resulting from intra-group sale of land

This adjustment results from the reversal of the intra-group profit (recognised in S Ltd) when the land was sold to P Ltd. The cost of the land to the group should be CU1 000 000 (its fair value at the date on which it was originally acquired by S Ltd) and the profit of CU500 000 recognised by the subsidiary should be reversed on consolidation. The financial statements of S Ltd (starting point) recognise the sale of the land and the profit, which should be reversed as the land is an asset for the group (end point).

This example does not take into account any tax implications.

Where an asset sold between a parent and a subsidiary is a depreciating asset, the cost to the group of that asset should be depreciated from the date on which it was acquired by the group over its expected useful life to its residual value. Any subsequent sale between the parent and subsidiary should be reversed.

Example

Intra-group sale of depreciating asset and deferred tax implication (parent sold to subsidiary)

P Ltd sold a factory building to S Ltd; the asset is a depreciable asset and will therefore be realised through depreciation (that is, through use).

A similar example, which illustrates the effects of a partially held subsidiary, is included on the accompanying CD. Refer to the CD after you have worked through Chapter 7, *Consolidation: Partly owned subsidiaries and other consolidation considerations*.

P Ltd acquired a new **factory building** on 1 January 20x0 at a cost of CU2 000 000. P Ltd immediately sold the factory building to S Ltd, a subsidiary, for CU3 000 000. S Ltd depreciates the building over its expected useful life of ten years. For tax purposes, wear and tear is deductible on the cost of the building over 20 years.

The carrying amount of the factory building is determined as follows at 31 December 20x0:

	P Ltd (starting point) CU'000	S Ltd (starting point) CU'000	Pro-forma journals CU'000	Group (end point) CU'000
1 January 20x0 (acquisition)	2 000	–		2 000
Profit on sale	1 000	–		–
Proceeds on sale	(3 000)	3 000	(1 000)	2 000
Depreciation (20x0)	–	(300)	100	(200)
31 December 20x0		2 700	(900)	1 800

Deferred taxation implications at 31 December 20x0

	S Ltd (starting point)				Group (end point)			
	Carrying amount CU'000	Tax base CU'000	Temporary difference CU'000	Deferred tax CU'000	Carrying amount CU'000	Tax base CU'000	Temporary difference CU'000	Deferred tax asset CU'000
Balance at 1 January 20x0	3 000	3 000	–	–	2 000	3 000	(1 000)	280 debit
Depreciation 20x0	(300)	(150)	(150)	42 debit	(200)	(150)	(50)	14 debit
Balance at 31 December 20x0	2 700	2 850	(150)	42 debit	1 800	2 850	(1 050)	294 debit

What are the implications for the group financial statements for the year ending 31 December 20x0?

Dr/(Cr)	P Ltd (starting point) CU'000	S Ltd (starting point) CU'000	Pro-forma adjustments (reversal of profit) CU'000	Pro-forma adjustments (depreciation adjustment) CU'000	Group (end point) CU'000
Statement of financial position:					
Factory building (cost)	–	3 000	(1 000)		2 000
Factory building (accumulated depreciation)	–	(300)		100	(200)
Deferred taxation (asset)	–	42	280	(28)	294
Profit or loss:					
Profit on sale of asset	(1 000)		1 000		–
Depreciation	300			(100)	200
Deferred taxation (P/L) (credit)		(42)	(280)	28	294

Pro-forma journal entries

			CU'000	CU'000
Dr		Profit on sale of asset (P/L) ①	1 000	
	Cr	Factory building (cost)		1 000

Elimination of unrealised profit

			CU'000	CU'000
Dr		Deferred taxation (asset)	280	
	Cr	Deferred taxation (P/L) ②		280

Related deferred taxation adjustment

			CU'000	CU'000
Dr		Accumulated depreciation (factory building)	100	
	Cr	Depreciation ③		100

Realisation of unrealised profit through group depreciation that is lower

			CU'000	CU'000
Dr		Deferred taxation (P/L)	28	
	Cr	Deferred taxation (asset) ④		28

Related deferred taxation adjustment

Comments

① The cost of the building to the group is CU2 000 000, being the cost to P Ltd (the entity that brought the asset into the group for the first time). The asset's cost in the starting point trial balance is CU3 000 000 (being the cost to S Ltd). The effect of the intra-group profit thus overstates the cost of the asset. The cost of the asset must be reduced (credited). In terms of double entry, there has to be a corresponding debit. In this case, the debit is to the profit or loss, reflecting the reduction in group net assets (and group profits) for the intra-group profit. Debiting the profit or loss makes sense: we are 'reversing' profits, so we would expect group profits to decrease.

② Deferred taxation implications: Even though we reduced the cost of the asset at a group level (to the group cost), the **tax base of the asset has not changed**. In other words, the tax base of the asset is the same as that recognised by S Ltd, the entity that legally owns the asset. As the asset is used to generate future economic benefits, the tax base is the amount that will be deductible in the future, in other words, the cost of the asset to S Ltd. There is a temporary difference on which deferred tax must be provided.

Deferred tax must be recognised based on the tax rate that best reflects the manner in which the asset will be recovered for tax purposes. The building is a depreciable asset that is expected to derive economic benefits through use. Those economic benefits will be taxed at the normal corporate tax rate; a tax rate of 28% is therefore appropriate.

The reduction of the cost of the asset (with no corresponding effect on the tax base) gives rise to a deductible temporary difference. A debit is therefore required to the group's deferred taxation balance. In terms of double entry, a credit is required to deferred taxation in profit or loss as the unrealised profit was eliminated from group profits.

Alternatively, you could also say that because of eliminating the unrealised profit, group profits (before taxation) have reduced, therefore group taxation must reduce. Consequently, a credit is required to deferred taxation in the profit or loss. (If you think about it, tax is an expense. If we wanted to reduce it, we would need to credit the expense.) In terms of a double entry, a debit is required to deferred taxation in the statement of financial position. There is no adjustment to current tax in the group. This is important for the following reasons:

- Firstly, the current taxation consequences for P Ltd are capital gains tax (as the asset was sold at an amount greater than the original cost). There is no recoupment for tax purposes as no wear-and-tear allowances were granted to P Ltd.
- No *pro-forma* journal entries are processed relating to current taxation as current taxation is not intra-group. In other words, it is a transaction between the entity and the tax authority (external party). This is one of the main distinctions between deferred and current taxation.
- *Pro-forma* journal entries are prepared for deferred taxation as the carrying amount of the asset has been adjusted (in preparing the group financial statements). Deferred taxation is based on the carrying amounts and tax bases of assets and liabilities. An adjustment to the carrying amount without a corresponding adjustment to the tax base will give rise to deferred taxation (unless specifically exempt in terms of IAS12: 15; this exemption does not apply here).
- Even though P Ltd paid taxation to the tax authority at the capital gains tax rate, deferred taxation is recognised at the normal tax rate. This is because the asset is a depreciable asset and is therefore expected to derive future economic benefits through use. These benefits will be taxed at the normal tax rate. Therefore, this is the rate that best reflects how management expects to recover the asset.

③ Because the cost to the group is lower, we would expect lower group depreciation. An adjustment is thus required to reduce the depreciation in our starting point trial balance to the depreciation that should be recognised in the group profit or loss section of the statement of profit or loss and other comprehensive income.

④ As per the alternate argument in comment 2 above, by reducing group depreciation, we are increasing group profits before tax, which makes sense if you think about: we are realising profits that were not recognised previously, so group profit must increase. Therefore, group taxation must increase. A debit is required to deferred taxation in profit or loss (with a corresponding credit to deferred taxation in the statement of financial position). The key principle here is to ensure that you distinguish between the effects of processing *pro-forma* journal entries and the actual balances or amounts that will be reflected in the group financial statements. This is a reinforcement of getting the correct starting point, identifying where you want to end up and processing *pro-forma* journal entries as a means of getting from your starting point to the end point.

7. Change in use of assets on transfer between group entities

In some cases, an item that is regarded by one entity in the group as inventory is transferred to another entity within the group that classifies it as a non-current asset. The key is to determine the appropriate adjustment entries in these cases and to prepare the consolidation adjusting journal entries for the intra-group transactions. In the group financial statements, there is no transfer or sale of the asset, just a reclassification from one asset group to another.

Example

Transfer from inventory to property, plant and equipment (parent sold to subsidiary)

This example illustrates the transfer of inventory that was first acquired by the parent to the subsidiary. The subsidiary uses the inventory as a depreciable asset (for example, a machine). Deferred tax implications are included.

A similar example, which illustrates the effects of a partially held subsidiary, is included on the accompanying CD. Refer to the CD after you have worked through Chapter 7, *Consolidation: Partly owned subsidiaries and other consolidation considerations.*

P Ltd sells an item of inventory to S Ltd (a wholly owned subsidiary) on 1 July 20x5 for CU36 000 cash. The inventory item cost CU30 000 (in P Ltd) when it was originally acquired. S Ltd intends to use the item as machinery with a useful life of ten years and no estimated residual value. The current reporting date is 31 December 20x5. Wear-and-tear allowances are deductible at 10% per annum for tax purposes. A tax rate of 28% applies.

The following facts are relevant for each of the individual legal entities:
- P Ltd: There has been a sale of inventory.
- S Ltd: There has been an acquisition of a depreciable asset, a machine.
- In the group: There has been no sale of inventory and no acquisition of a machine; instead, the asset that was previously classified as inventory is now classified as a depreciable asset: a machine with a cost of CU30 000.

The consolidation worksheet will include the following at 31 December 20x5:

Dr/(Cr)	P Ltd (starting point) CU	S Ltd (starting point) CU	Pro-forma journals (reversal of sale) CU	Pro-forma journals (correction of depreciation) CU	Group (end point) CU
Profit or loss:					
Sales	(36 000)		① 36 000		–
Cost of sales	30 000		① (30 000)		–
Depreciation		1 800		③ (300)	1 500
Deferred tax/current tax expense	1 680	(504)	② (1 680)	④ 84	(420)
Asset:					
Machine		36 000	① (6 000)		30 000
Accumulated depreciation		(1 800)		③ 300	(1 500)
Deferred tax liability/asset			② 1 680	④ (84)	1 596

① The following *pro-forma* journal entries are required to eliminate the sale between P Ltd and S Ltd:

			CU	CU
Dr		Sales	36 000	
	Cr	Cost of sales		30 000
	Cr	Machinery		6 000

Elimination of intra-group profit on transfer of inventory to depreciable asset

② From the group's perspective, the cost of the machine is CU30 000. This means that the carrying amount at the date of the transfer should be reduced by CU6 000, while the tax base is the cost of CU36 000 to S Ltd. This gives rise to a deductible temporary difference, with the recognition of a deferred tax asset and an adjustment to the deferred tax expense of CU1 680 (CU6 000 × 28%).

			CU	CU
Dr		Deferred tax (asset)	1 680	
	Cr	Deferred tax expense (P/L)		1 680

Tax adjustment relating to reduction in carrying amount of asset

③ S Ltd recognised depreciation based on its cost of the asset of CU36 000 at 10% per annum. Thus, depreciation expense in S Ltd for the six months since the asset was acquired amounts to CU1 800 (CU36 000/10 years × 6/12). From the group's perspective, the cost of the asset is CU30 000. Thus, depreciation in the group amounts to CU1 500 (CU30 000/10 years × 6/12). This implies that the depreciation in S Ltd should be reduced by CU300 from a group's perspective.

			CU	CU
Dr		Accumulated depreciation	300	
	Cr	Depreciation expense (P/L)		300

Reversal of excess depreciation on consolidation

④ The tax effect for consolidation purposes is CU84 (CU300 × 28%):

			CU	CU
Dr		Deferred tax expense (P/L)	84	
	Cr	Deferred tax (asset)		84

Tax adjustment relating to reversal of excess depreciation

 Think about it

What will the consolidation adjustments in the following reporting period be?

If the acquisition had taken place in the previous period, the sales and cost of sales of P Ltd for the current period would not be affected; instead, the adjustment would be against retained earnings. Furthermore, the depreciation adjustment for the previous period would also be against retained earnings.

Thus the adjustment against retained earnings would be as follows:

CU6 000 (decrease) – CU300 (increase) = CU5 700 × 72% = CU4 104.

In the current reporting period, the excess depreciation of CU300 would be adjusted together with the related deferred tax adjustment. This adjustment would be repeated each year until the end of the useful life of the asset.

In a similar way, if the subsidiary sold inventory to the parent to be used by the parent as a depreciable asset, you should consider the following key aspects of the transaction:

- In the subsidiary, the sale of the inventory was recognised as sales and cost of sales, and the profit is in the subsidiary.
- In the parent, the asset is recognised at its transfer price and accumulated depreciation is recognised based on the transfer price.
- In the group, the asset should be recognised at its cost (when it was first acquired by the subsidiary) and depreciation in the group is based on the cost to the group.
- Because the unrealised profit was made by the subsidiary, the non-controlling interest's share of profits (where applicable) should be adjusted for their share of removal of the unrealised profit and the subsequent realisation of the profit through decreased depreciation. Refer to Chapter 7 for a further discussion.

The same principles apply for intra-group **transfers from property, plant and equipment to inventory**. The entity transferring the asset recognises a sale when it disposes of the asset, while the entity acquiring the inventory recognises the transfer price as the cost of the inventory and no depreciation would be charged. From the group's perspective, there has been a change in the asset classification from property, plant and equipment to inventory. The consolidated adjustments would therefore include the following:

- The unrealised profit on the sale of the asset to another entity in the group must be reversed, resulting in the cost of the inventory being the carrying amount of the asset at the date when it was reclassified to inventory.
- As the carrying amount of the inventory is less in the group financial statements, a temporary difference arises which will give rise to a deferred tax asset in the group.

Note that when the inventory is sold to a third party, there is no asset in the group. The sales and cost of sales resulting from the sale of the inventory should then be recognised in the group and the unrealised profit should be recognised.

Test your knowledge

There is a list of learning objectives at the beginning of this chapter. Go back to this list and check whether you have achieved these outcomes. If not, reread the appropriate section.

Questions

Question 1

 A similar example, which illustrates the effects of a partially held subsidiary, is included on the accompanying CD. Refer to the CD after you have worked through Chapter 7, *Consolidation: Partly owned subsidiaries and other consolidation considerations.*

P Ltd purchased 100% of S Ltd on 1 July 20x4 for CU170 000. The equity of S Ltd consisted of share capital of CU50 000 and retained earnings of CU190 000. All of the assets and liabilities were considered fairly valued, except inventory, which was undervalued by CU14 000 at the acquisition date.

During the financial year ended 30 June 20x5, P Ltd earned profits of CU150 000 and paid dividends of CU60 000, while S Ltd earned profits of CU95 000 and paid dividends of CU15 000. All of the inventory on hand at 1 July 20x4 was sold during the year ended 30 June 20x5.

P Ltd charged S Ltd a management fee of CU18 000 for the year ended 30 June 20x5.

Ignore taxation.

You are required to do the following:

1. Explain how the management fee income should be treated in terms of the Conceptual Framework in the consolidated financial statements for the year ended 30 June 20x5.
2. Calculate the group profit for the year ended 30 June 20x5.

Suggested solution

1. **Explain how the management fee income should be treated in terms of the Conceptual Framework in the consolidated financial statements for the year ended 30 June 20x5.**

   Income is defined as an increase in net assets other than those relating to contributions from equity participants.

   The management fees are charged for assets being moved within the group, rather than an increase in net assets.

   Therefore, management fee income does not meet the definition of income in the group and cannot be recognised in the group profit or loss. Management fee income should be eliminated against the management fee expense when group financial statements are prepared.

2. **Calculate the group profit for the year ended 30 June 20x5.**

	CU
Profit of S Ltd	95 000
Less pre-acquisition adjustment relating to inventory	(14 000)
Profit of S Ltd	81 000
Profit of S Ltd relating to group	81 000
Plus: Profit of P Ltd	150 000
Less dividends received from S Ltd (15 000 × 100%)	(15 000)
Group profit	**216 000**

Question 2

A similar example, which illustrates the effects of a partially held subsidiary, is included on the accompanying CD. Refer to the CD after you have worked through Chapter 7, *Consolidation: Partly owned subsidiaries and other consolidation consid-erations.*

P Ltd acquired 100% of the ordinary shares in S Ltd on 1 January 20x5. S Ltd declared an ordinary dividend of CU100 000 on 2 January 20x5 and paid the dividend on 10 January 20x5. S Ltd earned after-tax profits of CU200 000 during the financial year ending 31 December 20x5.

Prepare the *pro-forma* **journal entry** arising from the dividend declared by S Ltd when preparing the group financial statements of P Ltd for the financial year ending 31 December 20x5.

Suggested solution

Pro-forma journal entry

			CU	CU
Dr		Dividend received	100 000	
	Cr	Dividend declared		100 000

Elimination of inter-co dividend declared from pre-acquisition profits

Note: The parent recognises the dividend once it was declared by the subsidiary (when the shareholder's right to receive payment has been established; see IAS27: 38A).

Question 3

P Ltd acquired a 100% controlling interest in S Ltd on 1 July 20x2 for CU2 700 000 when the share capital of S Ltd was CU500 000 and its retained earnings amounted to CU1 600 000. P Ltd considered all of the assets and liabilities of S Ltd to be fairly valued at the acquisition date, except for land that was considered to have a fair value of CU2 000 000 (cost to S Ltd of CU1 500 000). S Ltd sold the land to P Ltd on 1 February 20x4 for CU2 800 000.

S Ltd has always applied the cost model to land and did not make any adjustments to its carrying amount at the acquisition date.

Since the acquisition date, P Ltd has acquired inventory from S Ltd at a mark-up of 25% on cost. S Ltd sold inventory to P Ltd amounting to CU750 000 during the financial year ended 30 June 20x5 (20x4: CU687 500; 20x3: CU562 500). Inventories on hand at P Ltd, acquired from S Ltd, amounted to CU143 750 at 30 June 20x5 (20x4: CU112 500; 20x3: CU81 250).

The retained earnings of S Ltd amounted to CU3 540 000 at 30 June 20x4 and its current year's profit after tax was CU1 800 000. S Ltd declared a dividend of CU300 000 on 15 July 20x5.

You can assume that goodwill is not impaired. Ignore taxation.

You are required to do the following:

Show **all of the** *pro-forma* **journal entries** required (limited to the information in the question) to prepare consolidated financial statements for P Ltd for the financial year ending 30 June 20x5. Narrations are not required.

Suggested solution

Pro-forma journal entries

			CU	CU
Dr		Share capital	500 000	
Dr		Retained earnings	1 600 000	
Dr		Land	500 000	
Dr		Goodwill on consolidation	100 000	
	Cr	Investment in S Ltd		2 700 000

Elimination of investment in subsidiary at the acquisition date

			CU	CU
Dr		Retained earnings	1 300 000	
	Cr	Land		1 300 000

Reversal of intra-group profit on sale of the land

			CU	CU
Dr		Retained earnings	22 500	
	Cr	Cost of sales (w1)		22 500
Dr		Cost of sales (w2)	28 750	
	Cr	Inventory		28 750

Reversal of intra-group unrealised profit on sale of inventory

			CU	CU
Dr		Sales	750 000	
	Cr	Cost of sales		750 000

Elimination of intra-group sales during the current year

Workings
(w1): CU112 500 × 25/125
(w2): CU143 750 × 25/125

Question 4

> A similar example, which illustrates the effects of a partially held subsidiary, is included on the accompanying CD. Refer to the CD after you have worked through Chapter 7, *Consolidation: Partly owned subsidiaries and other consolidation consid-erations*.

P Ltd owns a controlling interest of 100% of S Ltd. The current financial year end is 31 December 20x5.

On 1 July 20x5, P Ltd sells equipment to S Ltd for CU800 000. The equipment originally cost P Ltd CU900 000 on 1 January 20x1. At that date, the equipment was expected to have a residual value of CU100 000 and a useful life of nine years. These estimates remain unchanged.

The tax authority allows the cost of equipment to be deducted over five years for tax purposes, not apportioned.

You are required to do the following:

1. Prepare the journal entries processed by P Ltd (in its separate general ledger) on the sale of the equipment to S Ltd. Ignore closing and tax-related entries.
2. Show the cost and accumulated depreciation relating to the equipment as it should appear in the P Ltd group statement of financial position as at 31 December 20x5.
3. Calculate the deferred tax asset or liability to be recognised in the P Ltd group statement of financial position as at 31 December 20x5.
4. Calculate the effect (if any) that the above inter-company transaction will have on the group profits after tax for the financial year ended 31 December 20x5.

Suggested solution

1. Prepare the journal entries processed by P Ltd on the sale of the equipment to S Ltd. Ignore closing and tax-related entries.

The journal entry in P Ltd is as follows:

			CU	CU
Dr		Bank	800 000	
Dr		Accumulated depreciation ([900 000 – 100 000] × 4.5/9)	400 000	
	Cr	Equipment (cost)		900 000
	Cr	Profit on disposal of equipment		300 000

Recording of profit on disposal of equipment

2. Show the cost and accumulated depreciation relating to the equipment as it should appear in the P Ltd group statement of financial position as at 31 December 20x5.

The cost of the equipment in the group is CU900 000 (that is, the cost when it was first acquired by the group).

	CU
Equipment: Cost	900 000
Less: Accumulated depreciation (w1)	(444 444)
Carrying amount	CU455 556

(w1): 900 000 – 100 000 (residual value) = 800 000 × 5/9 = CU444 444

3. Calculate the deferred tax asset or liability to be recognised in the P Ltd group statement of financial position as at 31 December 20x5.

The deferred tax in the group is as follows:

	Carrying amount CU	Tax base CU	Temporary difference CU
Equipment	455 556	(w2) 640 000	(184 444) deductible
			(184 444 × 28%)
Deferred tax (asset)			= CU51 644 debit

(w2): (800 000 × 4/5) = CU640 000

Note that the asset is in S Ltd and the tax base is therefore the cost to S Ltd less wear-and-tear allowances since the date when the asset was acquired by S Ltd.

4. **Calculate the effect (if any) that the above inter-company transaction will have on the group profits after tax for the financial year ended 31 December 20x5.**

In the group, profits will decrease by CU192 000, calculated as follows:

	CU
Reversal of inter-company profit, not realised	300 000
Less: Depreciation adjustment on consolidation (300 000 × 0.5/4.5)	(33 333)
Net adjustment against profit before tax	266 667
Less deferred tax (266 667 × 28%)	(74 667)
Group profits after tax will decrease by	192 000

Note that the equipment had a total estimated useful life of nine years. At the date when it was sold by P Ltd to S Ltd (1 July 20x5), the remaining useful life was confirmed at 4.5 years. A depreciation adjustment is required in the group for the six months.

Case study exercises

A similar example, which illustrates the effects of a partially held subsidiary, is included on the accompanying CD. Refer to the CD after you have worked through Chapter 7, *Consolidation: Partly owned subsidiaries and other consolidation considerations.*

Scenario 1

P Ltd acquired all of the issued ordinary share capital of S Ltd on 1 January 20x3. The identifiable assets and liabilities of S Ltd were considered fairly valued at the date of acquisition. You can assume that any goodwill arising on consolidation is not impaired. Ignore taxation.

None of the companies issued any further ordinary shares subsequent to the date of incorporation. The retained earnings of S Ltd amounted to CU200 000 at the acquisition date.

Statements of financial position of P Ltd and S Ltd on 31 December 20x5

	P Ltd CU'000	S Ltd CU'000
ASSETS		
Plant and machinery (carrying amount)	300	250
Investment in S Ltd	400	
Inventory	400	350
Other current assets	290	380
	1 390	**980**
CAPITAL AND LIABILITIES		
Share capital (CU1 shares)	290	160
Retained earnings	900	700
Shareholders' equity	1 190	860
Total liabilities	200	120
	1 390	**980**

Statements of profit or loss of P Ltd and S Ltd for year ended 31 December 20x5

	P Ltd CU'000	S Ltd CU'000
Revenue (including dividends and interest received)	2 320	1 700
Cost of sales	(1 050)	(875)
Gross profit	1 270	825
Net operating costs	(390)	(125)
Interest expense	(100)	(50)
Profit before taxation	780	650
Taxation expense	(300)	(250)
Profit after taxation	**480**	**400**

Extract from statements of changes in shareholders' equity of P Ltd and S Ltd for the year ended 31 December 20x5

	P Ltd CU'000	S LTD CU'000
Retained earnings 1 January 20x5	620	500
Profit after tax	480	400
Dividends declared	(200)	(200)
Retained earnings 31 December 20x5	**900**	**700**

Since 1 January 20x3, S Ltd has sold inventory to P Ltd at cost plus 50%. Inventory sold to P Ltd for the year ended 31 December 20x5 amounted to CU450 000 (20x4: CU300 000). Included in inventory on hand at 31 December 20x5 in the statement of financial position of P Ltd was inventory received from S Ltd amounting to CU270 000 (20x4: CU150 000).

You are required to do the following:
1. Answer the following questions before starting with the preparation of the consolidated financial statements:
   - What is the cost price of the inventory sold to P Ltd, still on hand at 31 December 20x5?
   - At what amount should the inventory be measured in the group statement of financial position at 31 December 20x5?
   - What is the effect on prior year profits?
   - What is the effect on current year group profit?
   - What is the amount of dividends declared and paid by the group?
2. Show the *pro-forma* journal entries required to prepare the consolidated financial statements of P Ltd Group for the year ended 31 December 20x5.
3. Prepare the consolidated statement of profit or loss and other comprehensive income, the consolidated statement of changes in equity and the consolidated statement of financial position for P Ltd and its subsidiary at 31 December 20x5.

Scenario 2
Use the same information given in the first scenario above and consider the taxation implications. Assume a current tax rate of 28%. Note that you are required to answer all of the questions included in the first scenario.

Scenario 3
Use the same information given in the first scenario above and add the following:
On 1 January 20x4, S Ltd sold a depreciable asset (plant and machinery) with an original cost price of CU100 000 to P Ltd for CU85 000. The asset had a total useful life of five years when it was originally

purchased by S Ltd. The remaining useful life of four years was confirmed on 1 January 20x4 when P Ltd acquired it from S Ltd. Ignore taxation.

You are required to do the following:

1. Answer the following questions before starting with the preparation of the consolidated financial statements:
   - What was the profit recognised in S Ltd when S Ltd sold the asset to P Ltd?
   - What is the carrying amount of the asset in the separate financial statements of P Ltd at 31 December 20x5?
   - What is the carrying amount of the asset in the group financial statements at 31 December 20x5?
   - What is the effect on prior year profits?
   - What is the effect on current year group profit?
2. Show the *pro-forma* journal entries required to prepare the consolidated financial statements of P Ltd Group for the year ended 31 December 20x5.
3. Prepare the consolidated statement of profit or loss and other comprehensive income, the consolidated statement of changes in equity and the consolidated statement of financial position for P Ltd and its subsidiary at 31 December 20x5.

Suggested solution

Scenario 1

1. **Answer the following questions before starting with the preparation of the consolidated financial statements:**
   - **What is the cost price of the inventory sold to P Ltd, still on hand at 31 December 20x5?**
     S Ltd sold inventory of CU450 000 to P Ltd during the current year. This is an intra-group transaction and should be eliminated by using *pro-forma* journal entries.
     Of the inventory sold to P Ltd, CU270 000 is still on hand in P Ltd at 31 December 20x5. This inventory is measured in P Ltd at its transfer price, which includes a mark-up of 50% on cost.
     Thus: Cost price of inventory still on hand in P Ltd: CU270 000 × 100/150 = **CU180 000**
     (Prior year: CU150 000 × 100/150 = CU100 000)
   - **At what amount should inventory be measured in the group statement of financial position at 31 December 20x5?**
     The inventory on hand in P Ltd includes an unrealised profit of CU90 000 (CU270 000 × 50/150). Inventory in the group financial statements should be measured at the cost price when it was first acquired by the group, as follows:
     - P Ltd: CU400 000 – 90 000 = CU310 000
     - S Ltd: CU350 000
     - Group: CU310 000 + CU350 000 = **CU660 000**.
   - **What is the effect on prior year profits?**
     Similarly, prior year profits are overstated by the unrealised profit in S Ltd relating to inventory not yet sold by the group: CU150 000 × 50/150 = CU50 000.
     This means that prior year's profits are overstated by **CU50 000**.
   - **What is the effect on current year group profit?**
     Current year profit in S Ltd is overstated by CU90 000. This is an unrealised profit in S Ltd as the inventory was sold to P Ltd (within the group) and not to a third party.
     The group profit should therefore be **reduced by CU90 000**. (Remember that in this scenario, we are ignoring taxation.)
     However, the inventory on hand at the end of the prior period affects the opening balance of inventory in the current period. The unrealised profit of CU50 000 is now realised as the inventory is sold.

Net effect on current year profit: Increase by CU50 000, decrease by CU90 000 = net decrease by **CU40 000**.

- **What is the amount of dividends declared and paid by the group?**
  The dividends declared by P Ltd to shareholders of the group: CU200 000.
  100% of the dividends declared by S Ltd was received by P Ltd, this represents an inter-company transaction and should be eliminated on consolidation.

2. **Show the *pro-forma* journal entries required to prepare the consolidated financial statements of P Ltd Group for the year ended 31 December 20x5.**

Pro-forma journal entries

			CU'000	CU'000
Dr		Share capital	160	
Dr		Retained earnings	200	
Dr		Goodwill arising on consolidation	40	
	Cr	Investment in S Ltd		400

Elimination of equity at acquisition, investment in S Ltd and raising non-controlling at acquisition

			CU'000	CU'000
Dr		Retained earnings	50	
	Cr	Cost of sales (opening inventory)		50

Elimination of unrealised profit in closing inventory of 20x4 and realisation of this profit in 20x5

			CU'000	CU'000
Dr		Dividends received	200	
	Cr	Dividends declared and paid		200

Elimination of inter-company dividend

			CU'000	CU'000
Dr		Sales	450	
	Cr	Cost of sales		450

Elimination of inter-company sales

			CU'000	CU'000
Dr		Cost of sales (closing inventory)	90	
	Cr	Inventory		90

Elimination of unrealised profit in closing inventory of 20x5

3. **Prepare the consolidated statement of financial position and consolidated statement of profit or loss and other comprehensive income for P Ltd and its subsidiary at 31 December 20x5.**

Consolidated statement of profit or loss and other comprehensive income for P Ltd and its subsidiary for the year ended 31 December 20x5

	Workings	CU'000
Gross revenue	(2 320 + 1 700 − 200 − 450)	3 370
Cost of sales	(1 050 + 875 − 450 + 90 − 50)	(1 515)
Gross profit		1 855
Net operating costs	(390 + 125)	(515)
Interest expense	(100 + 50)	(150)
Profit before tax		1 190
Taxation expense	(300 + 250)	(550)
Profit after tax		**640**

Consolidated statement in shareholders' interest for P Ltd and its subsidiary for the year ended 31 December 20x5

	Share capital CU'000	Retained earnings CU'000	Total CU'000
Opening balance	290	(w1) 870	1 160
Profit after tax		640	640
− Dividends		(200)	(200)
Closing balance	**290**	**1 310**	**1 600**

(w1): P Ltd: 620 000
S Ltd: (500 000 − 200 000 − 50 000) = 250 000
Group: 620 000 + 250 000 = CU870 000

Consolidated statement of financial position for P Ltd and its subsidiary at 31 December 20x5

	Workings	CU'000
ASSETS		
Non-current assets:		
Plant and machinery	(300 + 250)	550
Goodwill		40
Current assets:		
Inventory	(400 + 350 − 90)	660
Other current assets	(390 + 380)	670
		1 920
EQUITY AND LIABILITIES		
Share capital		290
Retained earnings		1 310
Total equity		1 640
Total liabilities	(200 + 120)	320
		1 920

Workings

Analysis of equity of S Ltd

		Total CU'000	P Ltd (100%)	
			At acquisition CU'000	Since acquisition CU'000
a)	**At acquisition:**			
	Share capital	160		
	Retained earnings	200		
		360	360	
	Investment		400	
	Goodwill		40	
b)	**Since acquisition:**	250		250
	Retained earnings	300		
	Inventory (opening balance)[1]	(50)		
	Current year:	360		360
	Profit after tax	400		
	Inventory (opening balance)	50		
	Inventory (closing balance)[2]	(90)		
	– Dividends	(200)		(200)
		770		410

Think about it

What if ...?

What if, instead of S Ltd selling the inventory to P Ltd, P Ltd sold the inventory to S Ltd? Does the inventory have a different cost? Is the adjustment to cost of sales different?

In this case, the same *pro-forma* journals would be processed:

		CU'000	CU'000
Dr	Sales	450	
	Cr	Cost of sales		450

Elimination of intra-group sales

		CU'000	CU'000
Dr	Retained income	50	
	Cr	Cost of sales		· 50

Elimination of unrealised profit at the end of the prior reporting period

		CU'000	CU'000
Dr	Cost of sales	90	
	Cr	Inventory		90

Elimination of unrealised profit resulting from intra-group sale of inventory still on hand in the group

---

[1] $150 \times 50/150 = 50$
[2] $270 \times 50/150 = 90$

The *pro-forma* journal entries are similar, however, in this case, the unrealised profit is in P Ltd and not in S Ltd.

Scenario 2

Use the same information given in the first scenario above and consider the taxation implications. Assume a current tax rate of 28%. Note that you are required to answer all of the questions included in the first scenario.

1. **Answer the following questions before starting with the preparation of the consolidated financial statements:**
   - **What is the cost price of the inventory sold to P Ltd, still on hand at 31 December 20x5?**
     S Ltd sold inventory of CU450 000 to P Ltd during the current year. This is an intra-group transaction and should be eliminated by using *pro-forma* journal entries.
     Of the inventory sold to P Ltd, CU270 000 is still on hand in P Ltd at 31 December 20x5. This inventory is measured in P Ltd at its transfer price, which includes a mark-up of 50% on cost.
     Thus: Cost price of inventory still on hand in P Ltd: CU270 000 × 100/150 = **CU180 000**
     (prior year: CU150 000 × 100/150 = CU100 000).
   - **At what amount should inventory be measured in the group statement of financial position at 31 December 20x5?**
     The inventory on hand in P Ltd includes an unrealised profit of CU90 000 (CU270 000 × 50/150). Inventory in the group financial statements should be measured at the cost price when it was first acquired by the group, as follows:
     - P Ltd: CU400 000 − 90 000 = CU310 000
     - S Ltd: CU350 000
     - Group: CU310 000 + CU350 000 = **CU660 000**.
   - **What is the effect on prior year profits?**
     Similarly, prior year profits are overstated by the unrealised profit in S Ltd relating to inventory not yet sold by the group: CU150 000 × 50/150 = CU50 000.
     This means that prior year's profits are overstated by CU50 000 × 72% = **CU36 000** (after tax).
   - **What is the effect on current year group profit?**
     Current year profit in S Ltd is overstated by CU90 000. This is an unrealised profit in S Ltd as the inventory was sold to P Ltd (within the group) and not to a third party yet.
     The group profit should therefore be reduced by CU90 000 × 72% = **CU64 800**.
     However, the inventory on hand at the end of the prior period affects the opening balance of inventory in the current period. The unrealised profit of CU36 000 is now realised as the inventory is sold.
     Net effect on current year profit: Increase by CU36 000, decrease by CU64 800 = net decrease by **CU28 800** (CU40 000 × 72%).
   - **What is the amount of dividends declared and paid by the group?**
     The dividends declared by P Ltd to shareholders of the group: CU200 000.
     100% of the dividends declared by S Ltd was received by P Ltd. This represents an inter-company transaction and should be eliminated on consolidation.
2. **Show the *pro-forma* journal entries required to prepare the consolidated financial statements of P Ltd Group for the year ended 31 December 20x5.**

   Pro-forma journal entries

			CU'000	CU'000
Dr		Share capital	160	
Dr		Retained earnings	200	
Dr		Goodwill arising on consolidation	40	
	Cr	Investment in S Ltd		400

   Elimination of equity at acquisition, investment in S Ltd and raising non-controlling at acquisition

			CU'000	CU'000
Dr		Retained earnings	36	
Dr		Deferred tax (P/L)	14	
	Cr	Cost of sales (opening inventory)		50

Elimination of unrealised profit in closing inventory of 20x4 and realisation of this profit in 20x5

			CU'000	CU'000
Dr		Dividends received	200	
	Cr	Dividends declared and paid		200

Elimination of inter-company dividend

			CU'000	CU'000
Dr		Sales	450	
	Cr	Cost of sales		450

Elimination of inter-company sales

			CU'000	CU'000
Dr		Cost of sales (closing inventory)	90	
	Cr	Inventory		90

Elimination of unrealised profit in closing inventory of 20x5

			CU'000	CU'000
Dr		Deferred tax (asset/liability)	25.2	
	Cr	Deferred tax (P/L) (90 × 28%)		25.5

Deferred tax implication relating to unrealised profit in inventory

3. **Prepare the consolidated statement of financial position and consolidated statement of profit or loss and other comprehensive income for P Ltd and its subsidiary at 31 December 20x5.**

Consolidated statement of profit or loss and other comprehensive income for P Ltd and its subsidiary for the year ended 31 December 20x5

	Workings	CU'000
Gross revenue	(2 320 + 1 700 − 200 − 450)	3 370
Cost of sales	(1 050 + 875 − 450 + 90 − 50)	(1 515)
Gross profit		1 855
Net operating costs	(390 + 125)	(515)
Interest expense	(100 + 50)	(150)
Profit before tax		1 190
Taxation expense	(300 + 250 + 14 − 25.2)	(538.8)
Profit after tax		**651.2**

Consolidated statement in shareholders' interest for P Ltd and its subsidiary for the year ended 31 December 20x5

	Share capital CU'000	Retained earnings CU'000	Total CU'000
Opening balance	290	(w1) 884	1 174
Profit after tax		651.2	651.2
− Dividends		(200)	(200)
Closing balance	290	1 335.2	1 625.2

(w1): P Ltd: 620 000
S Ltd: (500 000 − 200 000 − 36 000) = 264 000
Group: 620 000 + 264 000 = **CU884 000**

Consolidated statement of financial position for P Ltd and its subsidiary at 31 December 20x5

	Workings	CU'000
ASSETS		
Non-current assets:		
Plant and machinery	(300 + 250)	550
Goodwill		40
Current assets:		
Inventory	(400 + 350 – 90)	660
Other current assets	(290 + 380)	770
		1 920
EQUITY AND LIABILITIES		
Share capital		290
Retained earnings		1 335.2
Total equity		1 625.2
Total liabilities	(200 + 120 – [90 × 28%]*)	294.8
		1 920

* Assuming that deferred tax is included within total liabilities.

Workings

Analysis of equity of S Ltd

			P Ltd (100%)	
		Total CU'000	At acquisition CU'000	Since acquisition CU'000
a)	**At acquisition:**			
	Share capital	160		
	Retained earnings	200		
		360	360	
	Investment		400	
	Goodwill		40	
b)	**Since acquisition:**	264		264
	Retained earnings	300		
	Inventory (opening balance) (50³ × 72%)	(36)		
	Current year:	371.2		371.2
	Profit after tax	400		
	Inventory (opening balance) (50 × 72%)	36		
	Inventory (closing balance) (90⁴ × 72%)	(64.8)		
	– Dividends	(200)		(200)
		795.2		435.2

Note that the main difference between the first scenario and the second scenario is that Scenario 2 takes into account the effect of taxation. In the group financial statements, the carrying amount of inventory is changed, while its tax base remains unchanged. This gives rise to a temporary difference arising on consolidation, resulting in a deferred tax adjustment of 28% in the group. The elimination of the unrealised profits is thus after tax (profits × 72%) and as inventory in the group is lower, a net deferred tax asset is recognised at the reporting date.

---

³ 150 × 50/150 = 50
⁴ 270 × 50/150 = 90

Scenario 3

Use the same information given in the first scenario above and add the following:
On 1 January 20x4, S Ltd sold a depreciable asset (plant and machinery) with an original cost price of CU100 000 to P Ltd for CU85 000. The asset had a total useful life of five years when it was originally purchased by S Ltd. The remaining useful life of four years was confirmed on 1 January 20x4 when P Ltd acquired it from S Ltd. Ignore taxation.

1. **Answer the following questions before starting with the preparation of the consolidated financial statements:**
   - **What was the profit recognised in S Ltd when S Ltd sold the asset to P Ltd?**
     When S Ltd acquired the asset, it had a cost of CU100 000 and a total useful life of five years. When S Ltd sold the asset to P Ltd, its remaining useful life was confirmed at four years. This means that the carrying amount of the asset on 1 January 20x4 amounted to CU80 000 (CU100 000 × 4/5). S Ltd sold the asset to P Ltd for CU85 000, thus recognising a profit in its separate financial statements of **CU5 000**.

     However, remember that the cost of this asset to the group is still CU100 000 (that is, when it was first acquired by the group). From the group's perspective, the profit on S Ltd is unrealised. This profit is released over the remaining useful life of the asset through usage.

	P Ltd CU	S Ltd CU	Pro-forma adjustments CU	Group CU
Cost		100 000		100 000
Less: Accumulated depreciation		(20 000)		(20 000)
Carrying amount at 1 Jan 20x4		80 000		
Sold to P Ltd (remaining useful life of four years)	85 000	(85 000)		
Profit on disposal of asset		5 000	(5 000)	
Depreciation for year 20x4	(21 250)		1 250	(20 000)
Carrying amount at 31 Dec 20x4	63 750		(3 750)	60 000
Depreciation for year 20x5	(21 250)		1 250	(20 000)
Carrying amount at 31 Dec 20x5	**42 500**		**(2 500)**	**40 000**

   - **What is the carrying amount of the asset in the separate financial statements of P Ltd at 31 December 20x5?**
     CU42 500 (cost of CU85 000 less depreciation for two years at 25% per annum or 85 000 × 2/4). This is the starting point in the current year's consolidation.
   - **What is the carrying amount of the asset in the group financial statements at 31 December 20x5?**
     CU40 000 (cost of CU100 000 less depreciation for three years at 20% per annum or 100 000 × 2/5). This is the end point for the current year's consolidation.
   - **What is the effect on prior year profits?**
     In addition to the adjustments relating to inventory, (refer to Scenario 1 above): The profit in S Ltd of CU5 000 is unrealised and should be reversed on consolidation. This will result in a decrease in prior year profits. However, a further adjustment is required relating to the depreciation expense in the group relating to this asset of CU1 250. Thus: Effect on prior year's profits: Decrease of CU5 000, increase of CU1 250 = **CU3 750** decrease.
   - **What is the effect on current year group profit?**
     In addition to the adjustments relating to inventory, (refer to Scenario 1 above):
     Depreciation adjustment in the current year relating to this asset: **CU1 250** (increase in profits) (in this case, we are ignoring any tax implications).
     Total effect on current year profits:

Inventory: CU90 000 decrease less CU50 000 increase = CU40 000 net decrease
Plant and machinery depreciation: CU1 250 increase in profit
Total: CU38 750 decrease in profit.

2. **Prepare the *pro-forma* journal entries required to prepare the consolidated financial statements of P Ltd Group for the year ended 31 December 20x5.**

Pro-forma journal entries

			CU'000	CU'000
Dr		Share capital	160	
Dr		Retained earnings	200	
Dr		Goodwill arising on consolidation	40	
	Cr	Investment in S Ltd		400

Elimination of equity at acquisition, investment in S Ltd and raising non-controlling at acquisition

			CU'000	CU'000
Dr		Retained earnings	50	
	Cr	Cost of sales (opening inventory)		50

Elimination of unrealised profit in closing inventory of 20x4 and realisation of this profit in 20x5

			CU'000	CU'000
Dr		Plant and machinery	15	
Dr		Retained earnings	3.75	
	Cr	Accumulated depreciation (20 000 – 1 250)		18.75

Elimination of unrealised profit when asset was sold by S Ltd to P Ltd and depreciation adjustment in the prior year

			CU'000	CU'000
Dr		Dividends received	200	
	Cr	Dividends declared and paid		200

Elimination of inter-company dividend

			CU'000	CU'000
Dr		Sales	450	
	Cr	Cost of sales		450

Elimination of inter-company sales

			CU'000	CU'000
Dr		Cost of sales (closing inventory)	90	
	Cr	Inventory		90

Elimination of unrealised profit in closing inventory of 20x5

			CU'000	CU'000
Dr		Accumulated depreciation	1.25	
	Cr	Depreciation		1.25

Depreciation adjustment in current year relating to asset sold by S Ltd to P Ltd

3. **Prepare the consolidated statement of financial position and consolidated statement of profit or loss and other comprehensive income for P Ltd and its subsidiary at 31 December 20x5.**

Consolidated statement of profit or loss and other comprehensive income for P Ltd and its subsidiary for the year ended 31 December 20x5

	Workings	CU'000
Gross revenue	(2 320 + 1 700 – 200 – 450)	3 390
Cost of sales	(1 050 + 875 – 450 + 90 – 50)	(1 515)
Gross profit		1 855
Net operating costs (adjustment)	(390 + 125 – 1.25) (depreciation)	(513.75)
Interest expense	(100 + 50)	(150)
Profit before tax		1 191.25
Taxation expense	(300 + 250)	(550)
Profit after tax		**641.25**

Consolidated statement in shareholders' interest for P Ltd and its subsidiary for the year ended 31 December 20x5

	Share capital CU'000	Retained earnings CU'000	Total CU'000
Opening balance	290	(w1) 866.25	1 156.25
Profit after tax		641.25	641.25
– Dividends		(200)	(200)
Closing balance	290	1 307.5	1 597.5

(w1): P Ltd: 620 000
S Ltd: (500 000 – 200 000 – 50 000 – 5 000 + 1 250) = 246 250
Group: 620 000 + 246 250 = **CU866 250**.

Consolidated statement of financial position for P Ltd and its subsidiary at 31 December 20x5

	Workings	CU'000
ASSETS		
Non-current assets:		
Plant and machinery	(w2)	547.5
Goodwill		40
Current assets:		
Inventory	(400 + 350 – 90)	660
Other current assets	(290 + 380)	670
		1 917.5
EQUITY AND LIABILITIES		
Share capital		290
Retained earnings		1 307.5
Total equity		1 597.5
Total liabilities	(200 + 120)	320
		1 917.5

(w2): (300 000 + 250 000 + 15 000 – 20 000 + 1 250 + 1 250 = CU547 500)

Check your answer
- P Ltd: CU300 000
- S Ltd: CU250 000
- Less: Effect of unrealised profit resulting from intra-group sale: CU2 500
- Group: **CU547 500**.

Workings

Analysis of equity of S Ltd

| | | Total CU | P Ltd (100%) | |
			At acquisition CU	Since acquisition CU
a)	**At acquisition:**			
	Share capital	160	160	
	Retained earnings	200	200	
		360	360	
	Investment		400	
	Goodwill		40	
b)	**Since acquisition:**	246.25		246.25
	Retained earnings	300		
	Profit on sale of plant and machinery	(5)		
	Depreciation[5]	1.25		
	Inventory (opening balance)	(50)		
	Current year:	361.25		361.25
	Profit after tax	400		
	Depreciation	1.25		
	Inventory (opening balance)	50		
	Inventory (closing balance)	(90)		
	– Dividends	(200)		(200)
		767.5		407.5

---

[5] $5\,000 \times 1/4 = 1\,250$

Consolidation: Partly owned subsidiaries and other consolidation considerations

7

The following topics are included in this chapter:

- Basic consolidation process for a partly owned subsidiary with reference to the accounting equation
- Measurement of non-controlling interest at the acquisition date
- Recognition and measurement of goodwill and bargain purchase at the acquisition date
- Preparing basic group financial statements for a parent with a partly owned subsidiary in subsequent reporting periods, including:
  - Considerations when a subsidiary has a different reporting date
  - The use of uniform accounting policies
  - Insolvent subsidiaries.

Learning objectives

By the end of this chapter, you should be able to:

- Explain the consolidation process for a partly held subsidiary with reference to the accounting equation
- Identify the non-controlling interest and know how it is recognised
- Measure non-controlling interest at the acquisition date and at subsequent reporting dates
- Measure goodwill or gains on bargain purchase at the acquisition date
- Understand when the goodwill recognised represents the amount attributable to the parent equity holders and when the full goodwill amount is recognised
- Identify and recognise any impairment of goodwill in subsequent reporting periods
- Prepare *pro-forma* journal entries at the acquisition date in order to eliminate the investment in the subsidiary, recognise goodwill and allocate the appropriate portion to non-controlling interest
- Prepare consolidated financial statements for a parent and its partly held subsidiary, including for the following situations:
  - The controlling interest in the subsidiary was acquired during the financial year
  - The subsidiary has a reporting date that is different from that of the parent
  - The subsidiary uses an accounting policy that is different from the accounting policy for similar transactions in the group
  - The subsidiary has a loss at the acquisition date or is insolvent.

1. Introduction

In the previous chapters, you learnt the basic principles of consolidation for wholly owned subsidiaries. In this chapter, we will continue with our investigation of the consolidation process. We will consider the situation where the parent does not own all of the shares in a subsidiary, resulting in the recognition of non-controlling interest. Where the parent does not hold all of the shares of a subsidiary, the portion held by shareholders outside the group should be identified and recognised as non-controlling interest. Thus, **non-controlling interest** represents ownership interests in a subsidiary that are not held by the parent. The consolidation process requires that all of the **assets** and **liabilities** of the subsidiary be added to those held by the parent. However, the **equity** of the subsidiary should be split (allocated) between the different owners, the **equity** held by the parent, and the **equity** not held by the parent, referred to as non-controlling interest.

Following on from the measurement of non-controlling interest at the acquisition date, **goodwill** acquired is recognised either as the amount attributable to the parent or as full goodwill. Other considerations relating to the consolidation process are discussed later in this chapter, including when the subsidiary applies an **accounting policy that is different** from that of the parent for similar transactions or where the subsidiary's **reporting date is different** from that of the group. Finally, we discuss the consolidation of **insolvent subsidiaries**.

2. Non-controlling interest

Non-controlling interest is the equity in a subsidiary that is not attributable, directly or indirectly, to the parent. It is that portion of the profit or loss and net assets of a subsidiary that is attributable to equity interests that are not owned (directly or indirectly through subsidiaries) by the parent. Non-controlling interest arises when the parent does not hold all of the shares in a subsidiary that has been consolidated.

The portion of the fair value of the net assets of the subsidiary at the date of acquisition that is not held by the parent is identified as the non-controlling interest (also referred to as the 'outside or minority shareholders' interest'). The non-controlling interest also includes its interest in the post-acquisition reserves of the subsidiary earned after the date on which it first became a subsidiary. The result is that the total non-controlling interest is the sum of its interest in the fair value of the net assets at the acquisition date and its share of the increase in the net assets (equity) since the date of acquisition. The total represents the non-controlling interest in the net assets of the subsidiary at the current reporting date.

Total non-controlling shareholders' interest = Non-controlling interest at the acquisition date + Non-controlling interest in the reserves of the subsidiary accumulated since the acquisition date

The non-controlling interest at the acquisition date is measured either at its share of the fair value of the net assets of the subsidiary at that date or at the fair value of the non-controlling interest at that date. The non-controlling interest is the result of the consolidation process of combining all of the assets and liabilities of the subsidiary with those of the parent, and identifying the portion of the assets and liabilities of the subsidiary that are not held by the parent.

The non-controlling interest at the reporting date does not represent a liability of the group, as the non-controlling interest in the net assets of a subsidiary does not meet the definition of a liability (as per the Conceptual Framework). The reason is that it does not give rise to a present obligation of the group, the settlement of which is expected to result in an outflow of economic benefits from the group to the non-controlling shareholders. Instead, the non-controlling shareholders receive a share of the consolidated equity and are therefore **participants in the residual equity of the group**.

Non-controlling shareholders are not shareholders of the parent. They are the **holders of the shares in the subsidiary that are not held by the parent**. Their equity interest in the shares of the subsidiary does not form part of the total shareholders' interest of the parent. As a result, non-controlling interest should be disclosed as part of the **equity** of the group, but separately from the parent shareholders' equity. Non-controlling interest should be included as a separate column in the statement of changes in equity. This disclosure is based on the fact that a non-controlling interest represents the residual interest in the net assets of those subsidiaries held by some of the shareholders of the subsidiaries within the group. It therefore meets the Conceptual Framework's definition of equity, which states that equity is the residual interest in the assets of the entity after deducting all of its liabilities.

The non-controlling interest in the net assets of the subsidiary must be separately disclosed on the face of the statement of financial position as a credit balance. What you are doing, in effect, is combining all of the assets and liabilities of the subsidiary with those of the parent (to include all of the assets controlled by the group). However, as the parent does not hold all of the shares in the subsidiary, you need to identify the portion of the net assets of the subsidiary that are attributable to the non-controlling shareholders and disclose that as a separate balance within equity.

 ## Example

Illustrating non-controlling interest

P Ltd acquired 80% of the issued shares in S Ltd. The acquisition of these shares resulted in P Ltd obtaining control of S Ltd.

The shareholding in S Ltd can be illustrated as follows:

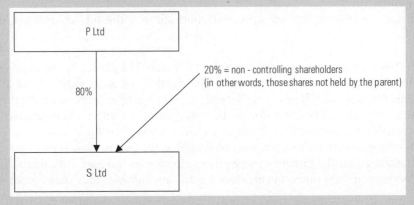

Figure 7.1 Group with partly held subsidiary and non-controlling interest

The table that follows illustrates the accounting equation principle when consolidated financial statements are prepared.

Table 7.1 The process of consolidation with reference to the accounting equation

S Ltd's financial statements (starting point)	Process of consolidation	Consolidated financial statements (end point)
Assets	Add 100% of assets and liabilities of the subsidiary to that of the parent	100% of assets of S Ltd
Liabilities		100% of liabilities of S Ltd
Equity	Equity is allocated based on ownership	80% of equity attributable to parent 20% of equity attributable to non-controlling interest

Note that the non-controlling interest is the result of the consolidation process of combining all of the assets and liabilities of the subsidiary with those of the parent, and of identifying the portion of the assets and liabilities of the subsidiary that are not held by the parent. There is no non-controlling interest recognised in the individual financial statements of the subsidiary. It only arises on consolidation.

2.1 How is non-controlling interest measured?

The non-controlling shareholders are entitled to a share of the consolidated equity of a subsidiary. This makes sense, as they are co-owners of the shares in the subsidiary. They are contributors of the equity of the consolidated group, and thus they are outside shareholders in the group (in other words, outside of the parent). Under the equity concept of consolidation, the group consists of the combined assets and liabilities of the parent and the subsidiary. There are two equity holders in this group: the **parent shareholders** and the **non-controlling shareholders**.

2.1.1 Non-controlling interest at acquisition date

At the acquisition date, IFRS3 requires the non-controlling interest to be measured in either of the following ways:
• At fair value
• As the non-controlling interest's proportionate share of the subsidiary's net identifiable assets.

Note that this choice is not an accounting policy choice. The choice between measuring non-controlling interest at fair value or at attributable net asset value is made on an investment-by-investment basis, with the choice often being influenced by the difficulty of getting a fair value. The fair value of the non-controlling interest is measured on the basis of an active market price for the equity shares not held by the acquirer (the parent). However, where an active share price is not available, the parent should measure the fair value of the non-controlling interest using other valuation techniques. If a valuation cannot be done, non-controlling interest is measured at the attributable share of net asset value.

Example

Recognising non-controlling interest at the acquisition date

P Ltd paid CU200 000 for 80% controlling interest in S Ltd on 1 January 20x4, when all identifiable assets and liabilities of the subsidiary were recorded at fair value of CU235 000.

The non-controlling interest proportionate share of the subsidiary's net identifiable assets at the acquisition date amounts to CU47 000 (20% of CU235 000).

This means that the **equity of the subsidiary at the acquisition date** (also equal to CU235 000; think about the accounting equation) is allocated as follows:

- 80% × CU235 000 = CU188 000 (represented by the investment by the parent in S Ltd)
- 20% × CU235 000 = CU47 000 (the non-controlling interest).

The measurement basis applied for non-controlling interest affects the measurement of **goodwill** at the acquisition date. This is because goodwill is measured as the residual balance. Where the non-controlling interest at the acquisition date is measured at its share of the fair value of the net assets of the subsidiary at that date, the goodwill recognised is only that of the parent. However, where the non-controlling interest is measured at fair value at the acquisition date, the portion of the value that exceeds its share of the fair value of the net assets of the subsidiary at that date relates to its share of goodwill. The non-controlling interest share of goodwill is included with that of the parent when goodwill is recognised in the consolidated financial statements. This is explained further in Section 3.2 below.

2.1.2 Non-controlling interest subsequent to the acquisition date

Non-controlling interests in the net assets consist of:
- The amount of those non-controlling interests at the date of the original acquisition (the pre-acquisition equity)
- The non-controlling interests' share of changes in equity since the date of the acquisition (the post-acquisition equity).

Because consolidated equity is affected by profits and losses made in relation to transactions within the group, the calculation of the non-controlling interest is affected by the existence of intra-group transactions.

The profits earned by the subsidiary after the date of acquisition should be included in the consolidated statement of profit or loss and other comprehensive income in the year in which they are earned, after adjusting for the effects of any intra-group transactions (refer to Chapter 6) and the effects on the current year of any adjustments to the fair value of assets or liabilities at the acquisition date (refer to Chapter 5). The profit for the year is then allocated between the amount attributable to the parent and the amount attributable to the non-controlling shareholders.

Example

Allocating profits between parent and non-controlling interest

Where a subsidiary's profit after tax for the year after the acquisition date amounts to CU35 000 and the parent has an 80% interest in this subsidiary, CU28 000 of the profits of the subsidiary is allocated to the group (CU35 000 profit for the year × the group's interest of 80%), while the remaining CU7 000 is allocated to the non-controlling interest.

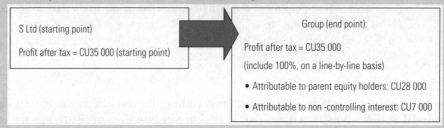

S Ltd (starting point)

Profit after tax = CU35 000 (starting point)

Group (end point):

Profit after tax = CU35 000

(include 100%, on a line-by-line basis)

• Attributable to parent equity holders: CU28 000

• Attributable to non -controlling interest: CU7 000

Figure 7.2 Allocation of profits in the subsidiary to parent equity holders and non-controlling interest

Where the subsidiary was acquired prior to the beginning of the current year, the opening balance of retained earnings for the group includes the group's share of profits earned by the subsidiary after the acquisition date until the beginning of the current year. The date of acquisition of the subsidiary is important because profits earned by the subsidiary prior to that date are pre-acquisition profits and form part of the equity purchased at acquisition, whereas profits earned by the subsidiary after that date are reflected as post-acquisition profits and should be included in the consolidated financial statements. The **retained earnings** on the group statement of financial position only include the group's share of the balance at the beginning of the year as well as the movement during the year. The share of prior year earnings attributable to non-controlling interest is recognised separately within the non-controlling interest credit balance within equity.

IFRS principles

Non-controlling interests since acquisition date (IFRS 10: B94, IFRS 10: B89)

A reporting entity attributes the profit or loss and each component of other comprehensive income to the owners of the parent and to the non-controlling interests. The proportion of profit or loss and changes in equity allocated to the parent and non-controlling interests are determined on the basis of present ownership interests.

As discussed in Chapter 4, where the parent owned shares in the subsidiary in the previous financial year, profits of the subsidiary would have been included in the prior year's statement of profit or loss and other comprehensive income and closing retained earnings. As the previous year's closing balance of retained earnings must equal the current year's opening balance, the opening balance of retained earnings in the statement of changes in equity must include the group's share of post-acquisition profits earned at the beginning of the current year. The current year's profits are recognised in the current year statement of profit or loss and other comprehensive income, and the balance is transferred to the closing balance of retained earnings.

The subsidiary accumulates profits (**retained earnings**) after its acquisition date as well as other reserves (for example, other comprehensive income in a **revaluation surplus**). In a similar way, the parent also shares in the increases in other reserves (other comprehensive income) recognised by the subsidiary after the acquisition date if these adjustments are in line with the group policy, for example, the subsidiary recognises owner-occupied land in accordance with the revaluation model and the group policy is to apply the revaluation model. Where the subsidiary has revalued its non-current assets after the acquisition date, the parent shares in the post-acquisition movement in the revaluation surplus. This also implies that the asset be recognised at its revalued amount in the group financial statements. The revaluation surplus is recognised as a group revaluation surplus when the value of the asset has increased after acquisition.

In each case where the equity of the subsidiary is increased, the increase is allocated between the parent and the non-controlling interest according to their ownership.

Example

Allocating profits in subsidiary to non-controlling interest

This example illustrates the allocation of the retained earnings of the subsidiary to the non-controlling interest, after allocating it between the pre-and post-acquisition periods.

When P Ltd acquired the controlling interest of 80% in S Ltd, the retained earnings of S Ltd amounted to CU115 000. The retained earnings of S Ltd recognised at 31 December 20x6 (three years since the acquisition date) amounts to CU390 000. The profit after tax for the current year, amounting to CU200 000, is included in this amount.

Summary of retained earnings of S Ltd

	CU
Retained earnings at acquisition date	115 000
Retained earnings after the date of acquisition, until the beginning of the current year (balancing figure)	75 000
Profit after tax for the current period	200 000
Retained earnings closing balance	**390 000**

The same figures are illustrated in the timeline that follows, which reflects the allocation of the closing retained earnings balance of CU390 000 into the relevant periods.

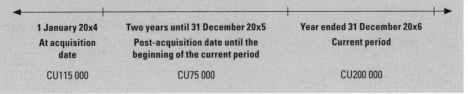

1 January 20x4	Two years until 31 December 20x5	Year ended 31 December 20x6
At acquisition date	Post-acquisition date until the beginning of the current period	Current period
CU115 000	CU75 000	CU200 000

How are the retained earnings of S Ltd recognised at the acquisition date?

The starting point for the consolidation includes 100% of the assets, liabilities and equity of the subsidiary. The total balance of CU390 000 is therefore included in the starting point. The adjustment that is required is therefore to remove the CU78 000 (20% of CU390 000) that belongs to the non-controlling interest. The remaining balance in retained earnings is correctly attributable to the parent, but should be split between the profits earned prior to the acquisition and the profits earned after the parent obtained control of the subsidiary.

The retained earnings of S Ltd at the acquisition date (CU115 000) is removed at the acquisition date. This makes sense as the retained earnings was earned prior to P Ltd's acquisition of the shares in S Ltd and was therefore included in the equity acquired by P Ltd. However, only 80% (CU92 000) of the retained earnings of S Ltd at the acquisition date was acquired by P Ltd and is included in the investment. This portion is eliminated against the investment, as was the case when the subsidiary was wholly owned. The remaining CU23 000 (20%) is attributable to non-controlling interest, and should be removed from retained earnings and recognised separately as non-controlling interest within equity.

What happens with the retained earnings of S Ltd since the acquisition date?

The consolidation process requires the adding together of all of the assets, liabilities and equity of the parent and its subsidiary. When all of the profits of the parent and the subsidiary are added together, the portion of retained earnings of S Ltd accumulated since its acquisition date is included in the group retained earnings.

However, as P Ltd acquired an 80% interest in S Ltd, only 80% of the retained earnings of S Ltd subsequent to the acquisition date should be included in the group financial statements. The portion attributable to the non-controlling interest should be allocated to it using a *pro-forma* journal entry.

Allocation of retained earnings of S Ltd subsequent to the acquisition date	Total (starting point) CU	Attributable to parent 80% CU	Non-controlling interest 20% CU
Retained earnings after the date of acquisition until the beginning of the current year	75 000	60 000	15 000
Profit after tax for the current period	200 000	160 000	40 000

The 80% of the retained earnings of S Ltd from after the acquisition date until the beginning of the current period, amounting to CU60 000, should be included in the **opening retained earnings** of the group. However, the starting point includes CU75 000 relating to the profits earned during this period. An adjustment of CU15 000 (CU75 000 − CU60 000) is therefore required. This amount is the portion of the prior-period profits that are attributable to the non-controlling interest.

The following *pro-forma* journal entry allocates the appropriate portion of the **prior year's profits** of S Ltd to the non-controlling interest:

			CU	CU
Dr		Retained earnings	15 000	
	Cr	Non-controlling interest (in equity)		15 000

Allocation of non-controlling interest in retained earnings

The **profit after tax** for the current period is included in the consolidated statement of profit or loss and other comprehensive income for the current year by including all of the income and expense items. The portion attributable to the interest not held by the parent of 20% (CU40 000) is then allocated to the non-controlling shareholders, resulting in the balance of 80% (CU160 000) being added to the closing retained earnings attributable to the parent equity holders.

The following *pro-forma* journal entry allocates the appropriate portion of the **current year's profits** of S Ltd to the non-controlling interest:

			CU	CU
Dr		Non-controlling interest in P/L	40 000	
	Cr	Non-controlling interest (in equity)		40 000

Allocation of share in current year's profit or loss to non-controlling interest

The **retained earnings balance attributable to the parent equity holders** includes the parent's share of the retained earnings of the subsidiary earned after the acquisition date, which amounts to (CU75 000 + CU200 000) × 80% = **CU220 000**.

This could also be calculated as follows:

CU60 000 + CU160 000 = CU220 000 or (CU390 000 – CU115 000) × 80% = CU220 000.

Note that the portion of the non-controlling interest balance within equity relating to the profits of the subsidiary includes its share of retained earnings and profit or loss post-acquisition as well as its share of pre-acquisition retained earnings, which is included in its share of the fair value of net assets at acquisition.

2.2 Presentation of non-controlling interest in equity

IFRS update

Non-controlling interests

A parent presents non-controlling interests (NCIs) in its consolidated statement of financial position within equity, separately from the equity of the owners of the parent (refer to IFRS10: 22).

Non-controlling shareholders are not shareholders of the parent; they are the **holders of the shares in the subsidiary that are not held by the parent**. Their equity interest in the shares of the subsidiary forms part of the total shareholders' interest of the group. As a result, non-controlling interest is disclosed as part of the **equity** of the group, but separately from the parent shareholders' equity. Non-controlling interest should be included as a separate column in the statement of changes in equity. This disclosure is based on the fact that a non-controlling interest represents the residual interest in the net assets of those subsidiaries that are only partially held by the group. It therefore meets the Conceptual Framework's definition of equity, which states that equity is the residual interest in the assets of the entity after all of its liabilities have been deducted.

Example

Recognising non-controlling interest

P Ltd purchased 80% and a controlling interest in S Ltd on 1 January 20x4 for CU220 000. On the acquisition date, P Ltd considered the identifiable net assets of the subsidiary to be fairly valued.

At the acquisition date, the equity of S Ltd consisted of the following:

	CU
Share capital	120 000
Revaluation surplus (land)	25 000
Retained earnings	115 000
Total equity	**260 000**

The following equity account was recognised in S Ltd's own financial statements at 31 December 20x6 (the current reporting period), including comparatives:

	31 December 20x6 CU	31 December 20x5 CU
Share capital	120 000	120 000
Revaluation surplus (land)	50 000	45 000
Retained earnings	390 000	190 000
Total equity	**560 000**	**355 000**

Assume that S Ltd has not declared any dividends since the acquisition date.

The **process of consolidation** requires the following:

- The adding together of all of the assets and liabilities of the parent and its subsidiary. This includes the inclusion of all of the assets acquired and liabilities assumed in the subsidiary. However, the equity of the subsidiary needs to be allocated based on the percentage interests of the parent. The portion that is not held by the parent is allocated to another classification of equity (non-controlling interest).
- The elimination of the investment in the subsidiary against the group share of equity of the subsidiary at the acquisition date. This makes sense as its represents an internal transaction (an investment in itself) from the group's perspective.

The increases in equity of S Ltd since the acquisition date are allocated to the **equity holders of the parent** and **non-controlling interest** when consolidated financial statements are prepared. This is illustrated by analysing the equity of S Ltd between the two different periods of time.

Analysis of the equity of S Ltd

	Total equity CU	Attributable to P Ltd (80%) CU	Non-controlling shareholders (20%) ⑤ CU
At acquisition date (1 January 20x4):			
Share capital	120 000	96 000	24 000
Revaluation surplus (land)	25 000	20 000	5 000
Retained earnings	115 000	92 000	23 000
Total equity	**260 000**	**208 000**	**52 000**
Investment in S Ltd (fair value)		(220 000)	
Goodwill acquired		**12 000**	
Since acquisition date:			
From 1 January 20x4 to 31 December 20x5:			
Retained earnings (190 000 – 115 000)	75 000	① 60 000	15 000
Revaluation surplus (45 000 – 25 000)	20 000	③ 16 000	4 000
From 1 January 20x6 to 31 December 20x6:			
Profit or loss (390 000 – 190 000)	200 000	② 160 000	40 000
Other comprehensive income (50 000 – 45 000)	5 000	④ 4 000	1 000
	560 000	**240 000**	**112 000**

In the above analysis of the equity of S Ltd, the different elements of equity (share capital, revaluation surplus and retained earnings) were allocated between the 'at acquisition period' and increases subsequent to the acquisition date until the reporting date. These amounts are included in the consolidated statement of changes in equity as follows:

① The parent's share of the retained earnings of S Ltd, amounting to CU60 000, is included in the group's retained earnings, specifically, opening retained earnings at the beginning of the current year. This represents the group's share of the profits of the subsidiary subsequent to its acquisition date until the beginning of the current period.

② The parent's share in the current year's profit or loss of the subsidiary of CU160 000 is allocated to retained earnings of the group in the consolidated statement of changes in equity. The full profit of the subsidiary of CU200 000 is included on a line-by-line basis in the consolidated statement of profit or loss and other comprehensive income, and is then attributed between the parent and non-controlling equity holders. The amount attributable to the parent equity holders is what is transferred to retained earnings of the group.

③ The parent's share of the revaluation surplus of S Ltd in prior periods, amounting to CU16 000, is included in the group's revaluation surplus as it represents increases in the carrying amount of the assets of the group since the acquisition date. This amount will be included in the opening revaluation surplus at the beginning of the current year.

④ Revaluation gains or losses in the current year are included in 'other comprehensive income'. The parent's share of the subsidiary's other comprehensive income of CU4 000 is allocated to the revaluation surplus in the consolidated statement of changes in equity as well as on a line-by-line basis in the consolidated statement of profit or loss and other comprehensive income with the same treatment as the profit for the year (②).

⑤ The non-controlling interest's share of the equity of the subsidiary is allocated in both the pre-acquisition and the post-acquisition period. Its share of equity at the date of acquisition as well as since the date of acquisition up to the beginning of the current year is included in the opening balance of the separate column within the consolidated statement of changes in equity for non-controlling interest.

The extract that follows is an illustration of the presentation of the parent's and non-controlling interest's share of the increases in the equity of the subsidiary for the current year, at the end of the **consolidated statement of profit or loss and other comprehensive income** (assume that the profit of P Ltd amounted to CU350 000 for the current year and that P Ltd has no 'other comprehensive income').

Extract from consolidated statement of profit or loss and other comprehensive income for the year ended 31 December 20x6

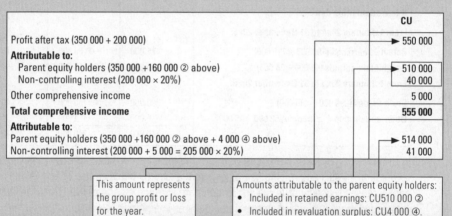

	CU
Profit after tax (350 000 + 200 000)	550 000
Attributable to:	
Parent equity holders (350 000 +160 000 ② above)	510 000
Non-controlling interest (200 000 × 20%)	40 000
Other comprehensive income	5 000
Total comprehensive income	**555 000**
Attributable to:	
Parent equity holders (350 000 +160 000 ② above + 4 000 ④ above)	514 000
Non-controlling interest (200 000 + 5 000 = 205 000 × 20%)	41 000

This amount represents the group profit or loss for the year.

Amounts attributable to the parent equity holders:
• Included in retained earnings: CU510 000 ②
• Included in revaluation surplus: CU4 000 ④.

The profit after tax for the year is closed off in the statement of changes in equity against retained earnings. Other comprehensive income is closed off against the revaluation surplus. These amounts are included in the **consolidated statement of changes in equity** as shown below.

Extract from consolidated statement of changes in equity for the year ended 31 December 20x6

	Share capital CU	Retained earnings CU	Revaluation surplus CU	Total parent interest CU	Non-controlling interest CU	Total group equity CU
Balance at 1 January 20x6						
Profit or loss for the year		510 000			40 000	550 000
Other comprehensive income			4 000		1 000	5 000
Closing balance at 31 December 20x6						

The non-controlling interest is presented as a separate column in the consolidated statement of changes in equity.

Note that the purpose of this extract is to illustration the inclusion of the subsidiary's changes in equity subsequent to the acquisition date. This extract from the consolidated statement of changes in equity is only presented for illustrative purposes and is not complete as it does not contain opening and closing balances. The completed consolidated statement of changes in equity is explained in more detail in the example below.

Example
Consolidating a partly owned subsidiary

This example illustrates the measurement of non-controlling interest at the acquisition date at its share of the net identifiable assets and recognising goodwill. The consolidated financial statements are prepared for a reporting period that is subsequent to the acquisition date.

The extracts that follow from the financial statements for P Ltd and its subsidiary, S Ltd, are presented at 31 December 20x4 (that is, at the reporting date, which is one year after the acquisition date). P Ltd acquired 80% of the issued share capital of S Ltd for a cash consideration of CU220 000 on 1 January 20x4. P Ltd considered the net assets of S Ltd to be fairly valued. Any excess paid is attributable to goodwill and non-controlling interest is measured at their share of the identifiable net assets at fair value. The retained earnings of S Ltd at the acquisition date amounted to CU115 000.

Statements of financial position of S Ltd and P Ltd at 31 December 20x4

	P Ltd CU	S Ltd CU
ASSETS		
Non-current assets	247 000	220 000
Current assets	213 000	130 000
Investment in S Ltd	220 000	
	680 000	**350 000**
EQUITY AND LIABILITIES		
Share capital	240 000	120 000
Retained earnings	300 000	150 000
Liabilities	140 000	80 000
	680 000	**350 000**

Statements of profit or loss for the year ended 31 December 20x4[1]

	P Ltd CU	S Ltd CU
Revenue	580 000	320 000
Cost of sales	(120 000)	(120 000)
Gross profit	460 000	200 000
Other operating expenses	(160 000)	(150 000)
Profit before tax	300 000	50 000
Taxation	(90 000)	(15 000)
Profit after tax	**210 000**	**35 000**

[1] Assuming that there is no 'other comprehensive income' in any of the entities

In order to be able to prepare the consolidated financial statements of the group, you need to identify the following information at the acquisition date (refer to IFRS3):

- The acquisition date: P Ltd acquired its controlling interest in S Ltd on **1 January 20x4**.
- The reporting date: Consolidated financial statements need to be prepared at the same reporting date as the parent, which is **31 December 20x4**.
- The purchase consideration: P Ltd paid **CU220 000** to acquire an 80% interest in S Ltd. This is recognised as the cost of the investment in the statement of financial position of P Ltd.
- The fair value of the net identifiable assets of the subsidiary: When P Ltd acquired the 80% controlling interest in S Ltd (1 January 20x4), it considered all of the assets and liabilities of S Ltd to be fairly valued. This implies that the fair value of the net assets at the acquisition date is equal to the equity balance of S Ltd at 1 January 20x4.
- Non-controlling interest: As P Ltd did not acquire all of the shares in S Ltd, the other 20% interest is attributable to the outside or non-controlling interest. Thus, CU235 000 × 20% = **CU47 000**.
- Goodwill acquired: The goodwill is determined as the excess paid. The goodwill acquired is the sum of the purchase consideration of CU220 000 (paid for the 80% interest) and the non-controlling interest of CU47 000 (in this case, it is equal to their share of the fair value of the identifiable net assets) less the fair value of the net identifiable assets acquired of CU235 000. Thus, goodwill acquired = (220 000 + 47 000) − 235 000 = **CU32 000**.

The *pro-forma* journal entry that follows eliminates the share capital and retained earnings of the subsidiary against the investment by the parent in the subsidiary at the acquisition date.

Pro-forma journal (1)

			CU	CU
Dr		Share capital	120 000	
Dr		Retained earnings	115 000	
Dr		Goodwill acquired	32 000	
	Cr	Non-controlling interest		47 000
	Cr	Investment in subsidiary		220 000

Elimination of investment in subsidiary at acquisition date

What is this?
The non-controlling interest is the equity that was not acquired by the parent at the acquisition date (20% × CU235 000).

As P Ltd acquired 80% of the interest in S Ltd, 80% of the **profit since acquisition date** is attributable to the parent and the remaining 20% is attributable to the non-controlling interest. As the process of consolidation requires the adding together of 100% of the assets and liabilities of the parent and its subsidiary, the related equity is split (allocated) between the different equity holders.

The appropriate portion of the profit since acquisition of S Ltd (in this case, 20% of CU35 000, amounting to CU7 000) is attributable to the non-controlling interest. The *pro-forma* journal entry that follows allocates the appropriate portion of the profits of S Ltd since acquisition date to the non-controlling interest.

Pro-forma journal (2)

			CU	CU
Dr		Non-controlling interest in P/L	7 000	
	Cr	Non-controlling interest (in equity)		7 000

Allocation of share in current year's profit or loss to non-controlling interest

> **What is this?**
> This is the non-controlling interest share in S Ltd's current year profit. See
> how it is presented in the consolidated statement of profit or loss below.

The consolidation worksheet containing the statements of financial position at 31 December 20x4 is presented below.

Consolidated statement of financial position at 31 December 20x4

	P Ltd CU	S Ltd CU	*Pro-forma* journal (1) CU	*Pro-forma* journal (2) CU	Group CU
ASSETS					
Non-current assets	247 000	220 000			467 000
Current assets	213 000	130 000			343 000
Goodwill			32 000		32 000
Investment in S Ltd	220 000		(220 000)		–
	680 000	**350 000**	**(188 000)**	**–**	**842 000**
EQUITY AND LIABILITIES					
Share capital	240 000	120 000	(120 000)		240 000
Retained earnings	300 000	150 000	(115 000)	(7 000)	328 000
Non-controlling interest			47 000	7 000	54 000
Liabilities	140 000	80 000			220 000
	680 000	**350 000**	**(188 000)**	**–**	**842 000**

> **What is the starting point?**
> The individual financial statements of the parent and its subsidiary at the reporting date, 31 December 20x4, are the starting point.

> **What is the end point?**
> The consolidated financial statements of the group at the reporting date, 31 December 20x4, are the end point.

Consolidated statement of profit or loss for the year ended 31 December 20x4

	P Ltd CU	S Ltd CU	Pro-forma journal (2) CU	Group CU
Revenue	580 000	320 000		900 000
Cost of sales	(120 000)	(120 000)		(240 000)
Gross profit	460 000	200 000		660 000
Other operating expenses	(160 000)	(150 000)		(310 000)
Profit before tax	300 000	50 000		350 000
Taxation	(90 000)	(15 000)		(105 000)
Profit after tax	**210 000**	**35 000**		**245 000**
Attributable to the parent equity holders			(7 000)	**238 000**
Attributable to the non-controlling interest			7 000	**7 000**

Note the allocation of the current year's profit between the parent equity holders and non-controlling interest.

Note that the group profit after tax amounts to CU245 000 (the combined profits of the parent and its subsidiary). However, this amount is not entirely attributable to the parent equity holders, as the parent only acquired an 80% interest in S Ltd and thus only has shares in 80% of the profits of S Ltd. The balance, being 20% of CU35 000 = CU7 000, is attributable to the non-controlling interest.

Consolidated statement of changes in equity for the year ended 31 December 20x4

	Share capital CU	Retained earnings CU	Attributable to the parent CU	Non-controlling interest CU	Total group equity CU
Balance at 1 January 20x5	240 000	90 000	330 000		330 000
Acquisition of subsidiary				47 000	47 000
Profit or loss for the year		238 000	238 000	7 000	245 000
Closing balance at 31 December 20x5	**240 000**	**328 000**	**568 000**	**54 000**	**622 000**

How is the retained earnings of the group determined?
- Retained earnings of P Ltd: CU300 000
- Retained earnings of S Ltd since acquisition date: CU35 000 × 80% = CU28 000
- Consolidated retained earnings: CU328 000.

Check your answer: Retained earnings
- Opening retained earnings of P Ltd: CU90 000
- Group profit from profit or loss: CU238 000
- Closing balance retained earnings: CU328 000.

How is non-controlling interest determined?
The non-controlling interest share in the net assets (or equity: 120 000 + 150 000 = 270 000) of S Ltd at the reporting date amounts to: 20% × CU270 000 = CU54 000.

Check your answer (refer to equity section in the consolidated statement of financial position)
- Share capital: CU240 000
- Retained earnings: CU328 000
- Non-controlling interest: CU54 000.

Acquisition of subsidiary
The group acquired its controlling interest in the subsidiary at 1 January 20x4, which is at the beginning of the current reporting period. This amount represents the non-controlling interest at the acquisition date. There is no opening balance because there was no subsidiary at the previous reporting date. Rather, the non-controlling interest balance is created as a result of the acquisition on the first day of the current reporting period. .

There is no balance for non-controlling interest in either the parent or the subsidiary's separate financial statements. **Non-controlling interest arises only from the process of consolidation.** Any balance required needs to be recognised by means of a *pro-forma* journal entry. A useful check is to ensure that the net debits and credits of adjustments to the non-controlling interest in the *pro-forma* journal entries are equal to the balance for non-controlling interest on the analysis of equity of the subsidiary.

 Think about it

What if the parent uses the fair value model to recognise its investment in S Ltd in its separate financial statements?

In order to eliminate the investment in the subsidiary (in P Ltd), we need to first reverse any fair value adjustment in the parent by using *pro-forma* journal entries before we can start with the consolidation adjustments. This makes sense as we need to calculate the correct goodwill and non-controlling interest at the acquisition date, and this will not be possible if the investment included in the starting point has been adjusted to its fair value in subsequent periods by the parent in its separate financial statements. (Refer to Chapter 1 for a discussion of this aspect.)

3. Goodwill recognised on consolidation

As required by IFRS3, the identifiable assets acquired and liabilities assumed of the subsidiary should be measured at fair value at the acquisition date. Where the fair value of an asset is different from its carrying amount in the separate financial statements of the subsidiary (the starting point), that asset is measured at fair value in the group (the end point) and the related adjustments are made as part of the consolidation process. Furthermore, where the consideration transferred (the amount paid by the parent) is more than the net fair value of the identifiable assets and liabilities of the subsidiary, the difference relates to **goodwill acquired by the group**.

As discussed in Chapter 4, a parent may pay more than its attributable share of the fair value of the identifiable assets and liabilities of the subsidiary at the acquisition date, the excess representing goodwill. Goodwill is an asset that is not individually identified and separately recognised by the parent in its separate financial statements at the acquisition date, but is recognised as a separate asset in the consolidated statement of financial position. Goodwill is the difference between the sum of the cost of the acquisition (the investment cost) and the value of the non-controlling interest at the date of acquisition, and the fair value of the identifiable assets and liabilities of the subsidiary.

The goodwill arising on consolidation can relate to various **intangible assets** that have been acquired, but that have not been recognised on the statement of financial position of the subsidiary (for example, a good customer base, loyal employees and market share). The mere fact that a controlling interest is obtained may result in the parent paying more than just the value of the net assets for an investment in a subsidiary.

3.1 Recognition of partial goodwill

The measurement of goodwill arising and recognised on consolidation depends on the measurement of the non-controlling interest at the acquisition date. Where the parent acquires less than all of the shares of a subsidiary, it acquires only a portion of the total equity or total net assets of the subsidiary. Hence, the consideration transferred (amount paid) is only for that portion of the net assets of the subsidiary. When the non-controlling interest is measured only at its share of the fair value of the net identifiable assets at the acquisition date (in other words, no additional amount is allocated to non-controlling interest for goodwill), the goodwill recognised will only be that portion that is attributable to the parent. This is also referred to as the **partial goodwill method**.

Goodwill (asset) = [Cost of investment + Non-controlling interest's proportionate share of net identifiable assets] – Fair value of net assets acquired

Example

Acquisition of a partly held subsidiary with goodwill

This example deals with the recognition of goodwill at the acquisition date in the consolidated financial statements using the partial goodwill method.

P Ltd acquired 80% of the ordinary share capital of S Ltd on 1 January 20x4. At that date, the equity of S Ltd comprised ordinary share capital of CU120 000 and retained earnings of CU115 000. P Ltd paid CU220 000 to acquire its 80% shareholding in S Ltd on 1 January 20x4.

Calculation of goodwill (in terms of IFRS3)

	CU
Cost of investment	220 000
Non-controlling interest ([CU120 000 + CU115 000] × 20%)	47 000
	267 000
Fair value of net identifiable assets of S Ltd at the acquisition date (equal to the equity of S Ltd at that date)	(235 000)
Goodwill (partial goodwill)	**32 000**

Summary of the *pro-forma* journal entry at the acquisition date

			CU	CU
Dr		Share capital	120 000	
Dr		Retained earnings	115 000	
Dr		Goodwill (residual balance)	32 000	
	Cr	Non-controlling interest		47 000
	Cr	Investment in S Ltd		220 000

Elimination of investment in subsidiary at acquisition date

In this case, non-controlling interest is measured at its share of the net assets of the subsidiary at the acquisition date, which amounts to CU47 000 (CU235 000 × 20%).

3.2 Recognition of full goodwill

Where the non-controlling interest is measured at its share of the net asset value, the goodwill relates only to the parent entity's investment. However, when the non-controlling interest is measured at fair value, the full goodwill of the subsidiary is measured and recognised on consolidation because both the parent's share and the non-controlling interest's share are recognised at a value above the fair value of the identifiable net assets, and the excess for both represents goodwill. This is referred to as the **full goodwill method,** as goodwill relating to 100% of the shares is recognised. The non-controlling interest in the subsidiary is measured at fair value, which is determined on the basis of the market prices for shares not acquired by the parent, or, if these are not available, a valuation technique is used.

Full goodwill = (Cost of investment + Fair value of non-controlling interest) − Fair value of net assets acquired

Example

Acquisition of a subsidiary, recognising full goodwill

This example deals with the recognition of non-controlling interest at fair value at the acquisition date, resulting in the recognition of full goodwill.

The details are similar to the example above, where P Ltd acquired 80% of the ordinary share capital of S Ltd on 1 January 20x4. At that date, the equity of S Ltd comprised ordinary share capital of CU120 000 and retained earnings of CU115 000. P Ltd paid CU220 000 to acquire its 80% shareholding in S Ltd on 1 January 20x4. The fair value of the non-controlling interest amounts to CU55 000 at the acquisition date.

Calculation of goodwill (in terms of IFRS3)

	CU
Cost of investment	220 000
Non-controlling interest (at fair value)	55 000
	275 000
Fair value of net identifiable assets of S Ltd at the acquisition date	(235 000)
Goodwill (full goodwill)	**40 000**

Summary of the *pro-forma* journal entry at the acquisition date

			CU	CU
Dr		Share capital	120 000	
Dr		Retained earnings	115 000	
Dr		Goodwill (residual balance)	40 000	
	Cr	Non-controlling interest (at fair value)		55 000
	Cr	Investment in S Ltd		220 000

Elimination of investment in subsidiary at acquisition date

In this case, the non-controlling interest is recognised and measured at a fair value of CU55 000, resulting in the recognition of the full goodwill amount of CU40 000 at the acquisition date.

All of the assets and liabilities of the subsidiary are added to those of the parent, while the non-controlling interest in the net assets of the subsidiary is reflected as a separate category of equity. If non-controlling interest is measured at fair value at the date of acquisition, both goodwill and non-controlling interest increase by the difference between the fair value and the attributable net asset value of the non-controlling interest at the date of acquisition.

Note that the choice between the partial goodwill method and the full goodwill method is not an accounting policy choice, but is made for each business combination. In choosing which method to use, you need to consider the amounts recognised for non-controlling interest and whether you are able to measure the fair value of the non-controlling interest reliably.

3.3 Gains on bargain purchase

When the net fair value of the identifiable assets and liabilities of the subsidiary is greater than the consideration transferred, the acquirer (parent) must first reassess the identification and measurement of the subsidiary's identifiable assets and liabilities as well as the measurement of the consideration transferred (refer to IFRS3, paragraph 36). This implies that the parent should first check and confirm that all of the identifiable assets and liabilities have been identified and are measured at their respective fair values in order to ensure that there are no measurement errors. When these have all been checked and confirmed, and an excess still exists, that excess is recognised in profit or loss as a **gain on bargain purchase**. The existence of a gain on bargain purchase is recognised at the acquisition date, when consolidated financial statements are prepared, and included in profit and loss. In subsequent years, the gain should be recognised as an adjustment to the retained earnings of the group.

Example

Acquisition of a subsidiary at a bargain

This example deals with the treatment of (negative) goodwill, referred to as a bargain purchase. Two scenarios are considered: when the non-controlling interest is measured at its share of the net identifiable assets at the acquisition date and when it is measured at fair value.

The details are similar to the example above, where P Ltd acquired 80% of the ordinary share capital of S Ltd on 1 January 20x4. At that date, the equity of S Ltd comprised ordinary share capital of CU120 000 and retained earnings of CU115 000. P Ltd paid CU180 000 to acquire its 80% shareholding in S Ltd on 1 January 20x4.

Calculation of goodwill (in terms of IFRS3)

	CU
Cost of investment	180 000
Non-controlling interest (CU120 000 + CU115 000) × 20%	47 000
	227 000
Fair value of net identifiable assets of S Ltd at the acquisition date	(235 000)
'Negative' goodwill or gain on bargain purchase	(8 000)

In terms of IFRS3, a gain on the bargain purchase exists when the fair value of the net assets of the subsidiary exceeds the cost of acquisition and the amount attributable to non-controlling interest (at the acquisition date). In this scenario, the cost of acquisition was CU180 000. The parent acquired its share of the net identifiable assets of S Ltd, amounting to CU188 000 (CU235 000 × 80%) at a discount of CU8 000. As mentioned above, in the case of a bargain purchase, the parent needs to review the identification and measurement of the assets acquired and liabilities assumed of the subsidiary as well as the measurement of the consideration transferred in order to confirm that the purchase was at a discount.

The bargain purchase amount is recognised in the group **profit or loss** at the acquisition date. In subsequent periods, the debit is against **retained earnings**.

Summary of the *pro-forma* journal entry at the acquisition date

			CU	CU
Dr		Share capital	120 000	
Dr		Retained earnings	115 000	
	Cr	Gain on bargain purchase (P/L)		8 000
	Cr	Non-controlling interest		47 000
	Cr	Investment in S Ltd		180 000

Elimination of investment in subsidiary at acquisition date

The calculation that follows assumes that the **fair value of the non-controlling interest** amounts to CU50 000 at the acquisition date and that the parent acquired its controlling share at a bargain, while goodwill is attributable to the non-controlling interest.

Calculation of goodwill (in terms of IFRS3)

	CU
Cost of investment	180 000
Non-controlling interest (at fair value)	50 000
	230 000
Fair value of net identifiable assets of S Ltd at the acquisition date	(235 000)
'Negative' goodwill	**(5 000)**

In this case, the parent acquired its investment in the subsidiary at a discount of CU8 000 (being CU180 000 − CU235 000 × 80%) and the goodwill that exists (CU3 000, being CU50 000 − CU235 000 × 20%) is attributable to the non-controlling interest. The net situation is a bargain purchase of CU5 000.

Summary of the *pro-forma* journal entry at the acquisition date

			CU	CU
Dr		Share capital	120 000	
Dr		Retained earnings	115 000	
	Cr	Gain on bargain purchase (P/L)		5 000
	Cr	Non-controlling interest (at fair value)		50 000
	Cr	Investment in S Ltd		180 000

Elimination of investment in subsidiary at acquisition date

This is a theoretical illustration, as it is unlikely in practice that the parent will acquire a controlling interest in a subsidiary at a bargain purchase where the fair value of the non-controlling interest is in excess of its share of the net identifiable assets of the subsidiary.

3.4 Subsequent treatment of goodwill: Impairment

IAS38, *Intangible Assets*, requires that the acquirer (parent) measure goodwill at the amount acquired at the acquisition date less any accumulated impairment. Goodwill acquired in a group arises on consolidation and should be considered for any impairment at each reporting date. The goodwill **impairment** is therefore also a consolidation adjustment; it has not been recognised by either the subsidiary or the parent as the goodwill is identified only when the cost of the investment is replaced by the underlying net assets (at a group level). The goodwill is recognised as part of the consolidation process and any adjustments to the goodwill balance should be adjusted to the consolidated retained earnings (if the impairment loss arose in previous years) or to the current year group profit or loss (if the impairment loss arose in the current year).

Example

Acquisition of a subsidiary with subsequent impairment of goodwill

The example deals with the recognition of goodwill at the acquisition date and its subsequent impairment. Two scenarios are considered: when the non-controlling interest is measured at its share of the net identifiable assets at the acquisition date and when it is measured at fair value.

The details are similar to the example above, where P Ltd acquired 80% of the ordinary share capital of S Ltd on 1 January 20x4. At that date, the equity of S Ltd comprised ordinary share capital of CU120 000 and retained earnings of CU115 000. P Ltd paid CU220 000 to acquire its 80% shareholding in S Ltd on 1 January 20x4. The current reporting period is 31 December 20x5. P Ltd recognises its investment in S Ltd using the **cost model** in its separate annual financial statements.

S Ltd earned profits of CU40 000 in the 20x5 reporting period (20x4: CU35 000) and no dividends have been declared since acquisition. Impairment tests on **goodwill** revealed that the goodwill arising from the acquisition of S Ltd had a recoverable amount of CU25 000 on 31 December 20x5 (31 December 20x4: CU28 000).

Analysis of equity of S Ltd

	Total 100% CU	P Ltd 60% CU	NCI 40% CU
At acquisition date 1 January 20x4			
Share capital	120 000		
Retained earnings	115 000		
	235 000	188 000	47 000
Cost		220 000	
Goodwill		**32 000**	
20x4 financial year			
Retained earnings	35 000	28 000	7 000
20x5 financial year			
Profit after tax	40 000	32 000	8 000
	310 000	60 000	62 000

Calculation of goodwill (in terms of IFRS3)

	CU
Cost of investment	220 000
Non-controlling interest (CU235 000 × 20%)	47 000
	267 000
Fair value of net identifiable assets of S Ltd at the acquisition date	(235 000)
Goodwill at the acquisition date	32 000
Impairment loss in retained earnings	① (4 000)
Carrying amount of goodwill at 31 December 20x4	28 000
Impairment loss in profit or loss	② (3 000)
Carrying amount of goodwill at 31 December 20x5	25 000

Goodwill is recognised at its recoverable amount, where the recoverable amount is less than its carrying amount, at each reporting date. An impairment loss of CU4 000 is recognised in group retained earnings in the prior year and a further impairment loss of CU3 000 is recognised in the group profit or loss in the current year.

Summary of the *pro-forma* journal entry at the acquisition date

			CU	CU
Dr		Share capital	120 000	
Dr		Retained earnings	115 000	
Dr		Goodwill (residual balance)	32 000	
	Cr	Non-controlling interest		47 000
	Cr	Investment in S Ltd		220 000

Elimination of investment in subsidiary at acquisition date

Pro-forma journal entry recognising the subsequent impairment of goodwill on consolidation

			CU	CU
Dr		Retained earnings	① 4 000	
Dr		Impairment loss (P/L)	② 3 000	
	Cr	Goodwill: Accumulated impairment losses		7 000

Recognition of impairment of goodwill in the prior and current periods

Think about it

Goodwill arises on consolidation

Goodwill is recognised as an asset on consolidation. It is not recognised in the separate financial statements of the parent or its subsidiary. This makes sense as goodwill was acquired on consolidation. Any subsequent adjustments to the carrying amount of goodwill are made on consolidation by using *pro-forma* journal entries.

3.5 Disclosure of goodwill

IFRS principles

Disclosure of goodwill

IFRS3 requires disclosure of information that will enable users to evaluate changes in the carrying amount of goodwill during the period, in other words, a reconciliation of the opening and closing carrying amounts of goodwill at the beginning and end of the period (refer to IFRS3: B67[d]).

Consolidated financial statements should include information that enables users of the financial statements to evaluate the nature and financial effect of a business combination. The disclosure requirements for business combinations are set out in IFRS3, paragraphs B64 to B67. Information about goodwill recognised on consolidation is normally presented in the form of a reconciliation, showing, for each reporting period, the gross amount and accumulated impairment losses at the beginning and end of the reporting period.

Example

Disclosure of goodwill

This example follows from the example in Section 3.4 above, where the goodwill was subsequently impaired.

The reconciliation of the opening and closing carrying amounts of goodwill as it would appear in the notes to the group annual financial statements of P Ltd for the financial year ended 31 December 20x5 are presented below.

Notes to the consolidated financial statements of P Ltd and its subsidiary for the year ended 31 December 20x5

Note 10: Goodwill	20x5 CU	20x4 CU
Carrying amount as at 1 January	28 000	–
Gross carrying amount	32 000	–
Accumulated impairment losses	(4 000)	–
Arising from the acquisition of a subsidiary (S Ltd)	–	32 000
Impairment	(3 000)	(4 000)
Carrying amount as at 31 December	**25 000**	**28 000**
Gross carrying amount	32 000	32 000
Accumulated impairment losses	(7 000)	(4 000)

4. Effect on non-controlling interest of fair value adjustments at acquisition

In Chapter 5, you learnt about the effect of fair value adjustments at the date of acquisition on the measurement of goodwill and the subsequent profits of the group. In that chapter, we only dealt with the situation where the subsidiary was wholly owned by the parent entity.

In the case where a subsidiary is partially owned, the adjustments at the date of acquisition will be adjusted for in exactly the same way, but the effect is shared between the parent equity holders and the non-controlling interest based on their shareholding. For example, if land was understated by CU100 000 when the parent acquired a 90% shareholding in the subsidiary, the net asset value of the subsidiary should be increased by CU100 000. When measuring the non-controlling interest at that date, their balance will be increased by CU10 000 (CU100 000 × 10%) in addition to their share of the net assets as recorded by the subsidiary.

Any adjustments to the group profit or loss or other comprehensive income subsequent to the acquisition date are also allocated between the parent equity holders and the non-controlling interest based on their respective shareholding.

Similar examples, which illustrate the effect of non-controlling interest, are included on the accompanying CD. Refer to the CD after you have worked through this chapter.

Example

The adjustment to fair value at acquisition and subsequent revaluation of an asset held by a partially owned subsidiary

This example illustrates the application of the revaluation model for property, plant and equipment in the context of a partially held subsidiary. In this case, the fair value of the revalued asset is higher than its carrying amount at the acquisition date and the subsidiary revalues the asset after the acquisition date. The example ignores any deferred tax implications relating to such a revaluation.

P Ltd acquired 80% of the ordinary shares in S Ltd on 1 January 20x4, when the retained earnings of S Ltd amounted to CU115 000 and there was a revaluation surplus of CU25 000. The trial balances of the two entities were as follows at 31 December 20x6:

	P Ltd		S Ltd	
	Debit CU	Credit CU	Debit CU	Credit CU
Ordinary share capital		240 000		120 000
Revaluation surplus (land)		200 000		50 000
Retained earnings (1 January 20x6)		500 000		190 000
Investment in S Ltd	320 000			
Land	500 000		110 000	
Other net assets (excluding investments)	470 000		450 000	
Revenue		840 000		600 000
Other expenses	325 000		314 000	
Tax expense	165 000		86 000	
	1 780 000	**1 780 000**	**960 000**	**960 000**

All of the assets and liabilities of S Ltd are considered fairly valued at the acquisition date, except for land, which had a carrying amount of CU100 000 and a fair value of CU110 000. Ignore deferred tax.

S Ltd revalued its land to CU120 000 at its next revaluation date, which was 31 December 20x5. Both P Ltd and S Ltd have always applied a policy of regular revaluation to non-current assets.

The balance on the revaluation surplus of S Ltd can be analysed as follows:

Revaluation surplus of S Ltd: Land

	CU
Balance at 1 January 20x4	25 000
Increases in valuation since acquisition date until 31 December 20x5	20 000
Increases in valuation during the current period	5 000
Closing balance at 31 December 20x6	**50 000**

The parent did not revalue any of its own assets during the current year. The increases in the revaluation surplus of the subsidiary subsequent to the acquisition date should be included in the analysis of equity as shown below.

Analysis of the equity of S Ltd

	Total of S Ltd's equity	P Ltd's interest		Non-controlling interest
		At acquisition	Since acquisition	
	100%	80%	80%	20%
	CU	CU	CU	CU
At acquisition (1 January 20x4):				
Share capital	120 000			
Revaluation surplus	25 000			
Land (excess over carrying amount)	① 10 000			
Retained earnings	115 000			
	270 000	216 000		54 000
Investment in S Ltd		(320 000)		
∴ Goodwill		104 000		
Since acquisition (January 20x4 to December 20x5):				
Retained earnings	75 000		60 000	15 000
(190 000 – 115 000)				
Revaluation surplus	② 10 000		8 000	2 000
(20 000 – 10 000)				
Current period (January 20x6 to December 20x6):				
Other comprehensive income	③ 5 000		4 000	1 000
Profit after tax	200 000		160 000	40 000
(600 000 – 314 000 – 86 000)				
Total equity of S Ltd	**560 000**		**232 000**	**112 000**

Check your workings

Analysis of the revaluation surplus of the subsidiary from the group's perspective:
- At acquisition date: CU35 000 (25 000 + 10 000)
- Since acquisition date: CU15 000 (10 000 + 5 000)
- Total revaluation surplus in S Ltd: CU50 000.

What is this?

The parent's interest in the equity of the subsidiary since the acquisition date (CU232 000) consists of the following:
- Retained earnings of CU60 000 + CU160 000 = CU220 000
- Revaluation surplus of CU8 000 + CU4 000 = CU12 000.

Check your workings

Non-controlling interest should be 20% of the total equity of the subsidiary from the group's perspective: CU560 000 × 20% = CU112 000.

Notes

① The revaluation surplus at the date of acquisition is included in the equity (or net assets) at the date of acquisition. This portion of the revaluation surplus is pre-acquisition equity and forms part of the equity of the subsidiary at the acquisition date, of which the appropriate portion (20%) is allocated to the non-controlling interest.

② The increase in the revaluation surplus subsequent to the acquisition date until the beginning of the current year (CU10 000) would have been recognised in the prior year's group financial statements and should be included as part of the opening balances in the current year. You should only include the group's portion (the 80% attributable to the equity holders of the parent) in the opening revaluation surplus balance. The other 20% is allocated to the non-controlling interest, as illustrated in the statement of changes in equity at the end of the example.

③ The current year's portion of the revaluation surplus has to be identified separately as it will be reflected in other comprehensive income.

Pro-forma journal entry at date of acquisition

			CU	CU
Dr		Share capital	120 000	
Dr		Revaluation surplus	25 000	
Dr		Retained earnings	115 000	
Dr		Land (fair value adjustment at acquisition date)	10 000	
Dr		Goodwill arising on consolidation	104 000	
	Cr	Non-controlling interest		54 000
	Cr	Investment in subsidiary		320 000

Elimination of investment in subsidiary at the acquisition date

This entry has the effect of reversing the equity that existed at the date of acquisition, specifically the revaluation surplus and the retained earnings, as that equity is purchased and not earned.

Pro-forma journal entries after the acquisition date

			CU	CU
Dr		Revaluation surplus	10 000	
	Cr	Land (fair value adjustment at acquisition date)		10 000

Reversing the fair value of the land at acquisition date, as the subsidiary has revalued its land since the acquisition date

As the statement of financial position of the subsidiary is added to that of the parent when consolidating (the starting point), the non-controlling interest in the reserves after the acquisition date until the beginning of the current period is allocated by transferring the portion applicable to the non-controlling interest. The balance remaining in each of the reserves after the *pro-forma* journal entries is the portion attributable to the parent equity holders.

			CU	CU
Dr		Revaluation surplus	2 000	
	Cr	Non-controlling interest (equity)		2 000

Allocating the non-controlling interest in revaluation since the acquisition date

			CU	CU
Dr		Non-controlling interest (other comprehensive income)	1 000	
	Cr	Non-controlling interest (equity)		1 000

Allocating the non-controlling interest in other comprehensive income in the current year

			CU	CU
Dr		Retained earnings	15 000	
	Cr	Non-controlling interest (equity)		15 000

Allocating the non-controlling interest in retained earnings since the acquisition date

			CU	CU
Dr		Non-controlling interest in profit for the year	40 000	
	Cr	Non-controlling interest (equity)		40 000

Allocating the non-controlling interest in profit or loss in the current year

The consolidation adjustments relating to the revaluation surplus are summarised as follows:

At 31 December 20x6	S Ltd (starting point)	Adjustments (*pro-forma* journal entries) above		Group (end point)
Revaluation surplus	CU50 000	Eliminate the balance at acquisition:	(CU25 000)	**CU12 000** ↑
		Reverse fair value adjustment relating to land, as subsidiary has subsequently recorded this entry:	(CU10 000)	
		Allocate appropriate portion of revaluation surplus to non-controlling interest: (CU15 000 × 20%)	(CU3 000)	

What is this?
The group's share of the revaluation surplus in the subsidiary at 31 December 20x6 amounts to CU12 000.

The *pro-forma* journal entries are recorded on the consolidation worksheet as follows:

	P Ltd	S Ltd	Pro-forma at acquisition	Pro-forma since acquisition	Group
	Dr/(Cr) CU	Dr/(Cr) CU	Dr/(Cr) CU	Dr/(Cr) CU	Dr/(Cr) CU
Equity:					
Ordinary share capital	(240 000)	(120 000)	120 000		(240 000)
Revaluation surplus	(200 000)	(50 000)	25 000	10 000	(212 000)
				2 000	
				1 000	
Retained earnings (1 January 20x6)	(500 000)	(190 000)	115 000	15 000	(560 000)
Assets:					
Land	500 000	110 000	10 000	(10 000)	610 000
Other net assets (excluding investments)	470 000	450 000			920 000
Investment in S Ltd	320 000		(320 000)		–
Non-controlling interest			(54 000)	►(58 000)	(112 000)
Goodwill			104 000		104 000
Profit or loss:					
Revenue	(840 000)	(600 000)			(1 440 000)
Expenses	325 000	314 000			639 000
Tax expense	165 000	86 000			251 000
Non-controlling interest in profit				40 000	40 000

Refer to analysis of equity:
(CU15 000 + 2 000+ 1 000 + 40 000) = CU58 000.

The total of all the adjustments in the *pro-forma* journal entry column should **balance out to zero** as all of the journal entries balance. The total of the adjustments to **non-controlling shareholders** is equal to the total on the analysis of equity.

The trial balances of the parent and subsidiary (**starting point**) do not include any balance relating to non-controlling shareholders and therefore *pro-forma* journal entries are required for every adjustment making up the balance of non-controlling interest on the consolidated statement of financial position (**end point**).

Consolidated statement of profit or loss and other comprehensive income for P Ltd and its subsidiary for the period ended 31 December 20x6

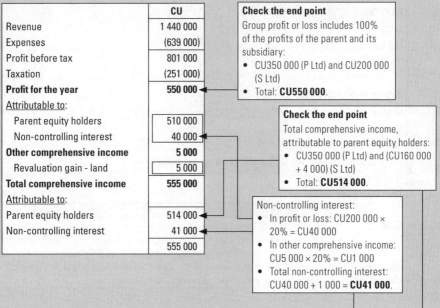

	CU
Revenue	1 440 000
Expenses	(639 000)
Profit before tax	801 000
Taxation	(251 000)
Profit for the year	550 000
Attributable to:	
Parent equity holders	510 000
Non-controlling interest	40 000
Other comprehensive income	5 000
Revaluation gain - land	5 000
Total comprehensive income	555 000
Attributable to:	
Parent equity holders	514 000
Non-controlling interest	41 000
	555 000

Check the end point
Group profit or loss includes 100% of the profits of the parent and its subsidiary:
- CU350 000 (P Ltd) and CU200 000 (S Ltd)
- Total: **CU550 000**.

Check the end point
Total comprehensive income, attributable to parent equity holders:
- CU350 000 (P Ltd) and (CU160 000 + 4 000) (S Ltd)
- Total: **CU514 000**.

Non-controlling interest:
- In profit or loss: CU200 000 × 20% = CU40 000
- In other comprehensive income: CU5 000 × 20% = CU1 000
- Total non-controlling interest: CU40 000 + 1 000 = **CU41 000**.

Consolidated statement of changes in equity for P Ltd and its subsidiary for the period ended 31 December 20x6

		Parent equity holders' interest			Non-controlling interest CU	Total CU
	Share capital CU	Revaluation surplus CU	Retained earnings CU	Total parent equity CU		
Opening balance at 1 January 20x6	240 000	208 000	560 000	1 008 000	71 000	1 079 000
Total comprehensive income		4 000	510 000	514 000	41 000	555 000
Closing balance at 31 December 20x6	240 000	212 000	1 070 000	1 522 000	112 000	1 634 000

Revaluation surplus (end point)
Opening balance: **CU208 000**
- P Ltd: CU200 000
- S Ltd: CU8 000 (refer to analysis of equity).
Closing balance: **CU212 000**
- P Ltd: CU200 000
- S Ltd: CU12 000 (refer to analysis of equity).

Retained earnings (end point)
Opening balance: **CU560 000**
- P Ltd: CU500 000
- S Ltd: CU60 000 (refer to analysis of equity).
Closing balance: **CU1 070 000**
- P Ltd: CU850 000
- S Ltd: CU220 000 (refer to analysis of equity).

Non-controlling interest (refer to analysis of equity and *pro-forma* journals)
- At acquisition date: CU54 000
- Since acquisition date: CU15 000 + 2 000 = CU17 000
- ∴ Opening balance = CU71 000.
- Current period: CU41 000
- ∴ Closing balance: **CU112 000**.

Consolidated statement of financial position for P Ltd and its subsidiary at 31 December 20x6

	CU
ASSETS	
Land	610 000
Net assets	920 000
Goodwill	104 000
	1 634 000
EQUITY AND LIABILITIES	
Share capital	240 000
Revaluation surplus	212 000
Retained earnings	1 070 000
Share capital and reserves attributable to parent equity holders	1 522 000
Non-controlling interest	112 000
Total equity and liabilities	**1 634 000**

Land

The land in the group statement of financial position is equal to the starting point (CU 500 000 + CU110 000), in other words, the balances in the current trial balances of P Ltd and S Ltd. This is because the fair value adjustment to land at acquisition was reversed when the subsidiary revalued the land. The group carrying amount for the land is now equal to the carrying amount of the subsidiary.

5. Effect on non-controlling interest of intra-group transactions

In Chapter 6, you learnt about the effect of intra-group transactions on the profits recognised by the group as well as the assets and liabilities. In that chapter, we only dealt with the situation where the subsidiary was wholly owned by the parent entity.

If a subsidiary is not wholly owned, intra-group transactions and balances should be reversed as usual, but the effect on non-controlling interest will depend on the nature of the transaction. In the case where an intra-group transaction is eliminated for disclosure purposes but the group profit or loss and net assets are not affected by the elimination, there will be no effect on the non-controlling interest.

However, if an unrealised profit was earned as a result of an intra-group transaction that is removed on consolidation, the non-controlling interest may be affected. This will depend on whether or not the unrealised profit was earned by the parent or the subsidiary in question. Where the unrealised profit was earned by the parent, the equity of the subsidiary is unaffected and therefore the non-controlling interest is not affected. However, if the unrealised profit was earned by the subsidiary, the equity of the subsidiary needs to be adjusted, together with the net assets, and the non-controlling interest is therefore also adjusted, based on their proportionate share of the unrealised profit (and the subsequent realisation of the profit).

Similar examples, which illustrate the effect of non-controlling interest, are included on the accompanying CD. Refer to the CD after you have worked through this chapter.

5.1 Effect on non-controlling interest of intra-group dividends

As discussed in Chapter 6, when a subsidiary distributes profits earned after acquisition (in other words, declares a dividend), the portion of the distribution relating to the parent's shareholding is recognised by the parent as dividends received. The parent includes any dividend income received from the subsidiary in revenue, together with any other dividends received. The subsidiary recognises dividends declared as an appropriation of the profits within retained earnings in the statement of changes in equity. The portion of the dividend declared by the subsidiary and received by the parent represents an intra-group transaction. From a group perspective, the only dividend declared or paid is the portion allocated to the non-controlling (outside) shareholders in the subsidiary. The intra-group portion of the dividend should thus be eliminated as with all intra-group transactions and the appropriate portion of the dividend that was declared should be allocated to non-controlling interest.

The dividend declared by the subsidiary to the parent must be eliminated in the consolidated financial statements as an intra-group transaction so that the only dividends that are reflected as being declared are those payable to the shareholders outside the group. In other words, the only dividends disclosed are those paid to the shareholders of the parent and the non-controlling shareholders of the subsidiary. The portion of the subsidiary's dividend attributable to the non-controlling shareholders is allocated to the non-controlling interest within equity, resulting in a reduction to the net credit balance for non-controlling shareholders representing their share of the net assets of the subsidiary. This adjustment to the non-controlling interest within equity represents the reduction in the net assets of the subsidiary resulting from a distribution of some of those net assets to the shareholders in the form of a dividend.

The *pro-forma* journal entry that follows is required to eliminate the intra-group dividends. In addition, it reflects the portion paid to the non-controlling interest.

Dr		Dividend income (parent's share)
Dr		Non-controlling interest (equity) (based on its shareholding)
	Cr	Dividends (100%)

The non-controlling shareholders' share of a dividend that has been declared but not paid should be shown as a liability, as there is an obligation to pay a party external to the group as a result of a past event (the declaration of the dividend).

Example

Dividends declared by a subsidiary

This example illustrates the elimination of intra-group dividends.

P Ltd acquired a controlling interest of 80% in S Ltd on 1 January 20x4, when the fair value of the identifiable net assets of S Ltd amounted to CU235 000. Non-controlling interest is measured at its share of the fair value of the net assets at the date of acquisition. At 31 December 20x4, the entities reported the profits and dividends shown below in their individual financial statements.

Statements of changes in equity for P Ltd and S Ltd for the year ended 31 December 20x4

	P Ltd			S Ltd		
	Share capital CU	Retained earnings CU	Total CU	Share capital CU	Retained earnings CU	Total CU
Balance at 1 January 20x4	240 000	90 000	330 000	120 000	115 000	235 000
Profit after tax		210 000	210 000		35 000	35 000
Less dividends		(150 000)	(150 000)		(10 000)	(10 000)
Balance at 31 December 20x4	240 000	150 000	390 000	120 000	140 000	260 000

P Ltd received 80% of the dividend declared by S Ltd, which is included in the profit after tax of P Ltd in the current reporting period. The effect of the elimination of the intra-group dividend results in a decrease in the profits of the parent. The portion of the dividend that was not received by the parent represents the profits of the subsidiary that have been distributed to the non-controlling interest. It should therefore be deducted from amounts distributable to non-controlling interest.

The following *pro-forma* journal entry eliminates the intra-group dividend declared by S Ltd:

			CU	CU
Dr		Dividend income	8 000	
Dr		Non-controlling interest (equity) (dividend)	2 000	
	Cr	Dividends (equity)		10 000

Elimination of dividend declared by S Ltd

In the consolidation worksheet, the effect of this *pro-forma* journal entry will be as follows:

	Dr/(Cr)	P Ltd (starting point) CU	S Ltd (starting point) CU	*Pro-forma* journals CU	Group (end point) CU
Dividend income		(8 000)		8 000	–
Dividend declared and paid			10 000	(10 000)	–
Non-controlling interest (equity)				2 000	2 000

Consolidated statement of changes in equity for the year ended 31 December 20x4

	Share capital CU	Retained earnings CU	Total equity attributable to parent equity holders CU	Non-controlling interest CU	Total equity CU
Balance at 1 January 20x4	240 000	90 000	330 000	–	330 000
Acquisition of subsidiary			–	① 47 000	47 000
Profit after tax		② 230 000	230 000	③ 7 000	237 000
Less dividends		(150 000)	(150 000)	(2 000)	►(152 000)
Balance at 31 December 20x4	**240 000**	**170 000**	**410 000**	**④ 52 000**	**462 000**

① CU235 000 × 20% = CU47 000 (non-controlling interest at acquisition of the subsidiary)

② (P: CU210 000 − 8 000 [dividend income]) + (S: CU35 000 × 80%) = CU230 000

③ Non-controlling interest in profit or loss of S Ltd: CU35 000 × 20% = CU7 000

④ Non-controlling interest in S Ltd: CU260 000 (equity of S Ltd) × 20% = CU52 000.

> **What is this?**
> The total dividends declared by the group include all dividends declared to equity holders outside the group, in other words, the parent's shareholders plus the non-controlling interest.

Think about it

Dividends in subsidiary attributable to non-controlling interest

The subsidiary was acquired on 1 January 20x4; thus the parent only shares in the profits of the subsidiary subsequent to the acquisition date. Group profit after tax of CU237 000 was determined as 100% of P Ltd, less the dividend received from S Ltd (CU8 000), plus 100% of the current year profit of S Ltd. This total profit includes the profit attributable to the non-controlling interest of CU7 000 (20% × CU35 000).

Notice that the group profit or loss for the year is reduced as a result of the elimination of the intra-group dividend, unlike other intra-group transactions, which have no effect on the group profit. This is because the one side of the adjustment reduces dividend income within profit or loss, but the other side is directly in retained earnings. However, the closing balance of retained earnings is unaffected by the elimination because the total group net assets are unchanged when dividends are paid from one group entity to another. The assets (usually cash) have simply changed location. The net assets of the subsidiary were in fact reduced, which is why it is appropriate that the non-controlling interest's share of the net assets be reduced as a result of the declaration of dividends.

Note that the dividend deducted from retained earnings is **only** that relating to the dividends of the parent. The dividend declared by S Ltd was partly eliminated against the profit of the parent. The other part was distributed to non-controlling interest and is shown as a reduction in their equity balance as opposed to a reduction of the group's retained earnings.

The total dividend declared by the group of CU152 000 is the parent's dividend of CU150 000 plus the portion of the subsidiary's dividend that was declared to the non-controlling interest of CU2 000.

5.2 Effect on non-controlling interest of intra-group inventory transfers

The sale of inventory between group entities was discussed in Chapter 6 in the context of wholly owned subsidiaries. It was illustrated that consolidation adjustments are required in a situation where one group entity has sold inventory to another group entity, resulting in the carrying amount of the inventory in the consolidated statement of financial position of the group being overstated by the mark-up on the sale. Where a parent owns 100% of the shares of a subsidiary, the unrealised profit on the transfer is eliminated in the group profit and the profit attributable to the parent equity holders will be adjusted by the full amount, regardless of whether the parent sold inventory to the subsidiary or vice versa because there are no non-controlling shareholders.

However, in a case where a subsidiary is partially owned, it becomes relevant which entity sold the inventory and therefore recognised the unrealised profit within its profit. The unrealised profit should be adjusted against the profit of the entity that recognised the profit on the intra-group sale. Where the parent sold inventory to the subsidiary at a mark-up, the unrealised profit should be adjusted against its profit. Consequently, the adjustments have no effect on the non-controlling shareholders. Where the subsidiary sells inventory at a mark-up to the parent, the same principles apply, but you should remember that the unrealised mark-up is included in the gross profit of the subsidiary. The adjustment for the unrealised profit should be made where the unrealised profit lies. Therefore, in this case of a sale from a subsidiary to the parent, the unrealised profit originated in the subsidiary and the adjustment should be done in the equity of the subsidiary. The non-controlling interest should be adjusted accordingly. This is illustrated in the example that follows, where the unrealised profit is in the subsidiary.

 Example

Elimination of intra-group inventory transactions (inventory sold by subsidiary to parent)

This example illustrates the elimination of inventory sold intra-group where the transfer is from the subsidiary to the parent. The unrealised profit is thus in the subsidiary, resulting in an adjustment to non-controlling interest. The example ignores any tax implications.

P Ltd acquired an 80% interest in the ordinary shares of S Ltd at 1 January 20x4, mainly with the purpose of obtaining control over an inventory purchase contract that S Ltd has had with an overseas supplier since its incorporation.

Since the date of acquisition, P Ltd has acquired inventory from S Ltd at its normal selling price less a discount of 20%. The normal selling price of inventory in S Ltd is determined to achieve a gross profit percentage of 50%.

During the financial year ending 31 December 20x4, S Ltd sold inventory to P Ltd for CU2 400. The entire balance of inventory was on hand in P Ltd at 31 December 20x4 and was sold in January 20x5.

The table that follows illustrates the relationships between the selling price, cost price and related gross profit of inventory transferred from S Ltd to P Ltd, and then to customers. This table illustrates what the amounts would be based on an item of inventory that originally cost the subsidiary CU50. These figures can also be used to express the ratio relationships between the various costs and the selling prices.

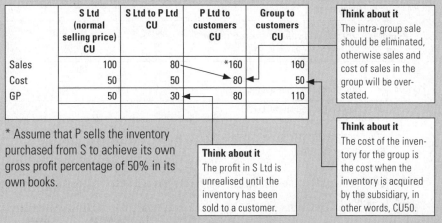

	S Ltd (normal selling price) CU	S Ltd to P Ltd CU	P Ltd to customers CU	Group to customers CU	**Think about it**
Sales	100	80	*160	160	The intra-group sale should be eliminated, otherwise sales and cost of sales in the group will be over-stated.
Cost	50	50	80	50	
GP	50	30	80	110	

* Assume that P sells the inventory purchased from S to achieve its own gross profit percentage of 50% in its own books.

Think about it
The profit in S Ltd is unrealised until the inventory has been sold to a customer.

Think about it
The cost of the inventory for the group is the cost when the inventory is acquired by the subsidiary, in other words, CU50.

The following consolidation worksheet represents the adjustments required for the reporting period ended 31 December 20x4:

	P Ltd (starting point)	S Ltd (starting point)	*Pro-forma* journals	Group (end point)
Sales	–	2 400	(2 400)	–
Cost of sales	–	(1 500)	(1 500)	–
O/Bal inventory	–	–		–
Purchases	2 400	1 500	(2 400)	(1 500)
C/Bal inventory	(2 400)	–	900	1 500
Gross profit	–	900		–

Think about it
How is the non-controlling interest's share of current year profits affected?
The unrealised profit is in the subsidiary. Thus, from the group's perspective, the profit of the subsidiary should be less in the current reporting period.
The non-controlling interest share of profits is therefore reduced by CU180 (CU900 × 20%).

Think about it
There are no sales or profit in the group as the inventory has not yet been sold to an outside customer.

The cost of the inventory (for the group) is CU1 500 (CU2 400 × 50/80). S Ltd sold this inventory to P Ltd for CU2 400. However, in the group, the cost is still CU1 500. The sale of the inventory by S Ltd to P Ltd should be eliminated as this is an intra-group sale. The end point should reflect that that the inventory is still held by the group, recognised at cost of CU1 500.

Pro-forma journal entries 20x4

			CU	CU
Dr		Sales	2 400	
	Cr	Cost of sales		2 400

Reversal of intra-group sales

			CU	CU
Dr		Cost of sales	900	
	Cr	Inventories		900

Removing unrealised profit in closing inventory

			CU	CU
Dr		Non-controlling interest (equity)	180	
	Cr	Non-controlling interest (P/L)		180

Reduction in non-controlling interest share of the subsidiary's profit or loss relating to the unrealised profit on inventory

The following consolidation worksheet represents the adjustments required for the reporting period ended 31 December 20x5:

	P Ltd	S Ltd	Pro-forma journals	Group
Sales	4 800	–	–	4 800
Cost of sales	(2 400)	–	900	(1 500)
O/Bal inventory	(2 400)	–	900	(1 500)
Purchases	–	–	–	–
C/Bal inventory	–	–	–	–
Gross profit	–	–		3 300

The inventory has now been sold to outside customers, thus a sale and profit should be recognised in the group. As consolidation adjustments are required to be repeated every year, it is necessary to repeat the adjustments relating to the prior year profits. The elimination of the sales and cost of sales is unnecessary as it would have no effect, but the decrease in the profits as well as the non-controlling interest's share of the profits needs to be repeated. The unrealised profit of CU900 that should be removed in the prior year should be recognised in the current year, because the inventory has now been sold to third parties.

The *pro-forma* journal entry that is used to reallocate the unrealised profit of CU900 from the prior year to the current year is shown below.

Pro-forma journal entries 20x5

			CU	CU
Dr		Retained earnings	900	
	Cr	Cost of sales		900

Recognising unrealised profit from the prior year

The non-controlling interest's share of prior year profits is also included in retained earnings. In order to reduce its share of prior year profits, it is therefore necessary to credit retained earnings and its share of current year profits are increased with a debit of CU180.

			CU	CU
Dr		Non-controlling interest (equity)	180	
	Cr	Retained earnings		180

Recognising non-controlling interest's share of unrealised profit from the prior year

It is not necessary to adjust the inventory asset because the inventory has been sold and is no longer included in the financial statements of either the parent or the subsidiary.

6. Other considerations when consolidating wholly or partly owned subsidiaries

The consolidation process results in the reporting of the financial information of the group as a single entity. Within this single entity, it is important that the same IFRS principles apply as for the separate financial statements of the individual legal entities, including the following requirements:

- The consolidated financial statements are prepared by the parent and must be reported at the same reporting date as that of the parent. Where the subsidiary then has a reporting date that differs from that of the parent, certain adjustments are required. Refer to Section 6.1 below.
- Transactions and events within the consolidated financial statements must be presented consistently in order to ensure faithful presentation and comparability of the information. Thus, where the subsidiary applies a different accounting policy for a specific transaction or event, an adjustment is required on consolidation in order to align the accounting policies to those of the group. Refer to Section 6.2 below.
- Consolidated financial statements must be prepared in line with the going concern principle and the parent needs to consider its share of a subsidiary with losses. Refer to Section 7 below.

6.1 Different reporting dates

Consolidated financial statements should be prepared for the same date as the reporting date of the parent. For example, if the parent has a 31 December reporting date, you should also prepare consolidated financial statements for that date.

 IFRS principles

Same reporting dates

The financial statements of the parent and its subsidiaries used in the preparation of the consolidated financial statements shall have the same reporting date (refer to IFRS10: B92, IFRS10: B93).

The reporting dates of subsidiaries are usually similar to the reporting date of their parent, which means that consolidated financial statements can be prepared at the same date. When the reporting date of a subsidiary is different from that of the parent, the subsidiary usually prepares additional financial statements at the same reporting date of the parent for consolidation purposes. However, the preparation of additional financial statements is costly and involves great effort. Where the preparation of additional financial statements for consolidation purposes is impractical and involves undue cost or effort, the financial statements of the subsidiary prepared for a different reporting date may be used, provided that the difference between the reporting dates is not greater than **three months**, and that the length of the reporting periods and the reporting dates are the same from period to period.

 Example

Subsidiary with a reporting date that is different from that of the parent

The parent's reporting date is 31 December. The parent acquired its 80% controlling interest in its subsidiary on 1 January 20x4. The subsidiary's reporting date is 30 June.
 The following is apparent from this scenario:
- The parent and its subsidiary do not have the same reporting date.
- The subsidiary's reporting date differs by more than three months from that of the parent.

In this case, the subsidiary has to change its reporting date to 31 December. This is feasible as the parent controls the subsidiary and therefore has the majority of voting rights to approve such a decision.

6.2 Uniform accounting policies

Where IFRS allows for alternative accounting policies to be adopted and an entity within the group uses accounting policies that differ from the accounting policies adopted in the consolidated financial statements for those types of transaction, that entity's financial statements should be adjusted **prior** to preparing consolidated financial statements. For example, if the parent accounts for investment property using the fair value model while a subsidiary uses the cost model, the parent will either instruct the subsidiary to change its accounting policy or on consolidation will adjust the investment property reported by the subsidiary to reflect the fair value model.

IFRS principles

Uniform accounting policies

Consolidated financial statements should be prepared using uniform accounting policies for similar transactions and other events in similar circumstances (refer to IFRS10:19).

Therefore, if a subsidiary applies an accounting policy that differs from that of the group, *pro-forma* journal entries are required to align the accounting policy (or policies) with that of the group. This is because the starting point (based on the subsidiary's accounting policy) and end point (based on the group accounting policy) differ.

Example

A subsidiary that applies the cost model for investment property when the group's policy is to use fair value

This example illustrates investment property in the subsidiary using the cost model and shows the consolidation adjustments necessary in order to apply the fair value model on consolidation. The example ignores any tax implications.

P Ltd owns 80% of the ordinary shares in S Ltd on 1 January 20x4. The group policy for investment property is fair value, while the subsidiary recognised its investment property at cost, less accumulated depreciation. S Ltd acquired the property on 2 January 20x4 at a cost of CU1 100 000 (of which CU200 000 related to the cost of the land and CU900 000 to the cost of the building). The useful life of the building was estimated at ten years and its residual value at CU100 000. These estimates have not changed. The annual depreciation relating to the building therefore amounts to CU80 000, while the land is not depreciated. The fair value of the property in S Ltd was estimated as follows at the respective reporting dates:
- At 31 December 20x5 (prior reporting date): CU1 600 000
- At 31 December 20x6 (current reporting date): CU1 850 000.

In the consolidated financial statements, the investment property of the subsidiary should be recognised at fair value since the acquisition date. This makes sense as the group policy is fair value and similar assets should be recognised using uniform accounting policies.

From the group's perspective, the cost of the property can be summarised as shown in the table below.

	S Ltd (starting point) (cost model) CU	Pro-forma adjustments CU	Group (end point) (fair value) CU
Cost (at 2 January 20x4)	1 100 000		1 100 000
Accumulated depreciation (for 2 years)	(160 000)	160 000	–
Prior year's fair value adjustments		500 000	500 000
Carrying amount at 31 December 20x5	940 000	660 000	1 600 000
Depreciation 20x6	(80 000)	80 000	–
Fair value adjustment 20x6		250 000	250 000
Carrying amount at 31 December 20x6	860 000	990 000	1 850 000

Pro-forma journal entries for the year ended 31 December 20x5

The subsidiary acquired its investment property after the acquisition date and therefore no adjustments are required relating to the fair value of the investment property at acquisition. The following *pro-forma* journal entries adjust the subsidiary's accounting policy to align with that of the group:

			CU	CU
Dr		Accumulated depreciation	160 000	
Dr		Investment property	500 000	
	Cr	Non-controlling interest (equity)		132 000
	Cr	Retained earnings		528 000

Adjustment to subsidiary's prior year profit, applying uniform accounting policy to investment property

> **What is this?**
> The credit to prior years' profits of the subsidiary includes the reversal of prior years depreciation of CU160 000 plus the fair value adjustments of CU500 000. The non-controlling interest receives a share of any increases in the value of the net assets of the subsidiary. Thus, attributable to non-controlling interest: CU660 000 × 20% = **CU132 000**.

The following *pro-forma* journal entry adjusts the accounting policy in the subsidiary to that applied in the group relating to the current year:

			CU	CU
Dr		Accumulated depreciation	80 000	
	Cr	Depreciation (P/L)		80 000

Reversal of current year's depreciation in subsidiary

			CU	CU
Dr		Investment property	250 000	
	Cr	Fair value adjustment (P/L)		250 000

Applying the group policy to investment property held by the subsidiary

The effect of the above transactions is that the subsidiary's profits for the current year increases by CU330 000 from the group's perspective. The effect of this adjustment on the non-controlling interest's share of the current year profits is an increase of CU66 000 (CU330 000 × 20%):

			CU	CU
Dr		Non-controlling interest (P/L)	66 000	
	Cr	Non-controlling interest (equity)		66 000

Allocation of non-controlling interest in current year profit

This example does not consider any tax implications. However, the increase in the carrying amount of investment property in the group financial statements may give rise to temporary differences, resulting in deferred tax adjustments on consolidation.

Example

A subsidiary that applies a different policy from that of the parent

This example illustrates the situation in which the subsidiary applies the revaluation model for owner occupied land and the group policy is to apply the cost model. The subsidiary's financial statements are therefore adjusted back to the cost model, including any related deferred tax that the subsidiary may have recognised.

P Ltd owns 80% of the ordinary shares in S Ltd. S Ltd acquired a property (comprising of its new head office and a plot of land) on 1 July 20x5. At that date, CU1 600 000 was attributed to the land. S Ltd revalued the land on 31 December 20x5 to its fair value (at that date) of CU2 000 000.

S Ltd would have processed the following journal entry to record the revaluation of the land:

			CU	CU
Dr		Land	400 000	
Dr		Deferred tax (OCI)	74 592	
	Cr	Deferred tax (liability) (CU400 000 × 28% × 66.6%)		74 592
	Cr	Revaluation gain (OCI)		400 000

Revaluation of land (and related deferred taxation)

> **What is this?**
> The subsidiary recognised deferred tax, resulting from the increase in the carrying amount of the land, at the capital gains tax inclusion rate of 66.6%.

As the group applies the cost model, the amounts recognised in the subsidiary (using the revaluation model) are adjusted on consolidation. The extracts that follow illustrate how the amounts recognised in the subsidiary (the starting point) are adjusted using *pro-forma* journal entries, resulting in the amounts in the group financial statements, using the cost model.

Land	S Ltd (starting point) CU'000	Pro-forma journals CU'000	Group (end point) CU'000
Cost	1 600		1 600
Revaluation (all post-acquisition)	400	(400)	–
Carrying amount	**2 000**		**1 600**

Related deferred taxation (liability)	S Ltd (starting point) CU'000	Pro-forma journals CU'000	Group (end point) CU'000
Balance at acquisition of land	–		–
Revaluation	74.6	(74.6)	–
Carrying amount	**74.6**		**–**

Revaluation surplus (equity)	S Ltd (starting point) CU'000	Pro-forma journals CU'000	Group (end point) CU'000
Balance as at 1 January 20x5	–		–
Other comprehensive income (OCI) (400 – 74.6)	325.4	(325.4)	–
Balance as at 31 December 20x5	**325.4**		**–**

Pro-forma journal entries

			CU	CU
Dr		Deferred tax (liability)	74 592	
Dr		Revaluation gain (OCI)	400 000	
	Cr	Land		400 000
	Cr	Deferred tax (OCI)		74 592

Reversal of revaluation (and related deferred taxation) as the policy is contrary to group policy

Think about it

Why is no adjustment to non-controlling interest required?

We have not allocated the non-controlling interest its share of the revaluation surplus. As the revaluation surplus balance should be nil, the non-controlling interests' share is nil.

By reversing the revaluation, the group revaluation surplus balance is nil. If we think about non-controlling interests:

- Starting point = Nil; no adjustment recorded by the subsidiary in its separate financial statements allocating the non-controlling interest share of revaluation
- End point = Nil
- Therefore no further *pro-forma* journals relating to non-controlling interests are required.

Think about it

What if the group applies the revaluation model?

Reserves relating to a subsidiary that are disclosed as part of the equity attributable to the shareholders of the parent must consist only of those reserves that are:
- Post-acquisition
- Attributable to the parent (in other words, in this case, the 80% attributable to P Ltd).

In the consolidated financial statements, the land is recognised at CU2 000 000. In addition to the *pro-forma* journal entries required to recognise the revaluation and related deferred tax, the portion of the revaluation surplus that is attributable to the non-controlling interest, amounting to CU65 082 ([CU400 000 − 74 592] × 20%) will be allocated separately, using the following *pro-forma* journal:

			CU	CU
Dr		Non-controlling interest (OCI)	65 082	
	Cr	Non-controlling interests (equity)		65 082

Allocation of revaluation surplus to non-controlling interests

7. Subsidiaries with accumulated deficits

A subsidiary is insolvent when the accumulated deficit (that is, an unfavourable balance on the retained earnings in the statement of financial position) exceeds the total equity, resulting in a net deficit in equity. This implies that the share capital and other reserves of the subsidiary are less than its accumulated deficit. A subsidiary may also be solvent, although it has an accumulated deficit if the share capital and other reserves exceed the accumulated deficit.

Depending on the commitments and arrangements made by the parent and other entities in the group, it is possible for some or all of the shareholders of an insolvent subsidiary to be held responsible for a part of the deficit, over and above the total shareholders' interest. This is possible where a shareholder (usually the parent) has guaranteed the liabilities or a certain liability of the subsidiary, or is also a creditor and has subordinated its claim as creditor until such time as the subsidiary becomes solvent again.

7.1 Accounting for an insolvent subsidiary

Where a parent has an insolvent subsidiary, it has to consider the most appropriate action after considering all of the factors and circumstances that gave rise to the insolvency. The parent may decide to take one of the following actions:
- Abandon the subsidiary
- Guarantee the liabilities of the insolvent subsidiary on its own
- Guarantee, with the non-controlling interest, the obligations of the subsidiary to third parties
- Subordinate its claim until such time as the subsidiary regains solvency

- Make loans to the subsidiary or increase the share capital investment in the subsidiary.

It is apparent that each of these situations will give rise to different accounting treatments and a different result. As with any financial decision, the accounting recording and reporting should result in a faithful representation of the facts and circumstances. For example, where the subsidiary is insolvent, consideration should be given to the recoverable amount of the investment in the subsidiary in the separate financial statements of the parent, resulting in the recognition of an impairment loss. Any impairment losses recognised by the parent in its separate financial statements are reversed on consolidation before any losses of the subsidiary are included, otherwise it would result in a double accounting of losses.

When consolidated financial statements are prepared, the same principles should apply. The parent should recognise the assets and liabilities of the subsidiary that it controls. Thus, if the parent lost control because the subsidiary is insolvent, consolidation is no longer appropriate.

Where a subsidiary becomes **insolvent after the acquisition date**, the accounting treatment of the subsidiary in the consolidated financial statements depends on the actual circumstances and actions taken by the parent. For example, if the parent decides to abandon the insolvent subsidiary in the sense that it does not provide any active financial support, the subsidiary will need to prepare its financial statements on the basis that it is no longer a going concern. This will result in the preparation of liquidation financial statements, where the assets and liabilities reflect their liquidation values. Alternatively, where the parent decides to provide support to the subsidiary, the subsidiary may be in a position to prepare its financial statements on a going concern basis. These statements can then be used for consolidation purposes.

7.2 Acquisition of an insolvent subsidiary

The parent must obviously have a very good reason for acquiring a controlling interest in an insolvent subsidiary. It may be that the parent is of the opinion that the unfavourable affairs of the subsidiary are only temporary and that the subsidiary can be converted into a profitable entity once it is supported by the group. Another reason may be that the parent wants to use the subsidiary as a vehicle for access into a specific market or to acquire control of a specific asset. It is thus logical to expect the parent to provide the unsecured creditors of the subsidiary with some or other form of security in order to prevent them from applying for the liquidation of the company. Such conditions and security should be recognised and disclosed in the separate financial statements of the parent.

The accumulated losses of a subsidiary are included in equity. The parent's share of such losses is eliminated at the acquisition date against the investment in the subsidiary. However, such losses may result in a negative (deficit balance) in non-controlling interest at the acquisition date. Even though the non-controlling interest is not required to cover the deficit, the fact is that **non-controlling interest** is an equity element and thus participates proportionately in the risks and rewards of the investment in the subsidiary. Thus, any negative total comprehensive income is attributable to the non-controlling interest, even if it results in a deficit balance.

IFRS principles

Non-controlling interest with deficit balance

The reporting entity attributes total comprehensive income to the owners of the parent and to the non-controlling interests, even if this results in the non-controlling interests having a deficit balance (refer to IFRS10: B94).

The net fair value of the identifiable assets and liabilities needs to be determined, as in the case of any other acquisition, in order to determine if the difference can be attributable to any specific asset or if it constitutes goodwill. Profits of the subsidiary after the acquisition date are treated as distributable profits in the consolidated financial statements insofar as the profits are available for distribution in the subsidiary to its shareholders. Refer to the example in the next section for an illustration of a situation where a subsidiary has post-acquisition profits.

7.3 Subsidiary with accumulated losses at the acquisition date

An accumulated loss in the subsidiary at the acquisition date forms a negative element in the equity of the subsidiary. The existence of such an unfavourable balance would certainly have influenced the price paid for the shares and the goodwill or gain on bargain purchase. The goodwill (or gain on bargain purchase) is determined by taking such an unfavourable balance into account.

The reserves relating to the subsidiary that are shown as part of the equity attributable to the shareholders of the parent consist of post-acquisition reserves and should only include the share attributable to the parent.

In addition, the retained earnings of the group (in other words, distributable reserves attributable to the shareholders of the parent) must reflect those reserves that could be distributed as a dividend by the group. Therefore, to the extent that these reserves arose in a subsidiary, they must reflect reserves that could be distributed as a dividend by the subsidiary. This is important because there are instances where the reserves may have arisen post-acquisition, but the subsidiary cannot distribute the reserves as a dividend.

Even though the group is entitled to these reserves and they should be presented as part of the group equity (that is, equity attributable to the shareholders of the parent), they cannot be reflected as part of retained earnings. Instead they are presented as part of **non-distributable reserves**. A transfer from retained earnings to a non-distributable reserve is thus required. This transfer arises at a group level and is facilitated through a *pro-forma* journal entry (or entries).

Example

A subsidiary with accumulated loss at acquisition date

This example illustrates the situation where a subsidiary has accumulated losses at acquisition, resulting in a transfer to non-distributable reserves when profits are subsequently earned.

P Ltd acquired 80% of the ordinary share capital of S Ltd on 1 January 20x4 for CU50 000. At that date, the equity of S Ltd comprised ordinary share capital of CU120 000 and an accumulated loss of CU60 000. The non-controlling interest was measured at its proportionate share of the net assets of S Ltd at the acquisition date. Note that the subsidiary is not insolvent at the acquisition date.

The trial balance of S Ltd for the financial year ended 31 December 20x5, which is the financial year end of S Ltd and P Ltd (and the P Ltd group), is presented below.

	Debit CU	Credit CU
Ordinary share capital (1 000 shares)	–	120 000
Retained earnings (1 January 20x5)	–	10 000
Sales	–	80 000
Cost of sales	20 000	–
Net operating costs	20 000	–
Taxation expense	10 000	–
Property, plant and equipment	130 000	–
Current assets	50 000	–
Current liabilities	–	20 000
	230 000	**230 000**

Note that S Ltd had an accumulated loss at acquisition. The following is an extract from the statement of changes in equity of S Ltd at 31 December 20x4 (prior year).

	Share capital CU	Retained earnings CU	Total CU
Balance at 1 January 20x4	120 000	(60 000)	60 000
Profit after tax		70 000	70 000
Balance at 31 December 20x4	120 000	10 000	130 000

Alternatively, you can consider the retained earnings general ledger account.

Retained earnings			
	CU		CU
As at 1 January 20x4	60 000		
		Profit for 20x4	70 000
As at 31 December 20x4	10 000		
	70 000		**70 000**

As can be seen from the above, there is a difference between the retained earnings of the subsidiary (CU10 000) and the post-acquisition retained earnings amounting to CU70 000 that can potentially be recognised by the group before allocating profits since the acquisition date to non-controlling interests. This difference is effectively the accumulated loss that existed at acquisition.

The retained earnings of the subsidiary (as recognised in its separate financial statements) represent the maximum amount that can be distributed by the subsidiary as a dividend. However, the full CU70 000 represents post-acquisition earnings and 80% thereof should be recognised as part of the equity attributable to the shareholders of P Ltd. As outlined above, this cannot be presented as part of retained earnings.

Analysis of equity of S Ltd

	Total CU	P Ltd (80%) CU	Non-controlling interest (20%) CU
At acquisition (1 January 20x4):			
Share capital	120 000	96 000	24 000
Accumulated loss	(60 000)	(48 000)	(12 000)
	60 000	48 000	12 000
Paid		50 000	
Goodwill		2 000	
Since acquisition:			
Profit for 20x4	70 000	56 000	14 000
Profit for 20x5 (CU80 000 – CU20 000 – CU20 000 – CU10 000)	30 000	24 000	6 000
Total	160 000	80 000	32 000

A transfer is required at an overall group level to a non-distributable reserve of CU48 000 (that is, CU60 000 × 80%, being P Ltd's share of the accumulated loss at acquisition).

Pro-forma journal entries at the acquisition date, thus at 31 December 20x4

			CU	CU
Dr		Ordinary share capital	120 000	
Dr		Goodwill	2 000	
	Cr	Retained earnings		60 000
	Cr	Investment in S Ltd		50 000
	Cr	Non-controlling interest (equity) (CU60 000 × 20%)		12 000

Elimination of equity at acquisition, investment in S Ltd and raising non-controlling interests at acquisition

Dr		Non-controlling interests (P/L) (CU70 000 × 20%)	14 000	
	Cr	Non-controlling interests (equity)		14 000

Post-acquisition prior year earnings allocated to non-controlling interests

Dr		Retained earnings	48 000	
	Cr	Non-distributable reserve		48 000

Transfer P Ltd's share of accumulated loss at acquisition date to non-distributable reserve

The accumulated loss at acquisition was a debit balance of CU60 000. In order to eliminate the equity at acquisition, a credit to retained earnings is required. The credit to retained earnings at acquisition of CU60 000 together with the retained earnings of the subsidiary of CU10 000 that is included in the starting point trial balance results in post-acquisition retained earnings of CU70 000. The portion that cannot be distributed as a dividend (in other words, CU48 000) needs to be transferred to a non-distributable reserve.

The other consolidation adjustments relating to the 20x5 reporting period and any subsequent periods would be performed in the usual way.

Test your knowledge

There is a list of learning objectives at the beginning of this chapter. Go back to this list and check whether you have achieved these outcomes. If not, reread the appropriate section.

Questions

Question 1

On 31 January 20x5, P Ltd acquired 60% (representing a controlling interest) of the issued share capital of S Ltd for CU40 000. The statements of financial position of the two companies at that date are set out below.

Statements of financial position at 31 January 20x5

	P Ltd CU	S Ltd CU
ASSETS		
Land	–	18 000
Plant	40 000	12 000
Investment in S Ltd	40 000	
Current assets	130 000	50 000
Inventory	50 000	30 000
Accounts receivable	42 000	20 000
Bank	38 000	
	210 000	80 000
CAPITAL AND LIABILITIES		
Share capital	100 000	50 000
Retained earnings	60 000	10 000
Shareholders' equity	160 000	60 000
Current liabilities	50 000	20 000
Accounts payable	50 000	15 000
Bank overdraft		5 000
	210 000	80 000

Assume that non-controlling interest is measured at its share of the net identifiable assets of the subsidiary at the acquisition date.

You are required to do the following:

1. Prepare the *pro-forma* journal entries for consolidation at 31 January 20x5.
2. Prepare the consolidated statement of financial position at 31 January 20x5, assuming that the identifiable assets and liabilities are fairly valued in the statement of financial position of the subsidiary at the date of acquisition.
3. Assume that S Ltd's profit for the period 1 February 20x5 to 31 December 20x5 amounted to CU20 000. What is the total non-controlling interest at 31 December 20x5?
4. In addition, assume that P Ltd's retained earnings amounted to CU80 000 at 31 December 20x5 (CU50 000 at 31 December 20x4). Determine the group profit for the year ended 31 December 20x5 and the profit attributable to the parent equity holders for the same period.

Suggested solution

1. Prepare the *pro-forma* journal entries for consolidation at 1 January 20x5.

			CU	CU
Dr		Share capital	50 000	
Dr		Retained earnings	10 000	
Dr		Goodwill	4 000	
	Cr	Non-controlling interest		24 000
	Cr	Investment in S Ltd		40 000

Elimination of investment in S Ltd at the acquisition date

Workings: Goodwill purchased

Non-controlling interest at acquisition date: (40% × CU60 000) = CU24 000
Goodwill = (Cash consideration + Non-controlling interest) – Fair value of net identifiable assets
CU40 000 + CU24 000 = CU64 000 – CU60 000 = CU4 000

2. Prepare the consolidated statement of financial position at 31 January 20x5, assuming that the identifiable assets and liabilities are fairly valued in the statement of financial position of the subsidiary at the date of acquisition.

P Ltd consolidated statement of financial position as at 31 January 20x5

	CU
ASSETS	
Non-current assets	74 000
Property, plant and equipment	70 000
Goodwill	4 000
Current assets	180 000
Inventories	80 000
Trade and other receivables	62 000
Cash and cash equivalents	38 000
Total assets	**254 000**
EQUITY AND LIABILITIES	
Capital and reserves	184 000
Share capital	100 000
Retained earnings	60 000
Non-controlling interest	24 000
Current liabilities	70 000
Trade and other payables	65 000
Bank overdraft	5 000
Total equity and liabilities	**254 000**

3. **Assume that S Ltd's profit for the period 1 February 20x5 to 31 December 20x5 amounted to CU20 000. What is the total non-controlling interest at 31 December 20x5?**

The equity of S Ltd will amount to CU80 000 at 31 December 20x5 (CU60 000 + CU20 000); the non-controlling interest in S Ltd will therefore amount to CU32 000 (CU80 000 × 40%).

Alternatively:

Non-controlling interest at 31 January 20x5:	CU24 000	(as above)
Share of profits of S Ltd since acquisition date:	CU8 000	(CU20 000 × 40%)
Total non-controlling interest at 31 December 20x5:	CU32 000	

4. **In addition, assume that P Ltd's retained earnings amounted to CU80 000 at 31 December 20x5 (CU50 000 at 31 December 20x4). Determine the group profit for the year ended 31 December 20x5 and the profit attributable to the parent equity holders for the same period.**

P Ltd's (the company) profit for the year: CU80 000 – CU50 000 = CU30 000

Note that P Ltd's retained earnings amounted to CU60 000 at 31 January 20x5. Refer to the statement of financial position at that date (per question). This means that P Ltd (the company) earned profit for the one-month period (1 January to 31 January 20x5) amounting to CU10 000 and the balance was earned for the period 1 February 20x5 to 31 December 20x5.

The group financial statements are prepared in accordance with the reporting date of the parent. Thus, the profit for the reporting period (year) ended 31 December 20x5 will be the full profit of P Ltd for the financial year plus S Ltd's profit since the acquisition date (for 11 months only).

		CU
P Ltd	12 months	30 000
S Ltd	11 months	20 000
Group profit for period		**50 000**
Attributable to:		
Parent equity holders		42 000
Non-controlling interest	(40% × CU20 000)	8 000

Check your answer

Profit attributable to parent equity holders:
P Ltd plus share of profits of subsidiary since acquisition date
CU30 000 + (60% × CU20 000) = CU42 000

Question 2

P Ltd paid CU560 000 for an 85% controlling interest in S Ltd on 1 July 20x0 (the acquisition date) ,when the total equity of S Ltd amounted to CU540 000. P Ltd considered the fair value of the net identifiable assets of S Ltd at CU600 000 at the acquisition date. The difference was attributable to the plant and machinery of S Ltd, which had a carrying amount at the acquisition date of CU90 000, a residual value of CU10 000 and four years of remaining useful life. The non-controlling interest is measured at its fair value of CU100 000. The goodwill is not impaired.

The following additional information is provided for the current reporting period, ending 30 June 20x5:

	P Ltd CU	S Ltd CU
Retained earnings at 1 July 20x0 (acquisition date)	100 000	50 000
Retained earnings for period 1 July 20x0 to 30 June 20x4	220 000	300 000
Total comprehensive income (current year)	480 000	150 000
Dividends declared and paid	(80 000)	(50 000)
Retained earnings at 30 June 20x5	720 000	450 000

P Ltd acquired some of its inventory from S Ltd subsequent to the acquisition date at a mark-up of 25% on cost. Inventory on hand in P Ltd at 30 June 20x5, acquired from S Ltd, amounted to CU11 875 (20x4: CU13 750).

You are required to do the following:
1. Calculate the total goodwill arising on consolidation at the acquisition date.
2. Show **only** the following *pro-forma* journal entries (including amounts attributable to non-controlling interest, if any) in order to prepare the consolidated financial statements of P Ltd for the year ended 30 June 20x5:
    a. Depreciation of S Ltd's plant and machinery since acquisition date
    b. Inventory of P Ltd acquired from S Ltd since acquisition date.
3. Calculate the total comprehensive income attributable to the non-controlling interest for the year ended 30 June 20x5.
4. Calculate the closing balance of retained earnings attributable to the parent equity holders at 30 June 20x5.

Suggested solution

1. **Calculate the total goodwill arising on consolidation at the acquisition date.**
    (CU560 000 + 100 000) = 660 000 − 600 000 = CU60 000 (full goodwill)

2. **Show only the following *pro-forma* journal entries (including amounts attributable to non-controlling interest, if any) in order to prepare the consolidated financial statements of P Ltd for the year ended 30 June 20x5:**

a. **Depreciation of S Ltd's plant and machinery since acquisition date**

			CU	CU
Dr		Retained earnings	60 000	
	Cr	Accumulated depreciation (w1)		60 000

Adjustment to group retained earnings since the acquisition date, relating to the increase in depreciation of plant and machinery

(w1): CU600 000 – CU540 000 = CU60 000

			CU	CU
Dr		Non-controlling interest (equity) (w2)	9 000	
	Cr	Retained earnings		9 000

Allocation of appropriate portion to non-controlling interest

(w2): CU60 000 × 15% = CU9 000

Note that the plant and machinery had an estimated remaining useful life of four years at the acquisition date, which was on 1 July 20x0. At 30 June 20x5, these assets are fully depreciated, thus there is no further adjustment to depreciation in the current year.

b. **Inventory of P Ltd acquired from S Ltd since acquisition date**

			CU	CU
Dr		Cost of sales (w1)	2 375	
	Cr	Inventory		2 375

Reversal of unrealised profit in inventory not yet sold at the reporting date

			CU	CU
Dr		Retained earnings	2 750	
	Cr	Cost of sales (w2)		2 750

Reversal of unrealised profit in opening inventory, realised in the current year

			CU	CU
Dr		Non-controlling interest (equity)	356	
Dr		Non-controlling interest in P/L (w3)	56	
	Cr	Retained earnings		412

Allocation of appropriate portion of unrealised profits in subsidiary to non-controlling interest

Workings

(w1): CU11 874 × $\frac{25}{125}$ = CU2 375

(w2): CU13 750 × $\frac{25}{125}$ = CU2 750

(w3): Net effect on current year profit: Increase of CU375 (CU2 750 – CU2 375)

CU375 × 15% = CU56.25 (rounded off to CU56)

3. **Calculate the total comprehensive income attributable to the non-controlling interest for the year ended 30 June 20x5.**

	CU
S Ltd profit (starting point)	150 000
Pro-forma journal entries: Cost of sales (opening inventory) (profit realised in current year)	2 750
Cost of sales (closing inventory) (profit unrealised at year end)	(2 375)
S Ltd from group perspective	150 375
Non-controlling interest in S Ltd profit (CU150 375 × 15%)	22 556

4. **Calculate the closing balance of retained earnings attributable to the parent equity holders at 30 June 20x5.**

	CU
P Ltd: Retained earnings (starting point)	720 000
S Ltd: Retained earnings (starting point) Less: Retained earnings at acquisition date	450 000 (50 000)
Pro-forma journal entries: Depreciation (cumulative)	(60 000)
Cost of sales (closing inventory) profit unrealised	(2 375)
S Ltd: Retained earnings from group perspective	337 625
Attributable to parent equity holders (CU337 625 × 85%)	286 981
Retained earnings closing balance attributable to parent equity holders (CU720 000 + CU286 981)	1 006 981

Question 4

P Ltd acquired 60% of S Ltd on 1 March 20x0 when the share capital of S Ltd was CU100 000 and retained earnings was CU10 000. S Ltd has always applied the first-in first-out (FIFO) method to measure the cost of its inventory. The group's accounting policy for similar inventories is weighted average.

The inventory carrying amounts in S Ltd can be summarised as follows:

	FIFO CU	WAC CU
At 28 February 20x3	45 000	42 000
At 28 February 20x4	48 000	49 000
At 28 February 20x5	55 000	51 500

Prepare the *pro-forma* journal entries relating to inventory that are required when preparing the group financial statements for the year ended 28 February 20x5 insofar as possible using the information provided. Assume that a tax rate of 28% applies in each of the reporting periods.

Suggested solution

		CU	CU
Dr	Cost of sales	1 000	
Cr	Deferred tax (P/L) (w1)		280
Cr	Retained earnings		720

Applying group accounting policy for inventory in S Ltd's prior year profits, including tax implications

(w1): CU1 000 × 28% = CU280

		CU	CU
Dr	Cost of sales (w2)	3 500	
Cr	Inventory		3 500

Applying group accounting policy for inventory in S Ltd's current year profits, before taxation
(w2): CU55 000 − CU51 500 = CU3 500

		CU	CU
Dr	Deferred tax (asset) (w3)	980	
Cr	Deferred tax (P/L)		980

Taxation implications resulting from applying group accounting policy for inventory in S Ltd
(w3): CU3 500 × 28% = CU980

		CU	CU
Dr	Retained earnings (w4)	288	
Dr	Non-controlling interest (equity)	1 008	
Cr	Non-controlling interest (P/L) (w5)		1 296

Allocation of attributable portion to non-controlling interest, relating only to the application of the group accounting policy for inventor, according to the pro-forma *journal entries above*
(w4): CU720 × 40% = CU288
(w5): [CU1 000 + CU3 500] × 72% × 40% = CU1 296

Workings

Illustration of adjustments required on consolidation, from the starting point (according to S Ltd's financial statements) to the end point, the group financial statements at 28 February 20x5

	S Ltd (starting point) FIFO	Adjustments (before tax)	Group (end point) WAC
Dr/(Cr)	CU	CU	CU
Equity:			
Retained earnings (prior year's cumulative profit)	(48 000)	(1 000)	(49 000)
Current year profit		4 500	
Retained earnings (cumulative at 28 February 20x5)	(55 000)	3 500	(51 500)
Assets:			
Inventory at 28 February 20x5	55 000	(3 500)	51 500

Extract from analysis of equity of S Ltd, relating only to the application of the group accounting policy for S Ltd's inventory

	Total CU	P Ltd CU	Non-controlling interest CU
Retained earnings	720	432	288
Change in inventory opening balance	1 000		
Less: Deferred tax	(280)		
Current profit	(3 240)	(1 944)	(1 296)
Change in inventory opening balance	(1 000)		
Change in inventory closing balance	(3 500)		
Less: Deferred tax	1 260		
			(1 008)

Case study exercises

Scenario 1

This scenario is the same as the case study in Chapter 4, except that this is a partly held subsidiary. You should think about how the process of consolidation is the same, but you need to recognise the non-controlling interest in the subsidiary separately.

P Ltd acquired 70% of the issued ordinary share capital of S Ltd on 1 January 20x5. The identifiable assets and liabilities of S Ltd were considered fairly valued at the date of acquisition.

Statements of financial position of P Ltd and S Ltd on 31 December 20x5

	P Ltd CU'000	S Ltd CU'000
ASSETS		
Plant and machinery (Cost: CU400 000; CU350 000)	300	200
Investment in S Ltd	280	–
Current assets	340	500
	920	700
CAPITAL AND LIABILITIES		
Share capital	200	100
Retained earnings	620	500
Shareholders' equity	820	600
Current liabilities	100	100
	920	700

Statements of changes in shareholders equity for the year ended 31 December 20x5

	P Ltd		S Ltd	
	Share capital CU'000	Retained earnings CU'000	Share capital CU'000	Retained earnings CU'000
Opening balance	200	400	100	200
Net profit for the year		370		300
Less: Dividends		(150)		–
Closing balance	**200**	**620**	**100**	**500**

Statements of profit or loss and other comprehensive income of P Ltd and S Ltd for the year ended 31 December 20x5

	P Ltd CU'000	S Ltd CU'000
Gross revenue	1 870	1 500
Net operating costs	(1 050)	(920)
Profit from ordinary activities before interest	820	580
Interest expense	(200)	(50)
Profit on ordinary activities before taxation	620	530
Taxation expense	(250)	(230)
Profit for the year	**370**	**300**

Net operating costs include depreciation of CU50 000 for P Ltd and CU50 000 for S Ltd for the year, respectively.

You are required to do the following:

1. Answer the following questions before starting with the preparation of the consolidated financial statements:
   - What is the non-controlling interest at the acquisition date?
   - What is the goodwill acquired, if any?
   - What is the reporting date?
   - What is the non-controlling interest at the reporting date?
2. Show the *pro-forma* journal entries required in order to prepare the consolidated statements of P Ltd and its subsidiary at 1 January 20x5 (the date of acquisition).
3. Prepare the consolidated statement of profit or loss and other comprehensive income, the statement of changes in equity and the consolidated statement of financial position for P Ltd and its subsidiary at 31 December 20x5. Your answer should include the note disclosure relating to property, plant and equipment.

Scenario 2

Refer to the abridged financial statements of P Ltd and its subsidiary S Ltd below.

Statements of financial position as at 30 June 20x5

	P Ltd CU	S Ltd CU
ASSETS		
Property, plant and equipment	240 000	450 000
At cost	400 000	600 000
Accumulated depreciation	(160 000)	(150 000)
Investment in S Ltd	330 000	
Trade receivables	405 000	105 000
Inventories	80 000	165 000
Bank	55 000	
Total assets	**1 110 000**	**720 000**
EQUITY AND LIABILITIES		
Share capital	300 000	240 000
Retained earnings	375 000	340 000
Long-term borrowings	225 000	
Trade and other payables	210 000	80 000
Bank overdraft		60 000
Total equity and liabilities	**1 110 000**	**720 000**

Statements of profit or loss and other comprehensive income for the year ended 30 June 20x5

	P Ltd CU	S Ltd CU
Revenue (including dividend income)	945 000	1 500 000
Cost of sales	(472 500)	(750 000)
Gross profit	472 500	750 000
Other expenses	(102 500)	(450 000)
Profit before tax	370 000	300 000
Income tax expense	(112 000)	(120 000)
Profit for the year	**258 000**	**180 000**

Extracts from statements of changes in equity for the year ended 30 June 20x5

	Retained earnings	
	P Ltd CU	S Ltd CU
Balance at 1 July 20x4	225 000	180 000
Profit for the year	258 000	180 000
Ordinary dividend	(108 000)	(20 000)
Balance at 30 June 20x5	**375 000**	**340 000**

Additional information

P Ltd acquired its 80% controlling interest in S Ltd on 1 January 20x2, when the equity of S Ltd consisted of share capital of CU240 000 and retained earnings amounted to CU135 000. Accumulated depreciation for S Ltd amounted to CU50 000 at the acquisition date.

The carrying amounts of the identifiable assets acquired and liabilities assumed at the acquisition date were shown at their acquisition-date fair values, as determined in terms of IFRS3, except for inventory, which was undervalued by CU10 000. All of the inventory was sold within the reporting period that followed. It is the entity's policy to measure any non-controlling interest at its proportionate share of the acquiree's identifiable net assets.

Ignore tax implications.

You are required to do the following:

1. Show all of the *pro-forma* journal entries necessary to prepare the consolidated financial statements of P Ltd and its subsidiary at 30 June 20x5.
2. Prepare the consolidated financial statements of P Ltd and its subsidiary for the year ended 30 June 20x5.

Suggested solution

Scenario 1

1. **Answer the following questions before starting with the preparation of the consolidated financial statements:**
   - **What is the non-controlling interest at the acquisition date?**
     The non-controlling interest at the acquisition date is its share of the fair value of the net identifiable assets, determined as follows:
     Fair value of net identifiable assets at the acquisition date: CU300 000 (equity at 1 January 20x5; no further adjustments are necessary, as the net assets were considered fairly valued at the acquisition date, thus net assets = equity at acquisition date)
     Non-controlling interest: CU300 000 × 30% = CU90 000.
   - **What is the goodwill acquired, if any?**
     Goodwill is the residual between the net consideration paid plus the non-controlling interest and the fair value of the net identifiable assets acquired. This is calculated as follows:
     Consideration paid: CU280 000 (investment in S Ltd)
     Non-controlling interest: CU90 000 (as calculated above)
     ∴ Goodwill acquired: (CU280 000 + CU90 000) = CU370 000 – CU300 000 = CU70 000.

Think about it

What is the equity acquired at the acquisition date?

	CU
Share capital	100 000
Retained earnings	200 000
FV of net assets	300 000
P Ltd's share of net assets (70% × CU300 000)	210 000
Investment	280 000
∴ Goodwill	70 000

- **What is the reporting date?**
  The current reporting date is 31 December 20x5. This means that we have to prepare the consolidated financial statements at this date and that S Ltd should be consolidated from 1 January 20x5 onwards.
- **What is the non-controlling interest at the reporting date?**
  As there are no other adjustments relating to the net assets of S Ltd arising on consolidation, the non-controlling interest in the subsidiary at the reporting date amounts to:
  CU600 000 (equity of S Ltd) × 30% = CU180 000.

2. **Show the *pro-forma* journal entries required in order to prepare the consolidated statements of P Ltd and its subsidiary at 1 January 20x5 (the date of acquisition).**

Pro-forma journal entries at 31 December 20x5

			CU	CU
Dr		Share capital	100 000	
Dr		Retained earnings	200 000	
Dr		Goodwill arising on consolidation	70 000	
	Cr	Non-controlling interest		90 000
	Cr	Investment		280 000

Elimination of investment in subsidiary, with equity of subsidiary at the acquisition date

			CU	CU
Dr		Accumulated depreciation (w1)	100 000	
	Cr	Plant and machinery		100 000

Elimination of accumulated depreciation relating to assets of subsidiary acquired at acquisition date
(w1): CU350 000 – (200 000 + 50 000) = CU100 000

3. **Prepare the consolidated statement of profit or loss and other comprehensive income, the statement of changes in equity and the consolidated statement of financial position for P Ltd and its subsidiary at 31 December 20x5. Your answer should include the note disclosure relating to property, plant and equipment.**

Consolidated statement of profit or loss and other comprehensive income for P Ltd and its subsidiary for year ended 31 December 20x5

		CU'000
Gross revenue	(1 870 + 1 500)	3 370
Net operating costs	(1 050 + 920)	(1 970)
Profit on ordinary activities		1 400
Interest expense	(200 + 50)	(250)
Profit before taxation		1 150
Taxation expense	(250 + 230)	(480)
Net profit for year		**670**
Attributable to:		
Parent equity holders	(370 + (70% × 300))	580
Non-controlling interest	(30% × 300)	90

Consolidated statement of changes in shareholders' equity for P Ltd and its subsidiary for year ended 31 December 20x5

	Parent equity interest			Non-controlling interest CU'000	Total equity CU'000
	Share capital CU'000	Retained earnings CU'000	Total CU'000		
Balance at the beginning of the year	200	400	600	–	600
Acquisition of subsidiary				90	90
Profit for the year		580	580	90	670
– Dividends		(150)	(150)		(150)
Balance at the end of the year	**200**	**830**	**1 030**	**180**	**1 210**

Consolidated statement of financial position for P Ltd and its subsidiary at 31 December 20x5

		CU'000
ASSETS		
Plant and machinery (carrying amount)	(See note disclosure)	500
Goodwill		70
Net current assets	(340 + 500)	840
Total assets		**1 410**
CAPITAL AND LIABILITIES		
Share capital		200
Retained earnings	(P: 620 + [70% of S]: 210)	830
Parent equity interests		1 030
Non-controlling interest		180
Total capital and reserves		1 210
Current liabilities	(100 + 100)	200
Total capital and liabilities		**1 410**

Extracts from the notes to the consolidated financial statements of P Ltd and its subsidiary for the year ended 31 December 20x5

Plant and machinery note:	CU'000
Cost:	
Balance at beginning of the year	400
Additions	250
Balance at end of the year	650
Accumulated depreciation:	
Balance at beginning of the year	50
Depreciation (50 + 50)	100
Balance at end of the year	150
Carrying amount at end of the year	**500**

Scenario 2

1. **Show all of the *pro-forma* journal entries necessary to prepare the consolidated financial statements of P Ltd and its subsidiary at 30 June 20x5.**

Pro-forma journal entries

			CU	CU
Dr		Share capital	240 000	
Dr		Retained earnings	135 000	
Dr		Inventory	10 000	
Dr		Goodwill acquired	22 000	
	Cr	Investment in S Ltd		330 000
	Cr	Non-controlling interest (equity)		77 000

Elimination of investment in subsidiary at acquisition date

			CU	CU
Dr		Accumulated depreciation	50 000	
	Cr	Property, plant and equipment		50 000

Elimination of accumulated depreciation relating to assets of subsidiary at acquisition date

			CU	CU
Dr		Retained earnings	10 000	
	Cr	Inventory		10 000

Reversal of fair value adjustment to inventory at acquisition when inventory was sold subsequently

			CU	CU
Dr		Retained earnings (w1)	7 000	
	Cr	Non-controlling interest (equity)		7 000

Allocation of retained earnings since acquisition date, to non-controlling interest in subsidiary
(w1): (CU180 000 – 135 000 – 10 000) × 20%

			CU	CU
Dr		Non-controlling interest (P/L) (w2)	36 000	
	Cr	Non-controlling interest (equity)		36 000

Allocation of current year profits of subsidiary to non-controlling interest
(w2): CU180 000 × 20%

			CU	CU
Dr		Dividend income	16 000	
Dr		Non-controlling interest (equity)	4 000	
	Cr	Dividends declared		20 000

Elimination of inter-company dividend and allocation of non-controlling interest portion

2. Prepare the consolidated financial statements of P Ltd and its subsidiary for the year ended 30 June 20x5.

Consolidated statement of financial position of P Ltd as at 30 June 20x5

	CU
ASSETS	
Property, plant and equipment	690 000
At cost (400 000 + 600 000 – 50 000)	950 000
Accumulated depreciation (160 000 + 150 000 – 50 000)	(260 000)
Goodwill	22 000
Trade receivables	510 000
Inventories	245 000
Bank	55 000
Total assets	**1 522 000**
EQUITY AND LIABILITIES	
Share capital (R1 ordinary shares)	300 000
Retained earnings (375 000 + 156 000)	531 000
Non-controlling interest (77 000 + 7 000 + 36 000 – 4 000)	116 000
Total equity	947 000
Long-term borrowings	225 000
Trade and other payables	290 000
Bank overdraft	60 000
Total equity and liabilities	**1 522 000**

Consolidated statement of profit or loss and other comprehensive income for the year ended 30 June 20x5

	CU
Revenue (945 000 + 1 500 000 – 16 000)	2 429 000
Cost of sales (472.500 + 750 000)	(1 222 500)
Gross profit	1 206 500
Other expenses (102.500 + 450 000)	(552 500)
Profit before tax	654 000
Tax expense (112 000 + 120 000)	(232 000)
Profit for the year (w1)	**422 000**
Attributable to:	
Parent equity holders	386 000
Non-controlling interest (w2)	36 000
Total comprehensive income	**422 000**

(w1): Proof of group profit: 258 000 – 16 000 (P) + 180 000 (S) = CU422 000

(w2): As per analysis of equity: 180 000 × 20% = CU36 000

Consolidated statement of changes in equity for the year ended 30 June 20x5

	Share capital CU	Retained earnings CU	Total parent equity interest CU	Non-controlling interest CU	Total equity CU
Balance at 1 July 20x4	300 000	(w3) 253 000	553 000	(w4) 84 000	637 000
Profit for the year		386 000	386 000	36 000	422 000
Ordinary dividends		(108 000)	(108 000)	(4 000)	(112 000)
Balance at 30 June 20x5	**300 000**	(w5) **531 000**	**831 000**	**116 000**	**947 000**

(w3): Retained earnings opening balance: 225 000 (P) + 36 000 – 8 000 (S) = CU253 000
(w4): Non-controlling interest opening balance: 77 000 + 9 000 – 2 000 = CU84 000
(w5): Proof of retained earnings closing balance: 375 000 (P) + 156 000 (S) = CU531 000

Workings

Analysis of equity of S Ltd

	Total CU	P Ltd's interest (80%)		Non-controlling interest (20%) CU
		At acquisition CU	Since acquisition CU	
At acquisition date:				
Share capital	240 000			
Retained earnings	135 000			
Inventory	10 000			
Total equity	385 000	308 000		77 000
Cost of investment		330 000		
Goodwill acquired		**22 000**		
Since acquisition date:				
Retained earnings	45 000		36 000	9 000
Inventory sold	(10 000)		(8 000)	(2 000)
Current year:				
Profit for the year	180 000		144 000	36 000
Dividends paid	(20 000)		(16 000)	(4 000)
Total	**580 000**		**156 000**	**116 000**

Consolidation: Subsidiary with preference shares

8

The following topics are included in this chapter:

- The different rights attached to preference shares
- The implications on consolidation when the subsidiary has different classes of shares
- How to recognise preference shares issued by the subsidiary in the group financial statements
- The implications on consolidation when the parent has acquired all, some or none of the preference shares
- The implications on consolidation when cumulative preference dividends are in arrears.

Learning objectives

By the end of this chapter, you should be able to:
- Identify the different rights attached to preference shares
- Explain the implications on consolidation when the subsidiary has different classes of shares
- Understand that, when preparing consolidated financial statements, it is necessary to allocate profits of the subsidiary to the different classes of shareholders
- Understand how preference shares issued by a subsidiary are recognised in the group financial statements
- Understand the implications on consolidation when cumulative preference dividends relating to preference shares in a subsidiary are in arrears
- Prepare consolidated financial statements when the subsidiary has issued preference shares and the parent has acquired all, some or none of the preference shares.

1. Subsidiaries with ordinary and preference shares

When preparing group financial statements, it is important to identify the nature of the shares that are outstanding because the subsidiary may have more than one class of shares. This may be relevant for determining whether control is established.

In addition, you need to be able to identify whether these different classes of shares are classified as debt or equity. Particular attention must be paid to the rights attached to the different classes of shares. For example, an entity may have outstanding ordinary and preference shares, with the preference shares comprising different types of preference shares, each attaching different preference rights with respect to receiving dividends. If the share capital of a subsidiary consists of **more than one class of shares**, which have been classified as equity, the total owners' equity must be allocated among the different classes of capital in accordance with the particular rights attached to them.

Example

Subsidiary with preference shares

S Ltd has 100 000 ordinary shares and 50 000 preference shares in issue. P Ltd acquired a controlling interest of 80% in S Ltd through its acquisition of 80 000 of the ordinary shares in S Ltd. P Ltd does not hold any of the preference shares in S Ltd.

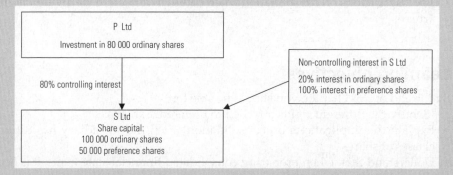

Figure 8.1 Group structure illustrating equity of subsidiary

Note that the voting rights are attached to the ordinary shares. The preference shareholders generally have no voting rights. (However, subject to the entity's memorandum of incorporation, preference shares may carry voting rights in certain circumstances.)

Preference shares may only be issued when an entity has previously issued shares with voting rights, which are usually referred to as ordinary shares. The rights attached to such preference shares are usually prescribed and may consist of the following:

- **Preferential rights in respect of dividends**: In this case, preference shareholders have a preferential claim to a dividend that is generally stipulated and fixed, whilst the balance is attributable to the ordinary shareholders. As is the case with ordinary shares, preference shareholders cannot legally lay claim to their share of the profit before a preference dividend has been declared. However, where the preference shares are cumulative, ordinary shareholders may not receive a dividend in the current reporting period unless a preference dividend is declared. The preference sharehold-ers can, therefore, lay claim to a portion of the profits of the entity until such time as the dividend is declared.

- **Cumulative dividends**: A cumulative preferential right exists to the current and arrears preference dividends that have not yet been declared, and such arrears dividends should be declared before a current dividend is declared to the preference equity holders as well as any other class of shares.
- **Non-cumulative dividends**: These shareholders are not entitled to payment of arrear dividends.

• **Preferential rights in respect of repayment of capital**: Preference shareholders usually enjoy preference to repayment of capital on liquidation. This should be an express provision relating to the shares when they are registered and issued.

• **Participating**: Preference shareholders are entitled to the fixed preference dividend as well as a share of the remaining portion of the profits of the entity. This implies that preference shareholders first receive the preference dividend, and then, after an ordinary dividend has been declared, the preference shareholders share in the remain-ing profits of the subsidiary. The profits of the subsidiary are, in the case of consolidation, allocated to both the ordinary and preference shareholders in accordance with the participation rights attached.

• **Voting rights**: Preference shares normally do not carry voting rights. However, in some cases and when specifically expressed, preference shares may have the right to vote while preference dividends are in arrears and remain unpaid. Such a situation may have significant consequences when you are establishing control as the additional voting rights of the preference shareholders may result in the existing parent not having a majority of voting rights and no longer having control (resulting in a loss of control). This situation seldom occurs in practice.

There are other types of preference shares as well, including the following:

• **Convertible preference shares**: The shareholder has the right, subject to certain stated conditions, to convert the shares into other shares of the company, usually ordinary shares.

• **Redeemable preference shares**: The shares are redeemable at a future date. Depending on the conditions of redemption, these shares should be classified as either equity or a liability. If the redemption conditions meet the definition and recognition criteria of a liability, in that there is a present obligation to redeem the shares (generally for cash) at a future date, and in that the amount can be measured and settlement is probable, the redeemable preference shares are classified as a **liability**. Any such redeemable shares are therefore not equity and should be recognised in the group financial statements as a liability. Refer to Chapter 8 in *Financial Accounting: IFRS Principles* (4e) by Lubbe, Modack and Watson for a further discussion of the classification of redeemable preference shares as a financial liability.

For consolidation purposes, the preferential claim of preference shareholders is probably the most important right attached to preference shares as the profits of the subsidiary need to be allocated between the different equity holders. This means that the profits are allocated to both ordinary and preference shareholders based on their respective rights.

In terms of paragraph B95 of IFRS10, if a subsidiary has issued **cumulative preference shares** that are held by non-controlling interests and classified as equity, the parent computes its share of profit or loss **after** adjusting for the dividends on such shares, irrespective of whether or not the dividends have been declared. This makes sense as the preference shareholders have the right to receive that portion of the profits of the subsidiary in the form of a dividend. Until such a dividend is declared and paid, that portion of the profits is attributable to the preference shareholders.

Think about it
Why is this important?

If the preference shares are equity, then the preference shares are another form of equity shares issued by the subsidiary. For the group entity, these are not preference shares, that is, shares of the parent entity. The starting point for the preparation of the group financial statements includes 100% of the trial balance of the subsidiary. This includes the subsidiary's preference share capital. The subsidiary's preference share capital should therefore be eliminated on consolidation through *pro-forma* journal entries.

- If the parent holds any of these preference shares, an amount should be eliminated against the investment in the parent.
- If any of these preference shares are not held by the parent, this amount represents equity of the subsidiary that is not held by the parent. This amount is reflected as the non-controlling interest and should be allocated to those equity holders. If the preference shares were issued before the date at which the parent acquires a controlling interest in the subsidiary, the fair value of the preference shares should be determined at the date of acquisition and should be included with the balance of non-controlling interest in equity.

Remember that dividends do not represent contractual amounts and also that equity represents the residual, that is, the amount left over that is attributed to the owners of the entity. However, where these preference equity holders have a right to a cumulative dividend, it implies that a portion of the profits of the subsidiary are attributable to the preference equity holders in the year that the subsidiary has earned those profits, irrespective of whether or not the related dividend has been declared. This means that you need to attribute the appropriate portion of the profits of the subsidiary to the preference equity holders (or preference owners) prior to attributing the rest of the profits to the ordinary equity holders (or ordinary owners).

2. Principle of attributable profits to preference equity holders

When preparing consolidated financial statements, you should pay particular attention to the **rights** attached to preference shares. Where the share capital of a subsidiary consists of more than one class of shares, the total owner's equity must be allocated between the different classes of capital in accordance with the particular rights attached to each. Thus, before allocating the equity between the parent and non-controlling interest, you must first allocate the equity between the different classes of shares, for example:

- Preference shareholders' equity (share capital and profits [only if they have a right to share in profits, otherwise only when dividends are declared]):
  - Attributable to the parent equity holders
  - Attributable to non-controlling interests
- Ordinary shareholders' equity (share capital and profits):
  - Attributable to the parent equity holders
  - Attributable to non-controlling interests.

When allocating profits, the portion attributable to the preference shareholders is allocated first. The balance is then attributable to the ordinary shareholders.

Example

Allocation of profits of an entity with cumulative preference shares

S Ltd issued 1 000 ordinary shares at its incorporation date of 1 January 20x3. On 1 January 20x5, it issued 200 preference shares at CU3 each, classified as cumulative preference shares, with no voting rights and a preferential right to receive 10% cumulative dividends per annum. The entity has retained earnings amounting to CU7 000 at 31 December 20x5 and current year profit after tax of CU5 000. The entity has not declared any dividends for the current and prior reporting periods.

As a first step, the profits of the entity should be allocated between its **ordinary** and **preference** equity holders. The reason for this is because the preference equity holders have a cumulative right to receive a portion of the profits of the subsidiary, limited to the annual dividend, even though a dividend has not been declared.

Allocation of profits of the entity since the acquisition date

	Total CU	Ordinary equity holders CU	Preference equity holders CU
Retained earnings to start of current year (3 years)	7 000	6 940	60
Profit after tax	5 000	4 940	60

Remember that equity is the residual. The profit and retained earnings of the entity therefore represent the amounts attributable to the entity's equity holders. These are the ordinary equity holders and the preference equity holders. The profits attributable to the ordinary and preference equity holders are allocated as follows:

- Preference equity holders: CU600 × 10% = CU60 per annum (limited to the annual dividend)
- Ordinary equity holders: The balance of the profits after the amount attributable to the preference equity holders; the ordinary equity holders, in essence, are last in line with claims against the entity.

Note that as no dividends have yet been declared, the preference equity holders have the right to arrear dividends, amounting to CU60 per year since the preference shares were issued on 1 January 20x5, which is only one year in this case. This amount has not yet been declared to the preference equity holders and as such is reflected in retained earnings as at the end of 20x5 (that is, profits that have been earned by the entity and are attributable to its equity holders, but have not yet been distributed because they are retained within the entity).

3. Treatment of non-cumulative preference dividends

If the subsidiary has declared the preference dividend, it should be accounted for in a similar way to ordinary dividends as discussed above in Chapter 6, Section 4. That means that the portion of the dividends received by the parent is eliminated against the dividends received, which is included in its revenue when consolidated financial statements are prepared, and the dividends relating to shares not held by the parent represent a distribution to non-controlling interest, which is removed from the balance of non-controlling interest in equity.

Unless the preference shares have participating rights, the preference shareholders' share of the profits of the subsidiary is limited to the preference dividend declared.

Example

Subsidiary with preference shares

This example illustrates the allocation of profits between the different classes of shares, where the preference shares are non-cumulative and not held by the parent.

P Ltd owns 60% of the 1 000 ordinary shares (total ordinary share capital of S Ltd of CU1 000) in S Ltd, purchased on 1 January 20x5.

On 1 January 20x5, S Ltd issues 200 non-cumulative preference shares at CU3 per share with a dividend rate of 10%. The parent does not hold any of the preference shares.

Summary of share capital of S Ltd

	20x6 CU	20x5 CU
Ordinary shares (1 000 shares)	1 000	1 000
Preference shares (200 shares)	600	600

S Ltd earned an after-tax profit of CU3 000 and CU5 000 during the 20x5 and 20x6 financial years respectively. The preference shares are non-cumulative. This means that the preference shareholders are not entitled to receive any arrear dividends.

S Ltd declares the following dividends:

	20x5 CU	20x6 CU
Ordinary dividend	120	100
Preference dividend (10% × CU3 × 200)	60	60

The profits of the subsidiary are therefore split between the two classes of shares and the profits attributable to these classes of shares are split accordingly, as follows:

	Total profit CU	Preference shares CU	Ordinary shares (residual) CU
Profit for 20x5	3 000	60	2 940
Less: Dividends	(160)	(60)	(100)
Retained earnings since acquisition date	2 840	–	2 840
Profit after tax for 20x6	5 000	⟶ 60	⟶ 4 940
Less: Dividends	(180)	(60)	(120)

Think about it
Of the profit attributable to the preference shareholders, 100% is attributable to the non-controlling interest, as the parent does not hold any preference shares.

Think about it
The non-controlling interest in the ordinary equity holders' share of the profits amount to CU4 940 × 40% = CU1 976.

Think about it
In this example, the preference shares are non-cumulative. If a preference dividend had not been declared in any of the years, the preference shareholders would not be entitled to a share of the profits in that year and all of the profits would be attributable to the ordinary shareholders, although an ordinary dividend could not have been declared in that year either because a preference dividend must always be declared first

Within the group worksheet, the following amounts are included:

Dr/(Cr)	P Ltd (starting point) CU	S Ltd (starting point) CU	Pro-forma journals CU	Group (end point) CU
Retained earnings since acquisition at 31 December 20x5		(3 000 – 160) = (2 840)	① 1 136	(1 704)
Profit after tax for 20x6 Dividend received (ordinary)	(120 × 60%) = (72)	(5 000)	② 2 036 ③ 72	(2 964) –
Ordinary dividend declared		120	③ (120)	–
Preference dividend declared		60	④ (60)	–
Non-controlling interest (equity)			① (1 136) ② (2 036) ④ 60 ③ 48	(3 064)

The following *pro-forma* journal eliminates the preference share capital against the non-controlling interest balance in equity:

			CU	CU
Dr		Preference share capital	600	
	Cr	Non-controlling interest (equity)		600

Elimination of preference share capital against non-controlling interest

> **Think about it**
> The preference share capital is not equity that is held directly by the equity holders of the parent. It would therefore not be appropriate to present it as a separate class of equity in the consolidated statement of financial position. The preference shares are all held by equity participants other than the parent and therefore belong to the non-controlling interest. It is therefore appropriate to reallocate the preference share capital to the non-controlling interest in equity.

> The retained earnings attributable to the non-controlling interest is after any dividends. Thus non-controlling interest is CU1 136 (CU2 840 × 40%).

The following *pro-forma* journal allocates the profits and dividends to the non-controlling interests:

			CU	CU
Dr		Retained earnings	① 1 136	
	Cr	Non-controlling interest (equity)		① 1 136

Allocation of prior year's profit to non-controlling interest

> **Check your answer**
> The amount attributable to the parent equity holders' share of retained earnings is CU1 704, calculated as CU2 840 × 60% or CU3 000 − 160 = 2 840 × 60%.

			CU	CU
Dr		Non-controlling interest (P/L) (w1)	② 2 036	
	Cr	Non-controlling interest (equity)		② 2 036

Allocation of current year's profit to non-controlling interest
(w1): CU60 × 100% (preference shareholders' share of profit) + CU4 940 × 40% (ordinary shareholders' share of profit)

			CU	CU
Dr		Ordinary dividend received (P/L)	③ 72	
Dr		Non-controlling interest (equity)	③ 48	
	Cr	Ordinary dividend declared		③ 120

Elimination of ordinary dividend received by parent and amount distributed to non-controlling interest

			CU	CU
Dr		Non-controlling interest (equity)	④ 60	
	Cr	Preference dividend declared		④ 60

Preference dividend distributed to non-controlling interest

> **Think about it**
> The closing balance of non-controlling interest in equity of CU3 064 (CU1 136 + CU2 036 − CU48 −CU60) is net of dividends. This is because the dividends have been paid and the non-controlling shareholders therefore no longer have a claim on the assets of the group.

4. Treatment of cumulative preference dividends

The profit attributable to the preference equity holders is limited to the amount of the dividend that they are entitled to receive. Thus, if a dividend has been declared, the preference shareholders are entitled to receive that portion of the profit, which is then in turn distributed as a dividend. If no preference dividend has been declared, they have no right to receive that portion of the profit as dividends are not contractual amounts. However, in the case of **cumulative preference shares**, the right to a dividend is specified. Where the shares are classified as **cumulative non-redeemable**, these shareholders have a right to arrear dividends not yet declared. This implies that the preference shareholders are entitled to that portion of the profits (limited to the dividend), even though a dividend has not been declared. The right ceases when the dividend is declared.

This means that in the case of **cumulative non-redeemable** preference shares, you have to attribute preference profits (equal to their dividends) to the parent and the non-controlling interest on consolidation based on their ownership of the preference shares, even if they have not been declared as a dividend. In addition, you need to eliminate the intra-group dividends when declared. The starting point for the consolidation will include any preference dividends paid by the subsidiary in the current year and if applicable, the parent will include the portion of preference dividends received as revenue. If the subsidiary did not declare a preference dividend in the current year, then the starting point will not include any amount relating to the dividends, but will include the full profit of the subsidiary before any allocation of profits was done.

The attribution of profits relating to the preference shares between the parent equity holders (if the parent owns a portion of the preference shares) and the non-controlling interest is simply an allocation of the profits attributable to the various equity participants. The *pro-forma* journal entries required to attribute the profits are done in exactly the same way. The existence of preference shares simply requires the calculation of the attribution to be done in a different way.

Example

Subsidiary with cumulative preference shares

This example illustrates the allocation of profits between the different classes of shares where the preference shares are cumulative and the parent holds some of the preference shares.

P Ltd owns 60% of the 1 000 ordinary shares (total ordinary share capital of S Ltd of CU1 000) in S Ltd, purchased on 1 January 20x3.

On 1 January 20x5, S Ltd issues 200 **cumulative non-redeemable** preference shares at CU3 per share. The preference shares entitle preference shareholders to an annual dividend (on 31 December) of 10%. The parent acquired 20% of the preference shares on 1 January 20x5, thus non-controlling interest in the preference shares is 80%.

S Ltd earned an after-tax profit of CU3 000 and CU5 000 during the 20x5 and 20x6 financial years respectively, and the total increase in retained earnings between the date of acquisition and 1 January 20x6 amounted to CU7 000 (including the CU3 000 profit earned in 20x5). No preference dividend is declared on 31 December 20x5. In other words, at that date, the preference dividends are in arrears. The arrear 20x5 and current preference dividend for 20x6 are paid on 31 December 20x6.

Summary of share capital of S Ltd

	20x6 CU	20x5 CU
Ordinary shares (1 000 shares)	1 000	1 000
Preference shares (200 shares)	600	600

Statement of profit or loss and other comprehensive income of S Ltd

	20x6 CU	20x5 CU
Profit after tax	5 000	3 000
Attributable to:		
Preference shareholders (CU600 × 10%) (note 1)	60	60
Ordinary shareholders (CU5 000 – CU60, CU3 000 – CU60)	4 940	2 940

Note 1: As the preference shares are cumulative, this is disclosed irrespective of whether or not the preference dividend is declared. When a dividend is declared, the declaration is disclosed in the statement of changes in equity as the preference shares are equity.

S Ltd has two classes of shares: ordinary shares and preference shares. The equity of the subsidiary should be allocated between the two classes of shares, as shown below.

Analysis of equity of S Ltd

	Total CU	P Ltd at acquisition CU	P Ltd since acquisition CU	Non-controlling interest CU
Preference shares:		(20%)		(80%)
Preference share capital	600	120		480
Dividend accrued for 20x5	60		12	48
Dividend accrued for 20x6	60		12	48
	720		24	576
Ordinary shares:		(60%)		(40%)
Ordinary share capital	1 000	600		400
Retained earnings 20x4	4 000		2 400	1 600
Profit for 20x5	2 940		1 764	1 176
Profit for 20x6	4 940		2 964	1 976
	12 880		7 128	5 152

Think about it

The preference shareholders are entitled to receive a portion of the profits each year, even though a preference dividend is not declared. On consolidation, a portion of the profits is allocated to non-controlling interest.

Pro-forma journal entries for 20x5 financial year focusing on the effects of the preference shares

			CU	CU
Dr		Preference share capital	600	
	Cr	Investment in S Ltd (CU600 × 20%)		120
	Cr	Non-controlling interest (equity) (CU600 × 80%)		480

Elimination of preference share capital, investment in S Ltd and raising non-controlling interests

			CU	CU
Dr		Non-controlling interest (P/L) (1 176 + 48)	1 124	
Dr		Retained earnings	1 600	
	Cr	Non-controlling interest (equity) (CU6 940 × 40% + CU600 × 10% × 80%)		2 824

Current year earnings allocated to non-controlling interests

In the following financial year, the *pro-forma* journal entries in 20x5 are repeated, followed by the consolidation adjustments in respect of 20x6:

			CU	CU
Dr		Preference share capital	600	
	Cr	Investment in S Ltd (CU600 × 20%)		120
	Cr	Non-controlling interest (equity) (CU600 × 80%)		480

Elimination of preference share capital, investment in S Ltd and raising non-controlling interests

			CU	CU
Dr		Retained earnings (CU6 940 × 40% + CU600 × 10% × 80%)	2 824	
	Cr	Non-controlling interest (equity)		2 824

Prior year earnings allocated to non-controlling interests in their capacity as ordinary and preference shareholders

			CU	CU
Dr		Non-controlling interest (P/L) (1 976 + 48)	2 024	
	Cr	Non-controlling interest (equity) (CU4 940 × 40% + CU600 × 10% × 80%)		2 024

Current year earnings allocated to non-controlling interests in their capacity as ordinary and preference shareholders

			CU	CU
Dr		Preference dividend income (CU600 × 10% × 20% × 2)	24	
	Cr	Non-controlling interests (equity) (CU600 × 10% × 80% × 2)	96	
	Cr	Preference dividends declared (×2, in other words, current and arrear)		120

Elimination of intra-group dividends

The profits attributable to the different classes of equity are based on how those classes of equity share in the profits. The profits attributable to the ordinary and preference equity holders are allocated based on the number of shares held:

- Assume that all of the preference shares are held by P Ltd: In this case, the profits attributable to the preference equity holders of CU60 are attributable to the parent equity holders in full.
- Assume that P Ltd holds none of the preference shares: This means that all of the preference shares are held by the other equity holders, that is, the non-controlling interest. All of the profits attributable to the preference equity holders of CU60 per annum are attributed to the non-controlling interest.

 ## Think about it

What if, when the preference dividend is in arrears, the preference shares attach voting rights?

To assess the nature of the investment, we have focused on voting rights. If the preference shares are cumulative and the dividend is in arrears, the preference shares may attach voting rights under certain circumstances. This may result in a change in the parent's controlling interest. Let's assume that the preference shares attach voting rights as of the date on which it is in arrears, which is 31 December 20x5. During the 20x6 financial year, there are the following numbers of shares:

- 1 000 ordinary shares, each attaching a voting right. Consequently, there are 1 000 voting rights.
- 200 preference shares, which now also each attach voting rights. Consequently, there are now 200 additional voting rights.
- Total shares attaching voting rights = 1 200.

P Ltd owns 600 (60% × 1 000) + 40 (20% × 200) = 640 = 53.33%. Therefore S Ltd is still a subsidiary, with 100% of its profits consolidated into P Ltd's group profit. However, as S Ltd is not a wholly owned subsidiary, profits are also attributable to the non-controlling interest. Remember that the non-controlling interest share is the equity that is not attributable to the parent. In this case, the equity of S Ltd comprises ordinary shares and preference shares:

- 80% of the profits attributable to the preference shareholders of S Ltd are attributable to the non-controlling interest (as they own 80% of the preference shares).
- 40% of the profits attributable to the ordinary shareholders of S Ltd are attributable to the non-controlling interest (as they own 40% of the ordinary shares).

This is important. As we can see from the example above, the cumulative preference dividends are in arrears and attach voting rights. Even though the non-controlling interest has 46.67% (100% − 53,33%) of the voting rights in S Ltd, that is not the same basis on which the profits of S Ltd are attributed to the non-controlling interest.

Test your knowledge

There is a list of learning objectives at the beginning of this chapter. Go back to this list and check whether you have achieved these outcomes. If not, reread the appropriate section.

Questions

Question 1

P Ltd owns 60% of the ordinary shares and 80% cumulative non-redeemable preference shares in S Ltd. These shares were acquired on 1 January 20x4. During the financial year ending 31 December 20x5, S Ltd earned after-tax profits of CU500 000 (20x4: CU300 000). Preference dividends (of CU10 000 per annum) have always been paid on time. No ordinary dividends were declared during 20x4 or 20x5. P Ltd earned after-tax profits of CU1 million during the financial year ending 31 December 20x5 (20x4: CU800 000).

You are required to do the following:

1. Calculate the group profit or loss of P Ltd and its subsidiary for the financial year ending 31 December 20x5, **before** attribution to non-controlling interests and the shareholders of P Ltd. Ignore comparatives.
2. Calculate the **profit attributable to the non-controlling interests** in the P Ltd group for the financial year ending 31 December 20x5. Ignore comparatives.

Suggested solution

1. **Calculate the group profit or loss of P Ltd for the financial year ending 31 December 20x5, before attribution to non-controlling interests and the shareholders of P Ltd. Ignore comparatives.**

	CU
Profit of parent: P Ltd	1 000 000
Less: Inter-co preference dividend (CU10 000 × 80%)	(8 000)
Profit of subsidiary: S Ltd	500 000
Group profit (before attribution)	**1 492 000**

2. **Calculate the profit attributable to the non-controlling interests in the P Ltd group for the financial year ending 31 December 20x5. Ignore comparatives.**

	CU
Preference profits (CU10 000 × 20%)	2 000
Ordinary profits (CU500 000 − CU10 000) × 40%	196 000
Profit attributable to non-controlling interest	**CU198 000**

Question 2

P Ltd acquired 100% of the ordinary shares and 40% of the CU2 000 000 10% cumulative preference shares in S Ltd on 1 January 20x5. At that date, S Ltd had retained earnings of CU2 million. As at 31 December 20x5 (the reporting date), S Ltd has retained earnings of CU2,8 million. No ordinary dividends have been declared.

You are required to do the following:

1. Assume that the preference shares pay dividends annually in arrears on 31 December and that all preference dividends were paid up to date on 31 December 20x5. Based on the information provided, **prepare the *pro-forma* journal entry** relating to non-controlling interest for the 20x5 reporting period.
2. Assume that the preference shares pay dividends annually in arrears on 30 September and that the 20x4 dividend was not declared on 30 September 20x4, but that all preference dividends were paid up to date on 30 September 20x5. **Calculate the post-acquisition retained earnings attributable to the ordinary shareholders** of S Ltd as at 31 December 20x5.

3. Assume that the preference shares pay dividends annually in arrears on 30 September and that the 20x4 dividend was not declared on 30 September 20x4, but that all preference dividends were paid up to date on 30 September 20x5. **Prepare the *pro-forma* journal entry** relating to the preference dividend declared on 30 September 20x5.

1. **Assume that the preference shares pay dividends annually in arrears on 31 December and that all preference dividends were paid up to date on 31 December 20x5. Based on the information provided, prepare the *pro-forma* journal entry relating to non-controlling interest for the 20x5 reporting period.**

			CU	CU
Dr		Non-controlling interest (equity) (w1)	120 000	
	Cr	Dividend declared		120 000

Preference dividend attributable to non-controlling interest
(w1): CU2m × 10% = CU200 000 × 60% = CU120 000

Note that the question only asked for the *pro-forma* journal entry relating to the non-controlling interest. If it had asked for the *pro-forma* journal entry relating to the preference dividend, the following entry would be appropriate:

			CU	CU
Dr		Dividend income (CU200 000 × 40%)	80 000	
Dr		Non-controlling interest (equity)	120 000	
	Cr	Dividend declared		200 000

Elimination of preference dividend received and preference dividend attributable to non-controlling interest

2. **Assume that the preference shares pay dividends annually in arrears on 30 September and that the 20x4 dividend was not declared on 30 September 20x4, but that all preference dividends were paid up to date on 30 September 20x5. Calculate the post-acquisition retained earnings attributable to the ordinary shareholders of S Ltd as at 31 December 20x5.**
At acquisition retained earnings:
CU2m – CU250 000 (arrear preference dividends of CU2 million × 10% × 15/12) = CU1 750 000
Since acquisition retained earnings:
(CU2.8m – CU2m) = CU800 000
Post-acquisition retained earnings attributable to the ordinary shareholders: CU800 000 + CU250 000 (arrear preference dividends now declared) – CU50 000 (preference dividends in arrears at 31 December 20x5) = **CU1 000 000**
OR
(CU2 800 000 – 50 000 [200 000 × 3/12]) – (2 000 000 – 250 000 [200 000 × 15/12])
= 2 750 000 – 1 750 000
= CU1 000 000
3. **Assume that the preference shares pay dividends annually in arrears on 30 September and that the 20x4 dividend was not declared on 30 September 20x4, but that all preference dividends were paid up to date on 30 September 20x5. Prepare the *pro-forma* journal entry relating to the preference dividend declared on 30 September 20x5.**

			CU	CU
Dr		Dividend income (CU200 000 × 2 × 40%)	160 000	
Dr		Non-controlling interest (equity) (× 60%)	240 000	
	Cr	Dividend declared		400 000

Elimination of preference dividend received and preference dividend attributable to non-controlling interest

Case study exercises

Scenario 1

P Ltd acquired 80% of the issued ordinary share capital of S Ltd on 1 January 20x3. The identifiable assets and liabilities of S Ltd were considered fairly valued at the date of acquisition. You can assume that any goodwill arising on consolidation is not impaired. Ignore taxation.

S Ltd has the following issued share capital, which remained unchanged since the acquisition date:
- 160 000 ordinary shares, issued at CU1 each
- 200 000 5% cumulative preference shares, issued at CU2 each (equivalent to the fair value).

Preference dividends are declared and paid annually on 30 December. The ordinary shares carry one voting right for every one share held, while the cumulative preference shares have no voting rights unless the dividends are in arrears. When preference dividends are not declared in any one year, each preference share receives one voting right until such time as the arrear preference dividends are declared and paid.

The retained earnings of S Ltd amounted to CU200 000 at the acquisition date. Non-controlling interest is measured at the attributable net asset value at the date of acquisition.

Statements of financial position of P Ltd and S Ltd on 31 December 20x5

	P Ltd CU'000	S Ltd CU'000
ASSETS		
Plant and machinery	560	650
Investment in S Ltd:		
128 000 ordinary shares (80% interest)	300	
20 000 cumulative preference shares (10% interest)	40	
Inventory	400	350
Other current assets	390	380
	1 690	**1 380**
CAPITAL AND LIABILITIES		
Ordinary share capital	290	160
Preference share capital	300	400
Retained earnings	900	700
Shareholders' equity	1 490	1 260
Current liabilities	200	120
	1 690	**1 380**

Statements of profit or loss of P Ltd and S Ltd for the year ended 31 December 20x5

	P Ltd CU'000	S Ltd CU'000
Revenue (including dividends and interest received)	2 320	1 700
Cost of sales	(1 050)	(875)
Gross profit	1 270	825
Net operating costs	(390)	(125)
Interest expense	(100)	(50)
Profit before taxation	780	650
Taxation expense	(300)	(250)
Profit after taxation	**480**	**400**

Extract from statements of changes in shareholders' equity of P Ltd and S Ltd for the year ended 31 December 20x5

	P Ltd CU'000	S Ltd CU'000
Retained earnings 1 January 20x5	620	500
Total comprehensive income	480	400
Dividends declared (and paid)		
Ordinary dividends	(185)	(180)
Preference dividends	(15)	(20)
Retained earnings 31 December 20x5	**900**	**700**

You are required to do the following:
1. Answer the following questions before starting with the preparation of the consolidated financial statements:
    • Does P Ltd have a controlling interest in S Ltd? Motivate your answer.
    • How would your answer above change if S Ltd did not declare any dividends in the current year?
    • What is the portion of current year profits of S Ltd that is attributable to the preference shareholders?
    • How would your answer above change if S Ltd did not declare any dividends in the current year?
    • What are the dividends received from S Ltd in P Ltd for the current year?
    • How would your answer above change if S Ltd did not declare any dividends in the current year?
    • Is there any adjustment necessary to opening retained earnings relating to the preference shares?
    • How would your answer above change if S Ltd did not declare any dividends in the current year?
2. Show the *pro-forma* journal entries required to prepare the consolidated financial statements of P Ltd Group for the year ended 31 December 20x5.
3. Prepare the consolidated statement of profit or loss and other comprehensive income, the consolidated statement of changes in equity and the consolidated statement of financial position for P Ltd and its subsidiary at 31 December 20x5.

Scenario 2

Use the same information given in the first scenario above. Assume that the ordinary and preference dividends are declared and paid annually on 30 June. As a result, P Ltd's investment in S Ltd consists of the following:
• Investment in ordinary shares: CU299 000
• Investment in preference shares: CU41 000.

You are required to do the following:
1. Answer the following questions before starting with the preparation of the consolidated financial statements:
    • What is the portion of current year profits of S Ltd that is attributable to the preference shareholders?

- Are there any preference dividends in arrears at the reporting date?
- Has any portion of the preference dividend accrued at 31 December 20x5?

2. Show the *pro-forma* journal entries required to prepare the consolidated financial statements of P Ltd Group for the year ended 31 December 20x5.
3. Prepare the consolidated statement of profit or loss and other comprehensive income, the consolidated statement of changes in equity and the consolidated statement of financial position for P Ltd and its subsidiary at 31 December 20x5.

Suggested solution

Scenario 1

1. **Answer the following questions before starting with the preparation of the consolidated financial statements:**
   - **Does P Ltd have a controlling interest in S Ltd? Motivate your answer.**
     Yes, P Ltd has 80% of the voting rights in S Ltd through its 80% interest in the ordinary shares in S Ltd. S Ltd's ordinary shares carry all of the voting rights as there are no arrears preference dividends.
   - **How would your answer above change if S Ltd did not declare any dividends in the current year?**
     When the preference dividends are in arrears, the preference shareholders have a voting right of one vote per preference share held. This means that if the preference dividend is not declared in the current year, P Ltd will have 80% of the ordinary voting rights and 10% of the preference voting rights.
     P Ltd will therefore have **41%** ([128 + 20]/[160 + 200]) of the voting rights. This means that P Ltd may lose control when the preference dividends are in arrears. However, should the preference shareholders not exercise their voting rights, P Ltd may still have *de facto* control of S Ltd.
     IFRS10 requires you to consider several factors when determining whether control exists, including decisions about other relevant activities of the investee and the nature of the relationship with the other parties (see IFRS10, paragraphs B2–B4). Thus a more detailed assessment of the factors is required before we can determine whether P Ltd will lose its controlling interest in S Ltd owing to undeclared preference dividends.
   - **What is the portion of current year profits of S Ltd that is attributable to the preference shareholders?**
     As the preference dividends are cumulative, CU20 000 (5% × CU400 000) of the current year profits of S Ltd is attributable to the preference shareholders.
   - **How would your answer above change if S Ltd did not declare any dividends in the current year?**
     The preference shareholders have a cumulative right to the preference dividend. So even if the preference dividend were not declared, CU20 000 of the profits per annum would still be attributable to the preference shareholders.
   - **What are the dividends received from S Ltd in P Ltd for the current year?**
     P Ltd received 80% of the ordinary dividend and 10% of the preference dividend, as follows:

	CU
Ordinary dividend (80% × CU180 000)	144 000
Preference dividend (10% × CU20 000)	2 000
Total dividends received from S Ltd:	**146 000**

- **How would your answer above change if S Ltd did not declare any dividends in the current year?**

  If S Ltd did not declare any dividends in the current year, then P Ltd would not receive any dividends. The answer would then be zero.

- **Is there any adjustment necessary to opening retained earnings relating to the preference shares?**

  As the preference dividends are cumulative, CU20 000 of the profits per annum is attributable to the preference shareholders. As the preference dividends have been declared and paid every year, the portion of the profits attributable to the preference shareholders has been distributed to them.

	CU
Annual share of profits attributable to preference shareholders	20 000
Annual preference dividend declared and paid	(20 000)
Net prior year profits attributable to the preference shareholders	**Zero**

- **How would your answer above change if S Ltd did not declare any dividends in the current year?**

  As stated above, CU20 000 of the profits per annum is attributable to the preference shareholders as the preference dividends are cumulative. If the preference dividend is not declared, that portion of the profits is still attributable to the preference shareholders as follows:

	CU
Annual share of profits attributable to preference shareholders	20 000
Annual preference dividend declared and paid	Not declared
Net prior year profits attributable to the preference shareholders	**20 000**

  For each year that the preference dividends are in arrears, we need to allocate CU20 000 of that year's profits to the preference shareholders. As P Ltd holds 10% of the preference shares, CU2 000 of the retained earnings attributable to the preference shareholders are attributable to P Ltd. The balance of CU18 000 is attributable to non-controlling interest. The following *pro-forma* journal entry allocated prior year retained earnings (for one year of arrear dividends) to the non-controlling interest:

			CU	CU
Dr		Retained earnings	18 000	
	Cr	Non-controlling interest (equity)		18 000

Allocation of prior year retained earnings to non-controlling interest

2. **Show the *pro-forma* journal entries required to prepare the consolidated financial statements of P Ltd Group for the year ended 31 December 20x5.**

Pro-forma journal entries

			CU'000	CU'000
Dr		Ordinary share capital	160	
Dr		Retained earnings	200	
Dr		Goodwill arising on consolidation	12	
	Cr	Investment in S Ltd (ordinary shares)		300
	Cr	Non-controlling interest (equity)		72

Elimination of equity at acquisition, investment in S Ltd and raising non-controlling at acquisition

			CU'000	CU'000
Dr		Preference share capital	400	
	Cr	Investment in S Ltd (preference shares)		40
	Cr	Non-controlling interest (equity)		360

Elimination of preference equity held by P Ltd and allocation of appropriate portion to non-controlling interest

			CU'000	CU'000
Dr		Retained earnings (CU300 000 × 20%)	60	
	Cr	Non-controlling interest (equity)		60

Post-acquisition prior year earnings allocated to non-controlling interest

			CU'000	CU'000
Dr		Dividends received (P/L)	144	
Dr		Non-controlling interest (equity)	36	
	Cr	Ordinary dividends declared		180

Elimination of inter-company ordinary dividend

			CU'000	CU'000
Dr		Non-controlling interest in profits (P/L) (CU380 000 × 20%)	76	
	Cr	Non-controlling interest (equity)		76

Current year's earnings allocated to non-controlling interest

			CU'000	CU'000
Dr		Dividends received (P/L)	2	
Dr		Non-controlling interest (equity)	18	
	Cr	Preference dividends declared		20

Elimination of inter-company preference dividend

			CU'000	CU'000
Dr		Non-controlling interest in profits (P/L) (CU20 000 × 90%)	18	
	Cr	Non-controlling interest (equity)		18

Current year's earnings allocated to non-controlling interest

3. **Prepare the consolidated statement of profit or loss and other comprehensive income, the consolidated statement of changes in equity and the consolidated statement of financial position for P Ltd and its subsidiary at 31 December 20x5.**

Consolidated statement of profit or loss and other comprehensive income for P Ltd and its subsidiary for the year ended 31 December 20x5

	Workings	CU'000
Gross revenue	(2 320 + 1 700 – 144 (ordinary dividend) – 2 (preference dividend)	3 874
Cost of sales	(1 050 + 875)	(1 925)
Gross profit		1 949
Net operating costs	(390 + 125)	(515)
Interest expense	(100 + 50)	(150)
Profit before tax		1 284
Taxation expense	(300 + 250)	(550)
Profit after tax		**734**
Attributable to:		
Equity holders of the parent		① 640
Non-controlling interest	(380 × 20%) + (20 × 90%)	94
Total comprehensive income		**734**

Check your answer

① P Ltd's profit for current year: CU480 000 – 144 000 (ordinary dividend) – 2 000 (preference dividend) = CU334 000

P Ltd's share of S Ltd's profit: CU304 000 (ordinary interest) + CU2 000 (preference interest) = CU306 000

Total profit attributable to parent equity holders: **CU640 000**

Consolidated statement in shareholders' interest for P Ltd and its subsidiary for the year ended 31 December 20x5

	Interest of parent equity holders				Non-controlling interest CU'000	Total CU'000
	Ordinary share capital CU'000	Preference share capital CU'000	Retained earnings CU'000	Total CU'000		
Opening balance	290	300	(w1) 860	1 450	492	1 942
Total comprehensive income			640	640	94	734
Less: Dividends						
Ordinary dividends			(185)	(185)	(36)	(221)
Preference dividends			(15)	(15)	(18)	(33)
Closing balance	290	300	1 300	1 890	② 532	2 422

(w1): P Ltd: 620 000
S Ltd: (500 000 – 200 000) × 80% = 240 000
Group: 620 000 + 240 000 = **CU860 000**

Check your answer

② The non-controlling interest includes their share of the ordinary and preference shares, calculated as follows:
Non-controlling interest in ordinary shares: CU860 000 × 20% = CU172 000
Non-controlling interest in preference shares: CU400 000 × 90% = CU360 000
Total non-controlling interest: **CU532 000**

Consolidated statement of financial position for P Ltd and its subsidiary at 31 December 20x5

		CU'000
ASSETS		
Non-current assets:		
Plant and machinery	(560 + 650)	1 210
Goodwill		12
Current assets:		
Inventory	(400 + 350)	750
Other current assets	(390 + 380)	770
		2 742
EQUITY AND LIABILITIES		
Ordinary share capital		290
Preference share capital		300
Retained earnings		1 300
Interest of parent equity holders		1 890
Non-controlling interest		532
Total equity		2 422
Current liabilities	(200 + 120)	320
		2 742

Workings

Analysis of equity of S Ltd

	Ordinary shares CU'000	Preference shares CU'000	P Ltd (80%) Ordinary shares At acquisition CU'000	Since acquisition CU'000	P Ltd (10%) Preference CU'000	Non-controlling interest CU'000
At acquisition:						
Ordinary share capital	160		128			32
Preference share capital		400			40	360
Retained earnings	200	–	160			40
	360	400	288		40	432
Investment			300		40	
Goodwill			12			
Since acquisition:						
Retained earnings	300	–		240		60
Current year:						
Profit after tax (400 – 20)	380	20		304	2	94
– Dividends	(180)	(20)		(144)	(2)	(54)
	860	400		400	–	532

Think about it

Why was there no allocation of the prior-year profits to the preference shareholders?

The preference dividends in the prior periods were declared and paid, and therefore they no longer have any claim on the retained earnings remaining in the subsidiary.

Think about it
What if ...?

- What if P Ltd held all of the cumulative preference shares?
  - On consolidation, P Ltd's investment in the preference shares of S Ltd would be eliminated in full.
- What if P Ltd did not hold any of the cumulative preference shares in S Ltd?
  - On consolidation, outside shareholders would hold the preference share capital of S Ltd. The full amount would then be allocated to non-controlling interest.

Scenario 2

Use the same information given in the first scenario above. Assume that the ordinary and preference dividends are declared and paid annually on 30 June.

You are required to do the following:

1. **Answer the following questions before starting with the preparation of the consolidated financial statements:**
   - **What is the portion of current year profits of S Ltd that is attributable to the preference shareholders?**
     At 30 June 20x5, the preference dividend of CU20 000 is payable. Thus, at that date, CU10 000 of the current year's profit and CU10 000 of the prior year's profit are attributable to the preference shareholders.
   - **Are there any preference dividends in arrears at the reporting date?**
     No. The declaration date is 30 June, and the most recent preference dividend was declared and paid on 30 June 20x5.
   - **Has any portion of the preference dividend accrued at 31 December 20x5?**
     Yes, six month's preference dividend has accrued at 31 December 20x5. Even though there is no accounting entry in the financial statements of S Ltd for the preference dividend until such time as it is declared, in the group financial statements, CU10 000 of the current year's profit (from 1 July to 31 December 20x5) accrues to the preference shareholders.

2. **Show the *pro-forma* journal entries required to prepare the consolidated financial statements of P Ltd Group for the year ended 31 December 20x5.**

Pro-forma journal entries

			CU'000	CU'000
Dr		Ordinary share capital	160	
Dr		Retained earnings	190	
Dr		Goodwill arising on consolidation	19	
	Cr	Investment in S Ltd (ordinary shares)		299
	Cr	Non-controlling interest (equity)		70

Elimination of equity at acquisition, investment in S Ltd and raising non-controlling at acquisition

			CU'000	CU'000
Dr		Preference share capital	400	
Dr		Retained earnings	10	
	Cr	Investment in S Ltd (preference shares)		41
	Cr	Non-controlling interest (equity)		369

Elimination of preference equity held by P Ltd and allocation of appropriate portion to non-controlling interest

			CU'000	CU'000
Dr		Retained earnings (CU300 000 × 20%)	60	
	Cr	Non-controlling interest (equity)		60

Post-acquisition prior year earnings allocated to non-controlling interest

			CU'000	CU'000
Dr		Non-controlling interest in profits (P/L) (CU380 000 × 20%)	76	
	Cr	Non-controlling interest (equity)		76

Current year's earnings allocated to non-controlling interest

			CU'000	CU'000
Dr		Non-controlling interest in profits (P/L) (CU20 000 × 90%)	18	
	Cr	Non-controlling interest (equity)		18

Current year's earnings allocated to non-controlling interest

			CU'000	CU'000
Dr		Dividends received	144	
Dr		Non-controlling interest (equity)	36	
	Cr	Ordinary dividends declared and paid (S Ltd)		180

Elimination of inter-company ordinary dividend

			CU'000	CU'000
Dr		Dividends received	2	
Dr		Non-controlling interest (equity)	18	
	Cr	Preference dividends declared and paid		20

Elimination of inter-company preference dividend

3. **Prepare the consolidated statement of profit or loss and other comprehensive income, the consolidated statement of changes in equity and the consolidated statement of financial position for P Ltd and its subsidiary at 31 December 20x5.**

Consolidated statement of profit or loss and other comprehensive income for P Ltd and its subsidiary for the year ended 31 December 20x5

		CU'000
Gross revenue	2 320 + 1 700 – 144 (ordinary dividend) – 2 (preference dividend)	3 874
Cost of sales	(1 050 + 875)	(1 925)
Gross profit		1 949
Net operating costs	(390 + 125)	(515)
Interest expense	(100 + 50)	(150)
Profit before tax		1 284
Taxation expense	(300 + 250)	(550)
Profit after tax		734
Attributable to:		
Equity holders of the parent		① 640
Non-controlling interest	(380 × 20%) + (20 × 90%)	94
Total comprehensive income		734

Check your answer
① P Ltd's profit for current year: CU480 000 – 144 000 (ordinary dividend) – 2 000 (preference dividend) = CU334 000
P Ltd's share of S Ltd's profit: CU304 000 (ordinary interest) + CU2 000 (preference interest) = CU306 000
Total profit attributable to parent equity holders: **CU640 000**

Consolidated statement in shareholders' interest for P Ltd and its subsidiary for the year ended 31 December 20x5

	Interest of parent equity holders				Non-controlling interest CU'000	Total CU'000
	Ordinary share capital CU'000	Preference share capital CU'000	Retained earnings CU'000	Total CU'000		
Opening balance	290	300	(w1) 860	1 450	499	1 949
Total comprehensive income			640	640	94	734
Less: Dividends Ordinary dividends			(185)	(185)	(36)	(221)
Preference dividends			(15)	(15)	(18)	(33)
Closing balance	290	300	1 300	1 890	② 539	2 429

(w1): P Ltd: 620 000
S Ltd: (500 000 – 200 000) × 80% = 240 000
Group: 620 000 + 240 000 = **CU860 000**

Check your answer
② The non-controlling interest includes their share of the ordinary and preference shares, calculated as follows:
- Non-controlling interest in ordinary shares: CU850 000 × 20% = CU170 000
- Non-controlling interest in preference shares: CU410 000 × 90% = CU369 000
- Total non-controlling interest: **CU539 000**

Consolidated statement of financial position for P Ltd and its subsidiary at 31 December 20x5

		CU'000
ASSETS		
Non-current assets:		
Plant and machinery	(560 + 650)	1 210
Goodwill		19
Current assets:		
Inventory	(400 + 350)	750
Other current assets	(390 + 380)	770
		2 749
EQUITY AND LIABILITIES		
Ordinary share capital		290
Preference share capital		300
Retained earnings		1 300
Interest of parent equity holders		1 890
Non-controlling interest		539
Total equity		2 429
Current liabilities	(200 + 120)	320
		2 749

Workings

Analysis of equity of S Ltd

	Ordinary shares CU'000	Preference shares CU'000	P Ltd (80%) ordinary shares CU'000		P Ltd (10%) preference CU'000	Non-controlling interest CU'000
			At acquisition	Since acquisition		
At acquisition (January 20x3):						
Ordinary share capital	160		128			32
Preference share capital		400			40	360
Retained earnings (200)						
Ordinary shares	190		152			38
Preference shares		③ 10			1	9
	350	410	280		41	439
Investment			299		41	
Goodwill			19		–	
Since acquisition:						
Retained earnings						
Ordinary shares	300			240		60
Preference shares						
30 June 20x3 dividend		(20)				
Profit for 20x3		20				
30 June 20x4 dividend		(20)				
Profit for 20x4		20				
Current year: (31 December 20x5)						
Profit after tax (400 – 20)						
Ordinary shares	380			304		76
Preference shares		20			2	18
– Dividends on 30 June 20x5						
Ordinary	(180)			(144)		(36)
Preference		(20)			(2)	(18)
	850	④ 410		400	–	539

③ Profit for six months accrued to preference shareholders
④ This amount consists of the preference shares of CU400 000 plus the dividend accrued of CU10 000 (for the period 1 July–31 December 20x5)

PART III

The equity method

9

Interests in associates and joint ventures

The following topics are included in this chapter:

- Identifying an investment in an associate and a joint venture
- Recognition of an investment in an associate and/or joint venture in the separate financial statements of the investor
- Recognition of interests in associates and joint ventures in group financial statements
- Intra-group transactions between the investor and associate when preparing group financial statements
- Interests in associates that have issued preference shares
- Preparing group financial statements when an associate owns a subsidiary or an investment in its own associate.

Learning objectives

By the end of this chapter, you should be able to:

- Identify an investment in an associate or a joint venture
- Recognise an investment in an associate in the separate financial statements of the investor
- Know how to identify an investment in a joint venture and explain how that is different from an investment in an associate
- Understand that when applying the equity method and group financial statements are prepared, the starting point does not include the financial statements of the associate or joint venture
- Recognise and measure the investment in an associate or joint venture at the acquisition date
- Prepare the *pro-forma* journal entries to include the investor's share of the equity of the associate and joint venture at the acquisition date and in subsequent reporting periods
- Explain what is meant by upstream and downstream intra-group transactions, and how these should be adjusted when applying the equity method
- Prepare group financial statements by applying the equity method for investments in associated and joint ventures
- Apply the equity method when the associate has issued preference shares
- Prepare group financial statements if an associate owns a subsidiary or an investment in its own associate.

1. Investments in associates and joint ventures

Even though an investor may not have control, it may still be able to participate in the decision-making processes of the investee. In this case, reflecting the investment at fair value in the investor's group financial statements and only recognising income in respect of dividends received from its investment may bear little relation to the performance of the investment. It would result in the group financial statements not adequately reflecting the impact of the investor's level of influence over the investee.

An investor may not have control, but may have joint control over an entity. Chapter 10 deals with joint control and distinguishes between two types of joint arrangement: joint ventures and joint operations. Refer to Chapter 10 before dealing with joint venture arrangements in this chapter.

In other cases, an investor may not have joint control, but may still be able to influence the decision-making of the investee as a result of the size of its shareholding, board representation and so on. We refer to such an investment as an **investment in an associate**. An investee is classified as an associate when the investor can exert **significant influence** over the decision-making of the entity. The investor does not have rights to the assets of the associate or joint venture and it should not combine the assets of the investee with its own (as done when consolidating a subsidiary). The assets of the investee are not assets of the group. However, the investor has an asset, which is represented by its interest in the associate or joint venture. This in turn is represented by its interest in the equity of the investee.

Owing to its significant influence over the activities of the associate, the investor should recognise any changes in the equity of the associate (or joint venture) as these arise, as opposed to when they are distributed. This is achieved by applying the equity method, which implies recognising the group's share of equity, as reflected in profit or loss and other comprehensive income in the period earned by the investee and therefore by the investor. Because the investor is able to exert significant influence or joint control, application of the equity method provides more informative reporting of the net assets and profit or loss of the investor.

The specific IFRS that deals with investments in associates is IAS28, *Investments in Associates and Joint Ventures*. This standard includes definitions of the terms an 'associate' and 'significant influence', as explained below. IFRS for SMEs, Section 14, *Investments in Associates*, contains similar descriptions of an associate and significant influence.

In this chapter, you will learn how to apply the equity method to the investor's investment in an investee that is an associate or a joint venture. Note that where examples illustrate the accounting treatment of an associate, the same principles apply to an investment in a joint venture.

2. Descriptions and definitions

2.1 Associate

IFRS principles

What is an associate?

An entity over which an investor has significant influence in the determination of financial and operating policy decisions is referred to as an associate.

An associate is 'an entity over which the investor has significant influence'. The investor has the power or capacity to affect the decisions made in relation to the investee. This means that the investor could either have significant influence directly (the investor owns the shares in the associate) or indirectly (through its subsidiaries). The specific power is that of being able to participate in the financial and operating policy decisions of the investee. Note that the investor cannot control the investee, but can significantly influence the investee.

2.2 Significant influence

Significant influence is 'the power to participate in the financial and operating policy decisions of the investee, but it is not control nor joint control over those policies'.

IAS28 provides guidance on how to determine whether an investor has significant influence. Where the investor holds 20% or more of the voting power of the investee, it is presumed that the investor has significant influence. On the other hand, where the investor holds less than 20% of the voting power of the investee, it is presumed that the investor does not have significant influence, unless such influence can be clearly demonstrated.

The fact that another entity holds a substantial or the majority interest in an investee does not necessarily preclude an investor from having significant influence. For example, the investee could be a subsidiary of another entity, but the investor that has a non-controlling interest could *still* have significant influence.

An investor may also be able to demonstrate that it has **significant influence** if:

- The investor has representation on the board of directors or an equivalent governing body of the investee
- The investor participates in the policy-making processes, for example, the associate's dividend policy
- There are material transactions between the investor and the investee
- The two parties interchange managerial personnel
- Essential technical information is provided by one party to the other.

The existence of potential voting rights that are currently exercisable or convertible should also be taken into account in assessing whether the investor has significant influence. As a practical guideline, you should also take into account the ability of the investor to obtain financial information regarding the associate (for example, where the investor has access to the investee's management accounts).

Significant influence is lost when the investor loses the power to participate in the financial and operating policy decisions of the investee. This can happen when the investor disposes of its interest in the associate, when there is a change in ownership (for example, if the investee issues more voting shares and the investor does not subscribe to these shares), or when the investee becomes subject to the control of a government, court, administrator or regulator (for example, if the investee is declared insolvent). Significant influence can also be lost as a result of a contractual agreement. The issue of changes in ownership is dealt with in Chapter 12.

2.3 Joint ventures

IFRS principles

What is a joint venture?

When an investor is involved in an investment where there is a contractually agreed sharing of control such that decisions require the unanimous consent of the parties sharing control, the investor has joint control over the investee, which is a joint venture.

Refer to Chapter 10 for a more detailed discussion of joint arrangements and the classification of such an arrangement as a joint venture.

IFRS principles

Relationship and levels of control

The level of control establishes the relationship between the investor and investee, as follows:
- Parent–subsidiary relationship: Dominant control
- Investor–associate relationship: Significant influence
- Investor–joint venture: Joint control.

3. Accounting for the investment in the investor's separate financial statements

Where the investor prepares separate financial statements in addition to the preparation of group or consolidated financial statements, the investor should account for its investment in the associate or joint venture by using one of the following models:
- The **cost model**
- The **fair value model** (in terms of IFRS9, *Financial Instruments*)
- The equity method (as a result of a narrow-scope amendment to IAS27).

See Section 4 of Chapter 1 regarding the recognition of investments in the financial statements of the investor.

The model that is applied to account for the investments in associates or joint ventures in the separate financial statements of the investor should be applied consistently for each category of investments; the investor cannot apply the cost model for some of its investments in associates or joint ventures and the fair value model for others.

The policy applied by the investor in its separate financial statements influences the carrying amount of the investment in the associate or joint venture, which is reflected in the starting point for the preparation of the investor's group financial statements.

3.1 Cost model

Under the cost model, an investor records its investment in the investee at cost, with no subsequent adjustments for the changes in the fair value of its investment. The cost comprises the purchase price plus any directly attributable costs incurred to acquire the investment. When applying the cost model, the investor recognises income only to the extent of dividend income earned.

Example

Recognising investment in an associate using the cost model

If P Ltd acquired a 25% interest in the share capital of A Ltd for CU90 000 on 1 January 20x4 and P Ltd incurred transaction costs of CU10 000, the following journal entry would be processed by P Ltd to record the acquisition:

			CU	CU
Dr		Investment in associate	90 000	
	Cr	Bank		90 000

Acquisition of shares in associate

			CU	CU
Dr		Investment in associate	10 000	
	Cr	Bank		10 000

Transaction costs relating to acquisition of shares in associate capitalised

3.2 Fair value

Alternatively, the investor may account for its investment in an associate or joint venture in accordance with IFRS9 in its separate financial statements. This implies measuring the investment at initial recognition at fair value plus transaction costs if the investment is not subsequently measured at fair value through profit or loss.

Subsequently, an equity investment is measured at fair value with fair value adjustments recognised either in profit or loss, or in other comprehensive income. In addition, the investor recognises dividend income in profit or loss when earned.

Example

Recognising investment in an associate using the fair value model with fair value gains and losses in profit or loss

Using the same information as above, P Ltd would process the following journal entry to record the acquisition of its investment in A Ltd on 1 January 20x4 if P Ltd classified the investment as at fair value through profit or loss in accordance with IFRS9:

			CU	CU
Dr		Investment in associate	90 000	
	Cr	Bank		90 000

Acquisition of shares in associate

			CU	CU
Dr		Transaction costs (P/L)	10 000	
	Cr	Bank		10 000

Transaction costs relating to acquisition of shares in associate expensed when incurred

Example

Recognising investment in an associate at fair value with fair value gains and losses in other comprehensive income

Using the same information as above, P Ltd would process the following journal entry to record the acquisition of its investment in A Ltd on 1 January 20x4 if P Ltd instead elected to measure the investment as at fair value and to present the fair value gains or losses in other comprehensive income in accordance with IFRS9:

			CU	CU
Dr		Investment in associate	90 000	
	Cr	Bank		90 000

Acquisition of shares in associate

			CU	CU
Dr		Investment in associate	10 000	
	Cr	Bank		10 000

Transaction costs relating to acquisition of shares in associate capitalised

Example

Subsequent measurement

The investor recognises the investment in the associate or joint venture at cost at the acquisition date. Depending on the accounting policy, the investor recognises its investment in the associate or joint venture at subsequent reporting dates, using either the cost model or the fair value model. The different accounting policies illustrated in the examples above each resulted in the measurement of the investment at the next reporting date as follows, assuming that the fair value of the investment amounts to CU120 000:

	Using cost model CU	At fair value recognised in profit or loss CU	At fair value recognised in other comprehensive income CU
Initial measurement at cost	90 000	90 000	90 000
Transaction costs capitalised	10 000	–	10 000
Carrying amount at acquisition date	100 000	90 000	100 000
Fair value adjustment		P/L: 30 000	OCI: 20 000
Carrying amount at subsequent reporting date	100 000	120 000	120 000

As mentioned earlier, the accounting policy applied by the investor in its separate financial statements influences the carrying amount of the investment in the associate or joint venture, which is reflected in the starting point for the preparation of the investor's group financial statements. When applying the **equity method** to investments in associates and joint ventures in preparation of group financial statements, you **first** need to **reverse any fair value adjustments** relating to the investment in the associate or joint venture (using *pro-forma* journal entries) in order to start with the original contribution at the acquisition date. From that point, you apply the equity method, which includes adding the investor's share of the post-acquisition equity of the associate or joint venture. The equity method is explained in the next section.

4. Applying the equity method in the investor's group financial statements

The investor should apply the **equity method to investments in associates or joint ventures** when preparing group financial statements. The equity method involves initially measuring the investment at cost, and then increasing or decreasing the carrying amount of the investment by recognising the investor's share of profit or loss and other comprehensive income after the date of acquisition. Under this method, the investor's share of the profit or loss of the investee after acquisition is included as a separate line item in the group profit or loss for the period. The investor's share of the post-acquisition other comprehensive income items of the investee is included as a separate component in other comprehensive income of the group.

IFRS principles

What is the equity method?

In terms of the equity method, an investor recognises an increase in the equity as well as an increase in the investment in an investee based on the investor's proportionate interest in the investee. The equity method is designed to provide more information about an investment than is generally supplied under the cost method, but less information than is supplied under the consolidation method.

The equity method results in recognising the group's share of the profits when the profits are earned and recognised by the investee, irrespective of when they are distributed to the investor in the form of dividends. Distributions received from the investee (in other words, dividends received by the investor) reduce the carrying amount of the investment. Essentially the carrying amount of the investment at a group level represents the investor's share of the net asset value (equity) of the investee. Distributions by the investee reduce its equity and consequently the investor's share of that equity at a group level.

As the associate or joint venture is equity accounted in the investor's group financial statements, any fair value adjustments recognised in the separate financial statements of the investor if the investor measures the investment in associate or joint venture at fair value are reversed through *pro-forma* journal entries when preparing the investor's group financial statements. This is to prevent any potential double-counting that may arise at a group level when recognising the investor's share of post-acquisition movement in the equity of the associate or joint venture and thus overstating the carrying amount of the investment.

However, IAS28 identifies certain circumstances where the equity method is not applied to the investment in an associate or joint venture:

- The same circumstances that were discussed in Chapter 3 apply, for example, where all the owners of the investor have agreed to the investor not presenting group financial statements
- Where the investor intends to dispose of the investment in the associate or joint venture and the investment is classified as held for sale in accordance with IFRS5, *Non-current Assets Held for Sale and Discontinued Operations*
- Where the investor is a venture capital organisation or a mutual fund, a unit trust or a similar entity that upon initial recognition has designated its investment as at fair value through profit or loss or as held for trading in accordance with IFRS9.

An investor should discontinue the use of the equity method in its group financial statements from the date that it ceases to have significant influence or joint control over the investee. Thereafter, the investor accounts for its interest on a basis that reflects the nature of its interest:

- If the investor has increased its shareholding such that it has control, the parent's group financial statements reflect a consolidated subsidiary.
- If the investor has reduced its shareholding such that the nature of its interest is not control, joint control or significant influence, then the investment is recognised at its fair value in accordance with IFRS9, *Financial Instruments*.

Changes in ownership are dealt with in more detail in Chapter 12.

IFRS for SMEs update

Section 14 (*Investments in Associates*) and Section 15 (*Investments in Joint Ventures*)

In an entity's group and separate financial statements, an entity may choose one of the following as the model applicable to all investments in associates and joint ventures:
- The cost model
- The fair value model
- The equity method.

4.1 Application of the equity method

In applying the equity method, many of the principles that are appropriate in the consolidation process, which was discussed in the previous chapters, may be applicable to the equity method as well:
- Identifying the difference between the cost of the investment and the investor's share of the fair value of the net assets of the associate or joint venture at the acquisition date as goodwill, which is included in the carrying amount of the investment, or a gain recognised in the investor's group profit or loss in the period in which the investment is acquired (refer to Chapter 4)
- Determining the fair value of the net assets of the associate or joint venture at the acquisition date (refer to Chapter 5)
- Appropriate adjustments to the investor's share of the profit or loss of the associate or joint venture after the acquisition date as a result of, for example, the depreciation of depreciable assets based on their fair values at the acquisition date (Chapter 5 and Chapter 6).

However, the most **significant difference between consolidation and the application of the equity method** is that the trial balance of the associate or joint venture is not added to that of the investor (as would be done in the case of a subsidiary) as the investor does not control its assets (it only has significant influence). The trial balance of the associate or joint venture is not in the starting point for preparing group financial statements. This implies that you do not include any of the assets or liabilities of the associate or joint venture, which makes sense as the investor does not control the net assets of the associate. The investor's share in the post-acquisition profit or loss and other comprehensive income of the investee is combined with the investor's profit or loss and other comprehensive income by way of *pro-forma* journal entries. This means that you add only the investor's portion of the associate's post-acquisition reserves to the trial balance of the investor using *pro-forma* journal entries. The application of the equity method is illustrated in the examples that follow.

IFRS principles

Basic principles when applying the equity method

Follow these basic principles when applying the equity method (IAS28:10):

- Recognise the initial investment in the investee at **cost**. If the investment is recorded at fair value, an adjustment must be made to return the investment back to original cost.
- Increase or decrease the carrying amount of the investment by the investor's share of the **profit or loss** of the investee after the acquisition date, in other words, the post-acquisition profit or loss.
- Increase or decrease the carrying amount of the investment for the investor's share of the changes in the **other comprehensive income** of the investee. This includes movements in reserves, such as the asset revaluation surplus.
- Reduce the carrying amount of the investment by **distributions**, such as dividends, received from the investee.

4.2 Recognising investment in an associate or joint venture at acquisition

The equity method requires that an investor recognise its share of the post-acquisition equity of the investee. At the acquisition date, the investor recognises its investment in the investee at the initial carrying amount (refer to Section 3 above). This means that the investment is recognised at the original cost of the investment. If the reporting date of the investor was the same as the acquisition date, the investment would be recognised at its cost.

The investor acquired its interest in the investee at a consideration (the investment in the associate) that took into account:

- The recorded equity of the investee, which is equal to the recorded carrying amounts of the assets and liabilities of the investee
- Any fair value adjustments that may be required resulting from differences between the carrying amounts of the assets and liabilities of the investee and the fair values of these assets and liabilities
- The fair values of any unrecorded assets and liabilities of the investee
- Any goodwill, being the difference between the cost of the investment and the investor's share of the fair value of the net assets of the investee.

The investment in the associate or joint venture at the acquisition date reflects all of these amounts. It therefore represents the pre-acquisition equity of the investee (recorded and unrecorded) and any goodwill acquired at the acquisition date. The principles when applying the equity method are the same, irrespective of whether the investment is in an associate or a joint venture. The examples that follow illustrate an investment in either an associate or a joint venture, and apply equally to both.

Example

Applying the equity method at the acquisition date of an associate

P Ltd acquired a 25% interest in the share capital of A Ltd for CU100 000 (including transaction costs of CU10 000) on 1 January 20x4 and is able to exert significant influence over A Ltd as of that date. P Ltd applies the cost model to investments in associates in its separate financial statements.

At the acquisition date, the equity of A Ltd comprised share capital of CU100 000 and retained earnings of CU200 000. The assets and liabilities of A Ltd were considered fairly valued at the date of acquisition, except for owner-occupied land that had a carrying amount of CU100 000 and a fair value of CU110 000. Ignore taxation.

The analysis of the equity of the associate is prepared in the same way as that of a subsidiary, but the investor recognises its interest in the associate in the statement of financial position only as a single line item called 'investment in associate'. There is no non-controlling interest as A Ltd is not a subsidiary. In order to summarise the investor's investment in the associate, a separate column may be added to the analysis of equity where all of the amounts to be included or deducted from the investment account are shown. The balance on that account is the amount that is recognised as the investment in an associate on the group statement of financial position.

Analysis of the equity of S Ltd

	Total equity CU	P Ltd's interest (25%) CU
At acquisition date (1 January 20x2):		
Share capital	100 000	25 000
Retained earnings	200 000	50 000
Fair value adjustment to land	10 000	2 500
Total equity	**310 000**	⟶ **77 500**

What is this?
The investment in associate is recognised at cost of **CU100 000**. The difference between the cost of CU100 000 and the investor's share of the net fair value of the identifiable assets of CU77 500 is goodwill, amounting to CU22 500.

From this summary of the analysis of the equity of the associate at the acquisition date, you will notice that P Ltd acquired a 25% interest in the fair value of the net identifiable assets of A Ltd, being 25% of CU310 000 = CU77 500. P Ltd paid CU100 000 for this investment. The difference represents the goodwill acquired, amounting to CU22 500 (CU100 000 − CU77 500).

Thus, on 1 January 20x4:
- P Ltd accounts for the investment in A Ltd on the cost basis in its separate financial statements. The cost of the investment in the separate statement of financial position of P Ltd is CU100 000.
- The carrying amount of the investment in the associate in the group statement of financial position is CU100 000. This includes the goodwill acquired of CU22 500. Thus, goodwill is not recognised separately; it is included in the cost of the investment in the associate.
- Consequently, no *pro-forma* journal entries are required.

- No adjustment is required for the fair value adjustment of the land as the land is not recognised in the group statement of financial position because the land is not an asset of P Ltd.

	P Ltd (starting point) CU	Pro-forma journals CU	Group (end point) CU
Investment in A Ltd	100 000	–	100 000

Goodwill implications

The cost of the associate or joint venture could include a portion paid for goodwill. Goodwill is calculated at the acquisition date using the same principles as would be applied to calculate goodwill on the acquisition of a subsidiary, but it is not recognised as a separate asset in the group statement of financial position as it is included in the carrying amount of the investment in the associate. Goodwill is calculated as the excess of the cost of the investment over the investor's share of the fair value of the net assets of the investee at the acquisition date. Any goodwill acquired is included in the cost of the investment and should not be recognised separately on the group statement of financial position (see the example above). This is really done as a check. If the net assets attributable to P Ltd exceeded the cost, this is a gain, which must be recognised in group profit or loss in the year in which it arises (see the example below).

Excess over the fair value of net assets of the associate attributable to the investor

As is the case with subsidiaries, the cost of the investment in the associate or joint venture may be less than the fair value of the net assets of the investee attributable to the investor. If this is the case, the investor recognises the **gain** immediately at a group level as part of the earnings from the associate or joint venture. In the above example, the cost of the investment is CU100 000. If we were to assume instead that the cost equalled CU70 000, then compared to the fair value of the net assets of A Ltd that are attributable to P Ltd (CU77 500), a gain of CU7 500 arises on acquisition. The following *pro-forma* journal entry would be processed to recognise the gain in P Ltd's group financial statements at 1 January 20x4:

			CU	CU
Dr		Investment in associate	7 500	
	Cr	Share of profits of associate (P/L)		7 500

Example

Equity accounting an investment in associate relating to arriving at a different fair value from the carrying amount of the net assets of the associate, including tax implications

P Ltd acquired 40% of the ordinary share capital of A Ltd on 1 January 20x4. At that date, the equity of A Ltd comprised ordinary share capital of CU1 000 000 and retained earnings of CU5 000 000. P Ltd paid CU2 750 000 to acquire its 40% interest in A Ltd. At acquisition, P Ltd considered that A Ltd's machinery was undervalued by CU1 000 000. The machinery had a remaining useful life of four years on 1 January 20x4. At that date, the machinery as recognised by A Ltd had a carrying amount of CU800 000 (cost of CU2 000 000 and accumulated depreciation balance of CU1 200 000).

P Ltd accounts for its investment in A Ltd using the cost method in its separate annual financial statements. Assume that a normal company tax rate of 28% applies and 66.6% of capital gains are included in taxable income.

What are the implications of the difference between the fair value and the carrying amount of the machinery at the acquisition date?

The fair value of the machinery is different from its carrying amount in A Ltd at the acquisition date. A fair value adjustment relating to the machinery is therefore required at the acquisition date. In terms of IAS12, paragraph 19, the fair value adjustment gives rise to deferred taxation (as specifically excluded from the IAS12, paragraph 15 exemption; note that even though this is not a business combination as it does not result in control, the principle is the same). This is because an adjustment has been made to the carrying amount of the machinery for accounting purposes (at a group level), but the tax base has not changed. In other words, it remains at the amount as recognised by A Ltd and for which A Ltd will continue receiving tax allowances.

Deferred taxation has been recognised at the applicable company tax rate as the machinery is a depreciable asset and as such is expected to be recovered through use unless it is sold or there is an intention to sell it. The company tax rate best reflects recovery through use as this is the tax rate that will apply to the future economic benefits to be derived from using the asset.

The equity of A Ltd at acquisition date is analysed below.

Analysis of the equity of A Ltd

	Total equity CU	P Ltd's interest (40%) CU
At acquisition date (1 January 20x4):		
Share capital	1 000 000	400 000
Retained earnings	5 000 000	2 000 000
Fair value adjustment to machinery	1 000 000	400 000
Deferred tax liability (at 28%)	(280 000)	(112 000)
Total equity	6 720 000	2 688 000

What is this?
The investment in associate is recognised at cost of **CU2 750 000**.
The difference between the cost of CU2 750 000 and the investor's share of the net fair value of the identifiable assets of CU2 688 000 is goodwill, amounting to CU62 000.

At a group level, the machinery of A Ltd was considered undervalued at acquisition, thus a fair value adjustment is required at acquisition.

At what amount should the investment in A Ltd be recognised in the group financial statements?

CU2 750 000 (Note that this amount includes the goodwill acquired of CU62 000.)

At what amount should the machinery be recognised in the group financial statements?

The machinery is not an asset that is controlled by the group. The equity method does not allow for the recognition of the assets and liabilities of the associate in the group financial statements.

What *pro-forma* journal entries are required at the acquisition date?

No *pro-forma* journal entries are required at the acquisition date. The calculations shown above are done in order to determine the goodwill and to identify the differences between the carrying amount of the machine (and deferred tax implications) in the associate for purposes of preparing group financial statements.

What is the effect of the fair value adjustment at the acquisition date on subsequent periods?

The difference between the carrying amount of the machine (and deferred tax implications) affects the profits of the associate after the acquisition date from a group's perspective. The fair value adjustment at the acquisition date reverses subsequent to acquisition. As the machinery is subsequently depreciated, the profits that are equity accounted at a group level differ from those recognised by the associate. This is because the fair value assigned to the machine differs from the carrying amount in the associate when the associate was acquired. As the future economic benefits of the machine are recovered through use (by depreciating the asset), the difference in the depreciation has deferred tax implications. This is explained in more detail in the section that follows.

4.3 Recognising post-acquisition earnings from associates and joint ventures

The investor's share of the recorded profit or loss of the investee since the acquisition date is included in the investor's group financial statements using the equity method. The investor has influenced the determination of the profits as a result of its ability to participate in the decision-making process of the investee, either through significant influence or through joint control. If the results of the investee were not equity accounted, this would result in an understatement of the results of the operations that are under the influence of the investor. Another reason for equity accounting is that it is a better application of the underlying assumption of the accrual basis, according to which profits should be recognised when they are earned as opposed to when they are received in cash in the form of a distribution.

4.3.1 Profit or loss of the associate and joint venture

The investor shares in the profit or loss of the associates or joint ventures that has been earned after the acquisition date in the same way that a parent shares in the profit or loss of a subsidiary that has been earned after the date of acquisition. However, when you prepare consolidated accounts, you add the statement of financial position of the subsidiary to that of the parent on a line-for-line basis (see Chapter 3 to Chapter 7). In the case of an associate or joint venture, the investor does not control the assets of the investee and this is therefore not done. It would be inappropriate to recognise the assets of the investee in the group statement of financial position as they do not meet the definition of an asset of the group. However, the investment in the associate or joint venture meets the definition of an asset for the group as the group controls that asset and the receipt of future economic benefits from it is probable. The equity method requires the investor to recognise its share of the profit or loss and other comprehensive income of the associate or joint venture after the acquisition date.

The investor's share in the profits of the investee within a reporting year is included in the investor's group profit or loss by disclosing it as a single line item called 'share of profit or loss of associates and joint ventures'. For example, where an investor has a 25% interest in an associate, the group profits of the investor include the investor's share in the profits of the associate. This is achieved through a single line item in profit or loss, as 'share of profit or loss from associate'. In this instance, the equity method differs from consolidation in that profit or loss items of the associate are not added to profit or loss line items of the investor as the investor does not control the assets of the associate that generate these profits, nor does it have obligations for the liabilities, whose settlement may have impacted on those profits.

As this line item is not reflected in the investor's separate financial statements, the investor's share of the profits of the associate and joint venture is recognised in the investor's group financial statements through the following *pro-forma* journal entry:

Dr		Investment in associate and joint venture
	Cr	Share of profit or loss of associate and joint venture (P/L)

Example

Applying the equity method in post-acquisition period for investment in an associate

P Ltd acquired a 25% interest (and significant influence) in the share capital of A Ltd on 1 January 20x4. The identifiable assets and liabilities of A Ltd were considered fairly valued at the date of acquisition. The retained earnings of A Ltd was R200 000 at 1 January 20x4.

Statements of financial position of P Ltd (the company) and A Ltd at 31 December 20x5

	P Ltd (separate financial statements) CU'000	A Ltd CU'000
ASSETS		
Plant and machinery	300	200
Investment in A Ltd	100	–
Current assets	820	710
	1 220	**910**
EQUITY AND LIABILITIES		
Share capital	220	110
Retained earnings	900	700
Total equity	1 120	810
Current liabilities	100	100
	1 220	**910**

Statements of profit or loss of P Ltd and A Ltd for the year ended 31 December 20x5

	P Ltd (separate financial statements) CU'000	A Ltd CU'000
Gross revenue	2 320	1 700
Net operating costs	(1 440)	(1 000)
Interest expense	(100)	(50)
Profit before taxation	780	650
Taxation expense	(300)	(250)
Profit for the year	480	400

On 31 December 20x5, the retained earnings of A Ltd amounted to CU700 000. This amount can be allocated between the respective periods as follows:

		Total CU	P Ltd's share 25% CU
At acquisition date	At 1 January 20x4	200 000	Pre-acquisition
From acquisition date until beginning of current year	From 1 January 20x4 to 31 December 20x4	100 000	25 000
Current year	From 1 January 20x5 to 31 December 20x5	400 000	100 000
Retained earnings	At 31 December 20x5	**700 000**	**125 000**

The equity of the associate is analysed at the acquisition date and for the period between acquisition and the current financial year. This makes sense as the equity at the acquisition date has been paid for and is included in the cost of the investment. None of this is earned by the investor group and is therefore not recognised as part of the equity attributable to its equity holders. The equity method requires recognising the investor's share of profit or loss and other comprehensive income of the associate or joint venture after the acquisition date. However, the amounts that have arisen after the acquisition date must be analysed further into those amounts that were earned in prior periods and those that arose in the current period. The amounts earned in prior periods are reflected as part of the relevant component of equity that prior period earnings and other comprehensive income may have been closed off to.

Analysis of equity of A Ltd

	Total CU'000	At acquisition 25% CU'000	Since acquisition 25% CU'000	Investment CU'000
At acquisition:				
Share capital	110			
Retained earnings	200			
	310	77.5		
Investment		100		100
Goodwill		22.5		
Since acquisition:				
Retained earnings	100		① 25	25
Current year earnings	400		② 100	100
	810		125	225

① The investor's share in the retained earnings of the associate earned after the date of acquisition until the beginning of the current year amounts to **CU25 000**. This is not reflected in the separate financial statements of P Ltd as those financial statements are not prepared applying the equity method to investments in associates or joint ventures. The *pro-forma* journal entry required when preparing the group financial statements of P Ltd as at 31 December 20x5 to account for the retained earnings after the acquisition date up to the beginning of the current year is as follows:

			CU	CU
Dr		Investment in associate	25 000	
	Cr	Retained earnings		25 000

Allocation of the investor's share of the profits of the associate in the prior period

② In addition, the investor's share in the profits of the associate in the current year amounts to **CU100 000** (CU400 000 × 25%).

			CU	CU
Dr		Investment in associate	100 000	
	Cr	Share of profit or loss of associate (P/L)		100 000

Allocation of the investor's share of the profits of the associate in the current period

These *pro-forma* journal entries are recorded in the group worksheet as follows in order to determine the group statement of financial position at 31 December 20x5:

	P Ltd (starting point) CU'000	Pro-forma journals CU'000	Group (end point) CU'000
ASSETS			
Plant and machinery	300		300
Investment in A Ltd	100	25	225
		100	
Current assets	820		820
	1 220	125	**1 345**
EQUITY AND LIABILITIES			
Share capital	220		220
Retained earnings	900	25	1 025
		100	
Total equity	1 120		1 245
Current liabilities	100		100
	1 220	125	**1 345**

Check your answer

The investment in the associate is recognised at the cost of the investment (CU100 000) plus the investor's share of the post-acquisition profits of the associate (CU125 000). Total: CU225 000.

Check your answer

Group retained earnings is the retained earnings of the investor (CU900 000) plus the investor's share of the retained earnings of the associate since the acquisition date (CU125 000). Total: CU1 025 000.

4.3.2 Other comprehensive income of the associate and joint venture

The investor's share in changes in the equity of the associate or joint venture after the acquisition date includes the investor's share of amounts recognised in other comprehensive income. The investee may have recognised amounts in other comprehensive income after the acquisition date (for example, the revaluation of land that is property, plant and equipment in terms of IAS 16, *Property, Plant and Equipment*). The carrying amount of the investor's interest in the associate or joint venture is adjusted by the investor's share of the other comprehensive income to the extent that is appropriate in accordance with the group accounting policy. So in this case, the group's accounting policy is to revalue land that is property, plant and equipment, and the associate applies the same accounting policy to its land.

As indicated earlier and similarly to accounting for the investor's share of the associate or joint venture's profit or loss, this is achieved through a single line item for other comprehensive income of associates or joint ventures being presented in the group statement of profit or loss and other comprehensive income. This line item is called 'share of other comprehensive income of associates or joint ventures' and includes the investor's share of the after-tax amount of the other comprehensive income of associates or joint ventures.

Example

Equity accounting a revaluation gain of an associate

P Ltd acquired 25% of the shares in A Ltd on 1 January 20x4 and has significant influence over the company. When P Ltd acquired its investment in A Ltd, the land recognised as property, plant and equipment in the statement of financial position of A Ltd at a cost of CU40 000 had a fair value of CU50 000. The land was therefore considered undervalued by CU10 000 on 1 January 20x4. A Ltd did not revalue the land on 1 January 20x4. Instead, A Ltd, in accordance with its policy and that of the P Ltd group, revalued the land to CU70 000 on 31 December 20x5. Ignore taxation.

In its individual financial statements, A Ltd recorded the revaluation on 31 December 20x5 as follows:

			CU	CU
Dr		Land	30 000	
	Cr	Revaluation gain (other comprehensive income)		30 000

Revaluation of land

None of the land is recognised by the P Ltd group as the asset is not controlled by P Ltd. However, there is an event that has arisen after the acquisition date that has changed the net assets and equity of A Ltd. This event is the revaluation of the land, which has resulted in an amount being recognised in other comprehensive income. Even though A Ltd revalued the land by CU30 000, only CU20 000 (CU70 000 – CU50 000) has arisen after the acquisition date, of which CU5 000 is P Ltd's share (CU20 000 × 25%).

P Ltd therefore processes the following *pro-forma* journal entry to equity account its share of A Ltd's revaluation gain on 31 December 20x5:

			CU	CU
Dr		Investment in associate	5 000	
	Cr	Share of other comprehensive income of associate (OCI)		5 000

Allocation of the investor's share in other comprehensive income of associate

As *pro-forma* journal entries are theoretically processed 'from scratch' annually, when you are processing the above *pro-forma* journal entry to prepare P Ltd's group financial statements for the financial year ended 31 December 20x6, the credit would be to the group 'revaluation surplus' account as that is the component of equity to which the amounts recognised in other comprehensive income in prior periods relating to revaluing property, plant and equipment would have been closed off to.

Example

Applying the equity method in the post-acquisition period for an investment in a joint venture

This example illustrates the application of the equity method for a joint interest where the joint venture applies the revaluation model for plant and machinery.

P Ltd entered into a joint venture agreement with Z Ltd where each of the companies acquired a 50% interest in the share capital of V Ltd on 1 January 20x4. The identifiable assets and liabilities of V Ltd were considered fairly valued at the date of acquisition.

The financial statements of V Ltd included the following balances at 1 January 20x4:

	CU'000
Share capital	130
Revaluation surplus (plant and machinery)	40
Retained earnings	200
Shareholders' equity	**370**

None of the companies has issued any further ordinary shares since the date of incorporation. Other comprehensive income for the current year relates to a revaluation of plant and machinery. Ignore taxation.

Statements of financial position of P Ltd and V Ltd on 31 December 20x5

	P Ltd CU'000	V Ltd CU'000
ASSETS		
Plant and machinery	300	250
Investment in V Ltd	200	
Current assets	790	730
	1 290	**980**
EQUITY AND LIABILITIES		
Share capital	250	130
Revaluation surplus (plant and machinery)	40	50
Retained earnings	900	700
Shareholders' equity	1 190	880
Current liabilities	100	100
	1 290	**980**

Statements of profit or loss and other comprehensive income of P Ltd and V Ltd for the year ended 31 December 20x5

	P Ltd CU'000	V Ltd CU'000
Revenue (including dividends received)	2 320	1 700
Net operating costs	(1 440)	(1 000)
Interest expense	(100)	(50)
Profit before taxation	780	650
Taxation expense	(300)	(250)
Profit for the year	480	400
Other comprehensive income (revaluation gain on plant and machinery)		4
Total comprehensive income	**480**	**404**

Extract from statement of changes in shareholders' equity of P Ltd and V Ltd for the year ended 31 December 20x5

	P Ltd CU'000	V Ltd CU'000
Retained earnings 1 January 20x5	620	500
Profit for the year	480	400
Dividends paid	(200)	(200)
Retained earnings 31 December 20x5	**900**	**700**

P Ltd prepares group financial statements and the investment in the joint venture is accounted for using the equity method. This means that the investor (P Ltd) shares in the increases in the equity (profit after tax and other comprehensive income) since the acquisition date. The equity method thus requires that we add the investor's share of the post-acquisition profits of the joint venture to the cost of the investment in the joint venture.

On 31 December 20x5, the **retained earnings** of V Ltd amounts to CU700 000. This amount can be allocated between the respective periods as follows:

		Total CU	P Ltd's share 50% CU
At acquisition date	At 1 January 20x4	200 000	Pre-acquisition
From acquisition date until beginning of current year	From 1 January 20x4 to 31 December 20x4	300 000	150 000
Current year Less: Dividends	From 1 January 20x5 to 31 December 20x5	400 000 (200 000)	200 000 (100 000)
Retained earnings	At 31 December 20x5	**CU700 000**	**CU250 000** ◄

Similarly, the **revaluation surplus** of V Ltd amounted to CU50 000 on 31 December 20x5. This amount can be allocated between the respective periods as follows:

		Total	P Ltd's share 50%
At acquisition date	At 1 January 20x4	CU40 000	Pre-acquisition
From acquisition date until beginning of current year	From 1 January 20x4 to 31 December 20x4	6 000	3 000
Current year	From 1 January 20x5 to 31 December 20x5	4 000	2 000
Retained earnings	At 31 December 20x5	**CU50 000**	► **CU5 000**

What is the investor's share in the increases in post-acquisition equity of the investee?

Retained earnings: CU150 000
Current year profit: CU200 000
Revaluation surplus: CU3 000
Other comprehensive income: CU2 000
Less: Dividends received: CU 100 000
Total: **CU255 000**.

The following *pro-forma* journal entries are recorded in application of the equity method:

			CU	CU
Dr		Investment in joint venture (asset)	153 000	
	Cr	Retained earnings (300 × 50%)		150 000
	Cr	Revaluation surplus ([10 – 4] × 50%)		3 000

Allocation of post-acquisition retained earnings and revaluation surplus in joint venture to investor

			CU	CU
Dr		Investment in joint venture (asset)	200 000	
	Cr	Share in profits of joint venture (P/L) (400 × 50% current year profit allocation)		200 000

Allocation of current year profit in joint venture to investor

			CU	CU
Dr		Dividend income (P/L)	100 000	
	Cr	Investment in joint venture (asset)		100 000

Elimination of dividend income from joint venture

			CU	CU
Dr		Investment in joint venture (asset) (4 × 50%)	2 000	
	Cr	Share of other comprehensive income of joint venture (OCI)		2 000

Allocation of other comprehensive income in joint venture to investor

When applying the equity method, the starting point is the investor's financial statements only. The investor's share of the increases in equity of the joint venture is then added using the *pro-forma* journal entries given above. The result is then the preparation of group financial statements, which includes the financial statements of the investor (P Ltd) and the investor's share in the increases in the equity of the joint venture since the acquisition date. The investor's share of the increases in the equity of the joint venture is included in the investment in the joint venture asset account.

Group statement of profit or loss and other comprehensive income for the year ended 31 December 20x5

	CU'000
Gross revenue (2 320 – 100)	2 220
Net operating costs	(1 440)
Interest expense	(100)
Profit before tax	680
Taxation expense	(300)
Share of profit of joint venture	200
Profit for the year	580
Share of other comprehensive income of joint venture	2
Total comprehensive income	**582**

What is this?
Revaluation surplus of P Ltd: CU40 000
P Ltd's share of retained earnings since acquisition date in V Ltd: CU3 000.
Total: **CU43 000**.

What is this?
Retained earnings of P Ltd: CU620 000
P Ltd's share of retained earnings since acquisition date in V Ltd: CU150 000.
Total: **CU770 000**.

Group statement of changes in shareholders' equity for the year ended 31 December 20x5

	Share capital CU'000	Revaluation surplus CU'000	Retained earnings CU'000	Total CU'000
Opening balance	250	43	770	1 063
Profit for the year			580	580
Other comprehensive income		2		2
– Dividends			(200)	(200)
Closing balance	**250**	**45**	**1 150**	**1 445**

Check your knowledge
Closing balance of retained earnings is the retained earnings of the investor (CU900 000) plus the investor's share in the retained earnings of the joint venture since the acquisition date (CU250 000).
Total: **CU1 150 000**.

Group statement of financial position at 31 December 20x5

	CU'000
ASSETS	
Plant and machinery	300
Investment in joint venture	455
Current assets	790
Total assets	**1 545**
EQUITY AND LIABILITIES	
Share capital	250
Revaluation surplus (40 + 5)	45
Retained earnings	1 150
Equity and reserves	1 445
Current liabilities	100
Total equity and liabilities	**1 545**

What is this?
Investment at acquisition date: CU200 000.
Plus investor's share in post-acquisition profit and other comprehensive income: C255 000
Total: **CU455 000**.
Note that this amount includes goodwill of **CU15 000**.

How was the goodwill calculated?
Fair value of net identifiable assets of V Ltd at the acquisition date: CU370 000
P Ltd's share: CU185 000 (50%)
P Ltd's investment in V Ltd: CU200 000
Excess represents goodwill: **CU15 000**.

Example

Equity accounting an investment in an associate with fair value adjustments at acquisition date and deferred tax implications

P Ltd acquired 40% of the ordinary share capital of A Ltd on 1 January 20x4. At that date, the equity of A Ltd comprised ordinary share capital of CU1 000 000 and retained earnings of CU5 000 000. P Ltd paid CU2 750 000 to acquire its 40% interest in A Ltd. At acquisition, P Ltd considered that A Ltd's machinery was undervalued by CU1 000 000. The machinery had a remaining useful life of four years on 1 January 20x4. At that date, the machinery as recognised by A Ltd had an original cost of CU2 000 000 and accumulated depreciation balance of CU1 200 000.

A Ltd sold the machinery at a profit of CU1 100 000 on 31 December 20x5. A Ltd has not revalued the machinery at any stage.

The trial balance of A Ltd for the financial year ended 31 December 20x5, which is the financial year-end of A Ltd and P Ltd (and the P Ltd group), is presented below.

	Debit CU'000	Credit CU'000
Ordinary share capital		1 000
Retained earnings (1 January 20x5)		10 000
Profit after tax		2 840
Property, plant and equipment	9 840	–
Current assets	5 000	–
Current liabilities	–	1 000
	14 840	14 840

P Ltd accounts for its investment in A Ltd using the cost method in its separate annual financial statements. Assume that a normal company tax rate of 28% and a capital gains tax inclusion rate of 66.6% apply.

The equity of A Ltd is analysed as follows from a group's perspective:

Analysis of equity of A Ltd

	100% CU'000	40% CU'000	P Ltd's investment CU'000
1 January 20x4			
Share capital	1 000		
Retained earnings	5 000		
Machinery	1 000		
Deferred tax liability (28%)	(280)		
	6 720	2 688	
Cost		2 750	2 750
Goodwill		62	
20x4 financial year			
Retained earnings	4 820	1 928	① 1 928
Post-acquisition (10 000 – 5 000)	5 000		
Reversal of fair value adjustment on machinery			
Adjustment to depreciation (CU1 000/4)	(250)		
Adjustment to deferred tax	70		
20x5 financial year			
Adjusted profit after tax	2 300	920	② 920
Profit after tax	2 840		
Reversal of fair value adjustment on machinery			
Adjustment to depreciation	(250)		
Adjustment to deferred tax (P/L)	70		
Reversal of fair value adjustment on machinery			
Adjustment to profit on sale (CU1 000 × 2/4)	(500)		
Adjustment to deferred tax (P/L)	140		
	13 840	2 848	5 598

The fair value of the machinery (CU1 800 000) is different from its carrying amount of CU800 000; therefore a fair value adjustment of CU1 000 000 is required. Deferred taxation has been recognised at the applicable company tax rate as the machinery is a depreciable asset and as such is expected to be recovered through use unless it is sold or there is an intention to sell it. The company tax rate best reflects recovery through use as this is the tax rate that will apply to the future economic benefits to be derived from using the asset. Thus: CU1 000 000 × 28% = CU280 000.

The starting point is the trial balance of P Ltd only. The equity method requires that the investor's share of the post-acquisition equity of the associate be included in the group financial statements. The following *pro-forma* journal entries are effecting this:

			CU	CU
Dr		Investment in associate	① 1 928 000	
	Cr	Retained earnings		1 928 000

Equity accounting prior year movement in post-acquisition profits

			CU	CU
Dr		Investment in associate	② 920 000	
	Cr	Share of profits of associate (P/L)		920 000

Equity accounting current year profits

Fair value adjustment at acquisition

The fair value adjustment of the machinery at the acquisition date had the following implications in the group:

- The machinery of A Ltd was considered undervalued at acquisition. Consequently, a fair value adjustment of CU1 000 000 is required at acquisition.
- This adjustment is necessary as the cost of the machinery in the P Ltd group is its fair value of CU1 800 000, compared to the cost or carrying amount as recognised by A Ltd of CU800 000. If the machinery was not adjusted to its fair value, the goodwill recognised by the group would be overstated.
- In this example, A Ltd has not adjusted the carrying amount of the machinery to its fair value in its own financial statements. The adjustment is made when the equity method is applied in the group financial statements.

Reversal of fair value adjustments

- Fair value adjustments are reversed (or realised) subsequent to acquisition.
- If you think about an asset, reversing or realising the carrying amount of an asset implies crediting the asset.

5. Uniform accounting policies

There are instances where IFRS allows entities to choose amongst different measurement bases for assets subsequent to initial recognition. For example, an entity may account for a class of property, plant or equipment on the cost model or the revaluation model. The investor may therefore apply one measurement basis in accounting for an asset in its separate financial statements. The associate or joint venture may apply a different basis in its individual financial statements.

Notwithstanding, the financial statements in which the associate or joint venture is equity accounted must be prepared using uniform accounting policies for similar transactions and/or events. It would not be appropriate for the investor's group financial statements to reflect 'other comprehensive income' relating to revaluing machinery when the group's policy is to account for machinery on the cost model. Therefore, where the associate or joint venture applies accounting policies in its separate financial statements that differ from those of the group, the *pro-forma* journal entries processed to apply the equity method should make adjustments to align the accounting policies of the investee with those of the group.

6. Transactions with associates and joint ventures

The group financial statements of the investor reflect the financial position as well as the performance of cash flows of the group as a single economic entity. The group recognises income that it has earned, expenses that it has incurred, and assets (initially at cost and subsequently using an appropriate measurement basis) and liabilities at the best estimate of amounts required to settle the obligation.

In Chapter 6, you looked at transactions between the parent and its subsidiaries, and the implications for the group. Essentially, the parent and its subsidiaries recognised the effects of the transactions in their respective separate and individual financial statements. The group does not recognise the transactions between the parent and its subsidiaries. The group financial statements therefore differ from what is reflected in the respective separate and individual financial statements. A correct reflection of the financial position and financial performance of the group is achieved through *pro-forma* journal entries.

IFRS principles

Adjusting for the effects of intra-group transactions (IAS28: 28)

Adjustments are made for transactions between an associate or a joint venture and the investor that give rise to unrealised profits and losses to the extent of the investor's share of the associate or joint venture. This means that where an investor (or a group) undertakes transactions with an associate or a joint venture, adjustments must be made for gains and losses on those transactions.

Unlike in the case of consolidation, there is no need to adjust for all transactions between the investor and the investee. You only need to adjust for those transactions where a profit or loss is earned by either the investor or the investee. This means that for transactions such as a loan between entities or the payment of interest on the loan, no adjustment is required under equity accounting. The following principles are important:

- Adjustments are done for transactions between an investor and an investee on a **proportional basis**, determined in accordance with the investor's ownership interest in the investee.
- Adjustments are made on an **after-tax basis**. This refers to the accounts 'share of profit or loss of associates', 'share of other comprehensive income of associate' and 'investment

in associate'. This is done because the equity method recognises a share of the after-tax profits only.

An investor may transact with its associates or joint ventures. The section that follows looks at the implications for the preparation of the investor's group financial statements as a result of possible transactions.

6.1 Dividends earned from associates and joint ventures

The distribution of dividends by the investee to its shareholders is an appropriation of profits. The investor recognises the distribution as dividend income when its right to receive payment is established, for example, when the dividend is declared. The distribution of dividends by an associate gives rise to a credit to dividend income in the accounts of the investor.

Example

Dividends received from an associate

P Ltd has a 25%-held associate and A Ltd earns a profit of CU50 000 during its financial year ended 31 December 20x5. A Ltd distributes all of the profit to its shareholders on 31 December 20x5.

P Ltd therefore processes the following journal entry to record the dividend income of CU12 500 (CU50 000 × 25%) in its separate accounts:

			CU	CU
Dr		Bank/dividend receivable	12 500	
	Cr	Dividend income (P/L)		12 500

Dividends received from the associate, A Ltd

We know that the equity method requires the investor to include its share of the profit or loss of the investee after the acquisition date. P Ltd therefore processes the following *pro-forma* journal entry (1) to equity account its share of A Ltd's profit for the 20x5 financial year (CU50 000 × 25%):

			CU	CU
Dr		Investment in associate	12 500	
	Cr	Share of profits of associate (P/L)		12 500

Allocation of the investor's share of the profit or loss of the associate

The equity method aims to recognise profits when they are earned by the group, irrespective of when they have been received in the form of dividends.

If both the profits that are equity accounted and the dividends were recognised, this would result in double-counting the same profits, as we can see in the example above. The group profit of P Ltd includes dividend income of CU12 500 and earnings from the associate of CU12 500.

When applying the equity method, the distribution of dividends by the investee reduces its net assets and the claim against the business by its shareholders (equity) as these have already been distributed in the form of the dividends. The carrying amount of the investment in the associate should also therefore be reduced as the carrying amount of the investment in an associate is essentially the investor's share of the net assets of the associate.

Distribution of dividends reduces the net assets (and the equity) and therefore should also reduce the carrying amount of the investment in the associate. Another way to think about it is that there is another asset at a group level that has increased as a result of the distribution, namely bank (if the dividend has been received in cash) or a receivable (if the cash is still owed at the reporting date).

As a result, the investor should eliminate any dividend income from the investee during the current reporting period against the investment in the associate account when preparing its group financial statements.

In our example, P Ltd would achieve this through the following *pro-forma* journal entry (2):

			CU	CU
Dr		Dividends income (P/L)	12 500	
	Cr	Investment in associate or joint venture		12 500

Elimination of dividend received from associate

	P Ltd (starting point) CU Dr/(Cr)	*Pro-forma* journal (1): Profit or loss CU	*Pro-forma* journal (2): Dividends CU	Group (end point) CU
Investment in A Ltd	CU100 000	12 500	(12 500)	CU100 000
Share of profit of associate		(12 500)		(12 500)
Dividend income	(12 500)		12 500	–
Bank	12 500			12 500

This makes sense as the profits have already been distributed in the form of dividends. The investor's share of the current year's retained profits is therefore zero and the investment in the associate is the cost of CU100 000. The overall effect at the investor's group financial statements level is that cash of CU12 500 has been received and is reflected as the investor's share of A Ltd's profit in profit or loss of CU12 500 or alternatively that this profit of CU12 500 has been received in cash.

Example

Earnings and dividends from associates

P Ltd acquired 40% of A Ltd on 1 January 20x4 for CU1m. During the 20x4 financial year, A Ltd earned profits (after tax) of CU500 000. It earned after-tax profits of CU600 000 in the 20x5 financial year. A Ltd declared a dividend of CU200 000 on 31 December 20x5.

What is the amount of dividend income that P Ltd received from A Ltd?
CU80 000 (CU200 000 × 40%)

> **Calculate the share of profits from the associate line item as it should appear in the group profit or loss of P Ltd for the year ended 31 December 20x5, including the comparative amount.**
>
> Year ended 31 December 20x5: CU240 000 (CU600 000 × 40%)
> Year ended 31 December 20x4: CU200 000 (CU500 000 × 40%)
>
> **Calculate the investment in associate amount as it should appear in the group statement of financial position of P Ltd at 31 December 20x5, including the comparative amount.**
>
> At 31 December 20x5: CU1 000 000 + CU200 000 + CU240 000 − CU80 000 = CU1 360 000
> At 31 December 20x4: CU1 000 000 + CU200 000 = CU1 200 000

6.2 Loans between the investor and associates and joint ventures

There is no need to adjust for transactions such as a loan between the entities or the payment of interest on the loan. This is because the equity method does not require that the assets and liabilities of the investee be added to those of the investee (as in the case of consolidation). The group financial statements only include the assets and liabilities of the investor.

For example, assume that P Ltd lends CU15 000 to a 25%-held associate, A Ltd, on 31 December 20x5. P Ltd processes the following journal entry to record the transaction in its separate accounts:

			CU	CU
Dr		Loan receivable	15 000	
	Cr	Bank		15 000

Loan to associate, A Ltd

A Ltd processes the following journal entry to record receipt of the cash:

			CU	CU
Dr		Bank	15 000	
	Cr	Loan payable		15 000

Loan from investor, P Ltd

- The group financial statements will reflect 100% of the assets and liabilities recognised by P Ltd and none of the assets and liabilities of A Ltd, as those assets and liabilities are not rights and obligations of the P Ltd group.
- In this case, the group financial statements of P Ltd will reflect a loan receivable, that is, the right to receive cash in the future of CU15 000. As this is already reflected in P Ltd's separate statement of financial position at 31 December 20x5, no *pro-forma* journal entries are required.

	P Ltd (starting point) CU	Pro-forma journals CU	Group (end point) CU
Investment in A Ltd	100 000	–	100 000
Loan receivable	15 000		15 000

Think about it this way: where the group is the economic entity, the group has a cash outflow of CU15 000, reflected as a credit to its bank balance. The cash has not come back into the group as the group does not control A Ltd and therefore does not control its bank balance. In terms of double entry, there has to be a balancing debit. The cash outflow now will be recovered in the future when the loan is settled. At this point, the group has the right to receive that amount in the future. This is represented by the loan receivable balance of CU15 000.

7. Transactions between the investor and its associate or joint venture that require adjustments

The investor should, on a similar basis, eliminate the effect of transactions with its associates or joint ventures that affect on the investor's group profit or loss. IAS28 refers to 'upstream' and 'downstream' transactions between the investor and its investee:
- 'Upstream' transactions are, for example, the sale of an asset from the investee to the investor.
- 'Downstream' transactions refer to the sale of an asset from the investor to the investee.

In the group financial statements, profits or losses resulting from both 'upstream' and 'downstream' transactions between an investor and its associate or joint venture should be eliminated to the extent of the investor's interest in the associate or joint venture, unless the asset is sold at a loss, which is an indicator that the asset sold could be impaired. The reason that the unrealised profits or losses are eliminated only to the extent of the investor's interest in the associate or joint venture is because that is the portion that is intra-group.

Effectively, the interest that is not held by the investor is held by third parties, in other words, the other investors of the associate or joint venture. This portion represents a transaction with third parties. At a group level, the earnings process in respect of this portion of the transaction is complete and any related profits or losses can be recognised. This is consistent with the accrual concept, which implies recognising income that has been earned and expenses that have been incurred.

7.1 Intra-group sale of depreciable assets

In Section 4 above, you learnt that in applying the equity method, adjustments are made to the equity balances as recorded by the investee at the acquisition date and that some of these adjustments may include fair value adjustments relating to non-current assets. The effect of such fair value adjustments on the post-acquisition profits of the investee may require adjustments from a group's perspective to the profits reported by the investee. Furthermore, adjustments are required for any intra-group sale of depreciable assets.

This is necessary as, from the group's perspective, at the time of the sale of the plant or equipment, the profit on the sale is unrealised. The profit is realised as the asset is consumed or used by the entity holding the asset. The consumption benefits are measured by the depreciation of the asset. Hence, as the asset is depreciated on a straight-line basis, a portion of the profit is realised in each year after the intra-group transfer.

Example
Intra-group sale of depreciable non-current asset

'Upstream' transaction

On 1 January 20x6, A Ltd (a 30%-held associate of P Ltd) sells a machine to P Ltd for CU100 000. At that date, the machine had a carrying amount in A Ltd's statement of financial position of CU80 000, and was expected to have a residual value of nil and a remaining useful life of four years. These estimates have been reviewed and confirmed annually. Ignore taxation.

During the financial year ended 31 December 20x6, A Ltd and P Ltd would have recognised the following amounts relating to this transaction:

A Ltd	CU
Profit on disposal of machine (CU100 000 – CU80 000)	20 000

P Ltd	CU
Depreciation (CU100 000/4)	25 000
Machine (at cost)	100 000
Accumulated depreciation	25 000

This is an upstream transaction as the associate has sold the machine to the investor. At a group level, the effect of this transaction can be summarised as follows:

- Our starting point trial balance for the preparation of the group financial statements of P Ltd for the 20x6 financial year includes 100% of all amounts recognised by P Ltd and none of the amounts recognised by A Ltd.
- A Ltd recognised a profit on disposal of CU20 000. To the extent of P Ltd's shareholding (30%), a portion of this profit is intra-group (CU20 000 × 30% = CU6 000).
- The profit or loss of A Ltd includes CU6 000 that cannot be recognised at a group level as it is intra-group and is therefore unrealised from a group perspective. The earnings from the associate are thus too high and a debit is required when preparing the *pro-forma* journal entries to reduce the earnings from the associate.
- The statement of financial position of P Ltd includes an asset (the machine) that is overstated by CU6 000.
- The following *pro-forma* journal entry is required to reflect the group financial statements of P Ltd correctly as a result of the intra-group transaction on 1 January 20x6:

			CU	CU
Dr		Share of profits of associate (P/L)	6 000	
	Cr	Machinery (cost)		6 000

Elimination of the intra-group portion of the profit included in the acquisition cost of the machine from associate, A Ltd

- The unrealised profit will be realised at a group level in the future reporting periods as the asset is subsequently depreciated or sold outside the group.
- The realisation of the profit is effectively a reversal of the *pro-forma* journal entry required when eliminating the unrealised profit.
- The machine is a depreciable asset. As it is depreciated over the next four years (assuming that the machine is not sold prior to the end of its useful life), 25% (one-quarter) of the unrealised profit of CU6 000 will be realised annually, which is 25% × CU6 000 = CU1 500. The effect of realising the profit is that group profits are increased for a transaction that originated in A Ltd's profit or loss, that is, the sale of the asset from A Ltd to P Ltd.
- In addition, the accumulated depreciation recognised by P Ltd is too high as this was based on the cost to P Ltd, including the effects of the CU6 000 unrealised profit.
- The following *pro-forma* journal entry is required to reflect the group financial statements of P Ltd correctly as a result of the realisation of the profit on 31 December 20x6:

			CU	CU
Dr		Accumulated depreciation (machinery)	1 500	
	Cr	Share of profits of associate (P/L)		1 500

Adjustment to profits in the associate resulting from release, through usage, of a portion of the intra-group profit included in the acquisition cost of the machine

'Downstream' transaction

Assume instead that the transaction is such that P Ltd sells the machine to A Ltd on 1 January 20x6. This is a downstream transaction as the investor has sold the machine to the associate.

During the financial year ended 31 December 20x6, A Ltd and P Ltd would have recognised the following amounts relating to this transaction:

P Ltd	CU
Profit on disposal of machine (CU100 000 – CU80 000)	20 000

A Ltd	CU
Depreciation (CU100 000/4)	25 000
Machine (at cost)	100 000
Accumulated depreciation	25 000

At a group level, the effect of the above transaction can be summarised as follows:

- Our starting point trial balance for the preparation of the group financial statements of P Ltd for the 20x6 financial year includes 100% of all amounts recognised by P Ltd and none of the amounts recognised by A Ltd.
- P Ltd recognised a profit on disposal of CU20 000. To the extent of P Ltd's shareholding (30%), a portion of this profit is intra-group, being CU20 000 × 30% = CU6 000. The profit on disposal recognised by P Ltd is therefore too high at a group level and needs to be reduced.
- The statement of financial position of A Ltd includes an asset, which is the machine that is overstated by CU6 000. The statement of financial position of A Ltd is represented by the investment in its associate, being P Ltd's share of the net assets of A Ltd. The CU6 000 cannot be recognised at a group level as it is intra-group. The investment in associate balance is therefore too high and a credit is required when preparing the *pro-forma* journal entries to reduce the investment in associate balance.

- The following *pro-forma* journal entry is required to reflect the group financial statements of P Ltd correctly as a result of the intra-group transaction on 1 January 20x6:

			CU	CU
Dr		Profit on disposal (P/L)	6 000	
	Cr	Investment in associate		6 000

Elimination of intra-group portion of profit resulting from sale of the machine to the associate

- The unrealised profit will be realised at a group level in the future reporting periods as the asset is subsequently depreciated or sold outside the group.
- The realisation of the profit is effectively a reversal of the *pro-forma* journal entry required when eliminating the unrealised profit.
- The machine is a depreciable asset. It is depreciated over the next four years (assuming that the machine is not sold prior to the end of its useful life); 25% (one-quarter) of the unrealised profit of CU6 000 will be realised annually, which is 25% × CU6 000 = CU1 500. The effect of realising the profit is that group profits are increased for a transaction that originated in P Ltd's profit or loss, being the sale of the asset from P Ltd to A Ltd. The portion of the profit on disposal that could not previously be recognised at a group level can now be recognised as it is realised.
- In addition, the accumulated depreciation recognised by A Ltd is too high as this was based on the cost to A Ltd, including the effects of the CU6 000 unrealised profit. As discussed above, P Ltd's share of the net assets of A Ltd is represented by the investment in its associate balance.
- As a result of the realisation of the profit on 31 December 20x6, the following *pro-forma* journal entry is required to reflect the group financial statements of P Ltd correctly:

			CU	CU
Dr		Investment in associate	1 500	
	Cr	Profit on disposal (P/L)		1 500

Adjustment to profit on disposal of asset in investor resulting from the use of the asset by the associate

7.2 Intra-group inventory transactions

If there are profits or losses that the investor cannot recognise at a group level, this also implies that the investor should eliminate the unrealised portion of a transaction included in the carrying amount of an asset in the group statement of financial position using *pro-forma* journal entries. For example, an investor has a 25% interest in an associate and acquires inventory from the associate at cost plus 10%. The profit of the associate includes the mark-up earned by the associate on inventory sold to the investor. The inventory on hand recognised in the group statement of financial position of the investor includes an unrealised profit between the investor and its associate. The investor should eliminate its interest in the unrealised profit (25% multiplied by 10% mark-up). The effect of this adjustment is that the investor will include its share in the profit or loss of the associate only after eliminating the unrealised profit. In addition, the investor will recognise the inventory in its group statement of financial position after eliminating the unrealised profit.

Example

Inventory transactions with an associate (and deferred tax implications)

'Upstream' transaction

A Ltd is a 25%-held associate of P Ltd. A sells inventory to P Ltd for CU50 000 during the financial year ended 31 December 20x5. The inventory had previously cost A Ltd CU40 000. None of the inventory had been sold by P Ltd by 31 December 20x5. P Ltd sold all of the inventory in the 20x6 financial year.

For the financial years ended 31 December 20x5 and 20x6, A Ltd and P Ltd would have recognised the amounts relating to the inventory in their respective individual and separate financial statements that are shown below.

A Ltd		31 December 20x5 CU	31 December 20x6 CU
Sales		50 000	–
Cost of sales		(40 000)	–
Gross profit		10 000	–

P Ltd		31 December 20x5 CU	31 December 20x6 CU
Inventory ◄		50 000	–

Consider the following for the 31 December 20x5 financial year:

- Our starting point trial balance for the preparation of the group financial statements of P Ltd for the 20x5 financial year includes 100% of all amounts recognised by P Ltd and none of the amounts recognised by A Ltd, as A Ltd is an associate and the equity method is applied.
- A Ltd recognised a gross profit of CU10 000. If that were the only profit it recognised, P Ltd would process a *pro-forma* journal entry to equity account its share of that profit, that is, CU10 000 × 25% = CU2 500.

Pro-forma journal entry (1)

			CU	CU
Dr		Investment in associate	2 500	
	Cr	Share of profit or loss of associate (P/L)		2 500

Allocation of investor's share of profit of associate in current year

However, this profit includes gross profit relating to the inventory, none of which has been sold by P Ltd. The earnings process is therefore not complete; if the inventory has not been sold, that profit cannot be recognised. This profit is therefore unrealised at the reporting date. P Ltd's share of this unrealised profit is CU10 000 × 25%, which amounts to CU2 500. A *pro-forma* journal entry is required to do the following:

- Eliminate the unrealised profit.
- Reduce the carrying amount of the asset that is overstated, in other words, in this case, the profit is unrealised because the inventory has not been sold by P Ltd. The asset that is overstated is inventory.

Pro-forma journal entry (2)

			CU	CU
Dr		Share of profit or loss of associate (P/L)	2 500	
	Cr	Inventory		2 500

Elimination of portion of intra-group profit relating to inventory acquired from associate

The effect is that the earnings from the associate is nil, which makes sense in this example. The gross profit all arose from the sales of inventory to P Ltd, none of which had been sold, so P Ltd's share of the earnings of A Ltd is nil. The investment of A Ltd has increased by CU2 500 because the net assets of A Ltd increased by CU10 000 (Bank), of which CU2 500 (CU10 000 × 25%) is attributable to P Ltd.

	P Ltd (starting point)	Pro-forma journal (1)	Pro-forma journal (2)	Group (end point)
Dr/(Cr)	**CU**	**CU**	**CU**	**CU**
Investment in A Ltd	CU100 000	2 500	–	CU102 500
Inventory	50 000		(2 500)	47 500
Profit or loss (before taxation)		(2 500)	2 500	–

What are the tax implications of these adjustments?

Because of eliminating the unrealised profit, A Ltd's profits (before taxation) have reduced. However, the investor shares in the **profit after tax** of the associate. The group's share of the profits of the associate amounts to CU10 000 × 72% × 25% = CU1 800.

Pro-forma journal entry (2) above should thus be replaced by the *pro-forma* journal entry that follows.

			CU	CU
Dr		Investment in associate	1 800	
	Cr	Share of profit or loss of associate		1 800

Allocation of investor's share in the profit after tax of associate

From a group's perspective, the carrying amount of inventory is reduced by CU2 500. However, its tax base remains the same. As the inventory is recovered through sale and the tax rate that best reflects recovering the inventory through sale is 28%, a deductible temporary difference arises. Thus, an adjustment is required for the tax effect of CU2 500 × 28% = CU700.

In the **31 December 20x5** financial year, the following *pro-forma* journal entry will give effect to the elimination of the unrealised profit and the deferred tax implications:

			CU	CU
Dr		Share of profit or loss of associate (P/L)	1 800	
Dr		Deferred taxation (asset)	700	
	Cr	Inventory		2 500

Elimination of portion of intra-group profit and tax implications relating to inventory acquired from the associate

Note that the investor's share of the profits of the associate is net of taxation.

Consider the following for the **31 December 20x6** financial year:

- Our starting point trial balance for the preparation of the group financial statements of P Ltd for the 20x5 financial year includes 100% of all amounts recognised by P Ltd and none of the amounts recognised by A Ltd.
- In the prior period, A Ltd earned profits of CU10 000, of which CU2 500 is attributable to P Ltd. *Pro-forma* journal entries relating to prior periods are theoretically reproduced annually. P Ltd would process the *pro-forma* journal entry that follows to equity account the prior period earnings, net of taxation (remember that last year's undistributed profits are accumulated in retained earnings).

Pro-forma journal entry (1)

			CU	CU
Dr		Investment in associate	1 800	
	Cr	Retained earnings (CU10 000 × 25% × 72%)		1 800

Allocation of investor's share in the retained earnings of the associate

The above *pro-forma* journal entry equity accounts profits that A Ltd recognised in 20x5, which the group can only recognise in 20x6 as P Ltd has sold the inventory (the profit is earned and is no longer 'unrealised'). Therefore the earnings from the associate that could not be recognised in 20x5 is recognised in 20x6. The *pro-forma* journal entry to reflect this is shown below.

Pro-forma journal entry (2)

			CU	CU
Dr		Retained earnings	1 800	
	Cr	Share of profit or loss of associate (P/L)		1 800

Allocation of investor's share in the profit after tax of the associate resulting from intra-group inventory sold in the current year

The cumulative effect on the group retained earnings attributable to the equity holders of P Ltd as at 31 December 20x6 is nil, but the impact of the above *pro-forma* journal entry is that profits are correctly reflected in group profit or loss in the period in which they were earned in line with the accrual basis.

	P Ltd (starting point) CU	*Pro-forma* journal (1) CU	*Pro-forma* journal (2) CU	Group (end point) CU
Dr/(Cr)				
Investment in A Ltd	CU100 000	1 800	–	CU101 800
Inventory	–			–
Retained earnings		(1 800)	1 800	–
Share of profit of associate			(1 800)	(1 800)

'Downstream' transaction

Assume the same information as the previous example except that the transaction is such that P Ltd sells the inventory to A Ltd. During the financial year ended 31 December 20x5, A Ltd and P Ltd would have recognised the following amounts relating to this transaction:

P Ltd	31 December 20x5 CU	31 December 20x6 CU
Sales	50 000	–
Cost of sales	(40 000)	–
Gross profit	10 000	–

A Ltd	31 December 20x5 CU	31 December 20x6 CU
Inventory	50 000	–

Consider the following for the **31 December 20x5** financial year:

- Our starting point trial balance for the preparation of the group financial statements of P Ltd for the 20x5 financial year includes 100% of all amounts recognised by P Ltd and none of the amounts recognised by A Ltd (see Section 4).
- P Ltd recognised a gross profit of CU10 000. If that were the only profit it recognised, P Ltd would have earned a profit of CU10 000.
- However, this profit includes gross profit relating to the inventory, none of which has been sold by A Ltd. The earnings process is therefore not complete; if the inventory has not been sold, that profit cannot be recognised. This profit is unrealised at the reporting date. P Ltd's share of this unrealised profit is CU10 000 × 25%, which amounts to CU2 500. A *pro-forma* journal entry is required to do the following:
    - Eliminate the unrealised profit. There is no account called 'unrealised profit', but we know that profit is reflected in the gross profit, which is the difference between the sales and the cost of sales. The implication is that at the P Ltd group level, there are some sales that cannot be recognised, that is, P Ltd's share of the sales that are effectively with itself (CU50 000 × 25%, which equals CU12 500). If the sale cannot be recognised, neither can the related cost of sale (being the cost of the inventory sold of CU40 000 × 25%, which equals CU10 000) be recognised. The difference between the sales that cannot be recognised and the cost of sales is CU2 500, which is P Ltd's share of the unrealised profit.
    - Reduce the carrying amount of the asset that is overstated. In this case, this refers to the profit that is unrealised because the inventory has not been sold by A Ltd. The asset that is overstated is inventory of A Ltd. However, none of this is reflected on P Ltd's group statement of financial position. The investment in associate reflects P Ltd's share of the net assets of A Ltd. It would make sense to adjust the investment in the associate account as follows:

Pro-forma journal entry (1)

			CU	CU
Dr		Sales	12 500	
	Cr	Cost of sales		10 000
	Cr	Investment in associate		2 500

Elimination of intra-group portion of the sale between the investor and the associate

Assume that the current year profit of A Ltd amounts to CU12 000. P Ltd's share of A Ltd's profit for the current year thus amounts to CU3 000 (CU12 000 × 25%).

Pro-forma journal entry (2)

			CU	CU
Dr		Investment in associate	3 000	
	Cr	Share of profit or loss of associate (P/L)		3 000

Allocation of the investor's share in the current year profit of the associate

Note that there is no inventory in the group financial statements as the inventory is in A Ltd. The asset that is overstated is the investment in the associate.

Dr/(Cr)	P Ltd (starting point) CU	Pro-forma journal (1) CU	Pro-forma journal (2) CU	Group (end point) CU
Investment in A Ltd	CU100 000	(2 500)	3 000	CU100 500
Share of profit of associate			3 000	3 000
Sales	(50 000)	12 500		(37 500)
Cost of sales	40 000	(10 000)		30 000

The effect is that the group profit of P Ltd includes only the sales and the cost of sales in respect of transactions with third parties, in other words, in this case, the other investors in A Ltd.

What are the tax implications of these adjustments?

Because of eliminating the unrealised profit, group profits (before taxation) have reduced compared to our starting point, therefore group taxation must reduce. Consequently a credit is required to deferred taxation in profit or loss. (Think about it: tax is an expense. If we wanted to reduce it, we would need to credit the expense.) As the inventory is recovered through sale and the tax rate that best reflects recovering the inventory through sale is 28%, an adjustment is required for the tax effect of the reduction in group profits, in other words, CU2 500 × 28% = CU700.

In terms of a double entry, a debit is required. This debit can either go to deferred taxation in the statement of financial position or to the investment in associate. (We are adjusting the group statement of financial position of P Ltd for an adjustment to the net assets of A Ltd.) All we have reflecting the net assets of A Ltd is the investment in associate line item.

In the **31 December 20x5** financial year, the following *pro-forma* journal entry will give effect to the deferred tax implications of these adjustments:

			CU	CU
Dr		Investment in associate/deferred taxation (asset)	700	
	Cr	Deferred tax expense (P/L)		700

Adjusting for the deferred tax implications resulting from the elimination of the intra-group portion of the sale of inventory

Consider the following for the **31 December 20x6** financial year:

- In the 20x6 financial year, the P Ltd group can now recognise the sales and related cost of sales that it could not previously as A Ltd has sold the inventory. The earnings process is now complete at a group level. However, we know that P Ltd has already recognised these amounts, but in the incorrect period (in other words, the prior period: 20x5). The starting point trial balance (that is, the separate financial statements of P Ltd) includes these amounts in retained earnings. An adjustment is required to remove the amounts from retained earnings (as we are starting with the separate financial statements of P Ltd) and recognise them in the profit or loss for 20x6:

			CU	CU
Dr		Retained earnings	1 800	
Dr		Deferred tax expense (P/L)	700	
Dr		Cost of sales	10 000	
	Cr	Sales		12 500

Elimination of intra-group portion of profits in current and prior periods resulting from the sale of inventory to the associate

- The cumulative effect on group retained earnings attributable to equity holders of P Ltd as at 31 December 20x6 is nil, but the impact of the above *pro-forma* journal entry is that profits are correctly reflected in group profit or loss in the period in which they were earned in line with the accrual basis.
- No adjustment is required to the investment in associate because the inventory has been sold and the remaining net assets do not include any unrealised profit as at 31 December 20x6.

8. Where the associate or joint venture has a different year end

Where the investee's reporting date is different from that of the investor, the investee often prepares a set of financial statements for the use of the investor with the same reporting date as the financial statements of the investor. This is a costly exercise and where it is impractical to do this, the financial statements prepared at the reporting date of the investee are used, irrespective of the fact that the date is different. However, the consistency principle dictates that the length of the reporting periods and the differences between the reporting dates be consistent from one period to another period, resulting in adjustments being made for the effects of any significant events or transactions that occurred between the investee's reporting date and the investor's reporting date. IAS28 requires that the difference between the reporting dates of the investee and investor should, in any case, be no more than three months.

9. Losses of associates and joint ventures

The equity method requires the investor's share in the profit or loss of the investee to be added to those of the investor in order to determine the group profits. This implies that if the investee incurs losses, the investor equity accounts its share of those losses.

However, the investor cannot share in the losses of an associate in excess of the carrying amount of its investment. This implies that the investor would therefore not reduce its investment in an investee below zero and the investment in an investee can never be a negative asset. The carrying amount of the **investment in the associate** would therefore be **reduced to zero** by recognising the attributable amount of losses, at which point recognition of losses ceases unless it is appropriate to recognise a liability. However, where the investor has incurred obligations **or** made payments on behalf of the investee, or where the investor has made certain guarantees or commitments, it would be appropriate to recognise these additional losses to the extent of its obligations by applying the definition and recognition criteria of a liability. This could occur where the investor has underwritten certain debt obligations of an investee.

Where, after incurring previous losses, the investee reports profits in subsequent periods, the investor should resume including its share of these profits, but only after its share of the profits equals its share of the losses not previously recognised. This prevents the investor from overstating the carrying amount of its investment.

10. Impairments

An investment in an associate or joint venture is an asset. An asset should not be recognised at a carrying amount that is in excess of the future economic benefits expected to be generated by that asset. At the end of each financial period, the investor must assess whether there is an indication that the carrying amount of the investment could be impaired. Indicators could be that the associate is in significant financial difficulty, may enter bankruptcy or is making continued losses.

An impairment test involves comparing the carrying amount of an investment in an associate or joint venture to its recoverable amount (which is the higher of its value-in-use or its fair value less costs to sell). An **impairment loss** should be recognised when the carrying amount is higher than the recoverable amount as the recoverable amount is the minimum future economic benefits expected to flow from the asset. You should determine the recoverable amount of an investment separately for each associate or joint venture, unless the associate or joint venture does not generate cash flows that are sufficiently independent from those of the other entities in the group.

As mentioned above, the **recoverable amount** of an investment is the higher of its value-in-use or its fair value less costs to sell. You should determine the value-in-use of an investment by estimating the entity's share in the present value of the estimated future cash flows expected to be generated by the investee as a whole, including the cash flows from the operations of the investee and the proceeds on the ultimate disposal of the investment. This implies that the investment should be valued at the present value of the future benefits that are expected to flow to the investor from this investment; these inflows arise from the dividends to be received and from the ultimate disposal of the investment.

If the recoverable amount of the investment subsequently increases such that it is no longer impaired, the investor recognises a reversal of the impairment loss.

Example

Impairment implications (ignoring tax implications)

Objective evidence indicates that the investment in the associate was impaired by CU1 000 and CU2 000 as at 31 December 20x4 and 31 December 20x5 respectively. The impairment losses should therefore be recognised in each of the two subsequent years.

The *pro-forma* journal entry that follows recognises the impairment in the year subsequent to the acquisition date (at 31 December 20x5). As the CU1 000 impairment loss arose in the 20x4 financial year and as that year's profit or loss has been closed off to retained earnings, the adjustment is recognised in retained earnings. The CU2 000 impairment loss that arose in 20x5 is recognised in the current year's (that is, 20x5) group profit or loss:

			CU	CU
Dr		Retained earnings	1 000	
Dr		Share of profits of associate (P/L)	2 000	
	Cr	Investment in associate		3 000

Recognising impairments in the investment in the associate in the prior and current periods

11. An associate or joint venture that has cumulative preference shares in issue

If an associate or joint venture has outstanding cumulative preference shares in issue that have been classified as equity, the investor computes its share of the profit or loss of the associate or joint venture after adjusting for the dividends on these preference shares, irrespective of whether or not they have been declared.

Example

Profits attributable to ordinary and preference shareholders

A Ltd earns a profit of CU100 000, of which CU15 000 is attributable to its cumulative preference equity holders. The remainder of CU85 000 (CU100 000 − CU15 000) is attributable to A Ltd's ordinary equity holders. P Ltd owns 25% of A Ltd's ordinary shares and none of the preference shares.

Applying the equity method, P Ltd's share of the profit of A Ltd is CU21 250 (CU85 000 × 25%).

Refer to Chapter 8 for a discussion of the allocation of the profits of a subsidiary that has cumulative preference shares. More complex group structures relating to associates, for example, vertical groups, or where an associate or joint venture owns subsidiaries, are discussed in Chapter 11.

12. Disclosure

IFRS12, *Disclosure of Interests in Other Entities*, requires disclosure of the following information for all material joint arrangements and associates:

- The name
- The nature of the entity's relationship
- The principal place of business
- The entity's proportion of ownership interest, participating share or voting rights (as applicable).

The following additional note disclosures are also required:

- Significant judgements and assumptions made in assessing whether the entity has joint control or significant influence and whether a joint arrangement is a joint operation or joint venture
- Where the investor holds less than 20% of the voting or potential voting power of the investee, but concludes that it has significant influence, the fact and the reasons that the investor is presumed to have significant influence should be disclosed
- Where the investor holds more than 20% of the voting or potential voting power of the investee, but concludes that it does not have significant influence, the fact and the reasons that the investor is presumed not to have significant influence should be disclosed
- On an individual basis or in appropriate groupings, summarised financial information regarding the assets, liabilities, revenues and profit or loss of the associates and joint ventures and reconciliations to the carrying amount of the investment in its associate or joint venture
- The fair value of investments in associates or joint ventures that are equity accounted for which there are published price quotations available
- The reporting date of the associate or joint venture, in instances where the reporting date is different from that of the investor, and the reason or reasons for using a different reporting date (and reporting period)
- The nature of any significant restrictions on the ability of the associate or joint venture to transfer funds to the investor, either as dividend payments or repayments of loans
- Unrecognised share of losses of the equity accounted joint venture or associate for the reporting period and cumulatively
- The investor's share of those contingencies and capital commitments of an associate or joint venture for which the investor is contingently liable and those contingencies that arise because the investor is severally liable for some or all of the liabilities of the associate or joint venture.

Example
Presentation of interests in associate and joint venture companies

In this example, we look at the presentation of interests in associate and joint venture companies, as included in the annual financial statements of The Super Group, June 2013.

Extract from accounting policies

Associate companies

An associate is an entity over which the Group has the ability to exercise significant influence, but not control, through participation in the financial and operating policy decisions of the investee, generally accompanying a shareholding embodying between 20% and 50% of the voting rights.

Joint venture companies

A joint venture is a contractual arrangement whereby the Group and other parties undertake an economic activity that is subject to joint control.

Equity accounted investees (associate and joint venture companies)

The Group's share of post-acquisition recognised profits or losses of equity-accounted investees is incorporated in the financial statements, using the equity method of accounting (initially recognised at cost), from the effective dates that significant influence was obtained until the effective dates that significant influence ceased, except when classified as held-for-sale where equity accounting ceases and the investment is measured at the lower of its carrying value and fair value less costs to sell.

Adjustments are made on consolidation to bring the associates' financial statements in line with the Group's accounting policies. Accumulated profits and movements on reserves are determined from the most recent audited financial statements of the equity-accounted investees and available information to the latest reporting date available.

Where the Group's share of losses of an equity-accounted investee exceeds its interest in the investment, the investment is carried at nil. Additional losses are only recognised to the extent that the Group has incurred legal or constructive obligations in respect of advances and commitments made to the equity-accounted investment.

Equity-accounted investees are carried in the statement of financial position at cost adjusted by cumulative post-acquisition changes in the Group's share of the net assets of the equity-accounted investees, less any impairment in the value of individual investments. If impaired, the carrying value of the Group's share of the underlying assets of associates is written down to its estimated recoverable amount in accordance with the accounting policy on impairment. The Group's equity-accounted investees includes goodwill (net of any accumulated impairment loss) identified on acquisition.

Extract from the notes to the financial statements

Notes to the annual financial statements *continued*
for the year ended 30 June 2013

	30 June 2013 R000	30 June 2012 R000
7 Equity-accounted investees and other non-current assets		
Equity-accounted investees	3 839	2 696
Other non-current assets	–	2 838
	3 839	5 534

7.1 **Equity-accounted investments**	% ownership	% ownership
The Group has the following significant unlisted equity-accounted investments:		
Moditouch (Proprietary) Limited	50	50

Current year transactions related to equity accounted investees
In the prior financial year, the Group acquired an equity investment in Moditouch Proprietary Limited for R2 588 500.

	R000	R000
Movement summary		
Balance at beginning of year	2 696	–
Equity-accounted investee acquired	–	2 589
Share of profit for the year	1 143	107
Balance at end of year	3 839	2 696

The Group's share in net assets and profit for the year in respect of its equity-accounted investee are R3 784 000 (2012: R2 642 000) and R1 143 000 (2012: R107 000) respectively.

Rental paid to equity-accounted investees during the 2013 year amounted to R6 712 000 (2012: R2 096 000).

The financial year-end of the equity-accounted investee is 30 June 2013.

The equity-accounted investee is not a publicly listed entity and consequentially does not have published price quotations.

Summary financial information for equity-accounted investees:

Summarised statement of financial position at 30 June 2013

	30 June 2013 R000	30 June 2012 R000
Current assets	492	1 866
Non-current assets	83 467	78 000
Total assets	83 959	79 866
Current liabilities	163	–
Non-current liabilities	76 227	74 583
Total liabilities	76 390	74 583
Net assets	7 569	5 283
Summarised statement of comprehensive income for the year ended 30 June 2013		
Income	11 089	3 521
Expenses	(7 915)	(3 184)
Taxation	(889)	(123)
Profit	2 285	214

Source: Super Group Ltd. 2013. Annual Financial Statements for the year ending 30 June 2013. [Online], Available: http://www.supergroup.co.za/downloads/2013_AFS.pdf Accessed 27 June 2014.

Test your knowledge

There is a list of learning objectives at the beginning of this chapter. Go back to this list and check whether you have achieved these outcomes. If not, reread the appropriate section.

Questions

Question 1

P Ltd acquired 40% (and significant influence) of A Ltd on 1 January 20x4 for CU1 500 000. During the 20x5 financial year, A Ltd earned profits (after tax) of CU600 000 (20x4: CU500 000). A Ltd declared a dividend of CU200 000 on 31 December 20x5 (20x4: CU180 000).

You are required to do the following:

1. Calculate the 'investment in associate' line item as it will appear in the group statement of financial position at 31 December 20x4 and 31 December 20x5 respectively.
2. Calculate the 'Share of profits from associate' line item as it should appear in the group statement of profit or loss of P Ltd for the financial year ended 31 December 20x5, including comparatives.

Suggested solution

1. Extract from group statement of financial position at 31 December 20x4 and 31 December 20x5:

	31 Dec 20x5 CU	31 Dec 20x4 CU
Non-current asset: Investment in associate	(w2) **1 788 000**	(w1) **1 628 000**

(w1): CU1 500 000 + (40% × [500 000 – 180 000]) = CU1 628 000
(w2): CU1 628 000 + (40% × [600 000 – 200 000]) = CU1 788 000

2. Extract from group statement of profit or loss for the years ended 31 December 20x4 and 31 December 20x5:

	31 Dec 20x5 CU	31 Dec 20x4 CU
Income from associate	(w4) **240 000**	(w3) **200 000**

(w3): (40% × CU500 000) = CU200 000
(w4): (40% × CU600 000) = CU240 000

Question 2

P Ltd owns 30% (obtaining significant influence) of A Ltd. The following information relates to A Ltd:

- On 1 January 20x5, P Ltd sold a delivery vehicle to A Ltd at a profit of CU15 000. The delivery vehicle had a remaining useful life of three years on 1 January 20x5.
- A Ltd earned profits during the 20x5 financial year of CU300 000 and declared a dividend of CU50 000 on 31 December 20x5.
- A Ltd revalued a plot of owner-occupied land by CU20 000 on 31 December 20x5 (the P Ltd group policy is to account for owner-occupied land on the revaluation model).

Assume a company tax rate of 28% and a capital gains inclusion rate of 66.6%.

You are required to do the following:

Based on the information provided, prepare all of the *pro-forma* journal entries to equity account A Ltd in the group annual financial statements of P Ltd for the financial year ended 31 December 20x5.

Suggested solution

			CU	CU
Dr		Investment in associate (CU300 000 × 30%)	90 000	
	Cr	Share of profits from associate (P/L)		90 000

Recognition of current year earnings

			CU	CU
Dr		Dividend received (CU50 000 × 30%)	15 000	
	Cr	Investment in associate		15 000

Elimination of inter-company dividend

			CU	CU
Dr		Investment in associate (CU20 000 × (1 − [66.6% × 28%]))	16 270	
	Cr	Share of associate's other comprehensive income (OCI)		16 270

Recognition of current year revaluation

			CU	CU
Dr		Profit on sale of vehicle (CU15 000 × 30%) (P/L)	4 500	
	Cr	Investment in associate		4 500

Elimination of inter-company profit

			CU	CU
Dr		Deferred tax (liability)/investment in associate	1 260	
	Cr	Deferred tax (P/L) (CU4 500 × 28%)		1 260

Deferred tax adjustment relating to elimination of inter-company profit

			CU	CU
Dr		Investment in associate (CU4 500/3)	1 500	
	Cr	Profit on sale of vehicle (P/L)		1 500

Realisation of profit

			CU	CU
Dr		Deferred tax (P/L) (CU1 500 × 28%)	420	
	Cr	Deferred tax (liability)/investment in associate		420

Deferred tax adjustment relating to realisation of profit

Question 3

P Ltd acquired 25% (representing significant influence) of A Ltd's ordinary shares on 1 January 20x5. At that date, the net asset value of A Ltd amounted to CU2 000 000, all of which was considered fairly valued, with the exception of A Ltd's machinery. The machine had an original cost of CU500 000, a carrying amount of CU300 000 and a fair value of CU400 000, with a remaining useful life of four years (all parties agreed with this assessment). P Ltd paid CU750 000 for its 25% interest in A Ltd.

A Ltd did not revalue the above-mentioned machine at any stage, but did sell it to a third party on 2 January 20x5 for CU410 000. During 20x5, A Ltd earned after-tax profits of CU1 200 000.

A normal tax rate and a capital gains inclusion rate of 28% and 66.6% respectively apply. Ignore VAT.

You are required to do the following:

1. Calculate the goodwill line item as it would appear in the group statement of financial position of P Ltd as at 31 December 20x5, giving supporting reasons.
2. Prepare the journal entry processed by A Ltd on the sale of the machine. Ignore all tax-related and closing entries.
3. Calculate the carrying amount of the machine as it would appear in the group statement of financial position of P Ltd as at 31 December 20x5.
4. Calculate P Ltd's share of the profits of A Ltd as it would appear in the group statement of profit or loss for the year ended 31 December 20x5.

Suggested solution

1. Nil. Goodwill is included in the investment in associate balance as the associate is equity accounted and not consolidated.
2. Journal entry in A Ltd:

			CU	CU
Dr		Bank	410 000	
Dr		Accumulated depreciation	200 000	
	Cr	Machine cost		500 000
	Cr	Profit on sale/disposal		110 000

Disposal of machine to third party

3. Nil. The assets of the associate are not included in the group statement of financial position.
4. CU282 000 ([CU1 200 000 − 72 000] × 25%)

Note that the 'cost to the group' of this asset was CU400 000 at the acquisition date. Thus, when A Ltd sold the machine, the profit attributable to the group is CU10 000 (CU410 000 − CU400 000). The balance of CU100 000 relates to the fair value adjustment of the asset at the acquisition date and needs to be reversed after tax amounting to CU72 000 (100 000 − [100 000 × 28%]).

Case study exercises

Scenario 1

You obtained the extracts that follow from the financial statements of P Ltd, X Ltd and Y Ltd, all for the current financial period that ended 31 December 20x5.

Statements of financial position of P Ltd, X Ltd and Y Ltd on 31 December 20x5

	P Ltd CU'000	X Ltd CU'000	Y Ltd CU'000
ASSETS			
Plant and machinery	440	250	285
Investment in X Ltd	150		
Investment in Y Ltd	100		
Inventory	320	350	275
Other current assets	380	380	170
	1 390	980	730
CAPITAL AND LIABILITIES			
Share capital (CU1 shares)	290	160	150
Retained earnings	900	700	300
Shareholders' equity	1 190	860	450
Current liabilities	200	120	280
	1 390	980	730

Statements of profit or loss and other comprehensive income of P Ltd, X Ltd and Y Ltd for the year ended 31 December 20x5

	P Ltd CU'000	X Ltd CU'000	Y Ltd CU'000
Revenue (including dividends and interest received)	2 320	1 700	1 080
Cost of sales	(1 050)	(875)	(560)
Gross profit	1 270	825	520
Net operating costs	(390)	(125)	(150)
Interest expense	(100)	(50)	(40)
Profit before taxation	780	650	330
Taxation expense	(300)	(250)	(130)
Profit after taxation	**480**	**400**	**200**

Extract from statements of changes in shareholders' equity of P Ltd, X Ltd and Y Ltd for the year ended 31 December 20x5

	P Ltd CU'000	X Ltd CU'000	Y Ltd CU'000
Retained earnings 1 January 20x5	620	500	240
Profit after tax	480	400	200
Dividends declared	(200)	(200)	(140)
Retained earnings 31 December 20x5	**900**	**700**	**300**

P Ltd acquired 40% of the issued ordinary share capital of X Ltd on 1 January 20x3. At the acquisition date, P Ltd entered into a contractual agreement with the only other shareholder in X Ltd, Z Ltd. In accordance with this agreement, both parties share control of X Ltd and decisions about the activities of X Ltd require the unanimous consent of both shareholders.

P Ltd further acquired 25% of the issued ordinary share capital of Y Ltd on 1 July 20x3. The identifiable assets and liabilities of X Ltd and Y Ltd were considered fairly valued at the respective dates of acquisition. You can assume that P Ltd is able to exert significant influence in the decisions of both entities.

Retained earnings of two entities at the respective acquisition dates

X Ltd (1 January 20x3)	CU200 000
Y Ltd (1 July 20x3)	CU210 000

None of the companies has issued any further ordinary shares since the date of incorporation. Ignore taxation.

You are required to do the following:

1. Answer the following questions before starting with the preparation of the group financial statements:
   - How would you classify P Ltd's interests in both X Ltd and Y Ltd? Motivate your answer.
   - How should P Ltd recognise the investments in X Ltd and Y Ltd in its separate financial statements?
   - What is the amount of dividends received in the separate financial statements of P Ltd?
   - What is the amount of dividends declared and paid by the group?
2. Show the *pro-forma* journal entries required to prepare the group financial statements of P Ltd Group for the year ended 31 December 20x5.
3. Prepare the group statement of profit or loss and other comprehensive income and the group statement of changes in equity for P Ltd for the year ended 31 December 20x5. Prepare the group statement of financial position at 31 December 20x5.

Scenario 2

P Ltd acquired 35% of the issued ordinary share capital of A Ltd on 1 July 20x3 for CU140 000, when A Ltd's retained earnings amounted to CU210 000. The identifiable assets and liabilities of A Ltd were considered fairly valued at the acquisition date, except for plant and machinery of A Ltd, which had a fair value of CU350 000 (carrying amount of CU300 000). The plant and machinery had a remaining useful life of five years and a residual value of CU50 000. These estimates were confirmed at each subsequent reporting period. A Ltd receives annual wear-and-tear allowances for tax purposes equal to the depreciation expense. Assume a normal tax rate of 28%.

You can assume that P Ltd is able to exert significant influence in the decisions of A Ltd. P Ltd recognises the investment in A Ltd in its separate financial statements at fair value, which amounted to CU150 000 at 31 December 20x5 (20x4: CU142 000). Fair value adjustments are recognised in profit or loss and deferred tax is recognised at the inclusive capital gains tax rate of 66.6%.

You obtained the extracts from the financial statements of P Ltd and A Ltd that follow, all for the current financial period that ended 31 December 20x5.

Statements of financial position of P Ltd and A Ltd on 31 December 20x5

	P Ltd CU'000	A Ltd CU'000
ASSETS		
Plant and machinery	540	285
Investment in A Ltd	150	
Inventory	320	275
Other current assets	380	170
	1 390	730
CAPITAL AND LIABILITIES		
Share capital (CU1 shares)	290	150
Retained earnings	900	300
Shareholders' equity	1 190	450
Current liabilities	200	280
	1 390	730

Statements of comprehensive income of P Ltd and A Ltd for the year ended 31 December 20x5

	P Ltd CU'000	A Ltd CU'000
Revenue (including dividends and interest received)	2 320	1 080
Cost of sales	(1 050)	(560)
Gross profit	1 270	520
Net operating costs	(390)	(150)
Interest expense	(100)	(40)
Profit before taxation	780	330
Taxation expense	(300)	(130)
Profit after taxation	**480**	**200**

Extract from statements of changes in shareholders' equity of P Ltd and A Ltd for the year ended 31 December 20x5

	P Ltd CU'000	A Ltd CU'000
Retained earnings 1 January 20x5	620	240
Profit after taxation	480	200
Dividends declared	(200)	(140)
Retained earnings 31 December 20x5	**900**	**300**

You are required to do the following:

1. Answer the following questions before starting with the preparation of the group financial statements:
   - What is the cost of the investment in A Ltd? Why is the cost different from the carrying amount in the separate financial statements of P Ltd at 31 December 20x5?
   - What is the cost to the group of the plant and machinery in A Ltd?
   - What is the carrying amount of the investment in A Ltd as it should be recognised in the group statement of financial position at 31 December 20x5?
2. Show the *pro-forma* journal entries required to prepare the group financial statements of P Ltd Group for the year ended 31 December 20x5.
3. Prepare the group statement of profit or loss and other comprehensive income and the group statement of changes in equity for P Ltd for the year ended 31 December 20x5. Prepare the group statement of financial position at 31 December 20x5

Scenario 3

You are the recently appointed accountant for P Ltd and are assisting in preparing the group financial statements for the year ended 31 December 20x5.

Extracts from the trial balances for the **three companies for the year ended 31 December 20x5** are presented below. (You can assume them to be correct in all respects.)

Dr/(Cr)	P Ltd CU	S Ltd CU	A Ltd CU
Sales	(785 000)	(200 000)	(160 000)
Cost of sales	458 000	80 000	45 000
Other income (including dividends)	(105 000)	(20 000)	–
Net operating costs	84 000	32 000	23 000
Taxation expense	62 000	28 000	22 000
Share capital	(175 000)	(150 000)	(100 000)
Retained earnings (at 1 January 20x5)	(980 000)	(115 000)	(38 000)
Revaluation surplus	(120 000)	(60 000)	(12 000)
Dividend (declared on 31 December 20x5)	60 000	20 000	30 000

P Ltd expanded its operations and, as a result, purchased shareholdings in S Ltd and A Ltd. Details of these investments are presented below.

S Ltd

P Ltd purchased 60% of the ordinary shares of S Ltd for CU210 000 on 1 January 20x4 and acquired control. At that date, the equity of S Ltd comprised share capital of CU150 000 and retained earnings of CU75 000. All assets and liabilities of S Ltd were considered to be fairly valued, with the exception of the following assets:

- An item of machinery, with a remaining useful life of three years from the date of acquisition with no residual value, which was considered undervalued by CU60 000
- Land that was considered to be undervalued by CU40 000
- Inventory with a cost of CU340 000 that was considered to be worth CU360 000.

Of the undervalued inventory on hand at the date of acquisition, 65% was sold during the 20x4 year and the remainder was sold during the 20x5 year. S Ltd did not revalue either of these assets in its own books.

The machinery that had been considered undervalued at the date of acquisition was sold on 30 June 20x5 to a third party for CU180 000.

Both P Ltd and S Ltd apply the revaluation method of accounting for land. On 31 December 20x5, P Ltd revalued its land by CU100 000 and S Ltd revalued its land by CU60 000.

P Ltd started selling inventory to S Ltd on 1 January 20x4. These sales were made at the standard mark-up of 25% on cost price. The details of the sales are as follows:

	20x4 CU	20x5 CU
Sales during the year	200 000	350 000
Inventory on hand at year end	15 000	25 000

Non-controlling interest is measured at their share of the attributable net assets at the acquisition date. You can assume that goodwill is not impaired.

A Ltd

P Ltd acquired 40% of the shares in A Ltd on 1 January 20x5 for CU80 000. P Ltd is able to exert significant influence over the decision-making processes of A Ltd and is using the equity method when including A Ltd in the group financial statements. The equity of A Ltd at this date was share capital of CU100 000, retained earnings of CU38 000 and a revaluation surplus of CU12 000. All of the assets and liabilities were considered to be fairly valued at the date of acquisition.

You can assume that there were no changes in share capital of any of the companies listed.

Ignore taxation.

You are required to do the following:

1. Show all of the *pro-forma* **journal** entries necessary to prepare the group financial statements for the year ended 31 December 20x5. Narrations are not required.

2. Calculate the following amounts that would be reflected in the **group annual financial statements** for the year ended 31 December 20x5:
   a. Cost of sales
   b. Profit attributable to non-controlling shareholders
   c. Non-controlling shareholders in the statement of financial position
   d. Share of profits from associate
   e. Investment in associate
   f. Goodwil
   g. Revaluation surplus
   h. Retained earnings as at 1 January 20x5

Suggested solution

Scenario 1

1. **Answer the following questions before starting with the preparation of the group financial statements:**
   - **How would you classify P Ltd's interests in both X Ltd and Y Ltd? Motivate your answer.**
     P Ltd acquired 40% of the issued shares in X Ltd and 25% of the issued shares in Y Ltd. P Ltd's interests are classified as follows:
     - In X Ltd: Joint venture
     - In Y Ltd: Associate.

     In terms of a contractual agreement with the other shareholder (Z Ltd) in X Ltd, P Ltd has joint control over X Ltd. The investment in X Ltd is therefore classified as a **joint venture** as X Ltd is a separate legal entity.

     Based on the information in the question and the assumption that one share represents one vote, P Ltd's investment in Y Ltd is classified as an **associate**. P Ltd has the power to participate in the financial and operating policy decisions of Y Ltd, thus representing significant influence.
   - **How should P Ltd recognise the investments in X Ltd and Y Ltd in its separate financial statements?**
     In P Ltd's separate financial statements, the investments in X Ltd and Y Ltd are recognised at cost or at fair value in terms of IFRS9, *Financial Instruments*. This means that P Ltd can decide (apply an accounting policy) to use either the cost model or the fair value model for both investments in an associate and joint venture in its separate financial statements.
   - **What is the amount of dividends received in the separate financial statements of P Ltd?**
     Dividends received from X Ltd: CU200 000 × 40% = **CU80 000**.
     Dividends received from Y Ltd: CU140 000 × 25% = **CU35 000**.
   - **What is the amount of dividends declared and paid by the group?**
     Total dividends declared and paid by the group (P Ltd only): **CU200 000**.

2. **Show the *pro-forma* journal entries required to prepare the group financial statements of P Ltd Group for the year ended 31 December 20x5.**

Pro-forma journal entries: P Ltd's interest in X Ltd (joint venture)

			CU'000	CU'000
Dr		Investment in X Ltd	120	
	Cr	Retained earnings (X Ltd) (500 – 200) × 40%		120

Share of post-acquisition profits of joint venture

			CU'000	CU'000
Dr		Investment in X Ltd	160	
	Cr	Share of profits of joint venture (P/L) (400 × 40%)		160

Share in current year earnings from joint venture

			CU'000	CU'000
Dr		Dividends received (P/L)	80	
	Cr	Investment in X Ltd		80

Elimination of dividends received from joint venture

Pro-forma journal entries: P Ltd's interest in Y Ltd (associate)

			CU'000	CU'000
Dr		Investment in Y Ltd	7.5	
	Cr	Retained earnings (Y Ltd) ([240 – 210] × 25%)		7.5

Share of post-acquisition profits of associate

			CU'000	CU'000
Dr		Dividends received (P/L)	35	
	Cr	Investment in Y Ltd		35

Elimination of dividends received from associate

			CU'000	CU'000
Dr		Investment in Y Ltd	50	
	Cr	Share of profits of associate (P/L) (200 × 25%)		50

Share in current year share of profits from associate

3. **Prepare the group statement of profit or loss and other comprehensive income and the group statement of changes in equity for P Ltd for the year ended 31 December 20x5. Prepare the group statement of financial position at 31 December 20x5.**

Group statement of profit or loss and other comprehensive income for P Ltd for the year ended 31 December 20x5

	Workings	CU'000
Gross revenue	(2 320 000 – 80 000 – 35 000)	2 205
Cost of sales		(1 050)
Gross profit		1 155
Net operating costs		(390)
Interest expense		(100)
Profit before tax		665
Taxation expense		(300)
Profit after tax		365
Share of profits of joint venture		160
Share of profits of associate		50
Total comprehensive income		**575**

Group statement of changes in equity for P Ltd for the year ended 31 December 20x5

	Share capital CU'000	Retained earnings CU'000	Total CU'000
Opening balance	290	(w1) 747.5	1 037.5
Total comprehensive income		575	575
– Dividends		(200)	(200)
Closing balance	**290**	**1 122.5**	**1 412.5**

(w1): P Ltd: 620 000
X Ltd: (500 000 – 200 000) × 40% = 120 000
Y Ltd: (240 000 – 210 000) × 25% = 7 500
Group: 620 000 + 120 000 + 7 500 = **CU747 500**

Group statement of financial position for P Ltd at 31 December 20x5

	CU'000
ASSETS	
Non-current assets	
Plant and machinery	440
Investment in joint venture	350
Investment in associate	122.5
Current assets:	
Inventory	320
Other current assets	380
	1 612.5
EQUITY AND LIABILITIES	
Share capital	290
Retained earnings	1 122.5
Total equity	1 412.5
Current liabilities	200
	1 612.5

Workings

Analysis of equity of X Ltd (joint venture, using the equity method)

	Total CU'000	P Ltd (40%)		Investment in X Ltd CU'000
		At acquisition CU'000	Since acquisition CU'000	
At acquisition:				
Share capital	160			
Retained earnings	200			
	360	144		
Investment		150		150
Goodwill		6		
Since acquisition:				
Retained earnings	300		120	120
Current year:				
Profit after tax	400		160	160
– Dividends	(200)		(80)	(80)
	860		200	350

Analysis of equity of Y Ltd (associate, using the equity method)

	Total CU'000	P Ltd (25%)		Investment in Y Ltd CU'000
		At acquisition CU'000	Since acquisition CU'000	
At acquisition:				
Share capital	150			
Retained earnings	210			
	360	90		
Investment		100		100
Goodwill		10		
Since acquisition:				
Retained earnings	30		7.5	7.5
Current year:				
Profit after tax	200		50	50
– Dividends	(140)		(35)	(35)
	450		22.5	122.5

Scenario 2

1. **Answer the following questions before starting with the preparation of the group financial statements:**
   - **What is the cost of the investment in A Ltd? Why is the cost different from the carrying amount in the separate financial statements of P Ltd at 31 December 20x5?**

     The initial cost of the investment in A Ltd was CU140 000 (in other words, this is the cost of the investment in its associate at the acquisition date).

     P Ltd recognises the investment in A Ltd using the fair value model. The investment is therefore recognised at its fair value of CU150 000 in the separate financial statements of P Ltd at 31 December 20x5.

- **What is the cost to the group of the plant and machinery in A Ltd?**
  At the acquisition date of the associate, the plant and machinery had a fair value of CU350 000. However, the group P Ltd does not have a controlling interest in A Ltd and therefore does not control the assets of A Ltd. The plant and machinery is not recognised as an asset in the group financial statements.
- **What is the carrying amount of the investment in A Ltd as it should be recognised in the group statement of financial position at 31 December 20x5?**
  The investment in A Ltd should be recognised at CU165 200, calculated as follows:

	Equity of A Ltd CU	Investment in A Ltd (35%) CU
Investment at cost		140 000
Share of equity in A Ltd since acquisition:	19 200	① 6 720
Retained earnings	30 000	
Less depreciation (50/5 × 1.5)	(15 000)	
Deferred tax	4 200	
Current year:	192 800	② 67 480
Profit after tax	200 000	
Less depreciation (50/5)	(10 000)	
Deferred tax	2 800	
– Dividends	(140 000)	③ (49 000)
Total investment in A Ltd (equity method)		**CU165 200**

2. **Show the *pro-forma* journal entries required to prepare the group financial statements of P Ltd Group for the year ended 31 December 20x5.**

Pro-forma journal entries: P Ltd's interest in A Ltd (associate)

			CU	CU
Dr		Retained earnings (w1)	1 627	
Dr		Fair value adjustment (P/L) (w2)	8 000	
Dr		Deferred tax (asset) (w3)	1 865	
	Cr	Deferred tax expense (P/L) (w4)		1 492
	Cr	Investment in A Ltd (w5)		10 000

Reversal of fair value adjustment of investment in A Ltd prior to application of equity method

(w1): (2 000 – [2 000 × 28% × 66.6%]) = CU1 627
(w2): (150 000 – 142 000) = CU8 000
(w3): (10 000 × 28% × 66.6%) = CU1 865
(w4): (8 000 × 28% × 66.6%) = CU1 492
(w5): (150 000 – 140 000) = CU10 000

			CU	CU
Dr		Investment in A Ltd	① 6 720	
	Cr	Retained earnings		6 720

Share of post-acquisition profits of associate

			CU	CU
Dr		Investment in A Ltd	67 480	
	Cr	Share of profits of associate (P/L)		② 67 480

Share in current year share of profits from associate

			CU	CU
Dr		Dividends received (P/L)	49 000	
	Cr	Investment in A Ltd		③ 49 000

Elimination of dividends received from associate

3. **Prepare the group statement of profit or loss and other comprehensive income and the group statement of changes in equity for P Ltd for the year ending 31 December 20x5. Prepare the group statement of financial position at 31 December 20x5.**

Group statement of profit or loss and other comprehensive income for P Ltd for the year ended 31 December 20x5

	Workings	CU
Gross revenue	(2 320 000 – 49 000)	2 271 000
Cost of sales		(1 050 000)
Gross profit		1 221 000
Net operating costs	(390 000 + 8 000 [fair value adjustment])	(398 000)
Interest expense		(100 000)
Profit before tax		723 000
Taxation expense	(300 000 – 1 492)	(298 508)
Profit after tax		424 492
Share of profits of associate		67 480
Total comprehensive income		**491 972**

Group statement of changes in equity for P Ltd for the year ended 31 December 20x5

	Share capital CU	Retained earnings CU	Total CU
Opening balance	290 000	(w1) 625 093	915 093
Total comprehensive income		491 972	491 972
– Dividends		(200 000)	(200 000)
Closing balance	**290 000**	**917 065**	**1 207 065**

(w1): P Ltd: 620 000 – 1 627 = 618 373
A Ltd: (240 000 – 210 000 – 15 000 + 4 200) × 35% = 6 720
Group: 618 373 + 6 720 = **CU625 093**

Group statement of financial position for P Ltd at 31 December 20x5

	CU
ASSETS	
Non-current assets	
Plant and machinery	540 000
Investment in associate	165 200
Deferred tax asset	1 865
Current assets:	
Inventory	320 000
Other current assets	380 000
	1 407 065
EQUITY AND LIABILITIES	
Share capital	290 000
Retained earnings	917 065
Total equity	1 207 065
Current liabilities	200 000
	1 407 065

Scenario 3

1. **Show all of the *pro-forma* journal entries necessary to prepare the group financial statements for the year ended 31 December 20x5. Narrations are not required.**

Investment in S Ltd (subsidiary)

			CU	CU
Dr		Share capital	150 000	
Dr		Retained earnings	75 000	
Dr		Inventory	20 000	
Dr		Land	40 000	
Dr		Machinery	60 000	
Dr		Goodwill	3 000	
	Cr	Investment in S Ltd		210 000
	Cr	Non-controlling interest (equity)		138 000

Elimination of investment in subsidiary at the acquisition date

			CU	CU
Dr		Retained earnings	13 000	
Dr		Cost of sales	7 000	
	Cr	Inventory		20 000

Elimination of fair value adjustment in inventory at acquisition date, subsequently sold

			CU	CU
Dr		Retained earnings	20 000	
Dr		Depreciation (P/L)	10 000	
	Cr	Accumulated depreciation		30 000

Adjustment to depreciation of machinery resulting from fair value adjustment at the acquisition date

			CU	CU
Dr		Profit on sale of machinery (P/L)	30 000	
Dr		Accumulated depreciation	30 000	
	Cr	Machinery		60 000

Elimination of profit on sale of machinery in subsidiary,subsequently sold

			CU	CU
Dr		Retained earnings	2 800	
	Cr	Non-controlling interest (equity)		2 800

Allocation of non-controlling interest in retained earnings

			CU	CU
Dr		Non-controlling interest (P/L)	13 200	
	Cr	Non-controlling interest (equity)		13 200

Allocation of non-controlling interest in current year profit of subsidiary

			CU	CU
Dr		Revaluation surplus	40 000	
	Cr	Land		40 000

Reversal of revaluation of land since the acquisition period

			CU	CU
Dr		Non-controlling interest (OCI)	8 000	
	Cr	Non-controlling interest (equity)		8 000

Allocation of non-controlling interest in other comprehensive income

			CU	CU
Dr		Dividend received (P/L)	12 000	
Dr		Non-controlling interest (equity)	8 000	
	Cr	Dividend paid		20 000

Elimination of intra-group dividends and allocation of appropriate portion to non-controlling interest

			CU	CU
Dr		Retained earnings	3 000	
	Cr	Cost of sales (P/L) (15 × 25/125)		3 000

Elimination of intra-group profit in opening balance inventory

			CU	CU
Dr		Cost of sales (25 × 25/125)	5 000	
	Cr	Inventory		5 000

Elimination of intra-group profit in inventory on hand at the reporting date

			CU	CU
Dr		Sales	350 000	
	Cr	Cost of sales		350 000

Elimination of intra-group sale of inventory in the current reporting period

P Ltd's interest in A Ltd (associate)

			CU	CU
Dr		Dividends received (P/L)	12 000	
	Cr	Investment in A Ltd		12 000

Elimination of dividends received from associate

			CU	CU
Dr		Investment in A Ltd	28 000	
	Cr	Share of profits of associate (P/L)		28 000

Share in current year share of profits from associate

2. **Calculate the following amounts that would be reflected in the group annual financial statements for the year ended 31 December 20x5:**
   a. **Cost of sales**

	CU
P Ltd (starting point)	458 000
S Ltd (starting point)	80 000
Elimination of intra-group sales	(350 000)
Elimination of unrealised profit included in closing inventory	5 000
Reversal of unrealised profit included in opening inventory	(3 000)
Inventory at acquisition sold in current period	7 000
	CU197 000

   b. **Profit attributable to non-controlling shareholders**
   CU13 200 (See analysis of equity of S Ltd.)
   c. **Non-controlling shareholders in the statement of financial position**
   CU154 000 (See analysis of equity of S Ltd.)
   d. **Share of profits from associate**
   CU28 000 (CU70 000 × 40%)
   e. **Investment in associate**
   CU96 000 (CU80 000 + 28 000 − 12 000)
   f. **Goodwill**
   CU3 000 (See analysis of equity of S Ltd.)
   g. **Revaluation surplus**
   CU120 000 (P Ltd) + CU12 000 (S Ltd) = CU132 000
   h. **Retained earnings as at 1 January 20x5**
   CU980 000 + CU4 200 − CU3 000 (opening balance inventory) = CU 981 200

Workings

Analysis of equity for S Ltd

	S Ltd Total CU 100%	At acquisition CU	Post-acquisition CU	Non-controlling interest CU 40%
		60%		
At acquisition:				
Share capital	150 000			
Retained earnings	75 000			
Inventory	20 000			
Land	40 000			
Machinery	60 000			
	345 000	207 000		138 000
Investment		210 000		
Goodwill		3 000		
Since acquisition				
Retained earnings (115 – 75)	40 000			
Depreciation	(20 000)			
Inventory	(13 000)			
Retained earnings	7 000		4 200	2 800
20x5 year				
Revaluation surplus	20 000		12 000	8 000
(60 – 40)				
Net profit	80 000			
Depreciation	(10 000)			
Profit on sale	(30 000)			
Inventory	(7 000)			
Profit after tax	33 000		19 800	13 200
Dividend	(20 000)		(12 000)	(8 000)
	385 000		**24 000**	**154 000**

Analysis of equity for A Ltd

	A Ltd Total CU	P Ltd's interest of 40% CU		Investment CU
At acquisition:				
Class A share capital	100 000			
Revaluation surplus	12 000			
Retained earnings	38 000			
	150 000	60 000		
		80 000		80 000
Paid				
Goodwill		20 000		
20x5 year				
Net profit	70 000		28 000	28 000
Dividend	(30 000)		(12 000)	(12 000)
	190 000		16 000	96 000

Joint arrangements

10

The following topics are included in this chapter:

- Identifying a joint arrangement
- How to determine that joint control exists
- The different types of joint arrangements
- The appropriate accounting treatment for each type of joint arrangement
- Preparing journal entries for transactions with and interests in joint operations
- Classifying a joint arrangement that is structured through a separate vehicle.

Learning objectives

By the end of this chapter, you should be able to:
- Identify and classify a joint arrangement
- State the key characteristics of a joint arrangement
- Determine whether or not joint control exists
- Classify a joint arrangement that is structured through a separate vehicle
- Explain the different types of joint arrangements
- Understand and apply the appropriate accounting treatment for each type of joint arrangement.

1. Introduction

In previous chapters, you were introduced to the concept of control. In the examples you looked at in those chapters, one entity was able to **control** another entity. This chapter looks at the financial reporting implications if a party is not able to exercise control alone, but does so **jointly with another party** such that no individual party is able to dominate decision-making relating to the financial and operational decisions of another business. The effect is that the decision-making process requires unanimous consent.

There are a number of different reasons why two (or more) parties would enter into an arrangement to have joint control over another business. These may be economic, with each party bringing different skills to the arrangement. There may be political reasons, for example, investments in certain countries may require partnering with local entities, communities and so on. In any event, the end result is that all parties involved benefit from the sharing of research and technology, the ability to achieve economies of scale and the opportunity to establish a new venture that would otherwise be beyond the capabilities of the individual participants.

IFRS 11, *Joint Arrangements*, is the International Financial Reporting Standard that deals with the accounting treatment of joint arrangements. A joint arrangement is an arrangement where two or more parties have joint control as a result of a contractual agreement. 'Joint control' implies that the parties, acting together (collectively), are able to control the operation, venture or project because decisions related to the operation, venture or project require their unanimous consent. Therefore no party has the right to make decisions without the consent of the other party or parties to the contractual arrangement.

 IFRS principles

What is a joint arrangement?

A joint arrangement is an arrangement between a number of parties in which two or more parties have joint control. A joint arrangement has two key characteristics:
- The parties are bound by a contractual agreement.
- This agreement gives two or more parties joint control over the arrangement.

 IFRS for SMEs update

Investments in joint ventures

Section 15, *Investments in Joint Ventures of the IFRS for SMEs*, deals with the accounting for interests in joint ventures by small and medium entities.

Whereas IFRS 11 defines joint ventures and joint operations as types of joint arrangements, the *IFRS for SMEs* treats all contractual arrangements that result in joint control as joint ventures, of which joint operations are a type.

2. Is there joint control?

Control exists when a party is exposed or has rights to variable returns from its investment and has the ability to affect those returns through its power (in other words, the current ability to direct the relevant activities of the investee). To have joint control, the parties sharing the decision-making power must together be able to control the entity. (See Chapter 1 and Chapter 3 for discussions of 'control'.)

Example
Who has control?

F Ltd was incorporated on 1 January 20x5. F Ltd's Memorandum of Incorporation stipulates that decisions about F Ltd are made by its shareholders, with each share attaching one voting right.

Five parties (A, B, C, D and E) each acquire 20% of F Ltd's shares on 1 January 20x5.

In this case, no party is able to control F Ltd as no individual party owns more than 50% of the shares and therefore the voting rights in F Ltd.

Joint control is the contractually agreed sharing of control of an arrangement. IFRS does not define the word 'joint', but the Oxford English Dictionary defines 'joint' when used as an adjective as 'shared, held or made by two or more people together; sharing in a position, achievement or activity; applied or regarded together'. The notion of sharing control is therefore evident. If one party is the dominant party and has the right to a final casting vote, then there is no joint or shared control.

IFRS principles

What is joint control?

Joint control exists when decisions about relevant activities require the unanimous consent of the parties sharing control.

Joint control is established by a contractual arrangement, which normally ensures that no single party to the arrangement is in a position to control the economic activities unilaterally. In terms of IFRS 11, joint control does not exist without a **contractual arrangement**. To determine whether a contractual arrangement actually exists, you should refer to various sources, such as the minutes of discussions between the parties or, if the joint arrangement takes the form of an incorporated company, the memorandum of incorporation. The contractual arrangement normally identifies those decisions that require the consent of all the parties that have joint control and those decisions that require the consent of the majority of those parties.

The **contractual arrangement** normally supplies the following details:
- The purpose, activity and duration of the joint arrangement
- The appointment of board members or an equivalent governing body and their respective voting rights·
- The decision-making process (the matters requiring decisions from the parties, the voting rights of the parties and the required level of support)
- The capital or other contributions by parties
- How the parties share the assets, liabilities, revenues, expenses and profits of the arrangement.

Example

Contractual agreement to have joint control

If the five parties A, B, C, D and E (refer to earlier example) enter into a contractual agreement that decisions about F Ltd require their unanimous consent, then F Ltd is a joint arrangement. This is because the parties own 100% of F Ltd's share, therefore establishing control. However, the control is exercised jointly.

In the example above, all five parties (A, B, C, D and E) entered into the contractual arrangement, but this need not be the case.

- If A and B entered into a contractual agreement that they would make decisions about their shareholding in F Ltd jointly, this would not result in a joint arrangement. This is because even though there is a contractual arrangement that establishes joint decision-making, the two parties do not have decision-making power of F Ltd as, collectively, they own 40% of the voting rights. Their combined shareholding of 40% does not establish control and therefore there is no joint control.
- If, however, A, B and C enter into a contractual arrangement that decisions about F Ltd require their unanimous consent, A, B and C own 60% of the F Ltd's voting rights collectively. Control is therefore established and in this instance is exercised jointly. F Ltd is therefore a joint arrangement, and A, B, and C will account for their respective interests in F Ltd as explained later in the chapter. D and E are parties to the joint arrangement that do not have joint control. This may be the case because they are merely providers of finance (for example, bankers) who have only provided finance to start up F Ltd without any involvement in the governance of F Ltd.

Joint control implies the nature of the decision-making power and is unrelated to the percentage shareholdings in the joint arrangement. For example, A Ltd owned 10% of the voting rights of F Ltd, B Ltd owned 10% and C Ltd owned the other 80%. Even though, on the face of it, C appears to control the entity, if it enters into a contractual arrangement with either A or B or both of them and they agreed contractually that they would make decisions jointly, there would be joint control. However, even if A and B entered into a contractual arrangement relating to their interests in the entity, they would not have control as they own less than 50% of the voting rights of the entity.

3. Types of joint arrangements

Joint arrangements may be structured in a number of different ways. The arrangement does not have to take the form of a separate entity (in other words, it does not necessarily involve the registration of a company, or the setting up of a partnership or another entity) and even if it were a separate entity, it does not have to be incorporated. The joint control may be over all of the operations of the business, or specific assets or a separate entity. All of these forms are included in the definition of a joint arrangement, provided that there is joint control.

IFRS 11 classifies joint arrangements into two types: **joint operations** and **joint ventures**. Having determined that a joint arrangement exists, you now need to classify it. The classification is dependent on the rights and obligations of the parties to the arrangement.

- A **joint operation** is an arrangement whereby the parties that have joint control of the arrangement have **rights to the assets and obligations for the liabilities** relating to the arrangement. In other words, the assets of the joint operation are those of the parties to the joint arrangement either because they have contributed those assets or because they own them jointly. Similarly the liabilities of the joint operation are those of the parties to the joint arrangement. The parties that have joint control are joint operators.
- A **joint venture** is an arrangement whereby the parties that have joint control of the arrangement have **rights to the net assets** of the arrangement. In this case, the assets and liabilities are those of the joint arrangement, and the parties to the joint arrangement have no rights to the assets and/or obligations for the liabilities of the joint arrangement. The parties that have joint control are joint venturers.
- There may also be other parties that participate in the joint arrangement, but do not have joint control of the arrangement.

The assessment of the classification of a joint arrangement is dependent on the rights and obligations of the parties to the arrangement, and requires some judgement. IFRS 11 provides guidelines to assist with the **classification of a joint arrangement**. We need to assess the rights and obligations in an arrangement by analysing the factors discussed below.

3.1 Structure of arrangement

The main factor here is whether or not the arrangement is structured through a separate vehicle.

IFRS principles

What is a 'separate vehicle'?

A separate vehicle is defined as 'a separately identifiable financial structure, including separate legal entities or entities recognised by statute, regardless of whether those entities have a legal personality' (refer to IFRS11: Appendix A).

Thus, a separate vehicle may constitute a company, but need not be one.

If the joint arrangement **is not structured** through a separate vehicle, the joint arrangement is a joint operation. This is because the contractual arrangement establishes the parties' rights to the assets and obligations for the liabilities relating to the operation.

Example

Not a separate vehicle

A and B require a component part that each entity uses in its manufacturing process. The component is imported and is expensive, but A and B could achieve economies of scale and reduce costs if they combined resources and expertise to manage the logistics of importing the component and distributing it to their respective manufacturing facilities. Each party may be responsible for a specific task using its own assets and incurring its own liabilities, and there may be tasks that they undertake jointly. In this case, a separate vehicle has not been established to manage the importation and distribution of the component.

A joint arrangement that **is structured through another vehicle** could be either a joint operation or a joint venture. Figure 10.1 illustrates how to analyse the factors when assessing the rights and obligations arising from an arrangement in order to classify the joint arrangement.

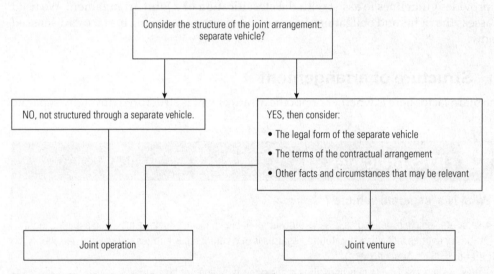

Figure 10.1 Classification of a joint arrangement (refer to IFRS11, Appendix B)

3.2 Legal form and terms of contractual arrangement

When considering the legal form of the separate vehicle, you need to determine how it affects the rights to the assets and obligations for the liabilities.

- Where the assets and liabilities are held in the separate vehicle but the legal form is such that the rights to the assets and obligations for the liabilities are those of the parties that have joint control, then the arrangement is a **joint operation**.
- Despite the arrangement being conducted through a separate vehicle, where the parties that have joint control structure the contractual arrangement between themselves such that the terms indicate that the parties have rights to the assets the joint arrangement, the arrangement is a **joint operation**.

- The activities of the separate vehicle may be primarily to provide output to the parties that have joint control. This indicates that these parties have rights to substantially all of the economic benefits of the assets of the arrangement. The liabilities incurred by the arrangement are satisfied by the cash flows received from the parties through purchasing the output and are substantially the only source of cash flows contributing to the arrangement. As such, the parties effectively have obligations for the arrangement's liabilities. Consequently, the arrangement is a **joint operation**.
- If none of these facts or circumstances is present, then the joint arrangement is a **joint venture**.

Example

Contractual agreement to have joint control (continued)

Refer to the previous example. Let's assume that A and B instead form a separate company, C Ltd, which will be responsible for managing the logistics of importing and distributing the component part. C Ltd can only import from suppliers approved jointly by A and B, and can only distribute the component to A and B. In this case, even though the joint arrangement is through a separate vehicle and may have been structured differently from the previous example legally, the substance is that the two arrangements are the same. A and B have rights to the assets of C Ltd, which are simplistically assumed to be the component parts. In addition, A and B are also effectively responsible for the obligations of C Ltd as they are its only source of cash flows.

Now instead assume that A and B form C Ltd. A and B are the only shareholders of C Ltd. C Ltd imports the component part, but only 20% of the imported components are sold to A and B. The remaining 80% of the parts are sold to third parties. A and B have a contractual agreement that indicates that they will jointly approve the suppliers from which C Ltd may import the component, the customers to which it may sell and the prices it charges customers. A and B jointly control C Ltd as they have decision-making power collectively. In other words, A and B jointly influence the relevant activities of C Ltd (suppliers, customers, selling prices and so on). C Ltd is a joint arrangement, but A and B do not have rights to its assets (the components parts are sold to other parties as well). A and B also do not have obligations for its liabilities as C Ltd has other sources of cash inflows. In this case, C Ltd is a joint venture. A and B only have an interest in the residual net assets of C Ltd.

4. Accounting for joint arrangements

The accounting for joint ventures is different from that of joint operations. In the case of a joint venture, the joint venturers have an interest in the investment in the joint arrangement. In this case, the investment is accounted for using the equity method (in accordance with IAS 28, *Investments in Associates and Joint Ventures*; refer to Chapter 9).

IFRS for SMEs update

Investments in joint ventures

The *IFRS for SMEs* allow three accounting models for interests in joint ventures: the cost model, the equity method and fair value.

The classification of a joint arrangement prescribes the accounting treatment, as described below. A joint venturer accounts for its interest in the **joint venture** as follows:
- In its separate financial statements, either on the cost model or at fair value as permitted by IAS27, *Separate Financial Statements* (see Chapter 1).
- In its group financial statements, using the equity method in accordance with IAS28, *Investments in Associates and Joint Ventures*, unless it is exempted from doing so by that standard. The equity method is dealt with in detail in Chapter 9.

As mentioned earlier, a **joint operation** may be undertaken outside a formal structure, thus separate accounting records are not specifically required for the joint operation. However, for accountability reasons, it makes sense that the joint operation agreement requires records of this nature. In addition, there may be instances where a joint operation is a separate vehicle and would have its own accounting records.

The joint operator recognises the following, in relation to its interest in the joint operation:
- Its assets, including its share of the assets held jointly
- Its liabilities, including its share of liabilities incurred jointly
- Its revenue from the sale of its share of the output by the joint operation
- Its expenses, including its share of any expenses incurred jointly.

The joint operator accounts for the assets, liabilities, revenues and expenses in relation to its interest in the joint operation in accordance with the relevant IFRS relating to those assets, liabilities, revenue and expenses in its separate financial statements.

A **party that participates in the joint arrangement, but that does not have joint control** accounts for its interest in the joint arrangement as follows:
- If the joint arrangement is classified as a joint operation, the party accounts for its interest in the joint operation on the same basis as a joint operator.
- If the joint arrangement is classified as a joint venture, the party must assess the nature of its interest. If it has significant influence, it accounts for its interest as an associate (see Chapter 9). Otherwise, it accounts for its interest as a financial asset in accordance with IFRS 9, *Financial instruments*.

4.1 Contributions of cash to joint operation

The key features of a joint operation are that each joint operator has an interest in the individual assets and liabilities of the joint operation. Where the joint operation produces an output that is distributed to the joint operators, each joint operator receives a share of the output of the joint operation and becomes responsible for its share of the related expenses. Usually the joint operation maintains a separate set of accounts, which include assets and liabilities as well as income and expenses, and as such, prepares separate financial statements. Each joint operator then views the accounts of the joint operation and calculates its share of each of the relevant accounts.

Example

Accounting records of joint operation

A Ltd and B Ltd signed an agreement to form a joint operation to manufacture a product that both entities use for the packaging of their products. The operation is conducted in the form of an unincorporated joint operation. The following transactions are typical examples of entries in the accounting system of the **joint operation**.

Contributions of cash
Each operator contributes CU500 000 in cash.

			CU	CU
Dr		Bank	1 000 000	
	Cr	A Ltd (contributor)		500 000
	Cr	B Ltd (contributor)		500 000

Cash contributions to the joint operation

This journal entry shows the contributions by each operator and the establishment of a separate bank account for the joint operation.

Acquisition of non-current asset
The cash is used and a loan is raised to buy equipment.

			CU	CU
Dr		Equipment	200 000	
	Cr	Bank		100 000
	Cr	Bank loan		100 000

Equipment acquired by the joint operation

Acquisition of inventory
The cash is used to buy raw materials.

			CU	CU
Dr		Inventory (raw materials)	150 000	
	Cr	Bank		150 000

Inventory acquired by the joint operation

These journal entries illustrate the establishment of the joint operation and the recording of its activities throughout the year. The joint operation's transactions further include the labour and overhead costs incurred to manufacture the packaging materials, the depreciation of the equipment and so on.

At the reporting date, financial statements are prepared for the joint operation.

Example

Accounting records of the joint operators

This example follows on from the previous example, where A Ltd and B Ltd signed an agreement to form a joint operation (sharing in a 50:50 ratio) to manufacture a product that both entities use for the packaging of their products. The information that follows was obtained from the financial statements of the joint operation at 31 December 20x5, its first reporting date.

Joint operation: Statement of financial position at 31 December 20x5 (extract)

	CU
ASSETS	
Equipment	180 000
Inventory (raw materials)	60 000
Inventory (finished goods)	45 000
Bank	480 000
	765 000
LIABILITIES	
Bank loan	(100 000)
Net assets	**665 000**

Joint operation: Payments and receipts ended 31 December 20x5

	Payments CU	Receipts CU
Cash contribution		1 000 000
Bank loan		100 000
Equipment	200 000	
Inventory (raw materials)	150 000	
Wages	90 000	
Overhead expenses	180 000	
Net bank balance: CU480 000	**620 000**	**1 100 000**

Joint operation: Costs incurred for the year ended 31 December 20x5

	CU
Raw materials used in production (150 000 – 60 000)	90 000
Depreciation (equipment)	20 000
Other overhead costs	180 000
Wages	90 000
	380 000
Less: Inventory (finished products) still on hand	(45 000)
Completed inventory transferred to joint operators	① **335 000**

① Completed finished products, amounting to CU335 000, are transferred to the joint operators. The contributions section of the statement of financial position of the joint operation thus includes the cash contribution for each operator, less any inventory transferred to the joint operators.

Joint operation: Contributions for the year ended 31 December 20x5

	A Ltd CU	B Ltd CU	Total CU
Initial cash contribution	500 000	500 000	1 000 000
Less: Inventory transferred	② (167 500)	(167 500)	① (335 000)
Net contributions (= to net assets)	**332 500**	**332 500**	**665 000**

What will be the entries in the records of A Ltd?

When A Ltd makes the initial contribution to the joint operation, it would record the following entry:

			CU	CU
Dr		Contribution to joint operation	500 000	
	Cr	Bank		500 000

Cash contribution to joint operation

② A Ltd also recognises the completed inventory of CU167 500 as and when it is transferred from the joint operation.

			CU	CU
Dr		Inventory (finished goods)	167 500	
	Cr	Contribution to joint operation		167 500

Inventory contribution to joint operation

As evidenced from the extracts of the financial statements of the joint operation, the cash has been used to acquire various assets, undertake loans, incur expenses and manufacture inventory. As a contributor of 50% of the cash into the joint operation, A Ltd is entitled to 50% of all of the assets, liabilities, expenses and output of the joint operation.

Thus, at 31 December 20x5, A Ltd records the entry that follows in order to replace the contribution to the joint operation with its 50% share of each of the assets and liabilities of the joint operation (JO).

			CU	CU
Dr		Equipment in joint operation	90 000	
Dr		Inventory (raw materials) in joint operation	30 000	
Dr		Inventory (finished goods) in joint operation	22 500	
	Cr	Bank loan in joint operation		50 000
	Cr	Contribution to joint operation		92 500

Recognising assets and liabilities in joint operation

Check your answer

What is A Ltd's net cash contribution (investment) in the joint operation at 31 December 20x5?

Initial cash contribution	CU500 000
Less: Completed inventory received from joint operation	(167 500)
Less: Cash used by joint operation to acquire assets, and incur liabilities	(92 500)
Contribution in joint operation	► CU240 000

At 31 December 20x5, A Ltd is still a 50% contributor to the cash balance of the joint operation: (CU480 000 × 50%) = CU240 000.

What will be the entries in B Ltd?

B Ltd will record the same entries as listed above for A Ltd.

Why are there no *pro-forma* journal entries?

Pro-forma journal entries are not required as there are no combinations of the different financial statements of the different operators in a single set of financial statements.

4.2 Contributions of assets to joint operation

In the example above, the joint operators each contributed cash to the joint operation. In some cases, a joint operation may contribute assets (other than cash) to the joint operations. Where an operator **contributes a non-current asset** to the joint operation, the value of the contribution is the fair value of that non-current asset. However, as the transaction is not an arm's length transaction, the transfer of such assets to the joint operation cannot result in the recognition of the full profit (gain or loss) on such transactions. The joint operator can only recognise gains and losses on such transactions to the extent of the other parties' interests in the joint operations (in other words, the joint operator that contributes the asset cannot recognise a profit based on the portion of the asset 'retained', that is, the portion not 'sold' to the other operator).

The accounting records of the operator that contributes the non-current asset cannot recognise the asset at fair value as the operator is effectively 'selling' a portion of the asset to the other joint operator and the other portion to itself. Thus, the operator makes a profit on selling the proportion of the asset to the other operators, but recognises its share of the asset at the carrying amount of the asset. This results in the asset being recognised at **different carrying amounts** in the records of the different operators. In the same way, any **depreciation** relating to that asset is then recorded at different amounts, where the other operators recognise depreciation based on the fair value of the asset and the operator that contributed the asset recognises depreciation based on its share of the carrying amount of the asset.

Example

Transfer of non-current asset to joint operation

Two operators contribute the following to the joint operation:
- A Ltd contributes cash of CU500 000.
- B Ltd contributes equipment with a fair value of CU500 000.

As one operator contributed CU500 000 in cash and the other operator contributed a non-current asset, both parties should agree that the non-current asset contributed to the joint operation has a fair value of CU500 000. This means that some form of valuation of contributions other than cash needs to be made by the parties involved.

In this case, each operator shares in the assets of the joint operation as follows:

	Total assets	A Ltd's share	B Ltd's share
Cash contributions	CU500 000	CU250 000	CU250 000
Equipment	CU500 000	CU250 000	CU250 000

This means that B Ltd shares in the cash and equipment of the joint operation in the same way as A Ltd shares in the net assets of the joint operation. However, you need to consider the carrying amount of the asset in B Ltd, as B Ltd's share of the equipment that it contributed to the joint operation cannot result in the recognition of an unrealised profit.

Thus, assume that the carrying amount of the equipment amounted to CU400 000 in B Ltd, then B Ltd's share of the equipment in the joint operation is CU200 000 (50% of its carrying amount).

On the other hand, A Ltd's share of the equipment is CU250 000.

What will be the entries in the records of the joint operation?

			CU	CU
Dr		Bank	500 000	
Dr		Equipment (at fair value)	500 000	
	Cr	A Ltd (contributor)		500 000
	Cr	B Ltd (contributor)		500 000

Contribution of cash (by A Ltd) and equipment (by B Ltd)

The joint operation records depreciation of the equipment based on its fair value of CU500 000.

What will be the entries in the records of A Ltd?

			CU	CU
Dr		Contribution in joint operation	250 000	
Dr		Equipment in joint operation	250 000	
	Cr	Bank		500 000

Contribution of cash to joint operation

Note that A Ltd recognises the equipment in its records at half of its fair value of CU500 000.

What will be the entries in the records of B Ltd?

			CU	CU
Dr		Contribution in joint operation	250 000	
Dr		Equipment in joint operation	200 000	
	Cr	Profit on sale of equipment		50 000
	Cr	Equipment (at carrying amount)		400 000

Contribution of equipment to joint operation

Note that B Ltd recognises the equipment in its records at half of its carrying amount of CU400 000, even though the fair value of the equipment is CU500 000. The profit recognised on the sale of the equipment relates to the portion that was 'sold' to the other operator, A Ltd, amounting to 50% of CU100 000.

The depreciation relating to the equipment is recognised in the records of the joint operation based on its fair value of CU500 000 and A Ltd includes depreciation expense based on 50% of this value, that is, CU250 000. However, B Ltd includes depreciation expense based on its share of the carrying amount of CU400 000.

Thus, the depreciation expense recognised in the records of A Ltd and B Ltd is not the same, as B Ltd originally held the asset and B Ltd could not recognise a profit on the sale of the portion of the asset to itself. B Ltd should continue to recognise depreciation on the proportionate carrying amount of CU200 000 (50% of CU400 000).

An alternative way of recording the equipment in the records of B Ltd is to transfer the asset at fair value first, and then to reverse (adjust) the proportionate unrealised portions of the profit and depreciation at each reporting date.

Think about it

What if the equipment was used in the production of inventory, as in the previous example?

Where the depreciation is capitalised into inventory and work in progress in the records of the joint operation, then B Ltd recognises its share of the assets of the joint operation after making a further adjustment to reduce the balances of the completed inventory. B Ltd's share of the inventory is overstated to the extent of the difference in the depreciation expense in the joint operation (based on the fair value of the equipment) and the depreciation expense based on the carrying amount of the equipment in B Ltd. Thus, the adjustment to depreciation is proportionately allocated to all inventory produced by the joint operation, recognised in B Ltd. This includes work in progress, completed inventory not yet transferred and completed inventory transferred to B Ltd.

4.3 Other charges to a joint operation

In some cases, one or more of the operators in a joint operation may charge for other services provided to the joint operation, such as management fees. For example, the joint operation pays a management fee to the joint operator for its management services. The joint operator that supplies the service normally incurs a cost relating to the service (salaries and so on). Thus, the operator supplying the service has to consider the following when accounting for its interest in the joint operation in its own accounting records:
- That the joint operator cannot earn a profit on supplying services to itself
- Where the cost of the service provided is included in the cost of an asset, for example, conversion costs of inventory, an adjustment is necessary to the inventory-related accounts of that operator because the cost of this asset is less to the operator supplying the service than to the other operators.

IFRS principles

Single economic entity

You should remember the principle that the operator records and reports its operations and activities as a single economic entity. A joint operator must recognise its share of the assets and liabilities of the arrangement as well as its revenues and expenses associated with the arrangement. In doing this, the reporting entity should not recognise any gains or losses that arise from transactions with itself.

5. Disclosure

Relevant information relating to the **joint arrangement** is disclosed in order to provide useful information to the users of the financial statements who wish to make assumptions about the risks and future cash flows of the reporting entity. IFRS 12, *Disclosure of Interests with Other Entities,* requires the reporting entity to disclose the nature, extent and financial effects of its interests in joint arrangements, including the nature and effects of its contractual relationship with the other investors with joint control of the joint arrangement. This is achieved by IFRS 12 requiring, for all material joint arrangements, disclosures of the following information:

• The name of the joint arrangement
• The nature of the entity's relationship with the joint arrangement
• The joint arrangement's principal place of business
• The entity's proportion of ownership interest, participating share or voting rights (as applicable).

Each joint operator includes the relevant amounts for assets, liabilities, revenues and expenses in its own records. The assets are actual assets of the joint operator and the operator is responsible for the liabilities recognised. There is no requirement to show these items separately for other assets and liabilities of the operator. However, some entities may consider these to be a separate class of assets and provide information in the notes to the financial statements regarding assets and liabilities associated with joint operations.

Additional disclosures are also required for joint ventures. These are dealt with in Chapter 9.

Test your knowledge

There is a list of learning objectives at the beginning of this chapter. Go back to this list and check whether you have achieved these outcomes. If not, reread the appropriate section.

Questions

Question 1

P Ltd owns 35% of X Ltd and enters into an agreement with another party that also owns 35% of X Ltd so that P Ltd and the other party vote in the same manner at X Ltd's shareholder's meetings. What is the nature of P Ltd's interest in X Ltd?

Suggested solution

P Ltd and the other party have entered into a joint arrangement; each has 35% of the voting rights in the arrangement with the remaining 30% being held by outside parties. Assuming that the contractually agreed sharing of control of this arrangement between P Ltd and the other party specifies that decisions about the relevant activities of the arrangement require both parties agreeing, then both parties own sufficient voting rights to have joint control.

As A Ltd is a separate entity (vehicle), it is classified as a joint venture and P Ltd recognises its interest in X Ltd using the equity method when preparing group financial statements.

Question 2

A Ltd enters into a joint agreement with B Ltd to establish an unincorporated joint operation to manufacture a lubrication used in equipment of both entities. It was agreed that the output of the operation would be shared as follows:
- A Ltd: 60%
- B Ltd: 40%.

Each entity contributed the following assets:
- A Ltd: Cash of CU560 000 and equipment with a fair value of CU40 000 (cost of CU48 000, carrying amount of CU35 000).
- B Ltd: Cash of CU400 000.

The operational manager of the joint operation provided the information that follows for the financial year ending 31 December 20x5.

Cash receipts and payments

	Payments CU	Receipts CU
Cash contributions		960 000
Plant purchased (expected useful life of five years, zero residual value)	300 000	
Wages paid	185 000	
Accounts payable (raw materials)	150 000	
Overhead costs	160 000	
	795 000	960 000
Bank balance	165 000	
	960 000	**960 000**

Assets and liabilities at 31 December 20x5

	Assets CU	Liabilities CU
Bank balance	165 000	
Raw materials on hand	80 000	
Completed inventory on hand	120 000	
Plant and equipment (300 000 + 40 000)	340 000	
Accumulated depreciation: New plant		60 000
Equipment from A Ltd		15 000
Accounts payable		150 000
Accrued expenses (overheads and other operating expenses)		40 000
	705 000	265 000
Net assets	**440 000**	

Costs incurred for the year ended 31 December 20x5

	CU
Raw materials purchased (150 000 + 150 000)	300 000
Wages	185 000
Factory overhead costs (160 000 + 40 000)	200 000
Depreciation	75 000
	760 000
Less: Raw materials on hand at 31 December 20x5	(80 000)
Cost of inventory produced	**680 000**

You are required to do the following:

Prepare the journal entries in the records of A Ltd relating to the joint operation for the year ended 30 June 20x5.

Suggested solution

Records of A Ltd

			CU	CU
Dr		Contribution in joint operation (960 000 × 60%)	576 000	
Dr		Equipment in joint operation (35 000 × 60%)	21 000	
	Cr	Bank		560 000
	Cr	Equipment		48 000
Dr		Accumulated depreciation	13 000	
	Cr	Profit on sale of equipment (5 000 × 40%)		2 000

Cash and equipment contribution to new joint operation

At 31 December 20x5

			CU	CU
Dr		Plant in joint operation (300 000 × 60%)	180 000	
	Cr	Accumulated depreciation (75 000 × 60%)		45 000
Dr		Raw materials in joint operation (80 000 × 60%)	48 000	
Dr		Completed inventory in joint operation (120 000 × 60%)	72 000	
Dr		Inventory from joint operation (560 000 × 60%)	336 000	
	Cr	Accounts payable (150 000 × 60%)		90 000
	Cr	Accrued expenses (40 000 × 60%)		24 000
	Cr	Contribution in joint operation (960 000 − 165 000) × 60%		477 000

Proportion of share of assets and liabilities in joint operation at reporting date

Note that the inventory completed and transferred to the operators amounts to CU560 000 (CU680 000 produced, less CU120 000 still on hand). However, as a portion of the depreciation relates to the equipment transferred by A Ltd and depreciation is capitalised to the production of inventory, an adjustment is required to accumulated depreciation and inventories:

- Depreciation in joint operation: CU15 000
- Depreciation of equipment based on cost in A Ltd: CU13 125 (CU15 000/CU40 000 × CU35 000)
- Adjustment required for depreciation: CU1 875, calculated as follows:

	CU		CU
Inventory in joint operation	120 000	(120 000/680 000 × CU1 875)	331
Inventory transferred to operators	560 000	(560 000/680 000 × CU1 875)	1 544
	680 000		**1 875**

			CU	CU
Dr		Accumulated depreciation	1 875	
	Cr	Completed inventory in joint operation		331
	Cr	Inventory from joint operation		1 544

Adjustment to accumulated depreciation and the cost of inventor relating to the equipment transferred to the joint operation

Case study exercises

Scenario 1
You obtained the extracts that follow from the financial statements of P Ltd for the current financial period that ended 31 December 20x5.

Statements of financial position of P Ltd on 31 December 20x5

	P Ltd CU'000
ASSETS	
Plant and machinery	590
Contribution in joint operation (note 1)	300
Inventory	320
Other current assets	180
	1 390
CAPITAL AND LIABILITIES	
Share capital	290
Retained earnings	900
Shareholders' equity	1 190
Current liabilities	200
	1 390

Statements of profit or loss and other comprehensive income of P Ltd for the year ended 31 December 20x5

	P Ltd CU'000
Revenue (including management fee received)	2 320
Cost of sales	(1 050)
Gross profit	1 270
Net operating costs	(390)
Interest expense	(100)
Profit before taxation	780
Taxation expense	(300)
Profit after taxation	**480**

Extract from statements of changes in shareholders' equity of P Ltd for the year ended 31 December 20x5

	P Ltd CU'000
Retained earnings 1 January 20x5	620
Total comprehensive income	480
Dividends declared	(200)
Retained earnings 31 December 20x5	**900**

Note 1

On 1 July 20x5, P Ltd entered into an arrangement with another operator, Y Ltd, to establish an unincorporated joint operation to supply distribution services to both entities. Each operator provided CU300 000 in cash and each operator will share equally in the distribution services supplied by the joint operation. P Ltd agreed to manage the project for a fee of CU20 000 per annum, which is equal to the cost for P Ltd to provide the service.

When the accountant of P Ltd prepared the above summarised financial statements, she only recorded the initial cash payment of CU300 000 and the management fee received of CU10 000. She did not consider any adjustments necessary relating to P Ltd's interest in the assets and liabilities of the joint operation.

The extracts of the statement of financial position of the joint operation at 31 December 20x5 appear below. Ignore taxation.

Statement of financial position of joint operation at 31 December 20x5

	Joint operator CU'000
ASSETS	
Delivery vehicles (carrying amount) (cost: CU750 000)	700
	30
	730
LIABILITIES	
Non-current liabilities	(420)
Net assets	**310**

The joint operation paid a management fee amounting to CU10 000 to P Ltd for the period 1 July to 31 December 20x5. The joint operation incurred the costs set out below relating to its distribution services.

Distribution expenses incurred by the joint operator

	CU'000
Delivery vehicles (depreciation)	50
Management fees	10
Salaries and wages	180
Interest expense	20
Other operating costs	30
	290

You are required to do the following:
1. Answer the following questions:
   - How would you classify P Ltd's share or investment in the joint operation?
   - How would you recognise P Ltd's share or investment in the joint operation?
2. Prepare the journal entries required to recognise P Ltd's share in the joint operation correctly in its financial statements for the year ended 31 December 20x5.
3. Prepare the statement of financial position for P Ltd at 31 December 20x5.

Suggested solution

Scenario 1
1. Answer the following questions:
   - **How would you classify P Ltd's share or investment in the joint operation?**
     P Ltd has entered into a contractual arrangement with another party to control the distribution activities of both parties jointly. This is a joint operation, which is undertaken outside a formal structure. The joint operation keeps separate accounting records.
   - **How would you recognise P Ltd's share or investment in the joint operation?**
     The joint operator that has an interest in the joint operation has an interest in the individual assets and liabilities of the joint operation. As the joint operation produces an output that is distributed to the joint operators, each joint operator receives a share of the output of the joint operation and becomes responsible for a share of the expenses of the operation that are not capitalised to the cost of the output. Hence, P Ltd needs to recognise the following in its own accounts:
     - Its share of the jointly held assets and liabilities of the joint operation
     - Its share of the expenses incurred by the joint operation.

2. **Prepare the journal entries required to recognise P Ltd's share in the joint operation correctly in its financial statements for the year ended 31 December 20x5.**

Records of P Ltd at 31 December 20x5

			CU	CU
Dr		Delivery vehicles (750 000 × 50%)	375 000	
	Cr	Accumulated depreciation (50 000 × 50%)		25 000
Dr		Distribution expenses in joint operation (290 000 × 50%)	145 000	
	Cr	Non-current liabilities (420 000 × 50%)		210 000
	Cr	Contribution in joint operation (600 000 – 30 000) × 50%		285 000

Proportion of share of assets and liabilities in joint operation at reporting date

P Ltd supplied the management services for the distribution service for a fee of CU10 000 for the current year. Half of this management fee was supplied to itself, so it should be eliminated against the fee income in P Ltd and the cost of the distribution supplied. This adjustment is necessary to eliminate the revenue and expense of supplying services to itself:

			CU	CU
Dr		Management fee income (10 000 × 50%)	5 000	
	Cr	Distribution expenses in joint venture (10 000 × 50%)		5 000

Adjustment for management fee supplied to itself

3. **Prepare the statement of financial position for P Ltd at 31 December 20x5.**

Statements of financial position of P Ltd on 31 December 20x5

	P Ltd CU'000
ASSETS	
Plant and machinery (carrying amount)	590
Delivery vehicles (carrying amount) (375 – 25)	350
Contribution in joint operation (300 – 285)	15
Inventory	320
Other current assets	180
	1 455
CAPITAL AND LIABILITIES	
Share capital	290
Retained earnings (900 – 145)	755
Shareholders' equity	1 045
Non-current liabilities	210
Current liabilities	200
	1 455

Statement of comprehensive income of P Ltd for year ended 31 December 20x5

	P Ltd CU'000
Revenue (2 320 – 5)	2 315
Cost of sales	(1 050)
Gross profit	1 265
Net operating costs	(390)
Distribution costs (145 – 5)	(140)
Interest expense	(100)
Profit before taxation	635
Taxation expense	(300)
Profit after taxation	**335**

Extract from statements of changes in shareholders' equity of P Ltd for the year ended 31 December 20x5

	P Ltd CU'000
Retained earnings 1 January 20x5	620
Total comprehensive income	335
Dividends declared	(200)
Retained earnings 31 December 20x5	**755**

PART IV

Complex issues

Direct and indirect interest

The following topics are included in this chapter:

- Different compositions of groups, including direct and indirect interests
- Determining the effective interest by a parent in an indirectly held subsidiary
- Vertical and horizontal groups
- Sequential and non-sequential ownership
- Preparing group financial statements for indirect interests and complex groups.

Learning objectives

By the end of this chapter, you should be able to:
- Identify directly held and indirectly held subsidiaries
- Determine the effective interest of a parent in an indirectly held subsidiary
- Understand the importance of the sequence of the acquisition of the controlling interest when there are a number of subsidiaries
- Prepare group financial statements for a 'vertical group'
- Prepare group financial statements for a 'horizontal group'
- Explain how you would determine the non-controlling interest in a complex group.

1. Different compositions of group companies

In the previous chapters, you learnt that a group is a single economic entity consisting of two or more entities and that we are required to prepare group financial statements where the parent has a controlling interest in another entity, which is called a subsidiary. The subsidiary is either wholly owned, which is when the parent acquires all of the shares in the subsidiary, or, in the case where the parent does not acquire all of the shares in the subsidiary, the parent has a partly held interest in the equity of the subsidiary. The equity of the subsidiary that is not attributable to the parent is known as the non-controlling interest. In Part II, the examples used mainly consisted of two entities: the parent and its subsidiary. This represents a **simple group** as it consists of a parent and a single subsidiary.

Where a parent has multiple subsidiaries and the subsidiaries are themselves parents (in other words, they control subsidiaries themselves), the group structure becomes more complex. In this chapter, we consider the effect that different forms of group structures have on the preparation of group financial statements. These include where the parent has a controlling interest in a subsidiary and that subsidiary has a controlling interest in a subsidiary of its own. In this case, the parent has an indirect controlling interest in the second subsidiary through its controlling interest in the first subsidiary. This form of group structure is referred to as a **vertical group** as it has multiple level structures. A **horizontal group**, by comparison, has a single level structure, where the parent has a controlling interest in two or more subsidiaries. The parent thus has a direct ownership in each of the subsidiaries. Where the parent has an interest in multiple subsidiaries, and the subsidiaries have further ownership interest in each other and in other entities, it is referred to as a **complex group**.

1.1 Controlling interest

A subsidiary is an entity that is controlled by a parent. IFRS10, *Consolidated Financial Statements*, provides numerous factors to be considered in making the decision concerning the existence of control (refer to Chapter 3). The three elements of control (an investor must hold all of them) include the following:
- Power over the investee
- Exposure, or rights, to variable returns from its involvement with the investee
- The ability to use its power over the investee to affect the amount of the investor's returns.

Ownership of shares normally provides **voting rights** that enable the holder of the majority of shares to dominate the appointment of directors or an entity's governing board. As mentioned earlier, the parent is the entity that controls one or more entities, an entity that is controlled by another entity is a subsidiary, and a group is a parent and its subsidiaries. Where the parent owns more than 50% of the shares of another entity and in the absence of other evidence, it is considered that the parent holds more than half of the voting power of an entity. This level of ownership constitutes **control** and a parent–subsidiary relation exists.

The parent consolidates the assets, liabilities and equity of the subsidiary into its group financial statements.

 IFRS principles

IFRS10: 4(a)

A parent need not present **consolidated financial statements** if and only if:
- The parent is itself a wholly owned subsidiary of another entity or where the owners of the non-controlling interests unanimously agree that the parent need not present consolidated financial statements
- The parent's securities are not publicly traded
- The parent is not in the process of issuing securities in the public securities markets
- The immediate or ultimate parent publishes consolidated financial statements so that the parent under discussion need not present consolidated financial statements.

There is only one parent in a group and the parent is required to prepare consolidated financial statements (unless the criteria as set out above are met). In this chapter, we will consider the preparation of consolidated financial statements for **multiple subsidiary structures**. In each case, it is important to identify the parent that is preparing consolidated financial statements.

1.2 Direct and indirect controlling interest

A **direct controlling interest** arises where the parent has a direct investment in the subsidiary (in other words, the parent owns the shares itself). An **indirect controlling interest** is where a parent has a controlling interest in a subsidiary that, in turn, is a parent (that is, controls another subsidiary). The parent controls the first subsidiary and is therefore able to control its shareholding in the second subsidiary.

Example

An illustration of different group structures

Assume that in the independent groups shown in Figure 11.1 below, the voting power is in proportion to shareholding.

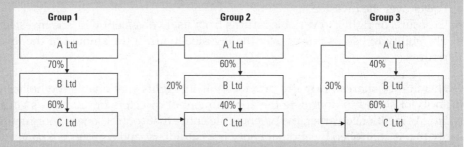

Figure 11.1 Illustration of different group structures

Group 1
A controls B and B is therefore a subsidiary of A. As A is able to control B, it is also able to control B's investment in C. As B is able to control C by virtue of its 60% shareholding, A is able to control both B and C. Therefore both B and C are subsidiaries of A. A has no direct shareholding in C, but has an indirect shareholding held through a controlled holding in B. The consolidated financial statements of A include 100% of A, B and C.

Group 2
A owns 20% of C directly. A controls B and therefore controls B's 40% investment in C. Consequently, A is able to control 60% of C (having a 20% direct interest and a 40% indirect interest through B). C is a subsidiary of A. The consolidated financial statements of A include 100% of A, B and C.

Group 3
A controls 30% of C directly. A does not control B because it has a shareholding of less than 50%. B's shareholding in C cannot be taken into account as indirect shareholdings can only be considered where held through a subsidiary. B and C are both equity accounted in A's group financial statements.

These examples illustrate the different forms of group structures as well as the concept of direct and indirect interest. In deciding whether an entity is controlled (and is therefore a subsidiary), direct holdings and indirect holdings through controlled entities should be taken into account. Indirect holdings through joint ventures or associates should be ignored.

A feature of multiple subsidiary structures, where the parent has an interest in a subsidiary that is itself a parent of another subsidiary, is the classification of the ownership in the subsidiaries into direct and indirect interest. A subsidiary arises because the parent has control. As indicated earlier, this is because the parent owns (directly or indirectly) **more than half of the votes** of the entity. This does not necessarily mean that the parent holds more than half of the issued shares or that it would receive more than half of the equity of the subsidiary. The subsidiary may have different classes of shares, there may be potential shares in the form of options or the shareholding in the subsidiary may be held indirectly through another subsidiary. There may therefore be a difference between the number of shares that attach voting rights and the number of shares outstanding (meaning the number of issued shares) that share in the equity of the subsidiary or alternatively the number of voting rights owned (directly or indirectly) compared to the profits attributable to the ultimate parent.

The percentage of profits that would be received is known as the 'effective interest' or the 'economic interest'. In any parent–subsidiary relationship, once you have established that control exists, you should determine the **parent's effective interest** in the subsidiary. The parent's interest in the equity of a subsidiary is determined by dividing the number of ordinary shares held by the parent in the subsidiary by the total outstanding ordinary share capital of the subsidiary. The effective interest not held by the parent is attributable to the non-controlling interest.

Example

An illustration of effective interest

A Ltd acquired 60 000 of the 100 000 issued shares of B Ltd. As A Ltd owns 60 000 shares in B Ltd (which represents a 60% interest and voting power), A Ltd controls B Ltd. Therefore B Ltd is a subsidiary of A Ltd.

B Ltd acquired 45 000 of the issued shares of C Ltd, which represents a 60% interest in C Ltd. As B Ltd owns 45 000 shares in C Ltd (a 60% interest and voting power), B Ltd controls C Ltd. C Ltd is therefore a subsidiary of B Ltd.

Through its controlling interest in B Ltd, A Ltd has control over 60% of the voting rights in C Ltd. A Ltd therefore has control over C Ltd (indirectly). C Ltd is therefore a subsidiary of A Ltd.

This multiple group structure is illustrated in Figure 11.2 below.

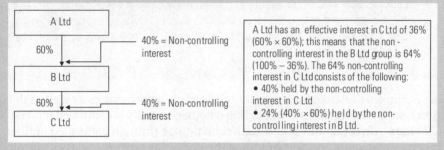

Figure 11.2 Illustration of effective interest in a vertical group

Effective interest

As indicated above, B Ltd and C Ltd are both subsidiaries of A Ltd. The group financial statements of A Ltd include the consolidated B Ltd and C Ltd. This implies that 100% of the assets, liabilities, income and expenses of B Ltd and C Ltd are recognised in A Ltd's group financial statements. However, not all of the equity of B Ltd or C Ltd is attributable to the equity holders of A Ltd. As neither B Ltd nor C Ltd is a wholly owned subsidiary, some equity is attributable to the non-controlling interest.

Assume the following profit after tax for the current year for each of the entities in the group:

	CU
A Ltd	800 000
B Ltd	550 000
C Ltd	380 000

What is the group profit recognised in the consolidated statement of profit or loss for the current reporting period?

	CU
A Ltd	800 000
B Ltd	550 000
C Ltd	380 000
Group profit after tax	**1 730 000**

As both B Ltd and C Ltd are subsidiaries of A Ltd, the group profit includes 100% of the profits of these subsidiaries.

What is the non-controlling interest in the current year's consolidated statement of profit or loss?

	CU
B Ltd (40% × CU550 000)	220 000
C Ltd (64% × CU380 000)	243 200
Non-controlling interest	**463 200**

The non-controlling interest is calculated separately for each subsidiary.

What is the group profit attributable to the parent equity holders of A Ltd in the current year's consolidated statement of profit or loss?

	CU
A Ltd	800 000
B Ltd (60% × CU550 000)	330 000
C Ltd (36% × CU380 000)	136 800
Profit attributable to parent equity holders in A Ltd	**1 266 800** ◀

Check your answer ─────────────

	CU
Group profit after tax:	1 730 000
Less attributable to non-controlling interest:	463 200
Profit attributable to parent equity holders:	**1 266 800**

Alternatively, let us prepare the consolidated profit or loss for the B Ltd group first:

B Ltd group	CU
Profit after tax (550 000 + 380 000)	930 000
Less: Non-controlling interest (40% × CU380 000)	(152 000)
Profit attributable to parent equity holders in B Ltd	**778 000** ◀

The B Ltd group is then consolidated into the A Ltd group, resulting in the following:

A Ltd group	CU
Profit after tax (800 000 + 550 000 + 380 000)	1 730 000
Less: Non-controlling interest (40% × 778 000) + 152 000	(463 200) ◀
Profit attributable to parent equity holders in A Ltd	**1 266 800**

Note that the non-controlling interest in B Ltd shares in the consolidated profit of B Ltd. This means the separate profit of B Ltd (the entity), amounting to CU311 200 (CU778 000 × 40%), plus its share of the profit in C Ltd, amounting to CU152 000.

2. Group structures

Group structures are designed to meet the objectives and strategies of the group. Identifying the group structure enables us to understand the correct processes to follow in order to prepare the group financial statements.

2.1 Horizontal groups

As stated earlier, a **horizontal group** has a single level structure. The parent owns the shares, forming the equity interest, in two or more subsidiaries. There is thus a direct interest by the parent in all of the subsidiaries in the group. A horizontal group is illustrated in Figure 11.3 below.

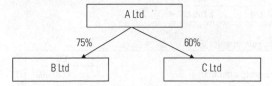

Figure 11.3 Illustration of a horizontal group

In a horizontal group, the parent has an interest in more than one subsidiary and holds that interest directly. The consolidation process is therefore similar to that of a simple group, as discussed in Part II. Each subsidiary should be consolidated at its acquisition date. You need to analyse the equity of each subsidiary individually in order to determine the correct goodwill acquired for each subsidiary as well as the non-controlling interest in that subsidiary.

Example

Consolidation of a horizontal group

This example illustrates the consolidation of two subsidiaries in a horizontal group, the measurement of goodwill acquired, profit for the year and non-controlling interest.

P Ltd holds a controlling interest in the following subsidiaries at 31 December 20x5, its current reporting date:

Subsidiary	Date of acquisition	Percentage interest acquired	Net fair value of identifiable assets and liabilities of subsidiary at acquisition date CU	Cost of investment in subsidiary CU
S1 Ltd	1 January 20x2	80%	800 000	680 000
S2 Ltd	1 July 20x4	75%	1 200 000	960 000

When P Ltd acquired its controlling interest in each of its two subsidiaries, the **goodwill** acquired and **non-controlling interest** are measured respectively, as shown below.

Acquisition of controlling interest in **S1 Ltd** (1 January 20x2)

	CU	CU
Purchase consideration (investment in subsidiary)	680 000	840 000
Non-controlling interest (measured at its share of the net identifiable assets) (see [w1])	160 000	
Less: Fair value of net identifiable assets		(800 000)
Goodwill acquired		**40 000**

(w1): (CU800 000 × 20%)

Acquisition of controlling interest in **S2 Ltd** (1 July 20x4)

	CU	CU
Purchase consideration (investment in subsidiary)	960 000	1 260 000
Non-controlling interest (measured at its share of the net identifiable assets) (see [w1])	300 000	
Less: Fair value of net identifiable assets		(1 200 000)
Goodwill acquired		**60 000**

(w1): (CU1 200 000 × 25%)

Assuming that the goodwill has never been impaired, the carrying amount of **goodwill** in the consolidated financial statements of P Ltd for the year ended 31 December 20x5 amounts to **CU100 000** (CU40 000 + CU60 000).

Each of the three entities had the following profits and dividends for the current period:

	P Ltd CU	S1 Ltd CU	S2 Ltd CU
Profit after tax	250 000	180 000	145 000
Ordinary dividend	(50 000)	(40 000)	(25 000)

An extract from the **consolidated statement of profit or loss** for the year ended 31 December 20x5 is shown below.

Extract from consolidated statement of profit or loss for the year ended 31 December 20x5

	CU
Profit after tax	▶ 524 250
Attributable to the parent equity holders	452 000
Attributable to non-controlling interest	72 250 ◀

What is this?
Group profit or loss is determined by adding 100% of the profit of the parent and 100% of each subsidiary. The dividends received by the parent are eliminated:
- Parent: CU250 000 – (80% × 40 000) – (75% × 25 000) = CU199 250
- S1: CU180 000
- S2: CU145 000.

What is this?
Non-controlling interest in each subsidiary:
- S1: CU180 000 × 20% = CU36 000
- S2: CU145 000 × 25% = CU36 250.

2.2 **Vertical groups**

In the case of a vertical group, the parent owns the controlling equity in a subsidiary. That subsidiary in turn owns the controlling interest in another subsidiary, which is referred to as a sub-subsidiary. The sub-subsidiary may in turn own the controlling interest in another entity. Thus, the vertical line of shareholding can extend even further downwards, resulting in multiple levels of shareholding structures.

This multiple **vertical** group structure is illustrated in Figure 11.4 below.

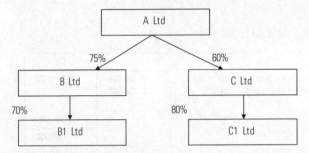

Figure 11.4 Illustration of a multiple group structure

This is just one example of a multiple group structure and many other possible combinations may exist in this type of group. In the example above, both B Ltd and C Ltd need to prepare consolidated financial statements, unless the criteria as set out in IFRS10, paragraph 4(a) are met.

There are essentially two methods whereby the consolidated financial statements for a vertical group can be prepared:

- Consolidated financial statements are first prepared for each sub-group. This means that you first prepare consolidated financial statements for the B Ltd group and for the C Ltd group. These consolidated financial statements are then consolidated further to prepare the group financial statements of A Ltd.
- One set of consolidated financial statements is prepared at the A Ltd group level. This may be the case because the criteria in IFRS10:4(a) have been met and neither B Ltd nor C Ltd prepares group financial statements.

On the assumption that we are required to prepare consolidated financial statements for the **ultimate parent** (in this case, A Ltd), we will apply the second method described above.

2.2.1 Sequential acquisition of subsidiaries and sub-subsidiaries

When consolidating multiple subsidiary structures, the accounting treatment used depends on the **sequence** in which the acquisitions occurred. Thus, the individual **acquisition dates** of each of the subsidiaries in the group is important as the parent only acquires the controlling interest in the sub-subsidiary when it acquires the direct controlling interest in its own subsidiary, if the newly acquired subsidiary already had a subsidiary. Attention should therefore be given to the sequence of acquisition of a subsidiary and sub-subsidiaries.

Think about it

What is sequential acquisition?

- Where the parent acquires its shares in a subsidiary **before** the subsidiary acquires its shares in a sub-subsidiary: This is a sequential acquisition as there are two business combinations. Refer to IFRS3, *Business Combinations*, and discussions in Chapter 2 and Chapter 3.
- Where the parent acquires its shares in a subsidiary after the subsidiary acquires its shares in a sub-subsidiary: In this case, there is one business combination, which is the date on which the parent acquires its shares in the subsidiary.

On consolidation, each subsidiary should be included in the consolidated financial statements when the group acquired its controlling interest and the increases in the reserves of each subsidiary are included in the group results since that date. This implies that we need to analyse the equity of each subsidiary separately from the perspective of preparing the consolidated financial statements of the ultimate parent

Example

Acquisition date of subsidiary in a vertical group

This example illustrates the calculation of the effective interest and non-controlling interest in a vertical group, and discusses the implications of different acquisition dates in the vertical group.

An illustration of the group structure for the P Ltd group is given in Figure 11.5 below.

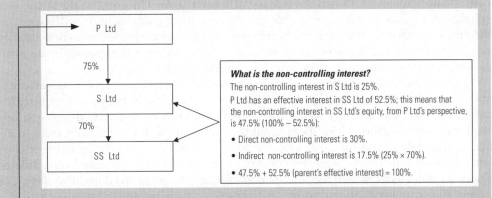

Figure 11.5 Illustration of vertical group structure

Consider the three scenarios that follow of P Ltd's acquisition date of S Ltd, while S Ltd acquired its controlling interest in SS Ltd on **1 January 20x2**.

Scenario 1: Same acquisition dates
P Ltd acquired its controlling interest in S Ltd on **1 January 20x2** and S Ltd acquired its controlling interest in SS Ltd on the same date. This means that the acquisition date (for preparing consolidated financial statements for P Ltd's group) is 1 January 20x2.

Scenario 2: Non-sequential acquisition
P Ltd acquired its controlling interest in S Ltd on 1 January 20x3, thus the acquisition date for preparing consolidated financial statements for the P Ltd group is **1 January 20x3**. This is the case even though S Ltd acquired its controlling interest in SS Ltd before that date. Should S Ltd prepare consolidated financial statements, its acquisition date of SS Ltd would be 1 January 20x2. P Ltd's acquisition date of its controlling interest in SS Ltd is 1 January 20x3, the date on which P Ltd acquired control of S Ltd.

Scenario 3: Sequential acquisition
P Ltd acquired its controlling interest in S Ltd on 1 July 20x1 and the acquisition date for preparing consolidated financial statements for the P Ltd group is **1 July 20x1**. From the group's perspective, P Ltd acquired its indirect controlling interest in SS Ltd when SS Ltd became a subsidiary of S Ltd, which is 1 January 20x2. This means that consolidated financial statements would be prepared (by P Ltd group) since it acquired its controlling interest in S Ltd (1 July 20x1) and that SS Ltd is a newly acquired subsidiary in the P Ltd group on 1 January 20x2.

From the ultimate parent's perspective, there are **two business combinations** when the parent acquired its controlling interest in its subsidiary and the subsidiary acquires a controlling interest in its sub-subsidiary **at a later date**. The combining of the two subsidiaries is exactly the same as that for any two-entity combination, as discussed in the previous chapters. The consolidation steps to follow include preparing a consolidation worksheet that includes both subsidiaries, thus adding together the financial statements of both subsidiaries from their individual acquisition dates.

However, when the parent acquires its controlling interest in a subsidiary **after** the subsidiary already has a controlling interest in a sub-subsidiary, the parent acquires the subsidiary as a group entity. From the ultimate parent's perspective, this is a **single business combination**, which means that the profits of the sub-subsidiary prior to the acquisition date of the subsidiary by the parent represents pre-acquisition profits on consolidation. The newly acquired subsidiary group will have prepared consolidated financial statements, which include its controlling interest in the sub-subsidiary. The parent therefore needs to determine the fair value of the net identifiable assets of the subsidiary-group in order to determine the measurement of goodwill.

The sequential or non-sequential acquisition of subsidiaries and sub-subsidiaries in a group are discussed and illustrated further in Section 5 of this chapter.

2.3 Complex groups

A complex group exists where the parent owns the controlling equity shareholding in at least one subsidiary, and that parent and the subsidiary together own the controlling interest in another entity. Where the parent has an interest in multiple subsidiaries, and the subsidiaries have further ownership interest in each other and in other entities, the group is referred to as a complex group.

Figure 11.6 is an example of a complex group.

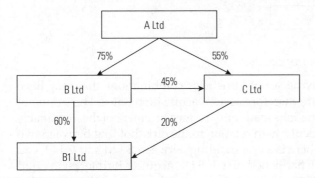

Figure 11.6 Illustration of a complex group

In the group structure illustrated above, there are several parent entities and subsidiaries. A further extension of the group may include associate entities and joint ventures. The results of **associate** and **joint venture** entities are included in the group financial statements by using the **equity method**. This is explained further in Chapter 9.

The complex area to consider when multiple subsidiaries are involved is the calculation of the non-controlling interest in the equity of the group.

2.4 **Reciprocal ownership**

Reciprocal shareholding exists when a parent and a subsidiary own shares in each other. This is also known as a **mutual holding** or **cross holding**. This type of ownership structure arises when a parent has more than one subsidiary and two or more of the subsidiaries own shares in each other. When a subsidiary holds shares in a parent company, such an interest is referred to as **treasury shares**, which is an investment by an entity in its own equity. This means that the group has acquired shares in another entity in the group. In some jurisdictions, entities are not allowed to hold their own shares. In some cases, subsidiaries are not allowed to hold shares in the parent entity or there may be a limit to the percentage shareholding that a subsidiary can hold in a parent. However, a crossholding between subsidiaries is usually allowed.

Figure 11.7 is an example of a reciprocal ownership between two entities.

Figure 11.7 Illustration of reciprocal interests

Figure 11.8 is an example of a reciprocal ownership between two subsidiaries (crossholding) where the parent holds shares in each subsidiary.

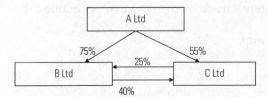

Figure 11.8 Illustration of reciprocal interest in a complex group

In such complex groups, there may be several business combinations that may have occurred at different dates. There are therefore several acquisition dates. The timing of these acquisitions will affect the valuations made and the measurement of the identifiable assets at each acquisition date, particularly in relation to the crossholding between two subsidiaries. In Figure 11.7, where there is a crossholding between B Ltd and C Ltd, you need to determine which acquisition happened first. If B Ltd acquires its interest in C Ltd before C Ltd acquires its interest in B Ltd, then, in determining the equity at the acquisition of the second interest (that is, C Ltd's interest in B Ltd), one of the assets in B Ltd is its investment in C Ltd. Particular adjustment needs to be made for the **cross investment**.

The preparation of group financial statements with reciprocal ownership is beyond the scope of this publication.

3. Identifying and recognising non-controlling interest

The non-controlling interest is the equity of a subsidiary that is not attributable to the **parent**. This means that if the parent and its wholly owned subsidiary together hold 100% of the sub-subsidiary, there are no outside shareholders, and if the sum of their holding is less than 100%, there are outside shareholders. As mentioned earlier, in multiple subsidiary structures, we need to classify the non-controlling ownership in the respective subsidiaries into the following types :
• Direct non-controlling interest
• Indirect non-controlling interest.

The **direct non-controlling interest** represents the proportionate share of all equity recorded by the subsidiary, and includes both **pre-acquisition** and **post-acquisition** equity, as discussed for a simple group. Indirect non-controlling interest represents the interest in the sub-subsidiary that is attributable to the non-controlling shareholders through its interest in the subsidiary. The **indirect non-controlling interest** receives a proportionate share of a subsidiary's **post-acquisition** equity only.

In analysing why the indirect non-controlling interest receives a share of post-acquisition equity of the sub-subsidiary, it is important to remember that an indirect non-controlling interest arises only when a partly owned subsidiary holds shares in another subsidiary. This makes sense, as the direct non-controlling interest in the parent–subsidiary is the same group of shareholders as the indirect non-controlling interest in the sub-subsidiary.

Think about it

What is the non-controlling interest?

Refer to the example above (see Figure 11.5), where P Ltd holds a 75% interest in S Ltd, and S Ltd, in turn, holds a 70% interest in SS Ltd.

- The **direct non-controlling interest** in the P Ltd group's interest in subsidiary S Ltd group is **25%**.
- The **direct non-controlling interest** in the S Ltd group's interest in SS Ltd is **30%**.

However, in the P Ltd group, the direct non-controlling interest in subsidiary S Ltd also shares in the profits of SS Ltd, hence giving it an **indirect non-controlling interest** in SS Ltd of 25% × 70% = **17.5%**.

The total non-controlling interest in the P Ltd group in SS Ltd is therefore **47.5%** (30% + 17.5%). This makes sense as the effective interest of P Ltd in SS Ltd is **52.5%** (75% × 70%) and the non-controlling interest has the remaining interest of **47.5%** (100% − 52.5%).

Example

Complex group structure and identifying non-controlling interest

This example illustrates the parent's effective interest in multiple subsidiaries and how to determine the non-controlling interest.

P Ltd owns 70% of the shares in B Ltd and 80% of S Ltd. B Ltd owns 60% of the shares in C Ltd and S Ltd owns 55% of G Ltd. Figure 11.9 below illustrates the group structure.

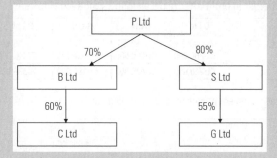

Figure 11.9 Illustration of group structure

All of the subsidiaries in the group were acquired in prior years. The profit for each entity in the group was obtained from the individual financial statements, as follows:

	P Ltd CU	B Ltd CU	C Ltd CU	S Ltd CU	G Ltd CU
Profit	1 000 000	800 000	750 000	900 000	600 000

Think about it

What is the group profit of P Ltd (ultimate parent) and the profit attributable to the non-controlling interest?

- The group profit is the sum of the profit of the parent and the subsidiaries of the group whose financial statements are being prepared. In this case, it amounts to **CU4 050 000** (1 000 000 + 800 000 + 750 000 + 900 000 + 600 000).
- In order to determine the non-controlling interest, we need to determine P Ltd's effective interest in each subsidiary:

	B Ltd	C Ltd	S Ltd	G Ltd
P Ltd's effective interest	70%	70% × 60% = 42%	80%	80% × 55% = 44%

Note that, even though P Ltd's effective interest in C Ltd and G Ltd is less than 50%, both C Ltd and G Ltd are sub-subsidiaries of P Ltd as they are each a subsidiary of another subsidiary in the P Ltd group.

- The direct and the indirect non-controlling interest are as follows:

For each subsidiary:	B Ltd	C Ltd	S Ltd	G Ltd
Direct non-controlling interest	30%	40%	20%	45%
Indirect non-controlling interest	–	30% × 60% = 18%	–	20% × 55% = 11%
Total non-controlling interest	30%	58%	20%	56%

Note that P Ltd's effective interest and the total non-controlling interest should equal 100% for each subsidiary, for example, for C Ltd: 42% (P Ltd's effective interest) + 58% (non-controlling interest) = 100%.

- Non-controlling interest in profit after tax is as follows for each subsidiary:

	B Ltd	C Ltd	S Ltd	G Ltd
Non-controlling interest	30% × CU800 000	58% × CU750 000	20% × CU900 000	56% × CU600 000
Total: **CU1 191 000** ①	**CU240 000**	**CU435 000**	**CU180 000**	**CU336 000**

Extract from consolidated statement of profit or loss for P Ltd group

	CU
Profit after tax, for the group	4 050 000
Attributable to:	
Parent equity holders	② 2 859 000◄
Non-controlling interest	① 1 191 000

What is this?

The profit attributable to the equity holders of the parent (that is, P Ltd) is the total profit of P Ltd plus P Ltd's share of the profits in each subsidiary. This amount is included in the retained earnings column in the consolidated statement of changes in equity.

② Profit attributable to parent equity holders: **CU2 859 000**
- P Ltd: CU1 000 000
- B Ltd: CU800 000 × 70% = CU560 000
- C Ltd: CU750 000 × 42% = CU315 000
- S Ltd: CU900 000 × 80% = CU720 000
- G Ltd: CU600 000 × 44% = CU264 000.

The non-controlling interest in each subsidiary is calculated based on consolidated equity and profits, rather than the reported equity and profit for each subsidiary. This means that you need to make adjustments to **eliminate any unrealised profits or losses** arising from transactions within the group **prior to** allocating the appropriate profit to non-controlling interest.

4. Intra-group transactions: Basic principles revisited

The principles discussed in Chapter 6 relating to the accounting treatment for intra-group transactions do not change. This implies that the effects of transactions within the group must be adjusted for in full. This is regardless of the combination of entities involved because the principle remains that you are reporting the group financial statements as if it is a single economic entity. However, careful consideration should be given to the treatment of dividends in multiple subsidiary structures.

4.1 Elimination of investment in sub-subsidiaries

As you know, the equity attributable to the non-controlling interest represents its share in the net assets of the subsidiary, unless it is measured at fair value at the acquisition date. By implication, the direct non-controlling interest thus shares in the equity of the subsidiary, which is represented by the net assets of the subsidiary. However, in a vertical group, one of the assets in the subsidiary is its **investment in the shares** of its sub-subsidiary. Because the direct non-controlling interest represents the same shareholders that have an indirect non-controlling interest in the sub-subsidiary, allocating the **at-acquisition equity** of the sub-subsidiary to the indirect non-controlling interest would lead to double counting because of the investment in the shares of the sub-subsidiary. The investment in the shares in the sub-subsidiary reflects the pre-acquisition equity (and net assets) of the sub-subsidiary at the acquisition date. When consolidated financial statements are being prepared, the indirect non-controlling interest thus only shares in the post-acquisition equity of the sub-subsidiary.

Example

Illustration of non-controlling interest in a vertical group

Refer to the example above, where P Ltd holds a 75% interest in S Ltd and S Ltd, in turn, holds a 70% interest in SS Ltd. The parent's interest as well as direct and indirect non-controlling interest can therefore be illustrated as shown in Figure 11.10.

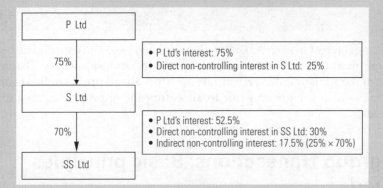

Figure 11.10 Illustration of a vertical group

Note that the direct non-controlling interest in S Ltd (25% interest) refers to the same shareholders that have an indirect non-controlling interest in SS Ltd of 17.5% (25% of 70%) because S Ltd has a 70% interest in SS Ltd.

The following extracts were obtained from the individual financial statements of S Ltd and SS Ltd immediately after the acquisition of shares:

	S Ltd CU	SS Ltd CU
Net assets:		
Investment in subsidiary	70 000	–
Other net assets	30 000	100 000
Total net assets	**100 000**	**100 000**
Equity	**100 000**	**100 000**

Shareholders in SS Ltd
- S Ltd's interest: 70%
- Direct non-controlling interest in S Ltd: 30%.

At the same acquisition date of P Ltd's investment in S Ltd, S Ltd acquired 70% of the equity of SS Ltd. The direct non-controlling interest has a 30% interest in SS Ltd. At that date, P Ltd and the non-controlling interest in S Ltd, who are also the indirect non-controlling interest in SS Ltd, do not share in any equity of SS Ltd.

Both P Ltd and the non-controlling interest in S Ltd share only in the equity (profits) of SS Ltd after the acquisition date.

The following *pro-forma* journal entry is therefore recorded in the P Ltd group, relating to its indirect interest in SS Ltd:

			CU	CU
Dr		Equity of SS Ltd	100 000	
	Cr	Investment in subsidiary (S Ltd)		70 000
	Cr	Non-controlling interest (direct)		30 000

Elimination of investment in subsidiary at acquisition date and recognising direct non-controlling interest

So far, you have learnt that when preparing consolidated financial statements, two important periods need consideration:

- The **acquisition date**: This is the date on which the parent acquired its controlling interest in the subsidiary. When consolidating, the investment in the subsidiary (by the parent) is eliminated against the equity of the subsidiary at the acquisition date in order to determine any goodwill acquired and to allocate the amount of equity attributable to the direct non-controlling interest. In terms of the accounting equation, the asset (investment in subsidiary) is eliminated and replaced by the underlying net assets of the subsidiary. As the parent did not acquire all of the equity of the subsidiary, the portion not acquired is attributable to the non-controlling shareholders. At this date, there is no indirect non-controlling interest in the sub-subsidiary, thus the indirect non-controlling interest does not receive a share of the equity of the sub-subsidiary at the acquisition date.
- The **subsequent period**: This is the period subsequent to the acquisition date until the reporting date. As the group shares in the increases (or decreases) in the equity of the subsidiary subsequent to the acquisition date, the appropriate portion of the profits in the sub-subsidiary is allocated to the parent as well as the direct and the indirect non-controlling interest.

Example

Vertical group structure and elimination of investment in sub-subsidiary

In this example, the parent acquired its controlling interest in subsidiary S Ltd at the same date on which S Ltd acquired its controlling interest in subsidiary SS Ltd. The consolidated financial statements are prepared one year after the acquisition date. There are no fair value adjustments at acquisition date and no other intra-group transactions. Ignore deferred tax.

P Ltd acquired its 75% controlling interest in S Ltd on 1 January 20x3 for CU800 000, when the fair value of the net identifiable assets of S Ltd was fairly valued at its carrying amounts of CU1 000 000. On the same day, S Ltd acquired its controlling interest of 80% in SS Ltd at a cost of CU120 000, when the fair value and carrying amounts of the net identifiable assets of SS Ltd amounted to CU150 000.

In this example, we are concerned about preparing group financial statements for **P Ltd and all of its subsidiaries** for the current reporting period that ended 31 December 20x3. Each group entity recognises its investment in subsidiaries at cost in its separate financial statements. Non-controlling interest, arising on consolidation, is measured at its share of the net identifiable assets at the acquisition date. Goodwill is recognised on the partial method and is not considered to be impaired. Ignore deferred tax implications.

The following extracts from the financial statements of the three individual entities are available at 31 December 20x3, the current reporting date:

	P Ltd CU	S Ltd CU	SS Ltd CU
ASSETS			
Non-current assets	900 000	800 000	120 000
Investment in subsidiary	800 000	120 000	–
Current assets	300 000	280 000	95 000
	2 000 000	1 200 000	215 000
EQUITY AND LIABILITIES			
Share capital	1 000 000	700 000	100 000
Retained earnings	800 000	400 000	65 000
Shareholders' equity	1 800 000	1 100 000	165 000
Liabilities	200 000	100 000	50 000
	2 000 000	1 200 000	215 000

The equity of SS Ltd is allocated between the **pre-acquisition** and **post-acquisition** periods as shown below.

Analysis of equity of SS Ltd

	Total CU	S Ltd's interest (80%) CU	Non-controlling interest (20%) CU
At acquisition date (1 January 20x3):			
Share capital	100 000	80 000	20 000
Retained earnings	50 000	40 000	10 000
	150 000	120 000	30 000
Investment in subsidiary		120 000	
Goodwill arising on consolidation		–	
Since acquisition date:			
Current year profit (65 000 – 50 000)	15 000	12 000	3 000
Total equity	**165 000**	**12 000**	**33 000**

What is this?

The equity of SS Ltd is analysed from S Ltd's group's perspective. S Ltd's share of the profits of SS Ltd for the period up to 1 January 20x3 represents **pre-acquisition** profits in the S Ltd group (as well as in the P Ltd group).

The method used in this example is to prepare the consolidated worksheet for the **S Ltd group**:

	S Ltd CU	SS Ltd CU	Pro-forma entries for SS Ltd CU	S Ltd group CU
ASSETS				
Non-current assets	800 000	120 000		920 000
Investment in subsidiary	120 000	–	(120 000)	–
Goodwill			–	–
Current assets	280 000	95 000		375 000
	1 200 000	215 000	(120 000)	1 295 000
EQUITY AND LIABILITIES				
Share capital	700 000	100 000	(100 000)	700 000
Retained earnings	400 000	65 000	(50 000) (3 000)	→ 412 000
	1 100 000	165 000	(153 000)	1 112 000
Non-controlling interest			30 000 3 000	33 000
Liabilities	100 000	50 000		150 000
	1 200 000	215 000	(120 000)	1 295 000

> **What is this?**
> The post-acquisition profit of SS Ltd, attributable to S Ltd (CU12 000), was earned after P Ltd acquired its controlling interest in S Ltd. Retained earnings in S Ltd group is CU412 000 (CU400 000 [S Ltd] plus S Ltd's share in SS Ltd since the acquisition date [CU12 000]).

The equity attributable to S Ltd group as identified in the worksheet above is used to analyse P Ltd's interest in S Ltd's consolidated owners' equity at 31 December 20x3 as shown below.

Analysis of equity of S Ltd

	Total CU	P Ltd's interest (75%) CU	Non-controlling interest (25%) CU
At acquisition date (1 January 20x3):			
Share capital	700 000		
Retained earnings S Ltd	300 000		
Equity of S Ltd (the entity) at acquisition date	1 000 000	750 000	250 000
Investment in subsidiary		800 000	
Goodwill arising on consolidation		50 000	
Since acquisition date:			
Current year profit	**112 000**	**84 000**	**28 000**
S Ltd (400 000 – 300 000)	100 000	75 000	25 000
SS Ltd (only S Ltd's share)	12 000	9 000	3 000
Total equity	**1 112 000**	**84 000**	**278 000**

The consolidated worksheet for the P Ltd group combines the assets and liabilities of the S Ltd group and P Ltd:

	P Ltd CU	S Ltd Group CU	Pro-forma entries for S Ltd CU	P Ltd group CU
ASSETS				
Non-current assets	900 000	920 000		1 820 000
Investment in subsidiary	800 000	–	(800 000)	–
Goodwill		–	50 000	50 000
Current assets	300 000	375 000		675 000
	2 000 000	1 295 000	(750 000)	2 545 000
EQUITY AND LIABILITIES				
Share capital	1 000 000	700 000	(700 000)	1 000 000
Retained earnings	800 000	412 000	(300 000) (28 000)	884 000
	1 800 000	1 112 000	(1 028 000)	1 884 000
Non-controlling interest		33 000	250 000 28 000	➤ 311 000
Liabilities	200 000	150 000		350 000
	2 000 000	1 295 000	(750 000)	2 545 000

> **What is this?**
> Total non-controlling interest is the non-controlling interest in SS Ltd of CU33 000 plus the non-controlling interest in S Ltd of CU278 000.

Summary of non-controlling interest

		CU	CU
At acquisition of interests in subsidiaries:			280 000
Direct non-controlling interest in SS Ltd	CU150 000 × 20%	30 000	
Direct non-controlling interest in S Ltd	CU1 000 000 × 25%	250 000	
Current year profit after tax:			31 000
Direct non-controlling interest in SS Ltd	CU15 000 × 20%	3 000	
Indirect non-controlling interest in SS Ltd	CU15 000 × 80% × 25%	3 000	
Direct non-controlling interest in S Ltd	CU100 000 × 25%	25 000	
			➤ 311 000

In this example, we prepared the consolidated statement of financial position for the S Ltd group first, and then used this to prepare the consolidated statement of financial position for the P Ltd group. In the examples later in the chapter, the consolidated financial statements are prepared without the intermediate consolidation.

4.2 Intra-group dividends

When a subsidiary distributes profits earned after acquisition (dividends declared), the portion of the distribution relating to the parent's shareholding is recognised by the parent as dividend income. The parent includes any dividend income received from the subsidiary in profit or loss together with any other dividends received. The portion of the distribution that is not earned by the parent is earned by the non-controlling interest. This represents a profit distribution to the non-controlling interest, hence the debit to non-controlling interest in equity.

Pro-forma journal entry

Dr		Dividend income (parent) (P/L)	Parent's share, for example, 70%	
Dr		Non-controlling interest (equity)	Based on its shareholding, for example, 30%	
	Cr	Dividends (subsidiary)		100 %

The portion of the subsidiary's dividend attributable to the non-controlling shareholders is allocated in the group statement of changes in equity, resulting in a reduction to the net credit balance for non-controlling shareholders representing their share of the net assets of the subsidiary.

The ultimate parent (P Ltd) receives its portion of the dividends of the subsidiary (S Ltd) and the portion not held by the parent is attributable to the direct non-controlling interest in S Ltd. When the sub-subsidiary (SS Ltd) declares a dividend, the parent–subsidiary (S Ltd) receives its portion of the dividend and the portion not held by the parent–subsidiary (S Ltd) is attributable to the direct non-controlling interest in SS Ltd. The **indirect non-controlling shareholders** in SS Ltd (in other words, the non-controlling interest in the S Ltd) do not share in the dividend of the sub-subsidiary (SS Ltd) as they are not shareholders of SS Ltd.

Example

Non-controlling interest in dividends in vertical group

Refer to the example above, where P Ltd holds a 75% interest in S Ltd and S Ltd, in turn, holds a 70% interest in SS Ltd. Assume that the three companies each declare a dividend of **CU100 000** at 31 December 20x5.

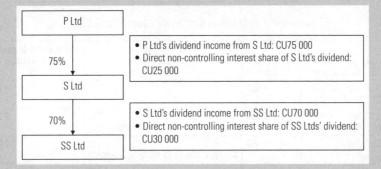

Figure 11.11 Illustration of vertical group

The direct non-controlling interest in S Ltd (25% interest) is the same shareholders that have an indirect non-controlling interest in SS Ltd of 17.5% (25% of 70%) through S Ltd's 70% interest in SS Ltd. However, as the indirect non-controlling interest in SS Ltd does not have a direct interest in SS Ltd (they are not shareholders in SS Ltd), no dividend is declared to it.

The indirect non-controlling interest receives its share of the profits and dividend through the direct non-controlling interest in the subsidiary, thus receiving a share of the profits of the sub-subsidiary, which is included in dividend revenue from the sub-subsidiary. When the direct non-controlling interest in the subsidiary receives a share of the profits of the subsidiary, it receives a share of the profit of the sub-subsidiary because of the dividend paid by the sub-subsidiary, which is included in the profit of the subsidiary. This raises a problem of double counting. This problem arises when there are multiple levels of subsidiaries, as a dividend paid or declared by one subsidiary is recognised as revenue by another subsidiary, both of which contain non-controlling interests. The risk of double accounting is avoided by following these two steps:

- First, reverse the dividend received from a sub-subsidiary in the profit of the subsidiary.
- Then allocate the portion of the profit, after the elimination of the dividend, to non-controlling interest.

Example

Complex group structure and intra-group dividends

This example illustrates the elimination of intra-group dividends received before allocating the remaining profit to non-controlling interest.

P Ltd owns a controlling interest of 80% in S Ltd. S Ltd owns 60% of SS Ltd. The following extracts were obtained from the separate financial statements of the individual entities in the group for the year ending 30 June 20x5:

	P Ltd CU'000	S Ltd CU'000	SS Ltd CU'000
Net profit after tax	4 400	3 100	2 150
Dividends declared	(250)	(500)	(400)

Extract from P Ltd Group statement of profit or loss for the year ended 30 June 20x5

Entity	Net profit, less dividend income	Group profit CU	Non-controlling share of profit CU	Attributable to parent equity holders CU
P Ltd	CU4 400 – CU400 (S: CU 500 × 80%)	4 000	–	4 000
S Ltd	CU3 100 – CU240 (SS: CU400 × 60%)	2 860	572 (2 860 × 20%)	2 288
SS Ltd	CU2 150	2 150	1 118 ([2 150 × 40%] + [2 150 × 20% × 60%])	1 032
Total		**9 010**	**1 690**	**7 320**

The following *pro-forma* journal entries eliminate the intra-group dividends and allocate the appropriate portion to non-controlling interest:

			CU	CU
Dr		Non-controlling interest in profit or loss	1 118	
	Cr	Non-controlling interest (equity)		1 118

Allocation of appropriate portion of the profit of SS Ltd to direct and indirect non-controlling interest

			CU	CU
Dr		Dividend income (P/L)	240	
Dr		Non-controlling interest (equity)	160	
	Cr	Dividend declared		400

Eliminating dividends received in S Ltd from its subsidiary SS Ltd and allocating an appropriate portion to non-controlling interest

			CU	CU
Dr		Non-controlling interest in profit or loss	572	
	Cr	Non-controlling interest (equity)		572

Allocation of appropriate portion of profit of S Ltd to direct non-controlling interest

			CU	CU
Dr		Dividend income (P/L)	400	
Dr		Non-controlling interest (equity)	100	
	Cr	Dividend declared		500

Eliminating dividends received in P Ltd from its subsidiary S Lt, and allocating an appropriate portion to non-controlling interest

4.3 Other intra-group transactions

One of the principles underlying group financial statements is that the financial statements reflect the financial performance of the group as **one economic entity**. An entity cannot make profits by entering into transactions with itself. Whenever related entities trade with each other or borrow and lend money from and to each other, the separate legal entities disclose the effects of these transactions in the assets and liabilities recorded and the profits and losses reported. The preparation of the consolidated financial statements of the parent starts with the separate financial statements of the parent and the individual financial statements of its subsidiaries, which are **added together**, without any adjustments for the effects of the intra-group transactions. This results in consolidated financial statements including not only the results of the group transacting with external parties, but also the results of transactions within the group. This is incorrect and conflicts with the purpose of the consolidated financial statements, which is to provide information about the financial performance and financial position of the group resulting only from its dealings with external entities.

The effects of transactions within the group must be adjusted for when preparing consolidated financial statements so that these statements only include transactions with third parties. In terms of the accrual basis, income and expenses can only be recognised when earned or incurred. Similarly, group financial statements should only reflect the results of transactions between the group as a whole and third parties.

In a group with multiple subsidiary structures, you should consider the effect of such intra-group adjustments on the non-controlling interest carefully. The principles of elimination of intra-group profits or losses that were discussed in Chapter 6 apply equally in a complex group structure:

- To the extent that profit or losses have been recognised by individual entities and are reflected in the starting point trial balance for preparing the group accounts, but these amounts have not been earned by the group, these **profits or losses should be eliminated on consolidation**. Generally, these profits or losses are said to be unrealised because the group as a single economic entity has not realised the carrying amount of the asset that has been sold between entities within the group and that gave rise to the profit in the individual entity.

- The profits of the individual entity are attributable to the equity holders of that entity. To the extent that there are profits at a group level that are not being recognised, this impacts on the amounts attributed to the equity holders of the group. Therefore, the amounts attributed to the non-controlling interest may be affected. Think about it this way: a subsidiary earns a profit of which some is attributed to the non-controlling interest of the subsidiary when drafting the parent's group financial statements. However, if the profit of the subsidiary includes amounts that the group has not earned, then adjusting the group accounts for those amounts impacts on the profits attributed to the non-controlling interest in that subsidiary.

 ## Example

Elimination of intra-group profit in complex group

This example illustrates the elimination of intra-group sale of inventory and the deferred tax implication.

P Ltd owns a controlling interest of 80% in S Ltd. S Ltd owns 60% of SS Ltd. During the current period, SS Ltd sold inventory with a cost to SS Ltd of CU20 000 to P Ltd for CU25 000. The inventory is still on hand at 31 December 20x5, the current reporting period. The current tax rate is 28%.

The following *pro-forma* entries are required in the P Ltd group:

			CU	CU
Dr		Sales	25 000	
	Cr	Cost of sales		20 000
	Cr	Inventory		5 000

Eliminating the intra-group sale and recognising inventory at cost to the group

			CU	CU
Dr		Deferred tax asset	1 400	
	Cr	Deferred tax expense (P/L)		1 400

Recognising deferred tax on the temporary difference arising on consolidation

The effect of these two *pro-forma* journal entries is that, from the group's perspective, the profit of SS Ltd is reduced by CU3 600 (CU5 000 × 72%).

The direct non-controlling interest in SS Ltd is 40% and the indirect non-controlling interest in SS Ltd is 12% (20% × 60%). The total non-controlling interest in SS Ltd is 52%. The amount attributable to non-controlling interest is **CU1 872** (CU3 600 × 52%).

			CU	CU
Dr		Non-controlling interest (equity)	1 872	
	Cr	Non-controlling interest in profit or loss		1 872

Recognising non-controlling interest relating to the reversal of the unrealised profit in inventory

Note that this *pro-forma* journal entry illustrates the allocation to non-controlling interest relating only to the unrealised profit in inventory, hence the credit to non-controlling interest in profit or loss. This entry only makes sense if the non-controlling interest in the current year's profits of the subsidiary has already been allocated.

Think about it

What is the effect of this intra-group transaction on the non-controlling interest?

In this example, the inventory was sold by the sub-subsidiary to the parent. The unrealised profit was therefore in the sub-subsidiary and the effect of the reversal of the unrealised profit on the profit attributable to the parent equity holders is as follows:

- CU5 000 × 72% = CU3 600 (after tax) × 48% (80% × 60% effective interest) = **CU1 728**.

If the subsidiary (S Ltd) sold the inventory to the parent, the unrealised profit is in the subsidiary and the effect of the reversal of the unrealised profit on the profit attributable to the parent equity holders is as follows:

- CU5 000 × 72% = CU3 600 (after tax) × 80% = **CU2 880**.

If the parent (P Ltd) sold the inventory to the subsidiary or sub-subsidiaries, the unrealised profit is in the parent. The effect of the reversal of the unrealised profit on the profit attributable to the parent equity holders is as follows:

- CU5 000 × 72% = **CU3 600**.

5. Preparing consolidated financial statements for different compositions of groups

The requirement to prepare consolidated financial statements for a complex group is similar to that of a single group, as discussed in Chapters 3 to 7. The **consolidated statement of financial position** is prepared by adding together the assets and liabilities of all of the subsidiaries to those of the parent and eliminating the effects of internal transactions or transactions that relate to amounts owing between group entities rather than to external parties. The group statement of financial position includes assets and liabilities that are the result of transactions with outside parties and not those that are the result of internal transactions between group entities. Assets should only be recognised in the statement of financial position of the group when they meet the definition and recognition criteria of an asset of the group (in other words, when the asset is a resource controlled by the group that can be measured and that would probably result in the inflow of future economic benefits to the group). Similarly, group liabilities should only be recognised when the definition and recognition criteria of a liability are met (where there is a present obligation of the group resulting from a past event that can be measured and the settlement of which would probably result in an outflow of future economic benefits from the group). In this section, we combine the knowledge that you acquired in earlier sections of this chapter and illustrate the preparation of consolidated financial statements for the different compositions of groups.

Example

Recognising assets (land) in a complex group

This example illustrates the recognition of 100% of an asset in the consolidated statement of financial position of a complex group.

Refer to the complex group in the example in Section 3 above, where P Ltd owns 70% of the shares in B Ltd and 80% of S Ltd. B Ltd owns 60% of the shares in C Ltd and S Ltd owns 55% of G Ltd.
  The following details relate to land held in the various group companies at the reporting date:
- P Ltd has land at a cost of CU800 000. The land was acquired from C Ltd, who purchased it from the developer for CU600 000.
- S Ltd has land at a cost of CU500 000. This land was owned by S Ltd when P Ltd bought the shares in S Ltd. At the date on which P Ltd bought the shares in S Ltd, P Ltd had the land valued and it was agreed that the land was worth CU650 000.
- G Ltd has a piece of land that has a cost of CU300 000 and that was considered to be worth CU450 000 when S Ltd acquired the shares in G Ltd.
- C Ltd has land with a cost of CU480 000.

Think about it

At what amount should land be recognised in the consolidated statement of financial position of the P Ltd group?

	CU
P Ltd's land should be included at the cost when it became **part of the group**, in other words, CU600 000. CU800 000 should be recognised as the amount that is in the **parent** company.	600 000
S Ltd is a **subsidiary company and therefore 100%** of the cost of the land should be included. The land should be included at the cost when it was first acquired by the group, which is the fair value of the land at the date on which the subsidiary company was acquired.	650 000
G Ltd is a subsidiary of S Ltd. Similar to S Ltd above, the land should be included at the cost when it was first acquired by the group, which is the fair value of the land at the date on which the subsidiary company was acquired.	450 000
C Ltd is a subsidiary company as more than half of its shares are **controlled by a controlled company** (B Ltd) and it should therefore be consolidated, which implies that **100% should be recognised**.	480 000
Land on the group statement of financial position	**2 180 000**

The **consolidated statement of profit or loss and other comprehensive income** is prepared by adding the income and expenses of the parent and all of the subsidiaries together on a line-by-line basis, and then eliminating any amounts that are 'internal' to the group. The consolidated profit (or loss) is the difference between the income and expenses of the parent and its subsidiaries. The profit or loss is attributed to the equity holders of the group, which are the **equity holders (owners) of the parent** and the **non-controlling interest**.

The income and expenses of a subsidiary are included in group profit or loss from the date of acquisition. If the **date of acquisition** is in the current year, the income and expenses relating to the current year but before the acquisition date should not be consolidated, but should be included in the equity acquired at the acquisition date. In this case, it is necessary for you to determine the total retained earnings of the subsidiary at the acquisition date.

The **consolidated statement of owners' equity** is prepared as a summary of the equity of the group as one economic entity. It divides the equity between the equity holders of the parent and the non-controlling interest. The **equity interest of the parent** includes the share capital of the parent only, as the equity of the subsidiary at the acquisition date is eliminated against the investment by the parent after allocating the portion of the equity attributable to the **non-controlling shareholders**.

The **reserves** of the group (those attributable to the equity holders of the parent) are determined by combining the retained earnings and other reserves of the parent with the parent's share of the changes in retained earnings and other reserves of the subsidiary since the date of acquisition.

The **dividends** declared by the subsidiary during the reporting period are eliminated against dividend income recognised by the parent. The consolidated statement of changes in equity should only include the dividends declared by the parent to its equity holders.

The dividends declared by the subsidiary that are attributable to the non-controlling interest are shown separately in the non-controlling interest column, reflecting the change in equity that has reduced the non-controlling interest's claims against the subsidiary (as amounts that it has earned have been distributed to it in the form of dividends).

5.1 Key issues to consider when consolidating multiple subsidiaries

You have learnt that there are **multiple forms of group structures**. A parent may have an interest in several subsidiaries and those subsidiaries may have interests in further subsidiaries. Such groups are identified as **horizontal groups**, **vertical groups** or **complex groups**. In the case of vertical groups, we identified the direct and indirect interest of the parent equity holders as well as the **non-controlling interest**. A complex group is a combination of a horizontal and vertical group, and may also include interests in associates and joint ventures (refer to Chapter 9 for the accounting treatment of these entities in the group financial statements).

There are certain complexities and principles relating to the sequence of acquisition of subsidiaries in a vertical group that require further consideration. These include the following:

- When the parent acquires its interest in a subsidiary and that subsidiary acquires another sub-subsidiary afterwards, there are **two business combinations**. Each of these acquisitions is accounted for in sequence.
- When the parent acquires its controlling interest in a subsidiary **after** the subsidiary already has a controlling interest in a sub-subsidiary, the parent acquires the subsidiary as a group entity. This is a **single business combination**, which means that the profits of the sub-subsidiary prior to the acquisition date of the subsidiary by the parent represents pre-acquisition profits on consolidation.

The newly acquired subsidiary has an asset described as 'investment in subsidiary' in its separate financial statements at the acquisition date. In the subsidiary's group financial statements, any goodwill acquired is recognised as an asset. The new parent therefore needs to determine the fair value of this asset at the acquisition date in order to determine the measurement of goodwill. Goodwill that exists in a subsidiary at the date of acquisition should be written off as it is not an identifiable asset. This reduces the net assets of the business acquired and increases the goodwill relating to the new acquisition. The cost of an asset to the group is its fair value when that asset is acquired by the group, which is when the group acquired control of its new subsidiary group. When a parent acquires a subsidiary, it also acquires control of all of the assets and other subsidiaries that that subsidiary controls. The fair value of all of those assets needs to be determined in order to establish the cost to the new group.

The equity of the new group is considered from the perspective of the reporting entity. This means that the consolidated financial statements include the group's share of the post-acquisition reserves of the new subsidiary group subsequent to the acquisition date of that subsidiary. Any profits in the sub-subsidiaries at that date are pre-acquisition profits and must be eliminated.

Think about it

Key questions to ask when preparing group financial statements for a vertical group

Think about these key issues:
* What goodwill should be recognised on the group statement of financial position?
* What is the cost to the group of an asset in the various group financial statements?
* What is post-acquisition equity?

Example

Illustration of these key principles in a vertical group

This example illustrates the following two situations:

* When the parent acquired its controlling interest in its subsidiary and the subsidiary then acquires a controlling interest in a sub-subsidiary
* The consolidation process when the parent acquired its controlling interest in a subsidiary that already has a controlling interest in a sub-subsidiary; this situation illustrates the elimination of goodwill when there is one business combination.

P Ltd owns 75% of B Ltd and B Ltd owns 60% of C Ltd. Ignore deferred tax.

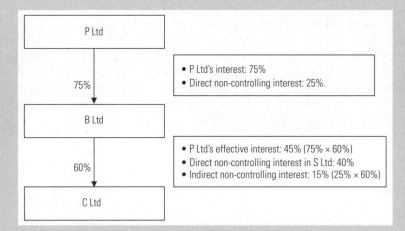

Figure 11.12 Illustration of vertical group structure

Scenario 1: P Ltd purchases B Ltd, and then B Ltd purchases C Ltd (sequential acquisition)

Assume that C Ltd's retained earnings is CU100 000 at the date of acquisition of C Ltd by B Ltd. At the reporting date, the retained earnings of C Ltd is CU300 000.

Note the following in respect of C Ltd:
* At the reporting date, B Ltd's group financial statements reflect retained earnings of CU120 000 (60% of (CU300 000 – CU100 000)).

- At the reporting date, P Ltd's group financial statements reflect retained earnings of CU72 000 (75% of 60% of [CU300 000 – CU100 000]).
- The cost of C Ltd's assets to the B Ltd and P Ltd groups is the same, being the fair value of the assets when B Ltd acquired C Ltd.
- B Ltd was part of the P Ltd group when it acquired C Ltd, which implies the following:
  - The goodwill relating to the acquisition of C Ltd recognised by B Ltd is recognised in the P Ltd group financial statements as it arose after B Ltd became part of P Ltd's group.
  - All of the equity of C Ltd earned after the acquisition by B Ltd is post-acquisition from the perspective of P Ltd and B Ltd.

Scenario 2: B Ltd purchased C Ltd first (on 31 December 20x2), and then P Ltd purchased B Ltd (on 31 December 20x4) (non-sequential acquisition)

B Ltd purchased 60% of C Ltd for CU30 000 on 31 December 20x2 when the net asset value of C Ltd was CU40 000. The non-controlling interest at acquisition was measured at its share of net asset value. All assets of C Ltd were considered to be fairly valued at its acquisition date, with the exception of land, with a fair value of CU12 000 (carrying amount of CU10 000). Retained earnings of C Ltd at 31 December 20x2 was CU15 000. Neither the company nor the B Ltd group revalued land.

P Ltd purchased 75% of the shares in B Ltd on 31 December 20x4 for CU90 000, at which date the non-controlling interest was measured at its fair value of CU28 000. The fair value of C Ltd's land on 31 December 20x4 was CU15 000. Retained earnings of C Ltd amounted to CU25 000 at 31 December 20x4. C Ltd earned profits of CU16 000 and declared a dividend of CU6 000 at 31 December 20x5. B Ltd (the company) earned profits of CU20 000 for the year ended 31 December 20x5.

B Ltd's group financial statements include goodwill relating to the acquisition of C Ltd and all of the equity of C Ltd earned after B Ltd purchased its controlling interest in C Ltd. When P Ltd purchases the controlling interest in B Ltd, it is purchasing the group of B Ltd, in other words, the group net assets (or equity as calculated in an analysis of equity of B Ltd, which includes its share of post-acquisition equity of C Ltd at the date of acquisition of B Ltd). B Ltd's goodwill relating to its acquisition of C Ltd is written off at acquisition. B Ltd's equity plus B Ltd's share of C Ltd's equity is treated as pre-acquisition from the perspective of P Ltd.

The equity of C Ltd can be analysed as follows:

	Total CU	B Ltd's share 60% CU	Non-controlling interest 40% CU
At acquisition date (31 December 20x2):			
Share capital	25 000		
Retained earnings	15 000		
Land (12 000 – 10 000)	2 000		
	42 000	25 200	16 800
Cost of investment		30 000	
Goodwill		4 800	
Since acquisition date:			
Retained earnings (25 000 – 15 000)	10 000	① 6 000	4 000
Net asset value of C Ltd: 31 December 20x4	52 000		② 20 800
Current year profit after tax	16 000	③ 9 600	6 400
Less dividends	(6 000)	④ (3 600)	(2 400)
Net asset value of C Ltd: 31 December 20x5	**62 000**	**12 000**	**24 800**

Note that the numbers in circles in the table above refer to the same amounts in the analysis of equity of B Ltd below and are intended to facilitate cross-referencing.

The net assets of B Ltd (the company) was CU80 000 (which includes its investment in C Ltd on the cost basis.) Assuming that the only adjustments in B Ltd are in relation to C Ltd, the net assets of the B Ltd group at 31 December 20x4 are CU106 800.

This can be calculated in either of the following ways:
- Focusing on the net assets controlled by the group
- Focusing on the group equity (this includes non-controlling interest, which must equal net assets).

The consolidation worksheet for the B Ltd group is as follows at **31 December 20x4**:

	B Ltd (the entity) starting point CU	C Ltd starting point CU	*Pro-forma* journal entries CU	B Ltd Group (end point) CU
ASSETS				
Land		10 000	2 000	12 000
Investment in subsidiary	30 000		(30 000)	–
Goodwill			4 800	4 800
Other net assets	50 000	40 000		90 000
	80 000	**50 000**	**(23 200)**	**106 800**
EQUITY				
Share capital	10 000	25 000	(25 000)	10 000
Retained earnings	70 000	25 000	(15 000)⎫ (4 000)⎭	76 000
	80 000	**50 000**	**(44 000)**	**86 000**
Non-controlling interest			16 800⎫ 4 000⎭	20 800
	80 000	**50 000**	**(23 200)**	**106 800**

The analysis of equity of B Ltd is:

	Total CU	P Ltd's share 75% CU	Non-controlling interest 25% CU
At acquisition date (31 December 20x4):			
Share capital	10 000		
Retained earnings of B Ltd	70 000		
Post-acquisition equity in C Ltd	① 6 000		
Non-controlling interest in C Ltd (equity)	② 20 800		
Group equity /net asset value	106 800		
Goodwill written off (not identifiable)	(4 800)		
Land (C Ltd) (15 000 – 12 000)	3 000		
B Ltd group equity	105 000	78 750	26 250
Cost of investment/fair value	118 000	90 000	28 000
Goodwill	13 000	11 250	1 750
31 December 20x5:			
Current year profit after tax:			
B Ltd (20 000 – 3 600) ④	16 400	12 300	4 100
C Ltd	③ 9 600	7 200	2 400
	144 000	19 500	34 500

④ The profits of B Ltd include dividend income earned from B Ltd's investment in C Ltd. The group profits of B Ltd of CU26 000 can therefore be calculated by adding the profits of B Ltd (in other words, including the dividend from C Ltd) to its share of the retained profits of C Ltd, that is, CU20 000 + CU6 000 (9 600 – 3 600).

The following extracts were obtained from the individual statements of financial position of the three entities at 31 December 20x5:

	P Ltd (the entity) CU	B Ltd (the entity) CU	C Ltd CU
ASSETS			
Land			10 000
Investment in subsidiary	90 000	30 000	
Other net assets	30 000	70 000	50 000
	120 000	100 000	60 000
EQUITY			
Share capital	20 000	10 000	25 000
Retained earnings	100 000	90 000	35 000
	120 000	100 000	60 000

The *pro-forma* journal entries that follow are prepared on the basis of using the individual financial statements of the different entities in the P Ltd group as opposed to using the consolidated financial statements of the B Ltd group. You can also prepare *pro-forma* journal entries that first consolidate C Ltd and B Ltd, and then use the consolidated financial statements of B Ltd group for consolidating that group. Some of these *pro-forma* journal entries may also be combined in one or two composite *pro-forma* journal entries.

Pro-forma journal entries at 31 December 20x5 arising from the consolidation of C Ltd

			CU	CU
Dr		Share capital	25 000	
Dr		Retained earnings	15 000	
Dr		Land	2 000	
Dr		Goodwill	4 800	
	Cr	Investment in C Ltd		30 000
	Cr	Non-controlling interest (equity)		16 800

Elimination of equity at the acquisition date of B Ltd's interest in C Ltd

			CU	CU
Dr		Retained earnings (31 December 20x4)	4 000	
	Cr	Non-controlling interest (equity)		4 000

Allocating prior years' profits to the non-controlling interest in C Ltd

			CU	CU
Dr		Non-controlling interest in profit and loss	6 400	
	Cr	Non-controlling interest (equity)		6 400

Allocating current year profits to the non-controlling interest in C Ltd

			CU	CU
Dr		Dividend income (P/L)	3 600	
Dr		Non-controlling interest (equity)	2 400	
	Cr	Dividend declared		6 000

Eliminating intra-group dividends received in B Ltd from C Ltd and amount distributed to non-controlling interest

Pro-forma journal entries at 31 December 20x5 arising from the consolidation of the B Ltd group

			CU	CU
Dr		Share capital	10 000	
Dr		Retained earnings (B Ltd)	70 000	
Dr		Retained earnings (C Ltd)	6 000	
Dr		Land (C Ltd)	3 000	
Dr		Goodwill in B Ltd group	13 000	
	Cr	Goodwill in C Ltd		4 800
	Cr	Investment in B Ltd group		90 000
Dr		Non-controlling interest (equity) in C Ltd	20 800	
	Cr	Non-controlling interest (equity) in B Ltd (at fair value)		28 000

Eliminating the group equity of B Ltd at the acquisition date of P Ltd's direct interest in B Ltd group

			CU	CU
Dr		Non-controlling interest in profit and loss	4 100	
	Cr	Non-controlling interest (equity) (direct in B Ltd)		4 100

Allocation of current year profit in B Ltd to non-controlling interest

			CU	CU
Dr		Non-controlling interest in profit and loss	2 400	
	Cr	Non-controlling interest (equity) (indirect in C Ltd)		2 400

Allocation of current year profit in C Ltd to indirect non-controlling interest

The **group statement of financial position** worksheet of P Ltd group is as follows at 31 December 20x5:

	P Ltd (the entity) CU	B Ltd (the entity) CU	C Ltd CU	Pro-forma entries (indirect) CU	Pro-forma entries (direct) CU	P Ltd Group (end point) CU
ASSETS						
Land			10 000	2 000	3 000	15 000
Investment in subsidiary	90 000	30 000		(30 000)	(90 000)	–
Goodwill				4 800	13 000 ⎫ (4 800)⎰	13 000
Other net assets	30 000	70 000	50 000			150 000
	120 000	100 000	60 000	(23 200)	(78 800)	178 000
EQUITY						
Share capital	20 000	10 000	25 000	(25 000)	(10 000)	20 000
Retained earnings	100 000	90 000	35 000	(15 000) ⎫ (4 000) ⎪ (6 400) ⎪ 2 400 ⎭	(70 000) ⎫ (6 000) ⎪ (4 100) ⎪ (2 400) ⎭	① 119 500
	120 000	100 000	60 000	(48 000)	(92 500)	139 500
Non-controlling interest				16 800 ⎫ 4 000 ⎪ 6 400 ⎪ (2 400)⎭	(20 800) ⎫ 28 000 ⎪ 4 100 ⎪ 2 400 ⎭	② 38 500
	120 000	100 000	60 000	(23 200)	(78 800)	178 000

Explanations

① From P Ltd's group perspective, the retained earnings of B Ltd and C Ltd at 31 December 20x4 are pre-acquisition. The P Ltd group's retained earnings consist of the retained earnings of P Ltd plus the group's share in the retained earnings of the B Ltd group in the 20x5 year:
P Ltd: CU100 000
B Ltd: CU19 500 (refer to the analysis of equity of B Ltd)
Total: CU119 500.

② The non-controlling interest is in both B Ltd and C Ltd, representing the interest not held by the parent, as follows:
B Ltd: CU34 500
C Ltd: CU4 000 (only relating to the profit of C Ltd in the current year; the profit of B is also only for the current year)
Total: CU38 500.

Assuming that P Ltd (the entity) earned a profit of CU25 000 for the year ended 31 December 20x5, the extract from the P Ltd group statement of profit or loss would be as follows:

	CU
Profit after tax	**57 400**
(25 000 (P Ltd) + 20 000 (B Ltd) + 16 000 (C Ltd) – 3 600 (C Ltd's dividend received by B Ltd))	
Attributable to:	
Parent equity holders (12 300 + 7 200 + 25 000) ③	44 500
Non-controlling interest (4 100 + 2 400 + 6 400) ④	12 900

③ Profit attributable to parent equity holders:
100% of P Ltd (25 000) + 75% of B Ltd (16 400 × 75% = 12 300) + 45% (75% × 60%) of C Ltd (16 000 × 45% = 7 200).

④ Non-controlling interest in current year profits:
25% of B Ltd (16 400 × 25% = 4 100) + 55% (40% + [25% of 60%] or 100% – 45%) of C Ltd (16 000 × 55% = 8 800).

Think about it

Summary of application of main principles in the example

The main principles applied in the example are as follows:
- The cost of C Ltd's land in C Ltd's entity financial statements is R10 000. In B Ltd's group financials, the land would be shown at a cost of CU12 000 and in P Ltd's group financials the land would be at a cost of CU15 000.
- If C Ltd were to revalue its land to CU18 000, the other comprehensive income in C Ltd would be CU8 000, B Ltd Group would be CU6 000 and P Ltd group would be CU3 000.
- Be careful of double counting. You cannot include all of the assets of C Ltd plus the assets of B Ltd in the group financial statements without eliminating the asset in B Ltd representing the cost of its investment in C Ltd. The consolidation process replaces the investment cost in C Ltd with the underlying net assets of C Ltd.
- Similarly, the consolidation process incorporates the profits of C Ltd and therefore any dividend income received by B Ltd from C Ltd must be eliminated to avoid double counting.
- The group share of B Ltd is 75% and the group share of C Ltd is 45%. That implies that 45% of C Ltd's and 75% of B Ltd's post-acquisition equity is included in P Ltd's group financial statements.
- Irrespective of the order of acquisition, you need to do the analysis of equity of the lowest company first in order to calculate the correct group profit. Note how B Ltd's 60% share of the profits in C Ltd is included in the 100% column of B Ltd's analysis of equity.
- Non-controlling interest is a class of equity. This implies that the non-controlling interest recognised by B Ltd in respect of C Ltd is eliminated on acquisition of B Ltd. Any post-acquisition increase is recognised.

5.2 **Where an associate or joint venture owns subsidiaries**

Where the investee is itself a parent (in other words, where the associate or joint venture has prepared group financial statements by consolidating its interests in its subsidiaries), the investor's attributable share is based on the profit of the investee's group profits after deducting the non-controlling interest in the subsidiary or subsidiaries of the investee. This makes sense as the investor is an equity holder of the parent, which in this case is the associate or joint venture.

Example

Investment in associate that has a subsidiary

An investor (P Ltd) acquired a 25% interest in an associate (A Ltd) that is itself a parent and has prepared the group statement of profit or loss that follows for the period ended 31 December 20x5.

Group statement of profit or loss for A Ltd for the period ended 31 December 20x5

	CU'000
Gross revenue	2 000
Net operating costs	(1 000)
Profit from ordinary activities	1 000
Interest expense	(220)
Profit before tax	780
Taxation expense	(300)
Profit for the year	**480**
Profit attributable to:	
Non-controlling interest	80
Equity holders of A Ltd	400
	480

Think about it
What is the profit attributable to the shareholders of A Ltd?
CU400 000

P Ltd owns a 25% interest in A Ltd.
Thus, using the equity method, P Ltd shares in 25% of the profits attributable to the equity holders of A Ltd: CU400 000 × 25% = CU100 000

The associate group earned profits of CU480 000 during the reporting period, of which CU400 000 is attributable to the equity holders of A Ltd (in other words, CU480 000 less the CU80 000 attributable to the non-controlling interest in the associate's group). P Ltd holds 25% of A Ltd's equity. As such, its share of the profit of the associate would amount to CU100 000, being 25% of CU400 000, which is the profit of A Ltd attributable to the equity holders (that is, after deducting the non-controlling interest).

The following *pro-forma* journal entry will thus record the investor's share in the associate's current year profits:

			CU	CU
Dr		Investment in associate	100 000	
	Cr	Share of profits of associate (P/L)		100 000

5.3 Vertical groups where a subsidiary acquires an investment in an associate or joint venture

In the sections above, we discussed the application of the equity method for interests in associates and joint ventures when preparing group financial statements. In more complex group structures, a parent may have an indirect interest in an associate or joint venture, for example, where the investor is a parent with a subsidiary and the subsidiary is the investor in the associate or joint venture. Thus, the parent has a controlling interest in the subsidiary and the subsidiary has significant influence in the associate. In this case, as the parent has control of the subsidiary, it has control of all of the assets and liabilities of the subsidiary, including its investment in the associate. This means that the parent has an indirect interest in the associate. When the parent then prepares group financial statements, it will consolidate its interest in the subsidiary and equity account its interest in the associate. Refer to Chapter 9 for a discussion of interests in associates and joint ventures.

As with any indirect interest, you have to consider the dates of acquisition of the respective entities in the group carefully. For example, if the subsidiary had the investment in the associate at the time when the parent acquires its controlling interest, the investment in the associate forms part of the assets and liabilities of the subsidiary at the acquisition date that need to be measured at fair value. On the other hand, if the subsidiary acquired its interest in the associate after the parent acquired its controlling interest in the subsidiary, the parent will recognise its indirect interest in the associate since the date that it was acquired in the group, using the equity method.

Example

Indirect interest in associate

P Ltd acquired 60% of S Ltd when S Ltd was incorporated on 1 January 20x4. S Ltd had ordinary share capital of CU1 000. S Ltd had retained earnings of CU20 000 on 31 December 20x4.

On 1 July 20x4, S Ltd acquired 40% of A Ltd for CU5 000. At that date, the shareholders' equity of A Ltd comprised ordinary share capital of CU1 000 and retained earnings of CU5 000. A Ltd's retained earnings balance as at 31 December 20x4 was CU10 000.

This is a vertical holding, where P Ltd first acquired its controlling interest in S Ltd and S Ltd subsequently acquired its investment in the associate, A Ltd.

The following information relates to the reporting period ended 31 December 20x5:

	P Ltd (the company) CU	S Ltd (the company) CU	A Ltd CU
Net profit before tax	6 000	4 000	3 000
Tax expense	(1 800)	(1 000)	(600)
Net profit	4 200	3 000	**2 400**
Dividends declared on 31 December 20x5	1 000	500	200

Both P Ltd and S Ltd account for investments in group companies on the cost basis in their separate annual financial statements.

What is the appropriate accounting treatment of S Ltd and A Ltd in the 20x5 group annual financial statements of P Ltd?

When preparing group financial statements, P Ltd will consolidate its interest in the subsidiary S Ltd and equity account its interest in the associate, A Ltd. As the consolidation process requires the inclusion of all of the assets and liabilities, income and expenses of the subsidiary in the group financial statements, the investment in the associate and the share of the associate's profits will also be included in the group financial statements. However, as the subsidiary has the investment in the associate and the parent does not own all of the shares of the subsidiary, the non-controlling shareholders share in the profits of the associate.

The group structure is illustrated in Figure 11.13 below.

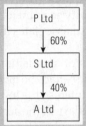

Figure 11.13 Diagram of vertical group

The starting point includes 100% of the trial balances of both P Ltd and S Ltd. In order to prepare the group financial statements (end point), we need to include the investor's (S Ltd) share of the post-acquisition profits of the associate, and then consolidate S Ltd. From Chapter 7, you will remember that non-controlling interest is determined as the equity not attributable to the equity holders of the parent. In this case, S Ltd is not a wholly owned subsidiary of P Ltd. Therefore, in the group financial statements of P Ltd, equity accounting A Ltd will result in recognising equity, some of which is attributable to the non-controlling interest.

Pro-forma journal entries necessary to produce the group annual financial statements of P Ltd as at 31 December 20x5 are shown below.

Equity accounting A Ltd

			CU	CU
Dr		Investment in associate	2 000	
	Cr	Retained earnings (CU10 000 – CU5 000) × 40%		2 000

Equity accounting group's share of post-acquisition prior year earnings

			CU	CU
Dr		Investment in associate	960	
	Cr	Share of profits of associate (CU2 400 × 40%)		① 960

Current year earnings allocated to group

			CU	CU
Dr		Dividend income	80	
	Cr	Investment in associate (CU200 × 40%)		80

Elimination of intra-group dividends

Consolidation of S Ltd

			CU	CU
Dr		Ordinary share capital (100%)	1 000	
	Cr	Investment in S Ltd (CU1 000 × 60%)		600
	Cr	Non-controlling interest (equity) (CU1 000 × 40%)		400

Elimination of equity at acquisition, investment in S Ltd and raising non-controlling interest at acquisition date

			CU	CU
Dr		Retained earnings	8 800	
	Cr	Non-controlling interest (equity) ([CU20 000 + CU2 000 ②] × 40%)		8 800

Post-acquisition prior year earnings allocated to non-controlling interest

			CU	CU
Dr		Non-controlling interest (P/L)	1 552 ◀	
	Cr	Non-controlling interest (equity) ([CU3 000 − CU80 (dividends from A Ltd) + CU960 ①] × 40%)		1 552

Current year earnings allocated to non-controlling interest

			CU	CU
Dr		Dividend income (CU500 × 60%)	300	
Dr		Non-controlling interest (equity)	200	
	Cr	Dividends declared		500

Elimination of intra-group dividends

> **What is the profit of S Ltd after equity accounting its interest in A Ltd?**
> CU3 000 + CU960 − CU80 = CU3 880
> The non-controlling interest shares in the profit of S Ltd:
> CU3 880 × 40% = CU1 552

Group statement of profit or loss for P Ltd group for the year ended 31 December 20x5

		CU
Net profit before tax	(6 000 [P] + 4 000 [S] – 300 [dividend from S] – 80 [dividend from A])	9 620
Tax expense	(1 800 + 1 000)	(2 800)
Share of profits from associate		960
Net profit for the year		**7 780**
Attributable to:		
Non-controlling interests		1 552
Equity holders of P Ltd		6 228

Proof of group profit attributable to equity holders of P Ltd

	CU
P Ltd	4 200
Less: Intra-group dividend from S Ltd	(300)
S Ltd (3 000 × 60%)	1 800
Less: Intra-group dividend from A Ltd (CU80 × 60%)	(48)
A Ltd share of profits of (CU960 x 60%)	576
Group profit attributable to parent equity holders	**6 228**

Test your knowledge

There is a list of learning objectives at the beginning of this chapter. Go back to this list and check whether you have achieved these outcomes. If not, reread the appropriate section.

Questions

Question 1
The following information relates to the reporting period ended 31 December 20x5:

	P Ltd	X Ltd	Y Ltd
Profit after tax	CU500 000	CU300 000	CU250 000
Less dividends declared and paid (31 December 20x5)	(80 000)	(50 000)	(30 000)

Assume that one share = one vote.

You are required to do the following:

Calculate the group profit for the year ended 31 December 20x5 as well as the profit attributable to parent equity holders and non-controlling interest of the P Ltd group in the following situations:
1. P Ltd owns 60% of X Ltd and P Ltd also owns 60% of Y Ltd.
2. P Ltd owns 60% of X Ltd and X Ltd owns 60% of Y Ltd.
3. P Ltd owns 60% of X Ltd and X Ltd owns 30% of Y Ltd.
4. P Ltd owns 30% of X Ltd and X Ltd owns 60% of Y Ltd.

(Note: For interest in associates and the equity method, refer to Chapter 9.)

Suggested solution

1. P Ltd owns 60% of X Ltd and P Ltd also owns 60% of Y Ltd.

Extract from group statement of profit or loss for the year ended 31 December 20x5

		Group CU
Group profit after tax	(w1)	1 002 000
Attributable to:		
Parent equity holders		782 000
Non-controlling interest	(w2)	220 000
(w1):		CU
P Ltd 500 000 – (50 000 × 60%) – (30 000 × 60%)		452 000
X Ltd		300 000
Y Ltd		250 000
Group profit		**1 002 000**
(w2):		CU
X Ltd (300 000 × 40%)		120 000
Y Ltd (250 000 × 40%)		100 000
Non-controlling interest		**220 000**

2. P Ltd owns 60% of X Ltd and X Ltd owns 60% of Y Ltd.

Extract from group statement of profit or loss for the year ended 31 December 20x5

		Group CU
Group profit after tax	(w1)	1 002 000
Attributable to:		
Parent equity holders		722 000
Non-controlling interest	(w2)	280 000
(w1):		CU
P Ltd 500 000 – (50 000 × 60%)		470 000
X Ltd 300 000 – (30 000 × 60%)		282 000
Y Ltd		250 000
Group profit		**1 002 000**
(w2):		CU
X Ltd (300 000 × 40%)		120 000
Y Ltd (250 000 × 60% × 40%) + (250 000 × 40%)		160 000
Non-controlling interest		**280 000**

3. P Ltd owns 60% of X Ltd and X Ltd owns 30% of Y Ltd.

Extract from group statement of profit or loss for the year ended 31 December 20x5

			Group CU
Group profit after tax		(w1)	836 000
Attributable to:			
Parent equity holders			689 600
Non-controlling interest		(w2)	146 400
(w1):			CU
P Ltd	500 000 – (50 000 × 60%)		470 000
X Ltd	300 000 – (30 000 × 30%)		291 000
Y Ltd	Equity account only (250 000 × 30%)		75 000
	Group profit		836 000
(w2):			CU
X Ltd	(291 000 + 75 000 = 366 000 × 40%)		146 400
	Non-controlling interest		146 400

4. P Ltd owns 30% of X Ltd and X Ltd owns 60% of Y Ltd.

Extract from group statement of profit or loss for the year ended 31 December 20x5

			Group CU
Group profit after tax		(w1)	614 600
(w1):			CU
P Ltd	500 000 – (50 000 × 30%)		485 000
X Ltd (group)	Equity account (432 000 × 30%)		129 600
	(300 000 – (30 000 × 60%) + [250 000 × 60%]) = 432 000		
	Group profit		614 600

Question 2

The following information was obtained from the **separate financial statements** of three entities at 31 December 20x5:

	P Ltd CU	A Ltd CU	S Ltd CU
Retained earnings (20x4)	3 000 000	1 100 000	1 600 000
Profit after tax	1 650 000	500 000	850 000
Dividends declared and paid	(250 000)	(80 000)	(100 000)
Retained earnings (20x5)	4 400 000	1 520 000	2 350 000

P Ltd owns a 30% interest in A Ltd (representing significant influence) and A Ltd owns a 70% controlling interest in S Ltd. Assume a normal tax rate of 28% and a capital gains tax inclusion rate of 66.6%.

Note: Answer each of the questions that follow independently.

You are required to do the following:

1. P Ltd charged interest of CU10 000 on a loan it has made to A Ltd. Calculate the group interest income.
2. A Ltd sold a plant (carrying amount of CU150 000) for CU180 000 to P Ltd on 1 July 20x3. At that date, the plant had a residual value of CU20 000 and a remaining useful life of five years. These estimates were confirmed at 31 December 20x5.

Calculate the carrying amount of the plant in P Ltd's group statement of financial position at 31 December 20x5, including comparatives.

Ignore the information in 1. and 2. above when answering 3. below.

3. S Ltd sold inventory to A Ltd subsequent to its acquisition date at a gross profit percentage of 20% on selling price (which is below the mark-up to customers). Inventory sold by S Ltd to A Ltd during the current reporting year amounted to CU240 000 and inventory still on hand in A Ltd at 31 December 20x5 amounted to CU50 000 (20x4: CU36 000).

   Calculate the group profit (after tax) to be recognised in P Ltd's group statement of comprehensive income for the year ended 31 December 20x5.

4. Show the amount that will be recognised in the P Ltd's group statement of changes in equity for the year ended 31 December 20x5 for dividends declared and paid.

Suggested solution

1. Group interest income: CU10 000 × 70% = CU7 000
2. Carrying amount of plant in group statement of financial position:

	31 December 20x5 CU	31 December 20x4 CU
Cost CU180 000 – (30% × CU30 000)	171 000	171 000
Less: Accumulated depreciation 20x4: CU171 000 – 20 000 = CU151 000/5 × 1.5		(45 300)
20x5: CU171 000 – 20 000 = CU151 000/5 × 2.5	(75 500)	
Carrying amount	**CU95 500**	**CU125 700**

Alternative workings

20x4:

In P Ltd: CU180 000 – (160 000/5 × 1.5) = CU132 000 (starting point)
Unrealised profit on sale of plant: CU30 000 × 30% = CU9 000
Group adjustment in *pro-forma* journal entry: CU9 000/5 × 3.5 = CU6 300
Group: CU132 000 – 6 300 = **CU125 700**

20x5:

In P Ltd: CU180 000 – (160 000/5 × 2.5) = CU100 000 (starting point)
Group adjustment in *pro-forma* journal entry: CU9 000/5 × 2.5 = CU4 500
Group: CU100 000 – 4 500 = **CU95 500**

3. Group statement of profit or loss for the year ended 31 December 20x5:

	Workings	CU
P Ltd:	CU1 650 000 – (30% × 80 000)	1 626 000
A Ltd:	CU500 000 – (70% × 100 000) = CU430 000 × 30%	129 000
S Ltd:	(CU850 000 – ((10 000 – 7 200) × 72%) = CU847 984 × 70% = CU593 589 × 30%	178 077
Group profit		**1 933 077**

4. Group statement of changes in equity: Dividend declared and paid:
   CU250 000

Case study exercises

Scenario 1

You obtained the extracts that follow from the financial statements of P Ltd, X Ltd and Y Ltd, all for the current financial period that ended 31 December 20x5.

Statements of financial position of P Ltd, X Ltd and Y Ltd on 31 December 20x5

	P Ltd CU'000	X Ltd CU'000	Y Ltd CU'000
ASSETS			
Plant and machinery	300	250	285
Investment in X Ltd	300		
Investment in Y Ltd	290		
Inventory	320	350	275
Other current assets	180	380	170
	1 390	980	730
CAPITAL AND LIABILITIES			
Share capital	290	160	150
Retained earnings	900	700	300
Shareholders' equity	1 190	860	450
Current liabilities	200	120	280
	1 390	980	730

Statements of comprehensive income of P Ltd, X Ltd and Y Ltd for the year ended 31 December 20x5

	P Ltd CU'000	X Ltd CU'000	Y Ltd CU'000
Revenue (including dividends and interest received)	2 320	1 700	1 080
Cost of sales	(1 050)	(875)	(560)
Gross profit	1 270	825	520
Net operating costs	(390)	(125)	(150)
Interest expense	(100)	(50)	(40)
Profit before taxation	780	650	330
Taxation expense	(300)	(250)	(130)
Profit after taxation	**480**	**400**	**200**

Extract from statements of changes in shareholders' equity of P Ltd, X Ltd and Y Ltd for the year ended 31 December 20x5

	P Ltd CU'000	X Ltd CU'000	Y Ltd CU'000
Retained earnings 1 January 20x5	620	500	240
Profit after tax	480	400	200
Dividends declared	(200)	(200)	(140)
Retained earnings 31 December 20x5	**900**	**700**	**300**

P Ltd acquired 80% of the issued ordinary share capital of X Ltd on 1 January 20x3. P Ltd then acquired 75% of the issued ordinary share capital of Y Ltd on 1 July 20x3. The identifiable assets and liabilities of X Ltd and Y Ltd were considered fairly valued at the respective dates of acquisition. You can assume that any goodwill arising on consolidation is not impaired. Ignore taxation.

The retained earnings of the subsidiary entities at the respective acquisition dates were as follows:

X Ltd (1 January 20x3)	CU200 000
Y Ltd (1 July 20x3)	CU210 000

None of the companies has issued any further ordinary shares since the date of incorporation. Non-controlling interest is measured at the attributable net asset value at the date of acquisition.

You are required to do the following:

1. Answer the following questions before starting with the preparation of the consolidated financial statements:
   - Prepare a group structure in which you clearly indicate P Ltd's effective interest and the non-controlling interest in the group.
   - Calculate the goodwill acquired when P Ltd acquired its controlling interest in X Ltd.
   - Calculate the goodwill acquired when P Ltd acquired its controlling interest in Y Ltd.
   - What is the amount of dividends received in the separate financial statements of P Ltd?
   - What is the amount of dividends declared and paid by the group?
2. Show the *pro-forma* journal entries required to prepare the consolidated financial statements of P Ltd Group for the year ended 31 December 20x5.
3. Prepare the consolidated statement of financial position and consolidated statement of profit or loss and other comprehensive income for P Ltd and its subsidiary at 31 December 20x5.

Scenario 2

You obtained the extracts that follow from the financial statements of P Ltd, X Ltd and Y Ltd, all for the current financial period that ended 31 December 20x5.

Statements of financial position of P Ltd and X Ltd on 31 December 20x5

	P Ltd CU'000	X Ltd CU'000	Y Ltd CU'000
ASSETS			
Plant and machinery	300	250	285
Investment in X Ltd	300		
Investment in Y Ltd		290	
Inventory	400	350	275
Other current assets	390	90	170
	1 390	**980**	**730**
CAPITAL AND LIABILITIES			
Share capital	290	160	150
Retained earnings	900	700	300
Shareholders' equity	1 190	860	450
Current liabilities	200	120	280
	1 390	**980**	**730**

Statements of comprehensive income of P Ltd and X Ltd for the year ended 31 December 20x5

	P Ltd CU'000	X Ltd CU'000	Y Ltd CU'000
Revenue (including dividends and interest received)	2 320	1 700	1 080
Cost of sales	(1 050)	(875)	(560)
Gross profit	1 270	825	520
Net operating costs	(390)	(125)	(150)
Interest expense	(100)	(50)	(40)
Profit before taxation	780	650	330
Taxation expense	(300)	(250)	(130)
Profit after taxation	**480**	**400**	**200**

Extract from statements of changes in shareholders' equity of P Ltd and X Ltd for the year ended 31 December 20x5

	P Ltd CU'000	X Ltd CU'000	Y Ltd CU'000
Retained earnings 1 January 20x5	620	500	240
Profit after tax	480	400	200
Dividends declared	(200)	(200)	(140)
Retained earnings 31 December 20x5	**900**	**700**	**300**

P Ltd acquired 80% of the issued ordinary share capital of X Ltd on 1 January 20x3. On 1 July 20x3, X Ltd acquired 75% of the issued ordinary share capital of Y Ltd. The identifiable assets and liabilities of X Ltd and Y Ltd were considered fairly valued at the respective dated of acquisition. You can assume that any goodwill arising on consolidation is not impaired. Ignore taxation.

The retained earnings of the subsidiary entities at the respective acquisition dates were as follows:

X Ltd (1 January 20x3)	CU200 000
Y Ltd (1 July 20x3)	CU210 000

None of the companies has issued any further ordinary shares since the date of incorporation. Non-controlling interest is measured at the attributable net asset value at the date of acquisition.

You are required to do the following:

1. Answer the following questions before starting with the preparation of the consolidated financial statements:
    - Prepare a group structure in which you clearly indicate P Ltd's effective interest and the non-controlling interest in the group.
    - Calculate the goodwill acquired when X Ltd acquired its controlling interest in Y Ltd.
    - Calculate the goodwill acquired when P Ltd acquired its controlling interest in X Ltd.
    - What is the amount of dividends received in the separate financial statements of P Ltd and X Ltd respectively?
    - What is the amount of dividends declared and paid by the group?
2. Show the *pro-forma* journal entries required to prepare the consolidated financial statements of P Ltd Group for the year ended 31 December 20x5.
3. Prepare the consolidated statement of financial position and consolidated statement of profit or loss and other comprehensive income for P Ltd and its subsidiary at 31 December 20x5.

Suggested solution

Scenario 1
1. **Answer the following questions before starting with the preparation of the consolidated financial statements:**
    - **Prepare a group structure in which you clearly indicate P Ltd's effective interest and the non-controlling interest in the group.**

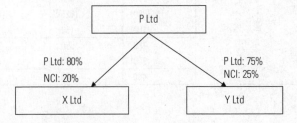

Figure 11.14 Group structure

- **Calculate the goodwill acquired when P Ltd acquired its controlling interest in X Ltd.**
  Goodwill acquired = Cash consideration + non-controlling interest − Fair value of net identifiable assets
  Fair value of net identifiable assets: CU160 000 + CU200 000 = CU360 000
  Non-controlling interest (share of net identifiable assets): CU360 000 × 20% = CU72 000
  Cash consideration: CU300 000
  ∴ Goodwill = (300 000 + 72 000) − 360 000 = **CU12 000**.
- **Calculate the goodwill acquired when P Ltd acquired its controlling interest in Y Ltd.**
  Goodwill acquired = Cash consideration + Non-controlling interest − Fair value of net identifiable assets
  Fair value of net identifiable assets: CU150 000 + CU210 000 = CU360 000
  Non-controlling interest (at share of net identifiable assets): CU360 000 × 25% = CU90 000
  Cash consideration: CU290 000
  ∴ Goodwill = (290 000 + 90 000) − 360 000 = **CU20 000**.
- **What is the amount of dividends received in the separate financial statements of P Ltd?**
  Dividends received from X Ltd: CU200 000 × 80% = CU160 000
  Dividends received from Y Ltd: CU140 000 × 75% = CU105 000.
- **What is the amount of dividends declared and paid by the group?**
  Dividends by P Ltd: CU200 000
  Dividends by X Ltd to non-controlling interest: CU200 000 × 20% = CU40 000
  Dividends by Y Ltd to non-controlling interest: CU140 000 × 25% = CU35 000
  Total dividends declared and paid by the group: CU275 000.

2. **Show the *pro-forma* journal entries required to prepare the consolidated financial statements of P Ltd Group for the year ended 31 December 20x5.**

Pro-forma journal entries: P Ltd's direct interest in X Ltd

			CU'000	CU'000
Dr		Share capital	160	
Dr		Retained earnings	200	
Dr		Goodwill arising on consolidation	12	
	Cr	Investment in X Ltd		300
	Cr	Non-controlling interest (equity)		72

Elimination of equity at acquisition, investment in X Ltd and raising non-controlling interest at acquisition

			CU'000	CU'000
Dr		Retained earnings	60	
	Cr	Non-controlling interest (equity)		60

Post-acquisition prior year earnings allocated to non-controlling interest

			CU'000	CU'000
Dr		Non-controlling interest in profits (P/L)	80	
	Cr	Non-controlling interest (equity)		80

Current year's earnings allocated to non-controlling interest

			CU'000	CU'000
Dr		Dividends received (P/L)	160	
Dr		Non-controlling interest (equity)	40	
	Cr	Dividends declared and paid		200

Elimination of inter-company dividend

Pro-forma journal entries: P Ltd's direct interest in Y Ltd

			CU'000	CU'000
Dr		Share capital	150	
Dr		Retained earnings	210	
Dr		Goodwill arising on consolidation	20	
	Cr	Investment in Y Ltd		290
	Cr	Non-controlling interest (equity)		90

Elimination of equity at acquisition, investment in Y Ltd and raising non-controlling at acquisition

			CU'000	CU'000
Dr		Retained earnings	7.5	
	Cr	Non-controlling interest (equity)		7.5

Post-acquisition prior year earnings allocated to non-controlling interest

			CU'000	CU'000
Dr		Non-controlling interest in profits (P/L)	50	
	Cr	Non-controlling interest (equity)		50

Current year's earnings allocated to non-controlling interest

			CU'000	CU'000
Dr		Dividends received (P/L)	105	
Dr		Non-controlling interest (equity)	35	
	Cr	Dividends declared and paid		140

Elimination of inter-company dividend

3. **Prepare the consolidated statement of financial position and consolidated statement of profit or loss and other comprehensive income for P Ltd and its subsidiary at 31 December 20x5.**

Consolidated statement of profit or loss and other comprehensive income for P Ltd and its subsidiary for the year ended 31 December 20x5

	Workings	CU'000
Gross revenue	(2 320 + 1 700 + 1 080 − 160 − 105)	4 835
Cost of sales	(1 050 + 875 + 560)	(2 485)
Gross profit		2 350
Net operating costs	(390 + 125 + 150)	(665)
Interest expense	(100 + 50 + 40)	(190)
Profit before tax		1 495
Taxation expense	(300 + 250 + 130)	(680)
Profit after tax		815
Attributable to:		
Equity holders of the parent		685
Non-controlling interest (80 + 50)		130
Total comprehensive income		**815**

Consolidated statement in shareholders' interest for P Ltd and its subsidiary for the year ended 31 December 20x5

	Interest of parent equity holders			Non-controlling interest CU'000	Total CU'000
	Share capital CU'000	Retained earnings CU'000	Total CU'000		
Opening balance	290	(w1) 882.5	1 172.5	(w2) 229.5	1 402
Total comprehensive income		685	685	130	815
− Dividends		(200)	(200)	(75)	(275)
Closing balance	**290**	**1 367.5**	**1 657.5**	**284.5**	**1 942**

(w1):

		CU
P Ltd:		620 000
X Ltd:	(500 000 − 200 000) × 80%	240 000
Y Ltd:	(240 000 − 210 000) × 75%	22 500
Group:	620 000 + 240 000 + 22 500	**882 500**

(w2):

		CU
X Ltd:	(72 000 + 60 000)	132 000
Y Ltd:	(90 000 + 7 500)	97 500
Opening non-controlling interest:		**229 500**

Consolidated statement of financial position for P Ltd and its subsidiary at 31 December 20x5

	Workings	CU'000
ASSETS		
Non-current assets		
Plant and machinery	(300 + 250 + 285)	835
Goodwill (12 + 20)		32
Current assets:		
Inventory	(400 + 350 + 275)	1 025
Other current assets	(390 + 90 + 170)	650
		2 542
EQUITY AND LIABILITIES		
Share capital		290
Retained earnings		1 367.5
Interest of parent equity holders		1 657.5
Non-controlling interest		284.5
Total equity		1 942
Current liabilities	(200 + 120 + 280)	600
		2 542

Workings

Analysis of equity of X Ltd

	Total CU'000	P Ltd (80%) At acquisition CU'000	P Ltd (80%) Since acquisition CU'000	20% Non-controlling interest CU'000
At acquisition:				
Share capital	160	128		32
Retained earnings	200	160		40
	360	288		72
Investment		300		
Goodwill		12		
Since acquisition:				
Retained earnings	300		240	60
Current year:				
Profit after tax	400		320	80
– Dividends	(200)		(160)	(40)
	860		**400**	**172**

Analysis of equity of Y Ltd

| | Total CU'000 | P Ltd (75%) | | 25% Non-controlling interest CU'000 |
		At acquisition CU'000	Since acquisition CU'000	
At acquisition:				
Share capital	150	112.5		37.5
Retained earnings	210	157.5		52.5
	360	270		90
Investment		290		
Goodwill		20		
Since acquisition:				
Retained earnings	30		22.5	7.5
Current year:				
Profit after tax	200		150	50
– Dividends	(140)		(105)	(35)
	450		67.5	112.5

Scenario 2

1. **Answer the following questions before starting with the preparation of the consolidated financial statements:**
   - **Prepare a group structure in which you clearly indicate P Ltd's effective interest and the non-controlling interest in the group.**

   This is a vertical group.

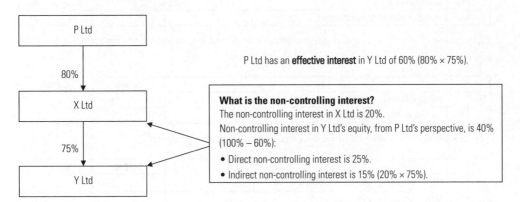

P Ltd has an **effective interest** in Y Ltd of 60% (80% × 75%).

What is the non-controlling interest?
The non-controlling interest in X Ltd is 20%.
Non-controlling interest in Y Ltd's equity, from P Ltd's perspective, is 40% (100% − 60%):
- Direct non-controlling interest is 25%.
- Indirect non-controlling interest is 15% (20% × 75%).

Figure 11.15 Group structure

   - **Calculate the goodwill acquired when P Ltd acquired its controlling interest in X Ltd.**
   Goodwill acquired = Cash consideration + Non-controlling interest − Fair value of net identifiable assets
   Fair value of net identifiable assets: CU160 000 + CU200 000 = CU360 000
   Non-controlling interest (at share of net identifiable assets): CU360 000 × 20% = CU72 000
   Cash consideration: CU300 000
   ∴ Goodwill = (300 000 + 72 000) − 360 000 = **CU12 000**.

- **Calculate the goodwill acquired when X Ltd acquired its controlling interest in Y Ltd.**
  Goodwill acquired = Cash consideration + Non-controlling interest – Fair value of net identifiable assets
  Fair value of net identifiable assets: CU150 000 + CU210 000 = CU360 000
  Non-controlling interest (at share of net identifiable assets): CU360 000 × 25% = CU90 000
  Cash consideration: CU290 000
  ∴ Goodwill = (290 000 + 90 000) – 360 000 = **CU20 000**.
- **What is the amount of dividends received in the separate financial statements of P Ltd and X Ltd respectively?**
  P Ltd: Dividends received from X Ltd: CU200 000 × 80% = CU160 000
  X Ltd: Dividends received from Y Ltd: CU140 000 × 75% = CU105 000
  Total dividends received: CU265 000.
- **What is the amount of dividends declared and paid by the group?**
  Dividends by P Ltd: CU200 000
  Dividends by X Ltd to non-controlling interest: CU200 000 × 20% = CU40 000
  Dividends by Y Ltd to non-controlling interest: CU140 000 × 25% = CU35 000
  Total dividends declared and paid by the group: **CU275 000**.

2. **Show the *pro-forma* journal entries required to prepare the consolidated financial statements of P Ltd Group for the year ended 31 December 20x5.**

Pro-forma journal entries: P Ltd's direct interest in X Ltd

			CU'000	CU'000
Dr		Share capital	160	
Dr		Retained earnings	200	
Dr		Goodwill arising on consolidation	12	
	Cr	Investment in X Ltd		300
	Cr	Non-controlling interest (equity)		72

Elimination of equity at acquisition, investment in X Ltd and raising non-controlling interest at acquisition

			CU'000	CU'000
Dr		Retained earnings (60 + 4.5)	64.5	
	Cr	Non-controlling interest (equity)		64.5

Post-acquisition prior year earnings allocated to non-controlling interest

			CU'000	CU'000
Dr		Non-controlling interest in profits (80 + 30)	110	
	Cr	Non-controlling interest (equity)		110

Current year's earnings allocated to non-controlling interest

			CU'000	CU'000
Dr		Dividends received (P/L)	160	
Dr		Non-controlling interest (equity)	40	
	Cr	Dividends declared and paid		200

Elimination of inter-company dividend

Pro-forma journal entries: X Ltd's direct interest in Y Ltd

			CU'000	CU'000
Dr		Share capital	150	
Dr		Retained earnings	210	
Dr		Goodwill arising on consolidation	20	
	Cr	Investment in Y Ltd		290
	Cr	Non-controlling interest (equity)		90

Elimination of equity at acquisition, investment in Y Ltd and raising non-controlling interest at acquisition

			CU'000	CU'000
Dr		Retained earnings (30 000 × 25%)	7.5	
	Cr	Non-controlling interest (equity)		7.5

Post-acquisition prior year earnings allocated to non-controlling interest

			CU'000	CU'000
Dr		Non-controlling interest in profits (P/L) (200 000 × 25%)	50	
	Cr	Non-controlling interest (equity)		50

Current year's earnings allocated to non-controlling interest

			CU'000	CU'000
Dr		Dividends received (X Ltd)	105	
Dr		Non-controlling interest (equity)	35	
	Cr	Dividends declared and paid (Y Ltd)		140

Reduction of P Ltd's share of profit in Y Ltd, relating to the dividend declared by Y Ltd to indirect non-controlling interest and elimination of inter-company dividend

3. **Prepare the consolidated statement of financial position and consolidated statement of profit or loss and other comprehensive income for P Ltd and its subsidiary at 31 December 20x5.**

Consolidated statement of profit or loss and other comprehensive income for P Ltd and its subsidiary for the year ended 31 December 20x5

	Workings	CU'000
Gross revenue	(2 320 + 1 700 + 1 080 − 160 − 105)	4 835
Cost of sales	(1 050 + 875 + 560)	(2 485)
Gross profit		2 350
Net operating costs	(390 + 125 + 150)	(665)
Interest expense	(100 + 50 + 40)	(190)
Profit before tax		1 495
Taxation expense	(300 + 250 + 130)	(680)
Profit after tax		815
Attributable to:		
Equity holders of the parent		655
Non-controlling interest	(80 + 30 + 50)	160
Total comprehensive income		**815**

Consolidated statement in shareholders' interest for P Ltd and its subsidiary for the year ended 31 December 20x5

	Interest of parent equity holders			Non-controlling interest CU'000	Total CU'000
	Share capital CU'000	Retained earnings CU'000	Total CU'000		
Opening balance	290	(w1) 878	1 168	(w2) 234	1 402
Total comprehensive income		655	655	160	815
– Dividends		(200)	(200)	(75)	(275)
Closing balance	**290**	**1 333**	**1 623**	**319**	**1 942**

(w1):

		CU
P Ltd:		620 000
X Ltd:	(500 000 – 200 000 + 22 500) × 80%	258 000
Group:	620 000 + 258 000	**878 000**

(w2):

		CU
X Ltd:	(72 000 + 60 000 + 90 000 + 7 500 + 4 500)	**234 000**

Consolidated statement of financial position for P Ltd and its subsidiary at 31 December 20x5

	Workings	CU'000
ASSETS		
Non-current assets:		
Plant and machinery	(300 + 250 + 285)	835
Goodwill (12 + 20)		32
Current assets:		
Inventory	(400 + 350 + 275)	1 025
Other current assets	(390 + 90 + 170)	650
		2 542
EQUITY AND LIABILITIES		
Share capital		290
Retained earnings		1 333
Interest of parent equity holders		1 623
Non-controlling interest		319
Total equity		1 942
Current liabilities	(200 + 120 + 280)	600
		2 542

Workings

Analysis of equity of X Ltd, including since-acquisition equity of Y Ltd

	Total CU'000	P Ltd (80%) At acquisition CU'000	P Ltd (80%) Since acquisition CU'000	20% Non-controlling interest CU'000
At acquisition:				
Share capital	160	128		32
Retained earnings	200	160		40
	360	288		72
Investment		300		
Goodwill		12		
Since acquisition:				
Retained earnings (X Ltd)	300		240	60
Retained earnings (X Ltd in Y Ltd) (30 × 75%)	22.5		18	4.5
Current year:				
Profit after tax (X Ltd)	400		320	80
Profit after tax (X Ltd in Y Ltd) (200 × 75%)	150		120	30
– Dividends	(200)		(160)	(40)
	1 032.5		**538**	**206.5**

Analysis of equity of Y Ltd

	Total CU'000	75% X Ltd at acquisition CU'000	75% Since acquisition CU'000	25% Non-controlling interest CU'000
At acquisition:				
Share capital	150	112.5		37.5
Retained earnings	210	157.5		52.5
	360	270		90
Investment		290		
Goodwill		20		
Since acquisition:				
Retained earnings	30		22.5	7.5
Current year:				
Profit after tax	200		150	50
– Dividends	(140)		(105)	(35)
	450		**67.5**	**112.5**

12

Changes in ownership

Learning objectives

By the end of this chapter, you should be able to:
- Understand what gives rise to changes in ownership of subsidiaries and associates, and the impact of such changes in ownership on the controlling interest of the parent
- Know how to recognise changes in ownership when preparing group financial statements
- Understand the implications for preparing group financial statements when the parent sells some of its interest, but control is retained
- Understand the implications for preparing group financial statements when an investor acquires additional shares in an investee to the extent that the investor has obtained the controlling interest
- Understand the implications for preparing group financial statements when control of a subsidiary is lost
- Know when a profit arising from changes in ownership is recognised in equity or when it is recognised in the statement of profit or loss and other comprehensive income.

1. Basic principles revisited: Controlling interest

In the previous chapters, we discussed the requirement for a parent to prepare and present consolidated financial statements when it has interests in subsidiaries. For an entity to be classified as a subsidiary, that entity must be controlled by another entity. In order to assess whether control exists, all available facts and circumstances must be considered, and professional judgement must be exercised. (Refer to IFRS10, *Consolidated Financial Statements*, for the meaning of the word 'control' and examples of the information required to determine whether control exists.)

If **the circumstances** that provided evidence of the existence of control **change**, an assessment of whether control still exists must be made. In this chapter, we will consider the implications for preparing consolidated financial statements that result from the following situations:
- Changes in ownership interests **without** the loss of control
- Changes in ownership interests that result in a loss of control.

Consolidated financial statements consist of a single set of financial statements in which the financial statements of the separate, individual entities in a group are combined so that they show the financial position and performance of the group of entities, presented as if they were a single economic entity. In consolidated financial statements (as required in IFRS10), there are **two groups of equity holders**: the parent equity holders and the non-controlling interest. In order to understand the principles of changes in ownership, you need to refer to the principles of control and the single economic entity.

The process of consolidation, which is the most important process used in the production of group financial statements, involves recognising all of the assets and liabilities **controlled by the group**. As the definition of a subsidiary implies, all of the assets and liabilities of the subsidiary are under the control of its parent. Group financial statements therefore include all assets and liabilities controlled by the group. The consolidated financial statements of the parent and its subsidiaries include information about a subsidiary from the date on which the parent obtains **control** of the subsidiary, that is, from the acquisition date. A subsidiary continues to be included in the parent's consolidated financial statements until the parent no longer controls that entity, that is, until the date at which control is lost. Changes to the economic entity's structure only occur when control over other entities is obtained or when control is lost.

Where the parent acquires **additional shares** in a subsidiary or where the parent sells shares in a subsidiary, but **retains control**, there is no change in the economic entity's structure. The economic entity still consists of the parent and the subsidiary. The substance of the transaction is that the parent (as an equity holder) transacted with the non-controlling interest (the other equity holders). These are transactions between owners and not with entities outside the group. These changes in ownership interest therefore cannot give rise to gains or losses to the economic entity.

Furthermore, where the parent acquires additional shares in a subsidiary, this transaction is not a business combination as control was obtained previously. As the parent already had control over the subsidiary, there is no need to adjust the identifiable assets and liabilities of the subsidiary to fair values or to measure goodwill in relation to the transaction involving the acquisition of additional shares.

IFRS principles

Obtaining and losing control

Consolidation of an investee shall begin from the date on which the investor obtains control of the investee and cease when the investor loses control of the investee (refer to IFRS10: 20).

2. Different forms of interest (ownership) in equity instruments

In order to understand the changes in ownership, it is useful first to revise the different forms of ownership and interests in equity instruments. Changes in an entity's shareholding in another entity may result in a new form of ownership to consider when preparing group financial statements. For example, assume a parent owns 60% of the issued shares of a subsidiary and subsequently sells half of its shareholding; the parent is now an investor with a 30% interest in an investee. If control is determined based on voting rights, this change in shareholding results in the parent entity losing control over the subsidiary, but maintaining significant influence over the entity, which is now an associate.

This change in shareholding will have a significant effect upon the group financial statements as the group will no longer consolidate the entity, but will now use the equity method to recognise its share of the post-acquisition changes in net assets of the associate.

This transaction raises a number of questions, including the following:

- Are the assets and liabilities of the subsidiary disposed of?
- How should the profits of the subsidiary before the change in ownership and the application of the equity method be accounted for?
- Is there any change in the net assets of the group? If so, how should it be recognised?

Example

Different forms of ownership

Consider the following group situation, where P Ltd owns a 42% shareholding in S Ltd as at 28 February 20x5. Given its 42% shareholding in S Ltd, there are four possibilities regarding the manner in which S Ltd should be accounted for in P Ltd's consolidated financial statements for the financial year ended 28 February 20x5.

What S Ltd is	Reason or reasons
Subsidiary	If these shares attribute voting rights, P Ltd could have *de facto* control if the remaining shareholders who own 58% of the voting rights are passive investors and/or have not collectively exercised control or prevented P Ltd from exercising control. There may be other arrangements that could indicate control, for example: Arrangements to vote on behalf of shareholders who own at least 8.01% of the voting rights in S Ltd (and therefore have access to 50.01% of the voting rights in S Ltd) The ability to appoint and/or remove the majority of directors to the board of S Ltd.
Associate	If these shares attribute voting rights, there is *prima facie* evidence that P Ltd exerts significant influence as it owns more than 20%, but less than 50% of the voting rights in S Ltd.
Joint venture	If these shares attribute voting rights, P Ltd could have a contractual arrangement with another shareholder (or shareholders) who owns at least 8.01% of the voting rights in S Ltd that the parties would jointly control S Ltd.
Financial asset	If these shares do not attribute any voting rights (for example, preference shares), then they may be insufficient to allow P Ltd to exercise control, significant influence or joint control. P Ltd would solely have the right to receive cash or another financial asset from dividends and/or the sale of its shareholding.

Changes in ownership may result in a change in the classification of the investee (for example, from being classified as a subsidiary to an associate or from being classified as an investment in a financial asset to a subsidiary). The accounting treatment of each entity in the group financial statements depends on its classification as a subsidiary, an associate, a joint venture or an investment in a financial asset. Subsequent to acquiring a controlling interest in a subsidiary, the parent's shareholding could change as a result of one of the following situations:
- The parent acquiring additional shares in the subsidiary from the non-controlling interest or from the subsidiary itself if the subsidiary issues shares subsequently
- The parent selling its shareholding or a portion thereof
- The subsidiary issuing additional shares to the non-controlling interest
- The subsidiary repurchasing shares from the non-controlling interest or the parent.

Where a parent acquires additional shares in a subsidiary subsequent to obtaining control or where the parent sells shares in a subsidiary but **retains control**, there is no change in the economic entity's structure (or the group's structure). Where the consideration paid to or received by the parent from the non-controlling interest on the acquisition or sale of shares in the subsidiary exceeds the carrying amount of the relevant non-controlling interest in the subsidiary, there is a change in the group's net assets. This difference (profit or loss) is recognised directly in equity in the consolidated financial statements.

The change in ownership is a transaction between two owners of a group: the parent and the non-controlling interest. When transactions of this nature occur, an adjustment reflecting the change in respective ownership interest must be made to the carrying amounts of the parent's controlling interest and the non-controlling interest. This adjustment is reflected directly in the consolidated statement of changes in equity, consistent with transactions with owners in their capacity as owners.

A parent may **lose control** of a subsidiary when it sells some or all of the shares in that subsidiary. The subsidiary should only be consolidated until the date that control is lost. When a parent has lost control and significant influence, but has retained an investment in the former subsidiary (in other words, still holds some shares in the entity), the investor will account for the remaining investment in accordance with IFRS9, *Financial Instruments*.

The fair value of the investment retained is part of the calculation of any gain or loss on disposal of the shares in the subsidiary.

An investor may acquire more shares in an existing investee, which may result in it being able to exert significant influence or control over the investee. This would result in the investment being accounted for as an investment in associate or a subsidiary in the investor's group financial statements, where previously the investment was simply a financial asset. For example, if an investor held an investment of 10% of the shares of an investee and subsequently acquired a further 20% of the shares, this 30% holding could, in isolation, result in the investor being able to exert significant influence over the investee as the investee is an associate of the investor. However, if a further 50% of the shares were acquired by the investor, the new shareholding could, in isolation, result in the entity being able to exert control over the investee as the investee is a subsidiary of the investor.

In this chapter, we will discuss the following scenarios:
- The acquisition of an associate or subsidiary (increase in shareholding from a previous investment in a financial asset)
- Increases in shareholding in a subsidiary without a change in control (acquisition of an additional shareholding from non-controlling interest)
- Decreasing shareholding in the subsidiary without a change in control (disposal of a portion of the parent's shareholding)
- Decreasing shareholding in the subsidiary as a result of the parent selling its shareholding in the subsidiary (control is lost).

2.1 Acquisition of an associate or subsidiary: Increase in shareholding from a previous investment in a financial asset

An investment in an investee that does not constitute significant influence or control is classified as a financial asset (investment in shares or equity instruments of another entity). In the separate financial statement of the investor, the investment in the financial asset is accounted for in accordance with IFRS9, *Financial Instruments*. Depending on the additional interest (shareholding) and voting power acquired, the investee can either be an associate (when significant influence is obtained) or a subsidiary (when control is obtained).

At a group level, when significant influence is obtained, the investment in the financial asset is derecognised and an investment in an associate is acquired.
- The 'sale' of the investment in the financial asset is recognised in the group financial statements.
- The acquisition of the associate is recognised and accounted for in accordance with the equity method.

Alternatively, at a group level, when control is obtained, the investment in the financial asset is derecognised and a subsidiary is acquired.
- The 'sale' of the investment in the financial asset is recognised in the group financial statements.

- A business combination is recognised. This means that the group acquired a controlling interest in a subsidiary, and that goodwill should be measured and recognised at the acquisition date.

2.2 Increases in shareholding in a subsidiary without a change in control: Acquisition of an additional shareholding from non-controlling interest

At a group level, the parent has transacted with an equity participant of the group: the non-controlling interest.

You should consider the following at the transaction date:

- There is no change to goodwill (and no bargain purchase gain recognised). Goodwill is recognised as a separate asset where there has been a business combination, in other words, control is gained. In this case, the parent already had control.
- No gain or loss (if the amount paid for the additional shares differs from the portion of the net asset value of the subsidiary that is being attained, in other words, the decrease in the non-controlling interest balance) is recognised in the statement of profit or loss and other comprehensive income. This transaction is a transaction with 'owners' and should be recognised directly in equity in the group statement of changes in equity as an equity adjustment.

2.3 Decreasing shareholding in the subsidiary without a change in control: Disposal of a portion of the parent's shareholding

As discussed above, at a group level, this is a transaction between the parent and an equity participant of the group: the non-controlling interest. Therefore, any profit or loss on disposal (being the difference between the proceeds and the portion of the net asset value of the subsidiary sold) cannot be recognised in the statement of profit or loss and other comprehensive income. Instead, the profit or loss on disposal is recognised directly to equity through the group statement of changes in equity.

There is no change to goodwill as control has not been lost.

2.4 Decreasing shareholding in the subsidiary as a result of the parent selling its shareholding in the subsidiary (control is lost)

As there is no longer any non-controlling interest (as the subsidiary is no longer part of the group), this is not a transaction between the parent and a class of equity holders.

Consequently, the parent will derecognise the assets and liabilities at their carrying amounts as well as derecognise the carrying amount of any non-controlling interest of the former subsidiary at the date when control was lost. The carrying amount of goodwill (if any) is also derecognised at that date; the goodwill no longer exists as control has been lost. If the parent retained any investment in the former subsidiary, the investment is recognised at its fair value at the date when control was lost. Any profit or loss on disposal can be recognised in the group profit or loss. In terms of IFRS10, paragraphs 25 and B98, this is calculated as follows:

- Fair value of the proceeds on disposal plus
- Fair value of the interest retained (which becomes the cost of the investment in the associate, joint venture or financial asset going forward) less
- Parent's share of the carrying amount in the group of the net assets at the date when control is lost.

In addition to the changes discussed above, there are several other outcomes (for example, the loss of control, but acquiring joint control, or the loss of control, but acquisition of significant influence). In these cases, the group no longer has a subsidiary, thus the subsidiary should be consolidated until the date on which control is lost. The joint venture or associate was 'acquired' and this remaining interest is measured at fair value.

3. Acquisition of control (business combination acquired in stages)

In the previous chapters, you have learnt that in order for a business combination to occur, there has to be an economic transaction between two entities in which the control of a business is obtained by another business. Such control exists when an investor has the right to variable returns from its involvement with the investee and has the ability to affect those returns through its power over the investee. Where an investor acquired shares in another entity and the investor does not have sufficient voting rights that result in it having control or significant influence over the other entity, the investment is classified as an investment in an equity instrument and accounted for in accordance with IFRS9, *Financial Instruments*.

If additional shares are acquired that enable the investor to obtain control of the other entity, that other entity is a subsidiary of the group. This means that in the group financial statements, the investment in the equity instrument is derecognised and the subsidiary is consolidated. Interests in subsidiaries that are consolidated are not in the scope of IFRS9.

In a business combination achieved in stages, or a step acquisition – where the investor had an investment in the subsidiary prior to obtaining control – the investor remeasures its previously held equity interest in the investee at its **acquisition-date fair value** and recognises the resulting gain or loss, if any, in profit or loss. In prior reporting periods, the investor may have recognised changes in the value of its equity interest in the investee in other comprehensive income. Where fair value adjustments were recognised in other comprehensive income, the acquisition-date fair value gain or loss is recognised in other comprehensive income. Effectively, this is done on the same basis as would be required if the investor had disposed directly of the previously held equity interest, the substance being that if an investor owned 10% of an investee and acquired a further 50% (so that the investor now owns 60%), the investor could have structured the transaction by selling its 10% shareholding and acquiring a 60% shareholding.

Step acquisitions need not only take the form of control arising in the situation mentioned above. For example, an entity could have an investment in equity instruments of another entity that it accounts in accordance with IFRS9. It could then acquire a further investment that results in the investor being able to exert significant influence. Thereafter, a further investment could be made resulting in the investor being able to control the investee.

It is also possible that the investor obtains control over the investee without an investment in shares of the investee. For example, the investee may repurchase some of its issued shares from other investors, resulting in a decrease in the total number of shares (and voting rights) in issue. The reduction in shares in issue may result in an increase in the percentage of voting rights held by the investor to an amount greater than 50%. Examples of circumstances where control is obtained without consideration being transferred include the following instances (refer to IFRS3, paragraph 43):

- The investee repurchases a sufficient number of its own shares from an existing other investor, resulting in the investor obtaining control.
- Minority veto rights that previously kept the investor from controlling an investee in which the investor held the majority voting rights lapse.
- The investor and investee agree to combine their businesses by contract alone. The investor transfers no consideration in exchange for control of an investee and holds no equity interests in the investee, either on the acquisition date or previously.

In the investor's **separate financial statements** (refer to Chapter 1), investments in subsidiaries, associates, and jointly controlled entities are accounted for by measuring them at either of the following (refer to IAS27, paragraph 10):

- Cost (taking into account any impairment)
- Fair value in accordance with IFRS9, *Financial instruments.*
- In accordance with the equity method (after the scope of IAS27 was amended).

In accordance with IFRS9, investments in **equity instruments** are measured at fair value at each reporting date with any fair value adjustments recognised in either of the following:

- Profit or loss
- Other comprehensive income (in certain circumstances).

Refer to Chapter 8 (Financial instruments) in *Financial Accounting: IFRS Principles* (4e) by Lubbe, Modack and Watson for a detailed discussion of the measurement and recognition of investments in equity instruments.

 IFRS principles

Recognition and measurement of equity instruments (IFRS9)

All equity investments that are in the scope of IFRS9 are to be measured at **fair value** in the statement of financial position, with changes in fair value to be recognised in profit or loss, except for those equity investments for which the entity has elected to recognise fair value changes in other comprehensive income.

'Other comprehensive income' option

If an equity investment is not held for trading, an entity can make an irrevocable election at initial recognition of that investment to recognise changes in its fair value in other comprehensive income.

When the investor purchases additional shares in the investee, there is **an increase** in the investment, which is recorded in the separate financial statements of the investor. The investor will therefore continue to recognise its investment at fair value (in accordance with IFRS9) or recognise its investment at cost (as allowed by IAS27: 10) using the equity method.

Example

Nature of investment changes to a subsidiary

Ignore all tax implications. P Ltd acquired 6% of the ordinary shares in S Ltd on 30 June 20x4 for a total cash consideration of CU500. On 31 December 20x4, P Ltd acquired a further 54% interest in S Ltd for a further cash consideration of CU7 000. All of the assets and liabilities of S Ltd were considered fairly valued at 31 December 20X4. The non-controlling interest was measured at its proportionate share of the net asset value of S Ltd at the acquisition date.

The shareholding in S Ltd was recognised at fair value through other comprehensive income in the separate financial statements of P Ltd . The fair value of the 6% shareholding in S Ltd on 31 December 20X4 was CU600 and the fair value of the 60% shareholding in S Ltd on 31 December 20x5 was CU9 000.

The trial balance of S Ltd for the financial year ended 31 December 20x5, which is the financial year end of S Ltd and P Ltd (and the P Ltd group), is presented below.

	S Ltd	
	Debit	Credit
	CU	CU
Ordinary share capital	–	1 000
Retained earnings (1 January 20x5)	–	10 000
Profit after tax	–	2 000
Property, plant and equipment	10 000	–
Current assets	4 000	–
Current liabilities	–	1 000
	14 000	14 000

From the above, the net asset value of S Ltd at 31 December 20x4 can be calculated as CU11 000.

In 20x4, the 6% shareholding was initially recognised at its fair value of CU500 (the cost of the investment) in the separate (and group if appropriate) financial statements of P Ltd and recognised at its fair value of CU600 on 31 December 20x4, with a fair value adjustment of CU100 recognised in other comprehensive income.

Journal entries in separate financial statements of P Ltd

Year ended 31 December 20x4

			CU	CU
Dr		Investment in S Ltd	500	
	Cr	Bank		500

Investment in S Ltd measured at cost when acquired on 30 June 20x4

			CU	CU
Dr		Investment in S Ltd	100	
	Cr	Gain on fair value adjustment (OCI)		100

Investment in S Ltd measured at fair value of CU600 at the reporting date

			CU	CU
Dr		Investment in S Ltd	7 000	
	Cr	Bank		7 000

Acquisition of additional 54% interest in S Ltd on 31 December 20x4

Year ended 31 December 20x5

			CU	CU
Dr		Investment in S Ltd	1 400	
	Cr	Gain on fair value adjustment (OCI)		1 400

Investment in S Ltd measured at fair value of CU9 000, less carrying amount of CU7 600

What is the carrying amount of the investment in S Ltd in the separate financial statements of P Ltd at 31 December 20x5?

Starting point

	31 December 20x5 CU	31 December 20x4 CU
Investment in S Ltd (at fair value)	9 000	7 600

The transactions above reflect a business combination achieved in stages. The acquisition date is the date when P Ltd acquired a controlling interest in S Ltd, which is 31 December 20x4. Thus, in the group financial statements, the investment in S Ltd should be consolidated from this date.

What is the goodwill (or bargain purchase gain) to be recognised at the acquisition date (31 December 20x4)?

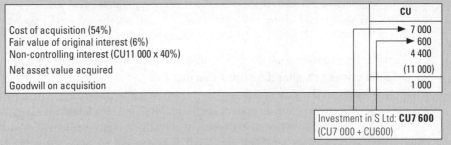

	CU
Cost of acquisition (54%)	7 000
Fair value of original interest (6%)	600
Non-controlling interest (CU11 000 x 40%)	4 400
Net asset value acquired	(11 000)
Goodwill on acquisition	1 000

Investment in S Ltd: **CU7 600**
(CU7 000 + CU600)

In the group financial statements, P Ltd is deemed to have 'sold' its investment in the financial instrument (the shareholding of 6% in S Ltd) and acquired a controlling interest in the subsidiary.

What *pro-forma* journal entries are required to consolidate S Ltd on 31 December 20x5?

			CU	CU
Dr		Gain on fair value adjustment (OCI)	1 400	
	Cr	Investment in S Ltd		1 400

Reversal of fair value adjustment in separate financial statements of P Ltd

What is this?
The parent recognises its investment in S Ltd at fair value in its separate financial statements. In the group financial statements, the fair value adjustments after the acquisition date are eliminated.

			CU	CU
Dr		Share capital	1 000	
Dr		Retained earnings	10 000	
Dr		Goodwill	1 000	
	Cr	Investment in S Ltd		7 600
	Cr	Non-controlling interest (equity) (CU11 000 × 40%)		4 400

Elimination of equity as at the date of acquisition of controlling interest (31 December 20x5)

			CU	CU
Dr		Non-controlling interest (P/L) (CU2 000 × 40% = CU800)	800	
	Cr	Non-controlling interest (equity)		800

Allocation of current year post-acquisition profits to the non-controlling interest

Note that the subsidiary is consolidated at the acquisition date, which is 31 December 20x4. This means that from this date, the assets and liabilities, income and expenses of the subsidiary are included in the group financial statements. When preparing the consolidated financial statements of the group at 31 December 20x5, the starting point is 100% of the parent's assets, liabilities and equity plus 100% of the subsidiary's assets, liabilities and equity balances. The above *pro-forma* journal entries result in a reversal of the fair value adjustment of the investment in the parent since the acquisition date, and then the elimination of the equity of the subsidiary at the acquisition date. 100% of the profit of the subsidiary in the current year (subsequent to the acquisition date) is included in the group's profit or loss and the appropriate portion, being 40% of this profit, is attributed to the non-controlling interest.

What if P Ltd decided to measure its investment in S Ltd at cost in its separate financial statements after the acquisition date?

In the example above, prior to the acquisition date of the subsidiary, P Ltd recognises the investment in S Ltd at fair value, in accordance with IFRS9, as it is a **financial asset** to P Ltd. Thus, P Ltd recognises the fair value adjustment of CU100 in other comprehensive income at 31 December 20x4. When, on 31 December 20x4, P Ltd acquired additional shares in S Ltd and S Ltd became a subsidiary, there is a change in circumstances. If P Ltd elects to account for the investment in S Ltd at cost in its separate financial statements (in accordance with IAS27), there will be no fair value adjustment in other comprehensive income in the separate financial statements of P Ltd. The investment is then recognised at CU7 600 (CU7 000 + CU 600). This means that the *pro-forma* journal entry eliminating the 20x5 fair value adjustment is not required.

4. Changes in ownership when control is maintained

IFRS principles

Changes in ownership

Changes in a parent's ownership interest in a subsidiary (refer to IFRS10: 23) that do not result in the parent losing control of the subsidiary are equity transactions (in other words, transactions with owners in their capacity as owners).

When the proportion of the equity held by non-controlling interests changes, an entity shall adjust the carrying amounts of the controlling and non-controlling interests to reflect the changes in their relative interests in the subsidiary. The entity shall recognise directly in equity any difference between the amount by which the non-controlling interests are adjusted and the fair value of the consideration paid or received, and attribute it to the owners of the parent (IFRS10: B96).

Where the parent **acquires additional shares** in the subsidiary subsequent to obtaining control, this transaction is not a business combination as the parent already has control of the subsidiary. As there is no new business combination, there is no adjustment to the identifiable assets and liabilities of the subsidiary to their respective fair values, and no remeasurement of goodwill.

Similarly, where the parent **sells shares in a subsidiary**, but **retains control**, there is no change in the group as an economic entity. The economic entity continues to exist, comprising of the parent and its subsidiary.

These changes in ownership interests are transactions amongst the different equity holders in their capacity as owners. They are accounted for as equity transactions and cannot give rise to gains or losses being recognised by the group as these transaction are merely 'transfers' within group equity.

In both of these cases, there are **changes in ownership interests** without the loss of control. When such transactions occur, the carrying amounts of the controlling interest and the non-controlling interest are adjusted to reflect the change in the respective ownership interests. As this is a transaction between the parent and non-controlling interest, these parties determine the **consideration to be paid**, based on an assessment of the fair value of the subsidiary. Any differences between the consideration paid or received by the parent to or from the non-controlling interest resulting from the acquisition or sale of the additional shares and the carrying amount of the relevant non-controlling interest in the subsidiary is recognised directly in equity.

Think about it

What is the gain or loss to be recognised in the parent's separate financial statements?

The parent recognises a gain or loss in its separate financial statements only when it has sold some of the shares it held (the investment) to other investors. The gain or loss is calculated as follows:

Gain/loss on disposal of shares = Consideration received – Carrying amount of the investment sold

What is the gain or loss to be recognised by the group?

The group does not recognise a gain or loss in profit or loss, but recognises a movement directly in equity. The movement can lead to an increase or a decrease in non-controlling interest's balance, depending on who acquired or disposed of shares in the transaction. This movement (equity transaction) is calculated as follows:

Equity transaction = Consideration received – Relative interest of non-controlling interest acquired or sold

The relative interest of non-controlling interest acquired or sold is based on the carrying amounts of the net assets of the subsidiary.

4.1 Acquisition of further interest with no change in control

When an entity (the subsidiary) is controlled, the acquisition of additional shares in the subsidiary does not change the group as an economic entity. The parent has acquired the additional shares in its subsidiary from another equity participant: the non-controlling shareholders. This means that the equity that was previously attributable to the non-controlling interest has now been acquired by the parent and is now attributable to the parent equity holders.

This transaction is **not** a business combination (as control already existed prior to this transaction). Therefore goodwill is not remeasured, and there is no gain or loss in the statement of profit or loss and other comprehensive income. This is a transaction between the owners in their capacity as owners and any gains or losses are recognised directly in equity through the group statement of changes in equity.

The following steps are appropriate:

1. The starting point (the parent's separate financial statements) has an increased shareholding and increased investment in the subsidiary than at the acquisition date.
2. Consolidate the subsidiary from the date on which control was acquired (the acquisition date). This means that the fair value of the net identifiable assets of the subsidiary, the amount attributable to non-controlling interest and goodwill, is determined at the acquisition date. This is eliminated against the original investment in the subsidiary when control was acquired.
3. Allocate its share of the post-acquisition equity of the subsidiary to the non-controlling interest up to the date on which additional shares are acquired.

4. At the date when additional shares were acquired, the parent acquired a greater interest in the subsidiary from the non-controlling interest. This will usually result in a decrease in non-controlling interest and an increase in the parent equity holders' interest.

5. The difference between the amount paid for the additional shares and the portion of the non-controlling interest acquired indicates whether the parent acquired these additional shares at an amount in excess of the net asset value at that date. This does not represent a gain or a loss in the group. Instead, this difference is recognised directly in equity.

Example

A parent increasing its shareholding in an existing subsidiary

On 1 January 20x4, P Ltd purchased a 70% shareholding in S Ltd for a total cash consideration of CU2.5m. This investment is a controlling interest in S Ltd. The fair value of the net assets of S Ltd at that date was CU3m. Non-controlling interest is measured at its attributable share of the net asset value of S Ltd at acquisition. P Ltd acquired an additional 10% in S Ltd for CU500 000 on 1 January 20x5, resulting in P Ltd holding an 80% controlling interest in S Ltd.

The equity of S Ltd was as follows at the respective dates:

	1 January 20x4 CU	31 December 20x4 CU
Share capital	100 000	100 000
Retained earnings	2 900 000	3 900 000
	3 000 000	4 000 000

No dividends were declared by S Ltd during 20x4.

The **investment in S Ltd** as recognised in the separate financial statements of P Ltd at 31 December 20x4 (the starting point) amounts to **CU3 000 000** (CU2 500 000 at acquisition and CU500 000 for the additional shares purchased).

At acquisition date, when control was acquired, the goodwill (or bargain purchase gain) to be recognised is as follows:

	CU
Investment in S Ltd: Cost of acquisition	2 500 000
Non-controlling interest (CU3 000 000 × 30%)	900 000
Net asset value acquired	(3 000 000)
Goodwill to be recognised on acquisition	400 000

The balance of non-controlling interest prior to P Ltd's additional investment is calculated as follows:

	CU
Non-controlling interest at acquisition date	900 000
Retained earnings since acquisition date	
(CU1 000 000 × 30%)	300 000
Non-controlling interest up to 31 December 20x4	1 200 000

Equity adjustment on acquisition of additional shareholding

	CU
Paid for additional 10% interest	500 000
Less: Non-controlling interest acquired (CU1 200 000/30% × 10%) or (CU4 000 000 × 10%)	(400 000)
Equity adjustment ('loss' on acquisition of additional shares)	100 000

The *pro-forma* journal entries required in the group financial statements of P Ltd for the financial year ending 31 December 20x4 are as follows:

			CU	CU
Dr		Share capital	100 000	
Dr		Retained earnings	2 900 000	
Dr		Goodwill	400 000 ◄	
	Cr	Investment in S Ltd		2 500 000 ◄
	Cr	Non-controlling interest (equity) (CU3m × 30%)		900 000

Elimination of equity as at the date of acquisition of controlling interest (1 January 20x4)

> **Pro-forma journal entry at acquisition date**
> Note that the investment (CU2 500 000) is eliminated at the acquisition date and goodwill of CU400 000 is recognised.

			CU	CU
Dr		Non-controlling interest (P/L) (CU1m × 30%)	300 000	
	Cr	Non-controlling interest (equity)		300 000

Allocation of current year post-acquisition profits to the non-controlling interest

			CU	CU
Dr		Non-controlling interest (equity) (CU4m × 10%)	400 000 ◄	
Dr		Loss on change in shareholding (equity)	100 000	
	Cr	Investment in S Ltd		500 000

Adjustment directly to equity for the additional 10% shareholding acquired

> **What is this?**
> The parent acquired a further 10% in B Ltd; this additional interest was acquired from the existing non-controlling interest. Non-controlling interest should therefore reduce by CU400 000.

In this case, P Ltd paid CU500 000 to acquire an additional 10% of S Ltd's equity, which at that date amounted to CU400 000, being CU4m × 10%. P Ltd has therefore incurred a loss at a group level, which is recognised directly in equity as it results from a transaction between shareholders.

Before and after the additional acquisition, S Ltd is a subsidiary of P Ltd as P Ltd owns more than 50% of the voting rights in S Ltd and is able to exercise control over S Ltd. Prior to the transaction in which P Ltd acquired an additional 10% of the shares in S Ltd, P Ltd owned 70% of S Ltd. After the transaction, P Ltd owned 80% of S Ltd. The non-controlling interest has therefore decreased its interest in S Ltd by selling shares to P Ltd in return for cash. This is effectively a transaction between P Ltd (as majority shareholder) and the non-controlling interest (as minority shareholders). The adjustment on the change in shareholding, therefore, does not meet the definition of income and must be recognised directly in equity (in other words, in the statement of changes in equity).

4.2 Partial disposal of interest with no change in control

If control is maintained, the disposal of some of the shares in the subsidiary does not change the group as an economic entity. The transaction involves the parent selling some of its shareholding in a subsidiary to other equity participants: the non-controlling shareholders. This means that the equity that was previously attributable to the parent equity holders is now attributable to the non-controlling interest. This is a transaction between the owners in their capacity as owners and any gains or losses are recognised directly in equity.

The following steps are appropriate:

1. The starting point (the parent's separate financial statements) has an investment in the subsidiary that is less than what it was at the acquisition date. Furthermore, the parent will have recognised a profit or loss on the disposal of these shares and this may have tax implications for the parent entity.
2. Consolidate the subsidiary from the date on which control was acquired (the acquisition date). This means that the fair value of the net identifiable assets of the subsidiary, the amount attributable to non-controlling interest and goodwill, are determined at the acquisition date as before. This is eliminated against the original investment in the subsidiary when control was acquired.
3. Allocate its share of the post-acquisition equity of the subsidiary to the non-controlling interest up to the date on which some of the shares are disposed of.
4. At the date on which some of the shares are sold by the parent, the non-controlling interest usually increases as a result of the sale. This means an increase in non-controlling interest and a decrease in the parent equity holders' interest.
5. The difference between the amount received for the sale of some of the shares and the increase in the non-controlling interest may result in either a gain or a loss in the group. This does not represent a profit or loss in the group and this difference is recognised directly in equity, including any taxation implications.

Example

A parent sells some of its shareholding in a subsidiary, but retains control

P Ltd acquired 60% of the ordinary shares in S Ltd on 30 June 20x4 for a cash consideration of CU2 500, when the share capital of S Ltd amounted to CU1 000 and its retained earnings amounted to CU3 000. All of the assets and liabilities of S Ltd were considered fairly valued at that date. The non-controlling interest was measured at its proportionate share of the net assets of S Ltd at the acquisition date.

The trial balance of S Ltd for the financial year ended 31 December 20x5, which is the financial year end of S Ltd and P Ltd (and the P Ltd group), is presented below.

S Ltd	Debit CU	Credit CU
Ordinary share capital (CU1 par value)		1 000
Retained earnings (1 January 20x5)		10 000
Profit after tax		2 400
Property, plant and equipment	10 400	
Current assets	4 000	
Current liabilities	–	1 000
	14 400	14 400

P Ltd accounts for its investment in S Ltd on the cost basis in its separate annual financial statements. P Ltd sold 10% of its shareholding in S Ltd on 31 December 20x5 for a cash consideration of CU900.

Number of shares in S Ltd sold by P Ltd

Total number of shares issued by S Ltd by 31 December 20x5	1 000
Total number acquired by P Ltd (1 000 × 60%) prior to sale of shares	600
Number of shares sold by P Ltd (600 × 10%)	60

Note that P Ltd sold '10% of **its** shareholding'. This is the same as saying that P Ltd sold '6% of the total number of shares in S Ltd'.

S Ltd is a subsidiary of P Ltd from the date on which P Ltd acquired its controlling interest (30 June 20x5). P Ltd sold 10% of its shareholding in S Ltd (in other words, 10% of 60% = 6% of the total issued shares of S Ltd) to other shareholders (non-controlling interest) on 31 December 20x5. As P Ltd retained a **54% controlling interest** in S Ltd, S Ltd remains a subsidiary in the P Ltd group.

What entries are recorded in P Ltd's separate annual financial statements?

	CU
Proceeds received on sale of 10% of the shareholding in S Ltd	900
Less: Carrying amount of investment sold (CU2 500 × 10%) Note: The carrying amount of the investment on the date of sale is the original cost (as per P Ltd's accounting policy) of the investment.	(250)
Profit on sale of shares	650

P Ltd would have processed the following journal entry in its separate accounting records:

			CU	CU
Dr		Bank	900	
	Cr	Investment in S Ltd		250
	Cr	Profit on sale of shares (P/L)		650

Recognition of sale of shares

Note that the **carrying amount of the investment in S Ltd** as recognised in the separate financial statements of P Ltd at 31 December 20x5 amounts to **CU2 250** (CU2 500 – CU250).

Analysis of equity of S Ltd

	Total CU	At acquisition 60% CU	Since acquisition 60%/54% CU	Non-controlling interest 40%/46% CU
At acquisition (30 June 20x4):				
Share capital	1 000			
Retained earnings	3 000			
Total equity at acquisition date	4 000	2 400		1 600
Investment in S Ltd at 30 June 20x4		2 500		
Goodwill		100		
Since acquisition date (1 July 20x4 – 31 December 20x4):				
Retained earnings (10 000 – 3 000)	7 000		4 200	2 800
Current year profit	2 400		1 440	960
	13 400		5 640	5 360
Sale of 6% interest to non-controlling shareholders			(804)	804
	13 400		4 836	6 164

The non-controlling interest has increased from 40% to 46%.
CU13 400 × 46% = CU6 164

What is the required equity adjustment as a result of the sale of the 10% shareholding in the group?

		CU
Proceeds received on sale of 10% of the shareholding in S Ltd		900
Less: Net asset value sold	(13 400 × 6%)	(804)
Prior to the sale, S Ltd was a 60%-held subsidiary. After the sale, S Ltd is a 54%-held subsidiary. From a group's perspective, P Ltd has therefore disposed of 6% of the net assets of S Ltd (that it previously controlled.)		
Equity adjustment ('profit' on disposal of shares)		96

What about goodwill?

Goodwill arises and is recognised as a separate asset because of control. Control has, however, not been lost as S Ltd is still a subsidiary after the sale of the shares. As the goodwill relates to P Ltd's 60% shareholding in S Ltd and as P Ltd will now only share in 54% of S Ltd's equity, the goodwill needs to be tested for impairment.

Pro-forma journal entries

Both before and after the sale of shares, S Ltd is a subsidiary of P Ltd as P Ltd owns more than 50% of the voting rights in S Ltd. The starting point for the preparation of the group annual financial statements of P Ltd for the 20x5 financial year is therefore 100% of P Ltd and 100% of S Ltd.

			CU	CU
Dr		Share capital	1 000	
Dr		Retained earnings	3 000	
Dr		Goodwill	100	
	Cr	Investment in S Ltd		2 500◄
	Cr	Non-controlling interests (equity)		1 600

Elimination of equity of S Ltd as at date of acquisition

> Note that the carrying amount of the investment in S Ltd as recognised in the separate financial statements of P Ltd at 31 December 20x5 amounts to **CU2 250** (CU2 500 – CU250).

			CU	CU
Dr		Retained earnings (CU7 000 × 40%)	2 800	
	Cr	Non-controlling interests (equity)		2 800

Allocation of prior year post-acquisition profits to non-controlling interest

			CU	CU
Dr		Non-controlling interests (P/L) (CU2 400 × 40%)	960	
	Cr	Non-controlling interests (equity)		960

Allocation of current profits to non-controlling interest

			CU	CU
Dr		Profit on sale (P/L)	650	
Dr		Investment in S Ltd	250	◄
	Cr	Non-controlling interests (equity)		804 ►
	Cr	Equity adjustment (equity)		96

Recognition of group profit on sale

> The non-controlling interest has increased from 40% to 46%.

Note that these *pro-forma* journal entries are based on the position at the acquisition date of 30 June 20x4. S Ltd was a 60%-held subsidiary as at 31 December 20x4 and for the 20x5 financial year (up until 31 December 20x5). Consequently, the non-controlling interest shared in 40% of S Ltd's post-acquisition profits and other reserves for those periods.

Prior to the sale of the shares, P Ltd owned 60% of S Ltd. After the sale of the shares, P Ltd owned 54% of S Ltd. P Ltd has therefore sold 6% of S Ltd's shares to the non-controlling interest. In other words, the non-controlling interest has increased its share of S Ltd (by paying P Ltd and acquiring an additional shareholding in S Ltd).

This is effectively a transaction between P Ltd and a class of equity holders that has increased the net assets of the group (profit on sale of shares at a group level), but has resulted in an additional contribution by the non-controlling interest (by paying P Ltd and acquiring an additional shareholding in S Ltd). The group profit on sale therefore does not meet the definition of income and must be recognised directly in equity as an equity adjustment.

 Think about it

Disposal of partial interest

When the parent sells a portion of its interest in a subsidiary, but retains control, from the group's perspective this represents a transaction between equity holders. Consolidation of that subsidiary should continue and the change in equity holding in the subsidiary is recorded in equity.

However, this is not the case when the parent sells a portion of its interest in a subsidiary and control is lost. In this case, from a group's perspective, the controlling interest is 'sold' and the subsidiary should no longer be consolidated (see Section 5).

What will be the tax implications when control is not lost?

If P Ltd is not a share dealer, P Ltd would pay capital gains tax when the investment was sold (depending on the tax legislation). Assuming a capital gains tax inclusion rate of 66.6% and a normal tax rate of 28%, the current tax expense in profit or loss of P Ltd amounts to CU121 (CU900 − CU250 = CU650 × 66.6% × 28%).

P Ltd would, therefore, have processed the following as part of its tax expense in its separate annual financial statements:

			CU	CU
Dr		Current tax expense (P/L)	121	
	Cr	Tax payable to the tax authority		121

Recognition of current tax expense

The following additional *pro-forma* journal entry (for the 20x5 financial year) is therefore required:

			CU	CU
Dr		Equity adjustment (equity)	121	
	Cr	Current tax expense (P/L)		121

Recognition of current tax expense directly in equity

The tax relating to the equity adjustment is recognised directly in equity.

5. Loss of control

Control is lost when the parent sells all or sufficient shares in the subsidiary, resulting in it not being able to control more than 50% of the voting rights in the subsidiary (assuming control is determined based on voting rights). However, there are a number of reasons that a parent may lose control, including the following:

- The parent may sell shares in the subsidiary such that another entity has the controlling interest.
- There may be a change in the 'spread' of the holding of shares by the different investors, resulting in a situation where a parent has less than a 50% voting right and thus loses control.
- A subsidiary may become subject to the control of a government, court, administrator or regulator.
- There may be a change in a contractual arrangement.

5.1 Disposal of interest when control is lost

When a parent sells its entire interest in a subsidiary, the parent recognises a profit on the disposal of its investment in the shares of the subsidiary. The profit recognised in the group financial statements is not the same as the profit in the separate financial statements of the parent. The parent would have recognised the investment in the subsidiary in its separate financial statements at cost or at fair value (see discussion in earlier sections). In the group financial statements, selling the subsidiary means that all of the assets and liabilities of the subsidiary are derecognised as the group no longer controls them.

When a parent loses control of a subsidiary, it should **derecognise** the assets and liabilities, including any related goodwill of the subsidiary at their carrying amounts on the date when control is lost and the carrying amounts of any non-controlling interest in the former subsidiary. The parent no longer controls the assets and liabilities of the former subsidiary, so consolidation is no longer appropriate.

The process of consolidation requires, as the starting point, that 100% of the subsidiary's assets and liabilities be added to those of the parent. In this case, as there is no subsidiary, the assets and liabilities of the subsidiary are **not included in the starting point**. However, the group's share of the profits of the subsidiary since the acquisition date until the date on which control was lost must be included in the group financial statements. This is achieved through the use of *pro-forma* journal entries.

Example

Sale of entire interest in subsidiary

P Ltd purchased 90% of the shares in S Ltd on 1 January 20x3 for a cash consideration of CU9.2m. At that date, the fair value of the net identifiable assets of S Ltd was CU8m and non-controlling interest was measured at its fair value of CU1m. P Ltd measures the investment in S Ltd at cost in its separate financial statements.

S Ltd earned the following profits after tax subsequent to the acquisition date:

- Year ended 31 December 20x3: CU400 000
- Year ended 31 December 20x4: CU800 000
- Year ended 31 December 20x5: CU600 000 (earned evenly over the year).

P Ltd sold its entire shareholding in S Ltd on 30 June 20x5 for CU12m. The current reporting date is 31 December 20x5.

For the year ended 31 December 20x5, what is the profit on disposal of the interest in S Ltd to be recognised in the separate financial statements of P Ltd?

The carrying amount of the investment in S Ltd immediately prior to the disposal amounted to CU9.2m (measured at cost in the separate financial statements of P Ltd). P Ltd sold this investment for proceeds of CU12m and therefore recognised a profit on the disposal of the investment of CU2.8m.

P Ltd records the following journal entry in its separate financial statements on 30 June 20x5:

			CU	CU
Dr		Bank	12 000 000	
	Cr	Investment in S Ltd		9 200 000
	Cr	Profit on disposal of investment (P/L)		2 800 000

For the year ended 31 December 20x5, what is the profit on disposal of the interest in S Ltd to be recognised in the group financial statements of P Ltd?

The profit on disposal of the interest in S Ltd as it would be included in the notes to the group financial statements of P Ltd for the year ended 31 December 20x5 can be calculated as follows:

	CU
Proceeds from sale of controlling interest	12 000 000
Net assets disposed of (w1)	(9 500 000)
From a group's perspective, P Ltd has disposed of the net assets of S Ltd (that it previously controlled)	
Goodwill derecognised (w2)	(2 200 000)
As per above, by selling its shareholding in S Ltd, P Ltd has also sold the related goodwill that arose at a group level	
Non-controlling interest derecognised (w3)	1 150 000
There is no longer any non-controlling interest at a group level	
Group profit on disposal of subsidiary	**1 450 000**

(w1): CU8 000 000 + 400 000 + 800 000 + 300 000 (six months' only) = CU9 500 000
(w2): (CU9 200 000 + CU1 000 000) − CU8 000 000 = CU2 200 000
(w3): CU1 000 000 + [(400 000 + 800 000 + 300 000) × 10%] = CU1 150 000

What *pro-forma* journal entries are required for the year ended 31 December 20x5?

As S Ltd is no longer a subsidiary, its assets and liabilities, income and expenses are not included in the starting point. This makes sense as P Ltd no longer controls the assets and liabilities of S Ltd. However, as P Ltd sold its controlling interest in S Ltd on 30 June 20x5, the income and expenses for the period 1 January 20x5 until 30 June 20x5 (up to when control was lost) are attributable to the shareholders of P Ltd based on P Ltd's ownership interest in S Ltd. Similarly, the comparative figures, including opening retained earnings (in the group statement of changes in equity), should include the profits of S Ltd after the original acquisition date until the date on which control was lost.

The *pro-forma* journal entries for the year ended 31 December 20x5 therefore recognise the attributable retained earnings in S Ltd after the acquisition date and the parent's share of the profits of S Ltd in the current year. The result is adjusted against the profit recognised on disposal in the parent's separate financial statements, as follows:

			CU	CU
Dr		Profit on disposal of investment (P/L)	2 800 000	
	Cr	Retained earnings (since acquisition date) (w4)		1 080 000
	Cr	Profit for current period (w5) ①		270 000
	Cr	Profit on disposal of subsidiary (P/L) (as above)		1 450 000

(w4): CU400 000 + 800 000 = CU1 200 000 × 90% = CU1 080 000
(w5): CU600 000 × 6/12 = CU300 000 × 90% = CU270 000

The profit in the separate financial statements of P Ltd is eliminated and replaced in the group financial statements with the group's share of the profits of the subsidiary from the acquisition date until the date on which control was lost. The difference is the group profit on the sale of the subsidiary.

① Note that as S Ltd was a subsidiary during the 20x5 financial year, the group profit or loss must include the **consolidated line items** of S Ltd for that period. These are accounted for using a *pro-forma* journal entry. As P Ltd only owned 90% of S Ltd, some of the current year profits are attributable to the non-controlling interest. These entries are not shown in this example, but the net effect of these entries is the credit to current year profit of CU270 000 (CU300 000 profit after tax less the amount attributable to non-controlling interest of CU30 000).

Think about it

Why are there no *pro-forma* journal entries relating to goodwill and non-controlling interest?

As S Ltd is no longer a subsidiary, goodwill should not be recognised. There is also no non-controlling interest. You can test this by first bringing all of the assets and liabilities of the subsidiary into account, and then derecognising them as the subsidiary has been sold. The overall effect is the same.

Think about it

What are the tax implications relating to the sale of the subsidiary?

In its separate financial statements, P Ltd will recognise a **current tax expense**. Depending on the tax legislation in its country of registration, this is likely to be at the capital gains tax inclusion rate of 66.6%. Thus P Ltd will recognise a current tax expense amounting to CU522 144 (CU2 800 000 × 28% × 66.6%) in profit and loss.

The group financial statements will recognise a profit amounting to CU1 450 000 on the sale of its subsidiary. Based on the assumption that the group is **not** a tax entity, the difference between the profit in the group financial statements and the profit in the separate financial statements, amounting to CU1 350 000, will result in a **deferred tax expense reversal** (credit) in the group statement of comprehensive income.

This makes sense as previous deferred tax liabilities resulting from the fair value adjustments of the net assets in the group will be reversed when the group sells these net assets.

Think about it

What *pro-forma* journal entries are required in the following financial year (in other words, 31 December 20x6)?

In the following financial year (that is, 31 December 20x6), there will be no *pro-forma* journal entries relating to S Ltd as S Ltd is not a subsidiary. The group share of post-acquisition profits of S Ltd, together with the group profit on the disposal of S Ltd, is equal to the profit on disposal recognised by P Ltd in its separate financial statements. The retained earnings is therefore correct and no adjustments are required.

5.2 Partial disposal of interest and control is lost

As discussed above, when an investor loses control, the investee is no longer a subsidiary and consolidation is not appropriate. Similarly, a partial disposal of an investment in a subsidiary that results in the loss of control triggers a remeasurement of the residual holding to fair value. Any difference between the fair value and the carrying amount of the investment is a gain or loss on the disposal of a subsidiary, and is recognised in the investor's (the parent's) profit or loss. Thereafter, the remaining investment is recognised as an investment in associate, a joint arrangement or a financial asset, depending on the nature of the investment.

IFRS principles

Loss of control

If a parent loses control of a subsidiary (refer to IFRS10: B98), it shall:
- Derecognise:
  - The assets (including any goodwill) and liabilities of the subsidiary at their carrying amounts at the date when control is lost
  - The carrying amount of any non-controlling interests in the former subsidiary at the date when control is lost (including any components of other comprehensive income attributable to them).
- Recognise:
  - The fair value of the consideration received, if any, from the transaction, event or circumstances that resulted in the loss of control
  - If the transaction, event or circumstances that resulted in the loss of control involves a distribution of shares of the subsidiary to owners in their capacity as owners, that distribution
  - Any investment retained in the former subsidiary at its fair value at the date when control is lost.
- Reclassify to profit or loss, or transfer directly to retained earnings if required by other IFRSs, the amounts recognised in other comprehensive income in relation to the subsidiary on the basis described in paragraph B99.
- Recognise any resulting difference as a gain or loss in profit or loss attributable to the parent.

Example

A parent decreasing its shareholding in a subsidiary, resulting in a loss of control

P Ltd acquired 60% of the ordinary shares in S Ltd on 30 June 20x4 for a cash consideration of CU5 000, when the share capital of S Ltd amounted to CU1 000 and its retained earnings amounted to CU3 000. All of the assets and liabilities of S Ltd were considered fairly valued at that date. The non-controlling interest was measured at its proportionate share of the net assets of S Ltd at the acquisition date.

P Ltd sold 60% of its shareholding in S Ltd on 30 June 20x5 for cash of CU10 000, with the effect that P Ltd's shareholding in S Ltd was reduced to 24%. At that date, a 24% shareholding in S Ltd had a fair value of CU6 000. P Ltd accounts for its investment in S Ltd on the cost basis in its separate annual financial statements. The fair value of the remaining investment in S Ltd amounted to CU7 500 at 31 December 20x5.

The trial balance of S Ltd for the financial year ended 31 December 20x5, which is the financial year end of S Ltd and P Ltd (and the P Ltd group), is presented below:

	S Ltd	
	Debit	Credit
	CU	CU
Ordinary share capital	–	1 000
Retained earnings (1 January 20x5)	–	10 000
Sales	–	8 000
Cost of sales	2 000	–
Operating costs	2 000	–
Taxation expense	1 120	–
Property, plant and equipment	10 000	–
Current assets	4 880	–
Current liabilities	–	1 000
	20 000	**20 000**

From the trial balance above, the profit after tax of S Ltd for the current year amounts to CU2 880. Based on the assumption that all profit or loss items of S Ltd arose evenly throughout the 20x5 financial year, the net asset value (total equity) of S Ltd at the date when P Ltd lost control (in other words, 30 June 20x5) amounted to **CU12 440** (CU1 000 + CU10 000 + [CU2 880 × 6/12]).

How many shares in S Ltd were sold by P Ltd and what is the interest that P Ltd retained?

Total number of shares as issued by S Ltd	1 000
Total number acquired by P Ltd (1 000 × 60%)	600
Number of shares sold by P Ltd (600 × 60%)	(360)
Number of shares retained by P Ltd (600 × 40%)	240 ◄

> Note that S Ltd is no longer a subsidiary of P Ltd. P Ltd now has a **24%** interest in S Ltd.

What is the appropriate accounting treatment of the remainder of the shares in S Ltd retained by P Ltd?

- If P Ltd is able to exert significant influence over the decision-making of S Ltd, then S Ltd is an associate. In this case, P Ltd will prepare group financial statements and account for the investment in S Ltd using the equity method.

- If P Ltd is not able to exert significant influence, P Ltd's investment should be recognised as a **financial asset** and accounted for in accordance with IFRS9.

What is the profit on sale of the investment in S Ltd that would be recognised in the separate financial statements of P Ltd for the year ended 31 December 20x5?

	CU
Proceeds	10 000
Less: Carrying amount of investment sold Carrying amount on the date of sale equals the original cost (as per P Ltd's accounting policy), in other words, CU5 000 × 60%.	(3 000)
Profit on sale	7 000

P Ltd processes the following journal entry in its separate financial statements on 30 June 20x5:

			CU	CU
Dr		Bank	10 000	
	Cr	Investment in S Ltd		3 000
	Cr	Profit on sale of shares (P/L)		7 000

Recognising profit on disposal of investment in subsidiary, S Ltd

Assume that after the sale of the shares, P Ltd has an investment in a **financial asset** (as P Ltd does not have significant influence) and recognises the investment at fair value, with fair value adjustments recognised in profit or loss (in accordance with IFRS9):

			CU	CU
Dr		Investment in S Ltd	4 000	
	Cr	Gain on fair value adjustment (P/L) (w1)		4 000

Recognition of investment in financial asset at fair value at 30 June 20x5

(w1): CU6 000 less carrying amount of CU2 000 (CU5 000 original cost less cost of portion sold of CU3 000)

And again at 31 December 20x5 (note that these journal entries can be combined):

			CU	CU
Dr		Investment in S Ltd	1 500	
	Cr	Gain on fair value adjustment (P/L) (w2)		1 500

Recognition of investment in financial asset at fair value at 31 December 20x5

(w2): CU7 500 less carrying amount of CU6 000 at 30 June 20x5

What is the carrying amount of the investment in S Ltd in the separate financial statements of P Ltd at 31 December 20x5?

Non-current assets

	31 December 20x5 CU	31 December 20x4 CU
Investment in financial asset: S Ltd (at fair value)	7 500	
Investment in subsidiary (at cost)		5 000

What is the profit on sale of the investment in the subsidiary, S Ltd, to be recognised in the group financial statements of P Ltd for the year ended 31 December 20x5?

		CU
Proceeds received for 36% interest sold on 30 June 20x5		CU10 000
Fair value of 24% retained interest at 30 June 20x5		6 000
Less: Net asset value sold at 30 June 20x5	①	(12 440)
From a group's perspective, P Ltd has therefore disposed of the net assets of S Ltd (that it previously controlled)		
As S Ltd is no longer a subsidiary, the non-controlling interest is derecognised (CU12 440 × 40%)		4 976 ◀
Less: Goodwill derecognised	②	(2 600)
Group profit on sale of subsidiary		**CU5 936**

① The **net asset value** (total equity) of S Ltd at the date on which P Ltd lost control (that is, 30 June 20x5) was as follows:

	100% CU
Share capital	1 000
Retained earnings at acquisition date	3 000
Fair value of net identifiable assets at acquisition date	4 000
Post-acquisition retained earnings (10 000 – 3 000)	7 000
Profit after tax for six months (2 880 × 6/12)	1 440
Net asset value on 30 June 20x5	▶ 12 440

> **What is the non-controlling interest in S Ltd at the date when control is lost?**
> CU12 440 × 40% = **CU4 976**

② **Goodwill** at the acquisition date amounted to:

	CU	CU
Cost of acquisition (60%)	5 000	
Non-controlling interest at acquisition date (40%)	1 600	6 600
Fair value of net identifiable assets at acquisition date		(4 000)
Goodwill on acquisition		2 600

What *pro-forma* journal entries are required for the year ended 31 December 20x5?

As S Ltd is no longer a subsidiary, its assets and liabilities, income and expenses are not included in the starting point when preparing consolidated financial statements. This makes sense as P Ltd no longer controls the assets and liabilities of S Ltd. However, as P Ltd sold its controlling interest in S Ltd on 30 June 20x5, the income and expenses for the period 1 January 20x5 until 30 June 20x5 (up to when control was lost) should be included in the group statement of profit or loss.

			CU	CU
Dr		Cost of sales (2 000 × 6/12)	1 000	
Dr		Operating costs (2 000 × 6/12)	1 000	
Dr		Taxation expense (1 120 × 6/12)	560	
Dr		Profit after tax in S Ltd ③	864◄	
Dr		Non-controlling interest (P/L) (CU1 440 × 40%)	576◄	
	Cr	Sales (8 000 × 6/12)		4 000

Consolidation of S Ltd's profit or loss for the six months until 30 June 20x5, when control is lost, and allocation of appropriate portion of current year profit in S Ltd to non-controlling interest

> **What is this?**
> S Ltd's profit for current year until control is lost = **CU1 440**.
> P Ltd's share: CU864 (60%)
> Non-controlling interest: CU576 (40%)

③ As S Ltd is not a subsidiary at 31 December 20x5, S Ltd's trial balance is not included in the starting point. This entry recognises the line items until control is lost. The balance is the group's share of the profit of S Ltd (CU1 440 × 60% = CU864), with the corresponding contra in the *pro-forma* journal entries that follow.

The *pro-forma* journal entries for the year ended 31 December 20x5 should recognise retained earnings in S Ltd since the acquisition date, allocate the appropriate portion to non-controlling interest and eliminate the parent's share of the profits on disposal of S Ltd, as follows:

			CU	CU
Dr		Profit on sale of shares	7 000	
Dr		Fair value gain on financial asset	4 000	
	Cr	Retained earnings (since acquisition date) ④		4 200
	Cr	Profit for current period ③		864
	Cr	Profit on disposal of subsidiary (as above)		5 936

Recognising group's share in retained earnings and current year profit of the subsidiary up to the date when control is lost

④ The group's share of the retained earnings of S Ltd after the acquisition date until the beginning of the current year amounts to CU10 000 – CU3 000 = CU7 000 × 60% = CU4 200. This amount needs to be credited (added) to retained earnings as the assets, liabilities and equity of S Ltd are not included in the starting point.

As P Ltd sold its entire shareholding in S Ltd on 30 June 20x5, our starting point for the preparation of the group annual financial statements for the 20x5 financial year is 100% of P Ltd and 0% of S Ltd.

However, S Ltd was a subsidiary during the 20x5 financial year, so the group profit or loss must include the consolidated line items of S Ltd for that period. We need to bring these amounts into the consolidated financial statements through a *pro-forma* journal entry.

As P Ltd only owned 60% of S Ltd, 40% of the prior year profits of S Ltd are attributable to the non-controlling interest.

> **What is this?**
> S Ltd was a subsidiary in the 20x4 financial year, thus the group's retained earnings as at 31 December 20x4 should include P Ltd's share of the post-acquisition retained earnings of S Ltd.

> **What is this?**
> As the group now has an investment in a financial asset, the investment should be recognised at fair value in the group financial statements at 31 December 20x5, in accordance with IFRS9.

Check your answer

Extract from a consolidation worksheet

Dr/(Cr)	P Ltd (starting point) CU	Pro-forma journals CU	Group (end point) CU
Investment in S Ltd	7 500		7 500 ◄
Retained earnings of subsidiary		► (4 200)	(4 200)
Profit or loss:			
Profit on sale of shares	(7 000)	7 000	–
Profit on disposal of subsidiary		(5 936)	(5 936)
Share of profit of subsidiary for six months:			
Sales		(4 000)	(4 000)
Cost of sales		1 000	1 000
Operating costs		1 000	1 000
Taxation expense		560	560
Non-controlling interest in P/L		576	576
Fair value gain on financial asset	(4 000) (1 500)	4 000	– (1 500)

What if, after selling 60% of its interest in S Ltd, P Ltd had significant influence over S Ltd through its remaining 24% interest?

S Ltd would be classified as an associate and group financial statements should be prepared in which the investment in S Ltd is equity accounted. Equity accounting the investment will require the following *pro-forma* journal entries to be processed:

		CU	CU
Dr	Investment in S Ltd	345.6	
	Cr	Share of profits of associate (P/L)		345.6

Profit of S Ltd for the period 1 July to 31 December 20x5 amounts to CU1 440 (see above). P Ltd's share of the profits of the associate since its acquisition date amounts to CU345.6 (CU1 440 × 24%).

The fair value adjustment in the separate financial statements of P Ltd at 31 December 20x5 should be reversed via the following *pro-forma* journal entry:

		CU	CU
Dr	Fair value gain (P/L)	1 500	
	Cr	Investment in S Ltd		1 500

The carrying amount of the investment in S Ltd in the group financial statements at 31 December 20x5 amounts to CU6 345.6 (CU6 000 + CU345.6).

Think about it

What if the group policy is to apply the revaluation model to its owner-occupied land?

If S Ltd owned land, the land would have been revalued in the group financial statements as the group should apply similar accounting policies for similar transactions (refer to IFRS10: 19). When S Ltd is no longer a subsidiary, the group no longer controls the assets and liabilities of the subsidiary, thus, in the group, these assets are derecognised.

A revaluation surplus amounting to the group's share of the revaluation of the land in S Ltd after the acquisition date would have been recognised in the group financial statements in accordance with IAS16, which permits a company (or group) a number of options when accounting for a revaluation surplus:

- It can be released to retained earnings as the underlying asset is depreciated.
- It can be realised when the underlying asset is disposed of.
- The amount can remain in equity without being transferred to retained earnings.

As a non-depreciable asset, land is realised through sale, and the related revaluation reserve may be 'realised' when the land is sold, depending on the group's policy.

If the group policy were to release the revaluation surplus on sale of the underlying asset, a *pro-forma* journal entry (at the after-tax amount, attributable to the parent equity holders ①) would be processed as follows:

			CU	CU
Dr		Revaluation surplus (equity)	①	
	Cr	Retained earnings (equity)		①

This makes sense as, from the group's perspective, the land has been sold and the revaluation surplus relating to S Ltd's land is then released to retained earnings.

What will be the tax implications when control is lost?

Assuming that P Ltd is not a share dealer, P Ltd would be liable for capital gains tax when the investment was sold (depending on the applicable tax legislation). Assuming a capital gains tax inclusion rate of 66.6% and a normal tax rate of 28%, the current tax expense in profit or loss of P Ltd amounts to CU1 305 (CU10 000 – CU3 000 = CU7 000 × 66.6% × 28%).

P Ltd would therefore have processed the following as part of its tax expense in its separate annual financial statements:

			CU	CU
Dr		Current tax expense (P/L)	1 305	
	Cr	Tax payable to tax authority (L)		1 305

Recognition of current tax expense

The group financial statements recognise a profit amounting to CU5 936 on the sale of its subsidiary. The difference between the profit in the group financial statements and the profit in the separate financial statements, amounting to CU1 064, results in a net **deferred tax expense reversal** (credit) in the group statement of profit or loss. This makes sense as previous deferred tax liabilities resulting from the fair value adjustments of the net assets in the group will be reversed when the group sells the net assets of S Ltd.

6. Disclosure of new acquisitions and disposals of subsidiaries

The disclosures relating to changes in ownership interests comprise the requirements included in IFRS3, *Business Combinations*, and IFRS12, *Disclosure of Interests in Other Entities*. The disclosure requirements included in IFRS12 emphasise the ability of users of financial statements to evaluate the nature of and the risks associated with the group's interests in other entities as well as the effects of those interests on the group's financial statements.

IFRS update

Disclosure where there are changes in ownership interest that do not result in a loss of control (IFRS12: 18)

An entity shall present a schedule that shows the effects on the equity attributable to owners of the parent of any changes in its ownership interest in a subsidiary that do not result in a loss of control.

IFRS update

Disclosure where a parent loses control of a subsidiary (IFRS 12: 19)

An entity shall disclose the gain or loss, if any, calculated in accordance with IFRS10: 25 and:
- The portion of that gain or loss attributable to measuring any investment retained in the forma subsidiary at its fair value at the date when control is lost
- The line item or items in profit or loss in which the gain or loss is recognised (if not presented separately).

In addition to the disclosure of changes in ownership, the investor is required to disclose information that enables users of its financial statements to evaluate the **nature** and **financial effect** of a **business combination** that has occurred either during the current reporting period or after the end of the period, but before the financial statements are authorised for issue (refer to IFRS3: 59). Among the disclosures required to meet the foregoing objective are the following (as set out in IFRS3: B64–66):
- Name and a description of the investee

- Acquisition date
- Percentage of voting equity interests acquired
- Primary reasons for the business combination and a description of how the investor obtained control of the investee
- Description of the factors that make up the goodwill recognised
- Qualitative description of the factors that make up the goodwill recognised, such as expected synergies from combining operations or intangible assets that do not qualify for separate recognition
- Acquisition-date fair value of the total consideration transferred and the acquisition-date fair value of each major class of consideration
- Details of contingent consideration arrangements and indemnification assets
- Details of acquired receivables
- The amounts recognised as of the acquisition date for each major class of assets acquired and liabilities assumed
- Details of contingent liabilities recognised
- Total amount of goodwill that is expected to be deductible for tax purposes
- Details of any transactions that are recognised separately from the acquisition of assets and assumption of liabilities in the business combination
- Information about a bargain purchase ('negative goodwill')

For each business combination in which the investor holds less than 100% of the equity interests in the investee at the acquisition date, the following disclosures are required:
- Details about a business combination achieved in stages
- Information about the investee's revenue and profit or loss
- Information about a business combination whose acquisition date is after the end of the reporting period, but before the financial statements are authorised for issue.

Test your knowledge

There is a list of learning objectives at the beginning of this chapter. Go back to this list and check whether you have achieved these outcomes. If not, reread the appropriate section.

Questions

In all of the questions below, assume that one share = one vote.

Question 1
P Ltd owns 30% of A Ltd as of 1 January 20x1 and acquires an additional 30% of A Ltd on 1 July 20x5. P Ltd (company) and A Ltd (company) earn after-tax profits of CU500 000 and CU300 000 respectively, evenly during their respective financial years ended 31 December 20x5. P Ltd and A Ltd each declare an ordinary dividend of CU100 000 and CU40 000 respectively on 31 December 20x5.

You are required to do the following:
Calculate the following amounts for the 31 December 20x5 financial year as they should appear in the P Ltd group statement of profit or loss:
1. Earnings from associate
2. Non-controlling interest.

Suggested solution

1. Earnings from associate: CU300 000 × 6/12 × 30% = **CU45 000**.
2. Non-controlling interest: CU300 000 × 6/12 × 40% = **CU60 000**.

Question 2

The following information relates to the reporting period ended 31 December 20x5:

	P Ltd CU	A Ltd CU
Profit after tax	500 000	300 000
Less dividends declared and paid (31 December 20x5)	(80 000)	(50 000)

All profits were earned evenly over the year.

You are required to do the following:

Calculate the profits attributable to the **non-controlling interest** of the P Ltd group in each of the following scenarios:

1. P Ltd owns 30% of A Ltd and acquires an additional 60% on 1 October 20x5.
2. P Ltd owns 80% of A Ltd and sells 20% of its shareholding on 31 August 20x5.

Suggested solution

1. P Ltd owns 30% of A Ltd and acquires an additional 60% on 1 October 20x5:
   CU300 000 × 3/12 × 10% = CU7 500
2. P Ltd owns 80% of A Ltd and sells 20% of its shareholding on 31 August 20x5:
   (20% × CU300 000 × 8/12) + (36% × CU300 000 × 4/12) = CU76 000

Question 3

P Ltd purchased 90% of the shares in S Ltd on 1 January 20x3 for CU9.2m. At that date, the fair value of the net identifiable assets of S Ltd was CU8m and non-controlling interest was measured at its fair value of CU1m.

S Ltd earned the following profits after tax subsequent to the acquisition date:

- Year ending 31 December 20x3: CU400 000
- Year ending 31 December 20x4: CU800 000
- Year ending 31 December 20x5: CU600 000 (earned evenly over the year)

P Ltd sold its entire shareholding in S Ltd on 30 June 20x5 for CU12m.

You are required to do the following:

Show your calculation of the profit on disposal of the interest in S Ltd as it would be included in the notes to the group financial statements of P Ltd for the year ended 31 December 20x5.

Suggested solution

Profit on disposal of subsidiary

	CU
Proceed from sale of controlling interest	12m
Net assets disposed (w1)	(9.5m)
Goodwill realised (w2)	(2.2m)
Non-controlling interest derecognised (w3)	1.15m
Group profit on disposal of subsidiary	**1.45m**

(w1): CU8m + 400 000 + 800 000 + 300 000 = CU9.5m
(w2): (CU9.2m + CU1m) − CU8m = CU2,2m
(w3): CU1m + ([400 000 + 800 000 + 300 000] × 10%) = CU1.15m

Question 4

Assume a corporate tax rate of 28%.

For each of the following **independent** scenarios, calculate the **goodwill or bargain purchase gain** that will be reflected in the group annual financial statements of P Ltd for the financial year ended 31 December 20x5 (ignore comparatives):

1. P Ltd owns 60% of S Ltd. On 1 January 20x5, S Ltd acquires 80% of A Ltd for CU2.2m. At that date, the net assets of A Ltd (as recognised by A Ltd) amount to CU2.5m. S Ltd (and P Ltd) consider A Ltd's plant to be undervalued by CU500 000. The non-controlling interest in A Ltd of 20% is measured at its fair value of CU1m on 1 January 20x5.

2. P Ltd acquires 70% of A Ltd for CU2.5m on 1 January 20x3. At that date, the net assets of A Ltd (as recognised by A Ltd) amount to CU2.6m. P Ltd considers A Ltd's plant to be undervalued by CU500 000. The non-controlling interest in A Ltd is measured at its fair value of CU800 000 on 1 January 20x3. P Ltd sells 60% of its shareholding in A Ltd on 30 June 20x5. On that date, the retained interest in A has a fair value of CU1m and A Ltd has net assets of CU6.5m (all fairly valued).

3. P Ltd acquires 70% of A Ltd for CU2.5m on 1 January 20x3. At that date, the net assets of A Ltd (as recognised by A Ltd and all fairly valued) amount to CU2.6m. The non-controlling interest in A Ltd is measured at its fair value of CU800 000 on 1 January 20x3. On 30 June 20x5, P Ltd sells 20% of its shareholding in A Ltd. On that date, the retained interest in A Ltd has a fair value of CU2.4m.

4. P Ltd acquires 60% of A Ltd for CU2.5m on 1 January 20x3. At that date, the net assets of A Ltd (as recognised by A Ltd) amount to CU2.7m. P Ltd consider A Ltd's plant to be undervalued by CU500 000. The non-controlling interest in A Ltd is measured at its fair value of CU1.25m on 1 January 20x3. P Ltd acquires an additional 20% shareholding in A Ltd for CU1m on 1 July 20x5. On that date, P Ltd's retained interest in A Ltd has a fair value of CU4.8m, A Ltd has net assets of CU4.2m and the non-controlling interest has a fair value of CU2m.

5. P Ltd acquires 30% of A Ltd for CU1.5m on 1 January 20x3. At that date, the net assets of A Ltd (as recognised by A and all fairly valued) amount to CU4.6m. On 1 January 20x5, P Ltd acquires a further 50% of A Ltd for CU5m. The net assets of A Ltd (as recognised by A Ltd and all fairly valued) amount to CU9.6m on that date (1 January 20x5). The non-controlling interest in A Ltd is measured at its fair value of CU2m on 1 January 20x5. At that date, P Ltd's previous shareholding in A Ltd has a fair value of CU2.9m.

Suggested solution

1. Goodwill at acquisition date

	CU
At acquisition date:	
Purchase consideration	2 200 000
Fair value of non-controlling interest	1 000 000
Less: Fair value of net identifiable assets of subsidiary (CU2.5m + [CU500 000 × 72%])	(2 860 000)
Goodwill	**340 000**

2. Goodwill = Nil (as P Ltd owns 28%, so is an associate)
3. Control is not lost. Goodwill is measured at the date of acquisition (1 January 20x4).

	CU
At acquisition date:	
Purchase consideration	2 500 000
Fair value of non-controlling interest	800 000
Less: Fair value of net identifiable assets of subsidiary	(2 600 000)
Goodwill	**700 000**

4. Goodwill is measured at the date of control (1 January 20x3):

	CU
At acquisition date:	
Purchase consideration	2 500 000
Fair value of non-controlling interest	1 250 000
Less: Fair value of net identifiable assets of subsidiary (CU2.7m + [CU500 000 × 72%])	(3 060 000)
Goodwill	**690 000**

5. Goodwill is measured at the date of control (1 January 20x5):

	CU
At acquisition date:	
Purchase consideration	5 000 000
Fair value of original interest in A Ltd	2 900 000
Fair value of non-controlling interest	2 000 000
Less: Fair value of net identifiable assets of subsidiary	(9 600 000)
Goodwill	**300 000**

Case study exercises

Scenario 1

The extracts that follow, which are from the financial statements of P Ltd and S Ltd, are presented to you.

Statements of financial position of P Ltd and S Ltd on 31 December 20x5

	P Ltd CU'000	S Ltd CU'000
ASSETS		
Land	360	250
Plant and machinery	300	120
Inventory	400	350
Other current assets	330	280
	1 390	**1 000**
CAPITAL AND LIABILITIES		
Share capital	290	170
Retained earnings	900	720
Shareholders' equity	1 190	890
Current liabilities	200	110
	1 390	**1 000**

Statements of profit or loss and other comprehensive income of P Ltd and S Ltd for the year ended 31 December 20x5

	P Ltd CU'000	S Ltd CU'000
Revenue (including dividends received)	2 320	1 700
Net operating costs	(1 440)	(1 000)
Interest expense	(100)	(50)
Profit before taxation	780	650
Taxation expense	(300)	(250)
Profit for the year	**480**	**400**

Extract from statements of changes in shareholders' equity of P Ltd and S Ltd for the year ended 31 December 20x5

	P Ltd CU'000	S Ltd CU'000
Retained earnings 1 January 20x5	620	500
Profit for the year	480	400
Dividends declared and paid on 30 December 20x5	(200)	(180)
Retained earnings 31 December 20x5	**900**	**720**

P Ltd acquired 80% (and control) of the issued ordinary share capital of S Ltd for CU365 000 on 1 January 20x3, when the financial statements of S Ltd included the following balances:

	CU
Share capital	170 000
Retained earnings	200 000
Shareholders' equity	370 000

At the date of acquisition, P Ltd considered the assets and liabilities of S Ltd to be fairly valued, except for land, which had a market value of CU310 000 (cost of CU250 000). S Ltd did not recognise any change in the carrying amount for land because of the fair value identified by P Ltd at the acquisition date. Ignore taxation.
   Non-controlling interest is measured at its attributable net asset value at the date of acquisition.
   P Ltd sold its entire interest in S Ltd for CU800 000 on 31 December 20x5.

You are required to do the following:
1. Answer the following questions before starting with the preparation of the consolidated financial statements:
   - Do you need to prepare group financial statements at 31 December 20x5?
   - What is the non-controlling interest at the acquisition date?
   - What is the goodwill acquired at the acquisition date?
   - Is there any goodwill at 31 December 20x5?
   - What is the carrying amount for land in the group statement of financial position at 31 December 20x5 (including comparative amount)?
   - What is the profit on the sale of the investment in S Ltd in the separate financial statements of P Ltd?
   - What is the group profit on the sale of the subsidiary?
   - What is the group profit for the year ended 31 December 20x5?
2. Show the *pro-forma* journal entries required to prepare the consolidated financial statements of P Ltd Group for the year ended 31 December 20x5.
3. Prepare the following extracts from the consolidated financial statements of P Ltd for the year ended 31 December 20x5:
   - Group statement of profit or loss and other comprehensive income showing the portions attributable to non-controlling interest and parent equity holders
   - Group statement of changes in equity.

Scenario 2

Assume the same information as for Scenario 1 above, except for the revised statements of financial position that follow for each of the entities.

Statements of financial position of P Ltd and S Ltd on 31 December 20x5

	P Ltd CU'000	S Ltd CU'000
ASSETS		
Land	360	250
Plant and machinery	260	120
Investment in S Ltd	255.5	
Inventory	300	350
Other current assets	214.5	280
	1 390	**1 000**
CAPITAL AND LIABILITIES		
Share capital	290	170
Retained earnings	900	720
Shareholders' equity	**1 190**	**890**
Current liabilities	200	110
	1 390	**1 000**

P Ltd sold 30% of its 80% interest in S Ltd for CU250 000 on 31 December 20x5. The result is that P Ltd still has a 56% interest in S Ltd and thus retained control. Ignore taxation.

You are required to do the following:

1. Answer the following questions before starting with the preparation of the consolidated financial statements:
   - What is the carrying amount for land in the group statement of financial position at 31 December 20x5 (including the comparative amount)?
   - What is the profit on the sale of the investment in S Ltd in the separate financial statements of P Ltd?
   - What is the group profit on the sale of the subsidiary?
   - What is the group profit for the year ended 31 December 20x5?
2. Show the *pro-forma* journal entries required to prepare the consolidated financial statements of P Ltd Group for the year ended 31 December 20x5.
3. Prepare the following extracts from the consolidated financial statements of P Ltd for the year ended 31 December 20x5:
   - Group statement of profit or loss and other comprehensive income showing the portions attributable to non-controlling interest and parent equity holders
   - Group statement of changes in equity.

Scenario 3

Assume the same information as for Scenario 1 above, except for the (revised) statements of financial position that follow for each of the entities.

Statements of financial position of P Ltd and S Ltd on 31 December 20x5

	P Ltd CU'000	S Ltd CU'000
ASSETS		
Land	360	250
Plant and machinery	260	120
Investment in S Ltd	480	
Inventory	230	350
Other current assets	60	280
	1 390	1 000
CAPITAL AND LIABILITIES		
Share capital	290	170
Retained earnings	900	720
Shareholders' equity	1 190	890
Current liabilities	200	110
	1 390	1 000

P Ltd acquired 60% (and control) of the issued ordinary share capital of S Ltd for CU280 000 on 1 January 20x3, when the financial statements of S Ltd included the following balances:

	CU
Share capital	170 000
Retained earnings	200 000
Shareholders' equity	370 000

At the date of acquisition, P Ltd considered the assets and liabilities of S Ltd to be fairly valued, except for land, which had a market value of CU310 000 (cost of CU250 000). S Ltd did not recognise any change in the carrying amount for land because of the fair value identified by P Ltd at the acquisition date. Ignore taxation.

Non-controlling interest is measured at its attributable net asset value at the date of acquisition.

P Ltd acquired an additional 20% interest in S Ltd for CU200 000 on 31 December 20x5.

You are required to do the following:

1. Show the *pro-forma* journal entries required to prepare the consolidated financial statements of P Ltd Group for the year ended 31 December 20x5.
2. Prepare the following extracts from the consolidated financial statements of P Ltd for the year ended 31 December 20x5:
   - Group statement of profit or loss and other comprehensive income showing the portions attributable to non-controlling interest and parent equity holders
   - Group statement of changes in equity.

Suggested solution

Scenario 1

1. **Answer the following questions before starting with the preparation of the consolidated financial statements:**
   - **Do you need to prepare group financial statements at 31 December 20x5?**
     Yes. As S Ltd was still a subsidiary during the 20x5 reporting period, group financial statements are still required until the date when control was lost, which was on 31 December 20x5.

- **What is the non-controlling interest at the acquisition date?**

	CU	CU
Fair value of net identifiable assets at acquisition date	430 000	
Net asset value per S Ltd's financial statements	370 000	
Fair value adjustment relating to land	60 000	
Non-controlling interest (CU430 000 × 20%)		**86 000**

- **What is the goodwill acquired at the acquisition date?**

	CU	CU
Fair value of net identifiable assets at acquisition date	430 000	
Net asset value per S Ltd's financial statements	370 000	
Fair value adjustment relating to land (310 000 – 250 000)	60 000	
Non-controlling interest (CU430 000 × 20%)		86 000
Cash consideration paid for 80% interest		365 000
		451 000
Goodwill acquired at acquisition date (CU451 000 – CU430 000)	**21 000**	

- **Is there any goodwill at 31 December 20x5?**
  No. When the subsidiary is sold, the goodwill is derecognised.
- **What is the carrying amount for land in the group statement of financial position at 31 December 20x5 (including the comparative amount)?**

	31 December 20x5 CU	31 December 20x4 CU
Land	360 000	(w1) 670 000

Note that as the group sold its subsidiary, the group sold the land as well as all of the other assets and liabilities of the subsidiary on 31 December 20x5.
(w1): CU360 000 + CU310 000 = CU670 000

- **What is the profit on the sale of the investment in S Ltd in the separate financial statements of P Ltd?**

	CU
Proceeds from disposal of subsidiary	800 000
Investment in subsidiary (cost)	(365 000)
Profit on disposal of investment in subsidiary	**435 000**

- **What is the group profit on the sale of the subsidiary?**

	CU
Proceeds from disposal of subsidiary	800 000
Net assets disposed of (890 000 + 60 000)	(950 000)
Goodwill derecognised	(21 000)
Non-controlling interest derecognised (950 000 × 20%)	190 000
Group profit on disposal of subsidiary	**19 000**

- **What is the group profit for the year ended 31 December 20x5?**
  As S Ltd was still a subsidiary for the 20x5 financial year, its profit for the current year should still be included in the group profit.

	CU	CU
P Ltd's profit (CU480 000 – [80% × 180 000]):	336 000	
S Ltd's profit	400 000	
Less: Profit on disposal of investment in subsidiary	(435 000)	
Plus: Group profit on disposal of subsidiary	19 000	
Group profit for the year		**320 000**
Attributable to parent equity holders		240 000
Attributable to non-controlling interest (CU400 000 × 20%)		80 000

2. **Show the *pro-forma* journal entries required to prepare the consolidated financial statements of P Ltd Group for the year ended 31 December 20x5.**

   Note that these *pro-forma* journal entries are prepared with the starting point being only the financial statements of P Ltd. This means that S Ltd is no longer in the starting point as S Ltd is not a subsidiary. The *pro-forma* journal entries therefore include the results of S Ltd subsequent to the acquisition date until the date of disposal.

   Pro-forma journal entry

			CU	CU
Dr		Operating costs	1 000 000	
	Cr	Revenue		1 700 000
Dr		Interest expense	50 000	
Dr		Taxation expense	250 000	
Dr		Non-controlling interest in profit or loss (400 000 × 20%)	80 000	
Dr		Dividends received	144 000	
Dr		Profit on disposal of investment in subsidiary	435 000	
	Cr	Profit on disposal of subsidiary (group)		19 000
	Cr	Retained earnings (300 × 80%)		240 000

Inclusion of profit and loss items of subsidiary until date of disposal and recognition of group profit

3. **Prepare the following extracts from the consolidated financial statements of P Ltd for the year ended 31 December 20x5:**
   - **Group statement of profit or loss and other comprehensive income showing the portions attributable to non-controlling interest and parent equity holders**

   Group statement of profit or loss and other comprehensive income of P Ltd and S Ltd for the year ended 31 December 20x5

	Group CU'000
Revenue (2 320 000 + 1 700 000 – 144 000)	3 876
Net operating costs (1 440 000 + 1 000 000 + 435 000 [profit in P Ltd] – 19 000 [group profit])	(2 856)
Interest expense	(150)
Profit before taxation	870
Taxation expense	(550)
Profit for the year	**320**
Attributable to:	
Non-controlling interest	80
Equity holders of the parent	240

- ## Group statement of changes in equity

Group statement of changes in equity for the year ended 31 December 20x5

	Share capital CU'000	Retained earnings CU'000	Total equity interest of the parent CU'000	Non-controlling interest CU'000	Total CU'000
Opening balance	290	(w1) 860	1 150	146	1 296
Profit for the year		240	240	80	320
– Dividends		(200)	(200)	(36)	(236)
Less disposal of subsidiary				(190)	(190)
Closing balance	**290**	**(w2) 900**	**1 190**	**–**	**1 190**

(w1): P: 620 000 + S: 240 000
(w2): P: 900 000 – 435 000 (profit in P) + 19 000 (group profit) + S: 416 000

Additional workings

Analysis of equity of S Ltd

	Total CU'000	P Ltd (80%)		20% Non-controlling interest CU'000
		At acquisition CU'000	Since acquisition CU'000	
At acquisition:				
Share capital	170	136		34
Retained earnings	200	160		40
Land (310 – 250)	60	48		12
	430	344		86
Investment		365		
Goodwill		21		
Since acquisition:				
Retained earnings	300		240	60
Profit after tax	400		320	80
Less: Dividends	(180)		(144)	(36)
	950		416	190

Scenario 2

1. **Answer the following questions before starting with the preparation of the consolidated financial statements:**
    - **What is the carrying amount for land in the group statement of financial position at 31 December 20x5 (including comparative amount)?**

	31 December 20x5 CU	31 December 20x4 CU
Land	(w1) 670 000	670 000

(w1): CU360 000 + CU310 000 = CU670 000

- **What is the profit on the sale of the investment in S Ltd in the separate financial statements of P Ltd?**

	CU
Proceeds from disposal of 30% interest subsidiary	250 000
Cost of portion of investment sold (30% × CU365 000)	(109 500)
Profit on disposal of portion of investment in subsidiary	**140 500**

- **What is the group profit on the sale of the subsidiary?**

  None. Even though P Ltd sold some of its interest in S Ltd, control was retained. S Ltd remains a subsidiary of P Ltd and should be consolidated. The sale of some of the interest to the non-controlling shareholders represents a transaction between shareholders.

- **What is the group profit for the year ended 31 December 20x5?**

  As S Ltd was still a subsidiary for the 20x5 financial year, its profit for the current year should still be included in the group profit.

	CU	CU
P Ltd's profit (CU480 000 – (80% × 180 000)	336 000	
S Ltd's profit	400 000	
Less: Profit on disposal of portion of investment in subsidiary	(140 500)	
Group profit for the year		**595 500**
Attributable to parent equity holders		515 500
Attributable to non-controlling interest (CU400 000 × 20%)		80 000

2. **Show the *pro-forma* journal entries required to prepare the consolidated financial statements of P Ltd Group for the year ended 31 December 20x5.**

Pro-forma journal entries

			CU	CU
Dr		Share capital	170 000	
Dr		Retained earnings	200 000	
Dr		Land	60 000	
Dr		Goodwill	21 000	
	Cr	Investment in S Ltd		365 000
	Cr	Non-controlling interest (equity)		86 000

Elimination of equity at acquisition, investment in S Ltd and raising non-controlling interest at acquisition

			CU	CU
Dr		Retained earnings	60 000	
	Cr	Non-controlling interest (equity)		60 000

Post-acquisition prior year earnings allocated to non-controlling interest

			CU	CU
Dr		Non-controlling interest (P/L)	80 000	
	Cr	Non-controlling interest (equity)		80 000

Current year's profits allocated to non-controlling interest

			CU	CU
Dr		Dividends received (P/L)	144 000	
Dr		Non-controlling interest (equity)	36 000	
	Cr	Dividends declared and paid		180 000

Elimination of subsidiary's dividends

			CU	CU
Dr		Investment in subsidiary (365 000 – 255 500)	109 500	
Dr		Profit on disposal of interest in subsidiary (P/L)	140 500	
	Cr	Group profit on disposal of share of subsidiary (equity) (w1)		22 000
	Cr	Non-controlling interest (equity) (24% × 950 000)		228 000

Elimination of profit on sale of portion of interest in subsidiary and recognition of group profit in equity
(w1) CU250 000 (proceeds) – CU228 000 (net asset value sold to non-controlling shareholders) = CU22 000

3. **Prepare the following extracts from the consolidated financial statements of P Ltd for the year ended 31 December 20x5:**
   - **Group statement of profit or loss and other comprehensive income showing the portions attributable to non-controlling interest and parent equity holders**

Group statement of profit or loss and other comprehensive income of P Ltd and S Ltd for the year ended 31 December 20x5

	Group CU'000
Revenue (2 320 000 + 1 700 000 – 144 000)	3 876
Net operating costs (1 440 000 + 1 000 000 + 140 500 [profit in P Ltd])	(2 580.5)
Interest expense	(150)
Profit before taxation	1 145.5
Taxation expense	(550)
Profit for the year	**595.5**
<u>Attributable to</u>:	
Non-controlling interest	80
Equity holders of the parent	515.5

- **Group statement of changes in equity**

Group statement of changes in shareholders' equity for the year ended 31 December 20x5

	Share capital CU'000	Retained earnings CU'000	Total equity interest of the parent CU'000	Non-controlling interest CU'000	Total CU'000
Opening balance	290	(w1) 860	1 150	146	1 296
Profit for the year		515.5	515.5	80	595.5
– Dividends		(200)	(200)	(36)	(236)
Disposal of interest in subsidiary to non-controlling shareholders		22	22	228	250
Closing balance	**290**	**(w2) 1 197.5**	**1 487.5**	**418**	**1 905.5**

(w1): P: 620 000 + S: 240 000
(w2): P: 900 000 – 140 500 (profit in P) + 22 000 (group profit) + S: 416 000

Group statement of financial position of P Ltd and S Ltd on 31 December 20x5

	Group CU'000
ASSETS	
Land	670
Plant and machinery	380
Goodwill	21
Inventory	650
Other current assets	494.5
	2 215.5
CAPITAL AND LIABILITIES	
Share capital	290
Retained earnings	1 197.5
Shareholders' equity	1 487.5
Non-controlling interest	418
Total equity	1 905.5
Current liabilities	310
	2 215.5

Additional workings

Analysis of equity of S Ltd

	Total CU'000	P Ltd (80%)		20% Non-controlling interest CU'000
		At acquisition CU'000	Since acquisition CU'000	
At acquisition:				
Share capital	170	136		34
Retained earnings	200	160		40
Land (310 – 250)	60	48		12
	430	344		86
Investment		365		
Goodwill		21		
Since acquisition:				
Retained earnings	300		240	60
Profit after tax	400		320	80
Less: Dividends	(180)		(144)	(36)
	950		416	190
			56%	**44%**
Disposal of 24% ① to non-controlling shareholders			(228)	228
	950		**188**	**418**

① P Ltd disposed of 30% of its interest in S Ltd: 30% of 80% = 24%; P Ltd retained a 56% controlling interest.

Scenario 3

1. Show the *pro-forma* journal entries required to prepare the consolidated financial statements of P Ltd Group for the year ended 31 December 20x5.

Pro-forma journal entries

			CU	CU
Dr		Share capital	170 000	
Dr		Retained earnings	200 000	
Dr		Land	60 000	
Dr		Goodwill	22 000	
	Cr	Investment in S Ltd		280 000
	Cr	Non-controlling interest (equity)		172 000

Elimination of equity at acquisition, investment in S Ltd and raising non-controlling interest at acquisition

			CU	CU
Dr		Retained earnings	120 000	
	Cr	Non-controlling interest (equity)		120 000

Post-acquisition prior year earnings allocated to non-controlling interest

			CU	CU
Dr		Non-controlling interest (P/L)	160 000	
	Cr	Non-controlling interest (equity)		160 000

Current year's profits allocated to non-controlling interest

			CU	CU
Dr		Dividends received (P/L)	108 000	
Dr		Non-controlling interest (equity)	72 000	
	Cr	Dividends declared and paid		180 000

Elimination of subsidiary's dividends

			CU	CU
Dr		Non-controlling interest (equity) (20% × 950 000)	190 000	
Dr		'Loss' on acquisition of additional interest in subsidiary (equity)	10 000	
	Cr	Investment in subsidiary		200 000

Elimination of additional interest in subsidiary and recognition of group profit in equity

2. **Prepare the following extracts from the consolidated financial statements of P Ltd for the year ended 31 December 20x5:**
   - **Group statement of profit or loss and other comprehensive income showing the portions attributable to non-controlling interest and parent equity holders**

Group statement of profit or loss and other comprehensive income of P Ltd and S Ltd for the year ended 31 December 20x5

	Group CU'000
Revenue (2 320 000 + 1 700 000 – 108 000)	3 912
Net operating costs (1 440 000 + 1 000 000)	(2 440)
Interest expense	(150)
Profit before taxation	1 322
Taxation expense	(550)
Profit for the year	**772**
Attributable to:	
Non-controlling interest	160
Equity holders of the parent	612

   - **Group statement of changes in equity**

Group statement of changes in shareholders' equity for the year ended 31 December 20x5

	Share capital CU'000	Retained earnings CU'000	Total equity interest of the parent CU'000	Non-controlling interest CU'000	Total CU'000
Opening balance	290	(w1) 800	1 090	292	1 382
Profit for the year		612	612	160	772
– Dividends		(200)	(200)	(72)	(272)
Additional interest in subsidiary		(10)	(10)	(190)	(200)
Closing balance	**290**	**(w2) 1 202**	**1 492**	**190**	**1 682**

(w1): P: 620 000 + S: 180 000
(w2): P: 900 000 – 10 000 (group profit) + S: 312 000

Statements of financial position of P Ltd and S Ltd on 31 December 20x5

	Group CU'000
ASSETS	
Land	670
Plant and machinery	380
Goodwill	22
Inventory	580
Other current assets	340
	1 992
CAPITAL AND LIABILITIES	
Share capital	290
Retained earnings	1 202
Shareholders' equity	1 492
Non-controlling interest	190
Total equity	1 682
Current liabilities	310
	1 992

Additional workings

Analysis of equity of S Ltd

	Total CU'000	P Ltd (60%, increased to 80%)		40% decrease to 20% Non-controlling interest CU'000
		At acquisition CU'000	Since acquisition CU'000	
At acquisition:				
Share capital	170			
Retained earnings	200			
Land (310 – 250)	60			
	430	258		172
Investment		280		
Goodwill		22		
Since acquisition:				
Retained earnings	300		180	120
Profit after tax	400		240	160
Less: Dividends	(180)		(108)	(72)
	950		312	380
			80%	**20%**
Acquisition of an additional 20% interest in subsidiary			190	(190)
	950		**291.2**	**190**

13

Foreign operations

The following topics are included in this chapter:

- The presentation and functional currency of an entity
- Identifying and recording a foreign currency transaction
- Recognition and measurement of a foreign currency transaction at the reporting date when the transaction results in the recognition of a:
  - Monetary item
  - Non-monetary item
- Recognition and measurement of transactions of a foreign operation
- Consolidation of a controlling interest in a foreign entity.

Learning objectives

By the end of this chapter, you should be able to:

- Explain what is meant by the presentation and functional currency of an entity
- Identify a foreign currency transaction
- Know when and how to record a foreign currency transaction
- Describe how to measure a foreign currency transaction at the reporting date when the transaction results in the recognition of:
  - Monetary item
  - Non-monetary item
- Describe how you would recognise and measure transactions of a foreign operation
- Explain why it is necessary to consolidate a controlling interest in a foreign entity
- Prepare group financial statements when the parent has an interest in a foreign subsidiary and/or a foreign associate.

1. Introduction

Entities transact with other entities throughout the world on a daily basis. In many instances, these transactions occur in a currency that is different from the entity's local or domestic currency. For example, a South African retailer imports clothes from Europe and pays for them in euros. In South Africa, the local currency is the rand. The South African entity has transacted in a foreign currency, namely the euro. An entity may undertake these foreign currency transactions directly as in the example above or indirectly through another entity, which may be a subsidiary, an associate, a joint arrangement or a branch whose activities are based in another currency. This other entity is referred to as a **foreign operation**.

 IFRS principles

What is a foreign operation? (IAS21: 8)

A foreign operation is a subsidiary, an associate, a joint venture or a branch whose activities are based in a country or currency other than that of the reporting entity.

In the preceding chapters, you looked at investees that report in the same currency as that of the investor or parent. This chapter looks at how to include the financial statements of a foreign operation into that of the reporting entity. The chapter does not deal with the detailed procedures for consolidating a subsidiary or applying the equity method to investments in associates or joint ventures, as those principles are the same as dealt with in previous chapters. The focus in this chapter is on the presentation of **foreign exchange differences** relating to the foreign operation in the reporting entity's group financial statements, and in particular, a **foreign subsidiary**.

An entity may carry on foreign activities in two ways:
- It may have **transactions in foreign currencies**, for example, where a South African company purchases inventory from the US and pays for the inventory in US dollars.
- It may have **foreign operations**, for example, where a South African entity has a subsidiary in the United States of America.

IAS21, *The Effects of Changes in Foreign Exchange Rates*, provides outlines as to how you should account for foreign currency transactions and operations in financial statements as well as how to translate financial statements into a presentation currency.

2. Functional and presentation currencies

It is important that you are able to distinguish between the three different types of currency: local currency, functional currency and presentation currency.
- The **local currency** is the country's domestic currency.
- The **functional currency** is the currency of the primary economic environment in which the entity operates. This is typically the currency in which the entity generates and spends cash.

- The **presentation currency** is the currency in which the financial statements are presented. This need not be the same as the functional currency.

Not all foreign subsidiaries experience all three currencies.

An entity is required to determine a **functional currency** (for each of its operations if necessary) based on the primary economic environment in which it operates and generally records foreign currency transactions using the spot conversion rate to that functional currency on the date of the transaction. This means that the financial statements of a foreign operation need to be translated to the currency of the primary economic environment in which the entity operates, which is referred to as the **functional currency**. In order to account for transactions denominated in another currency, an entity first needs to identify its functional currency. This is typically the currency in which the entity generates and spends cash.

Where the financial statements of a foreign subsidiary are prepared in a foreign currency (that is, a currency that is different from the presentation currency of the parent), it is necessary to translate the financial statements of the foreign subsidiary to the currency used by the parent entity in order to be able to prepare consolidated financial statements for the group. An entity is not required to prepare its financial statements in its functional currency. It may select a presentation currency that is different from its functional currency. Refer to Section 4 below for a detailed discussion of the translation to presentation currency. The principles provided in IAS21 relate to the translation of a set of financial statements into the **presentation currency** and the resulting foreign exchange translation adjustments that arise from this transaction.

IFRS principles

Functional and presentation currencies

IAS21 notes the following two areas of application of functional and presentation currencies (refer to IAS21: 3):
- Translating the results and financial position of foreign operations that are included in the financial statements of the entity by consolidation or the equity method
- Translating an entity's results and financial position into a presentation currency.

2.1 Identifying the functional currency

In deciding on its functional currency, an entity looks at the currency in which the sales price of its goods and services is denominated and settled, the cost of providing goods and services or the currency in which it retains cash from its main operations. Therefore, you could have a South African entity where the selling price of all or most of its goods is denominated in US dollars. In that case, the entity's **functional currency** could be US dollars, even though its **local (domestic) currency** is rands. This is typical of mining entities, where resources such as gold, platinum and other minerals are routinely sold on the international market at prices determined in US dollars. Then, should this entity be a subsidiary of an Australian parent, the **presentation currency** of the parent may be the Australian dollar. This means that the consolidated financial statements are presented in Australian dollars. As the accounts are maintained in South African rands, they may first have to be translated into the functional currency, US dollars, and then translated again to the Australian dollar for presentation purposes.

> ### Think about it
> **Determining the functional currency**
>
> An entity's functional currency is the currency of the primary economic environment in which it operates. The assessment of the functional currency requires judgement by giving priority to the primary indicators of the following:
> - The currency in which the entity generates and expends cash, for example, the currency influencing sales prices for goods and services, the currency of the country whose competitive forces and regulations determine sale prices or the currency that mainly influences input costs
> - If there is no clear answer to the above, then consider the currency in which funds from financing activities are generated or receipts from operating activities are retained.
> - If there is no clear answer from the above two points, consider the level of autonomy for the subsidiary from the parent. If it is not autonomous, then the functional currency is the same as the parent.

3. Foreign currency transactions

Once the entity's functional currency has been identified, any other currency is a foreign currency for financial reporting purposes. Therefore, any transaction (buying or selling of goods and services or borrowings) denominated in a foreign currency is a foreign currency transaction. Such transactions need to be translated into the functional currency of the reporting entity.

3.1 Initial recognition and measurement of foreign currency transactions

The foreign currency transaction is translated into the entity's functional currency by applying the spot exchange rate ruling at the transaction date. The use of the **spot rate** makes sense as the spot rate is the rate on that day, which is the transaction date. The transaction may not necessarily take place on one particular date, but perhaps over a period of time. In that case, the average spot exchange rate for the period may be more appropriate.

3.2 Subsequent measurement of foreign currency

Subsequently the treatment depends on whether the transaction results in the recognition of **monetary** or **non-monetary items**. Monetary items are units of currency held (for example, cash) and assets and liabilities to be received or paid in a fixed or determinable number of units of currency (for example, foreign receivables and payables that will be settled in cash). Monetary items therefore represent the right to receive or the obligation to deliver a fixed or determinable number of units of currency; in other words, they will be settled in cash.

IFRS principles

Subsequent measurement

At each subsequent reporting date (refer to IAS21: 23):
- Foreign currency monetary amounts should be reported using the closing rate at the reporting date.
- Non-monetary items carried at historical cost should be reported using the exchange rate at the date of the transaction.
- Non-monetary items carried at fair value (revaluation) should be reported at the rate that existed when the fair values were determined.

Any translation gains or losses on assets and liabilities are recognised in profit or loss.

The table below identifies monetary and non-monetary items. This is followed by a more detailed discussion of these items.

Table 13.1 Examples of monetary and non-monetary items

Monetary items	Non-monetary items
Cash and bank accounts	Property, plant and equipment
Long-term receivables or payables	Inventory
Trade and other receivables	Pre-payments
Trade and other payables	Intangible assets
Deferred tax	
Provisions to be settled in cash	

3.2.1 Monetary items

One of two things can happen to a monetary item (for example, a foreign creditor or a foreign debtor) after initial recognition: it can either be settled (in cash) or is still outstanding at the reporting date.

When the monetary item is **settled**, the settlement is recorded at the spot rate on the settlement date as that is the amount paid or received in the functional currency.

If the monetary item is **still outstanding** at the reporting date, it is translated at (or restated to) the closing rate. The closing rate is the spot rate at the reporting date (in other words, the exchange rate on the date on which the financial statements are closed off). Translation at the closing rate for amounts still outstanding at the reporting date is appropriate as the statement of financial position represents the financial position of the entity at a point in time (in other words, the future economic benefits to be derived from an asset [say the foreign customer settles a receivable] or the amounts that will need to be paid to settle the entity's obligations [say to the foreign creditor]). Even though settlement will take place only after the reporting date, the closing rate reflects the exchange rate that would be used if the cash flows were to occur at the reporting date, that is, if the reporting date were the date on which the monetary item were to be settled.

3.2.2 Non-monetary items

A non-monetary item, such as property, plant and equipment or inventory, is initially measured at cost. The exchange rate movements that arise relate to the amount payable (creditor or loan) arising from the acquisition of the asset rather than from the asset itself.

The cost of an asset should be the same, irrespective of whether payment was settled on the transaction date or a few months later.

Depreciation is based on the spot exchange rate on the date on which the machine was initially recognised and not the spot exchange rate that applies to the period during which the machine was used. The machine is recognised at **cost in the functional currency** at the date of acquisition. Depreciation is an allocation of that cost. The cost of the machine (and consequently the depreciation) is not affected by how exchange rates have moved subsequently.

If an asset is subsequently measured at fair value and if that fair value is measured in a foreign currency, the amount at which the fair value is presented in the entity's financial statements in the entity's functional currency is calculated by applying the exchange rate when the fair value is measured. In this case, even though a different exchange rate is applied to the fair value compared to when the non-monetary item was originally recognised, the reason that the item is remeasured is because the entity measures the item at fair value subsequently, as opposed to because of subsequent changes in the exchange rates.

For the rest of the chapter, we will assume that the functional currency of the entities that we look at is **LC** ('local currency' units). Therefore, any other currency is a foreign currency, which in this chapter is denoted by **FC**.

3.3 **Exchange differences**

Exchange differences arise when an amount is recognised or settled in a currency (say a payable of FC100 or a loan to an offshore entity of FC50 000) that differs from the currency that is used to measure the amount payable or receivable for accounting purposes (functional currency). Exchange differences arise only in relation to monetary items, that is, amounts that are payable or receivable (in cash). A monetary item denominated in a foreign currency gives rise to a different rand equivalent amount as the exchange rate moves. This difference is a **foreign exchange gain or loss** and reflects a change in the net assets of the entity. The spot rate on settlement date or the reporting date is likely to be different from that used when the monetary item was originally recognised. Depending on the subsequent moves in exchange rates, the amount received or settled may be different from the amount recognised at the reporting date

Monetary items that are denominated in a foreign currency are directly influenced by how exchange rates have moved. Thus only monetary items in a foreign currency give rise to exchange differences as a result of applying different exchange rates used on initial recognition and subsequent measurement in the functional currency.

These foreign exchange gains or losses are recognised in **profit or loss** as that is where changes in net assets that are non-owner related are recognised (unless IFRS allows or requires recognition in other comprehensive income). The exchange differences may be recognised in other comprehensive income when an entity applies cash flow hedge accounting to a foreign currency transaction (this topic is beyond the scope of this publication).

3.3.1 Changes in functional currency

When the transactions, events and conditions that result in an entity's selection of an appropriate functional currency change such that the entity's functional currency changes, this is accounted for prospectively from the date of the change. Prior periods are therefore not restated.

More information and examples on foreign currency transactions can be found in Chapter 20 of *Financial Accounting: IFRS Principles* (4e) by Lubbe, Modack and Watson.

4. Translation to presentation currency

Thus far, we have looked at the concepts of a functional currency and a foreign currency, and how to measure transactions and amounts in a foreign currency in the entity's functional currency. Having decided what its functional currency is, an entity may present its financial statements in that functional currency or any other currency. The currency in which the entity presents its financial statements is its **presentation currency**.

Example

Presentation currency that is different from functional currency

A mining entity in South Africa has a functional currency of US dollars, but because its investors are predominantly South African and are the main users of its financial statements, the mining entity presents its financial statements in rands. In this example, the mining entity's presentation currency differs from its functional currency. If the presentation currency differs from its functional currency, the entity needs to translate amounts that are recognised in its functional currency into its presentation currency so as to present its financial statements.

As mentioned earlier, a foreign operation or entity identifies its functional currency and accounting records are kept in the functional currency. However, the foreign entity may decide to present its financial statements in a currency that is different from its functional currency. When the functional currency is different from the presentation currency, the financial statements of the entity are translated to the presentation currency, using the **translation method** as prescribed in IAS21.

Different exchange rates are used to translate the various line items in the trial balance from the functional currency into the presentation currency. Therefore, in order for the trial balance to balance in the presentation currency, there has to a **balancing amount**. This amount is known as exchange difference. This exchange difference is presented in **other comprehensive income** and accumulated in a separate component of equity, which is called the **foreign currency translation reserve** (often abbreviated to 'FCTR').

IFRS principles

Translation from the functional currency to the presentation currency

The results and financial position of an entity are translated into a different presentation currency using the following procedures (refer to IAS21: 39–47):

1. Assets and liabilities in the functional currency are translated into the presentation currency using the closing rate at the date of the statement of financial position. This includes any goodwill arising on the acquisition of a foreign operation. Any fair value adjustments to the carrying amounts of assets and liabilities arising on the acquisition of that foreign operation are treated as part of the assets and liabilities of the foreign operation.
2. Income and expenses are translated at the exchange rate at the date of transaction, although an average may be used for transactions that arise over a period.
3. Other movements in equity are translated at the exchange rate at the date of the transaction
4. All resulting exchange differences are recognised in other comprehensive income.

5. Application to consolidating foreign operations

The principles discussed for the application of the **translation method** above are applied to translate the financial performance and financial position of a foreign operation for presentation as part of the group financial statements of the parent for consolidation purposes in the case of a foreign subsidiary, where the foreign operation has a functional currency that differs from that of the group's presentation currency. This makes sense. For example, in order to consolidate a foreign subsidiary, the financial statements of that subsidiary need to be translated into the presentation currency of the group.

IFRS principles

What is the presentation currency?

The presentation currency (refer to IAS21: 8) is the currency in which financial statements are presented.

The consolidation procedures discussed in the previous chapters apply equally to foreign subsidiaries. The focus here is on the additional adjustments that may be required because of the translations of the financial performance and the position of the foreign operation.

5.1 Acquisition date

At the acquisition date of the controlling interest in a foreign subsidiary, the investment is recorded in the parent's separate financial statements at the net consideration transferred (refer to IFRS3, *Business Combinations*). The parent recognises the investment in its separate financial statements in accordance with IAS27, *Separate Financial Statements*, using the presentation currency of the parent. This means that when the foreign subsidiary is consolidated, the assets, liabilities and equity of the subsidiary are translated to the presentation currency prior to its elimination at the acquisition date. Any goodwill arising on acquisition date is recognised as an asset. In the case of a partly held foreign subsidiary, non-controlling interest is recognised in equity.

5.2 Subsequent reporting periods

The consolidation process requires, as the starting point, that the assets, liabilities, income and expenses of the subsidiary be added to that of the parent. When the financial statements of the foreign subsidiary is prepared using a currency that is different from the presentation currency of the group, the individual items in the trial balance need to be translated to the presentation currency, using the **translation method** described above. As different exchange rates are used to translate the various line items in the trial balance to the presentation currency, the resulting exchange difference is recognised in other comprehensive income and accumulated in equity, using the **foreign currency translation reserve**.

Example

Wholly owned foreign subsidiary

P Ltd acquired 100% of S Ltd for FC10 000 on 1 January 20x4 on incorporation of the latter company. P Ltd's functional and presentation currency is LC. S Ltd's functional currency is FC.

Trial balance of S Ltd at 31 December 20x5

	FC	
	Debit	**Credit**
Share capital		10 000
Retained earnings on 31 December 20x4		60 000
Profit for the 20x5 period		110 000
Dividends declared on 31 December 20x5	30 000	
Machinery	70 000	
Inventory	20 000	
Bank	30 000	
Trade receivables	40 000	
Trade payables		10 000
	190 000	**190 000**

The trial balance given above is in FC units. As S Ltd is a foreign operation that is a subsidiary, 100% of amounts recognised by S Ltd should be presented in the P Ltd group financial statements. The presentation currency of the group is LC units. We therefore need to translate the amounts recognised by S Ltd into LC units for presentation as part of the group financial statements. To do this, we need spot exchange rates, which are provided on the next page.

The following spot exchange rates applied:

	1FC = LC
At 1 January 20x4	5
At 31 December 20x4	6
At 31 December 20x5	7
Average for the period	
20x4	5.50
20x5	6.50

In addition, this translation process yields an exchange difference. Essentially, there are two ways of calculating this exchange difference:

1. Translate the trial balance of the foreign operation, applying the applicable spot exchange rates to the assets, liabilities, income, expenses and other equity of the subsidiary.
2. Prepare an analysis of equity, applying the closing rate to the equity balance (that is, the net assets) at the relevant reporting date and the applicable spot exchange rates to the changes in the equity balance

Method 1: Translating S Ltd's trial balance (as at 31 December 20x5)

	Notes	FC	Exchange rate	LC
Share capital	① a.	(10 000)	5	(50 000)
Retained earnings	① a.	(60 000)	5.5	(330 000)
Profit for period	① a.	(110 000)	6.5	(715 000)
Dividends declared and paid	① a.	30 000	7	210 000
Machinery	① b.	70 000	7	490 000
Inventory	① a.	20 000	7	140 000
Bank	① a.	30 000	7	210 000
Trade receivables	① a.	40 000	7	280 000
Trade payables	① a.	(10 000)	7	(70 000)
				165 000
Exchange difference	②			**(165 000)**
		–		–

In the trial balance presented above, the credit balances are reflected in brackets (). The trial balance of S Ltd is prepared and balances in FC units, as we would expect it to.

Notes

① To translate the account balances from FC units into LC units, different spot exchange rates are applied to the amounts denominated in FC units.

a. Equity is translated using the spot exchange rate on the date on which the change in equity arose to the change in equity denominated in FC units:
- Share capital: On the date on which the shares were acquired by P Ltd, which in this example is also the date on which they were issued by S Ltd
- Dividends declared: To closing rate on 31 December 20x5 as the dividends were declared on that date; the assumption is that no dividends were declared in 20x4
- The profit for 20x4 at the average exchange rate for the 20x4 financial year and the profit for the 20x5 financial year at the average for that period.

b.   Assets and liabilities are translated into LC units at the closing rate.
② The trial balance does not automatically balance in LC units as we would expect given that different amounts are translated using different exchange rates.

The amount that is required for the trial balance to balance in LC units is the exchange difference and it arises only in the trial balance denominated in LC units. In this case, the 'balancing' amount is a credit of LC165 000. This is therefore an exchange gain.

This approach has the following shortcomings:
- The amount reflected in the trial balance as the exchange difference of LC165 000 is the cumulative balancing figure to date, in other words, the combination of exchange differences arising in the current and prior period. This split is important for presenting amounts in the statement of profit or loss and other comprehensive income for 20x5 (and the comparative in respect of 20x4) as well as in the statement of changes in equity.
- There may be adjustments, amounts and line items that ought to appear in the group financial statements, but that do not appear in the trial balance of the foreign operation (for example, goodwill arising on the acquisition of a foreign subsidiary or adjustments at the date of acquisition to reflect the net assets acquired at the cost to the group that are not recognised by the foreign operation in it separate financial statements).

Using an analysis of equity may be useful in addressing the shortcomings highlighted above.

Method 2: Using an analysis of equity

	Notes	FC	Exchange rate	LC ①
At the acquisition date:				
Share capital		10 000	5	50 000
After the acquisition date:				
20x4 financial year				
Profit for 20x4	②	60 000	5.5	330 000
Exchange difference	③			40 000
31 December 20x4		**70 000**	**6**	**420 000**
20x5 financial year				
Profit for the period	②	110 000	6.5	715 000
Dividends declared	②	(30 000)	7	(210 000)
Exchange difference	③			125 000
31 December 20x5		**150 000**	**7**	**1 050 000**

Notes
① The principle of restating assets and liabilities at the closing rate is achieved by translating the equity of S Ltd at each reporting date, which makes sense as assets less liabilities (net assets) equal equity.
② The changes in equity are translated using the spot exchange rate when the change occurred.
③ The cumulative exchange difference that arises is a gain of LC165 000, of which LC40 000 arose in 20x4 and LC125 000 arose in 20x5. So in 20x5, the exchange difference arises because opening net assets, the change in net assets during 20x5 and closing net assets at 31 December 20x5 are translated using different exchange rates.

Pro-forma journal entries

The following *pro-forma* journal entries are required to consolidate S Ltd in P Ltd's group financial statements for the 20x5 financial year:

			LC	LC
Dr		Share capital	50 000	
	Cr	Investment in S Ltd		50 000

Elimination of investment in subsidiary at the acquisition date

			LC	LC
Dr		Dividend income	210 000	
	Cr	Dividends declared		210 000

Elimination of intra-group dividends received

			LC	LC
Dr		Foreign exchange gain (OCI)	40 000	
	Cr	Foreign currency translation reserve (equity)		40 000

Allocation of cumulative exchange gain between current and prior periods

Notes

The first two *pro-forma* journal entries are the same as what you have seen before in respect of the position at the acquisition date (1) and the elimination of intra-group dividends (2).

The third *pro-forma* journal entry is required to split the cumulative exchange gain of LC165 000 correctly between the current (20x5) and prior (20x4) periods. Remember that the starting point for the preparation of the group financial statements is the aggregated trial balance, which comprises 100% of the parent (in this case, P Ltd) and 100% of the subsidiary (in this case, S Ltd). The trial balance of S Ltd included in that starting point is the trial balance denominated in LC units (that is, the translated trial balance). This includes the cumulative exchange difference, but not all was earned (or arose) in the 20x5 financial year. A *pro-forma* journal entry is therefore required. It is debatable as to whether the starting point includes the exchange differences in other comprehensive income, that is, before being closed off (as in the example above) or whether the cumulative exchange differences have already been closed off to the foreign currency translation reserve and the equity amount is what is reflected in the starting point trial balance. If this were the case, then *pro-forma* journal entry (3) would look as follows instead:

			CU	CU
Dr		Foreign currency translation reserve (equity)	125 000	
	Cr	Foreign exchange gain (OCI)		125 000

Allocation of exchange gain in other comprehensive income

In this instance, a journal entry is required to show that LC125 000 arose in the 20x5 financial year and is reflected in the 20x5 group statement of profit or loss and other comprehensive income.

5.2.1 Goodwill

For translation purposes, goodwill is treated as an asset of the foreign operation and is therefore expressed in the functional currency of the foreign operation (FC units in this case). It is translated at the closing rate at each reporting date (if there is a carrying amount) and the resulting exchange difference is presented in other comprehensive income.

In the example above, the subsidiary (S Ltd) was acquired on incorporation for an amount that equalled the net assets. This resulted in a goodwill balance of nil.

If P Ltd had instead paid FC20 000 to acquire its interest in S Ltd on 1 January 20x4, the acquisition would have resulted in goodwill of FC10 000, being the consideration transferred of FC20 000 less the net assets of S Ltd of FC10 000.

In the example above, this would have resulted in exchange differences of LC10 000 in 20x4 and LC10 000 in 20x5, calculated as follows:

	FC	Exchange rate	LC
Goodwill on 1 January 20x4	10 000	5	50 000
Exchange difference			10 000
31 December 20x4	10 000	6	60 000
Exchange difference			10 000
31 December 20X5	10 000	7	70 000

5.2.1.2   *Pro-forma* journal entries relating to goodwill

The following *pro-forma* journal entries are required to consolidate S Ltd in P Ltd's group financial statements for the 20x5 financial year (relating specifically to the goodwill):

				LC	LC
①	Dr		Share capital	50 000	
	Dr		Goodwill	50 000	
		Cr	Investment in S Ltd (FC20 000 × 5)		100 000

Elimination of investment at acquisition date and recognising goodwill

				LC	LC
②	Dr		Goodwill	20 000	
		Cr	Foreign currency translation reserve		10 000
		Cr	Foreign exchange gain (OCI)		10 000

Recognising changes in the carrying amount of goodwill, as a result of movements in exchange rates in current and prior periods

The first *pro-forma* journal entry relates to the position at the acquisition date, including the goodwill that arose (in this example)

Goodwill is recognised as a separate asset at a group level through the consolidation process, which implies that the goodwill is not recognised in the starting point aggregated trial balance. If the goodwill is not recognised, the related exchange differences are not recognised in the starting point aggregated trial balance either. However, as indicated previously, the goodwill that arises on the acquisition of a subsidiary is treated as an asset of the foreign operation for translation purposes. As such, the goodwill must be translated at the closing rate at each reporting date. To the extent that exchange differences arose in 20x4, which is the prior period, this is accumulated in the foreign currency translation reserve (as prior period exchange differences presented in other comprehensive income are closed off to that component of equity) and to the extent that the exchange gain arose in 20x5, this amount is presented in the 20x5 group statement of profit or loss and other comprehensive income.

5.2.2 Non-controlling interest

In the example above, S Ltd is a wholly owned subsidiary. Therefore none of its equity was attributable to the non-controlling interest as there was none. If S Ltd was not a wholly owned subsidiary, a portion of the exchange difference that arose in each reporting period would be attributed to the non-controlling interest on the same basis that the non-controlling interest shares in the profit or loss of the subsidiary. For example, if S Ltd were an 80%-held subsidiary of P Ltd, 80% of the exchange differences would be attributed to P Ltd in the year in which they arose and 20% to the non-controlling interest. This means that the amount accumulated in the foreign currency translation reserve would only be the portion attributable to the parent's equity holders. This is consistent with other group reserves such as retained earnings and revaluation surpluses.

Further, there may be implications for the goodwill recognised as a separate asset at the acquisition date because IFRS allows a measurement choice regarding the non-controlling interest at the acquisition date:

- If the non-controlling interest is measured at fair value, there may be an additional component of goodwill as a result of the difference between the fair value of the non-controlling interest and its proportionate share of the fair value of the net assets of the subsidiary.
- If non-controlling interest is measured at its proportionate share of the fair value of the net assets of the subsidiary, there is no additional impact on goodwill.

The way in which the non-controlling interest is measured at the acquisition date may affect the attribution of exchange differences recognised in respect of goodwill:

- If the non-controlling interest is measured at fair value at the acquisition date, the exchange difference relating to translating goodwill is attributed to the non-controlling interest on the same basis on which the interest shares in the profit or loss of the subsidiary.
- If the non-controlling interest is measured at proportionate share of the fair value of the net assets, then no exchange differences relating to the subsequent translation of goodwill are attributed to the non-controlling interest.

5.3 An asset is undervalued at the date of acquisition

We know that an asset must be measured initially at cost, which is generally fair value. The same principle applies to assets acquired when acquiring a subsidiary. We also know that the fair value may be different from the carrying amount of the asset in the subsidiary at the acquisition date.

Example

Foreign subsidiary with fair value adjustment to assets at acquisition date

P Ltd acquired 100% of S Ltd for FC11 000 on 1 January 20x4 when S Ltd's net assets had a fair value of FC11 000. The carrying amount of the net assets as recognised by S Ltd were represented by share capital of FC8 000 and retained earnings of FC2 000. In addition, P Ltd considered a plot of land of S Ltd to be undervalued by FC1 000. P Ltd's functional and presentation currency is LC. S Ltd's functional currency is FC. Ignore taxation.

Trial balance of S Ltd at 31 December 20x5

	FC	
	Debit	Credit
Share capital		8 000
Retained earnings on 31 December 20x4		62 000
Profit for the 20x5 period		110 000
Dividends declared on 31 December 20x5	30 000	
Machinery	70 000	
Inventory	20 000	
Bank	30 000	
Trade receivables	40 000	
Trade payables		10 000
	190 000	**190 000**

The above trial balance does not reflect any revaluation by S Ltd of its land.
    The following spot exchange rates applied:

	1FC = LC
At 1 January 20x4	5
At 31 December 20x4	6
At 31 December 20x5	7
Average for the period	
20x4	5.50
20x5	6.50

Using an analysis of equity

	Notes	FC	Exchange rate	LC
At the acquisition date:				
Share capital		8 000	5	40 000
Retained earnings		2 000	5	10 000
Land		1 000	5	5 000
After the acquisition date:				
20x4 financial year				
Profit for 20x4	2	60 000	5.5	330 000
Exchange difference	3			41 000
31 December 20x4	1	**71 000**	6	**426 000**
20x5 financial year				
Profit for the period	2	110 000	6.5	715 000
Dividends declared	2	(30 000)	7	(210 000)
Exchange difference	3			126 000
31 December 20x5	1	**151 000**	7	**1 057 000**

From the above example, you will notice that the net assets of the subsidiary differ by FC1 000 from the first example. They also differ from the net assets of S Ltd as per its trial balance as at 31 December 20x5. This amount relates to the adjustment made to the land of the subsidiary at the acquisition date, which the subsidiary did not recognise in its individual accounts (in other words, it is not in the starting point).

You will also notice that the cumulative exchange differences are now LC167 000. The additional LC2 000 arises from the fair value adjustment to the land at the acquisition date. This amount does not appear in the translated trial balance of S Ltd as S Ltd did not recognise the land at its fair value on 1 January 20x5.

These adjustments to the land, including the exchange differences, therefore need to be brought to account through *pro-forma* journal entries.

5.3.1 *Pro-forma* journal entries

The following *pro-forma* journal entries are required to consolidate S Ltd in P Ltd's group financial statements for the 20x5 financial year (relating specifically to the land):

			LC	LC
Dr		Share capital	40 000	
Dr		Retained earnings	10 000	
Dr		Land	5 000	
	Cr	Investment in S Ltd		55 000

Elimination of investment in subsidiary and adjusting land at the acquisition date

			LC	LC
Dr		Land	2 000	
	Cr	Foreign currency translation reserve		1 000
	Cr	Foreign exchange gain (OCI)		1 000

Recognising changes in the carrying amount or land, relating to movements in the exchange rates

6. Investment in associates or joint ventures

As indicated at the start of this chapter, if the foreign operation were an associate or a joint venture, the investor would still apply the equity method to its investment in the associate or joint venture in its group financial statements (see Chapter 9, Interests in associates and joint ventures).

In addition, the investor would apply the same principles as outlined in this chapter to translate the equity (net assets) of the associate or joint venture that are denominated in a functional currency different from the presentation currency used to prepare the investor's group financial statements.

As the investor does not control the associate or joint venture, the investor's group financial statements do not include any of the assets or liabilities of the associate or joint venture. The investor's group financial statements reflect the investment, initially at cost plus the changes in the profit or loss and other comprehensive income of the investee after the acquisition attributable to the investor. This includes the investor's share of the exchange difference relating to the investment in the foreign associate or joint venture.

As the investor's group financial statements do not include the individual assets and liabilities of the associate, it may make more sense to calculate the exchange difference using an analysis of equity.

Example

Investment in foreign associate

Assume that P Ltd acquires 30% (and significant influence) of A Ltd on 1 January 20x4, when A Ltd is incorporated. A Ltd is a foreign operation with a functional currency of FC units. P Ltd has a functional and presentation currency of LC units.

P Ltd pays FC3 000 to acquire its 30% interest and accounts for the investment in A Ltd on the cost basis in its separate financial statements.

The following analysis of equity has been prepared relating to the equity of A Ltd and P Ltd's interest in A Ltd:

	Notes	FC	Exchange rate	LC	LC	Investment in A Ltd
				100%	30%	
At the acquisition date:						
Share capital	①	10 000	5	50 000	15 000	15 000
After the acquisition date:						
20x4 financial year						
Profit for 20x4		60 000	5.5	330 000	99 000	99 000
Exchange difference	②			40 000	12 000	12 000
31 December 20x4		70 000	6	420 000	126 000	126 000
20x5 financial year						
Profit for the period		110 000	6.5	715 000	214 500	214 500
Dividends declared		(30 000)	7	(210 000)	(63 000)	(63 000)
Exchange difference	②			125 000	37 500	37 500
31 December 20x5		150 000	7	1 050 000	315 000	315 000

Notes

① P Ltd acquired its interest in A Ltd on the date of A Ltd's incorporation. In this example, P Ltd paid an amount equal to the equity (share capital) of A Ltd attributable to P Ltd at the acquisition date. There is therefore no goodwill component (refer to Chapters 4 to 7).

② The exchange difference for the 20x4 and 20x5 financial years is calculated on the same basis as the previous examples in this chapter.

Pro-forma journal entries

The following *pro-forma* journal entries are required to apply the equity method to the investment in A Ltd when preparing P Ltd's group financial statements for the 20x5 financial year:

			LC	LC
Dr		Investment in associate	111 000	
Dr		Retained earnings		99 000
	Cr	Foreign currency translation reserve		12 000

Recognising investor's share of prior years' profits in associate

			LC	LC
Dr		Investment in associate	252 000	
Cr		Share of profits in associate		214 500
	Cr	Foreign exchange gain (OCI)		37 500

Recognising investor's share in current year's profit or loss and other comprehensive income in associate

			LC	LC
Dr		Dividend income	63 000	
	Cr	Investment in associate		63 000

Reversing dividends received from associate

If you refer to the *pro-forma* journal entries above, you should note the following:

1. The *pro-forma* journal entries are the same, in principle, to those that were prepared in Chapter 9 to apply the equity method.
2. The starting point for the preparation of the group financial statements of P Ltd is the aggregated trial balance, which includes all of the assets and liabilities of P Ltd, and none of A Ltd's individual assets and liabilities. P Ltd's trial balance includes the investment in A Ltd at cost.
3. This *pro-forma* journal entry equity accounts P Ltd's share of the change in equity of A Ltd that arose in the prior period.
4. This *pro-forma* journal entry equity accounts P Ltd's share of the current year profits and the exchange difference.
5. Note that the exchange difference is recognised in other comprehensive income of the group in the year that it arises. The exchange rate difference results from the translation process in that year and the accumulated amount is recognised in the foreign currency translation reserve ('closed off to the foreign currency translation reserve'). In addition, the amount accumulated in the foreign currency translation reserve is P Ltd's share of the exchange difference. However, the amount recognised in other comprehensive income is only P Ltd's share of the exchange difference.
6. The last *pro-forma* journal entry is adjusting for the effects of the intra-group dividend.

The above example did not include the effects of goodwill. Remember from Chapter 9 that under the equity method, the goodwill is not recognised as a separate asset in the investor's group financial statements.

The above example focused on an investment in an associate. If A Ltd were a joint venture that is a foreign operation, P Ltd would, when drafting its group financial statements, apply the equity method as outlined above to its investment in the joint venture.

7. Disposal of a foreign operation

An entity may dispose of its interest in the foreign operation in various ways, for example, by selling its shares, or as a result of the foreign operation going into liquidation or the foreign operation repurchasing its share capital (share buy-back). The effect of a disposal is that it results in a loss of control, joint control or significant influence.

On the disposal of the foreign operation, the cumulative amount of the foreign exchange differences relating to that foreign operation recognised in other comprehensive income and accumulated in a separate component of equity is reclassified from equity to profit or loss when the gain or loss on disposal is recognised. A reclassification is the recognition in profit or loss of amounts previously recognised in other comprehensive income. This implies that the amount accumulated in the foreign currency translation reserve (that is, the parent's share of the cumulative exchange difference) is reclassified to profit or loss in the period in which the disposal occurs. This means a debit (or credit) to other comprehensive income and a credit (or debit) in profit or loss.

IFRS principles

Disposal of a foreign operation

When a foreign operation is disposed of, the cumulative amount of the exchange differences recognised in other comprehensive income and accumulated in the separate component of equity relating to that foreign operation shall be recognised in profit or loss when the gain or loss on disposal is recognised (refer to IAS21: 48).

Example
Disposal of an interest in a foreign subsidiary

If a parent owned 80% of a foreign subsidiary:
* The parent's group statement of profit or loss would reflect 100% of the exchange differences in other comprehensive income in the period they arose as a result of consolidating the subsidiary.
* However, only the parent's share of the exchange differences (that is, 80%) would be accumulated in the foreign currency translation reserve. The remaining 20% would have been attributed to the non-controlling interest.
* If the parent sells the subsidiary, the reclassified amount is the 80% accumulated in the foreign currency translation reserve.

Alternatively, there may only be a partial disposal. This is a change in the entity's interest in the foreign operation other than a disposal.

For example, the entity sells some of its shares in a foreign subsidiary, but retains significant influence. In this case, no amount is reclassified, although a proportionate amount reflected in the foreign currency translation reserve is reattributed to the non-controlling interest. This treatment is consistent with the treatment of transactions that do not result in the loss of control, where amounts are recognised directly in equity (refer to Chapter 12).

Example

What if an entity sells some shares in a foreign associate?

If an investor owned 30% of a foreign associate:
- The investor's group statement of profit or loss would reflect 30% of the exchange differences in other comprehensive income in the period they arose as a result of applying the equity method.
- This amount (that is, 30%) would be accumulated in the foreign currency translation reserve.
- If the investor sells a portion of the associate, but retains significant influence, that is a partial disposal. If, for example, the investor sells 10% of the shares in the associate (or alternatively 33.3% of the shares that the investor owns), the investor has reduced its shareholding in the associate to 20%. The reclassified amount is a proportionate share of the foreign currency translation reserve that relates to the shareholding disposed of (in this case, 33.3%).

8. Net investment in a foreign operation

A parent or investor (or another entity in the group) may lend cash to or borrow cash from the foreign operation in a foreign currency. For example, a parent entity with a functional currency of rands lends money to a foreign subsidiary with a functional currency of US dollars and the loan is denominated in US dollars. This results in a monetary item that is receivable from the foreign operation (or payable by the foreign operation) in US dollars. As indicated previously, restatement of monetary items at the reporting date or when settled results in exchange differences, which are recognised in profit or loss in the entity's separate financial statements. In this case, the foreign subsidiary has a functional currency of US dollars and as such, will not recognise any exchange difference. The parent entity has a functional currency of rands, but has a receivable that will be settled in US dollars. The restatement of the receivable to the spot rate at the reporting date results in a foreign exchange difference in the parent entity's separate financial statements.

However, where settlement of the monetary item is not planned nor likely in the foreseeable future, then the monetary item is similar in substance to an equity investment in the foreign operation. So, in the example above, the loan to the foreign subsidiary may not have a planned repayment date. However, the receivable is still a monetary item that results in an exchange difference when restated to the closing rate. As the loan to the foreign operation is in substance similar to an investment in the equity of the foreign operation, the resulting exchange difference is presented in other comprehensive income in the group financial statements of the parent (or investor). This is consistent with the treatment of the exchange differences relating to the translation of the foreign operation's net assets in the group financial statements of the parent (or investor).

Example
Wholly owned foreign subsidiary with inter-group loan

P Ltd lends FC100 000 to its 100%-held foreign subsidiary on 1 January 20x5. The loan is not expected to be repaid in the foreseeable future. On 1 January 20x5, 1 FC = 5 LC. At 31 December 20x5 (the reporting date), 1 FC = 6 LC. Ignore interest relating to the loan.

S Ltd records the following journal entries in its individual financial statements:

			FC	FC
Dr		Bank	100 000	
	Cr	Loan payable		100 000

Long term loan received from P Ltd

P Ltd records the following journal entries in its separate financial statements:

			LC	LC
Dr		Loan receivable	500 000	
	Cr	Bank		500 000

Recording cash lent to foreign subsidiary (FC100 000 × 5)

			LC	LC
Dr		Loan receivable	100 000	
	Cr	Foreign exchange gain (P/L)		100 000

Restating loan receivable to closing rate (FC100 000 × 6 – LC500 000)

The following *pro-forma* journal entries are required when drafting P Ltd's group financial statements:

			LC	LC
Dr		Loan payable	600 000	
	Cr	Loan receivable		600 000

Elimination of intra-group loan on consolidation

The loan between P Ltd and its foreign subsidiary is intra-group and as such is eliminated. Remember that the loan receivable is a monetary item and is therefore restated in LC using the closing rate in P Ltd's separate statement of financial position. The loan payable is a liability of S Ltd and as S Ltd is a foreign operation, the liability would have been translated at the closing rate at 31 December 20x5 for inclusion in the aggregated starting point trial balance used to prepare P Ltd's group financial statements.

			LC	LC
Dr		Foreign exchange gain (P/L)	100 000	
	Cr	Foreign exchange gain (OCI)		100 000

Exchange difference relating to loan in parent (starting point) recognised in other comprehensive income in group (end point)

The foreign exchange gain relates to how exchange rates have moved. The exchange difference is not intra-group. Consequently, the gain is not eliminated. In the parent's separate financial statements, the exchange difference is recognised in profit or loss. However, as the receivable in substance forms part of P Ltd's investment in the foreign subsidiary, the foreign exchange is presented in other comprehensive income. A *pro-forma* journal entry is therefore required to present the exchange difference in other comprehensive income correctly.

9. Disclosure

Disclosure of the following information is required:
- Exchange differences recognised in profit or loss (except those relating to financial instruments measured at fair value in accordance with IFRS9, *Financial Instruments*) must be identified.
- The net exchange differences recognised in other comprehensive income and accumulated in a separate component of equity must be identified. A reconciliation of the opening and closing balances of the component of equity is also required. This is generally presented as part of the statement of changes in equity.
- If the presentation currency differs from the functional currency, a statement to that effect is required as well as an explanation of why a different presentation currency is being used.
- If the functional currency of the entity or a significant foreign operation has changed, an explanation of why there has been a change is required.

Test your knowledge

There is a list of learning objectives at the beginning of this chapter. Go back to this list and check whether you have achieved these outcomes. If not, reread the appropriate section.

Questions

Question 1
P Ltd purchased 60% of the shares of S Plc, a company registered in a foreign country with a foreign functional currency (FC), on 1 January 20x3 for FC700 000, at which date the equity of S Plc was FC1 020 000. All of the identifiable assets and liabilities of S Plc were considered to be fairly valued at their carrying amounts in the financial statements of S Plc at the date of acquisition. All entities have a 31 December financial year end.
   You are presented with the analysis of the equity of S Plc (in FC units) that follows.

Analysis of equity: S Plc

	FC	FC	FC
	100%	60%	40%
Share capital	10 000		
Revaluation surplus	340 000		
Retained earnings	670 000		
	1 020 000	612 000	408 000
Cost at 1 January 20x3		700 000	
Goodwill		88 000	
Retained earnings (1 January 20x3–31 December 20x4)	160 000	96 000	64 000
Profit after tax	240 000	144 000	96 000
	1 420 000	**852 000**	**568 000**

The presentation currency of P Ltd is CU. The following exchange rates applied:

	FC1 = CU
At 1 January 20x3	1.13
At 31 December 20x3/1 January 20x4	1.15
At 31 December 20x4/1 January 20x5	1.10
Average 20x4	1.14
At 31 December 20x5/1 January 20x6	1.12
Average 20x5	1.11

You are required to do the following:
1. Determine at what amount P Ltd will recognise its investment in S Plc in its separate financial statements at 31 December 20x5.
2. Calculate the following amounts to be recognised in the group financial statements of P Ltd for the year ended 31 December 20x5:
   a. Goodwill
   b. Non-controlling interest
   c. Foreign currency translation reserve (FCTR)

Suggested solution

1. Initially, P Ltd will recognise the investment at the spot rate when the investment was made, which is on 1 January 20x3. Thus, in the separate financial statements of P Ltd, the investment is recognised initially at: FC700 000 × 1.13 = **CU791 000**
   The investment is a non-monetary item and is therefore not restated for changes in exchange rates. Assuming that P Ltd measures the investment on the cost basis in its separate financial statements, the carrying amount of the investment on 31 December 20x5 is CU 791 000.
2. a. Goodwill (group asset, translated at the closing exchange rate)
      FC88 000 × 1.12 = **CU98 560**
   b. Non-controlling interest:
      CU461 040 + CU72 960 – CU14 800 + CU106 560 + CU10 400 = CU636 160 (non-controlling interest is measured at its proportionate share of the net assets at the acquisition date plus changes in equity of S Plc post-acquisition)
   c. Foreign currency translation reserve (FCTR):
      –CU37 000 + CU 26 000 = –CU11 000 × 60% = –CU6 600

Plus: Translation of goodwill: (CU98 560 – CU97 680) = –CU880

FCTR: **CU7 480** (debit)

As the non-controlling interest was measured at its share of the net assets of S Plc at the acquisition date, no translation gains or losses relating to goodwill are attributed to the non-controlling interest.

Workings: Analysis of equity translated into presentation currency

	FC	Exchange rate	CU 100%	CU 60%	CU 40%
At the acquisition date:					
Share capital	10 000				
Revaluation surplus	340 000				
Retained earnings	670 000				
	1 020 000	1.13	1 152 600	691 560	461 040
Investment in S Plc				791 000	
Goodwill				99 440	
After the acquisition date					
20x4 financial year					
Profit for 20x4	160 000	1.14	182 400	109 440	72 960
Exchange difference			(37 000)	(22 200)	(14 800)
31 December 20x4	**1 180 000**	**1.10**	**1 298 000**	**778 800**	**519 200**
20x5 financial year					
Profit for the period	240 000	1.11	266 400	159 840	106 560
Exchange difference			26 000	15 600	10 400
31 December 20x5	**1 420 000**	**1.12**	**1 590 400**	**954 240**	**636 160**

Case study exercises

P Ltd purchased 60% (representing control) of Foreign Ltd on 1 January 20x3 for CU1 800. The retained earnings of Foreign Ltd at that date was FC1 000. Share capital has remained unchanged since then and no property, plant and equipment have been bought or sold by Foreign Ltd except as noted below. Non-controlling interest is measured at the attributable share of the fair value of the net assets at the acquisition date.

Foreign Ltd purchased its plant on 1 January 20x3 and is depreciated at 25% per annum on the straight-line basis with no residual value. Land and buildings were purchased on 1 January 20x3. Buildings are not depreciated. Goodwill is not impaired.

You received the extract that follows from the trial balance of Foreign Ltd.

Foreign Ltd trial balance as at 31 December 20x4

	FC Debit	FC Credit
Share capital		1 000
Share premium		500
Retained earnings: Pre-acquisition		1 000
Retained earnings: Post-acquisition		1 000
Long-term loan		2 500
Creditors		1 500
Bank overdraft		2 500
Land and buildings	3 000	
Plant, at cost	4 000	
Accumulated depreciation (plant)		2 000
Inventory	2 000	
Trade receivables	2 000	
Cash	1 000	
Sales		10 000
Cost of sales	5 000	
Depreciation (plant)	1 000	
Interest expense	1 000	
Dividends (30 September 20x4)	3 000	
	22 000	22 000

The following exchange rates are relevant:

	1CU = FC	1FC = CU
At 1 January 20x2	1.20	0.833
At 1 January 20x3	1.00	1.00
At 1 January 20x4	0.80	1.250
At 30 September 20x4	0.60	1.667
At 31 December 20x4	0.50	2.00
Average 20x2	1.10	0.909
Average 20x3	0.90	1.111
Average 20x4	0.70	1.429

Ignore taxation.

You are required to do the following:

1. Translate the results of Foreign Ltd assuming that its functional currency is FC (in other words, using the closing rate method). Assume that the translated closing retained earnings were as follows:
   - CU1 000 at 31 December 20x2
   - CU2 111 at 31 December 20x3.
     (In other words, CU1 111 [the FC1 000 translated at 20x3 average of 1.111] + CU1 000 = CU2 111.)
2. Prepare the *pro-forma* journal entries necessary to consolidate the translated results of Foreign Ltd with P Ltd at 31 December 20x4.

Suggested solution

1. Translation of trial balance of Foreign Ltd:

Foreign Ltd: Trial balance as at 31 December 20x4 (translation into presentation currency [CU])

	FC	Rate	CU
Share capital	(1 000)	1.00	(1 000)
Share premium	(500)	1.00	(500)
Retained earnings: Pre-acquisition	(1 000)	Given	(1 000)
Retained earnings: Post-acquisition	(1 000)	Given	(1 111)
Long-term loan	(2 500)	2.00	(5 000)
Creditors	(1 500)	2.00	(3 000)
Bank overdraft	(2 500)	2.00	(5 000)
Land and buildings	3 000	2.00	6 000
Plant, at cost	4 000	2.00	8 000
Accumulated depreciation (plant)	(2 000)	2.00	(4 000)
Inventory	2 000	2.00	4 000
Debtors	2 000	2.00	4 000
Cash	1 000	2.00	2 000
Sales	(10 000)	1.429	(14 290)
Cost of sales	5 000	1.429	7 145
Depreciation (plant)	1 000	1.429	1 429
Interest	1 000	1.429	1 429
Dividends	3 000	1.667	5 000
Foreign currency translation reserve (FCTR)			(4 102)
	0		0

① The CU4 102 is a cumulative balance. As disclosure is required of the opening balance and current year's transfer, these amounts will need to be calculated on the analysis of equity.

2. *Pro-forma* journal entries: Closing rate method:

(Note that the starting point is 100% of the CU trial balance, that is, it includes a foreign currency translation reserve of CU4 102.)

			CU	CU
Dr		Share capital	1 000	
Dr		Share premium	500	
Dr		Retained earnings (pre-acquisition)	1 000	
Dr		Goodwill (* translated at historic rate)	300	
	Cr	Investment in subsidiary		1 800
	Cr	Non-controlling interest (equity)		1 000

Reversal of equity at acquisition

			CU	CU
Dr		Retained earnings - post acquisition	444	
Dr		Foreign currency translation reserve (equity)	306	
	Cr	Non-controlling interest (equity)		750

Allocation of 40% of post-acquisition retained earnings + foreign currency translation reserve to non-controlling interest

			CU	CU
Dr		Goodwill	300	
	Cr	Foreign currency translation (OCI)		225
	Cr	Foreign currency translation reserve (equity)		75

Restatement of goodwill to closing rate; resulting adjustment recognised in foreign currency translation reserve

			CU	CU
Dr		Foreign currency translation reserve (equity)	3 338	
	Cr	Foreign currency translation (OCI)		3 338

Recognition of 100% of current year gains in OCI

			CU	CU
Dr		Non-controlling interest (P/L)	1 715	
	Cr	Non-controlling interest (equity)		1 715

Allocation of 40% of net income to non-controlling shareholders

			CU	CU
Dr		Dividend income	3 000	
Dr		Non-controlling interest (equity)	2 000	
	Cr	Dividends paid/retained earnings		5 000

Reversal of intra-group dividends

			CU	CU
Dr		Non-controlling interest (OCI)	1 335	
	Cr	Non-controlling interest (equity)		1 335

Allocation of 40% of foreign currency translation reserve non-controlling shareholders

Analysis of equity

	FC	Rate	100% CU	60% CU	40% CU
Share capital	1 000	1.00	1 000	600	400
Share premium	500	1.00	500	300	200
Retained earnings (pre-acquisition)	1 000	1.00	1 000	600	400
Equity at acquisition date	2 500	1.00	2 500	1 500	1 000
Cost				1 800	
Goodwill				300	
Retained earnings (post-acquisition)	1 000	1,111	1 111	667	444
Foreign currency translation reserve (equity)			② 764	458	306
Equity 31 December 20x3	3 500	1,250	4 375	2 625	1 750
Current year:					
Profit after tax	3 000	1,429	4 287	2 572	1 715
Dividends	(3 000)	1,667	(5 000)	(3 000)	(2 000)
Foreign currency translation reserve (other comprehensive income)			② 3 338	2 003	1 335
Equity 31 December 20x4	**3 500**	**2,00**	**7 000**	**4 200**	**2 800**

②   764 + 3338 = 4102 per translated trial balance

Group statements of cash flows

14

The following topics are included in this chapter:

- Basic methodology for preparing a group cash flow statement , including cash flows from operating activities, investing activities and financing activates
- Recognising cash and cash equivalents in group statements of cash flows
- Recognition of the purchase consideration for the acquisition of a controlling interest in a subsidiary in the group cash flow statements
- Recognition of the proceeds on the sale of a subsidiary in the group cash flow statement
- Recognition of the purchase consideration paid for an interest in an associate in the group statement of cash flows
- Recognition of intra-group dividends received and paid in the group statement of cash flows.

Learning objectives

By the end of this chapter, you should be able to:

- Prepare the statement of cash flows from the group's perspective, thereby reporting the cash flows of the group with third parties
- Explain how the group statement of cash flows is affected when a new subsidiary is acquired, and identify and present the net cash outflow in investing activities
- Explain and understand how the group statement of cash flows is affected when the controlling interest in a subsidiary is sold, and identify and present the net cash inflow from the disposal in investing activities
- Explain how cash flows relating to changes in interests in subsidiaries that do not represent a change in control affect the group statement of cash flows, and identify and present the related cash inflow or outflow in financing activities
- Explain how you would recognise the acquisition of an interest in an associate in the group statement of cash flows.

1. Introduction and basic principles

In this chapter, we will consider the preparation and presentation of a group statement of cash flows. The group statement of cash flows is based on the same basic principles and concepts as a statement of cash flows in an entity's separate financial statements. Therefore, as an introduction and to refresh your knowledge and understanding, you should refer to Chapter 27 of *Financial Accounting: IFRS Principles* (4e) by Lubbe, Modack and Watson before considering this chapter. If you understand the statement of cash flows in an entity's separate financial statements, and are comfortable with the principles and mechanics of group accounting addressed in earlier chapters of this textbook, you are well prepared to tackle a group statement of cash flows.

The preparation and presentation of the statement of cash flows is the subject of IAS7, *Statement of Cash Flows*. The objective of a statement of cash flows is to provide information about an entity's cash flows that allows the users of that information to assess its ability to generate cash and cash equivalents, and to determine how the entity utilises such cash flows. In the case of a **group entity**, the statement of cash flows provides information about the cash flows of the group as a single economic entity.

When preparing a group statement of cash flows, it is vital to consider the nature of the parent entity's investments in all other entities that form part of the group. In other words, are there investments that give rise to control, significant influence or joint control of other entities by the parent entity? Once the nature of all investments has been determined, the accounting treatment of such entities in the group financial statements can be established and, with this, an understanding can be acquired of which cash flows should be included in the group statement of cash flows.

For example, if the acquiring entity (or the investor) is able to exert control over the acquired entity (or the investee) as a result of its investment, the acquired entity is consolidated in the group financial statements. This means that 100% of the acquired entity's assets and liabilities (including its cash and cash equivalents) are included in the starting point when the group financial statements are being prepared. In the group statement of cash flows in this situation, 100% of the acquiring entity's cash flows and 100% of the acquired entity's cash flows are included in the starting point for preparing the group statement of cash flows. However, consistent with group principles that you have dealt with previously, only those cash flows to and from entities outside the group are presented in the actual group statement of cash flows (or the end point).

Table 14.1 summarises the treatment of cash flows depending on the nature of the investor's investment in another entity.

Table 14.1 Treatment of cash flows between group entities

Nature of investment	Accounting treatment of investment	Cash flows of investor to be included	Cash flows of investee to be included	Other considerations
Subsidiary (in other words, there is control)	Consolidate	100%	100%	All cash flows between the investor and the investee are to be eliminated (not included in group statement of cash flows)

Nature of investment	Accounting treatment of investment	Cash flows of investor to be included	Cash flows of investee to be included	Other considerations
An associate (in other words, there is significant influence)	Equity method (in accordance with IAS28, *Investments in Associates and Joint Ventures*)	100%	Zero (the equity method recognises the investor's post-acquisition share in the investee's equity; none of the investee's cash flows are recognised by the investor)	See treatment of distributions and payments or receipts between investor and investee in later sections of this chapter (see Section 4.5 below)
Joint venture	Equity method (in accordance with IAS28, *Investments in Associates and Joint Ventures*)	100%	Zero (application of the equity method as above)	See treatment of distributions and payments or receipts between investor and investee in later sections of this chapter (see Section 4.5 below)
Joint operation	Limited to investor's contributions to the joint operation	100%		All cash flows between the investor and investee are to be eliminated (not included in group statement of cash flows)

The group statement of cash flows is a component of the group annual financial statements. As such, the group statement of cash flows includes all cash that arises from transactions with entities that are outside the group.

2. Group cash flows versus changes in group equity

As discussed in the preceding chapters of this textbook, the nature of a reporting entity's investment in another entity determines the accounting treatment of that investment in the group financial statements of the reporting entity. The accounting treatment dictates how to determine the effects of changes in equity (in other words, assets less liabilities) of the investee or investees in the group financial statements. When an investor is able to exert significant influence upon another entity, that other entity is an associate of the investor and the investment is accounted for in accordance with the equity method in the group financial statements. This entails recognition of the changes in the entity's equity after acquisition based on the shareholding of the investor. No assets or liabilities of the investee are recognised in the group statement of financial position.

In previous chapters, you have learnt that the starting point for a group or consolidated statement of financial position is 100% of the assets and liabilities of the parent and subsidiary entities, and that the parent equity holders share in changes in the equity of the subsidiary since its acquisition date based on the parent's shareholding in the subsidiary entity. It makes sense, therefore, that cash flows relating to the subsidiary's assets and liabilities be included in the consolidated statement of cash flows.

Think about it

Before you continue ...

Before you continue with this chapter, make sure that you fully understand the principles, concepts and mechanics of group accounting outlined in the earlier chapters of this textbook as well as the basic principles, concepts and mechanics of the statement of cash flows. Without a solid foundation, you will struggle to understand the cash flow implications for groups as discussed in this chapter.

3. Basic methodology for preparing a group statement of cash flows

There are at least two approaches to take when preparing a consolidated statement of cash flows. The first is based on the same concept that is used in the preparation of other consolidated financial statements (which have been addressed in other chapters): combining the cash books (or cash transactions) of the parent and subsidiary entities (this is the starting point) and adjusting for any of the cash flow effects of any intra-group transactions.

The second is an extension of the approach that is often used to prepare a statement of cash flows of a separate entity. A statement of cash flows for an entity for a specific reporting period is usually prepared based on movements that occurred in that entity's statement of financial position, in other words, the movement in balances from the beginning to the end of the reporting period. The same thought process and approach are used when preparing a consolidated statement of cash flows. However, the movement in the balances of the consolidated statement of financial position is used as a basis for the calculation of cash flows for the group in the consolidated statement of cash flows.

Cash flow information is provided in the same format regardless of whether the information relates to a single entity or to group–cash flow information (whether cash has been generated or utilised). It is presented as one of the following activities: **operating activities**, **investing activities** or **financing activities**. In addition, the basic premise is the same: the statement of cash flows shows the changes in the opening and closing cash balances of the reporting entity. In this chapter, the reporting entity is the group.

The overriding principle is as follows: **Has the group's cash balances changed?** If the answer is, 'Yes', the group statement of cash flows needs to reflect this inflow or outflow. If not, there is no movement to be reflected in the group statement of cash flows.

3.1 Cash flows from operating activities

Group cash flows from operating activities are primarily derived from the principal revenue-producing activities of the group. As a starting point, these cash flows result from the transactions taken into account to determine the consolidated profit or loss for the reporting period. Because the group profit or loss is determined in accordance with the accrual basis as opposed to the cash basis on which the statement of cash flows is prepared, non-cash items that are included in the profit or loss for the period need to be identified in order to determine the cash flow resulting from operating activities. The group statement of cash flows is prepared for the group entity. The cash flow effects of any intra-group transactions between the parent and subsidiary (for example, an intra-group sale of inventories) are excluded from the group cash flows from operating activities as they do not represent changes in the group's cash. The group has not generated or utilised cash as a result of this intra-group transaction.

IAS7, *Statement of Cash Flows*, permits the operating activities to be presented using two different formats. The two formats differ only in the way in which the amount of cash generated from operations is presented. The remaining parts of the statement of cash flows are identical for both formats. The cash flows from operating activities are reported by using either the **direct method** or the **indirect method**.

3.2 Cash flows from investing activities

Group cash flows relating to investing activities are shown as a separate category on the group statement of cash flows. Cash flows arising from investing activities provide information about expenditures (which result in a recognised asset on the statement of financial position) made by the group to generate future income and cash flows.

Examples of group cash flows from **investing activities** include the following:
- Cash payments to acquire non-current assets
- Cash receipts from the sale of non-current assets
- Cash payments to acquire other entities and other equity or debt instruments
- Cash receipts from the sale of equity or debt instruments, or interests in other entities
- Cash advances and loans made to other parties or cash receipts from the repayment of such loans or advances.

Separate disclosure of investing activities to expand operations is encouraged as it is an indication of management's growth plans.

3.3 Cash flows from financing activities

The group cash flows from financing activities provide information about the cash flows to and from the providers of capital to the group. This is particularly useful to investors wishing to predict any future claims on the cash of the group. Separate disclosure is required of group cash flows from financing activities.

Examples of group cash flows arising from **financing activities** include the following:
- Cash proceeds from the issue of shares or other equity instruments
- Cash payments arising from the entity acquiring or redeeming the its own shares
- Cash proceeds from the issue of debentures, loans, bonds and other short- or long-term debt
- Cash repayments of amounts borrowed.

3.4 Cash and cash equivalents

The purpose of the group statement of cash flows is to **reconcile the cash and cash equivalents** of the group as a single economic entity at the beginning of the reporting period to the balance at the end of the reporting period (as reported in the group statement of financial position).

All of the cash and bank balances of the group as well as any other deposits or funds that are highly liquid (for example, call deposits) should be included as cash or cash equivalents.

3.5 Cash flow effects within the group

Movements between bank accounts (or cash resources) within the group should not be identified separately in the statement of cash flows as they do not represent inflows or outflows of cash from an external party to the group entity. For example, where the parent has transferred CU100 000 to its subsidiary as a loan, there is a decrease in the bank balance in the separate financial statements of the parent and an increase in the bank balance in the financial statements of the subsidiary. However, from the perspective of the group (a single economic entity), there is no change in cash resources. There is therefore no need for separate identification of this transaction on the group statement of cash flows.

In this section, we will focus on the preparation of a consolidated statement of cash flows for a group that consists of the parent entity and one subsidiary entity. The preparation of the group statement of cash flows when there are investments in associates and joint arrangements is discussed in Section 4.5 below.

Based on the assumption for this section, the consolidated statement of cash flows therefore includes the following as a starting point:
- 100% of the cash flows of the parent entity
- 100% of the cash flows of the subsidiary.

However, only those cash flows that have flowed outside of the group should ultimately be presented.

When the consolidated statement of cash flows is being prepared, either of the following approaches may be used:
- Use the information provided in the statements of cash flows of each entity in the group.
- Use the consolidated statement of financial position and consolidated statement of profit or loss and other comprehensive income as the starting point and adjust the accrual-based information to determine the relevant cash flows.

The approach selected is determined based on the information provided to you and how the reporting systems for the group are set up. However, the second approach is more popular as the intra-group transactions have already been eliminated. This approach is illustrated by the example that follows.

 Example

Preparing a consolidated statement of cash flows

The extracts that follow from the consolidated financial statements for P Ltd are presented at 31 December 20x5 (its reporting date). P Ltd acquired 60% of the issued share capital of S Ltd for a cash consideration of CU180 000 on 1 January 20x5.

Consolidated statement of financial position at 31 December 20x5

	20x5 CU	20x4 CU
ASSETS		
Non-current assets	467 000	279 500
Goodwill	39 000	39 000
Accounts receivable	107 000	167 500
Inventories	172 000	65 000
Cash and cash equivalents	104 000	53 000
	889 000	**604 000**
EQUITY AND LIABILITIES		
Share capital	240 000	240 000
Retained earnings	321 000	90 000
Non-controlling interest	108 000	94 000
Liabilities	220 000	180 000
	889 000	**604 000**

Consolidated statement of profit or loss for the year ended 31 December 20x5 (extract)

	20x5 CU
Profit before tax	350 000
Taxation	(105 000)
Profit after tax	**245 000**
Attributable to the parent equity holders	231 000
Attributable to the non-controlling interest	14 000

The following items are included in profit before tax:
- Depreciation on non-current assets: CU45 000
- Profit on sale of machinery: CU2 300
- Accrued interest expense relating to the long-term loan liability (included as part of 'Liabilities'): CU18 000.

Plant and equipment with a cost price of CU10 000 and a carrying amount of CU7 500 on the date of sale was sold for CU9 800. All non-current asset acquisitions by the group during the period were for the purpose of expansion.

As the consolidated statement of financial position and consolidated statement of profit or loss are used to prepare the consolidated statement of cash flows, all of the consolidation adjustments have already been included. The **indirect method** is used for the preparation of the consolidated statement of cash flows, as shown below.

Consolidated statement of cash flows for the year ended 31 December 20x5

	CU
Cash flows from operating activities	
Profit before taxation	350 000
Adjustments for:	
Depreciation	45 000
Profit from disposal of non-current assets	(2 300)
Interest expense	18 000
Adjustments for changes in working capital:	
Decrease in accounts receivable	60 500
Increase in inventories	(107 000)
Taxation paid (assume all tax are current tax and have been paid)	(105 000)
Net cash from operating activities	**259 200**
Cash flows from investing activities	**(230 200)**
Purchase of non-current assets for expansion ①	(240 000)
Proceeds from disposal of non-current assets	9 800
Cash flows from financing activities	**22 000**
Increase in long-term loan (220 000 – [180 000 + 18 000])	22 000
Net increase in cash and cash equivalents	**51 000**
Cash and cash equivalents at beginning of period	53 000
Cash and cash equivalents at end of period	**104 000**

① In order to determine the purchase of non-current assets in the group, we 'reconstruct' the general ledger account for non-current assets (at their carrying amount) from the group's perspective:

Non-current assets			
Balance at beginning of year	279 500	Carrying amount of asset disposed	7 500
		Depreciation	45 000
∴ Additions	① 240 000	Closing balance	467 000
	519 500		**519 500**
Balance at end of year	467 000		

Note that there are no adjustments for non-controlling interest or goodwill. The non-controlling interest is in equity and changes in equity do not represent any cash flows.

3.5 Dividends paid by a subsidiary

Dividends paid by a subsidiary only have an effect on the group cash flows to the extent of the amount paid to the non-controlling interest since these are equity holders outside the group. In the previous chapters, you learnt that the dividends declared by the parent as well as the non-controlling interest's share in the subsidiary's dividends declared are presented in the consolidated statement of changes in equity. Similarly, only the dividends declared and paid by the parent and the subsidiary's dividends declared and paid to the non-controlling interest are included in the consolidated statement of cash flows.

Example

Dividends declared and paid in the group

P Ltd owns 60% of S Ltd. The following dividends were paid in cash by the two entities during the financial year ending 31 December 20x5:

	CU
P Ltd	800 000
S Ltd	550 000

What is the dividend income recognised in P Ltd?

In P Ltd's separate financial statements, dividend income (from S Ltd) is recognised at **CU330 000** (60% × CU550 000).

What is the dividend income recognised in the consolidated financial statements?

None, as the dividend income is eliminated by the following *pro-forma* journal entry:

			CU	CU
Dr		Dividend income (P/L)	330 000	
Dr		Non-controlling interest (equity)	220 000	
	Cr	Dividend declared (equity)		550 000

Elimination of intra-group dividend

What is the dividend declared that is included in the consolidated statement of changes in equity?

P Ltd's dividend of CU800 000 plus S Ltd's dividend attributable to the non-controlling interest of CU220 000 = **CU1 020 000**.

What are the cash flow implications of the dividends received and paid?

Dividends received: There is no dividend received in the consolidated statement of cash flows. This is because the dividends were received from other entities in the group, thus there were no cash inflows from outside the group.

Dividends paid:

- P Ltd paid its dividend of CU800 000 to the parent equity holders.
- S Ltd paid its dividend of CU550 000, of which CU330 000 was received by P Ltd, thus this cash remained within the group.
- The portion of S Ltd's dividend attributable to the non-controlling and paid outside the group amounts to CU220 000.
- Total dividends paid in the consolidated statement of cash flows amounts to **CU1 020 000**. This represents the amount paid to equity holders of the group, in other words, the cash outflow from the group relating to dividends paid to the reporting entity's equity holders.

4. Cash flow effects of changes in ownership

As mentioned earlier, the accounting treatment of an investment in another entity in the statement of cash flow is dependent on the nature of this investment. In other words, does the investment in another entity result in the acquiring entity having control, significant influence or joint control over the other entity? When the initial acquisition of an interest in a subsidiary, associate or joint arrangement is acquired for cash, it represents a cash outflow for the group. Similarly, when an investment in a subsidiary, associate or joint arrangement is disposed of for cash, the proceeds received (cash) represents an inflow of cash. The sections that follow explain the different changes in ownership and the resulting cash flow implications.

IFRS principles

Changes in ownership interests in subsidiaries and other businesses (IAS7: 39 and 40)

The aggregate cash flows relating to acquisitions and disposals of subsidiaries and other business units should be presented separately and classified as **investing activities**. Specified additional disclosures should also be presented.

The aggregate cash paid or received as consideration should be reported net of cash and cash equivalents acquired or disposed of. When a subsidiary is acquired, one of the assets acquired may be cash and cash equivalents. The net cash consideration paid for the acquisition of the controlling interest in the subsidiary is thus the amount paid by the parent for its controlling interest, less any cash balances of the subsidiary. There are two things happening here:

First, the reporting entity acquires control (for which a cash consideration is paid) or loses control (for which cash is received).

Then the reporting entity either obtains control of the cash and cash equivalent balances of the subsidiary or (when the controlling interest is lost) loses control of the cash and cash equivalent balances of the subsidiary.

When a parent entity obtains control of an operating entity or loses control of an existing subsidiary, the comparative consolidated statement of the financial position before and after the acquisition or disposal reflects significant changes in the assets and liabilities arising from the acquisition or disposal. When an entity acquires an investment in another entity that is settled in cash, such an investment is reflected as a **cash outflow** in the **investing activities** of the acquiring entity's separate statement of cash flows. This treatment is consistent with that which is applicable when acquiring a non-current asset such as a building.

Think about it

Non-cash purchase of investment

What happens when an investment in another entity is settled by the acquiring entity issuing a number of its own shares to the previous shareholders of the acquired entity? Does this represent a cash flow? Should there be an effect on the acquiring entity's statement of cash flows?

Answer: No, there is no cash payment for the acquisition of the interest in the other entity. The acquiring entity's statement of cash flows is therefore not affected unless the subsidiary has cash and cash equivalents as one of its assets.

Similarly, when the original acquiring entity decides to dispose of all or a portion of its investment in another entity, if the disposal results in the receipt of cash, this cash is reflected as a **cash inflow** in the **investing activities** section of the acquiring entity's separate statement of cash flows.

Example

Cash flow implications in separate financial statements of investor

Assume that P Ltd acquired 100 shares in S Ltd in 20x4 for a total cash consideration of CU1 000. In 20x5, P Ltd disposed of all of these shares for CU1 200 in cash. Consider the separate financial statements of the investor, P Ltd.

Did P Ltd generate a profit on disposal of these shares?

Yes, P Ltd sold an asset that had an original cost of CU1 000 for CU1 200, thus generating a profit of CU200.

Where is this profit recognised in the financial statements of P Ltd?

In the separate financial statements of P Ltd, the profit is recognised in profit or loss (assuming that the investment is recognised at cost or at fair value, with fair value adjustments in profit or loss).

If P Ltd prepares its statement of cash flows using the indirect method, what effect will the disposal of the shares have in the 20x5 financial year?

The profit on the disposal of the investment (CU200) will be excluded (or deducted) from the cash flows from operating activities and the proceeds of CU1 200 will be included in cash flows from investing activities.

4.1 Acquisition of a controlling interest in an entity

At the acquisition date on which an investor acquires control of another entity, the assets and liabilities of that entity are consolidated when preparing the group financial statements. From the group's perspective, the assets (including cash and cash equivalents) of the subsidiary have been acquired and its liabilities have been assumed, and if the group paid for this acquisition in cash, there is an outflow of cash resources.

The assets and liabilities in the consolidated statement of financial position include all of the assets and liabilities of the parent and its subsidiary from the date of acquisition of a controlling interest in the subsidiary. None of the subsidiary's assets or liabilities is included in the comparative amounts in the consolidated statement of financial position as it was not a subsidiary in the prior period. As the acquisition of the individual assets and liabilities of the subsidiary represents a **business combination**, these assets and liabilities should not be shown separately as 'new' assets acquired and liabilities assumed in the consolidated statement of cash flows. They should rather be combined in one line item: 'acquisition of subsidiary'.

If the investment is settled in cash, this investment is included as part of the investing activities section in the consolidated statement of cash flows as a cash outflow. This makes sense as this is a transaction with a third party (the seller who was the previous owner of the shares in the investee) that is not part of the group and must therefore be reflected on the consolidated statement of cash flows.

Once control of a subsidiary has been obtained, the process for determining cash flow amounts is the same as that in separate cash flow statements. However, as a result of consolidation (of the assets and liabilities of the subsidiary), the process for determining cash movements (generally through the reconstruction of 'group' general ledger accounts) includes the effect of the assets and liabilities of the acquired entity. The additional assets acquired and liabilities assumed should be included in the relevant group general ledger accounts at their respective fair values at the date of acquisition before calculating any group operating, investing and financing cash flows.

Example

Cash flow effects of the acquisition of an asset through the acquisition of a subsidiary

P Ltd acquired a controlling interest in S Ltd during the 20x5 financial year. On acquisition date, S Ltd owned investment property with a fair value of CU27 000. P Ltd owned investment property with a fair value of CU70 000 at the end of the previous reporting period. On the last day of the financial period, P Ltd and S Ltd's investment properties had fair values of CU110 000 and CU39 000 respectively. No investment properties were disposed of during the year and a fair value adjustment relating to investment property of CU22 000 was recognised in group profit or loss for the 20x5 financial year.

The following is an extract from the group statement of financial position at 31 December 20x5:

	Dr/(Cr)	Group 20x5 CU	Group 20x4 CU
Investment property (20x5: CU110 000 + 39 000)		149 000	70 000

The 'group' investment properties general ledger account can be reconstructed as follows:

Investment properties			
	CU		CU
Balance at beginning of year	70 000		
Subsidiary acquired	27 000		
∴ Additions	30 000		
Fair value adjustments	22 000		
	149 000		**149 000**

From the reconstructed 'group' general ledger account above, we determined that additional investment property amounting to CU30 000 was acquired by the group during 20x5. This excludes the investment property of CU27 000 acquired as part of the business combination involving S Ltd.

The acquisition of investment property for cash of CU30 000 is included in the 'cash flows from investing activities' section in the consolidated statement of cash flows for the financial year ending 31 December 20x5. The acquisition of the investment property of S Ltd amounting to CU27 000 is included in the net acquisition cost of the subsidiary as well as in the 'cash flows from investing activities' section in the consolidated statement of cash flows for the financial year ending 31 December 20x5.

If, at the date of acquisition, the investee has a balance for cash and cash equivalents, this must be considered when preparing the consolidated statement of cash flows as it forms part of the net assets in the subsidiary acquired. Therefore, the **net effect** upon acquisition of a controlling interest in an entity (reflected in the investing activities section) is the outflow relating to the investment **less** the inflow (the cash and cash equivalents of the investee at the acquisition date).

Cash flows that result from the transaction in which control over a subsidiary is obtained is presented as a single line that represents the net payment (that is, net of any cash and cash equivalent balances of the subsidiary acquired) for **interests in subsidiaries acquired**. This is included as an **investing activity**. A summary of the business combination transaction is provided in the notes to the financial statements in order to support and explain the net cash consideration paid. This summary should include the following information (refer to IAS7: 40):

- The total consideration paid
- The portion of the consideration consisting of cash and cash equivalents
- The amount of cash and cash equivalents in the subsidiaries or other businesses over which control is obtained
- The amount of the assets and liabilities other than cash or cash equivalents in the subsidiaries or other businesses over which control is obtained, summarised by each major category.

Example

Acquisition of subsidiary

P Ltd acquired 60% of the issued share capital of S Ltd for a cash consideration of CU180 000 on 31 December 20x5. (This represents a controlling interest in S Ltd.) The extract that follows is from the financial statements of P Ltd and S Ltd at **31 December 20x5** (in other words, the acquisition date of S Ltd is the same as the reporting date).

Consolidated statement of financial position at 31 December 20x5

	P Ltd CU	S Ltd CU	Pro-forma journal CU	Group 20x5 CU	Group 20x4 CU
ASSETS					
Non-current assets	247 000	220 000		467 000	210 000
Other current assets	203 000	100 000		303 000	75 000
Cash and cash equivalents	50 000	30 000		80 000	155 000
Goodwill			18 000	18 000	–
Investment in S Ltd	180 000		(180 000)	–	–
	680 000	350 000	(162 000)	868 000	440 000
EQUITY AND LIABILITIES					
Share capital	240 000	120 000	(120 000)	240 000	240 000
Retained earnings	300 000	150 000	(150 000)	300 000	90 000
Non-controlling interest			108 000	108 000	
Liabilities	140 000	80 000		220 000	110 000
	680 000	350 000	(162 000)	868 000	440 000

The controlling interest in S Ltd was acquired on 31 December 20x5. Thus, at 31 December 20x4, the prior reporting period, S Ltd was not a subsidiary and, based on the information provided, P Ltd had no other subsidiaries. The group acquired the net assets of S Ltd on 31 December 20x5 and paid CU180 000 in cash for this investment.

What amount or amounts should be included in the consolidated statement of cash flows of P Ltd for the financial year ended 31 December 20x5?

The cash consideration paid for the controlling interest amounts to CU180 000. In P Ltd's separate financial statements, this amount should be recognised as 'investment in subsidiary' under investing activities.

In the **consolidated statement of cash flows**, the net cash consideration should be presented. This amount is calculated as follows:

	CU
Cash consideration paid/investment in subsidiary	180 000
Less: Cash and cash equivalents acquired	(30 000)
Net cash consideration paid for purchase of subsidiary	150 000

This amount is included in the cash flows from investing activities.

Detailed information relating to the acquisition of the net assets in the subsidiary is presented in the notes to the group statement of cash flows, as shown below.

Acquisition of subsidiary

	CU
Non-current assets	220 000
Other current assets	100 000
Cash and cash equivalents	30 000
Less: Liabilities	(80 000)
Total equity of S Ltd at acquisition date	270 000
Attributable to non-controlling interest (40%)	(108 000)
Goodwill acquired	18 000
Total purchase price	180 000
Less: Cash and cash equivalents acquired	(30 000)
Net cash consideration paid for purchase of subsidiary	**150 000**

The group statement of financial position reflects these new assets acquired and liabilities assumed individually. However, as these net assets were acquired as a business combination, the net cash consideration paid for this investment is shown as a single line under the investing activities in the group statement of cash flows.

4.2 Loss of controlling interest through disposal of shares for cash

Similar to the acquisition of a controlling interest in a subsidiary, the cash flow effects of the loss of control through the disposal of an interest in another entity are reported as a single cash flow transaction in the consolidated statement of cash flows. When a parent loses control of a subsidiary, any cash and cash equivalents held by that subsidiary at the time of its disposal are deducted from the cash consideration received when reporting the cash flow effects of losing control.

The following detailed information relating to the **loss of control** of subsidiaries during a financial period should be presented (refer to IAS7: 40):

- The total consideration received
- The portion of the consideration consisting of cash and cash equivalents
- The amount of cash and cash equivalents in the subsidiaries over which control is lost
- The amount of the assets and liabilities other than cash or cash equivalents in the subsidiaries over which control is lost per major category.

Example

Sale of entire interest in subsidiary

P Ltd purchased 90% of the shares in S Ltd on 1 January 20x3 for CU920 000. This represents a controlling interest. At that date, the fair value of the net identifiable assets of S Ltd was CU800 000. P Ltd sold its entire shareholding in S Ltd on 31 December 20x5 for cash of CU1 400 000. The current reporting date is 31 December 20x5.

The net assets of S Ltd amounted to CU1 150 000 at 31 December 20x5 and comprised of the following:

	CU
Non-current assets	520 000
Other current assets	300 000
Cash and cash equivalents	480 000
Less: Liabilities	(150 000)
	1 150 000

What is the profit on the disposal of the interest in S Ltd in the separate financial statement of P Ltd?

P Ltd acquired this investment for CU920 000 and sold it for CU1 400 000. Thus, in the separate financial statements of P Ltd, a profit on disposal of investment in subsidiary amounting to CU480 000 should be recognised.

What are the cash flow implications in the separate financial statements of P Ltd?

At 31 December 20x5, when P Ltd disposed of its interest in S Ltd, P Ltd will show the proceeds from the disposal of its interest in S Ltd, amounting to CU1 400 000, in the statement of cash flows under investing activities.

For the year ended 31 December 20x5, what is the profit on disposal of the interest in S Ltd in the group financial statements of P Ltd?

	CU
Proceeds from sale of controlling interest	1 400 000
Less: Net assets disposed of	(1 150 000)
Less: Goodwill recognised at acquisition (w1)	(200 000)
Less: Non-controlling interest derecognised (w2)	115 000
Group profit on disposal of subsidiary	**165 000**

(w1): (CU920 000 – (CU800 000 × 90%) = CU200 000
(w2): CU1 150 000 × 10% = CU115 000

What is the amount in the group statement of cash flows relating to the sale of the subsidiary?

In the **group statement of cash flows**, the net cash consideration should be presented, calculated as follows:

	CU
Cash consideration received	1 400 000
Less: Cash and cash equivalents of subsidiary disposed of	(480 000)
Net cash consideration received from sale of subsidiary	920 000

This amount is included in the cash flows from investing activities.

The detailed information relating to the sale of the subsidiary is presented in the notes to the consolidated statement of cash flows, as shown below.

Sale of controlling interest in subsidiary

	CU
Non-current assets	520 000
Other current assets	300 000
Cash and cash equivalents	480 000
Less: Liabilities	(150 000)
Total assets of subsidiary sold	1 150 000
Non-controlling interest derecognised (10%)	(115 000)
Goodwill derecognised	200 000
Profit on disposal of subsidiary	165 000
Total proceeds from sale of subsidiary	1 400 000
Less: Cash and cash equivalents sold	(480 000)
Net cash consideration received from sale of subsidiary	920 000

At 31 December 20x5, the group statement of financial position no longer includes these assets and liabilities as the controlling interest in the subsidiary has been sold.

The net proceeds received (in cash) for the sale of the controlling interest, amounting to CU920 000, is shown as a single line under the investing activities in the consolidated statement of cash flows.

4.3 **Acquisition of an operation**

In some cases, an entity may acquire an operation or 'business' directly through the acquisition of assets, as opposed to acquiring control of another entity's assets through the investment in the shares of another entity. The principles of a business combination apply equally to the acquisition of a business's assets.

IFRS principles

What is a business?

A business is an integrated set of activities and assets that is capable of being conducted and managed for the purpose of providing a return in the form of dividends, lower costs or other economic benefits directly to investors or other owners, members or participants (refer to Appendix A to IFRS3, *Business Combinations*).

When the assets of another entity are acquired directly, these assets are included in both the separate and, if applicable, the group financial statements of the investor (the entity that has acquired the assets). The principles of IFRS3, *Business Combinations*, apply to the acquisition of a business (as defined). The identifiable assets acquired and liabilities assumed are recognised and measured at fair value at the acquisition date. The business acquisition is settled with the transfer of a consideration, which can be in the form of cash, other monetary assets, non-monetary assets or equity instruments, or a combination of these. When payment is in the form of a cash consideration, this payment is reported in the statement of cash flows.

The cash consideration paid for the acquisition of a business is reported as a separate purchase and is classified under **investing activities** in the statement of cash flows. If one of the assets acquired in the business operation represents cash and cash equivalents, the aggregate cash paid should be reported net of such cash and cash equivalents acquired. The acquisition is presented in the separate financial statements of the investor as this is a direct acquisition of the business operation by the investor. (Note that if a consolidated statement of cash flows is presented, this cash flow will be presented in the same way as in the separate statement of cash flows.)

Example

Acquisition of a business

P Ltd acquired the assets and liabilities listed below from X Ltd on 30 June 20x5. It paid CU800 000 in cash for the business.

Fair value of identifiable net assets at 30 June 20x5

	CU
Machinery	350 000
Inventory	180 000
Trademarks	300 000
Cash	20 000
Accounts payable	(80 000)
Total	**770 000**

P Ltd acquired the individual net assets from X Ltd, instead of acquiring a controlling interest through a purchase of shares of X Ltd. This transaction is accounted for as a business combination in accordance with IFRS3. The excess of consideration paid over the fair value of the net assets acquired represents goodwill.

What goodwill should be recognised?

P Ltd paid CU800 000 for the net identifiable assets, which amount to CU770 000. The excess of CU30 000 represents goodwill to be recognised.

What amount or amounts should be included in the separate statement of cash flows of P Ltd for the financial year ended 31 December 20x5?

P Ltd, the separate entity, acquired a business. The net cash consideration paid by P Ltd amounts to CU780 000 (CU800 000 paid less CU20 000 cash acquired). CU780 000 should be reported as the 'purchase of the business' and classified under investing activities.

The detailed information relating to the acquisition of the business is presented in the notes to the statement of cash flows, as shown below.

Purchase of business operation

	CU
Machinery	350 000
Inventory	180 000
Trademarks	300 000
Cash	20 000
Accounts payable	(80 000)
Total equity of S Ltd at acquisition date	770 000
Goodwill recognised	30 000
Total purchase price	800 000
Less: Cash and cash equivalents acquired	(20 000)
Net cash consideration paid for business operation	**780 000**

What amount or amounts should be included in the consolidated statement of cash flows for the financial year ended 31 December 20x5?

Consolidated financial statements will only be prepared if P Ltd has interests in subsidiaries. Despite being accounted for similarly to the acquisition of a subsidiary, the investment in a business does not represent a subsidiary. The reported cash flow and disclosure will be the same as in the separate financial statements of P Ltd.

4.4 Changes in ownership when control is retained

In Chapter 12, you learnt that changes in ownership that do not result in a change in control are not business combinations. Therefore, if the shareholding of the parent in the subsidiary increases or decreases, but control in the subsidiary is retained, the parent continues to consolidate the subsidiary. As a result, the group statement of financial position includes all of the assets and liabilities of the parent and the subsidiary, and the transaction that gave rise to a change in ownership does not change this. When preparing the consolidated statement of cash flows, the cash flow movements reported relate to all of the assets and liabilities of the group.

When transactions that change ownership interest but do not impact on control occur, the carrying amounts of the controlling interest and the non-controlling interest are adjusted to reflect the change in respective ownership interests. This is a transaction between the parent and the non-controlling interest, and any differences between the consideration paid or received by the parent to the non-controlling interest resulting from the acquisition or sale of the additional shares and the carrying amount of the relevant non-controlling interest in the subsidiary is recognised directly in equity. This is known as an 'equity adjustment'.

IFRS principles

Changes in ownership that do not result in a loss of control

Cash flows arising from changes in ownership interest in a subsidiary that do not result in a loss of control shall be classified as cash flows from financing activities (refer to IAS7: 42A).

The amount paid for the additional interest in the subsidiary or the amount received for the portion of the interest sold in the subsidiary represents a cash outflow or inflow to the group. Cash flows arising from changes in ownership interests in a subsidiary that do not result in a loss of control should be classified as cash flows from **financing activities**. This makes sense as such cash flows represent payments or receipts relating to transactions with equity participants, therefore the cash flows are classified in the same way as other transactions with equity participants. When additional shares in a subsidiary are acquired or some shares are sold, the payment is between the parent (investor) and the non-controlling interest (holder of equity in a group entity).

Example

A parent selling some of its shareholding in a subsidiary while retaining control

P Ltd acquired 60% of the ordinary shares (and control) of S Ltd on 30 June 20x4 for CU25 000, when the share capital of S Ltd amounted to CU10 000 and its retained earnings amounted to CU30 000. All of the assets and liabilities of S Ltd were considered fairly valued at acquisition date. The non-controlling interest was measured at its proportionate share of the net assets of S Ltd at the acquisition date. P Ltd sold 5% of its shareholding in S Ltd on 31 December 20x5 for CU9 000 in cash.

What amount or amounts should be included in the separate statement of cash flows of P Ltd for the financial year ended 31 December 20x5?
P Ltd reports the cash flow from the sale of its 5% interest in S Ltd as a 'proceeds from sale of shares' amounting to CU9 000, classified under **investing activities**.

What amount or amounts should be included in the consolidated statement of cash flows for the financial year ended 31 December 20x5?
On consolidation, this is a transaction between the equity participants, as P Ltd sold 5% of its shares in a subsidiary to the non-controlling shareholders.
  Thus, the cash flow from the sale of its 5% interest in S Ltd is reported as 'proceeds from sale of partial interest in subsidiary'. It amounts to CU9 000 and is classified under **financing activities**.

This is effectively a transaction between P Ltd and a class of equity holders that has increased the cash balance of the group from the proceeds received, but has resulted in an additional contribution by the non-controlling interest (by paying P Ltd and acquiring an additional shareholding in S Ltd).

4.5 Cash flow effects of applying the equity method

Where an investor is able to exert significant influence over the investee (in other words, the investee is an associate of the investor) or where the investor has joint control over an investee (that is a joint venture), this investment is accounted for by applying the equity method (refer to Chapter 9 for a detailed discussion of the equity method) in the group financial statements.

The equity method does not include any of the assets or liabilities of the associate or joint venture in the group financial statements as there is no control. Furthermore, no cash flows of the associate or joint venture are reflected at a group level. The group statement of financial position recognises the investor's share of the post-acquisition equity of the investee in the **investment** in the associate or joint venture. Therefore, the associate's (or joint venture's) cash is not included in the group's cash balances. Thus it makes sense that none of the associate's (or joint venture's) changes in cash balances are reflected in the investor's group statement of cash flows.

Any cash flows of the investor relating to the actual investment in the associate or joint venture (such as receipts, payments and distributions between the entities) are reported in the group statement of cash flows as they represent cash that has been received (or paid out) by the investor. Similarly, these amounts represent cash that has flowed from or into the group.

 IFRS principles

Cash flows of associates and joint ventures

Where the equity method is used, the statement of cash flows should report only cash flows between the investor and the investee. Reporting is restricted to the cash flows between the investor and investee, for example, to dividends and advances (refer to IAS7: 37–38).

Cash flows between the investor and the associate (or joint venture) arise from the acquisition of the investment, loans to and from associates and joint ventures, proceeds from the sale of the investment and dividends received. Any other assets sold to an associate or joint venture are reported in the same way as a cash flow transaction with a third party. For example, when the investor sells a machine to an associate, the proceeds from the sale are reported in the same way the sale of any other property, plant and equipment items.

The example that follows illustrates the cash flow implications relating to intra-group dividends and loans when the group statement of cash flows relating to investments in both subsidiaries and associates is being prepared.

Example

Cash flows relating to intra-group dividends and loans

P Ltd owns the following investments:
- 60% of S Ltd, a subsidiary
- 30% in A Ltd, an associate
- 50% in JV Ltd, a joint venture.

The following dividends were declared and paid in cash by the different entities during the financial year ending 31 December 20x5:

	CU
P Ltd	800 000
S Ltd	550 000
A Ltd	320 000
JV Ltd	150 000

In addition, the following cash loans were made during the current financial year:
- P Ltd lent CU1 000 000 each to S Ltd and A Ltd.
- S Ltd lent CU500 000 to JV Ltd.
- JV Ltd borrowed CU300 000 from a bank (an independent third party).

What is the dividend income recognised in P Ltd?

In P Ltd's separate financial statements, dividend income is recognised as follows:

		CU
From S Ltd:	(60% × CU550 000)	330 000
From A Ltd:	(30% × CU320 000)	96 000
From JV Ltd:	(50% × CU150 000)	75 000
Total:		**501 000**

What is the dividend income recognised in the group financial statements?

None, since the dividend income is eliminated as follows:
- The dividend received from S Ltd is an intra-group transaction. It is eliminated against the dividend declared by S Ltd.
- The dividends from A Ltd and JV Ltd are eliminated in accordance with the equity method. Income from these entities is recognised as 'earnings from associates and joint ventures' (refer to Chapter 9).

What dividend declared should be included in the consolidated statement of changes in equity?

P Ltd's dividend of CU800 000 plus S Ltd's dividend attributable to the non-controlling interest (a party outside of the group) of CU220 000 = CU1 020 000.

What are the cash flow implications of the dividends received and paid?

Dividends received (cash inflow):

		CU
From A Ltd:	(30% × CU320 000)	96 000
From JV Ltd:	(50% × CU150 000)	75 000
Total:		**171 000**

The dividends received from the subsidiary do not reflect cash that has come into the group. The cash flows of an equity accounted interest are not included in the group statement of cash flows as none of the dividends paid by the associate and joint venture is a cash outflow to the group. Dividends received from the associate and joint venture are a cash inflow to the group.
Dividends paid (cash outflow):

		CU
P Ltd		800 000
S Ltd (paid to non-controlling interest)	(40% × CU550 000)	220 000
Total:		**1 020 000**

Dividends paid to non-controlling interest in a subsidiary represent a cash outflow to the group.

What are the cash flow implications of the loans received and paid?
Loans received (cash inflow): None.
Note that JV Ltd's borrowings from the bank of CU300 000 are not cash controlled by the group.
Loans granted (cash outflow):

		CU
To A Ltd	(Cash no longer controlled)	1 000 000
To JV Ltd	(Cash no longer controlled)	500 000
Total:		**1 500 000**

Note that the loan from P Ltd to S Ltd is not reflected on the consolidated statement of cash flows as the cash remained in the group.

5. Disclosure in the consolidated statement of cash flows

A consolidated statement of cash flows is one of the statements that forms part of a complete set of consolidated financial statements. The presentation and layout of the group statement of cash flows is illustrated in Illustrative Example A to IAS7.

Additional information included in the notes to the statement of cash flows relates to the components of cash and cash equivalents, changes in ownership interests of subsidiaries and other businesses, and non-cash investing and financing transactions.

IAS7 requires separate disclosure of the following for investments in subsidiaries, associates and joint ventures:
- The total cost of acquisition of the investment or investments
- The portion of the cost of acquisition settled in cash and cash equivalents
- The amount of cash and cash equivalents in the acquired subsidiary at the date of acquisition
- The amount of assets and liabilities (other than cash and cash equivalents) in the acquired subsidiary (summarised by each major category) at the date of acquisition.

Refer to the extracts from the annual financial statements of Super Group (June 2013) that follow.

Consolidated statement of cash flows

for the year ended 30 June 2013

	Note	Year ended 30 June 2013 R000	Year ended 30 June 2012 R000
Cash flows from operating activities			
Cash generated from operations	28	1 155 366	1 844 342
Finance costs paid		(154 143)	(189 397)
Investment income and interest received		81 501	107 184
Cash dividends paid	29	–	(399)
Income tax paid	30	(349 011)	(232 496)
Net cash generated from operating activities		733 713	1 529 234
Cash flows from investing activities			
Additions to land, buildings and leasehold improvements	2	(191 987)	(49 258)
Additions to plant and equipment	2	(369 177)	(358 329)
Additions to full maintenance lease assets	4	(361 523)	(396 586)
Additions to intangible assets	5	(19 896)	(17 622)
Proceeds on disposal of land, buildings and leasehold improvements		14 063	16 606
Proceeds on disposal of plant and equipment		129 229	76 847
Proceeds on disposal of full maintenance lease assets		219 776	536 761
Proceeds on disposal of intangible assets		–	1 208
Long-term receivable loans granted		(23 235)	(2 838)
Long-term receivable loans repaid		1 281	4 747
Acquisition of businesses	31	(217 619)	(82 464)
Other investing activities		(9 224)	(1 958)
Net cash outflow from investing activities		(828 312)	(272 886)
Cash flows from financing activities			
Share repurchases		(59 127)	(227 962)
Interest-bearing borrowings raised		848 759	289 774
Interest-bearing borrowings repaid		(664 801)	(217 784)
Full maintenance lease borrowings raised		190 286	128 196
Full maintenance lease borrowings repaid		(215 550)	(753 890)
Net cash inflow/(outflow) from financing activities		99 567	(781 666)
Net increase in cash and cash equivalents		4 968	474 682
Net cash and cash equivalents at beginning of the year		1 776 430	1 210 456
Effect of foreign exchange on cash and cash equivalents		91 147	91 292
Cash and cash equivalents at end of the year	12	1 872 545	1 776 430

Figure 14.1 Example of consolidated statement of cash flows of Super Group, June 2013

Source: Super Group Ltd. 2013. Annual Financial Statements for the year ended 30 June 2013. [Online], Available: http://www.supergroup.co.za/downloads/2013_AFS.pdf Accessed 29 June 2014.

31 Net cost on acquisition of businesses

During the year, the Group acquired various subsidiaries and businesses.
The fair value of the net assets acquired and liabilities assumed were:

	Digistics R000	Dealerships R000	Safika Oosthuizens R000	30 June 2013 R000	30 June 2012 R000
Property, plant and equipment	(106 989)	(887)	(504 737)	(612 613)	(48 938)
Intangible assets	(72 200)	–	(144 232)	(216 432)	–
Trade and other receivables	(435 116)	–	(196 762)	(631 878)	(2 023)
Provision for impairment of trade receivables	2 000	–	–	2 000	–
Inventories	–	(13 730)	(17 378)	(31 108)	(31 639)
Cash and cash equivalents	(100 486)	–	(91 169)	(191 655)	–
Non-controlling interest	58 063	–	100 293	158 356	–
Deferred tax liability	18 137	–	95 768	113 905	–
Interest-bearing borrowings	89 513	–	384 757	474 270	2 023
Trade and other payables	480 828	–	68 849	549 677	18 187
Provisions	7 657	1 181	6 115	14 953	115
Taxation	297	–	(2 371)	(2 074)	–
Fair value of assets acquired	(58 296)	(13 436)	(300 867)	(372 599)	(62 275)
Goodwill	(62 104)	(12 948)	38 377	(36 675)	(20 189)
Cash paid on acquisition	(120 400)	(26 384)	(262 490)	(409 274)	(82 464)
Cash acquired	100 486	–	91 169	191 655	–
Cash outflow	(19 914)	(26 384)	(171 321)	(217 619)	(82 464)

The Group acquired 50,1% of the shares and voting interests in Digistics Proprietary Limited on 1 October 2012, a procurement and food distribution business in the Quick Service Restaurant industry. The non-controlling interest at acquisition date was 49,9%. The acquisition agreement gives rise to a put option in the hands the non-controlling interests and a call option in the hands of the Group for the remaining 49,9% exercisable between 1 and 30 October 2017. This put option resulted in a financial liability of R105 707 000 as at 30 June 2013. The Group performed a purchase price allocation exercise whereby intangible assets acquired were independently valued by EY. The valuation, using projected financial information, was performed on 1 October 2012 resulting in the recognition of R72 200 000 in respect of customer relationships. The negative goodwill arose as a result of customer contracts that were identified and recognised as part of the purchase price allocation exercise that were not included in the acquiree's statement of financial position.

Acquiring control of Digistics has enabled the Group to take advantage of synergies in the supply chain division as well as to enter into new markets.

The Group acquired 75% of the shares and voting interests in Safika Logistics Holdings Proprietary Limited Transport on 1 March 2013, a logistics service company that provides hauling of dry bulk goods such as coal, chrome and "run of mine minerals" in tipper trucks. The non-controlling interest at acquisition date was 25%. The acquisition agreement gives rise to a put option in the hands on the non-controlling interests and a call option in the hands of the Group for the remaining 25% exercisable between 1 and 30 March 2016. This option resulted in a financial liability of R101 649 000 as at 30 June 2013. The Group performed a purchase price allocation exercise whereby intangible assets acquired were separately valued. The valuation, using projected financial information, was performed on 1 March 2013 resulting in the recognition of R144 232 000 in respect of customer relationships, trade name and customer contracts, this has also resulted in negative goodwill of R38 377 000 arising on acquisition.

The acquisition of Safika Oosthuizens has enabled the Group to enter into new Supply Chain markets.

Super Group's Dealership division acquired a Nissan dealership in Alberton (effective date 1 August 2012), a Fiat Alfa dealership in the East Rand and a Renault dealership at The Glen (effective date 1 October 2012) for R13 638 000, R4 713 000 and R8 033 000 respectively. These acquisitions will enable the Group to expand the Dealerships division.

Goodwill is attributable mainly to the skills and technical talent of the workforce and synergies expected to be achieved from integrating the acquired businesses into the Group's various operations. None of the goodwill recognised is expected to be deductible for tax purposes.

The Group measured the acquisition date components of non-controlling interests at its proportionate share in the recognised amounts of the acquiree's identifiable net assets.

The acquisition related costs of R3 621 000 are included in other operating expenses in the consolidated statement of comprehensive income.

The pre-acquisition carrying amounts were determined based on applicable IFRS statements immediately preceding the relevant acquisition. The contribution to the Group's results, made by the businesses acquired is provided in the summary below:

	30 June 2013 R000	30 June 2012 R000
Revenue	1 002 954	268 438
Operating profit	127 187	5 623
Profit before tax	116 328	3 446
Attributable profit to equity holders of Super Group[1]	37 238	(550)
Attributable profit[2]	57 793	651

[1] Profit after tax, after non-controlling interest
[2] Profit after tax

If the above acquisitions had occurred on 1 July 2012 the contribution to revenue would have been R1 954 289 000, profit attributable to equity holders of the Group for the year would have been R100 528 000 and attributable profit for the year would have been R145 071 000.

Source: Super Group Ltd. 2013. Annual Financial Statements for the year ended 30 June 2013. [Online], Available: http://www.supergroup.co.za/downloads/2013_AFS.pdf Accessed 29 June 2014.

Figure 14.2 Example of note disclosure of acquisitions of various subsidiaries and business by Super Group Limited

Test your knowledge

There is a list of learning objectives at the beginning of this chapter. Go back to this list and check whether you have achieved these outcomes. If not, reread the appropriate section.

Questions

Question 1

The group, A Ltd, owns a 60% controlling interest in B Ltd and a 30% interest in D Ltd, an associate company. Furthermore, B Ltd owns 75% of Z Ltd.

The following dividends were paid in cash by group companies during the financial year ending 31 December 20x4:

	CU
A Ltd	700 000
B Ltd	400 000
D Ltd	350 000
Z Ltd	400 000

The following cash loans were made during 20x4 in the A Ltd group:
- Z Ltd lent CU500 000 to A Ltd.
- A Ltd lent CU150 000 to D Ltd.

Assume that, apart from the information given in the question, there are no dividends received or paid and no loans received or granted by any of the companies in the group.

You are required to do the following:

Calculate the amounts that will be included in the group statement of cash flows of A Ltd for the 31 December 20x4 year end for the following:
- Dividends received
- Dividends paid
- Loans received
- Loans granted.

Where relevant, your solution should include **brief** explanations.

Suggested solution

Dividends received

CU350 000 × 30% = **CU105 000**

Dividends received from an associate company are a cash inflow to the group. The cash flows of an equity accounted company are not included in the group statement of cash flows.

The group controls 100% of the cash of a subsidiary. Dividends received from a subsidiary do not have any impact on group cash flows. The portion of dividends paid to non-controlling shareholders is cash going out of the group's control and is therefore a cash outflow.

Dividends paid

		CU
A Ltd		700 000
B Ltd	(40% × CU400 000)	160 000
Z Ltd	(25% × CU400 000)	100 000
		960 000

Dividends paid to non-controlling shareholders of a subsidiary represent a cash outflow to the group. 75% of the dividend paid by Z Ltd is received by B Ltd and the cash has therefore remained within the control of the group.

Loans received (cash inflow)

Z Ltd to A Ltd	Cash remained in group	–

Loans granted (cash outflow)

A Ltd to D Ltd	Cash no longer controlled	CU150 000

Question 2

P Ltd acquired 80% of S Ltd for CU60 000 during the year ended 31 December 20x5. The assets and liabilities of S Ltd at acquisition were as follows:

	CU
Non-current assets	25 000
Inventories	45 000
Accounts receivable	30 000
Cash at bank	10 000
Accounts payable	(10 000)
Long-term liabilities	(30 000)
	70 000

The consolidated financial statements of P Ltd and S Ltd for the year ended 31 December 20x5 are given below.

Consolidated statement of profit or loss for P Ltd for the year ended 31 December 20x5

	CU	CU
Gross revenue		1 520 000
Cost of sales		(1 040 000)
Gross profit		480 000
Interest income		12 000
Depreciation	(20 000)	
Interest received	(15 000)	
Other operating costs	(186 000)	(221 000)
Profit before tax		271 000
Taxation expense (current tax)		(130 000)
Profit after taxation		**141 000**
Attributable to:		
Parent equity shareholders		136 000
Non-controlling shareholders		15 000

Consolidated statement of financial position for P Ltd at 31 December 20x5

	20x5 CU	20x4 CU
ASSETS		
Non-current assets		
Property, plant and equipment	125 000	70 000
Goodwill	4 000	–
Current assets		
Accounts receivable	70 000	35 000
Inventories	105 000	40 000
Cash at bank	20 000	–
	324 000	**145 000**
EQUITY AND LIABILTIES		
Share capital	50 000	50 000
Retained earnings	113 000	25 000
Parent equity interest	163 000	75 000
Non-controlling interest	21 000	–
Total equity	184 000	75 000
Long-term liabilities	90 000	40 000
Trade payables	50 000	30 000
	324 000	**145 000**

The following information should also be taken into account:
- S Ltd declared and paid dividends of CU40 000 on 31 December 20x5. Dividends paid by P Ltd amounted to CU38 000 for the current reporting period.
- There was no tax or dividends unpaid at the beginning or end of the 20x5 financial year.

Assume that there have been no disposals of non-current assets or repayment of long-term liabilities throughout the year.

You are required to do the following:
1. Prepare the consolidated statement of cash flows for the year ended 31 December 20x5 using the indirect method. Relevant notes to the statement of cash flows are required.
2. Prepare the consolidated statement of cash flows for the year ended 31 December 20x5 using the direct method.

Ignore all VAT implications.

Suggested solution

1.

Consolidated statement of cash flows for P Ltd for the year ending 31 December 20x5

	Note	CU
Cash flows from operating activities		
Profit before tax		271 000
Adjustments for:		
Depreciation		20 000
Interest income		(12 000)
Interest expense		15 000
		294 000
Increase in accounts receivable (see w1)		(5 000)
Increase in inventories (see w2)		(20 000)
Increase in trade payables (see w3)		10 000
Cash generated from operations		**279 000**
Interest received		12 000
Interest paid		(15 000)
Dividends paid		
• To shareholders of the parent		(38 000)
• To non-controlling shareholders (40 000 × 20%) (see w7)		(8 000)
Income tax paid		(130 000)
Net cash inflow from operating activities		**100 000**
Cash flows from investing activities		
Acquisition of subsidiary S Ltd, net of cash acquired	2	(50 000)
Purchase of property, plant and equipment (see w5)		(50 000)
Net cash outflow from investing activities		**(100 000)**
Cash flows from financing activities		
Proceeds from long term borrowings		20 000
Net cash inflow from financing activities		20 000
Net increase in cash and cash equivalents		**20 000**
Cash and cash equivalents at beginning of period	1	Nil
Cash and cash equivalents at end of period	1	**20 000**

Notes to the statement of cash flows

1   Cash and cash equivalents: Cash and cash equivalents included in the statement of cash flows comprise the following balance sheet amounts:

	20x5 CU	20x4 CU
Cash at bank	20 000	Nil

2   Acquisition of subsidiary: During the year, the group acquired subsidiary S Ltd. The fair value of the assets and liabilities assumed was as follows:

	20x5 CU
Property, plant and equipment	25 000
Accounts receivable	30 000
Inventories	45 000
Cash	10 000
Trade payables	(10 000)
Long-term debt	(30 000)
	70 000
Non-controlling interest (20%)	(14 000)
	56 000
Goodwill acquired	4 000
Total purchase price	60 000
Less: Cash of S Ltd	(10 000)
Net cash flow on acquisition of subsidiary	50 000

Workings 1

Accounts receivable	CU		CU
Balance 1 January 20x5	35 000		
Acquisition of S Ltd	30 000		
∴ Increase (w1)	**5 000**	Balance 31 December 20x5	70 000
	70 000		**70 000**
Balance brought forward	70 000		

Workings 2

Inventories	CU		CU
Balance 1 January 20x5	40 000		
Acquisition of S Ltd	45 000		
∴ Increase (w2)	**20 000**	Balance 31 December 20x5	105 000
	105 000		**105 000**
Balance brought forward	105 000		

Workings 3

Trade payables	CU		CU
		Balance 1 January 20x5	30 000
		Acquisition of S Ltd	10 000
Balance 31 December 20x5	50 000	∴ Increase (w3)	**10 000**
	50 000		**50 000**
		Balance brought forward	50 000

Workings 4

Cash at bank			
	CU		CU
Balance 1 January 20x5	Nil		
Acquisition of S Ltd	10 000		
∴ Increase	**10 000**	Balance 31 December 20x5	20 000
	20 000		**20 000**
Balance brought forward	20 000		

Workings 5

Property, plant and equipment			
	CU		CU
Balance 1 January 20x5	70 000		
Acquisition of S Ltd	25 000	Depreciation	20 000
∴ Bank (acquisitions) (w5)	**50 000**	Balance 31 December 20x5	125 000
	145 000		**145 000**
Balance brought forward	125 000		

Workings 6

Long-term loans			
	CU		CU
		Balance 1 January 20x5	40 000
		Acquisition of S Ltd	30 000
Balance 31 December 20x5	90 000	∴ Bank (raised) (w6)	**20 000**
	90 000		**90 000**
		Balance brought forward	90 000

Workings 7

Non-controlling interest			
	CU		CU
		Balance 1 January 20x5	Nil
∴ Dividend paid (w7)	**8 000**	Acquisition of S Ltd	14 000
Balance 31 December 20x5	21 000	Share of profits	15 000
	29 000		**29 000**
		Balance brought forward	29 000

2. Direct method statement of cash flows:

Cash flows from operating activities

	CU
Cash flows from operating activities	
Cash receipts from customers (see w8)	1 515 000
Cash paid to suppliers and employees (see w10)	(1 236 000)
Cash generated from operations	279 000
Interest received	12 000
Interest paid	(15 000)
Dividends paid:	
• To shareholders of the parent	(38 000)
• To non-controlling shareholders (see w7)	(8 000)
Income tax paid	(130 000)
Net cash inflow from operating activities	**100 000**

The rest of the cash flow and notes are the same as for the indirect method. However, an additional note to show the reconciliation of net profit before taxation to cash generated from operations must be shown.

Workings 8: Cash received from customers

	CU
Accounts receivable 1 January 20x5	35 000
Add: Sales	1 520 000
Add: Receivables purchased in subsidiary	30 000
Accounts receivable 31 December20x5	(70 000)
Cash receipts from customers (w8)	**1 515 000**

Workings 9: Purchases

	CU
Opening inventory	40 000
Subsidiary inventory acquired	45 000
∴ Purchases (derived) (see w10 below)	**1 060 000**
Amount available	1 145 000
Less: Closing inventory	(105 000)
Cost of sales (given)	1 040 000

Workings 10: Cash paid to suppliers and employees

	CU
Trade payables 1 January 20x5	30 000
Add: Purchases (per w9)	1 060 000
Add: Trade payables of subsidiary purchased	10 000
Less: Trade payables 31 December 20x5	(50 000)
	1 050 000
Operating costs	186 000
Cash paid to suppliers and employees (w10)	**1 236 000**

Case study exercises

Scenario 1

P Ltd acquired 80% (and control) of the issued ordinary share capital of S Ltd for CU365 000 on 1 January 20x3, when the financial statements of S Ltd included the following balances:

	CU
Share capital	170 000
Retained earnings	200 000
Shareholders' equity	370 000

At the date of acquisition, P Ltd considered the assets and liabilities of S Ltd to be fairly valued, except for land, which had a market value of CU310 000 (cost of CU250 000). S Ltd did not recognise any change in the amount of land because of the fair value identified by P Ltd at the acquisition date. Ignore taxation.

Extracts from the group financial statements for the year ended 31 December 20x5 are presented below.

Group statement of profit or loss and other comprehensive income for the year ended 31 December 20x5

	Group CU'000
Revenue (including interest income: CU280 000)	3 876
Net operating costs	(2 580)
Interest expense	(150)
Profit before taxation	1 146
Taxation expense	(550)
Profit for the year	**596**
Attributable to:	
Non-controlling interest	80
Equity holders of the parent	516

Group statement of changes in shareholders' equity for the year ended 31 December 20x5

	Share capital CU'000	Retained earnings CU'000	Total equity interest of the parent CU'000	Non-controlling interest CU'000	Total CU'000
Opening balance	290	860	1 150	146	1 296
Profit for the year		516	516	80	596
– Dividends		(200)	(200)	(36)	(236)
Disposal of interest in subsidiary to non-controlling shareholders		22	22	228	250
Closing balance	**290**	**1 198**	**1 488**	**418**	**1 906**

Group statements of financial position at 31 December 20x5

	20x5 CU'000	20x4 CU'000
ASSETS		
Land	670	670
Plant and machinery	580	460
Goodwill	21	21
Inventory	350	300
Accounts receivable	400	340
Cash and cash equivalents	195	59
	2 216	1 850
CAPITAL AND LIABILITIES		
Share capital	290	290
Retained earnings	1 198	860
Shareholders' equity	1 488	1 150
Non-controlling interest	418	146
Total equity	1 906	1 296
Non-current liabilities	200	390
Current liabilities (accounts payable)	110	164
	2 216	1 850

Additional information

- P Ltd sold 30% of its 80% interest in S Ltd for CU250 000 on 31 December 20x5. The result is that P Ltd still has a 56% interest in S Ltd and thus retained control.
- Non-controlling interest is measured at its attributable net asset value at the date of acquisition.
- There were no changes in the issued share capital for both entities.
- Plant and machinery in the group had a cost price of CU1m at 31 December 20x5 (20x4: CU800 000). New machinery for expansion amounting to CU200 000 was acquired in the current year. This was the only change in non-current assets.

You are required to do the following:

Prepare the group statement of cash flows for the year ended 31 December 20x5 using the indirect method for cash flows from operating activities.

Scenario 2

Assume the same information as for Scenario 1 above, except that P Ltd sold its entire interest in S Ltd for CU800 000 on 31 December 20x5.

Extracts from the group financial statements for the year ended 31 December 20x5 are presented below.

Group statement of profit or loss and other comprehensive income for the year ended 31 December 20x5

	Group CU'000
Revenue (includes interest income: CU280 000)	3 876
Net operating costs	(2 856)
Interest expense	(150)
Profit before taxation	870
Taxation expense	(550)
Profit for the year	320
Attributable to:	
Non-controlling interest	80
Equity holders of the parent	240

Group statement of changes in shareholders' equity for the year ended 31 December 20x5

	Share capital CU'000	Retained earnings CU'000	Total equity interest of the parent CU'000	Non-controlling interest CU'000	Total CU'000
Opening balance	290	860	1 150	146	1 296
Profit for the year		240	240	80	320
– Dividends		(200)	(200)	(36)	(236)
Less disposal of subsidiary				(190)	(190)
Closing balance	**290**	**900**	**1 190**	**–**	**1 190**

Group statements of financial position on 31 December 20x5

	20x5 CU'000	20x4 CU'000
ASSETS		
Land	360	670
Plant and machinery	475	460
Goodwill	–	21
Inventory	100	300
Accounts receivable	230	340
Cash and cash equivalents	405	59
	1 570	1 850
CAPITAL AND LIABILITIES		
Share capital	290	290
Retained earnings	900	860
Shareholders' equity	1 190	1 150
Non-controlling interest	–	146
Total equity	1 190	1 296
Non-current liabilities	350	390
Current liabilities (accounts payable)	30	164
	1 570	1 850

Statement of financial position of S Ltd at 31 December 20x5 (the date of disposal)

	CU'000
ASSETS	
Land	250
Plant and machinery	120
Inventory	350
Accounts receivable	200
Cash and cash equivalents	80
	1 000
CAPITAL AND LIABILITIES	
Share capital	170
Retained earnings	720
Shareholders' equity	890
Current liabilities (accounts payable)	110
	1 000

You are required to do the following:

Prepare the group statement of cash flows for the year ended 31 December 20x5 using the indirect method for cash flows from operating activities.

Suggested solution

Scenario 1
Prepare the group statement of cash flows for the year ended 31 December 20x5 using the indirect method for cash flows from operating activities.

Group statement of cash flows for the year ending 31 December 20x5

	Note	CU
Cash flows from operating activities		
Profit before tax		1 146 000
Adjustments for:		
Depreciation (see w1)		80 000
Interest income		(280 000)
Interest expense		150 000
		1 096 000
Increase in accounts receivables		(60 000)
Increase in inventories		(50 000)
Decrease in trade payables		(54 000)
Cash generated from operations		**932 000**
Interest received		280 000
Interest paid		(150 000)
Dividends paid:		
To shareholders of the parent		(200 000)
To non-controlling shareholders		(36 000)
Income tax paid		(550 000)
Net cash inflow from operating activities		**276 000**
Cash flows from investing activities		
Purchase of plant and machinery for expansion (see w1)		(200 000)
Net cash outflow from investing activities		**(200 000)**
Cash flows from financing activities		
Proceeds from sale of interest in subsidiary		250 000
Repayment of non-current liabilities		(190 000)
Net cash inflow from financing activities		**60 000**
Net increase in cash and cash equivalents		**136 000**
Cash and cash equivalents at beginning of period	1	59 000
Cash and cash equivalents at end of period	1	**195 000**

Notes to the statement of cash flows

1   Cash and cash equivalents: Cash and cash equivalents included in the statement of cash flows comprise the following balance sheet amounts:

	20x5 CU	20x4 CU
Cash at bank	195 000	59 000

Workings 1

Plant and machinery			
	CU		CU
Opening balance	460 000		
Bank (new machinery) (w1)	200 000	∴ Depreciation expense	80 000
		Closing balance	580 000
	660 000		**660 000**
Closing balance	580 000		

Scenario 2

Prepare the group statement of cash flows for the year ended 31 December 20x5 using the indirect method for cash flows from operating activities.

Group statement of cash flows for the year ending 31 December 20x5

	Note	CU
Cash flows from operating activities		
Profit before tax		870 000
Adjustments for:		
Profit of disposal of subsidiary (see w5)	2	(19 000)
Depreciation (see w1)		65 000
Interest income		(280 000)
Interest expense		150 000
		786 000
Increase in accounts receivables (see w3)		(90 000)
Increase in inventories (see w2)		(150 000)
Decrease in trade payables (see w4)		(24 000)
Cash generated from operations		**522 000**
Interest received		280 000
Interest paid		(150 000)
Dividends paid:		
To shareholders of the parent		(200 000)
To non-controlling shareholders		(36 000)
Income tax paid		(550 000)
Net cash inflow from operating activities		**(134 000)**
Cash flows from investing activities		
Proceeds from sale of subsidiary	2	720 000
Purchase of plant and machinery for expansion (see w1)		(200 000)
Net cash outflow from investing activities		**520 000**
Cash flows from financing activities		
Repayment of non-current liabilities		(40 000)
Net cash inflow from financing activities		**(40 000)**
Net increase in cash and cash equivalents		**346 000**
Cash and cash equivalents at beginning of period	1	59 000
Cash and cash equivalents at end of period	1	**405 000**

Notes to the statement of cash flows

1 Cash and cash equivalents: Cash and cash equivalents included in the statement of cash flows comprise the following balance sheet amounts.

	20x5	20x4
Cash at bank	405 000	59 000

2 Disposal of subsidiary: The group sold its entire interest in S Ltd on 31 December 20x5. The fair value of the assets and liabilities was as follows:

	20x5 CU
Land	310 000
Plant and machinery	120 000
Inventory	350 000
Accounts receivable	200 000
Cash and cash equivalents	80 000
Accounts payable	(110 000)
Net assets disposed	950 000
Non-controlling interest	(190 000)
Goodwill derecognised	21 000
Profit on disposal (see w5)	19 000
Proceed received	800 000
Less: Cash and cash equivalent disposed of	(80 000)
Net cash inflow from disposal of entire interest in subsidiary	**720 000**

Workings 1

Plant and machinery			
	CU		CU
Opening balance	460 000		
Bank (new machinery) (w1)	200 000	∴ Depreciation expense (w1)	65 000
		Disposal of subsidiary	120 000
		Closing balance	475 000
	660 000		**660 000**
Closing balance	475 000		

Workings 2

Inventory			
	CU		CU
Opening balance	300 000		
Net increase/bank (w2)	150 000	Disposal of subsidiary	350 000
		Closing balance	100 000
	450 000		**450 000**
Closing balance	100 000		

Workings 3

Accounts receivable			
	CU		CU
Opening balance	340 000		
Net increase/bank (w3)	90 000	Disposal of subsidiary	200 000
		Closing balance	230 000
	430 000		**430 000**
Closing balance	230 000		

Workings 4

Accounts payable			
	CU		**CU**
		Opening balance	164 000
Disposal of subsidiary	110 000		
Net decrease/bank (w4)	24 000		
Closing balance	30 000		
	164 000		**164 000**
		Closing balance	30 000

Workings 5

Group profit on the sale of the subsidiary

	CU
Proceed from disposal of subsidiary	800 000
Net assets disposed (890 000 + 60 000)	(950 000)
Goodwill derecognised	(21 000)
Non-controlling interest derecognised (950 000 × 20%)	190 000
Group profit on disposal of subsidiary	**19 000**

Index

540